THE ECONOMIC ORGANIZATION
OF WAR COMMUNISM, 1918–1921

SOVIET AND EAST EUROPEAN STUDIES

THE ECONOMIC ORGANIZATION OF WAR COMMUNISM, 1918–1921

SILVANA MALLE

Associate Professor, University of Verona

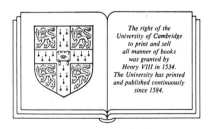

The right of the
University of Cambridge
to print and sell
all manner of books
was granted by
Henry VIII in 1534.
The University has printed
and published continuously
since 1584.

CAMBRIDGE UNIVERSITY PRESS

CAMBRIDGE

LONDON   NEW YORK   NEW ROCHELLE

MELBOURNE   SYDNEY

Published by the Press Syndicate of the University of Cambridge
The Pitt Building, Trumpington Street, Cambridge CB2 1RP
32 East 57th Street, New York, NY 10022, USA
10 Stanford Road, Oakleigh, Melbourne 3166, Australia

First published 1985

Printed in Great Britain at the University Press, Cambridge

Library of Congress catalogue card number: 84–29197

British Library Cataloguing in Publication Data

Malle, Silvana
The economic organization of war communism,
1918–1921. – (Soviet and East European studies)
1. Soviet Union – Economic policy – 1917–1928
I. Title II. Series
330.947′0841   HC335.2
ISBN 0 521 30292 7

To Minh
dark light

E molti si sono immaginati repubbliche e principati, che non si sono mai visti nè conosciuti essere in vero; perchè elli è tanto discosto da come si vive a come si doverebbe vivere, che colui che lascia quello che si fa per quello che si doverebbe fare, impara piùtosto la ruina che la preservazione sua: perchè uno uomo, che voglia fare in tutte le parte professione di buono, conviene rovini infra tanti che non sono buoni. Onde è necessario a uno principe, volendosi mantenere, imparare a potere essere non buono, et usarlo e non usare secondo la necessità.

N. Machiavelli, Il principe, par. 15

C'est le marxisme, non le bolchevisme, qui fonde les interventions du Parti sur des forces qui sont déjà là et la praxis sur une vérité historique. Quand, dans la seconde moitié du XIXe siècle, Marx passe au socialisme scientifique, cette idée d'un socialisme inscrit dans les faits vient cautionner plus énergiquement encore les initiatives du Parti. Car si la révolution est dans les choses, comment hésiterait-on à écarter par tous les moyens des résistances qui ne sont qu'apparentes? Si la fonction révolutionnaire du prolétariat est gravée dans les infrastructures du capital, l'action politique qui l'exprime est justifiée comme l'Inquisition par la Providence.

M. Merleau-Ponty, Les Aventures de la dialectique

Contents

vii

Figures

x

Tables

xi

Preface

This book is the result of years of research and redrafting based on materials in the libraries of the Hoover Institution (Stanford), the British Museum and in particular the Bibliothèque de Documentation et Information Contemporaine (BDIC, Paris Nanterre).

During the initial research I was fortunate to have received comments on my drafts from Professors B. Ward, G. Grossman and M. Lewin. In the final stages, the stimulating remarks of Professors R.W. Davies, O. Crisp, L. Szamuely and L. Sirc were of considerable help. The initial English editing was undertaken with much sensitivity and respect for the content by Mr Jacob Miller, without whose aid and enthusiasm the script would never have been ready for printing.

My gratitude goes also to Dr J.M. Cooper and Mrs Bo Richter, who have in different degrees but with the same spirit of friendship helped me in the editing of the final version. In this they displayed much patience and a cheerful disregard for my intermittent objections to their justified corrections. I am also indebted to Dr Cooper for bringing my attention to additional sources and information contained in his remarkable collection of early Soviet literature.

I wish to express my thanks to all these scholars and at the same time to apologize for any weaknesses which may remain; I assume full responsibility for them.

Miss Jean Fyfe performed the valuable task of decoding my illegible handwriting and translating it into a neatly typed text.

All through my work I have been encouraged by Professor D. Cantarelli while he was the Director of the Institute of Economic Science at Verona University.

My friend Dr Girolamo Sciullo, although not an expert in the subject matter, has been always ready to listen patiently to my lucubrations and to cheer me up at times of pessimism with an exhilarating glass of champagne.

Finally I wish to mention the financial help awarded by the Italian Ministry of Public Education and by the Cassa di Risparmio of Verona.

S.M.

I

Introduction

I.I THE LITERATURE ON WAR COMMUNISM

A large number of scholars have been concerned with the history of war communism in the Soviet Union. Broadly, two interpretations have emerged. The first, which originated in the twenties, when the political implications of the revolution were still being worked out, tends to focus on the ideological origins of the new system. The second, which is the result of a cooler perspective on past events, tends to emphasize the emergency character of the economic measures adopted in connection with the civil war and relegates the ideological aspect to *ex post facto* rationalizations.

A characteristic of the first kind of interpretation is the lack or scattered nature of evidence to prove the point of ideological bias or inspiration of the economic policy adopted in the early years of the revolution. There is no systematic scrutiny of the Marxist literature produced before and after the revolution, and whenever any attempt in this direction is made, the reader is confronted with limited excerpts and with a literal interpretation of the content, deprived of historical perspective. Economic policy is often confused with declaration of principles. Vice versa, excessive focus on emergency as the immediate cause of all measures in the economic field tends to a neglect of the impact of the ideological framework which conditioned the number of possible choices and produced a bias in the evaluation of effective choices.

These remarks apply to the Western as well as to the Soviet literature. A peculiarity which is common to both is the emphasis on a single explanatory key for all sorts of events affecting economic organization, either the Marxist ideology incarnated in the party leadership or the civil war interpreted as an exogenous, objective factor conditioning economic choices. What is striking in the Soviet literature is the sacrifice of a dialectical interpretation of the continuous changes which characterized war communism in all fields, in favour of a deterministic approach resting

1

on the assumption of Lenin's exclusive role and infallibility. The Stalinist purges of the thirties, which removed from the political scene most of the communist leaders of war communism, thus depriving history of their specific contributions, partially explain the bias that even modern Soviet literature maintains on this subject. But there is an additional element. The effort to build an epic of the Soviet revolution, emphasizing its success and minimizing its mistakes, corresponds to the need of intellectuals who have not renounced the Marxist credo to identify themselves with those pages of history full of enthusiasm, sacrifice, idealism and hope, which, after the ideological crisis opened by the repudiation of the Stalinist period, still maintain the appeal of a unifying element for the several sects of Marxist derivation, whensoever their divorce from Soviet orthodoxy may be dated.

Because of an opposite ideological bias, as well as of partial information and lack of adequate methodology, most of the Western literature places a particular emphasis on Lenin's impact on economic choices, leaving in the shade the influence of the economic leadership as well as the traditions and legacies of the Russian economy and society. Study of the actual working of the new Soviet system suggests that both sympathizers and opponents tend to attribute too much to Lenin and to the hasty pamphlet activity which preceded and accompanied the Red October, rather than focusing attention on the Russian Marxist ideology as such, which was the filter through which an entire new political leadership screened the immediate goals and the means to attain them. The myth of the leader is likely to obscure the complexities of the decision-making process and transform it into something coordinated, harmonious, predetermined and unidirectional; in fact, most decisions were the result of a precarious compromise between antagonistic drives and the ephemeral mirror of an anxious search for stability and consolidation of power in a shifting context.

A further difficulty which the literature has not yet been able to overcome is that of discriminating between immediate goals of the government's policy and a proclaimed orthodoxy of Marxist principles used as charisma to gain uncritical consensus. This practice, which still strikes many observers as analogous with religious attitudes, should not lead us to take for granted the dogmatism of the choices, but should rather be an incentive for confronting concrete issues with their immediate objectives and constraints and an incentive to evaluate in such a perspective the process of decision-making. The Party Congress debates which remained quite alive even during the most acute phases of the civil war, bearing no analogy with the miserable conformism of the Stalinist period and the present mode, are more instructive for a correct appraisal of the alternatives than is mere reference to the ideological matrix of the protagonists, though the latter must not be disregarded.

This survey of the literature on war communism is an experiment in the search for bias – though possibly it is not going to cancel out the bias of the author – rather than a comprehensive scrutiny of the existing works on this topic.*

1.2 SOVIET LITERATURE

Two approaches may be distinguished in the Soviet literature on war communism. The first focuses on the heroic performance of the re-volution, on the originality of the Soviet system, on the coherence of the 'ensemble' of policies aimed at the rapid construction of socialism. The alternative approach, developed in the thirties, tends to appraise the features of war communism as a forced temporary break in the Leninist plan of construction of socialism, due to exogenous factors like civil war and foreign intervention. Recent access to archive materials seems to have provided support for the extension and deepening of both interpretations. On one side, some of the literature has tried to find additional arguments to distinguish even more sharply than before the first months of Soviet power from the crucial period of civil war, by identifying in the former policies an anticipation of NEP. On the other side, the axiom of the exogeneity of civil war has been questioned by a subtle reading of Bolshevik policies which focuses on their ideological roots. Thus a thesis of the continuity of the policies which ended up in the organization of the war communism economy emerges. The novelty of this approach in Soviet literature, combined with the availability of archive documents,

---

*For a broader panorama on Soviet revolution as viewed by some minor, though keen observers, the reader may find of interest the following: L. Pasvolsky, *The Economics of Communism*, New York, 1921, who focused on the gap between theory and reality in some fields, like income distribution (p. 16); J. Lescure, *La Révolution Russe et le Bolchevisme*, Paris, 1929, who grasped that the essence of war communism was the logic of distribution (p. 222); N. Zvorikine, *La Révolution et le Bolchevisme en Russie*, Paris, 1920, for whom the Bolshevik doctrine has never been implemented, nor had the government any principles (p. 211); P. Ryss, *L'Expérience Russe*, Paris, 1922, who was impressed by the Bolsheviks as true children of Russia, psychologically estranged from the Marxian evolutionary theory and convinced that the light would come from the East (pp. 119–20). For both G. Welter, *Histoire de la Russie Communiste 1917–1935*, Paris, 1935 (p. 97) and D. Gavronsky, *Le Bilan du Bolchevisme Russe*, Paris, 1920, coercion rather than persuasion was the necessary issue of the Bolshevik doctrine; for G. Aleksinskij, *Les Effets économiques et sociaux de la Révolution Bolcheviste et son échec*, Bruxelles, 1920, the backwardness of the country was the main hindrance to efforts to improve economic standards (p. 20). L. H. Guest, *The Struggle for Power in Europe (1917–1921)*, London, 1921, p. 81, gives a description of Communist Party members as picked soldiers enjoying considerable privileges, but called to volunteer for dangerous and disagreeable duties.

opens a new perspective not only on war communism, but also on the origins and nature of the Soviet system.

The most important theoretical synthesis of the war communist system is the *Ekonomika perekhodnogo perioda (The Economics of the Transformation Period)*, written by Bukharin, a direct protagonist of the revolution, and published early in 1920. Bukharin emphasizes the impact of a given stage of development on economic organization with regard to methods of management and means of labour discipline. Rationalizing the Russian experience, he affirms that the initial phase of the revolutionary process is one of destruction, which corresponds to the seizure of the strategic points of the economy. The break-up of the former system into a number of factory-committees is the outcome of the political struggle for power. Such a phase is a necessary one, since the bourgeoisie and the technical intelligentsia have no interest in the reorganization of production. But this system is not the best from a technical point of view. In wartime, argues Bukharin, one-man management is the most concrete and condensed form of proletarian administration of industry. One-man management should not imply restriction of class rights or reduction of the role of class organizations. Likewise, the replacement of the principle of electivity from below by the principle of selection from above of the managerial staff should not be a hindrance to the further development of a collective–socialist form of management and control of economic life. This is because the dictatorship of the proletariat is the guarantee that leaders may not go beyond the functions they are expected to perform on behalf of the proletariat.[1] But, how would a society based on the methods of war communism during the transition period evolve towards a socialist society, where no coercion will be needed and the highest form of 'administration of things' will replace the 'administration of people'? Bukharin envisages such a development, but does not explain why and how it should occur. The most serious shortcoming of the *Ekonomika* is its failure to draw a clear distinction between the disequilibrium period and the period following the installation of equilibrium. In Marxist terms, this deficiency, which has been stressed by one of the most serious studies of Bukharin's personality,[2] would be regarded as a product of his use of a mechanist, non-dialectical method.[3] The following excerpt is an example:

The transformation of the process of creating surplus value into a process of systematic satisfaction of social needs finds its expression in the regrouping of the relation of production, in spite of the formal maintenance of the same place in the hierarchical system of production, which, as a whole, bears a different character, the character of the dialectical negation of the capitalist structure; and which leads in so far as it destroys the social caste character of the hierarchy, to the abolition of the hierarchy as a whole.[4]

There is no place in Bukharin's concept of the process of 'systematic satisfaction of social needs' for the possible evolution of the new relations of production into institutions endowed with their own rationality and, consequently, no place for the potential development of antagonism between them. Thus, for Bukharin, the crux of the matter becomes one of correct methods of management and training for administrative tasks:

in further phases of development, insofar as the positions of the working class as a ruling class have stabilized themselves and insofar as a secure foundation for a competent administration of industry has arisen the base of which is already a group of selected workers-administrators, insofar as, on the other hand, the technological intelligentsia turns back like the lost son into the process of production, insofar does the function of administration separate itself from the function of schooling for this administration.[5]

The problem of constructing an alternative society thus becomes only a technical problem. Since Bukharin does not see the possibility that the interests of workers as such may not coincide with the goals of their managers, that is, since his analysis rules out the possibility of this or any other form of antagonism occurring in the new system and becoming the possible catalyst of future evolution (or revolution), the only dynamic element capable of transforming the negative power of the proletarian anarchy into a conscious will is the coercive power of the state. In order to transform the spontaneous disequilibrium process caused by revolution into an equilibrium phase, a social and conscious regulator is needed, through which commodities are transformed into products.[6] There are two reasons for coercion in the transition period. First, a re-education process is required to eliminate the residuals of the former individualistic, non-proletarian mentality, and the harshness of this process is proportional to the former social status of those concerned. Second, the lack of unity of the proletariat necessitates a process of revolutionary education, in the sense of a steady raising of the working class to the level of the vanguard. Bukharin argues that the presumption of the unity of the working class may be held only in theory, whereas, in practice, the imprint of the capitalist commercial world is such as to affect even wide circles of the working class and its vanguard. Coercion must be imposed on the working class from outside, while self-discipline applies within the party.[7] Bukharin does not see that, by taking his own theory to its logical conclusion, the party is bound to become a new caste. The separation between ends and means is taken for granted. Bukharin admits that freedom of personality (*svoboda lichnosti*)[8] will exist only in the communist society. In the mean time:

From a broader point of view, i.e. from the point of view of a historical scale of greater scope, proletarian compulsion in all its forms, from executions to compulsory labour constitutes, as paradoxically as it may sound, a method of the formation of a new communist humanity from the human material of the capitalist epoch.[9]

How long the transition period will last, Bukharin does not say. The legacies of the former system which made it easier for the revolution to succeed – a weak state apparatus, the limited diffusion of capitalism, the agrarian economy and military defeat – turn out to be the major hindrances to its further development. In a tragic anticipation of the ideological grounds for the Stalinist policy of the thirties, Bukharin affirms that the large peasantry which helped the proletariat to gain victory is going to be the greatest obstacle in the period of construction of new productive relations.[10]

The ideological requisites of the new society are the only novelty of the revolution in the first phase. Bukharin maintains that the tasks of the proletariat in power are not dissimilar to the tasks of the bourgeoisie in the phase of expanded reproduction: frugality with all resources, and so systematic utilization and maximal centralization, since capitalism has already prepared the specific methods of labour organization.[11] Bukharin agrees with Kritsman's periodization of the revolutionary process into a sequence of ideological, political, economic and technical phases. This periodization puts the emphasis on the process of formation of the 'consciousness' of the working class as the future leading class. The revolution of technical methods, the change and rapid improvement of the rationalized social techniques, come later.[12] Conversely, Bukharin reproaches Tsyperovich, a prestigious Russian trade unionist, for having misunderstood the originality of the new system. Against Tsyperovich's focus on the continuity of the new organization with respect to the former bourgeois system, Bukharin stresses that 'our productive associations are a completely *different* organizational apparatus' and that 'they have grown up *on the skeleton* of the dead, decayed, disintegrated capitalist apparatus' (Bukharin's italics).[13] The problem of filiation of the new institutions from the former is not explored, because Bukharin considers the political and ideological dimension as the ultimate check on the correspondence of institutions to revolutionary goals. The mutual influence of structure and superstructure, which was a most powerful tool of analysis in Marxism, is lost completely in the post-revolutionary accounts of Soviet history.

Bukharin's approach was not an isolated one among the Bolsheviks. His essay was carefully read by Lenin, who praised several parts of it, including the chapter on extra-economic coercion.[14] Nor was any significant disagreement expressed on Bukharin's appraisal of war communism from the ranks of the communist leadership. In reality, Bukharin's conclusion on the need for coercion was the logical outcome of the rejection of the Marxian method of analysis as a useful tool for the understanding not only of the functioning of capitalism, but also of the transformation period following the revolution. Bukharin (but he was not the only one) interpreted the change of power as the crucial element of the new system, whereas Marx assumed the transformation of social relations, i.e. the change of power, to be the consequence of the development of the productive relations, i.e. the final phase of a process of growth. The extemporaneous nature of the Bolshevik Revolution with respect to the Marxian hypothesis did not bring about an explicit revision of Marxism, but rather an adaptation of it to the Russian reality. Any phenomenon which did not fit the model of a new society intended first of all as the negation of capitalism was interpreted as a residual of past behaviour, mentality and feelings. These residuals were not considered the expression of real relations, but mere appearances of them. The chapter on the economic categories of capitalism in the transition period is an instructive indication of such an approach to the Soviet economic system. This chapter was written in collaboration with Iu. Piatakov. The authors rejected the possibility of making use of the concepts of commodity, value, price and wage in the economy of the transition period. The argument was as follows: the commodity as a category presupposes the social division of labour, or its fragmentation, which imply the lack of a conscious regulator of the economic process. To the extent that the irrationality of the production process disappears, that is a conscious social regulator takes the place of spontaneity, the commodity loses its commodity character and turns into a product.[15] About value the authors argued in a different way. The law of value presumes a state of equilibrium. Value is the law of equilibrium of the 'anarcho-mercantile' system. Therefore, it is not adequate in the period of transition, when commodity production disappears and there is no equilibrium. It follows that price becomes a form deprived of content, a pseudo-form, totally detached from value. This fact is connected with the collapse of the monetary system. Money as such goes through a process of self-negation. Inflation and the distribution of money tokens independent of, and inversely proportionate to, product distribution are expressions of the annihilation of money, which ceases to be the general equivalent and becomes only a conventional and highly imperfect sign of product circulation. The wage keeps only its external, monetary form, which will disappear together with money. Since wage labour disappears through the transformation of the working class into the dominant class, workers will receive, not a wage, but an allocation proportional to the contribution of their work to society. Bukharin's conclusion is that as the natural (i.e. non-monetary) system of economic relations grows, the corresponding ideological categories will also explode and it will become necessary to go over to a natural economic type of reasoning.[16]

Bukharin offers a rationalization of the economic organization of war communism, but not a convincing one. No hint is given about the new rules or regulators which society has to employ to get things done. He mentions the conscious social regulator taking the place of the anarchy of the market, a sort of planning board, but no attention is paid to the criteria by which production, supply and distribution should be regulated to satisfy the needs of society.

In the postscript to the German edition of his book, Bukharin declared that he had not been writing an economic history of Soviet Russia, but a general theory of the transition period. Therefore the principles stated in the *Ekonomika* did not need to be revised in the light of the new economic policy undertaken after war communism. 'I openly admit (said Bukharin in polemics against German Social Democracy) objectively speaking, the inevitably destructive effect of the revolution as such.'[17] The central point of Bukharin's essay was, in fact, the 'negation' side of the revolution. However, evidence for this had been abundantly drawn from the Soviet experience, the generalization of which could not but provide a very strange model of the first phase of the revolution. The postscript, written in December 1921, reduced the effective significance of Bukharin's essay. When he wrote the *Ekonomika*, Bukharin believed that the phase of transition represented by war communism was going to last, with all its implications in the economic field, until the world revolution put an end to the fundamental task of repression of the bourgeoisie. Only then would 'the externally coercive norms' become extinct.[18]

Bukharin's message went beyond war communism. The cold portrait of a society based on coercion, the only dynamic force in the transition phase,[19] was the definite legacy that war communism impressed on the theoreticians of the new society. An ideology which succeeded in embodying coercion as a means of development was going to provide the communist leadership with justification for all sorts of deviation from the original ideals.

Bukharin's *Ekonomika* does not say much about the criteria of economic organization, since the goal of the essay is to show the need for the suppression of all former categories and criteria of performance. A better source of information about the economic organization of war communism is Kritsman's *Geroicheskii period Velikoi Russkoi Revoliutsii*.[20] Kritsman, who was first the head of the chemical section, and then head of the Utilization Committee of VSNKh, the Supreme Council of the

National Economy, elaborated his essay as a challenge to Lenin's repudiation of the war economic organization at the Tenth Congress of the Russian Communist Party in March 1921. Lenin acknowledged that mistakes had been made in the economic programme, but argued that war had imposed its own necessity. War communism – said Lenin at the congress – was not a harmonious system.[21] Kritsman evoked, instead, a glorious image of the recent past. 'In reality, the so-called "war communism" has been the first great example of a proletarian–natural economy... *an experiment in the first steps of transition to socialism.*' Kritsman added that war communism was by no means an error made by a people or by a class, but 'though not clearly and with well known perversities, an *anticipation of the future*, a breaking through of this future into the present (now already gone), made possible thanks to the exceptional and specific conditions of development of the Russian Revolution'.[22] Kritsman singled out two peculiarities of the war communism system, the principle of collegiality and the principle of rationality. The multiform reality of war communism was forced into an all-encompassing synthesis. Forgetting the diffusion of one-man management in the militarized sector of industry, Kritsman affirmed that collegiality spread over all forms of the economy: in organization of management and labour remuneration, in collective supply and reward, in collective exchange between town and countryside. Neglecting the overlapping of institutions operating in the same field, which during war communism was also the outcome of rapid changes, Kritsman asserted that the rationale of war communism was a new principle of organization, by which 'what is necessary will be realized; what is not, will be abolished'.[23] In conformity with Bukharin's theory, Kritsman considered positive the tendency of the new system to abolish fetishistic relations, that is, the market, monetary and credit relations, a fact which went along with the formation of the natural economy.

Written when the first steps towards NEP had already been made, Kritsman's book was an apologia on behalf of those who had given their devotion to the revolutionary drive. Kritsman's account of the war communist organization, highly commendable as it is for the amount of data and information supplied, embodies the bias of any heroic chronicle which justifies the success of military operations fought in such a tough context that only self-denial and faith appear to be responsible for victory. The effort of rationalization is here the source of a voluntaristic approach to the origin of the Soviet system. This seems excessive, even taking into account the ideological drive of its protagonists. Signs of this approach may still be found in some later literature.[24] The party history of 1930 interpreted war communism as a system of measures directed toward the most rapid construction of socialism.²⁵ Its successor of 1938 still focused on the initiative of the leadership, though its goals were reshaped in a cruder way more consistent with the developments of the Stalinist regime; the Soviet leadership was determined from the beginning to implement a communist policy, identified with state control over production, distribution and trade with labour mobilization.²⁶ This approach ignores the conflictive nature of the transition from collective management to one-man management and the controversial nature of several decisions, such as the structure of the administration, labour conscription, the extension of nationalization and so forth.

The revision of the voluntaristic approach to the origin of the organization of the Soviet economy began in the late twenties. Emphasis began to be put on exogenous factors. The *Bol'shaia Sovetskaia Entsiklopediia* of 1928 presents war communism as a war economy employing centralization as a means of achieving military efficiency and gradually evolving under the constraints imposed by war.²⁷ Kritsman's approach is turned upside down. Kritsman emphasized the derivation of the political system from the economic system: the political system was organized after the economic system and, likewise, had been built upon a 'productive' principle.²⁸ The *Entsiklopediia* concludes that 'the historical meaning of war communism consists essentially in the fact that, by operating on the basis of military and political power, it mastered the economic basis'.²⁹ The food-procurement policy is considered a development of the Provisional Government's policy, which decreed the grain monopoly in 1917. The problem of control over distribution is indicated as the crux of economic policy in a context of falling output. The point is made that 'war communism' intended as a system never came fully to life, since sizeable amounts of commodities flowed through the channels of the black market, which the authorities tolerated.³⁰

The cooler perspective (from 1928) of the early days of the revolution, as compared with the passionate account of Kritsman, does provide a better framework for a critical evaluation of war communism. But some ideological factors, which were important in party circles, are not given appropriate weight. Nor does the neglect of the social pressures, which interposed definite obstacles of a political as well as a material nature with regard to the efforts of directing the economy from a single centre, seem justified. Excessive focus on necessity deprives history of its human dimensions; ideals, goals, mentality, and passions provided the grounds for what Lenin defined in March 1921 as the mistakes of war communism.

The tendency to confine the war communism experience to a mere military policy, justified exclusively by the exigencies of war, emerged fully in the historiography of the thirties. Lomakin identifies war communism with compulsion, the essence of which had been the extraction of the surplus and even part of the necessaries from the peasantry to finance war. Following Stalin's interpretation, Lomakin sharply rejects the thesis that elements of the war communism economy were present before the autumn of 1918, and identifies the Soviet of Workers' and Peasants' Defence as the institutional framework, created in November 1918 in connection with war, where the policy of war communism was originated.[31]

The Soviet interpretation of the necessary nature of war communism could and did find support in Lenin's words. In the margin of the plan of substitution a tax in kind for the surplus appropriation system, Lenin wrote 'difficult' (*trudno*)! This indicates that what Lenin said about the former economic policy at the Tenth Congress of the party was inspired by the necessity of finding a consensus for change in a hostile environment. It was Lenin who for the first time defined the economic organization of 1918–20 as 'war' communism, when he wrote the draft of his pamphlet 'The Tax in Kind'. By this device Lenin emphasized the transitory, military nature of the system, to justify the need for its transformation into '*proper* (Lenin's italics) socialist foundations'.[32] In 'The Tax in Kind' Lenin proposed the first 'necessity' interpretation of war communism:

...a peculiar war communism... was forced on us by extreme want, ruin and war... it was not, and could not be, a policy that corresponded to the economic tasks of the proletariat.

It was 'a makeshift', he concluded.[33] At the same time, at the Tenth Congress of the party, Lenin acknowledged that 'quite a few mistakes' had been made in carrying out the former policy.[34] Through this politically brilliant 'reconciliation of opposites', Lenin was able to strike simultaneously at the Mensheviks, Socialist-Revolutionaries and Kautskyists, and at the Workers' Opposition, against which most of his efforts were directed at the Party Congress.[35] If war communism had been necessary, it could not be mistaken. Vice versa, if mistakes had been made in the choice of policies, the chosen policies were not necessary, but on the contrary, perverse. Lenin laid the foundations for both interpretations of war communism. But the literature on war communism, particularly the Soviet literature, preferred to focus on emergency. This approach stimulates an excessive emphasis on the exogeneity of the factors which affected economic organization, and relegates to the role of accidents the elements which would help to clarify the motivations and goals of specific measures. The focus on the rationality of necessity lays the basis for an interpretation of facts according to the theory of 'deviation', which happens to be essential for absolving the decision-makers and isolating the allegedly guilty individual from the responsibility of his group. Furthermore, this approach presupposes the existence of a correct line, in spite of the deviations from it. Recent interpretations of the Stalinist period in Marxist literature show that this attitude towards history is not conducive to getting to the root of facts, and raises before the secular observer the spectre of dogmatism and the evil of metaphysical certainties capable of absolving any aberration.

The presumption that intentions were good and that the goals were just is implicit in most of the Soviet literature of the fifties, which looks for analogies between the economic policy of the first months of 1918 and NEP.[36]

Baevskii points out that facts like the efforts to restore the monetary power of the ruble in May 1918 by reducing the rate of currency emission, the use of fiscal policy, the policy of compromise with private commerce and concessions, and the leasing of the nationalized enterprises to their former owners, show that economic policy until June 1918 was on the lines of NEP.[37] He assumes that an economic programme existed, though not the one imposed by war. VSNKh was created to prepare the organization of the centralized and planned economy, and workers' control should have prepared the way for the later expropriation of private factories and plants. This peaceful programme was interrupted by the counter-revolution and was replaced by war communist policies, which otherwise would not have been inevitable.[38]

Baevskii mentions that the revolutionary destruction of the old discipline went on more successfully than the creation of a new one, but he ascribes this fact mainly to counter-revolution.[39] In this way, a further explanatory variable for the policy of coercion undertaken from the spring of 1918, i.e. what Kritsman called the 'proletarian anarchy', is sacrificed in favour of an apologetic attitude attributing to Lenin and the Bolshevik circles more authority and consensus than they in effect had. Analogous remarks can be applied to Gladkov's *Ocherki sovetskoi ekonomiki 1917–1920 gg*, which shares the idea that the economic policy was initially in the spirit of NEP.[40] The assertion of the existence of an economic plan to establish socialism rests on Lenin's *April Theses* of 1917, which contained a programme for the nationalization of the land and the banking system and also for the extension of workers' control over production.[41] The expropriation of the means of production is interpreted by Gladkov as a means of class struggle and as a prerequisite for state intervention in the economy. Workers' control is considered a step towards nationalization of industry and nothing more.[42] Gladkov disregards any evaluation of the role of factory-committees other than that of Lenin, both inside and outside the Bolshevik Party. This authorizes the false impression that there was a general consensus on the further development of such organs. In fact, the whole question of management was a burning question for the leadership after the seizure of power. Even in 1920, when one-man management had already taken the place of collective management in several undertakings, the collegiality principle in management found wide support among authoritative members of the party. The reduction of the role of factory-committees to a mere preparation for nationalization, i.e. their transitory character, implies the belief that the Bolsheviks were ready to undertake nationalization of industry at short notice. There is evidence, on the contrary, that until March 1918 the economic leadership was quite reluctant to extend the scope of state intervention. After the signing of the Brest–Litovsk Treaty, even Lenin, who had initially urged VSNKh to behave as the leading authority for industry and who had urged VSNKh's attention to his programme of nationalization of industry, did not hesitate to call for moderation in economic policy, damping down the excitement of the left wing of the party.

Overall, Gladkov's approach suffers from an unduly personalized interpretation of history, a fault which is common to a large part of the literature on Soviet Russia. An excessive belief in the foresight and degree of authority of Lenin does not help in understanding the economic developments. The role of other party members of recent or older formation should not be underestimated. By and large the moving balance of political forces conditioned Lenin's attitude toward economic problems, too, and did exert an impact on choices. It does not seem correct to isolate a historical period, when decisions are supposed to have followed a preconceived plan, from another period in which decisions are supposed to have been exogenously determined. A sharp line should not be traced to separate the time in which, according to most of the recent Soviet literature, the foundations of NEP were laid, from the time in which the economy of war communism was built in response to military necessities. This approach may lead to quite arbitrary conclusions, like those reached by Gladkov in a further essay, about an alleged plan of Lenin's for nationalization of the *whole wealth* (my italics) of the country, for which no evidence may be found before or after the revolution.[43] To avoid this bias, the chronology of economic policy is crucial in the evaluation of both subjective and objective factors.

Gradualness in the formation of the Soviet system has recently received attention in part of the literature on the subject. This approach, if accompanied by a correct appreciation of the conflicts which conditioned crucial decisions and affected their implementation, may in future give a better understanding of the peculiar form that the socialist ideal assumed at that time. Using this approach, Gimpel'son reaches the conclusion that the Bolshevik Party worked out only general principles about the soviets, without producing a concrete scheme of organization.[44] The one-party organization developed only gradually as a consequence of the conflicting roles that other parties and factions assumed during civil war.[45] Gimpel'son's essay on the policy of war communism ridicules the historiography which 'juggling in the term "communism", strives to exhibit the civil war organization as the image of a Soviet experiment in a communist economy'.[46] Gimpel'son presents the chronological escalation and partial implementation of the economic policy of war communism as evidence for the dependence of the selected alternatives on the needs of war. Destruction and disorganization are not ascribed to such measures.

Gimpel'son offers several arguments in support of his thesis. The surplus-appropriation system was never so all-embracing as to exclude the possibility that many products could be sold freely in the market. In several cases the government declared inadmissible arbitrary requisition by local organs. Only in 1920 was surplus-appropriation extended to the consuming provinces and to all necessities. Nationalization was also gradual. Private enterprises were excluded from nationalization by the April 1919 decree which limited nationalization to cases decided by the Presidium of VSNKh. Only in September 1920 was the usual criterion for nationalization – the technical importance of enterprises expressed by the number of workers per prime mover – modified in favour of social criteria, i.e. the distinction between undertakings employing wage labour and household handicrafts.[47]

These arguments are appreciable. However, the conclusions are not quite satisfactory. Although a great deal of expediency can be detected in the war communism experience, the ideological framework of the leadership also imposed a certain logic. There were some constants, like centralization of economic decisions, collective commodity-exchange, and the ability to make use of financial means of control, which preceded the major involvement in war and prepared the way for some later economic developments. On the other hand, the argument that war communism never really came to life[48] claims too much. If legislation ran far ahead of implementation, it is valid to ask whether the communist ideology, affected also by war, urged for more rapid changes in the economic organization than were objectively possible given the overall situation. On the whole, Gimpel'son provides a stimulating approach to the nature and goals of war communism, to the extent of questioning the credibility of war 'communism' itself as a coherent system. The earliest Soviet accounts of the span of time between November 1917 and June 1918 repeatedly stressed the anarchical development of the first economic measures, the punitive character of nationalization, and the lack of an economic plan. Only later did Soviet literature try to emphasize facts which could provide evidence for an initial coherent programme of construction of socialism. For much of the time, war communism also evolved through the trial and error adoption of workable measures, whose implementation could not be centrally controlled.

The anarchical developments of the first months are stressed in an original essay by Nasyrin, whose approach has been coolly received by the official historiographers. Among the numerous Soviet studies on this subject, Nasyrin's thesis remains an isolated attempt to explore the disruptive effects of the revolution in connection with the effective capacity of the Bolshevik leadership to master them. Nasyrin recalls that the factory–shop committees were not under the full control of the Bolsheviks, but in great part were also under the influence of Mensheviks and Socialist-Revolutionaries, both before and after the revolution.[49] Nasyrin challenges the official approach represented by Gladkov, both on the goals attributed to the October Revolution platform and on the reasons for nationalization. The Bolshevik platform at the Sixth Congress of Soviets concerned only the nationalization of banks and syndicates (and not of large-scale industry). Nasyrin blames Gladkov for mixing different notions when the latter affirms that the early economic measures were directed towards transforming private ownership of the means of production into collective ownership.[50] The acceleration of nationalization occurred as a response to sabotage and to the aggression of German imperialism – argues Nasyrin against Gladkov's version that the two factors hampered this policy.[51] Nasyrin makes three points: first, for the Bolsheviks, workers' control represented a peculiar form of state capitalism; second, for Lenin, state capitalism consisted not only in leasing factories to private managers and inviting foreign concessionaires, but also in accounting and control following the example of capitalism; third, the principle of NEP was affirmed as early as 1918. Nasyrin's conclusion is that elements of socialism were introduced gradually and that for some time the question of the forms of property in the means of production was not confronted. The Soviet Republic was called socialist because Soviet power directed the country on to the path of socialism, making use for this purpose of capitalist economic forms.[52] The main shortcoming of Nasyrin's essay is that it challenges the official historiographers on the basis of poor documentation, almost exclusively derived from Lenin's works. This confines Nasyrin's version to the field of suggestive hypotheses, rather than enabling it to breach the compact wall of orthodoxy.

The only approach to the Bolshevik policy from the point of view of the eventual *mistakes* committed on the morrow of the revolution is R. Medvedev's. Medvedev affirms that in the spring of 1918, inebriated by the success of the first reforms, the Bolsheviks went ahead with more reforms and decrees than the political, social and economic reality could bear.[53] The most serious mistakes were committed in the commodity exchange policy with the peasantry. According to Medvedev, the food situation was not so catastrophic as to demand special measures. A policy such as that undertaken in 1921 would have been better suited to face the problem.[54] Wrong policies were inspired by sectarianism and dogmatism: 'Marxists in general and the Bolsheviks in particular held the never demonstrated belief that socialism excluded commercial production, purchase, selling, money, etc.'[55] A further reproach is that of lack of realism. 'The Bolsheviks should not have ignored the fact that masses adopt in the first place the slogans which respond to their interests', and the peasants' interest was in free trade.[56] According to Medvedev the bases of war communism were laid in the spring of 1918, not only through the system of grain requisition, but also through state intervention in enterprises, starting from the most important ones and ending with small medium undertakings. State intervention in industry was the consequence of the adoption of forced commodity exchange.[57] Medvedev's conclusion is that 'the historical responsibility for civil war falls not only on the Russian counter-revolution and on intervention, but on the Bolsheviks themselves who, through a premature introduction of socialism, raised against themselves a large part of the population'.[58] It is unfortunate that Medvedev, even in a further contribution on the same subject, does not provide sufficient evidence for his very strong assertions.[59] His suggestions, however, in particular the focus on the Bolshevik mistakes that Lenin denounced in March 1921 without making them explicit, are a very important contribution to an original approach to Soviet history, which may give very fruitful results if additional evidence is provided for the understanding of the early Bolshevik economic and social policy.

1.3 WESTERN LITERATURE

Western literature, though on the whole more critical of the war communism experience than its Soviet counterpart, also shows two different approaches. Some authors prefer to focus on ideological motivations; others stress the emergency element.

Leites, in a work of 1922, recalls that the real programme for the reorganization of economic life was contained in the fifth chapter of the Declaration of the Rights of the Toiling and Exploited Peoples. The sections referred to by the author concern the socialization of land, the abolition of private property, the introduction of workmen's control and the establishment of a Supreme Economic Council. The Declaration did not mention any distribution policy, any specific organization of management or any monetary policy. Nevertheless, it is on the basis of the points mentioned that Leites attributes to the Bolshevik doctrine, as well as to the inconsistencies of their policy, the economic failure of war communism.[60]

A similar impatience in characterizing the Bolsheviks as doctrinaires is manifested by Lawton, who devotes a whole chapter to theories and tactics[61] without ever referring to dates, or to the public to which the speeches or writings were addressed. Lawton refers to 'State and Revolution' as if to the political programme of the Bolsheviks, but even in so doing he does not question the reasons for nationalization, abolition of commercial secrecy, etc. So he concludes that: 'as fast as they could be committed to paper, all reforms of which the Bolsheviks had dreamt in exile were translated into decrees'.[62] The proof of the fanaticism of the Bolsheviks is, for Lawton, that their economic measures were adopted in the midst of the chaos arising from the civil war. As later became a ritual for many scholars, the charge of fanaticism is backed by reference to the famous passage in 'State and Revolution' where Lenin claims that the operations of accounting and control will become so simple that they could be performed by anybody.[63]

Chamberlin, who is more inclined to interpret the policy of war communism as an outcome of the war, defines it as 'a compound of war emergency and socialist dogmatism'.[64] His approach seems more appropriate; however, for the charge of dogmatism no satisfactory evidence is adduced, apart from a short uncritical reference to Larin's and Preobrazhenskii's articles at the end of 1920 on the abolition of money as a means of exchange.

Larin's role in the shaping of economic organization is stressed by Wiles. This author accepts the idea of a model of war communism shaped by the intentions of the most extreme members of the party, namely Larin and Kritsman. The model was a rigidly centralized economy, which represented, according to Wiles, the embodiment of the dreams of a certain kind of communist. All choices were to be made by the centre, and central power had to penetrate everywhere.[65] This interpretation may be attractive, but it takes for granted the rationalization of war communism presented by some leading protagonists of the revolution, while ignoring the unlinear evolution of the economic policy after the seizure of power and the ardent debates and contrasts among the Bolsheviks which accompanied its course.

A recent endeavour to identify war communism with a premeditated policy conceived by Lenin has been made by Roberts. He rescues the old interpretation, but goes even further in asserting the existence before war communism of the clearly defined body of economic policy. He does not attempt, however, to examine the events under consideration in relation to their material and mental environment to see whether they were simply ideas or real facts. The writings of Lenin are carefully examined and all sentences containing a formal connection with the economic measures of war communism are cited as proofs of Roberts' hypothesis.[66] However, the points raised by Roberts belonged to the Marxist tradition in general and were already clearly defined in the *Communist Manifesto* of 1848.[67] Roberts does not pay attention to the specific connotations of the measures advocated and to their timing. He also seems to ignore the role of the other Bolshevik leaders in shaping Soviet institutions and policies.

A more interesting approach to the problem of a critical interpretation of the Marxist literature in relation to the Russian Revolution is furnished by Barrington Moore Jr. Moore rejects the type of approach focusing on the purely political and demagogical aspects of Lenin's writing and suggests a historical approach, within a broad acceptance of Marxist ideology, which could allow an analysis of the development at any point of time of Lenin's theory.[68] However, this does not eliminate the ambiguity stemming from the undifferentiated assessment of literature written for different purposes, but which appeared at the same time. The problem of reconciling conflicting statements on the organization of the proletariat and the peasantry in communes versus centralization and planning, or wage differentiation versus the egalitarian schemes of 'State and Revolution', requires that an attempt is made to distinguish between theory and politics, aspirations and immediate objectives, ideology and tactics.

Meyer, on the other hand, fails to single out these apparent contradictions in his chapter on the Leninist state in theory and practice, where he tries to follow the coherence of Lenin's thought, distinguishing three periods after the October Revolution in which Lenin's mood and activity took different aspects.[69] But this search for historical coherence which is not coupled with a critical analysis of the two levels of activity, theory and practice, between which Lenin easily moved, leads to further, rather unconvincing hypotheses about errors in strategy, which Lenin seemingly committed in the belief that 'communism was just around the corner'.[70]

Nove's opinion is that the Bolsheviks did not have any idea what to do after seizing power. He correctly distinguishes between the presence of strong statements on principles and the absence of ideas and methods concerning the actual management of industry. His review of Lenin's ideas on economic organization indicates that some of the writings of Lenin were demagogical, whereas others contained some practical programmes.[71] Nove remarks that nationalization did not mean to Lenin more than 'a control over the syndicates, rather than expropriation'. Overall, Lenin is depicted as a fairly realistic political figure, while charges of utopianism, anarcho-syndicalism, fanaticism and dogmatism are reserved for other members of the party, whose role and doctrines are, however, not explored. The comparative approach that Nove generally has toward the policies of the Soviet Union leads him to point out the similarity between some Bolshevik policies and some measures taken in analogous circumstances by other countries. This approach helps to de-mystify in part the epic or terrifying accounts presented in some of the literature. Nove acknowledges the existence of a process of interaction between reality and ideas,[72] but this insight gets somewhat lost in the subsequent analysis. Emphasizing the role of ideology in the process that led to a natural economy, he writes: 'This entire process reached its apogee at the end of 1920 and was undoubtedly deeply influenced by the ideology which was so widespread among the party during the period of war communism.'[73] This comment deserves a deeper analysis than is presented by Nove. The theorizing of Bukharin in 1920 may not be useful as a proof that ideology influenced the process of naturalization of the economy, rather than vice versa. Nove's conclusion that war communism was a response to war emergency and collapse, and at the same time an all-out attempt to leap into socialism, is, however, an attractive hypothesis to test.

M. Dobb and E.H. Carr consider war communism as the product of an emergency situation and tend to disregard the adventurous literature of 1920 as a by-product of the situation itself or as later rationalization. Dobb mentions that the allegations of utopianism were to a certain extent supported by the actions and expressed opinions of some Bolsheviks in those years. A distinction is made between Lenin and the group of leftists, Preobrazhenskii, Larin and Bukharin, whom Dobb calls the 'leftist fancy'. Around the end of 1920 the leftists began to regard war communism as a partial embodiment of their ideals.[74] Although he claims that con-tradictions and conflicts existed between the centralized administration and the functioning of the whole economic apparatus, as well as between Soviet institutions in general,[75] Dobb does not attempt an adequate explanation of the inconsistency between aims and poor implementation, nor does he provide satisfactory answers to the very crucial questions concerning the maintenance of the war communist organization after the end of civil war and the sudden change in policy in early 1921. Carr also distinguishes two schools of thought inside the party with respect to war communism.[76] One considered it as a series of steps correctly conceived though unduly hastened as a result of the civil war. The other saw it not as an advance on the road to socialism, but as a result of emergency. Carr recalls that Lenin himself was not always consistent in his evaluation of war communism. However, while Dobb finds it appropriate not to go further into the reasons for the utopianism within the left, considering it somewhat like an aberration within the party, Carr gives a psychological explanation, which is of interest and could be elaborated upon. Referring to *The ABC of Communism*, written by Preobrazhenskii and Bukharin as a commentary on the new Party Programme of March 1919, Carr writes: 'It was a period during which the energies of politicians and administrators were absorbed by the civil war and by problems of survival ... Such periods commonly inspire, side by side with the harsh realism of the current experience, and by way of compensation for it, far ranging vision of a future social order to be attained through the present turmoil of exertion and suffering, visions embodying the ideals for which the struggle is being waged.'[77] Elsewhere Carr rejects the hypothesis that war communism ended up as a natural economy because it embodied the Marxist doctrine of the disappearance of money in the future communist society. Carr uses two arguments against this view. First, he analyses many statements from Lenin to Bukharin and Preobrazhenskii during the crucial years, stressing the need for money in the transition period. Second, in so far as contrary statements were made, for example by Zinoviev, Carr is careful to stress in which circumstances and to whom the statements were made, and finally he concludes that they do not prove that the policy of abolition of money was initially desired.[78] However, he tends to neglect the impact that the constant pursuit of central control over trade and distribution may have had on the progressive demonetization of the economy. Carr suggests that civil war, more than industrial administration, was responsible for increasing disorganization.[79] He also suggests that the centralized control of industry was a practicable proposition in the summer of 1919 when the territory of the RSFSR had shrunk to the size of the ancient Muscovy. Carr's conclusion is that the cause of the industrial collapse was due 'not so much to the breakdown of industry as to the failure to evolve any agricultural policy capable of obtaining from the peasants food surpluses adequate to feed the cities and factories'.[80]

Both Dobb and Carr seem to remain prisoners of the axiom that the economic organization under war communism responded, in fact, to the needs of war; therefore, they are bound to conclude that war communism could not outlast the war period. Alternatives which were discussed before and during war communism, thus, do not receive adequate attention.

Some authors, like Baykov,[81] on the contrary, blame overcentralization for the poor performance of industry, transport and productivity; while others, like Prokopovitch,[82] ascribe the breakdown of the economy to the radical principles which inspired Soviet policy. Both approaches seem to take for granted that the performance of the economy depended, in fact, on the implementation of a set of coherent, though unsuitable, policies. An isolated voice is Zagorsky's, who singles out the contradictions between the Bolshevik policy and the organic social process which was taking place in the country in spite of it. He defines the Soviet reforms as paper reforms, but fails to provide adequate evidence for the very strong assertion that war communism was 'externally communist, internally capitalist'.[83] Mention must be made of Bettelheim's recent contribution on the development and fate of war communism, although the subject is tackled merely from the viewpoint of the ideological foundations of Bolshevism. Bettelheim believes that the policy of war communism was justified by war,[84] and ascribes to it the victory of the revolution, without providing any evidence for this assertion. Nonetheless, more than any other scholar, he dwells on the nature of the mistakes which were made at that time. Briefly dismissing what he defines as 'practical mistakes', on the ground that no matter who implemented the Bolshevik political directives, the latter were, indeed, the only guidelines for action, Bettelheim chooses to focus on the dominant 'ideological and political' aspects of such mistakes. He concludes, then, that 'what was mistaken was to consider that measures of state coercion could be substituted for action by the masses and for the revolutionary transformation of ideological relations in the struggle for a radical transformation of production relations'.[85] Unfortunately, no facts are offered in support of this bold conclusion, while the superficial dismissal of the mistakes made in implementation deprives his comments of any real basis for serious consideration and confines the possible diagnoses to the nebulous realm of endless ideological disputes on the true essence of Marxism.

1.4 A HUNGARIAN VIEW

The exploration of the ideological world of war communism has recently stimulated another, very interesting, endeavour to define the principles and the theoretical roots of the initial Soviet experience.[86] East European socialist countries, and particularly Hungary, are nowadays seeking a new path of socialist economic development, giving an important role to the market. The first economic model of socialism abolished market relations. Moving from this perspective, Szamuely raises the following questions: first, was war communism really brought about by the requirements of the war economy alone, as most of the literature maintains? Second, did war communism have an internal logic?

The author gives an affirmative answer to the second question and an articulate, substantially negative, answer to the first question, which is the core of his work. Szamuely outlines five principles of war communism: maximum extension of state ownership; forced allocation of labour; far-reaching central management of economic activity; class and social principles of distribution; and naturalization of economic life.[87] He does not enquire into the circumstances in which these principles were affirmed and the degree to which they were implemented. However, he recalls that 'the state deliberately aimed at eliminating every element of market relations from economic activity', but all efforts ended up in the formation of an illegal market economy. The 'defetishization' of economic life, argues Szamuely, did affect, but superficially, the sphere of distribution as well as that of production. Though supply was supposed to be channelled to the state sector without monetary transactions, increasing rates of currency emission were used to cover the expenses of the legally non-existent free market. In spite of the gap between principles and implementation, Szamuely asserts that there was a logic to the war communism system,[88] i.e. that this experience was not only due to war, but to the theories and aims of the protagonists. The features of war communism provide the basis for an interesting enquiry into their ideological foundations.

Szamuely affirms that some theoretical antecedents of the war communist ideology can be found in Marx and Engels. From scattered observations it would be possible to argue that they believed in the central allocation of means of production, labour and consumer goods in natural form within the economic organization of socialism. But the responsibility for driving the theory to absurd conclusions, like the immediate liquidation of commercial exchange and monetary economy, falls, according to Szamuely, on the leaders of German Social Democracy, particularly on Kautsky. Kautsky affirmed the incompatibility of commodity production with socialism, the necessity of central control and a self-sufficient economy and of natural economic relations even in the transition period.[89] Since these features occurred partly as a consequence of the war economy, the Bolsheviks in 1920 believed that a communist economy was taking shape precisely because it manifested some similarities with Kautsky's formulation of the socialist economic system. Szamuely asserts that Bukharin's *Ekonomika perekhodnogo perioda* well represented the prevailing ideas of Russian and foreign communists at that time.[90] Bukharin put forward two essential criteria of organization: first, naturalized (i.e. non-monetary) relations; second, state coercion. On the basis of such criteria, a specific economic model was outlined which, argues Szamuely, was not considered as temporary by its ideologues.[91]

Szamuely also rejects the theory that the foundations of NEP were already set in 1918, for which support is usually sought in Lenin's works on 'state capitalism'. Szamuely argues that, even taking into account that Lenin's approach to economic problems changed over time, his theoretical conception could not be distinguished from the basic tenets of the ideology of war communism. Only his practical approach came into sharp conflict with the later ideologues of war communism in relation to quite a few problems.[92]

Szamuely's book offers an extremely important contribution to the evaluation of the sources, principles and ideological influence of war communism, both for the questions raised and for the evidence, documents and materials provided in support of a quite original approach to the subject. The chronology of events, however, which a model-orientated approach such as Szamuely's is bound to disregard, cannot be avoided if one tries to discriminate between choices which were more affected by ideological bias and those which were determined by emergency or the political appreciation of emergency, between the influence of legacies and the pressure for change, between immediate aims and programmes of gradual organization.

1.5 THE PURPOSE OF THE WORK

The survey of the main literature on war communism indicates the major questions which remain unanswered and which justify the present attempt to give order and an interpretation to the available material. A first question, the importance of which is related not only to the emergence of the new Soviet system, but also to the nature of change from a capitalist into a socialist system in general, concerns the motivations and real pressures for change which characterized the shaping of the economy of war communism. This question can be answered by examining both decisions and the context in which they were adopted. There are decisions that the Bolsheviks took at different moments, which may be explained without recourse to abstract principles. In some fields, decisions responded to long-standing aims, but were also conditioned by current circumstances. In other fields, the Bolshevik policy may have been inspired by ideological bias as well as by erroneous evaluations of political and economic factors. Moreover, some goals were proclaimed, but they were not really pursued. A further incentive to explore in detail the post-revolutionary policies arises from the conviction that the protagonists were, indeed, ideologically motivated, but had different cultural and social backgrounds which affected their approach to economic policy and administration, in which most of them lacked any experience. When confronted with actual problems, the Bolsheviks often disagreed among themselves as to the adoption of the most suitable policies. Compromises on acceptable options were often sought, despite the fact that emergency dictated rapid decisions. Ideology acted as a filter for acceptable alternatives, but not as a blind prescription of necessary measures. Some choices, which may be referred to a broader category of coercion, which ideology did not reject, but did not prescribe either, were rationalized in ideological terms by a few Bolsheviks, passionately opposed by others and opportunistically ignored by some. The chronology of the military situation, which affected the size of the territory under Soviet rule and compelled the leadership rapidly to review and reshape the original programmes, and to resort increasingly to means of compulsion and political control, cannot be ignored. Nor should the influence of past history be disregarded in so far as the continuity in institutional as well as mental frameworks may have been stronger than ingenuity and the desire for innovation.

Another, but equally important, question to be illuminated concerns the degree of correspondence between legislation and its implementation, i.e. the effectiveness of the decrees and instructions in achieving their aims in the light of both the changing nature of the aims themselves and the play of conflicting forces that preceded and followed the enacted legislation.

It is often implicitly assumed that whatever happened under war communism was due to the enforcement of the Bolshevik legislation. This has led many scholars to emphasize dogmatism as an essential component of war communism and to disregard the gap between legislative activity, which was feverish at that time, and its implementation. The same approach has led, on the other hand, to neglect of the very relevance of those radical choices, which, in fact, could not be implemented because they were rejected as incompatible implantations into a socio-economic context which was not ready or not capable of assimilating them, but which remained potential policy options for the future.

This book tries to pay both legislation and practical policies the attention they deserve, in order to lay down some basic grounds for an assessment of the conditions and limits not only of the nature, but also of the possibility, of revolutionary change of an economic system in general.

Following the outlined approach, the book examines the economic situation of production and distribution, taking into account the existing pre-requisites for the transformation of the economic system, the origin and quality of decision-making in each field, as well as their outcomes. Chronology is paid particularly close attention in fields where it would be otherwise difficult, if not impossible, to distinguish immediate aims from long-standing goals, in order to check the consistency of the adopted policies. Institutional innovations, which are the main concern of the book are interpreted not only as empirical, but also as mental frameworks. The path to innovation is analysed through the main features of nationalization, management, financial policy, industrial organization, planning and food procurement policy.

Some readers may find inconvenient the fact that, interrupting a well-established tradition, the author provides no definition of war communism. An explanation is due for what could be interpreted as a lack of boldness. The belief acquired by the author is that no definition can encompass in a meaningful way the main attributes of the revolutionary phase of a transition from one system into another which aims at its negation, without compromising a genuine full description. Any definition focusing on the novelty introduced into a system which undergoes a revolutionary change would necessarily distort its image, since it would disregard the very nature of the negation that the revolution embodies, while trying to model a false taxonomic consistency from that compound of inherited and vital institutions and emerging, but often empty, structures which characterizes the destructive and substantially incoherent phase inherent in any abrupt change forced upon society.

NOTES

1 All quotations are taken from the English translation: N. Bukharin, *The Economics of the Transformation Period, with Lenin's Remarks*, New York, 1971, p. 131.
2 S.F. Cohen, *Bukharin and the Bolshevik Revolution*, Oxford, 1980, p. 94.
3 C. Bettelheim, *Class Struggles in the USSR, First Period: 1917–1923*, Brighton, 1976, p. 204, n31.
4 Bukharin, p. 75.
5 *Ibid.*, p. 131.
6 *Ibid.*, p. 145.

7 *Ibid.*, p. 156.
8 *Ibid.*, p. 157.
9 *Ibid.*, p. 160.
10 *Ibid.*, p. 166.
11 *Ibid.*, p. 67.
12 *Ibid.*, pp. 70–71.
13 *Ibid.*, p. 78 and pp. 184–5, n 64.
14 *Leninskii sbornik*, vol. 11, pp. 348–403. Only Olminskii, one of the oldest members of the Moscow executive committee, accused Bukharin of having abandoned the Marxist political economy for the 'Bukharinist method of penal servitude and shooting' (quoted by S.F. Cohen, p. 96.)
15 Bukharin, p. 145.
16 *Ibid.*, p. 147.
17 *Ibid.*, p. 203.
18 *Ibid.*, p. 161.
19 In Bukharin's essay there is not 'the faintest allusion to, or mention of, the material interest of workers in building socialism', as pointed out by L. Szamuely, *First Models of the Socialist Economic Systems, Principles and Theories*, Budapest, 1974, p. 39.
20 L. Kritsman, *Geroicheskii period Velikoi Russkoi Revoliutsii*, Moscow (no date, probably 1924).
21 V.I. Lenin, *Collected Works*, 4th edn., London, 45 vols., 1964–70, vol. 32, 1965, pp. 233–4.
22 Kritsman, p. 75.
23 *Ibid.*, pp. 81–2.
24 See, for instance, the critical appraisal of war communism by L.N. Iurovskii, *Denezhnaia politika Sovetskoi Vlasti (1917–1927)*, Moscow, 1928, pp. 47–63.
25 *Istoriia VKP (b)*, pod red. Iaroslavskogo, Moscow, 1930, p. 399.
26 *Istoriia VKP (b), kratkii kurs*, Moscow, 1938, p. 219.
27 *Bolshaia Sovetskaia Entsiklopediia*, vol. 12, Moscow, 1928. The section 'War communism' is signed by Aukhenbakh.
28 Kritsman, p. 76.
29 *Bol'shaia Sovetskaia Entsiklopediia*, p. 376
30 *Ibid.*, p. 375.
31 A. Lomakin, 'Ob osnovnykh etapakh istorii SSSR (1917–1934)', *Vestnik kommunisticheskoi akademii*, 1934, nos. 5–6, 70–81.
32 Lenin, *Collected Works*, vol. 32, p. 321. 'The draft of The Tax in Kind' was written between March and April 1921.
33 Lenin, *Collected Works*, vol. 32, pp. 342–3. 'The Tax in Kind' was published as a pamphlet in May 1921.
34 Lenin, *Collected Works*, vol. 32, p. 168 ('Speech at the Opening of the X Congress of the Party, March 8, 1921'). Soviet historiography nowadays shows a broader appreciation of archival documents and the writings of the early years of the revolution: cf. T.A. Ignatenko, *Sovetskaia istoriografiia rabochego kontrolia i natsionalizatsii promyshlennosti v SSSR (1917–67)*, Moscow, 1971.
35 Lenin, *Collected Works*, vol. 32, pp. 192–207.
36 On this thesis, see the survey of current Soviet literature by V.E. Iustuzov, 'K voprosu o preemstvennosti novoi ekonomicheskoi politiki i ekonomicheskoi politiki vesny 1918 g.', in *Problemy istoriografii i istochnikovedeniia istorii KPSS*,

vyp. 1, Izd. Leningrad, 1971, pp. 107–20.

37 D.A. Baevskii, *Ocherki po istorii khoziaistvennogo stroitel'stva perioda grazhdanskoi voiny*, Moscow, 1957, pp. 20–3.

38 *Ibid.*, pp. 12–14, 24.

39 *Ibid.*, p. 15.

40 I.A. Gladkov, *Ocherki Sovetskoi ekonomiki 1917–1920 gg*, Moscow, 1956, p. 140.

41 *Ibid.*, p. 19.

42 *Ibid.*, pp. 22, 36, 55–6.

43 I.A. Gladkov, 'Leninskie printsipy rukovodstva sotsialisticheskoi ekonomiki', *Voprosy istorii KPSS*, no. 3, 1969, 48.

44 E.G. Gimpel'son, 'Kak slozhilas Sovetskaia forma proletarskogo gosudarstva', *Voprosy istorii*, no. 9, 1967, 14–15.

45 *Ibid.*, p. 24

46 E.G. Gimpel'son, 'O politike voennogo kommunizma', *Voprosy istorii*, no. 5, 1963, 36; the same approach is pursued in Gimpel'son's *Velikii Oktiabr' i stanovlenie Sovetskoi sistemy upravleniia narodnym khoziaistvom (Noiabr 1917–1920 gg)*, Moscow, 1977 and '*Voennyi kommunizm*', *politika, praktika, ideologiia*, Moscow, 1973.

47 *Ibid.*, pp. 38–9.

48 *Ibid.*, pp. 43–4.

49 V.P. Nasyrin, 'O nekotorykh voprosakh sotsialisticheskogo preobrazovaniia promyshlennosti v SSSR', *Voprosy istorii*, no. 5, 1956, 91.

50 I.A. Gladkov, *Ocherki Sovetskoi ekonomiki 1917–1920 gg*, Moscow, 1956, p. 20.

51 I.A. Gladkov, *Ocherki Sovetskoi ekonomiki*, 1956, p. 76 and *Ocherki stroitel'stva Sovetskogo planovogo khoziaistva v 1917–1918 gg*, Moscow, 1950, p. 121.

52 Nasyrin, p. 99.

53 R. Medvedev, *La Révolution d'Octobre était-elle inéluctable?* Paris, 1976, pp. 117–18.

54 *Ibid.*, pp. 122–3, 131.

55 *Ibid.*, p. 122.

56 *Ibid.*, p. 127.

57 *Ibid.*, pp. 128–31.

58 *Ibid.*, p. 134.

59 R. Medvedev, *Dopo la Rivoluzione*, Roma, 1978, pp. 85–92.

60 K. Leites, *Recent Economic Development in Russia*, Oxford, 1922, pp. 80, 63–128.

61 L. Lawton, *An Economic History of Soviet Russia*, London, 1928, pp. 31–5.

62 *Ibid.*, p. 78.

63 *Ibid.*, p. 104.

64 W.H. Chamberlin, *The Russian Revolution*, New York, 1935, p. 96.

65 P. Wiles, *The Political Economy of Communism*, Oxford, 1962, p. 30.

66 P.C. Roberts, *Alienation and the Soviet Economy*, Albuquerque, *NM*, 1971, pp. 20–47.

67 K. Marx and F. Engels, *Selected Works*, vol. 1, Moscow, 1962, p. 53.

68 B. Moore Jr, *Soviet Politics: The Dilemma of Power*, New York, 1965, p. 39.

69 A. Meyer, *Leninism*, Cambridge, Mass., 1957, pp. 185–216.

70 *Ibid.*, p. 194. An analogous approach is R.V. Daniels' ('The State and Revolution: a Case Study in the Genesis and Transformation of Communist Ideology', *The American Slavic and East European Review*, vol. 12, February 1953, 22, 24) who defines Lenin's essay as a monument to its author's intellectual

deviation during the year of the 1917 Revolution and 'an aberration'.

71 A. Nove, *An Economic History of the USSR*, Harmondsworth, 1969, pp. 40–5.
72 *Ibid.*, pp. 47–8.
73 *Ibid.*, p. 64.
74 M. Dobb, *Soviet Economic Development after 1917*, London, 1951, p. 122.
75 *Ibid.*, pp. 106–24.
76 E.H. Carr, *The Bolshevik Revolution, 1917–1923*, 3 vols., London, 1952, vol. 2, pp. 274–5.
77 E.H. Carr, *The October Revolution*, New York, 1971, p. 84.
78 Carr, *The Bolshevik Revolution*, vol. 2, pp. 260–8.
79 *Ibid.*, vol. 2, pp. 179–80.
80 *Ibid.*, vol. 2, pp. 197–8.
81 A. Baykov, *The Development of the Soviet Economic System*, Cambridge, 1946, p. 47.
82 S.N. Prokopovitch, *The Economic Condition of Soviet Russia*, London, 1924, pp. 59–61.
83 S. Zagorsky, *La République des Soviets*; Bilan économique, Paris, 1921, pp. 313–14, 317.
84 Bettelheim, p. 455.
85 *Ibid.*, pp. 458–9.
86 Szamuely's study.
87 *Ibid.*, pp. 10–22.
88 *Ibid.*, p. 22.
89 *Ibid.*, pp. 24–8.
90 *Ibid.*, p. 29.
91 *Ibid.*, p. 44.
92 *Ibid.*, p. 62.

2

Nationalization of industry

2.1 THE APPROACH TO NATIONALIZATION
AND STATE CONTROL

Marxist literature has generally focused on the expropriation of the means of production as a decisive step towards socialism. The aim of abolishing private property, however, did not in itself provide positive indications regarding the operation of the new institutions. Nor did Marxist literature ever systematically examine the possible alternatives. This neglect may be ascribed to the composite nature of Marxism: on the one side, its attachment to an empirical approach to economic problems; on the other, a deep-rooted faith in the creative imagination of the proletariat. The first aspect was responsible for a sort of self-censorship in the face of alternatives of a speculative nature. The second aspect, rooted in the tradition of humanitarian socialism, provided an incentive to postpone the solution of concrete problems to a point at which the liberated proletariat would display its full potential in organizing a more just society. The basic tenet of the Marxian analysis – the necessary transition from one mode of production to a higher one, once the former had achieved its full development – provided the theoretical framework for faith in an inevitably more progressive society together with an uncritical acceptance of the neutrality of technology.

Of the few hints given by Marx on the possible form of the new mode of production, some can be derived *a contrario* from the criticism of capitalism and others from the prescriptions of communist programmes. Marx stressed the importance of the financial setting. Money and monetary institutions were central to his refutation of Say's law,[1] as well as to his analysis of the internal process of accumulation – expanded reproduction – or in modern terms the process of growth.[2] In the *Grundrisse*, Marx affirmed that '*Money as capital* [Marx's italics] is an aspect of money which goes beyond its simple character as money. It can

29

be regarded as a higher realization; as it can be said that man is a developed ape.'[3]

From the political point of view, the focus on the monetary aspect of capital meant that the socialist society had to put under control, first of all, financial capital. In the *Communist Manifesto*, one of his few elaborations on the transition to a communist society, Marx points to the necessity of nationalization of the banking system as well as the basic means of production.[4] The events of 1848 in France strengthened Marx's belief that banking was the core of the capitalist system. His attention centered on the fact that banks stopped payments and credits whenever capitalist power was endangered.[5] The *Critique of the Gotha Programme*[6] indicated in outline how capitalist institutions could be transformed and how they could work. The *Critique* emphasized the following points:[7] 1. Common property in the means of production; 2. Deduction of a capital depreciation fund, net investments, general costs of administration, an insurance fund, social services and other costs, such as the official poor relief fund, before the distribution of the social product among individual producers; 3. Distribution criteria granting each producer his exact contribution to society in terms of individual labour time (after deduction of the aforementioned costs); 4. The right of each producer to draw from the social consumption fund a quantity of products corresponding to the amount of labour spent in production, as certified by society. 'From each according to his ability, to each according to his needs', were criteria of distribution for a further, more advanced, stage of development.

The *Critique* focused on the need for a transition period, when the proletariat would exert its dictatorship, before the communist stage was reached. Defects would be inevitable in the first phase of communism 'when it has just emerged after prolonged pangs from capitalist society'.[8] But the *Critique* was nebulous on the crucial question of which criteria would replace capitalist criteria of production. The only indication was that deductions for productive use should be determined 'by available means and forces, and partly by calculation of probabilities'.[9] Marx said nothing about decision-making under socialism. He did not raise any significant criticism concerning the forms of cooperation, which the Gotha programme mentioned, but he had probably in mind a 'state' framework for economic organization, since he emphasized – against the Gotha programme – that the surplus should not be distributed to producers. Although it offered no profound analysis, the *Critique* provided Marxists – and Lenin above all – with some basic principles, important because they were accepted as the main guidelines for the shape of socialist institutions during the transition.

Kautsky emphasized the aspect of *state socialism* which could be derived from Marx's approach. The process of concentration of production, which Marx had shown to be one of the outcomes of the competitive system, was focused upon by Kautsky as a necessary stage. 'Without the development of large-scale industry', he declared to the audience of the Socialist Reading Club of Amsterdam in 1902, 'socialism is impossible'.[10] Large-scale techniques, higher productivity of labour, improved utilization of capacity, and lower costs of transport, administration, marketing and procurement of raw and auxiliary materials were for Kautsky the most attractive aspects of concentration. *The Erfurt Programme* stressed that socialist production required the aggregation of all plants into a single large association. Only the modern state was capable of providing the institutional framework for the socialist society. Against the *utopia* of the phalansteries or similar socialist settlements of the early nineteenth century, Kautsky adduced two points: firstly, the huge dimensions of modern enterprise-plants; secondly, the strong economic relations between capitalist nations.[11] Consequently, the process of concentration was to be pursued by shutting down small enterprises and concentrating the labour force in the large ones.[12] Whilst Marx had not ventured any specific hypothesis about the functioning of the socialist economy, Kautsky stressed that 'orders' should replace 'market'; he focused on the problem of control, rather than on the question of property. Kautsky even suggested that the means of production could be owned by individuals – alongside other forms of ownership – provided that the market had been crushed: 'What will disappear [in socialist society] is our feverish excitement – the struggle for life or death, the struggle which is imposed by our present competitive system; what will ultimately disappear is the antagonism between exploiters and exploited.'[13] Passionate dislike of the market was common to all Marxists. This feeling turned out to be the most powerful motive for state intervention.

Kautsky's influence on Lenin's approach to socialism remained even after the war had sharpened the divergences between the two leaders of the Marxist movement. While Lenin argued against Kautsky that the socialist organization would not necessarily be bureaucratic,[14] he did not repudiate the German emphasis on the role of the state. 'State and Revolution' represented Lenin's effort to reach a synthesis between the soviets, spontaneous forms of workers' organization, and the dictatorship of the proletariat, which embodied both elements of coercion and the necessity of guidance:

The proletariat needs state power, a centralized organization of force, an organization of violence, both to crush the resistance of the exploiters and to *lead* the enormous mass of the population – the peasants, the petty-bourgeoisie and the semi-proletarians – in the work of organizing a socialist economy.[15]

Lenin's specification that the proletariat needs 'only a state which is withering away'[16] was based on a quantitative rather than qualitative distinction, which seriously impaired its credibility. The *special machine* of suppression (Lenin's italics) would begin to fade in so far as

> the suppression of the minority of exploiters by the majority of wage slaves of yesterday is comparatively so easy, simple and natural a task that it will entail far less bloodshed than the suppression of the risings of serfs or wage-labourers, and it will cost mankind far less.[17]

Should antagonism remain, the state would remain. By this argument, Lenin emphasized the need for the state in the transitional phase. Would this state be a looser form of state as compared with the bourgeois institution? On what basis could the assertion be made that 'State power as a centralized organization of violence' did not need a special apparatus, but merely 'the simple organization of the armed people (such as the Soviets of Workers' and Soldiers' Deputies)'? At least on three elements, which were to become the pillars of Leninism: the party, the nature of the dominant class, and the merging of legislative and executive functions.[18]

The theory of the vanguard party[19] affirmed that the party, expressing the ideology of the proletarian revolution, would of itself guarantee the democratic character of the new state. The replacement of the old cadres by new revolutionary members coming from the worker and peasant strata, by definition, for a Marxist, ensured a new mode of governing. The social character of the ownership of the means of production was to be consolidated by merging legislative with executive functions performed by the elected bodies. The model of state socialism which resulted from these elements was legitimized by the implicit belief that the state would be subordinated to society. Lenin did not refute Kautsky's theory of the need for centralized institutions competent in the economic domain, but, on the contrary, added a political justification for them. The problem of finding new devices for the direction of the economy was shifted from the economic field, as such, into the political sphere. Lenin's comment on the *Critique of the Gotha Programme*[20] was directed not to exploring and developing the few Marxian guidelines it offered, but only to reaffirming the unquestionable necessity of a state organization in the transition period. To this extent, however, the stress on legitimizing the new proletarian state was to have an impact on economic organization. This ideological framework offered a better soil for nationalization of industry, banks and land, than for municipalization or cooperation. It was also a determining factor in the identification of nationalization – in a state ruled by communists – with *socialization*. Lenin's emphasis on *political control* allowed, at the same time, some room for workers' control. In

Lenin's model of power, workers' control would not evolve in any decentralized institutional form, but, on the contrary, would facilitate the flow of information to the centre and the correct implementation of central guidelines. Lenin's political realism in capturing the positive elements in the spontaneous phenomenon of factory committees, which characterized the tumultuous fall of Tsarism, emerges better if it is compared with Bukharin's merely economic approach to socialist organization:

It is essentially wrong to define the difference between socialists and anarchists by stating that the former are supporters of the state and the latter are not. The difference consists in the fact that revolutionary social democracy may organize a new social production in a centralized way, i.e. in a technically more productive way, while decentralized anarchic production may be looked upon as a step backwards to the old technique, to the old production form.[21]

Lenin's terse comment was that the first sentence was true, but the second wrong and the third incomplete.[22] What Bukharin did not take into account was the importance of political control. Bukharin questioned state power before Lenin,[23] but he still had in mind a centralized model of economic organization.[24] Lenin was ready to accept any institutional form in so far as it could be subjected to political control by the party.

Before October 1917, the Bolsheviks had not formulated any concrete alternative to the existing economic institutions. This fact was stigmatized by Sukhanov, a sharp but not hostile observer of Bolshevik policy.[25] Nonetheless, economic disorganization and social unrest, two by-products of war and bureaucratic inefficiency, strengthened the belief that only the expropriation of finance capital would help to enforce order in the economy.

In April 1917, Lenin proposed the nationalization of the banks and capitalist syndicates. These measures, according to Lenin's Tasks of the Proletariat in our Revolution', had been resorted to frequently during the war by a number of bourgeois states; thus they were indispensable to avert the impending total economic disorganization and famine, but they were also steps toward socialism.[26] Following the 7 April Conference of the Russian Social-Democratic Labour Party, these measures were inserted in the revised party programme. According to Lenin, they were not revolutionary:

Under no circumstances can the party of the proletariat set itself the aim of 'introducing' socialism in a country of small peasants so long as the overwhelming majority of the population has not come to realize the need for a socialist revolution.[27]

In his first 'Letter from Afar' on 20 March 1917, Lenin put the first problems to be tackled as giving peace, bread, freedom and land to the proletariat, and to the semi-proletarian and small peasant population.[28] Besides state control over finance capital, Lenin envisioned, at that time, only one basically new institution: a progressive income tax.

The radicalization of the Bolshevik opposition to the Provisional government occurred after Lenin's return to Petrograd on 3 April 1917, and materialized in the summer and autumn of 1917. However, Lenin did not renounce the division of aims into a minimum and maximum programme, which had been characteristic of the RSDLP since its origin.[29] At the Extraordinary Congress of the Party convoked for 17 October, Lenin's stand on the party programme was more moderate than that of the left wing of the Bolshevik faction, led by Bukharin, Smirnov and Osinskii. Since July 1917, Bukharin had seemingly deepened his belief that war had accelerated the concentration and centralization of capital in capitalist countries to such an extent that small producers and the petty-bourgeoisie were rapidly losing any significant economic function.[30] At the congress, Bukharin and Smirnov proposed the abolition of the minimum programme, on the ground that the time had come to elaborate measures for the transition to socialism.[31] The view that war had favoured the evolution of capitalism into state capitalism which in a revolutionary situation could be 'directly transformed into socialism', did not encounter objection from Lenin. Both Bukharin and Lenin had just examined the cartels and trusts characteristic of monopoly capitalism, focusing on their impressive number 'even in a backward country scarce in capital as is Russia'.[32] But Lenin was more circumspect. When he wrote 'A Caricature of Marxism and Imperialist Economism' in October 1916, he had considered Russia among the underdeveloped countries, embracing 'the whole of Eastern Europe'. These undeveloped countries had still to accomplish 'mainly democratic tasks, the tasks of overthrowing foreign oppression', unlike Western Europe and North America, which he considered ready for socialism.[33] At the Extraordinary Congress of the Party, Lenin tried to persuade his young colleagues to be cautious:

We all agree that the most important of the first steps to be taken must be such measures as the nationalization of banks and syndicates. Let us first realize this and other similar measures, and *then we shall see*. Then we shall be able to see *better*; for, practical experience, which is worth a million times more than the best of programmes, will considerably widen our horizon. It is possible and even probable, nay, indubitable, that without transitional 'combined types' the change will not take place. We shall not, for instance, be able to nationalize petty enterprises with one or two hired labourers at short notice or subject them to real workers' control. Their role may be insignificant, they may be bound hand and foot by the nationalization of banks and trusts, but so long as there are even odds and ends of bourgeois relations, why abandon the minimum programme?[34]

Lenin was convinced that nationalization alone would not alter the nature of the system and its internal mechanism. This explains why he defined these reforms as 'bourgeois'.[35] State banks were supposed to allow indirect control over capital so long as capital remained in part in private hands. The nationalization of land was assumed to favour the spread of capitalist methods in agriculture.

The crucial issue for all parties of Marxist inspiration was the nationalization of the means of production in the industrial field. This concerned mainly basic industry. About a month before the revolution, in the newspaper *Rabochii put'*, Lenin published the lines of what he believed should be done in order to make effective the programme of reforms promised by the February Revolution. Alongside nationalization of banks and insurance companies, he demanded the nationalization of the most important branches of industry (oil, coal, metallurgy, sugar, etc.) and the immediate introduction of workers' control over production and distribution.[36] From these measures Lenin expected an improvement of labour productivity, the return to the Treasury of the money hoarded by the rich and the realization of state control over the exchange of grain for manufactured goods, that is, price control. From a political point of view, Lenin wanted to stress that the Bolsheviks were ready to engage in radical policies if the situation demanded. He was challenging the Provisional Government and inviting workers and the marginal sections of society to adhere to the Bolshevik programme. While affirming that only the support of the majority would permit the peaceful development of the revolution, Lenin anticipated punishment, confiscation of property and arrest in order to overcome the capitalists' resistance.[37]

Lenin's programme assumed the possibility of mastering the state apparatus. This problem was examined in 'Can the Bolsheviks Retain State Power?', written by Lenin at the end of September 1917.[38] This pamphlet had some points in common with 'State and Revolution'. The bourgeois state was identified with the army, police and bureaucracy, which ought to be replaced by the Soviets of Workers' and Peasants' Deputies. The soviets were to be the vehicle for the party's will and guidance. Lenin remarked that the soviets provided an organization for the vanguard, through which this latter would 'elevate, train, educate and lead the entire mass of people which had remained up to now completely outside political life and history'.[39] Honesty and efficiency were expected from the system of election and recall and from close contact with various occupations through the soviets, a system which, according to Lenin, was likely to facilitate the most radical reforms without red tape. Lenin stated frankly that the first aim of Bolshevik strategy was to get a firm hold of the crucial posts of control. He focused on the political alternative, and not on an economic one:

The modern state possesses an apparatus which has extremely close connections with banks and syndicates, an apparatus which performs an enormous amount of accounting and registration work, if it may be expressed in this way. This apparatus must not, and should not be smashed. It must be wrested from the control of the capitalists; the capitalists and the wires they pull must be *cut off, lopped off, chopped away from* the apparatus; it must be *subordinated* to the proletarian Soviets; it must be expanded, made more comprehensive, and nation-wide. And this *can* be done by utilizing the achievements already made by large-scale capitalism (in the same way as the proletarian revolution can, in general, reach its goal by utilizing these achievements).[40]

The ground for this approach was that the old institutions would, under the vigilance of the soviets and the guidance of the party, perform the tasks they were not able to perform under bourgeois management. For the same reason Lenin rejected the hypothesis of general expropriation, substituting for it 'country-wide, all-embracing workers' control over the capitalists and their possible supporters':

Confiscation alone leads nowhere, as it does not contain elements of organization and accounting for proper distribution. Instead of confiscation, we could easily impose a *fair* tax, taking care, of course, to preclude the possibility of anyone evading assessment, concealing the truth, evading the law. And this possibility can be *eliminated only* by workers' control of the workers' state.[41]

By 'workers' control', Lenin meant a sort of political supervision of the activity of managerial staff, rather than workers' management. 'We are not utopians', he wrote in 'State and Revolution', 'we do not dream of dispensing at once with all administration and all subordination.'[42] 'Can the Bolsheviks Retain State Power?' again emphasized this point: 'We are not utopians, we know that an unskilled labourer or a cook cannot immediately get on with a job of state administration.'[43]

The elements of utopianism in Lenin's approach to the administration of the economy did not concern workers' management, but the capacity of the proletariat politically organized around the party to exert an effective supervision of business requiring a high degree of competence and expertise. To Bazarov,[44] who had objected that the soviets could not be a suitable apparatus for all activities, Lenin replied that the Bolsheviks were centralists, by conviction, by their programme and by the entire tactics of their party. The Bolsheviks believed in centralization and in the need for a plan, Lenin argued, but this plan should operate within the framework of a proletarian state where specialists would work 'under the control of workers' organizations on drawing up a "plan", on verifying it, on decisions, on labour-saving methods, on centralization, on devising the simplest, cheapest, most convenient and universal measures and methods of control'.[45]

But Lenin did not want to commit the party to detailed programmes.[46] The explicit reason for this was the relative backwardness of Russia. In his April Draft for the revision of the party programme, Lenin stressed that 'in the case of Russia, it would be wrong to present imperialism as a coherent whole ... since in Russia there are not a few fields and branches of labour that are still in a state of transition from natural to semi-natural economy to capitalism'.[47] The whole idea of a transitional stage between capitalism and communism was based on the assessment of the discrepancy between a given stage of development of material resources and techniques, their non-uniform diffusion over the country's economy and persistence of the old superstructures, amongst which education, expertise and mentality played a fundamental role. This approach was not peculiar to Lenin. In fact, it had deep roots in the analytical framework which the Russian Social Democratic Labour Party borrowed from Marx. For Marxists, the transition to a further stage implied realization of the complete potential of the old social order, in order to establish the material conditions necessary for the transformation of social relations.

This contradiction confined the Mensheviks to defence of the stage of the bourgeois revolution, which, politically, meant their passive support of the Provisional Government.[48] The Bolsheviks were indeed able to free themselves from the political impasse, but remained caught within the contradiction between goals and means in the economic field. The seizure of power did not exempt the Bolsheviks from confronting the problems of efficiency and growth, but on the contrary compelled them to assume tasks and goals which they believed to be beyond the capacities of the Provisional Government to solve. Thus, full-fledged capitalism provided the image of the economy which the Bolsheviks endeavoured to realize. After observing their performance in government, Bertrand Russell commented: 'the Bolsheviks are industrialists in all their aims; they love everything in modern industry, except the excessive rewards of the capitalists'.[49] This admiration and uncritical preference for large dimensions, the belief in the organizational efficiency of trusts and combines, the trend towards integration of independent units and the extension of state control over the economy, brought about by war, reflected the firmly held conviction that all the latest features of the capitalist system in the economic field should be adopted in order to advance toward the new society. This approach was especially characteristic of the technicians. Kritsman's creed was expressed in this way:

> The task of the proletariat in revolution is not only to reshape the organization of the national economy, but to complete and continue the organizational work of the former system, not only in a revolutionary way, but also in the sense of an evolution.[50]

The productivist approach – inherent in Marxist ideology [51] – provided in general the basic guidelines for future policies. Bukharin's elaboration of the Party Programme in March 1919 stressed that the Bolsheviks were supporters of *productive communism* and that the development of the productive forces was the foundation of this programme.[52] Radek[53] insisted: 'the communist economy is the utilization of all the productive forces according to a predetermined plan, in the interests of working people'.[54]

Forms of monopoly capitalism were breaking through the nineteenth-century competitive system. From the viewpoint of supporters of the market system, cases of concentration and the formation of trusts and unions were to be interpreted as a perversion of the competitive system, leading to waste and distorted price signals, to be counteracted by adequate legislation. In some countries this interpretation favoured the introduction of anti-trust laws. The anarchist movement, fearing the power that a combination of economic concentration and control from above would give to the state, proposed the organization of a federal system as a way of coordinating the autonomous activities of each productive unit.[55] From the perspective of the European Marxists, however, the process of concentration represented a positive expression of mature capitalism. Marx had often characterized capitalism as an anarchic mode of production, since it was based on market laws.[56] To Marxists, industrial concentration seemed to provide the background for a political economy aimed at transforming the anarchic, competitive mode of production into a coordinated and programmed process of growth, whose expression later became central planning. Kautsky's *Die Soziale Revolution* stressed that one could learn from the American trusts how to increase production at a stroke 'simply by concentrating production in the most advanced enterprises and leaving idle the factories which had not reached such a degree of perfection'. According to Kautsky, Germany could have achieved this progress by shutting down all factories having less than 200 workers.[57] Lenin was much impressed by Kautsky's pamphlet, which he edited in Russian, adding some comments of his own about concentration of production in Russia. Lenin concluded that productivity of labour and wages would increase and working time decrease 'if we expropriated all the manufactures, closed down the small enterprises and left only 1,500 big factories working two eight-hour shifts or three five-hour shifts'.[58] Later, Bukharin pointed out that finance capitalism had abolished the anarchy of production in countries of high capitalist development, through a system of share control, participation and financing which substituted a technical division of labour within a 'national' organized economy for individual economic relations.[59]

Confronted with problems of implementing an economic policy, the Bolsheviks had as a main goal the acceleration of what was already occurring. In the new edition of Bogdanov's *Short Course of Economic Science*, published in 1919, the organization of the socialist society was to be inspired by 'scientific centralism', as opposed to the 'authoritarian centralism', of capitalism.[60] Kritsman's approach to development embodied Marxian determinism:

Each further phase of revolution is possible only if the former has gone far enough..., as long as any revolutionary phase has not yet been completed it is necessary to keep the *old* relations on in other fields. In particular, the transformation of technical relations is impossible, as long as all phases of the revolution are not concluded. Revolution, therefore, advances on the basis of old techniques, the methods of which remain essentially unchanged.[61]

Bukharin praised Kritsman for this approach to transformation.[62] Lenin's development of the idea of state capitalism, as a suitable method of economic policy in the phase of transition,[63] was definitely dependent on the image of organization offered by the developed West European countries. When seizing power, therefore, the crucial problem seemed only one of furthering the process of concentration, enlarging the scope of price control policies and substituting guidelines from above for market incentives, while leaving to controlled distribution the task of implementing communist principles.

2.2 THE INDUSTRIAL SITUATION IN RUSSIA BEFORE THE REVOLUTION

Did the degree of concentration of Russian industry justify the idea that the nationalization of trusts and syndicates together with bank nationalization would provide the means of control over the economy? An answer depends on certain specific features of the Russian economy, as well as on the approach of contemporaries to them.

Around the turn of the century, competitive capitalism was already turning into oligopolistic capitalism, particularly in the domain of heavy industry. The diffusion of finance capital and the consequent separation between ownership and management, as well as the socialization of the latter, were the crucial points of Hilferding's analysis. From him both Lenin and Bukharin borrowed much for their analysis of imperialism. Concentration was interpreted as an extraordinary advantage for the overthrow of capitalism. Control over the production and initial processing of raw materials and over transportation was sufficient, according to Hilferding, for control and indirect socialization of medium- and small-scale enterprises.[64]

Though not as developed as Germany, Russia had gone through a rapid process of concentration. Lenin remarked that in 1894–5 one-tenth of Russian factories employed three-quarters of the total labour force and produced seven-tenths of total industrial output.[65] This feature was emphasized not only by Marxists, but also by most of the Russian economists, whose tendency was to stress those aspects of Russian development which most resembled European patterns, neglecting traditional features to a greater extent than an impartial approach would have justified. Basing his calculations on 1908 data (which he considered the most complete until 1919), Grinevetskii maintained that Russian industry was more concentrated than the German:

Table 2.1. *Distribution of enterprises by number of workers employed in 1908*
(per cent of total)

Number of workers	Russian enterprises	German enterprises
More than 1,000	24.5	8.1
501–1,000	9.5	6.1
201–500	10.9	11.2
101–200	5.8	9.9
51–100	5.4	10.2
21–50	4.8	11.6
5–20	6.2	13.4
less than 5	32.9	29.5

Source: V.I. Grinevetskii, *Poslevoennye perspektivy Russkoi promyshlennosti*, Kharkov, 1919, pp. 139–40

In Russia, the participation of the state in industrial activities had stimulated the formation of large enterprises and speeded up the entire process of industrialization.[66] The mining, engineering, textile and food-processing industries offered a picture of industrial concentration which, despite differences in overall development when compared with other European countries, presented some similarities to the most developed

Table 2.2. *Industrial output and imports, 1912 (million rubles)*

Industry	Large-scale industry	Small-scale industry [a]	Imports	Total
Mining	520	—	62	580
Metal	715	165	373	1,250
Textiles	1,158	260	147	1,550
Food-processing	1,350	120	338	1,800
Various	822	520	220	1,560
Total	4,565	1,150	1,140	6,750

[a] errors: $\pm 25\%$
Source: Grinevetskii, p. 166

capitalist economies. From Grinevetskii's pre-First World War data on total output (large- and small-scale industry, see Table 2.2), one can calculate that, besides the large-scale mining industry providing 100 per cent total output, the large-scale metal, textile, and food-processing industries produced respectively 83, 82, and 92 per cent of total output.

The degree of concentration of Russian industry before the First World War appears quite high in the light of Grinevetskii's and other data on the distribution of labour force and capital (by enterprises). Fifty-four per cent of the industrial labour force was estimated to be engaged in five per cent of the total number of enterprises, and there were a fairly large number of giant concerns with a foundation capital of over five million rubles.[67] But both criteria may be misleading. The number of workers engaged in handicrafts was undervalued in Russian statistics, as was their share of total output. Statistics did not take into account the enterprises with fewer than twenty workers. *Kustar'* (handicraft) industry was not statistically recorded at all and urban artisan industry (*remeslo*) was recorded, in general, only for large urban centres. Grinevetskii acknowledged that the number of *kustari* might have oscillated between two and ten millions. Nonetheless, he took the lower figure as significant, thus allowing for a very high margin of error in total output and, consequently, in the output share of large-scale industry. On the other hand, foundation capital may not be a reliable index of concentration because its expansion could be dictated by company or taxation laws; thus it did not correspond necessarily to the scale of the firm's productive operations or to its value of output.[68] Thus the features of a 'traditional' economy, by the available statistics, were likely to be overlooked by the intelligentsia ready to grasp any sign of capitalist development.

Though remaining heavily dependent on imports of finished products,

Table 2.3. *Structure of output of large-scale industry*
(% of total)

Branches	1908	1912
Mining	10	11
Metal	14	16
Textiles	26	25
Food-processing	32	30
Various	18	18
Total	100	100

Source: Grinevetskii, pp. 30–1

Russia manifested between 1908 and 1912 the characteristics of economic take-off.[69] Mining and the iron and steel industry grew faster than other branches.

Another feature which impressed the young Bolsheviks was the increasing degree of monopoly of Russian industry. With the growth of Russian industry before the First World War, agreements of various kinds were concluded between firms. However, these agreements did not always indicate aggressive dynamism. More often, in the Russian case, they represented attempts to reduce the impact of economic crises on developing, not yet firmly established, industrial undertakings. Soviet literature has often confused the meaning of 'trust' with that of 'cartel' (which the Russians called 'sindikat').[70] In the same way, neither Lenin nor Bukharin, in their essays on imperialism, made a distinction between the two forms of cooperation, since in their opinion they both resulted, in any case, in a form of monopoly.[71] If, indeed, one does mean by 'trust' an agreement, of greater or lesser importance, by which competitors in a given branch of industry are tied through financial links with a controlling company, it is possible to affirm that this form of monopoly almost did not exist in pre-war Russia.[72] Instead, cartels (or syndicates), whose members kept their financial autonomy but agreed on a parity status in price fixing, sales quotas and production quotas, were formed particularly in iron and steel and in oil. In iron and steel the origin of the powerful cartels *Prodameta* and *Krovlia* lay in the economic crisis of 1900–3. In 1908 *Prodameta* controlled 90 per cent of the iron and steel output of South Russia and 45 per cent of the total national output. In 1909 *Krovlia* controlled 52 per cent of steel plate.[73] The control of *Prodameta* over the market and the integration of an increasing number of activities, from fuel and minerals to specialized products, provided on the eve of the war grounds for considering it a monopoly. Nonetheless, it

Table 2.4. *Participation of foreign capital in industry, excluding banking capital, 1916–17 (million rubles)*

	Total capital in stocks and securities	Foreign capital in stocks and securities	%
Mining	917.8	834.3	91
Metal-working	937.8	392.7	42
Textiles	685.4	192.5	28
Chemicals	166.9	83.6	50
Wood-working	68.8	25.7	37

Source: P.I. Liashchenko, *Istoriia narodnogo khoziaistva SSSR*, vol. 2, Gos. Izd. Politicheskoi Literatury, 1948, p. 378

could not evolve into a trust, because of conflicting pressures both inside and outside its organization.[74] Cartels also dominated other sectors, including coal and sugar. By a sales agreement concluded in 1905, two corporations, *Nobel* and *Mazout*, attained by 1914 control over 77 per cent of total oil sales.[75]

Concentration was mainly an outcome of the financial policy of Western banks. Iron and steel, mining, tobacco and sugar were heavily dependent on finance capital under bank control. Foreign and Russian capital, through the intermediation of a fairly well developed banking system, dominated the principal industries. Of fifty joint-stock banks, twelve controlled 80 per cent of the banking capital.[76] Foreign capital was particularly important in the mineral, metal-working, chemical and wood-working industries.

Though German capital played a smaller role than French or English (20 per cent of total foreign capital, as against 33 and 23 per cent respectively,[77]) it was more evenly distributed over a wide range of activities. Moreover, the German participation in industry was characterized by dependence of the enterprises concerned on raw materials, semi-manufactures and auxiliary materials provided by the German parent company.[78] As a consequence, the measures of control adopted during the war over enemy enterprises favoured a sort of state participation in the financing of a number of undertakings whose shares held by enemy citizens were subject to compulsory sale. However, most of these undertakings were cut off from their normal sources of raw and auxiliary materials and were affected by the interruption of directives from their foreign controlling company. Electrical and electrical engineering plants, chemical plants, mineral and mineral processing enterprises, as well as the Russko Baltiskii plants (thereafter known as the Putilov works) were sequestered and put under state management.[79]

Cut off by the war from its normal sources of supply, Russian industry could not be easily supplied by alternative domestic sources. The transport system was disorganized and over-burdened by army movements and military supply. The southern industrial centres, where mining and oil production were concentrated, were not able to supply the metallurgical and engineering centres around Petrograd and Moscow. The state railways, covering 43,000 versts (about 30,000 miles), had 15,000 engines, of which about a quarter were at least 25 years old. In 1915 the production of wagons was reduced to half the pre-war level and the number of engines in service was lower than in 1912. An additional cause of the incapacity of Russian industry to adapt itself to war needs was the mobilization of industrial workers for the army. The employment of female unskilled labour lowered the average labour productivity.[80] In 1917 the total output of European Russia was already only about two-thirds that of 1916, as can be seen from Table 2.5. The increase in output of war industry as compared with other sectors occurred at the expense of production for the market, which decreased by about 9 per cent between 1913 and 1916.[81]

Government policy aimed at introducing some form of regulation of industrial activity, particularly in trade. In 1915 four special commissions were instituted for defence, fuel, transport and provisions: their basic goal was to facilitate material and financial supplies to war industry, by means of price control and privileged quotas. These forms of control did not evolve into state monopoly. They did provide, however, the initial framework for the organization of the economy around 'chief committees' (*glavki*), which were to become the characteristic economic agencies of war communism. Between July 1915 and May 1916 supply committees for cotton, leather, flax, jute and paper were formed. Among the duties assigned to them were: fixing ceilings on prices of raw and semi-manufactured materials and manufactured goods; determination of productive capacity and distribution of raw materials among individual production units, purchase of raw materials, and other supervisory tasks.[82] As a consequence of control over supply, a black market in raw materials developed. Meanwhile, sellers of raw materials tried to conceal their stocks, thereby adding to the wartime inflationary pressure. The number and rigidity of controls were increased, until it became necessary to create centres concentrating all transactions, even in branches, like the cotton and wool centres (*tsentry*), characterized by a relatively large number of medium- and small-scale enterprises.[83]

To the Bolsheviks, ready to grasp any form of evolution towards central

Table 2.5. *Industrial output and employment (pre-war rubles)*

Branches of industry	1913		1916		1917	
	no. employed (thous.)	output (mill.)	no. employed (thous.)	output (mill.)	no. employed (thous.)	output (mill.)
Quarrying, clay, earth-moving	177.4	154.3	106.8	89.3	99.4	65.8
Mining and metallurgy	695.8	1,003.9	635.0	941.3	691.3	528.1
Metal working and machine building	347.9	628.1	697.2	1,888.4	766.3	1,212.9
Timber	104.0	171.2	92.2	106.3	92.3	93.3
Chemicals	70.8	333.7	128.3	853.5	108.3	564.1
Food-processing	332.9	1,505.8	354.5	1,176.0	359.7	734.8
Organic materials processing	45.2	134.6	73.9	182.5	72.9	128.9
Cotton	491.6	1,090.3	472.9	892.5	462.5	596.4
Wool	92.1	195.1	89.3	187.2	96.5	134.4
Silk	33.3	49.2	28.8	38.9	25.5	21.8
Flax and hemp	85.9	115.3	110.7	130.6	100.7	90.7
Various fibrous materials	26.4	44.6	42.6	146.0	40.2	27.2
Paper and printing	87.4	152.0	84.0	126.6	85.8	99.2
Energy and water supply	7.9	38.7	11.8	72.9	18.4	46.5
Total for Russia	2,598.6	5,620.8	2,976.0	6,832.4	3,024.3	4,344.1
Total for European Russia	2,498.8	5,429.9	2,839.3	6,668.0	2,932.6	4,232.9

Source: Sbornik statisticheskikh svedenii po Soiuzu SSSR 1918–1923, Moscow, 1924, pp. 168–9

state administration as a necessary path of capitalist development, these forms of control – in addition to the existing cartels – seemed to provide good grounds and prerequisites for nationalization and price control. In spite of initial objections,[84] *glavki* and *tsentry* (chief and central committees), partially purged of their former staff, were kept on and assigned increasing functions. Other *glavki* were also formed according to the rules of the former committees. Under war communism, they became the foundation of the organization of production.

2.3 FROM PROJECTS TO REALITY: ECONOMIC DIRECTION AND NATIONALIZATION

In the 'Inevitable Catastrophe and Extravagant Promises', published in *Pravda* on 29 and 30 May 1917, Lenin proposed the establishment of control over banks and the gradual introduction of more just, progressive taxation of incomes and properties as a way out of the crisis.[85] War had brought about a large increase in profits, particularly in branches such as the copper industry, textiles and food-processing,[86] which left-wing parties found outrageous in the face of increasing distress in the urban centres.

Lenin, however, did not believe that new institutions and extraordinary measures could counteract economic disruption. He ridiculed Skobelev, the Menshevik Minister for Labour, for threatening a 100 per cent levy on profits and the introduction of labour conscription[87] for shareholders, and characterized the economic council proposed by Groman as a new bureaucratic institution.[88] Though demagogy was no doubt present, Lenin's unresponsiveness to the technical side of any economic measure[89] was not only a polemical shrewdness. It was also one aspect of the Marxist belief that the effectiveness of institutions depended on the rigour of administrative supervision over them, and on who exerted this supervision, rather than on correct methods and institutions. An illuminating example of this attitude was the Declaration of the Bolshevik Group read out at the All-Russian Democratic Conference held on 1 October 1917:

Only a power resting on the proletariat and the poor peasantry which controls all the country's material wealth and economic capability, whose measures do not stop as soon as they touch the selfish interests of property-owning groups, which mobilizes all the scientific and technically valuable resources to social and economic ends is capable of bringing as much order as can be attained now into a disintegrating economy, of helping the peasantry and rural workers to use the available means of agricultural production to the greatest effect, of limiting profit, of fixing wages, and of securing true work discipline in a context of regulated production, based on self-administration by the workers and their centralized control over industry: only this kind of authority can ensure the demobilization of the whole economy with the least amount of stress.[90]

This faith was shared also by technically trained Marxists. Soon after the revolution, Kritsman affirmed with enthusiasm: 'the proletarian revolution, by transferring to the working class the power over the national economy, impregnates the whole organization of the proletariat and regenerates the [economic system], converts it into its substantial opposite, from a capitalist to a socialist one'.[91]

One of the first decrees issued by the Bolshevik Government was the Decree on Workers' Control of 27 November 1917. By this decree workers' control was institutionalized, that is, extended to all factories.* It consisted in the limitation of the rights of ownership and disposal of property, under the assumption that production and delivery of products ought not to be left to the discretional decisions of owners and managers in a time of economic crisis. Workers' control implied the persistence of private ownership of the means of production, though with a 'diminished' right of disposal. It meant the introduction of a political constraint into business. The organs of workers' control, the factory-committees, were not supposed to evolve into workers' management organs after the nationalization of the factories. The hierarchical structure of factory work was not questioned by Lenin, who affirmed that the socialist revolution would not dispense with subordination, control, 'foreman and accountants'. The fact that Lenin's statement was written in 'State and Revolution' is relevant, because this pamphlet was conceived by him as a theoretical essay, in which he tried for the first time to formulate a coherent institutional framework of the future socialist society, to oppose his own Marxist project to the 'distortions' of Marxism produced by Kautsky.[92] To the Bolshevik leadership the transfer of power to the working class meant power to its leadership, i.e. to the party. Central control was the main goal of the Bolshevik leadership. The hasty creation of the VSNKh (the Supreme Council of the National Economy) on 1 December 1917, with precise tasks in the economic field, was a significant indication of the fact that decentralized management was not among the projects of the party, and that the Bolsheviks intended to counterpose central direction of the economy to the possible evolution of workers' control toward self-management. Osinskii, the first president of VSNKh, and one of the

---

*I use the standard translation 'workers' control' for *rabochii kontrol'*. However, the meaning of the Russian word *kontrol'* is very wide, ranging from audit and general supervision, to the exercise of authority in detail over an institution or activity. In this book the particular meaning of *kontrol'* is indicated where necessary.

supporters of the largest participation of workers in management, observed that 'workers' control' was one of those transitory slogans, not entirely fitting, not quite consistent with other more consequential ones of the pre-October period. Socialist appropriation, he added, was going to be reinforced only by a developed state socialism, i.e. by a centralized system of socialized production, monopoly distribution of products and planned utilization of labour resources.[93] The main alternative to workers' control was nationalization. It entailed 'state control' over the means of production, that is, direction and disposal of these means in favour of the interests of society as a whole. But a crucial barrier to nationalization was the lack of Bolshevik cadres at the top levels. This was a further reason for limiting the programme of nationalization to banks and syndicates, the only institutions where the process of concentration was presumed to prevent the dispersion of managerial cadres. On the basis of Hilferding's analysis, too, Lenin believed that the socialization of management in the joint-stock companies, determined by the separation of ownership from administration, made the transition to socialism easier. This approach comes through almost incidentally in 'State and Revolution':

> The question of control and accounting should not be confused with the question of the scientifically trained staff and engineers, agronomists and so on. These gentlemen are working today in obedience to the wishes of the capitalists, and will work even better tomorrow in obedience to the wishes of the armed workers.[94]

Lenin's approach to this question was superficial. It might have been partially justified by the war trend towards equalization of wages, depressing higher salaries,[95] which could have been interpreted as a form of 'proletarianization'. But, whether aware or not of such a trend, Lenin's presumption that white-collar staff would keep offering their services to Soviet Power at 'salaries no higher than a workman's wage'[96] was oddly optimistic. In a rapidly deteriorating situation, under the banner of the revolution, not only were economic disparities going to be resented, but also prestige and authority. Some months of experience in power convinced Lenin that the services of 'bourgeois specialists' should be paid at higher salaries.[97]

What occurred in the first months after the seizure of power is evidence of the fact that the Bolsheviks were not able to determine the tempo of their economic reforms. They had a programme of nationalization of key branches, but they did not intend to apply it immediately, without preparatory work, which also meant preparation of cadres. In December 1917 Lenin instructed VSNKh to prepare the nationalization of large-scale industry, as one step towards implementation of the party programme in the economic field. But there were no deadlines, nor did VSNKh consider it necessary to start immediately on this project.[98]

Before June 1918 nationalization did not follow a plan. In the absence of a definite hierarchy among administrative powers, local authorities often decided confiscation of factories and requisition of products, independently of the scale or importance of industry from the general point of view. Confiscation was a punitive measure, which implied no compensation or obligation on the part of the state to the owner.[99] The chaotic way in which nationalization of industry proceeded preoccupied the leadership of VSNKh and was criticized by contemporary Soviet economists,[100] as well as by the opposition.[101] Pressures for nationalization from below were strong. It may be interesting to note that the first production units to be nationalized did not belong to the sugar, coal, iron and steel or oil syndicates, the control of which Lenin considered necessary before October 1917, but were single factories, of no particular national relevance.

The first factory to be nationalized was a textile mill belonging to a former minister of the Provisional Government. This factory, which was situated in the Moscow Region, had stopped working before the October Revolution. The Textile Trade Union presented a petition for confiscation to the Moscow Soviet. *Sovnarkom* decreed nationalization, adducing that it was inadmissible to shut down a factory working for the army and for the needs of the poorest consumers, that the owner had sabotaged production and that nationalization was necessitated by 'the interests of the national economy, of the large masses of consumers and of the 4,000 workers and their families'.[102]

State subsidies and lock-outs were additional causes for petitioning for nationalization. In the case of a textile factory which was kept working thanks to funds and supplies from public authorities,[103] the workers claimed that it was highly undesirable to supply funds and increase profits at their own expense for the advantage of the owner rather than of any collective organization.[104] The waste of government subsidies was adduced as motivation for the confiscation of an electrical company on 29 December 1917.[105] The nationalization of water transport was demanded by workers of various Soviet institutions and the Trade Unions Control Committees of Kostroma.[106]

But state intervention was claimed not only in cases of disruption. At the end of January 1918, the Conference of the Factory-Plant Committees in Petrograd demanded not only immediate confiscation of factories which did not apply workers' control, showed no concern for improvement of working conditions, committed sabotage or stopped working; but also that steps be taken to nationalize the best equipped factories in a good financial position. The conference affirmed that 'the proletarian revolution not only receives from the hands of the plunderers a disrupted economy, which represents a burden on the state budget, but also those enterprises which may work intensively, producing economic goods for the country, thereby helping the good maintenance of national wealth'.[107]

The Soviet government was not eager to burden the state budget with the losses of private enterprises. For the leadership, nationalization implied preparatory work, in order to avoid halting the production process, and did not exclude compensation. This is why in November 1917 *Sovnarkom* instructed the local soviets to slow down their initiatives of confiscation and requisition and to verify preliminarily the technical and financial position of enterprises.[108] In addition, lack of public funds available to finance industry alarmed Menshevik circles even in cases of projects for partial nationalization.[109] People in charge of economic affairs were cautious. VSNKh tried to stop the wave of confiscations and to bring order into the process of nationalization. On 16 February 1918 VSNKh decreed that nationalization was to be decided by itself, with the approval of *Sovnarkom*, and that no other institution had the right to confiscate enterprises.[110] Two months later VSNKh had to resort to financial weapons to make this rule effective. Soviet institutions were informed that enterprises nationalized without approval would not be financed through public funds.[111]

Between 15 November 1917 and 6 March 1918, eighty-one enterprises were expropriated by *Sovnarkom* decree or by VSNKh. In this period, emphatically reported by the Soviet literature as the 'red attack on capital', of the thirty expropriation decrees signed by *Sovnarkom*, twenty-five referred to confiscation; three, to transfer to state ownership; and two, to nationalization.[112] The Soviet literature, by and large, stresses that nationalization had a rationale, for more than half of the expropriated enterprises belonged to the mining industry and a third to the metal working and electrical industries.[113] But this is not by itself evidence of the implementation of a plan. Nationalization often sanctioned autonomous initiatives by workers or local soviets. Of the thirty-four decrees of expropriation signed by *Sovnarkom* and by VSNKh between December 1917 and February 1918, only five mentioned the national importance of the undertaking. Refusal by the management to apply workers' control led to nationalization in eight cases and stoppage of production in twelve.[114] In addition, important undertakings were expropriated without preparatory work, in order to put a barrier against politically undesirable developments. The confiscation of the joint-stock company Bogolovskii in the mining district of the Urals was decided at the request of a delegation of workers and was motivated by sabotage by the managerial staff, for which Lenin demanded arrest.[115] Other factories of the same region were confiscated by *Sovnarkom* at about the same time for not applying workers' control or the decree on land.[116] For twenty-four out of thirty-four factories in the Urals, the reason for expropriation was that stocks were deteriorating after the owners had stopped production.[117]

The Bolsheviks had also to cope with anarchical twists. A soviet in Irkutsk province decided in January 1918 to take ownership of the mines and their inventories located in fifteen *raiony* of the province. The 'factory-plant committees' of the mines were declared to be the management *in loco* (*khoziain*). An analogous decision was taken in the Glukhov province in the Donbass, where industrial cooperatives were formed.[118] Also in the Donbass the workers spontaneously formed local economic councils and proclaimed those mines which were ownerless, for whatever reason, to be the property of the Republic. They directly assumed the management.[119] In this case, nationalization was declared without any participation of the higher authorities; it covered half of the mines. The VSNKh Commissar, Osinskii, who had been sent to this area, observed that nationalization was necessary because most of the coal mining industry had lived upon state financing since the Kerenskii government (wages and all sorts of subsidies), and that private bank credits were no longer available after the nationalization of banking. But the ultimate reason for nationalization, concluded Osinskii, was that if it were not decreed by the competent organs, it would be carried out anyway locally.[120] By the end of March 1918, 230 mines had already been nationalized locally.[121]

The tempo and scale of nationalization up to the autumn of 1918 have recently been analysed by a comprehensive Soviet survey of the process of 'socialization' (*obobshchestvlenie*) of industry.[122] Figures produced show that, after an initial period of hesitation, the central government increased the rate of nationalization. Not only large-scale industry, but a fair quantity of medium- and small-scale enterprises, the nationalization of which had not been foreseen by the Bolshevik theoreticians, were nationalized.

From a detailed examination of the expropriated enterprises by branch, no conclusive observations may be reached as to the existence of an order of priorities as between heavy and light industry in the process of nationalization.

The highest percentage of nationalized enterprises was in the agrarian regions (Central Black Earth Region and Volga Region), where more than 51 per cent of the 3,221 examined enterprises were expropriated before the autumn of 1918. About 1,000 enterprises (23.3 per cent of the

Table 2.6. *Time of 'socialization' of industrial units according to number employed*[a]

Number employed	Expropriated (% of total) 1 + 2 + 3	Nationalized 1	Sequestered or confiscated 2	Municipalized 3	Nov.–Dec. 1917	Jan.–Mar. 1918 (percentage)	Apr.–July 1918	After July 1918
Less than 50	38.9	1,369	71	412	10.8	19.6	30.9	38.7
51–200	31.9	560	41	87	5.9	13.8	44.8	35.5
201–500	33.3	155	14	32	7.0	11.9	47.8	33.3
501–1000	50.2	123	3	3	3.1	4.6	57.4	34.9
1001–5000	51.9	117	—	5	2.5	9.2	47.5	41.8
Over 5000	82.6	17	2	—	15.8	—	52.6	31.6
Unknown	21.6	271	19	37	10.1	11.9	31.8	46.2
Total	35.0	2,612	150	576	8.9	16.1	36.6	38.4

Note: [a]The total number of enterprises recorded by the census of autumn 1918, from which these data have been computed, was 9,542.
Source: V.Z. Drobizhev, 'Sotsialisticheskoe obobshchestvlenie promyshlennosti v SSSR', *Voprosy istorii*, 1964, no. 6, 58

Table 2.7. *Time of 'socialization' of industrial units according to branch of production*

Branch of production	Number of enterprises	Expropriated enterprises	(%)	Nov.–Dec. 1917	Jan.–Mar. 1918 (percentage)	Apr.–July 1918	After July 1918
Ferrous metals	32	28	87.5	—	10.7	64.3	25.0
Fuel	218	118	51.7	5.1	11.0	59.3	24.6
Electrical energy	63	34	53.9	7.1	44.1	20.6	26.5
Chemicals	344	71	20.6	7.0	25.3	23.9	43.8
Machine building and metal working	875	317	36.2	8.5	19.9	38.5	33.1
Timber and woodworking	946	365	38.6	10.9	11.4	23.4	55.3
Paper	301	79	26.2	7.6	7.6	68.4	16.4
Building materials	371	131	35.3	3.1	13.0	58.0	25.9
Textiles	1,059	234	22.1	3.4	9.0	45.7	41.9
Leather	939	136	14.6	5.1	9.5	42.7	42.7
Food-processing	3,252	1,150	47.7	11.1	18.0	33.5	37.4
Printing	663	141	21.3	5.7	20.5	30.5	43.3
Railway transport	36	29	80.6	6.9	37.9	10.3	44.9
Glass and china	140	72	51.4	11.1	9.7	41.7	37.5
Other	158	33	20.8	6.1	6.1	42.4	45.4
Total	9,542	3,338	35.0	8.9	16.1	36.6	38.4

Source: Drobizhev, p. 61.

Table 2.8. *Number of industrial units 'socialized' by initiative of various institutions*

Institution	November–December 1917			January–March 1918			April–July 1918			After July 1918			Total
	N[a]	S	M	N	S	M	N	S	M	N	S	M	
Sovnarkom	10			17	1		247	3		177	1		456
VSNKh	4	11	61	12	1	76	104	4	147	164	3	88	292
Local soviets	136	2	4	208	16		251	24	31	197	10	28	1,225
Local *Sovnarkhozy*	18	2	4	56	6	4	264	13	26	417	18	18	861
Trade unions	3	3	17	14	2	17	24	10	12	20	1	30	141
Other	23			94	1	13	56	6		96	12		363
Total	194	18	86	401	27	110	946	60	216	1,071	45	164	3,338

[a]N = Nationalized
S = Sequestered or confiscated
M = Municipalized
Source: Drobizhev, p. 63

total recorded number) in the Moscow Region, and 201 (21.5 per cent of the enterprises examined) in the North-West European part of the RSFSR, were nationalized before the autumn.[123]

Lack of data on the volume of output nationalized prevents one drawing conclusions about effective control over the economy made possible by nationalization up to mid 1918. The fact that expropriation was often decided independently of central authority suggests, however, that central control over the economy was far from achieved by June 1918. Until March of that year, nationalization by *Sovnarkom* or VSNKh concerned only 28.1 per cent of cases. This percentage represented 63.8 per cent of industrial enterprises with over 1,000 workers, but included only 4.2 per cent of the total enterprises (141 of the 3,338) expropriated by the end of the year[124] (see Table 2.8). Local soviets and *sovnarkhozy* helped the process of nationalization to get out of the control of the centre. The economic organs registered the existing disorganization. In November 1918 VSNKh stated again that the right to nationalization belonged exclusively to it and to *Sovnarkom* and concerned only joint-stock companies.[125] In spite of this declaration, *Tsentrotekstil'* in December ordered nationalization of all textile factories purchasing wool,[126] while its local organs urged the nationalization of textile factories so as to have them subsidized by the government.[127]

Implementation of a steady programme of nationalization was also hindered by lack of agreement among the leaders. The common opinion that finance capital ought to be expropriated did not entail an agreement on methods, priority and schedules of nationalization. The institutional gap determined by the revolution, therefore, favoured the spontaneous outburst of initiatives from below, which could not be overcome by the leadership. A resolution of the Fourth Conference of Factory-Plant Committees in Petrograd, held in January 1918, demanded the transition of 'all the means of production, factories and workshops' into the hands of the State.[128] In the same month, the First Trade Union Congress approved unanimously the thesis that 'the insufficiency of technical forces and the financial exhaustion of the country dictates a definite gradualism' in the matter of state organization and trustification. An agreement was reached about starting with the trustification of the coal mining industry, which was the most concentrated and the one on which all other industries depended.[129] The contrast between factory committees and trade unions not only reflected different positions on this question by Bolsheviks, largely represented in the former, and Mensheviks, who were more important in the trade unions. It also echoed the lack of consensus within the Bolshevik leadership, of which the Meshchersky Trust and Stakhaev Trust affairs are instructive examples. After ratification of the

Brest–Litovsk peace negotiation on 25 March 1918, the divergences within the Bolshevik Party became sharper. While Lenin tried to persuade his comrades to interpret the peace agreement as a respite, to be used for restoration of the country's economy, the left wing manifested its opposition by abandoning leading posts and starting a campaign against Lenin's proposal on the utilization of bourgeois specialists in industrial management.[130] The outcome of the negotiations with the representatives of the two powerful metallurgical trusts indicates that the arguments of the left wing had no small impact. The initial project concerned the formation of a trust combining twenty enterprises, which could have controlled from 50 to 60 per cent of Russia's machine-building and metallurgical industries. For this purpose, contacts had been maintained with the director of the railway wagon works of the Sormovo–Kolomna metallurgical complex, Meshchersky, since January 1918. Complex negotiations were conducted between representatives of VSNKh and the Association of Moscow Factory Owners.[131] In the course of the negotiations the industrialists offered to the government 100 per cent of the shares and complete control over the trust, provided that 20 per cent of the shares were held in reserve to be returned to the original owners with accumulated dividends, should the government sell the trust's shares in the future.[132] In March 1918 similar negotiations were undertaken with the Stakhaev group controlling a powerful metallurgical trust in the Urals. From the initial proposal concerning the division of finance capital into three main parts (two-fifths held by Russian capitalists, one-fifth by American shareholders and two-fifths by the Soviet government), the financial group came even closer to more unfavourable terms proposed by VSNKh: full nationalization with joint participation in a commission entrusted with reorganization of the metallurgical complex. The Stakhaev group declared itself ready to accept these terms if the representatives of the group were granted the status of 'official representatives of the agglomerate', rather than the status of specialists as proposed by VSNKh.[133]

Both negotiations were interrupted and the industrialists' offers rejected on 14 April, when VSNKh decided on full nationalization of the metallurgical complex.

The Meshchersky project had encountered the opposition of some local trade unions, which demanded full nationalization and participation of their representatives in the bargaining.[134] But the fate of these projects must be evaluated in the light of the Brest–Litovsk agreements and the left-wing position on them. The left-wing communists challenged Lenin's concept of 'respite' on several grounds. Firstly, the hypothesis that Germany, busy fighting England and France, would not attack Russia was rejected by the argument that Germany had not only conquered the Ukraine, but she also would restore factories and fields to the original owners. Secondly, the left-wing communists observed that the respite was not of much help, since the organization of the economy required not only time, but points of departure, such as control of iron, machines, coal, fabrics and food. The final argument – and the crucial one for its political implications – was that Russia capitulated to Germany because the government's efforts had been directed at gaining the services of the bourgeoisie, rather than the people's support against Germany.[135] At the 4 April Session of the Central Committee, Osinskii argued that if the Meshchersky proposal and similar projects had been accepted, 'all initiative in organizing and managing the enterprise would have remained in the hands of the organizers of the trust'.[136] This and similar objections were probably decisive for the final outcome, at a time when the Bolsheviks were endeavouring to solve the food crisis by a scheme of collective commodity exchange, which presumed full control over basic industrial and agricultural products.

The First Congress of *Sovnarkhozy*,* held between 26 May and 4 June 1918, reflected the preoccupations of the leadership on what had to be done first in the field of nationalization. The theses on moderation and gradualness were adopted by a small majority, while a substantial group of left-wing communists opposed them with cogent arguments.

2.4 NATIONALIZATION AFTER BREST–LITOVSK: TIMING AND SCOPE

The recent experience of nationalization, the need for a new strategy after the German occupation of the Ukraine, and the contrasting appreciation of the economic consequences of the Brest–Litovsk agreement furnished the political background for discussion of the economic theses presented at the congress of *sovnarkhozy*.

Two main lines, each concluding with the presentation of separate resolutions to be voted on, reappraised the terms of the debate and singled out the major divergences on the subject.

The official position of VSNKh was presented by Miliutin. He observed that 50 per cent of the enterprises of the mining and metal working industries had already been nationalized. In the Urals, nationalization had proceeded even faster than elsewhere, since 80 per cent of all

*The congress consisted of 252 delegates from several institutions (VSNKh, *Sovnarkom*, trade unions, workers' cooperatives, etc.) who elected the leading organs of VSNKh, the Presidium of sixty-seven people and a smaller bureau of nine.

mining–metallurgical and metal working industries had been expropriated. Nationalization, he continued, occurred without preparatory
work, in the atmosphere of class struggle. Nonetheless, this process had
taken place in the field of heavy industry, where it was most desirable. On
behalf of VSNKh he proposed the complete nationalization of the
mining–metallurgical, metal working, fuel and textile industries on the
basis of a systematic plan. He noted as immediate preoccupations the
possible shut-down of non-profitable enterprises by the capitalists, as had
happened with some of the oil wells. The scale and concentration of these
branches should be taken into account in nationalization policy.[137] He
proposed gradual nationalization. Before it took place, the preliminary
work of accounting and registration of inventories should be done.

Miliutin's theses aroused sharp criticism from the left wing, who
demanded rapid nationalization. Their overall analysis of the political
and economic situation formed the dramatic basis of their radical
alternative proposals. Some speakers reminded the congress that much of
the domestic capital was in the hands of foreigners and economic
initiatives were in many cases dictated by Germany.[138] Osinskii argued
that the preliminary work of accounting and control, which workers were
supposed to carry out according to Miliutin's project, was blocked, in
fact, by the survival of private ownership. Should private ownership not
be abolished, balance-sheets could not be checked and nationalization
would be deferred indefinitely. From this standpoint, Osinskii proposed
the straightforward nationalization of all the means of production and the
division of industry into two departments. Means of production, basic
industrial materials, means of transport and goods for the peasant market
should be included in the first department. The second department would
function as a buffer section of the economy, since it included non-essential
output, which could be suspended without affecting overall economic
growth.[139]

In his proposal for the two departments of industry, Osinskii's
development of the Marxian scheme of reproduction was a partial
anticipation of Preobrazhenskii's analysis in the mid twenties as well as of
the Soviet-type planning of the thirties. The division of the economy into
two departments gave a guideline for priority in investment. Osinskii
proposed allocation of adequate financial and productive resources
together with consumption funds to the first department, production in
which had to be speeded up. From this point of view, he opposed Lenin's
project of electrification, which risked freezing investments for too many
years.[140]

The rapid and decisive industrial collectivization proposed by the left
wing presumed extensive participation of workers in management.

Smirnov stressed that nationalization was but a change of ownership, entailing nothing from a socialist point of view. This approach had already been Lenin's stand on nationalization before the revolution. But, while according to Lenin's theory of the vanguard party the mere seizure of power by the Bolsheviks produced a socialist framework, the left wing focused on the composition of management at the factory level. It was the left wing's merit to point out clearly the relation between nationalization and management, and to propose the radical – though questionable – solution of collective management in the early stages of socialism. By emphasizing the connection between nationalization and managerial composition, the left wing wanted to show that nationalization was feasible. If there was to be one-man management – an idea which attracted both Lenin and Trotskii at that time – the lack of centrally appointed, reliable managers could have become decisive for opposing the rapid programme of nationalization.

At the congress of the *sovnarkhozy*, Lenin's stand on workers' participation in decision-making was quite moderate. Lenin concentrated on the problem of productivity and labour discipline. His proposal to apply Taylorism in industry aroused a passionate controversy in the assembly. The most recent conquests of the working class were at stake. Left-wing communists and anarcho-syndicalists imputed the fall in productivity to sabotage by bourgeois specialists. Technicians were indeed granted a conspicuous role in management by the first decree on management, which at the time was a source of internal conflicts and political debate.[141] The official line, which had the authoritative support of Lenin, on the contrary, singled out other factors of inefficiency, such as poor discipline, disorganization and mistakes due to local interference in the economic field, often ending in punitive confiscations, undesired by the centre.[142]

The majority of the voters voted for Miliutin's theses (twenty-five votes for, seven against and thirteen abstentions). Osinskii's resolution got nine votes for and twelve abstentions. The large number of abstentions shows that, though prevalent, the official position had not sufficient support to create a basis for stable future policies and preclude opposition.

On 28 June 1918, *Sovnarkom* promulgated the decree on nationalization of joint-stock companies.[143] This decree did not correspond to the programme of gradualism defended by Miliutin, nor to the criteria of priority for the nationalization of the means of production and exchange which were at the basis of Osinskii's proposals. It concerned joint-stock companies, i.e. large-scale industry. Conjectures have been expressed to explain the suddenness of this decision, with reference to the fact that the capital of joint-stock companies was primarily German.[144] Unlike other decrees, indeed, the June decree came into force from the moment of its signature. The thesis that political reasons were the determining factors behind the sudden nationalization of large-scale industry receives strong support from the available material. At the First Congress of *Sovnarkhozy*, an eminent personality of the party, Radek, had expressed his fear that the Russian capitalists could obtain the support of Germany to carry out the counter-revolution by selling their stocks and shares to German citizens, through simulated contracts. He proposed, therefore, the forced sale to the state of all stocks and shares in the possession of German citizens,[145] a measure which the Provisional Government had already begun to implement.

Joint-stock companies had been a matter of concern throughout the world war. Between July 1915 and October 1916 measures of liquidation and compulsory administration of joint-stock companies incorporated under Russian law, but controlled by German capital, had been adopted. In 1917, under the pressure of public opinion, the government decreed the compulsory sale of shares held by enemy nationals. The difference between the real value of the shares, which was used as the basis of the selling price to Russian citizens, and the purchase price, based on the price of the stock of reissue according to the last pre-war balance-sheet, was to be paid into the Treasury budget.[146]

After the Brest–Litovsk agreement, the question of the enemy's shares again acquired strong relevance. One of the economic clauses of the agreement stated that 'land, mines, industrial and commercial establishments and shares are restored to enemy nationals... except property which has been taken over by the State'.[147] During the negotiations, the German representative accepted that nationalizations taking place before 1 July 1918 could be paid in redemption money, but claimed that all nationalizations taking place after that date, concerning German-owned industries, had to be fully and immediately indemnified. This claim induced Larin and Krasin, the Soviet representatives in the joint financial commission sitting in Berlin, to draw up a draft of the industrial branches included in the plan of nationalization before July. Krasin's dispatch to Moscow warned that publication of the decree of nationalization should not be deferred to after 29 June since otherwise, Germany would demand payment in cash for the German shares in the given enterprises, thus making nationalization in effect impossible. Krasin urged the Presidium of VSNKh to check the list of enterprises subject to nationalization.[148] The degree of improvisation which accompanied the drafting on expropriation (the most far-reaching decisions in this field taken up to then by any country) has been revealed vividly in the published memoir of Shotman, who was at the time secretary of the VSNKh Presidium.[149] On 27 June Lenin convened a meeting of economic experts. The economists were urged to draw up a list of enterprises in all industrial sectors within twenty-four hours. No excessive precision was requested. Next day the list was completed. The Presidium of VSNKh declared the nationalization of all listed enterprises and submitted the decree for Lenin's approval. At 1 a.m. on the 29th, Lenin sent Shotman to *Izvestiia*, to make sure of the publication of the decree on the same day. The editorial office had to change the stereotype in order to make possible immediate publication of the decree. Lenin's telegram to the Soviet embassy in Berlin concluded the three-day epic of nationalization by the glorious assertion that the law 'was expected impatiently by the Russian people and its publication had been deferred by events independent of the will and wishes of Soviet Power'.[150]

This improvisation explains why the decree on nationalization of large-scale industry affirmed that the former owners could keep their enterprises under free lease from the state, invest in them and get a benefit from them, as well as why the managerial staff were obliged to remain at their posts. Though the June decree was the pretext for some epic' interpretations of Bolshevik history, both by contemporaries and by later literature, nationalization maintained a random and unplanned character even after June. The decree represented a political act and a legal decision. Effective nationalization required the issue of individual decrees for each expropriated factory or industrial complex. Such decrees depended on contingent reasons and were frequently the outcome of conflicting pressures between central and local administrations. The June decree concerned 215 enterprises of heavy industry. In the course of war communism, this number was far exceeded. Individual decrees of nationalization were issued throughout 1918 to 1920.

On 30 June 1918, VSNKh decreed nationalization of the Sormovo–Kolomna works, which together with some other works formed the first large union of machine building factories, GOMZA (state union of machine building plants). Some months elapsed before decisions of analogous weight were taken. In October 1918 two large enterprises of competing financial groups in the copper industry, the Kolchugin and Tula, were nationalized. *Tsentromed'* (Central Administration for Copper), controlling eight enterprises falling under the June decree, was created in January 1919.[151] By the end of 1919 the number of enterprises of the metal-processing industry kept in the records of VSNKh was 1,191 (with the exception of the Southern Regions and the Urals). Out of this number, 434 had been nationalized and put under direct control of VSNKh and 158 had been united into fourteen unions.[152]

The number of enterprise nationalizations in each branch has never been precisely determined. Contrasting figures are indicated by the official statistics and by further investigations on this subject. On 1 October 1919, VSNKh recorded 2,522 nationalized enterprises employing 750,619 workers. These enterprises represented 37 per cent of the total recorded enterprises.[153] On 1 November 1920, VSNKh reported to the Congress of Soviets 4,547 nationalized enterprises, employing one million workers, and presented the following division by branches:

Table 2.9. *Nationalized enterprises, 1 November 1920*

Branches	Number of enterprises	Number of workers	Number of nationalized enterprises	% total Nationalized
Quarrying, clay, earth-moving	998	187,487	445	44.5
Metal working	1,155	243,547	582	50.4
Wood working	242	9,984	157	64.9
Chemicals	261	45,735	244	93.5
Food-processing	2,639	161,551	1,946	73.7
Organic materials	421	43,322	228	54.1
Textiles	847	454,639	629	74.2
Paper and printing	146	32,684	146	100.0
Mineral–metal	133	91,963	127	95.5
Various	66	6,600	43	65.1
Total	6,908	1,277,515	4,547	65.7

Source: Report of VSNKh to the 8th All-Russian Congress of Soviets, December 1920, quoted in I.E. Ankudinova, *Natsionalizatsiia promyshlennosti v SSSR (1917–1920)*, Moscow, 1963, p. 70

The VSNKh estimates suggest that both large and small enterprises were nationalized, since the average number of workers in some branches was rather low.

VSNKh's figures do not coincide with the number of enterprises recorded by the census of August 1920 as 'state enterprises'. The census recorded 26,156 state (*gosudarstvennyi*) enterprises employing hired labour out of a total of 58,074.[154] An explanation for this discrepancy between official data may be that VSNKh included only enterprises which were subject to nationalization by a decree of a competent organ, while the census included all enterprises which, in one form or another, were dependent on public subsidies and public institutions such as the local soviets or *sovnarkhozy*.[155] From this point of view, one may also argue that nationalization under war communism did not ensure full central control over the country's resources and means of production, though such was certainly the intention of the leadership. Fully operative centralization was precluded by several factors, among which the location of raw materials, the changeability of the frontiers, and the resistance of local organs to central directives played the major role. The nationalization of large-scale industry was to make possible the formation of unions of enterprises directed by central administrations or under the direct control of VSNKh. But the geographical distribution of raw materials and fuel was particularly unfavourable to this programme. Industrial activities were concentrated around a few centres, such as Petrograd, Vladimir, Ivanovo-Voznesensk and Moscow, while coal (which in 1913 accounted for 67.1 per cent of the fuel consumed by industry) was provided to the extent of 86.9 per cent by the Donets Basin and 3.9 per cent by the Urals. The other coal sources were in the Caucasus, Turkestan and Siberia. Under war communism, the loss of the territory where most of the fuel and raw materials were concentrated increased the inefficiency of large-scale industry as compared with enterprises of average and small dimensions less dependent on capital-intensive techniques. The Moscow industrial district, where before the war 26 per cent of the metal working and machine building output and 88 per cent of the textiles output were produced, was cut off from the regions of the South which supplied before the war 73.7 per cent of the total output of cast iron and 63.1 per cent of iron and steel, in addition to coal and oil. At the same time, the Moscow Basin, which in 1919 was the only source of coal under Soviet control, provided only 0.9 per cent of the 1913 total supply. The Baku and Groznyi Basin – which together supplied 96.3 per cent of the total output of oil (representing in 1913 11.7 per cent of the total industrial demand for fuel) – were not available.[156]

The mobility and uncertainty of the frontiers made impossible any alternative location of industry and furthered the process of nationalization of all the available resources. Alternative locations were, indeed, looked for by the first congress of *sovnarkhozy*, which took place when the central regions had already been cut off from the South-West mines. A plan was made to transfer industry to the East, in order to exploit the resources of the Urals and Eastern Russia.[157] But in the autumn of 1918 the loss of the Urals nullified this project. Scarcity of raw materials and disruption of transport became powerful factors justifying centralized direction of the economy. The drive towards industrial concentration and shut-down of small units, which had been one of the basic tenets of the Bolshevik industrial policy for rapidly increasing productivity, received an additional impulse. The concentration of the industrial labour force in the old industrial centres under Soviet control facilitated it. The total labour force on 31 August 1918 was 1,175,549 in thirty-three provinces:

30 per cent of this was settled in Moscow and its province, 11 per cent in the province of Petrograd and 21 per cent in the two provinces of Vladimir and Ivanovo-Voznesensk.[158]

The Soviet choice for concentration and centralization of production was consistent with short-term goals, such as control over existing stocks of raw materials and fuel. But perverse effects were manifested as soon as materials and fuel used by the technologically advanced works were exhausted and had to be replaced. The substitution of wood fuel and peat could not help the technologically best equipped factories; while, conversely, it made traditional methods of production comparatively more efficient. The Bolshevik government could not rely on imports. Foreign trade almost ceased: the foreign blockade, which during the world war was aimed at Germany, by diverting shipments to the distant ports of Archangel and Vladivostok, was turned – after the revolution – against Soviet Russia. Wood fuels, which in 1913 provided only 16.5 per cent of the total energy consumed by industry, became the principal source of power. In November 1920 they represented 82.9 per cent of total industrial fuel consumption.[159]

Given this context, one main reason for the decree on overall nationalization of industry, which was passed in November 1920, was the hope of settling once for all the contradictory mechanisms set in motion by the policy of concentration and centralization in a dispersive economic framework restive at any effort of control. This decree had been preceded by a number of regulations issued between 1919 and 1920 restricting the scope for market production and trade. It concerned all industrial enterprises employing more than five workers with mechanical power, or more than ten without, that is, mainly, *kustar'* undertakings that until now had been almost ignored in the nation-wide statistics.[160] Coming at the end of the unresolved conflict of interests which opposed the centre to the provinces during the civil war, the decree on nationalization of small industry was aimed at the incorporation of the local economy into the overall plan of supply of raw materials and funds, in money and in physical terms. The economic experts of the party believed that in this way illegal commodity exchange would cease and a central plan of supply in physical terms could replace it.[161]

The full nationalization of small industry could not be implemented, though some small-scale units were in fact nationalized. The most comprehensive figures on nationalization under war communism remain those of the 1920 census. The overall number of recorded enterprises in 1920 was 278,043. About 11 per cent, that is 29,804, were classified as state enterprises. There were 185,727 enterprises not employing hired labour: not one of these was numbered among state enterprises. Of the

Table 2.10. *Nationalized and non-nationalized enterprises according to number employed, 1920*

State enterprises		Other enterprises	
Number of workers	Number of enterprises	Number of workers	Number of enterprises
1	3,492	1	15,733
2	3,676	2	6,449
3–5	4,909	3–5	5,407
6–10	3,668	6–10	2,220
11–15	1,902	11–15	783
16–20	1,281	16–20	348
21–30	1,631	21–30	395
31–50	1,655	31–50	295

Source: *Sbornik statisticheskikh svedenii po Soiuzu SSR 1918–1923*, p. 165

58,074 employing hired labour, 26,156 or 45 per cent were classified as state enterprises.[162] A fairly large number of small undertakings were considered state property (see Table 2.10).

If any trend may be discerned from reading the official data, it is one towards nationalization of all enterprises employing hired labour, i.e. those forms of production which Marxian analysis considered as producing 'surplus value'. Though the last decree on nationalization concerned only enterprises employing a minimum of five workers with power, the census recorded a fairly high number among state enterprises employing fewer than five workers. Nor was there any sign that this trend would be reversed after the conclusion of hostilities. The extension of nationalization and the restriction of the market sphere occurred in the second half of 1920, when the Bolsheviks had already won on all the fronts, and regions providing agricultural raw materials and the mining and metal working industries were returning to Soviet control.[163]

When emergency ceased to command specific measures of economic policy and economic organization, the ideology of emergency started to get the upper hand. Programmes were not respected. Only one year before, in the summer of 1919, Bukharin and Preobrazhenskii – following the instructions of the Eighth Party Congress of March – were writing in *The ABC of Communism*:

The nationalization of small scale industry is absolutely out of the question: first of all, because it is beyond our powers to organize the dispersed fragments of petty industry; secondly, because the Communist Party does not and cannot wish to alienate the many millions of small masters. Their adhesion to socialism will be quite voluntary, and will not result from their forcible expropriation. This fact must be especially borne in mind in those regions where small scale production is widely prevalent.[164]

These principles were not put into practice: firstly, because small-scale industry manifested a higher comparative efficiency than large-scale industry; secondly, because central power was not strong enough to resist autonomous actions in this sphere; thirdly, because an 'ideology of war communism' emerged out of an extremely hard – but successful – military experience. The success of the Red Army not only against the counter-revolution, but also against foreign intervention, vested the civil war with a patriotic aura which disarmed the opposition and strengthened Bolshevik power. From the political standpoint, this turned out to be a powerful motivation for furthering the process of reorganization according to the authoritative models imposed by the most radical leaders.

Contrary to the intentions expressed in *The ABC of Communism*, expropriation of small undertakings was higher in the regions where their number was greater.[165] The inclusion of unplanned units in the state sphere was the result of autonomous impulses coming from the state sector, where central administrations, *glavki* and *tsentry* endeavoured to get control of that part of output which went into the black market. The sphere of state economy expanded more rapidly than was forecast. Within a Marxist framework this fact could not but be welcome, as were other features peculiar more to a war economy than to communist organization. Rationing and central distribution of foodstuffs and consumer goods much reduced market operations. The progressive naturalization (de-monetization) of the economy, which was favoured by inflation, seemed to work for the extrusion of money out of the system. The realm of 'product exchange' as opposed to 'commodity exchange' – that is, the conscious distribution of the social product instead of market distribution, as indicated by Marx – seemed to be at hand, if only the state could get total control and disposal of the mass of goods, which would be necessary to create a *national wage fund in kind*, adequate to the supply of *all hired workers*, that is, the new dominant class.

Rationing, annihilation of the purchasing power of money, the substitution for market regulators of military orders, barter – interpreted through the filter of Marxist ideology – seemed only to need a politically and rationally directed social and economic organization in order to become consistent parts of the new society. It was in this framework that the idea of central planning materialized.

By 1920 the nationalization of the means of production was formally completed. The large-scale enterprises were all nationalized and subject to the direction of central administrations directly dependent on VSNKh. Ninety-two per cent of medium-scale industry, that is, firms employing from 51 to 1,000 workers, was nationalized; 90 per cent of the total labour force, as reckoned by the 1920 census, belonged to the nationalized sphere.[166] Although the total value of output of the industry of Central Russia – the only region where Soviet Power maintained control during the civil war – was a mere 18 per cent of 1912 in real terms,[167] the expropriation of the means of production gave to the new dominant class expressed by the Communist Party a real and permanent mastery over the economy. Even if the revision of economic policy, which started at the beginning of 1921, led to the interruption of the process of nationalization of small-scale industry in May 1921,[168] and some months later to the decree on de-nationalization of this sector,[169] control over the potential output of large-scale state industry was the permanent achievement and the foundation of the new economic system based on the dictatorship of the proletariat.

2.5 SUMMARY

The Bolshevik approach to nationalization and state control was heavily influenced by the contributions of Marx and Kautsky. The core of Marx's analysis of capitalism was his criticism of market competition. Kautsky added a further reason for the suppression of market competition: the comparatively higher efficiency of monopoly, as exemplified by the concentrated large-scale industry of Germany. The concentration of production in a few large-scale enterprises was a manifest goal of the Bolshevik leaders, whose programme consisted in furthering what was considered a natural historical process, by shutting down small-scale enterprises, introducing market control measures and replacing market incentives by guidelines from above.

This theoretical approach was to have an impact on the understanding of the economic dynamic of Russia, characterized at the beginning of the century by a process of concentration in some industrial branches, the importance of which was exaggerated by most progressive intellectuals. The available statistics neglected the existence of a fairly large number of small-scale enterprises and handicrafts, concealing the size and importance of the traditional economy, which was, in fact, essential in consumer goods production. The First World War added new incentives to the enforcement of policies of control over prices and stocks of raw materials and finished goods through the creation of branch control committees, called *glavki* or *tsentry*. The emerging structure of the economy, thus, from the point of view of the revolutionary leadership, became even more favourable to the pursuit of state control. But nationalization, as such, was a programme which the Bolshevik leadership had intended to pursue gradually, had they not been pushed to speed up the schedules by pressures from below and by other circumstances related to war. In the first months of power, nationalization was often the result of confiscation of industrial property by local bodies, which acted independently of central guidelines or orders. It was politically defined as *punitive* nationalization. After the Brest–Litovsk Treaty, two contrasting approaches to nationalization emerged even within the leadership itself. Although many still supported gradualness and moderation in economic organization, the policy of rapid nationalization of all means of production supported by the left-wing communists began to gain conspicuous support. Thus, the decree on nationalization of joint-stock companies promulgated by *Sovnarkom* on 28 June, under the threat that nationalization of German enterprises after 1 July would have to be compensated, was welcomed by those Bolsheviks who wanted to speed up the process of change initiated by the revolution. Thereafter there was an increasing number of decrees on the nationalized enterprises far above that foreseen by the June 1918 Decree. If financial disorganization, anti-market polices, civil war and the need for control over supply all accounted for the increasing pace of nationalization in 1919–20, the reasons for the decree on overall nationalization of November 1920 have to be found, instead, in the conception of a central plan of supply of raw materials and consumer goods, which started taking shape in the course of civil war, along with the rising rate of inflation and progressive demonetization of the war economy.

NOTES

1 K. Marx, *Theories of the Surplus Value*, Moscow, 1969, vol. 2, pp. 499–505.
2 K. Marx, *Capital*, 3 vols., Moscow, 1957, vol. 2, pp. 492–523.
3. K. Marx, *Grundrisse*, Harmondsworth, 1973, pp. 250–1.
4. K. Marx and F. Engels, *Selected Works*, vol. 1, Moscow, 1962, p. 53.
5 Marx and Engels, *Collected Works*, London, 1978, vol. 10, p. 60.
6 Marx's criticism was directed to the 1875 programme of unification of the two German workers' organizations.
7 K. Marx, *Critique of the Gotha Program*, New York, 1966, pp. 5–6, 7–10.
8 *Ibid.*, p. 10.
9 *Ibid.*, p. 7.
10 K. Kautsky, *La Révolution sociale*, Paris, 1921, p. 173.

11 K. Kautsky, *Das Erfurter Programm*, Stuttgart–Berlin, 1922, pp. 114–15.
12 Kautsky, *La Révolution sociale*, pp. 165–6, 167–8, 174–5.
13 *Ibid.*, p. 197.
14 V.I. Lenin, *Collected Works*, 4th edn, 45 vols., London, 1964–70, vol. 25, 1965, p. 481: 'State and Revolution'.
15 *Ibid.*, p. 404.
16 *Ibid.*, p. 402.
17 *Ibid.*, p. 463.
18 W. Brus, *Socialist Ownership and Political Systems*, London–Boston, 1975, pp. 42–5, defines these three elements as *genetic, socio-economic* and *political* systemic factors respectively.
19 Lenin started formulating this theory at the turn of the century, in commenting on the programme of the Russian Social Democratic Party: 'Zamechaniia na pervyi proekt Programmy Plekhanova' and 'Proekt Programmy Rossiiskoi Sotsialisticheskoi Rabochei Partii', *Polnoe sobranie sochinenii*, vol. 6, 5th edn, Moscow, 1959, pp. 195–202, 198, 205.
20 Lenin, *Collected Works*, vol. 25, pp. 456–74.
21 Quoted by Lenin, *Polnoe sobranie sochinenii*, vol. 33, p. 333.
22 *Ibid.*, p. 333.
23 See S.F. Cohen, *Bukharin and the Bolshevik Revolution*, Oxford, 1980, p. 39.
24 Cf. also N. Bukharin, *Anarchia e Comunismo Scientifico*, Società editrice del P.C. d'Italia, 1922, p. 5.
25 N.N. Sukhanov, *The Russian Revolution 1917: An Eyewitness Account*, vol. 2, New York, 1962, pp. 420–1, 554–5.
26 Lenin, *Collected Works*, vol. 24, pp. 73–4.
27 *Ibid.*, p. 73.
28 Lenin, *Collected Works*, vol. 23, pp. 306–8.
29 On the distinction between a minimum and maximum programme see E.H. Carr, *The Bolshevik Revolution, 1917–1923*, 3 vols., London, 1952, vol. 2, pp. 14–15.
30 Cf. Cohen, p. 55.
31 Lenin defined as 'ostensibly "very radical", but really very groundless' Bukharin's and Smirnov's proposal (V.I. Lenin, 'Revision of the Party Programme', *Collected Works*, vol. 26, pp. 169–70).
32 Cf. N. Bukharin, *Imperialism and World Economy*, London, 1972, p. 59, and Lenin, *Polnoe sobranie sochinenii*, vol. 27, pp. 364–73.
33 Lenin, *Collected Works*, vol. 23, p. 59.
34 Lenin, *Collected Works*, vol. 26, p. 172.
35 Lenin, *Collected Works*, vol. 24, pp. 150, 194, 282–7, 306–7, 502.
36 Lenin, *Collected Works*, vol. 26, 'The Tasks of the Revolution', p. 65.
37 *Ibid.*, p. 67.
38 However, the pamphlet was not published until January 1918.
39 Lenin, *Collected Works*, vol. 26, 'Can the Bolsheviks Retain State Power?', pp. 103–4.
40 *Ibid.*, pp. 105–6.
41 *Ibid.*, pp. 107–8.
42 Lenin, *Collected Works*, vol. 25, p. 425.
43 Lenin, *Collected Works*, vol. 26, p. 110.

44 V.A. Bazarov (Rudnev) (1874–1939) was in 1917 one of the editors of the Menshevik newspaper *Novaia Zhizn'*. From 1921 onwards he worked in the State Planning Commission of the USSR.

45 Lenin, *Collected Works*, vol. 26, pp. 116–18.

46 He told the October 1917 Congress of the Party that it would be inexpedient to venture into a discussion of separate and concrete measures (*Collected Works*, vol. 26, p. 173).

47 Lenin, *Collected Works*, vol. 26, p. 465.

48 The difference between the Menshevik and Bolshevik stands on revolution after 1905 has been thoughtfully analysed by L.H. Haimson, *The Russian Marxists and the Origins of Bolshevism*, Cambridge, Mass., 1955, pp. 198–208.

49 Bertrand Russell, *The Practice and Theory of Bolshevism*, London 1920, p. 80.

50 *Narodnoe Khoziaistvo*, 1919, no. 3, 14.

51 For this feature of Marxism see E.H. Carr, *The October Revolution*, New York, 1971, pp. 5–6.

52 *8i S"ezd RKP (b), 18–23 marta 1919 g*, Moscow, 1933, pp. 42–4.

53 Karl Radek (1885–1939) joined the Bolshevik Party in 1917. From 1923 he became a member of the Trotskii faction. He was expelled from the party in 1936. Before joining the Bolsheviks, Radek had been active in the RSDLP and in the faction of the internationalists.

54 K. Radek, 'L'evoluzione del socialismo dalla scienza all' azione', *Documenti della Rivoluzione*, no. 13 (Reprint Feltrinelli), 1970, p. 17.

55 Cf. G.D.H. Cole, *A History of Socialist Thought. Marxism and Anarchism: 1850–1890*, vol. 2, London, 1954, pp. 219–36 on Bakunin's thought and his project of 'federalism' as a component of his rejection of Marxian determinism.

56 Marx, *Capital*, vol. 1, chapter 12, par. 4; chapter 13, par. 8; vol. 2, pp. 172, 469; vol. 3, p. 858; and *Theories of the Surplus Value*, vol. 2, pp. 507–24.

57 Kautsky, *La Révolution sociale*, pp. 165–6, 172–3.

58 Lenin, *Collected Works*, vol. 43, p. 114 and 71, p. 650.

59 Bukharin, *The Economics of the Transformation Period, with Lenin's Remarks*, New York, 1971, pp. 14–15.

60 A. Bogdanov, *A Short Course of Economic Science*, London, 1925, p. 383.

61 L. Kritsman, *Geroicheskii period Velikoi Russkoi Revoliutsii*, Moscow (no date, probably 1924), p. 26.

62 N. Bukharin, *The Economics*, pp. 182–3, n. 182, and 70–1.

63 An illuminating discussion of Lenin's writings on state capitalism is provided by L. Szamuely (*First Models of the Socialist Economic Systems, Principles and Theories*, Budapest, 1974, pp. 45–62).

64 *Das Finanz Kapital, Marx Studien* vol. 3, Vienna, 1923, pp. 472–4.

65 Lenin, *Collected Works*, vol. 43, p. 650.

66 A. Gerschenkron, *Economic Backwardness in Historical Perspective*, New York, 1965, pp.128–9.

67 Cf. O. Crisp, *Studies in the Russian Economy before 1914*, London, 1976, pp. 36–44. *Statisticheskii sbornik za 1913–1977 gg*, Moscow, 1921, pp. 36–7, on the basis of 1913 data computed for fifty provinces, gives the following distribution:

Number of workers	Enterprises	%	Workers	%
Up to 10	2,366	13.2	17,314	0.7
11–20	3,782	21.1	58,513	2.5
21–50	5,411	30.3	177,720	7.7
51–100	2,707	15.2	196,197	8.5
101–200	1,484	8.3	213,566	8.2
201–500	1,233	6.9	403,028	17.4
501–1,000	502	2.8	350,682	15.1
Above 1,000	392	2.2	902,557	38.9
Total	17,877	100.0	2,319,577	100.0

68 V.I. Grinevetskii, *Poslevoennye perspektivy Russkoi promyshlennosti*, Kharkov, 1919, p. 166. Satisfactory estimates of the pre-war output of small-scale industry have not yet been produced. The industrial census excluded timber (logging), fishing and railway repair shops. In 1926 Voroboev estimated that total industrial output at 1913 prices (including excises) for the census industry was 7526.1 million rubles, of which 1904.7 million rubles belonged to small-scale industry, i.e. 25 per cent of total output. Voroboev's estimates did not include salt, peat and stone breaking (see *Trudy TsSU, XXVI*, first part, Moscow, 1926, pp. 69–73 and *Trudy TsSU, XXIX*, second part, Moscow, 1926, p. 92). New estimates produced in 1929–30 increased the absolute volume of both census industry output and small-scale industry output (which was estimated at 2040 million rubles, i.e. 24.1 per cent of total output), cf.: *Piatiletnii plan*, I, 1930, p. 15 and *Ekonomicheskoe Obozrenie*, no. 9, 1929, 114. I am indebted to Prof. R.W. Davies for allowing me to use his 'Soviet Industrial Production, 1928–1937. The Rival Estimates', *CREES Discussion Papers*, Birmingham, no. 18, 1978, pp. 14–15, 58, from which the above figure and references have been taken. Doubts have also been thrown on the assertion that in Russia a large enterprise labour force was evidence of mature capitalism, suggesting that, on the contrary, it was a sign of immaturity. Large concerns often had their own machine repair shops, workers' houses, hospitals, baths, schools, bakeries, etc., because these services were not otherwise provided (cf. Crisp, p. 41).

69 W.W. Rostow, *The Stages of Economic Growth*, 7th edn, Cambridge, 1969, pp. 93–105, considers the period 1880 to 1913 as that of take-off for the Russian economy. See also C.E. Black, ed., *The Transformation of Russian Society: Aspects of Social Change Since 1861* Cambridge, Mass. 1, 1960, on Russian development (1861–1917). Soviet literature nowadays maintains that prerevolutionary Russia was a medium-developed country, where the high concentration of capital and banking, however, justified the outbreak of the revolution according to the Marxian scheme (cf. L.S. Gaponenko, A.N. Sakharov, G.L. Sobolev, 'Velikii Oktiabr' i ego sovremennye burzhuaznye kritiki', *Voprosy Istorii*, no. 1, 1969, 21). An analysis of the contradictions stemming from the historiography of the Russian stage of development and

the material foundations for the revolution is provided by B.D. Wolfe, 'Backwardness and Industrialization in Russian History and Thought', *Slavic Review*, vol. 25, no. 2, June 1967, 177–203.

70 See, for instance, P.I. Liashchenko, *Istoriia narodnogo khoziaistva SSSR*, Gos. izd. politicheskoi literatury, 1948, vol. 2, p. 292.

71 Bukharin, *Imperialism and World Economy*, p. 69 and p. 64. Only in a footnote does Bukharin, having mentioned that trusts are only a more centralized form of the same phenomenon, seem to agree with Hilferding's distinction that 'contrary to the process of trustification, cartelization by no means signifies the elimination of the conflict of interests between the individual enterprises belonging to the cartel'; Lenin, *Polnoe sobranie sochinenii*, vol. 27, pp. 317–20, considered that price agreements and control of the terms of sale practised by trusts and cartels indicated the definite monopolistic nature of the latter.

72 For this distinction see R. Portal, *La Russie industrielle de 1881 à 1927*, Paris, 1976, p. 128.

73 *Ibid.*, pp. 130–7. See Liashchenko, pp. 294–324 on the evolution of *Prodameta*.

74 Portal, pp. 130–5.

75 *Ibid.*, pp. 142, 129.

76 *Ibid.*, p. 143.

77 P.V. Ol', *Inostrannye kapitaly v Rossii*, Petrograd, 1922, p. 9.

78 V. Sarabianov, *Ekonomika i ekonomicheskaia politika SSSR*, Moscow, 1926, p. 46.

79 B.B. Grave, 'Militarizatsiia promyshlennosti i rossiiskii proletariat v gody pervoi mirovoi voiny' *Iz istorii rabochego klassa i revoliutsionnogo dvizheniia*, Moscow, 1958, p. 419.

80 Portal, pp. 149–51.

81 Sarabianov, pp. 50–4. According to Sarabianov's data, military industrial output in 1916 was 222.1 per cent and civil industrial output 90.9 per cent of the 1913 levels.

82 S. Zagorsky, *State Control of Industry in Russia during the War*, New Haven, 1928, pp. 145–9; and Portal, pp. 155–6.

83 Zagorsky, p. 149.

84 When the discussion opened on the role and functions of a supreme economic council (VSNKh), Bukharin's proposal to use the institutions inherited from the Kerensky Government, as well as Larin's project aiming at the bringing together in VSNKh of a large number of capitalist and public organizations, were both rejected. *The History of the Civil War in the USSR*, ed. M. Gorkii *et al.*, 2 vols., 1946, vol. 2, pp. 578–9.

85 Lenin, *Collected Works*, vol. 24, pp. 424–5.

86 Grinevetskii, p. 13. This author adds, however, that there was not much left, after depreciation, of investment funds and private dividends, and that wage increases in 1917 were financed out of profits.

87 An excerpt of Skobelev's public speech on these issues was reported by Lenin in the 'Inevitable Catastrophe and Extravagant Promises'. For this and Lenin's comments see Lenin, *Collected Works*, vol. 24, pp. 424–8.

88 On Groman's proposal see V.P. Miliutin, *Sovremennoe ekonomicheskoe razvitie Rossii i diktatura proletariata (1914–1918gg)*, Moscow, 1918, pp. 31–2; for Lenin's comments see *Collected Works*, vol. 24, pp. 525–6.

89 On this aspect of Lenin's personality see A. Nove, *An Economic History of the USSR*, Harmondsworth, 1969, p. 42; and M. Hoschiller *Le Mirage du Soviétisme*, Paris, 1921, p. 146.

90 *The Bolsheviks and the October Revolution. Central Committee Minutes of the Russian Social-Democratic Labour Party (bolsheviks), August 1917–February 1918*, London, 1974, p. 53.

91 *Narodnoe Khoziaistvo*, 1919, no. 3, 10–11; cf. also N. Bukharin, *The Economics*, p. 61, 179, n 42. Bukharin qualifies Kritsman's statement by pointing out that the revolution destroys the former capitalist hierarchical ties, but not the technological relations, which remain as a temporary legacy of capitalism.

92 See the preface to 'State and Revolution', Lenin, *Collected Works*, vol. 25, pp. 383–4.

93 N. Osinskii, *Stroitel'stvo sotsializma*, Moscow, 1918, pp. 33, 38.

94 Lenin, *Collected Works*, vol. 25, p. 473.

95 In 1917, in real terms, manual workers received 85 per cent and clerical workers 38 per cent of their corresponding remunerations in 1913. Managers and technicians received respectively 30 and 39 per cent of their corresponding salaries in 1913. In industries working for the war, such as engineering, wage equalization was even stronger: while, in real terms, in 1917 the wages of metal manual workers were 35 per cent lower than in 1913, the salaries of clerical workers in the lowest category were 65% lower. In absolute terms, the latter dropped below the wages of manual workers. (*cf. Sbornik statisticheskikh svedenii, 1918–1923*, pp. 191, 189).

96 Lenin, *Collected Works*, vol. 25, 'State and Revolution', p. 427.

97 Lenin, *Collected Works*, vol. 27, 'Speech at the session of the All-Russian Central Executive Committee', 29 April 1918, pp. 310–11; 'Six Theses on the Immediate Tasks of the Soviet Government', approved by the party on 3 May 1918, p. 316; 'Left-Wing Childishness', 5 May 1918, p. 350.

98 Cf. Osinskii at the First Congress of *Sovnarkhozy: Trudy I Vserossiiskogo S''ezda Sovetov narodnogo khoziaistva (26 Maia-4 Iunia 1918g)*, stenogr. otchet, Moscow, 1918, p. 102.

99 On the distinction between confiscation, sequestration and nationalization see N.N. Razumovich, *Organizatsionno-pravovye formy sotsialisticheskogo obobshchestvleniia promyshlennosti v SSSR, 1917–1920gg*, Moscow, 1959, pp. 58–9, 66–7.

100 Cf. Miliutin's theses at the First Congress of *Sovnarkhozy, Trudy I Vserossiiskogo S''ezda Sovetov*, p. 53; R. Arskii and A. Kaktyn in *Narodnoe Khoziaistvo*, 1919, nos. 9–10, 8, 16; Osinskii and Miliutin in *Oktiabr'skii perevorot i diktatura proletariata, sbornik statei*, Moscow, 1919, pp. 87, 101.

101 Cf. speech by Dalin (a Menshevik representative) in *Za god, sbornik statei*, Moscow, 1918, p. 58.

102 *Uprochenie Sovetskoi Vlasti v Moskve i Moskovskoi gubernii, dokumenty i materialy*, Moscow, 1958, document no. 172.

103 That is, through the Moscow Military Revolutionary Committee.

104 This case is produced by D.A. Baevskii, *Rabochii klass v pervye gody Sovetskoi Vlasti (1917–1921gg)*, Moscow, 1974, pp. 40–1.

105 *Uprochenie Sovetskoi Vlasti*, document no. 178.

106 *Rabochii kontrol'i natsionalizatsiia promyshlennosti v Kostromskoi Gubernii. Sbornik dokumentov 1917–1918 gg*, Kostroma, 1960, p. 29.

107 Quoted by A.A. Voronetskaia, 'Organizatsiia Vysshego Soveta Narodnogo Khoziaistva i ego rol' v natsionalizatsii promyshlennosti', *Istoricheskie Zapiski*, 1953, no. 43, 6.

108 Cf. Razumovich, pp. 58–9.

109 *Novyi Luch*, no. 20, 3 January 1918, 1–2.

110 *Sbornik dekretov i postanovlenii po narodnomu khoziaistvu*, 2 vols., Moscow, 1918–21, vol. 1, 1917–1918, p. 203.

111 I.E. Ankudinova, *Natsionalizatsiia promyshlennosti v SSSR (1917–1920)*, Moscow, 1963, p. 68. Some soviets were compelled by VSNKh to restore former owners to management of the illegally nationalized factories (cf. E. Antonelli, *La Russie Bolcheviste*, Paris, 1919, pp. 228–9 and *Pravda*, no. 84, 30 April 1918, 4). But these were probably isolated cases.

112 Razumovich, p. 39.

113 Amongst others: A.V. Venediktov, *Organizatsiia gosudarstvennoi promyshlennosti v SSSR*, vol. 1, Moscow, 1957, pp. 186, 193–4; I.A. Gladkov, *Ocherki sovetskoi ekonomiki 1917–1920 gg*, Moscow 1956, p. 22; Baevskii, *Rabochii klass*, pp. 39–40, 44–5; I.A. Ankudinova, p. 49.

114 *Narodnoe Khoziaistvo*, 1918, no. 1, 38–9.

115 This case is described by Baevskii, *Rabochii klass*, pp. 33–5.

116 *Ibid.*, p. 36.

117 *Ibid.*, pp. 44–5.

118 V.Z. Drobizhev and A.B. Medvedev, *Iz istorii sovnarkhozov*, Moscow, 1964, p. 155.

119 *Biulleten' VSNKh*, 1918, April, no. 1, 37.

120 *Ibid.*, 37–9.

121 V.Z. Drobizhev, 'Sotsialisticheskoe obobshchestvlenie promyshlennosti v SSSR', *Voprosy Istorii*, 1964, no. 6, 59.

122 *Ibid.*, 58.

123 *Ibid.*, 62.

124 *Ibid.*, 163.

125 *Ekonomicheskaia Zhizn'*, no. 2, 9 November 1918, 2.

126 *Ekonomicheskaia Zhizn'*, no. 2, 1 December 1918, 4.

127 *Ekonomicheskaia Zhizn'*, no. 25, 6 December 1918, 5.

128 *Novyi Put'*, 1918, nos. 4–5, p. 13.

129 *Putevoditel' po rezoliutsiiam Vserossiiskikh S"ezdov i Konferentsii Professional'nykh Soiuzov* (Sos. Iu. Milanov), Moscow, 1924, p. 118.

130 The left-wing communists produced their own organ *Kommunist (ezhegodnyi zhurnal ekonomiki, politiki i obobshchestvlennosti)*, in which they presented their theses against the policy of the government.

131 On the Meshchersky affair see H.R. Buchanan, 'Lenin and Bukharin on the Transition from Capitalism to Socialism: the Meshchersky Controversy', *Soviet Studies*, vol. 28, no. 1 January 1976, 72–5; and P.V. Volobuev and V.Z. Drobizhev, 'Iz istorii goskapitalizma v nachalnyi period sotsialisticheskogo stroitel'stva v SSSR', *Voprosy Istorii*, 1957, no. 9, 113–21.

132 Buchanan, pp. 73–4.

133 Voronetskaia, p. 23; see also *Ekonomicheskaia Zhizn' SSSR, khronika sobytii i faktov 1917–1965 v dvukh knigakh*, vol. 1, Moscow, 1967, p. 20.

134 Buchanan, p. 73. On the opposition of the *fabzavkom* to the Meshchersky

project, see S.I. Liberman, *Dela i liudi (na sovetskoi stroike)*, New York, 1944, pp. 119–21.

135 Buchanan, p. 73.

136 Quoted by Buchanan, p. 75.

137 *Trudy I Vserossiiskogo S"ezda Sovetov*, pp. 53–5; Miliutin's programme was presented to the Party Congress for the first time in March 1918: V.P. Miliutin, *Istoriia ekonomicheskogo razvitiia SSSR*, Moscow–Leningrad, 1929, pp. 151–64.

138 *Trudy I Vserossiiskogo S"ezda Sovetov*, p. 69.

139 *Ibid.*, pp. 88–9.

140 This project was cherished by Lenin who, personally, in April 1918, asked the Academy of Sciences to set up a number of expert commissions, which he asked, *inter alia*, to give 'special attention to the electrification of industry and transport and the application of electricity to farming': Lenin, *Collected Works*, vol. 27, pp. 320–1; *Trudy I Vserossiiskogo S"ezda Sovetov*, p. 89.

141 *Sbornik dekretov i postanovlenii*, vol. 1, pp. 311–15 and N. Osinskii's criticism of it in *Stroitel'stvo sotsializma*.

142 *Trudy I Vserossiiskogo S"ezda Sovetov*, p. 92.

143 *Sobranie uzakonenii*, 1917–18, no. 47, art. 559.

144 Cf. M. Dobb, *Soviet Economic Development after 1917*, London, 1951, p. 95 and Carr, *The Bolshevik Revolution, 1917–1923*, vol. 2, p. 99.

145 *Trudy I Vserossiiskogo S"ezda Sovetov*, p. 16.

146 Boris E. Nolde (Baron), *Russia in the Economic War*, New Haven, 1928, pp. 91, 98–100.

147 *Ibid.*, p. 180.

148 Quoted by D.A. Kovalenko, *Oboronnaia promyshlennost' Sovetskoi Rossii v 1918–1920*, Moscow, 1970, pp. 153–5.

149 *V.I. Lenin: vo glave velikogo stroitel'stva* (collection of memoirs), Moscow, 1960, pp. 63–4.

150 *Leninskii sbornik*, vol. 35, p. 27, and n.

151 *Narodnoe Khoziaistvo*, 1918, no. 12, 25.

152 Razumovich, pp. 101–11.

153 *Ibid.*, p. 111.

154 *Sbornik statisticheskikh svedenii po Soiuzu SSR, 1918–1923*, vol. 18, pp. 166–7.

155 This was also the conclusion of Vainshtein, who made an investigation into the total number of enterprises under the control of the central organs of VSNKh in May 1921. He reported 25,900 nationalized enterprises, plus 350 in a special territorial category (*Narodnoe Khoziaistvo*, March 1922, 56).

156 For data on distribution of resources, see Sarabianov, p. 154 and *Sbornik statisticheskikh svedenii . . . 1918–1923*, pp. 193–5. On the economic situation of Russia during the world war, see A.L. Sidorov, *Ekonomicheskoe polozhenie Rossii v gody pervoi mirovoi voiny*, Moscow 1973, p. 372, and *passim*.

157 Miliutin, *Sovremennoe ekonomicheskoe razvitie*, p. 59.

158 *Sbornik statisticheskikh svedenii . . . 1918–1923*, pp. 70–1.

159 Sarabianov, p. 155.

160 *Sobranie uzakonenii*, 1920, no. 93, art. 512. The question of *kustar'* production is discussed in more detail in the Appendix to this chapter.

161 Kritsman, pp. 130–3, 137.

162 *Sbornik statisticheskikh svedenii*... *1918–1923*, pp. 165–6. The discrepancy between the total number of state enterprises and the number employing hired labour was not explained.

163 War against Poland ended in October 1920, but the 1920 March Congress of the Party was already celebrating military victory over the enemy.

164 N. Bukharin and E. Preobrazhensky, *The ABC of Communism*, Harmondsworth 1969, p. 315; the impracticability of the nationalization of small industry was asserted by *Ekonomicheskaia Zhizn'* too (n. 156, 18 July 1919, 1).

165 *Sbornik statisticheskikh svedenii*... *1918–1923*, p. 165; out of thirteen *raiony*, whose average number of state enterprises employing from 1–5 workers was 30 per cent of the total number of such enterprises, the Moscow Industrial Region, where 23 per cent of small undertakings were located, had a higher percentage of state enterprises.

166 *Sbornik statisticheskikh svedenii*... *1918–1923*, p. 165.

167 *Statisticheskii spravochnik po narodnomu khoziaistvu*, vyp. 2, *Promyshlennost'*, Moscow, 1923, Table 8.

168 *Sobranie uzakonenii*, 1921, no. 48, art. 240.

169 *Sobranie uzakonenii*, 1921, no. 79, art. 684.

Nationalization of *kustar'* industry

The Second Congress of *Sovnarkhozy* focused on centralization of the economy and the amalgamation of industry. Small-scale industry and handicrafts attracted only an incidental curiosity and a concern affected by ideological bias. Nogin affirmed that a way had to be found to integrate the *kustar'* economy into the state economy, for otherwise such undertakings would develop in number and ambition and that would make it harder to deal with them. To the obvious objections that *kustari*, unlike large-scale industry, were not easy to organize, because of their number and geographical dispersion, Nogin replied only that the aim was correct, though a mode of implementation had not yet been discovered.[1] The draft resolution foresaw the formation of a special *kustar'* section attached to VSNKh and affirmed the principle that the development of private property should be resisted by means of a policy of incentives and cooperation. The final resolution, however, embodied the arguments of the opposition. The goal of unifying *kustari* was maintained, but for the time being only the organization of *kustar'* sections at the level of the *sovnarkhozy* was proposed. Decentralization was approved essentially because the representative of *Narkomzem* (People's Commissariat for Agriculture), who was also responsible for *kustari*, pointed out with common sense that priority had to be given to the needs of the army, for which *kustar'* output was necessary. In this field, added the *Narkomzem* official, theoretical speculations did not help.[2]

Kustar' output had a traditional place in the Russian national product. Taking countryside and town together, *kustar'* industrial output was estimated at between 24 and 27 per cent of total industrial output in 1913 prices before the First World War. In some fields like the wood-working industry, cloth, haberdashery and flour milling, the productivity of small industry was definitely greater than that of large-scale industry. Even in metal production and the processing of organic products, however, *kustari* showed great strength.[3] In 1913 there were almost four million *kustari* and small producers officially registered in several fields.[4]

Economic disorganization, after the revolution, was an incentive to *kustar'* activity. State monopoly of trade together with the falling productivity of industry, particularly in the field of finished products, spurred small producers to sell goods on the black market, which in the large towns was very active and in the countryside helped the peasantry to overcome the oppressive rules of collective commodity exchange. The peasants themselves organized their own handicraft activities or endeavoured to improve the existing ones. The lack of fuel and raw materials which hindered the activity of large industry was relatively less detrimental to handicrafts, which made use of traditional and less sophisticated techniques. Beside the usual handicraft production of household goods, wooden articles, fabrics, etc., small producers developed or went back to the production of raw materials and building materials, coal and charcoal, dyeing, etc.[5] Reports showed that the production of salt by the old methods of evaporation reached a fairly significant output.[6] By the beginning of 1919, about three and a half million people were reckoned to be working in *kustar'* industry.[7] Local handicrafts enjoyed the collaboration and assistance of the *uezd sovnarkhozy*. The latter organized central workshops by assembling small shops making agricultural implements, repair shops and *artels* producing bricks and lime. In the more agricultural provinces, *kustari* milled grain and produced bricks, rope, iron implements, etc., and processed agricultural products.[8] In the province of Cherepovets, ten thousand people were engaged in *kustar'* processing of wood.[9] In 1919 the number of *kustari* in the wood-working industry, producing bast, birch bark, wood equipment, barrels, furniture, etc., was much higher than the number of people working under the Chief Committee for Timber, *Glavleskom*: 180,000 people as against 37,690 in thirty-one provinces.[10] In the peripheral provinces, like Olonets, only *kustar'* enterprises remained active in wood-processing.[11] Other auxiliary activities concerned packing for *Narkomprod* (People's Commissariat for Food Procurement) and making brooms, shovels, etc., for the People's Commissariat of Transport.[12] The local organs promoted the formation of *artels* of production, especially when *kustari* had to work on army orders.

Kustar' production was not limited to the provinces. In Moscow, 20,000 people worked in associations of *kustari*, whose number more than doubled in one year. The average number of people per *artel* was about twelve to fifteen. However, some organizations consisted of 100–200 and even 350. The largest association of *kustari* in Moscow consisted of 815 people.[13] In 1919, raw materials to the value of five million rubles were turned over to the Moscow *kustari* by the central administrations. The value of *kustar'* output in this town reached fifty million rubles. The major customers were reported to be the All-Russian Council of Trade Unions, consumers' cooperatives, *Narkomprod* and *Narkomzdrav* (the People's Commissariat for Health). Output for the army was estimated at more than three million rubles.[14] In Moscow, the central administrations of VSNKh fulfilled only 35 per cent of the total industrial orders. The remainder fell to the local undertakings controlled by the town *sovnarkhoz*. Towards the end of 1919, small-scale and craft industry in Moscow produced 120,000 arshin of fabrics a month, whilst large-scale industry stopped working for lack of power.[15] The decline of large-scale industry as compared with small undertakings is shown by the fact that in May 1919 the average number of people working per production unit in industry was only 75.[16]

Raw materials were sometimes supplied by the *kustari* themselves;[17] sometimes by the local *sovnarkhozy*.[18] Output was delivered on the basis of sales contracts with customers,[19] while prices were negotiated between customers and producers. Financial means were advanced by the customers upon the signed contract.[20]

VSNKh's initial plan of economic organization ignored the *kustari*. The organization by *glavki* was intended to group the advanced productive plants, in order to form industrial amalgamations which could more easily be directed by the centre. Independently of the intentions of the leadership, *kustar*' economy increased its relative importance during the civil war, when it was one of the few elements of continuity with the past. This fact induced party and government to turn their attention to this economic sector and gradually extend to it the economic measures applying to large-scale industry in order to include the *kustari* in the realm of the state economy. At the beginning, this policy was essentially aimed at preventing the provinces from capturing *kustar*' output and eventually municipalizing *kustari*. Nationalization of this sector was not in the programme of 1919. *The ABC of Communism*, which appeared when the enemy attack was being directed against Petrograd and Moscow in one of the most critical moments of the civil war, declared that the forcible expropriation of small producers was quite inadmissible. The purpose was, instead, to reduce the margins of autonomy of small producers in decision-making with regard to the quantity and quality of output. The programme envisaged the gradual inclusion of the *kustari* in the socialist economy through the extension of the central regime of supply of fuel, raw materials and financial aid to the sector, in order to make the individual producers work 'for the proletarian State in accordance with a plan prescribed for them by the instruments of the proletarian State'. The establishment of production cooperatives among *kustari* was considered as the condition for state aid and as a technical means to encourage 'the painless transformation [of *kustari*] into workers of the great united organized, "mechanized" system of social production'.[21]

Although nationalization was excluded, central control over *kustar'* output was considered an attainable goal by *The ABC of Communism*. Nonetheless, the directives issued by the Eighth Party Congress in March 1919 stressed that small and *kustar'* industry was to be used to fulfil state orders and was to be included, for this reason, in the national plan of distribution of raw materials, fuel and finance.[22] Such guidelines inspired the regulations on *kustar'* industry issued in April 1919.[23] To avoid local municipalization of small undertakings, the decree established that small enterprises, employing up to ten workers without mechanical power or five workers with mechanical power, could be nationalized only in special cases and on the decision of VSNKh. If raw materials had been supplied by state or cooperative organizations, the latter had the right to decide the quantity and range of the output and to obtain the output itself. If raw materials had been provided by *kustari* themselves, the output was to be 'purchased' by state organs or cooperative unions. The latter were subordinated for this matter to State Control. The decree also defined the sphere of products which *kustari* could sell in the local market and the nearby villages. It may be interpreted, therefore, as a preparation for the August 1919 decree which extended obligatory commodity exchange to the whole country. Its immediate aim was hence to extend central control over local output in order to squeeze the existing local markets which benefited peasants' transactions and at the same time increase the central fund for exchange. But centralization encountered many obstacles partly related to the geographical dispersion of *kustar'* activities, partly to the structure of the organization itself. According to *kustar'* representatives, however, the April decree did not bring about an improvement, since local agencies went on hindering trade in *kustar'* products, in spite of the rules governing the sale of some products in the market.[24] Conflicts between *glavki* and *sovnarkhozy* for the control over *kustar'* output went on. The agents of *Glavleskom* (Chief Committee for Timber) in the province of Kazan imposed the rule that *kustar'* output should be collected in central storehouses of each *uezd*, and be delivered to other institutions like the local agencies of *Glavprodukt* (the Chief Administration for Supply of consumer goods attached to *Narkomprod*) and of the *tsentry* and the provinces, only by authorization of *Glavleskom* or its local agents. Moreover, such an authorization was to be given only on the basis of central production plans and prices.[25] The *sovnarkhozy* were alarmed. A rapid approval of a decree granting juridical status to *kustar'* activity and the protection of communal activities had been demanded before the issue of the April 1919 decree.[26] A congress of the local *sovnarkhozy* of the

Northern Region, which met in September 1919 to debate the problem of cooperation, maintained that *kustari* had to be treated as auxiliary producers for large-scale industry.[27] But it was taken for granted that any form of centralized organization was not practicable. The congress agreed, instead, on regional indirect control over *kustar'* output exercised through finance granted on condition that the terms of delivery were respected and fixed prices applied when it was turned over to the distribution centres. *Kustar'* cooperatives which tried to convince the *sovnarkhozy* representatives that bank financing would be the most suitable form of financing in the sector did succeed, but only partially. The *oblast sovnarkhoz* of the Northern Region imposed the principle of financing upon estimates for state orders, through the intermediary of the *kustar'* cooperatives section of VSNKh. Industrial credit for activities which did not depend on state order was to be released by the cooperative section of the People's Bank and its local divisions. These funds could eventually be integrated by special public industrial loans.[28] In December 1919, the *sovnarkhoz* of the Northern Region demanded from VSNKh a fund of 100 million rubles for the *kustar'* industry (a substantial sum if compared with the request for 120 million rubles for nationalized factories).[29]

During war communism, the principle of centralization which inspired economic organization prevented a fair transitional solution for small enterprises. Laws and regulations were inspired by the aim of putting under control *kustar'* output and disposing of it. But the dispersion of *kustar'* activities and the small size and wide range of output from the numerous individual enterprises made any form of central control impossible. A possible solution would have been the inclusion of *kustar'* economy in the local economy, under the control of the *sovnarkhozy*, with precise rules on financing. But this solution found an obstacle in *glavkism*. The broad rights which were granted to *glavki* in the matter of regulation of their economic branches, together with their limited financial budgets and bureaucratic attitude to production problems, had an adverse effect both on the search for a transitional workable regime for the *kustari* and on industrial activity as a whole. The *glavki* laid claim on *kustar'* output, but were not interested in the promotion of *kustar'* activity. Several reports indicate that this policy may have provoked production losses. In some cases the application of non-remunerative prices caused the bankruptcy of small enterprises and losses in terms of output foregone, in so far as former activities were not replaced.[30] In other cases, compulsion did not bring any positive results. *Glavki* which tried to impose orders and unfair prices on *kustari* were not able to obtain their output.[31] In some provinces, strong competition developed for the appropriation of *kustar'* output and the regulation of *kustar'* activity between the local organs of *glavki* and the local military state purchase sections.[32] Even the *kustar'* output which the April decree and VSNKh instructions allowed to be sold in the market was subject in some cases to expropriation by the *glavki*.[33] In the midst of the transport crisis, the Chief Committee for Leather approved a resolution concerning the immediate stoppage of supply of raw materials to small factories working up to 250 skins a month, and the closure within a month of factories working up to 500 skins a month, in order to concentrate production in the largest factories.[34] This policy was condemned by the local *sovnarkhozy*, which claimed they could have improved the supply of raw materials and increased the output volume if the *raion* committees for tanning had been put under their control.[35] In 1920, the second congress of timber committees, which one year before had decided to close down 204 factories and to stop production in 294 factories, demanded the inclusion of *kustar'* activity in their organization. The blatant contradiction between the arguments for closure, that is, concentration of industrial production, and the request for control of *kustar'* activity, had a meaning only in the *glavkis'* logic of distribution, for which the taking over of the output of the non-state sector was but one way to hide the acute inefficiency of the state sector. Timber was the only raw material of which shortage could not be claimed to hinder production of the woodworking industry. The mechanized enterprises in this branch could hardly claim to have had a higher productivity than others in wartime, because a lack of specialized labour and a shortage of spare parts had adverse effects on productivity. At the end of 1920 their output was estimated at one third of the pre-war level.[36]

The lack of precise understanding of the role that the *kustari* could play in a centralized economy was reflected in the conflict between *kustari* *Narkomzem* and VSNKh. Since the *kustari* consisted mainly of peasants, whose activity had a seasonal character, *Narkomzem* had developed its own *kustari* sections. VSNKh, on the other hand, striving for market control, argued that *Narkomzem kustar'* sections were a duplication of its own and that they hindered central policy.[37] The war environment was not propitious to a rapid settlement of conflicts about responsibility. At the end of December 1919, *Narkomzem* obtained a decision that all draft laws by VSNKh had to be submitted to a council of the People's Commissariats of Agriculture, Labour, Communications and Trade, and to the All-Russian Council of Trade Unions, for their approval before submission to *Sovnarkom* or the All-Russian Central Executive Committee.[38] But VSNKh found a way round this obstacle. At the beginning of 1920 it formed a central administration for *kustar'* industry, *Glavkustprom*, with the purpose of merging the *kustar* section of *Narkomzem*, which up to then had been concerned with the productive activity of *kustari*, and the *kustar'* cooperative administration of VSNKh, which had regulatory tasks in this sector.[39] VSNKh, in fact, had already intervened in this sector by providing credits and subsidies approved by *Narkomfin*.[40] Both *Narkomzem* and VSNKh were represented by four members each on the board of *Glavkustprom*, which included also one representative of the Trade Unions; it was VSNKh, however, which dominated the policy-making of the board.[41] An active policy of amalgamation of the *kustari* through production cooperatives was carried out in order to include this sector in the centrally controlled state economy. *Glavkustprom* had what Kritsman defined as a 'functional' activity.[42] The weakest part of this programme, of course, was the implementation of central control. The central institutions, which had no particular difficulty in requisitioning the *kustar'* output or their raw materials, were unable to formulate general production programmes for millions of dispersed craftsmen all over the country and control their fulfilment. The *kustari* thus remained exposed to an unstable regime regarding the disposal of their output, depending on the increasing requirements of the state economy. In September 1920 the craft industry was divided into three groups.[43] The first group included single-owner artisan undertakings working without hired labour, and cooperative associations of single artisans. Such enterprises could be nationalized only in very special cases. Free selling of the output was authorized if raw materials had been supplied by private customers and on the basis of a predetermined nomenclature. In any case, the production orders could be fulfilled only if such *kustari* respected the priority of state agencies, which had a claim on the output, whether raw materials had been supplied by them or by the producers themselves. The second group concerned undertakings with mechanical power employing hired labour of up to five workers. These enterprises were registered at the cooperative-*kustar'* section of the provincial *sovnarkhoz*, from which they were supposed to receive instructions on the further conduct of their undertakings. Accounting and distribution of orders and materials were to be carried out exclusively through *Glavkustprom* and its local organs. The output was to be delivered directly to *Glavkustprom* and its agencies. Purchase by other institutions and cooperatives was subject to the authorization of *Glavkustprom*.

Undertakings with mechanical power and employing more than five workers, or more than ten without mechanical power, had to work exclusively for the production centres of VSNKh and their local organs, which were supposed to supply raw materials, fuel and equipment. The *glavki* were to draw up production plans for them, to determine prices and to collect the output. This group of enterprises was nationalized only two months later, on 26 November 1920.[44]

The trend towards the nationalization of small-scale industry, which the Party Programme had excluded in March 1919, was partially determined by the inefficiency of *glavkism* and partially by the conscious effort of the economic leadership in 1920 to achieve stricter control over distribution of final products in order to put an end to legal and illegal market transactions. Some of the most powerful central economic organs had already taken decisive steps in this direction. In October 1920 the Metal Section of the Petrograd *Sovnarkhoz* decided to nationalize and include in the corresponding unions of enterprises nine small metal works. Thirteen other small undertakings were shut down and their output and equipment were transferred to other plants.[45] The need to control auxiliary output might have been one of the reasons in some cases, but it was not the primary one. The directors of the Metal Section acknowledged that there was not one healthy large enterprise in the metal industry.[46] The Metal Section of the Moscow *Sovnarkhoz* fulfilled the 1919 production plan by only 35 per cent. The managers affirmed that the reason for making use of small undertakings was their relatively better performance.[47]

This was true for the whole of industry. Thanks to the utilization of traditional techniques and local resources, small-scale industry developed proportionately more than large-scale industry during war communism (see Table A1.1).

Small-scale industry's proportion of total output almost doubled since 1913. Evidence of this performance may be also indirectly obtained by comparing the number of active and inactive enterprises in 1920 and their respective average mechanical power. Active enterprises had an average of 39.5 horse power per enterprise; inactive enterprises had an average of 43.3 horse power.[48] In spite of the original plans, production was gradually concentrated in enterprises which were not large. An additional reason for the comparatively better performance of small-scale

Table A1.1. *Output of small- and large-scale industry (millions of rubles at 1913 prices)*

	1913	1920	1920 as % of 1913
Large-scale industry	5,620	1,001	18
Small-scale industry	1,528	660	43

Source: L. Kritsman, *Geroicheskii period Velikoi Russkoi Revoliutsii*, Moscow, n.d., probably 1924, pp. 54–5

Table A1.2. *Number of hired and dismissed workers in four months of 1919 in the province of Vladimir (of 37 surveyed enterprises)*

		Enterprises employing	
Months		less than 50 workers	51–500 workers
September	hired	17	58
	dismissed	2	223
October	hired	62	48
	dismissed	10	29
November	hired	5	79
	dismissed	1	62
December	hired	22	54
	dismissed	5	117
Total	hired	106	239
	dismissed	18	431

Source: E.G. Gimpel'son, 'Izmeneniia v sotsial'nom sostave rabochego klassa Sovetskoi Respubliki v 1918–1920 gg', *Iz istorii grazhdanskoi voiny i interventsii 1917–1922 gg*, Moscow, 1974, p. 287.

industry and *kustar'* undertakings was the greater stability of labour, which consisted mainly of women. The case of thirty-seven enterprises in the province of Vladimir could be indicative also for other regions. In four months of 1919 the balance of hired and dismissed workers was positive in the enterprises employing less than fifty workers and negative in the larger ones (see Table A1.2).

It has been suggested that, if things had not gone so badly with large-scale industry, VSNKh might not have interfered with handicrafts.[49] The Party Programme of 1919, which excluded the nationalization of small undertakings, could be cited in support of such a view. However, the decision to nationalize all industry was taken only one year later, when the civil war was over. The reasons for it must be sought not only in the situation of emergency determined by the breakdown of large-scale industry – since the acquisition of the traditional sources of raw materials and fuel under Soviet control might have been supposed to eliminate one of the major causes of breakdown – but also in the emerging system of economic organization based on central distribution of products.

On the one hand, the crisis of large-scale industry, whose production fell to less than 20 per cent the pre-war level, no longer allowed command over national resources, which it was presumed to entail in 1918. On the other hand, the progressive naturalization of the economy, which was initially unforeseen, then accepted and finally promoted, required maximum control over goods and products necessary for the subsistence of labour as soon as the problem of reconstruction was faced. In 1920 a national fund of consumer goods could not be formed, unless the last margins of freedom in the utilization of output, that is, private enterprise and the black market, were prohibited. The utilization of *kustari* was considered to be necessary to satisfy, at least partially, the demand for finished products and the requirements of the bonus system adopted in key sectors to increase the productivity of labour. It may not be accidental that nationalization was decreed in November, a time when agricultural labour was idle. The inclusion of the *kustari* into the state economy occurred not only through nationalization of their undertakings or state purchase of their products, but also in the form of manpower. At the beginning of 1921, by a decision of the People's Commissar of Labour, all *kustari* registered by the local organs of *Glavkustprom* working on the orders of state organs and responsible for a given output norm were called to labour conscription according to norms fixed for each province by a special commission. This commission was formed by representatives of *Glavkustprom*, of the provincial labour committees, and members of the trade unions' provincial councils (*Gubprof*).[50] The inclusion of the *kustari* in labour conscription meant extension of the system of payments in kind for *kustari* output, under the supervision of *Glavkustprom*. For sixty pairs of felt boots, for instance, the *kustari* received six funt of salt, one funt of kerosene and one arshin of cotton cloth.[51]

Overall nationalization was based on the assumption that the system of allocation of foodstuffs and raw materials would be maintained and would ensure the regular flow of basic materials and means of subsistence from the countryside. This plan was ambitious if compared with available resources, inconsistent with the constraints imposed by decreasing availability of industrial products, and unrealistic in the face of the size and dispersion of the production units which were to be subject to central control. The model of 'exchange of products' that Marx had reserved for the imaginary communist society, the realm of plenty, was forced upon its exact opposite, an economy at the edge of exhaustion and intolerable distress.

Some years later, Kritsman commented that when the mass of small enterprises came under the ownership of the state, it proved impossible to organize them.[52] The failure of centralized allocation and the peasants' revolts did the rest. At the beginning of 1921 the ideology of war communism was an empty box, if one had to find in it the prescriptions capable of pushing the economy out of its impasse. Soon after approving the tax in kind, *Sovnarkom* undertook immediate steps to put an end to the extension of the sphere of the state economy. On 17 May 1921, *Sovnarkom* stopped the process of nationalization which had been set in motion by the decree of 29 November 1920, and decided that the proper economic policy was to adopt measures for the development of small-scale and *kustar'* industry, in the form of cooperative as well as private undertakings.[53]

NOTES

1 *Trudy II Vserosiiskogo S"ezda Sovetov narodnogo Khoziastva, 19 Dekabria-27 Dekabria 1918g,* Moscow, 1919, pp. 320–4.
2 *Ibid.,* pp. 330, 337, 396.
3 Cf. S. Rozenfeld', *Promyshlennaia politika SSSR,* Moscow, 1926, p. 40. Other estimates of *kustar'* output are discussed by R.W. Davies in *CREES Discussion Papers,* Series SIPS, Birmingham, no. 18, 1978, pp. 14–18: see chapter 1, n68.
4 A.F. Chumak, 'K voprosu o vovlechenii kustarei i resmeshlennikov v sotsialisticheskoe stroitel'stvo', *Voprosy istorii KPSS,* no. 7, 1967, p. 58.
5 *Ekonomicheskaia Zhizn',* no. 265, 26 November 1919, 4; *Narodnoe Khoziaistvo,* 1919, no. 7, p. 85; *Narodnoe Khoziaistvo,* 1919, nos. 9–10, p. 90.
6 *Ekonomicheskaia Zhizn',* no. 280, 13 December 1919, 1.
7 *Narodnoe Khoziaistvo,* 1919, nos. 1–2, p. 36.
8 *Narodnoe Khoziaistvo,* 1919, no. 7, p. 65.
9 *Narodnoe Khoziaistvo,* 1919, nos. 1–2, pp. 39–40.
10 *Narodnoe Khoziaistvo,* 1920, nos. 11–12, pp. 32–3.
11 *Ekonomicheskaia Zhizn',* no. 265, 26 November 1919, 3.
12 *Narodnoe Khoziaistvo,* 1920, nos. 15–16, 33.
13 *Ekonomicheskaia Zhizn',* no. 289, 24 December 1919, 2.
14 *Ibid.*
15 *Ekonomicheskaia Zhizn',* no. 231, 17 October 1919, 2.
16 *Ekonomicheskaia Zhizn',* no. 102, 14 May 1919, 3.
17 *Ekonomicheskaia Zhizn',* no. 289, 24 December 1919, 2.
18 *Narodnoe Khoziaistvo,* 1919, no. 7, 85.
19 *Ekonomicheskaia Zhizn',* no. 289, 24 December 1919, 2.
20 *Ekonomicheskaia Zhizn',* no. 261, 21 November 1919, 1.
21 N. Bukharin and E. Preobrazhensky, *The ABC of Communism,* Harmondsworth, 1969, pp. 328–30.
22 *8i S"ezd RKP (b). 18–23 Marta 1919g,* Moscow, 1933, p. 392.
23 *Sobranie uzakonenii,* 1919, no. 14, art. 190.
24 *Narodnoe Khoziaistvo,* 1919, nos. 9–10, p. 18; *Narodnoe Khoziaistvo,* 1920, nos. 1–2, p. 36.
25 *Ekonomicheskaia Zhizn',* no. 259, 19 November 1919, 2.
26 *Materialy po istorii Sovetskogo stroitel'stva: Sovety v epokhu voennogo kommunizma, Sbornik dokumentov,* part one, 1928, p. 156.

27 *Narodnoe Khoziaistvo*, 1920, nos. 1–2, p. 37.
28 *Ibid.*, p. 38.
29 *Natsionalizatsiia promyshlennosti i organizatsiia sotsialisticheskogo proizvodstva v Petrograde (1917–1920 gg)*. *Dokumenty i materialy*, vol. 2, Leningrad, 1960, pp. 373–4.
30 *Ekonomicheskaia Zhizn'*, no. 260, 20 November 1919, 4.
31 *Ekonomicheskaia Zhizn'*, no. 261, 21 November 1919, 2.
32 *Ekonomicheskaia Zhizn'*, no. 280, 13 December 1919, 2.
33 *Narodnoe Khoziaistvo*, 1919, nos. 9–10, pp. 18–19.
34 *Narodnoe Khoziaistvo*, 1919, no. 4, 49–50 and no. 9, 50; VSNKh, *Plenum*, September 1918, p. 99: at a plenum of VSNKh the president of the Leather Committee declared that 35.6 per cent of the tanneries in European Russia produced more than fifty skins per month, which amounted to 90% of total output, and 64 per cent less than 150 skins, which amounted to 10 per cent of total output.
35 *Narodnoe Khoziaistvo*, 1920, nos. 15–16, p. 33.
36 *Narodnoe Khoziaistvo*, 1920, nos. 11–12, pp. 31–2.
37 *Ekonomicheskaia Zhizn'*, no. 285, 19 December 1919, 1.
38 *Ekonomicheskaia Zhizn'*, no. 288, 24 December 1919, 1.
39 *Sobranie uzakonenii*, 1920, no. 50, art. 218; *Izvestiia*, no. 240, 27 October 1920, 2.
40 *Izvestiia NKF*, no. 10, 7 November 1919, 74–5.
41 *Izvestiia*, no. 240, 27 October 1920, 2.
42 L. Kritsman, *Geroicheskii period Velikoi Russkoi Revoliutsii*, Moscow, n.d., probably 1924, p. 104.
43 *Sobranie uzakonenii*, 1920, no. 78, art. 366.
44 *Sobranie uzakonenii*, 1920, no. 93, art. 512.
45 A.V. Venediktov, *Organizatsiia gosudarstvennoi promyshlennosti v SSSR*, vol. 1, Leningrad, 1927, pp. 473–74 n.
46 *Narodnoe Khoziaistvo*, 1920, nos. 9–10, 3.
47 *Izvestiia*, no. 88, 25 April 1920, 2.
48 *Sbornik statisticheskikh svedenii po Soiuzu SSR, 1918–1923*, Moscow, 1924, pp. 154–5.
49 Rozenfeld', p. 109.
50 *Izvestiia*, no. 10, 16 January 1921, 3.
51 *Izvestiia*, no. 19, 29 January 1921, 4.
52 Kritsman, *Geroicheskii period*, p. 127.
53 *Sobranie uzakonenii*, 1921, no. 47, arts. 230 and 240. For other measures on *kustari* cf. also E.H. Carr, *The Bolshevik Revolution, 1917–1923*, 3 vols., London, 1952, vol. 2, pp. 299–309.

3

Management

Management was one of the hardest issues the leadership had to tackle. Lack of cadres sympathetic to the new government was a major problem which jeopardized the possibility of establishing a competent administration conforming to the political views of the Bolsheviks. This peculiar situation led to an unstable framework for management, which went through three stages: workers' control, state control, party control. Each stage, however, must be interpreted not as a coherent set of institutions, but rather as an unbalanced and precarious equilibrium of forces, none of which was able, so long as war communism lasted, to assert its prevalence over the others. Weakness, lack of experience and inadequate support from the unions all served to isolate the Bolshevik leadership in its effort to master the levers of economic power.

When the Seventh Congress of the Party met on 6–8 March 1918 to decide the question of concluding peace with Germany, Lenin declared in polemics with the left-wing communists that the question of organization could not be solved by the 'hurrah' methods by which the Bolsheviks had solved the problems of civil war.[1] The peculiarity of Russia was, added Lenin, that the class which had conquered political power had no means of administering economic power. The bourgeois French Revolution – a recurrent reference for Marxists – had occurred as the outcome of an opposite process. A class excluded from political power, but which had come to hold the economic levers of the country, was able, through a revolutionary upheaval, to oust the aristocracy and firmly take over state administration. Lenin remarked that, while in France capitalism had reached a synthesis of economic and political power, starting from a situation of economic power,

the difference between a socialist revolution and a bourgeois revolution is that in the latter case there are ready made forms of capitalist relationships; Soviet power

89

does not inherit such ready made relationships, if we leave out of account the most developed forms of capitalism, which, strictly speaking, extended to but a small top layer of industry and hardly touched agriculture.[2]

The recent formation of an industrial working class and the precarious and weak presence of scattered trade unions provided evidence of the basic unpreparedness of the proletariat to take over the direction of the economy.

Most trade unions were formed after the February Revolution. Two thousand unions were organized in the first two months after February 1917.[3] Between March and April 1917, seventy-four trade unions uniting 100,000 workers were formed in Petrograd. The Metal Workers' Union, which in February 1917 had no more than 200–300 members in Moscow, already had 40,000 there in May 1917.[4] In July 1917 there were about half a million organized workers in Moscow and Petrograd and 145 trade unions in the provinces with a membership of 150,000–160,000.[5] Side by side with, but independently of, the trade unions, workers' councils were formed in the most important industrial centres. There were 1,251 factory-shop committees (*fabzavkomy*) before the October revolution.[6]

At the Second All-Russian Conference of Trade Unions, 21–8 July, 1917, where 976 trade unions were represented, the Bolsheviks had 73 delegates with right of vote, against 36 Mensheviks, 31 uncommitted social-democrats and 25 Socialist-Revolutionaries and representatives of other parties.[7] The Bolsheviks started gaining popularity in the trade unions in the summer of 1917, when the central administration of the Moscow Textile Workers' Union and of the Metal Unions of Petrograd, Moscow, Samara, Kharkov and some Urals towns, passed into their hands. However, it was among the *fabzavkomy* that the Bolsheviks gathered most of their supporters.[8] At the Central Council of the Petrograd *fabzavkomy*, elected by the first conference of Petrograd factory committees, held 30 May–3 June 1917, 90 per cent of the delegates were Bolsheviks.[9]

Lenin tried to gain the agreement of the factory workers for his revolutionary policy, directed at breaking the compromise which the Mensheviks had found with the Provisional Government. Rejecting control from above over business, which he judged impossible under a government 'fettered by a thousand chains which safeguard the interests of capital',[10] Lenin developed the slogan of control from below 'exercised by the workers themselves'.[11]

To Lenin, workers' control did not mean workers' management of the factories, but supervision or vigilance over business. Lenin believed that the spontaneous workers' organizations within the factories could be stimulated to operate in such a way as to disclose the real financial budgets and make possible a proper application of the progressive income tax. The revolutionary role of workers' organizations was emphasized by Lenin in 'Can the Bolsheviks retain State Power?', written on the eve of the revolution, to demonstrate that the Bolsheviks would be able to master the state apparatus. Foreseeing the resistance of the managers, board members and large shareholders, Lenin proclaimed:

the proletarian state, with the apparatus of the Soviets, of the employees unions, etc., will be able to appoint ten or even a hundred supervisors to each of them, so that instead of 'breaking resistance' it may even be possible, by means of '*workers' control*' [over the capitalists], to make all resistance *impossible*' [Lenin's *emphasis*].[12]

Workers' control was necessary to the extent to which the maintenance of the former officials and managers at their posts was considered by Lenin necessary in the phase of transition:

we shall give all these specialists work to which they are accustomed and which they can cope with: in all probability we shall introduce complete wage equality only gradually and shall pay these specialists higher salaries during the transition period. We shall place them, however, under comprehensive workers' control and we shall achieve the complete and absolute operation of the rule 'He who does not work, neither shall he eat.' We shall not invent the organizational form of the work, but take it ready made from capitalism.[13]

In contrast to *State and Revolution*, where he had favoured greatly reduced wage differentials, when he was presenting alternative forms of organizations as practical measures Lenin assumed a flexible attitude on economic criteria and a rigid stand on political control.

Like most of the parties of the left, the Bolsheviks believed that a great deal of the 1917 economic disorganization, closures and social conflicts were due to the uncompromising attitude of the industrialists to the changes and expectations that the February Revolution had brought about. The conference of industrialists in June 1917, representative of the main industries, had approved a resolution against 'workers' interference in industrial management' through 'the formation of all sorts of control economic commissions' which stimulated anarchy in the enterprises.[14] Neither the one side nor the other fully realized the complex factors affecting the economic situation.

Closures during March–July 1917 involved 568 enterprises, employing more than 100,000 workers.[15] The Ministry of Trade and Industry commented that closures were due to lack of materials and fuel, and excessive demands by the workforce.[16]

The decline of productivity and increases in costs were also affected by the rising cost of working capital. The higher proportion of working capital in Russia as compared with other countries (about six months of production costs) had several reasons, such as climate, distances and terms of payment, which made it increasingly difficult for enterprises to keep up with cost increases.[17] Furthermore, not all the enterprises were able to increase wages out of high profits, as was the practice in military supply industries.[18] From the first half of 1914 to the second half of 1917 money wages increased about six times, while real wages decreased by about 50 per cent in the Moscow *Oblast*.[19] Inflation, which provided the reason for most labour claims, affected the real value of wages to an extent depending on the local relative price indexes. The industrial centres which were situated further from the grain-producing regions were more heavily affected. The metal workers' union claimed that real wages in 1917 had fallen 6–8 times below pre-war levels;[20] in Petrograd the fall of real wages was higher than in Moscow.[21] A further reason to demand wage increases was the tendency to wage levelling brought about by war, which skilled workers opposed, fighting to maintain the pre-war differentials.[22]

The outburst of workers' councils under Kerenskii's government was a spontaneous phenomenon of collective action for the safeguarding of labour rights. But it was there that the Bolsheviks saw the platform for political activity, grasping their revolutionary potential, rather than their immediate reasons for unrest. In some cases, workers' councils took over management, namely when the administrative staff had left their post. But in most cases the activity of the factory committees was directed towards preventing firing and closures and to demanding wage increases and social insurance.[23] This fact emerged even at the feverish meetings of the Bolshevik faction which preceded the Bolshevik takeover. Reports from the metal workers' unions indicated that workers did not feel ready to take over management and that the issue of workers' control had to be tied to wage increases to find support.[24]

Lenin did not simply theorize the *de facto* situation in 1917. His 'draft regulations on workers' control' contain three elements which show the meaning he attributed to this institution. First, Lenin *extended* and *institutionalized* the application of workers' control to all industrial, commercial, banking, agricultural and other enterprises employing not less than five people, or having an annual turnover of not less than 10,000 rubles. Second, he *limited* the functions of the elected representatives to *access* to all books and documents and to all warehouses and stocks. Third, he *affirmed a hierarchy* between the organs of workers' control and the trade unions, since to the latter and their congresses was attributed the right to annul the decisions of the elected representatives of the workers and employees.[25]

Lenin's attempt was to transform the spontaneous workers' organizations into state organs at the service of power, rather than for defence of labour interests as such. Their functions were restricted to vigilance over business activity in its financial and commercial aspects. Thus Lenin's clause on the obligatory character of their decisions on the owners is to be interpreted as concerning workers' rights of inspection, rather than their eventual competence in managerial functions. Finally, the subordination of the workers' committees to the trade unions (from which the *fabzavkomy* had up to then been quite independent) was meant to circumscribe and coordinate the multiform expressions of workers' activity, trying to channel them towards superior interests.

Lenin's draft regulations on workers' control were discussed at the meeting of the Petrograd Council of Factory Committees, which consisted almost entirely of Bolsheviks, and were then submitted to Miliutin and Larin, who had been charged by *Sovnarkom* to draw up the Decree on Workers' Control.[26] The final draft was far less moderate than Lenin's proposals. The Decree on Workers' Control was issued on 27 November 1917.[27] Workers' control was institutionalized for *all* enterprises employing hired labour, including outworkers, 'in the interests of systematic regulation of the national economy'. Workers' rights were extended beyond those proposed in Lenin's draft. They concerned supervision of production, fixing of minimum output and determining the cost of production, besides access to all documents. The principle of hierarchy was approved, but within the institution of workers' control, rather than within the trade union organization. Councils of workers' control were to be established in every large city, province or industrial region. An All-Russian Council of Workers' Control was to formulate general plans and instructions for workers' control, to issue binding decisions and to coordinate the regional councils with other economic institutions.

The decree embodied Lenin's intention to keep *in loco* a workers' militia as a support of Soviet power, but it also specified workers' rights in the domain of production. This responded not only to anarcho-syndicalist positions, but also to the aspirations of the Bolshevik members at the factory level. In this way the door was opened to the evolution of workers' control with greater intervention in management. The extension of the rights of workers' control, together with the maintenance of Lenin's clause on the binding force of their decisions,[28] jeopardized the possibility, if any, of installing within the factory a workable compromise between management and subordinate labour,[29] by which Lenin had intended to get through the difficult initial stages of the revolution. Larin and Miliutin, who were opposed to the binding character of decisions on owners, probably agreed with the Mensheviks on this issue. The Menshevik arguments were, first, that workers' control was not democratic, since the peasantry and other strata were excluded from exercising it. Second, if workers' control over industry was meant to be collective, it would be fruitless and shortlived since workers would decide products and prices without concern for the interests of the rest of the population.[30] Third, the owners, who might have accepted government control, would not accept any form of workers' control.[31]

The composition of the All-Russian Council of Workers' Control did, indeed, suggest some of these worries. Besides the representatives of the All-Russian Bureau of Factory-Shop Committees and the All-Russian Council of Trade Unions, a conspicuous number of representatives were allowed to other groups, such as the Central Executive Committee of Peasants' Deputies, the All-Russian Central Executive Committee of Soviets, the Union of Engineers and Technicians, and the Union of Agronomists. Furthermore, owners were granted the right to lodge complaints with the higher organs of workers' control against the decisions of the lower organs.[32] It is likely that the arguments for centralization in economic policy, which were prevalent among Marxists,[33] determined the short life of the All-Russian Council of Workers' Control. Its instructions never became operative, and finally it totally disappeared from the political scene.[34]

The Decree on Workers' Control applied to private enterprises. It was mainly because of inertia, and because of the symbolic importance of the power that workers' councils had conquered in 1917, that workers' control organs remained within the factories, even after nationalization. The fact that several decisions on nationalization were motivated by reference to the decree on workers' control does not necessarily support the interpretation met in Soviet literature that the latter was intended to be a step towards the full nationalization of industry.[35] When the first decree on nationalization was passed, there was no mention of workers' control as any prerequisite. On the contrary, nationalization implied the possibility of dismissing most of the rights of workers' committees, and coincided with the creation of a different hierarchy of organs and competences. When nationalization was decided by higher organs, a commissar was appointed to management.[36] Workers' control was an incentive to nationalization, in so far as it was not effective along the lines Lenin had in mind, that is, management by owners under the vigilance of a workers' militia.

In January 1918, Lenin made it clear at the Congress of Soviets that the formation of other institutions made it possible to dispense with workers' control. 'From workers' control we passed on to the creation of a Supreme

Economic Council.'[37] Lenin's statement was intended to show a continuity in the evolution of economic organization, which, in fact, did not exist. Lenin wanted to rationalize the role of workers' control, as if it were only a preparatory step to the formation of central organs of economic control. It was not quite so. From before October, the Bolshevik leadership inherited the factory-shop committees as they were, with all their claims. Demands for higher wages, interference with management, hostility to the administrative staff, all the facts which could be and were exploited as political arguments in polemics with the Provisional Government and the parties supporting it,[38] turned out, after October, to be uncontrollable sources of conflicts and pressures to the Bolshevik power. The Supreme Council of the National Economy, VSNKh, was instituted on 1 December 1917, shortly after the approval of the Decree on Workers' Control, not as an evolution of it but independently of it. Whereas the workers' control committees were expected to exert a control from below over business, VSNKh was supposed to provide general guidelines for the coordination and regulation of economic life, and in this field its decisions were given the force of law.[39] Workers' control was a tribute paid to reality from a political point of view by a power seeking to extend its area of support. VSNKh was an expression of the principle of centralization and control from above which was peculiar to the Marxist ideology. Though workers' control implied a great deal of decentralization and VSNKh embodied centralization, the formal coexistence of the two institutions did not appear to be necessarily contradictory, since their tasks were distinct. Workers' control aimed at defining the limits of activity of workers' committees and at channelling them towards the formation of self-discipline and responsibility for the protection of premises, prevention of closures and interruptions of production. VSNKh was to provide the directives in economic policy and to work out the alternative forms of economic organization in the transition to socialism.

In practice, the dividing-line between workers' control and workers' management was not respected. The Decree on Workers' Control left a large potential for workers' intervention in management, for the rights of managers had not been given specific attention, and explicit connections with the other Soviet institutions were deferred to forthcoming regulations, leaving no guideline for a transitional hierarchy between the existing institutions. On the other hand, VSNKh was the result of a compromise between a line which emphasized the consultative character of the central economic council and a line, expressed by Lenin which opted for an active body, capable of administering industry.

The potential for conflict embodied in the two decrees was displayed, first of all, on the question of nationalization. While pressures for immediate nationalization were exerted by several workers' organs, on different grounds, *Sovnarkom* and VSNKh endeavoured to slow down the wave of nationalization until a workable solution for management and financing could be found.

Two months of experience in administration were sufficient for Lenin to grasp the necessity for an option between the decentralistic and disruptive potential of workers' control and central command over the economy. The Congress of Councils of Workers' Control, which was intended to elect the All-Russian Council of Workers' Control, was never called, nor were regulations defining relations between the latter and other economic institutions ever issued. When Lenin announced that workers' control was over, he implicitly admitted the failure of an alternative – control from below – which the party leadership had shown itself to be incapable of mastering.

3.2 WORKERS' CONTROL: THE WORKERS' UNDERSTANDING AND PRACTICE

During the phase of spontaneous 'punitive' nationalizations, the *fabzavkomy* often took over factories and mines whose managements had been removed or who had abandoned the firms. A direct observer commented: 'Instead of a rapid adjustment of public production and distribution, instead of measures representing a step toward the socialist organization of society, we see a practice which reminds one of the dreams of anarchists about autonomous production-communes.'[40]

The Decree on Workers' Control, indeed, did not provide those elements of coordination which some writers consider to have been the goal of the Bolsheviks after the October Revolution.[41] The failure depended not only on the unequal distribution and authority of Bolshevik elements within the *fabzavkomy*,[42] but also on the different interpretation of workers' control within the Bolsheviks themselves, between the leadership and the local cadres.[43]

The draft instruction on workers' control drawn up in November 1917 by the Central Council of Factory-Shop Committees, where the Bolshevik representation was predominant, interpreted workers' control as a transitional stage towards the organization of the overall economic life of the country on socialist foundations. Workers' control was not intended, as in Lenin's project, to be a form of vigilance over business, but an intervention in management, an *active surveillance* and a *participation in the organization of production*, 'the first essential step taken from below and paralleling the work going on in the central organs of the national economy'.[44] This draft distinguished three basic functions of the factory-shop committees: (1), control over organization of production, (2), control over supply of essential materials, and (3), protection of the interests of workers and employees of the enterprise. Rights pertaining to the first function concerned determination of the cost of the end product, computation of inventories and distribution of instructions among the various shops. In the financial sphere, rights of the factory committees included ascertainment of the available cash of the enterprise, of its payments and receipts, and making decisions on which orders to accept. If a particular order was not found to be in the interest of the enterprise, the factory committee could halt its execution, pending final decision by higher economic organs. In the field of labour relations, the *fabzavkomy* could decide hiring and firing of workers, dismissals and taking on of managerial staff, and working time.

Gladkov maintains that the draft, unofficially, circulated everywhere and was taken as a basis for the issue of local instructions on workers' control.[45] There is indirect evidence for this assertion. The instruction of the Moscow Union of Textile Workers, issued in December 1917, invited workers' organs to apply 'the strictest control, immediately passing on to workers' management'.[46] In one case the factory committee found that a large part of the factory outlays had been incurred 'illegally' and 'unproductively' and refused to approve payment.[47] Decisions on dismissal were taken by the factory committee without informing the administration.[48] The factory committee of a textile mill ejected the owner and his management who had refused to increase output, and introduced piece-rates and minimum output norms.[49] Against the decision of owners to stop production, factory committees took over management, making themselves responsible for the supply of raw materials and continuation of production.[50] The Yaroslav factory committees decided not only on wages, working time and disputes with the administration, but also on hiring and firing.[51] The Samara Council of Factory Committees empowered these committees to decide on production costs, prices and terms of sale. In some cases *fabzavkomy* decided the distribution of profits.[52] Some firms were not allowed to conclude any contract without the consent of the control commission.[53] Some factory committees were particularly strict in controlling cash flows. There is evidence from foreign reports that no money was paid for goods delivered or work done without their consent.[54] The factory committee of a machine-tool workshop in Moscow discussed and settled questions pertaining to holidays, sick pay, overtime; all real grievances were settled by the vote of all, rules and regulations were discussed and approved. This factory elected the manager on the principle of one person, one vote.[55] Some factories of Kostroma province claimed the right of intervention in management and controlled all aspects of enterprise activity. At the Third Conference of workers' control of Kostroma province, in September 1918, many reports focused on the role of workers' control over material and financial matters. In some cases, workers' committees found the financial means to keep an undertaking going.[56] Some factory committees kept a register of customers and decided terms of delivery.[57] The workers' organs of a print shop distributed orders among shops, determined the number of workers and their wages, issued payment orders and fixed dividends.[58] This case seems rather exceptional in the variegated panorama of post-revolutionary workers' control. But it indicates how discretional was the interpretation of the Decree on Workers' Control and how much its application responded to real situations rather than to law.

3.3 TRADE UNIONS VERSUS WORKERS' CONTROL

The attempts to bridle reality were expressed in regulations reducing the capacity of workers' control committees to intervene in managerial activities, and in the effort to gain trade union support in counteracting unwanted spontaneous workers' initiatives from below.

At the First Congress of Trade Unions (7–14 January 1918), where the Bolsheviks had the majority of delegates with voting rights (217 delegates out of 402 representing party and non-party factions),[59] the resolution on workers' control presented by Lozovskii (at that time a non-party delegate) and worded in its final form by a commission composed of three Bolshevik delegates and two non-Bolsheviks, was adopted unanimously. The resolution stated that, in the interests of the proletariat itself, 'any idea of atomization of workers' control by way of granting to the workers of each enterprise the right to take final decisions on questions affecting the very existence of the enterprise ought to be rejected', and that 'control over production does not mean transfer of an enterprise into the hands of the workers of that enterprise'; 'workers' control is not equivalent to socialization of production and exchange, but represents only a preparatory step towards it'.[60]

The congress debated two major points. First, the specific tasks and limits of factory workers' control organs. Second, the coordination of workers' control at the union level. Solutions were found in a compromise which was to pave the way for institutional changes without touching what already existed. The congress approved the formation of control commissions at the factory level and economic control commissions at the union level.[61] The relations between existing *fabzavkomy* and control commissions were not defined. Nowhere was it said that the control commissions were to replace the *fabzavkomy*, but the final resolution mentioned that the latter might be included as a whole in the control commissions. The choice of the word *komissiia* instead of *komitet*, by which originally the factory councils were designated, raises the question of whether the congress intended to stress the nature of advisory technical boards of workers' control organs, rather than their potentially permanent leading role. Regardless of this, the impression remains that the congress was not able or did not want to settle clearly the issue of workers' control from the institutional point of view.

The rights and duties of the control commissions as defined in the resolution corresponded to the trade unions' understanding of the political and social situation, which was not the same as that of the Bolshevik Party leadership. Though the Bolsheviks comprised the majority of delegates with voting rights, the political orientation of trade-union members was still quite varied and not necessarily congruous with that of the Bolshevik leadership, even among Bolshevik trade unionists. Trade unionists did not necessarily identify the Bolshevik Revolution with a revolution in the sphere of labour relations. To experienced trade unionists it was not at all evident that the role of labour in the new society had changed and that wage labour had disappeared or was bound to disappear in a short time. Owing to this approach on social relations, the trade unions disliked any solution close to co-management, either in private or public enterprises. However, in the latter the trade unions admitted that workers' control should operate in order to counteract the formation of a state bureaucracy.

The trade unions' resolution on workers' control rejected joint responsibility for the enterprise of workers' representatives and owners, which could be derived from the Decree on Workers' Control, and explicitly stated that 'the right to give instructions on management of the enterprise, its course and actions, remains with the owner', and that 'the control commission does not take part in management of the enterprise and does not assume any responsibility for its course and actions, which remains with the owner'.[62]

The trade unions foresaw that workers' control might be abolished or nullified in industries entrusted to the state, through the syllogism implicit in the slogan of the dictatorship of the proletariat. For this reason, the congress affirmed that workers' control ought to be 'the basis of state regulation' since 'the absence of such control could bring about a new industrial bureaucracy'.[63]

While restricting the scope of workers' control, the congress took care that room should be left for the intervention of control organs in managerial decisions affecting labour. In the first draft, the control commissions were to watch over the implementation of output norms set by state institutions, or in the absence of such norms, to determine them on the basis of the equipment and actual conditions of the enterprise. To be able to do this the control commissions were to have access to all documents and meetings of management as well as the right to raise questions.

The defence of labour rights did not rest only on a trade unionist partial view of economic problems. An effort at coordination was made in order to avoid the danger of the atomization of workers' control organs. The resolution on workers' control subordinated control commissions and factory committees to 'control economic' commissions (*kontrol'no-khoziaistvennyi*) which were to be established by the trade unions at the level of the whole industrial branch. One or two members of the trade union concerned who were not employed at a given enterprise were to take part in all the work of the control commissions and factory committees in the enterprise and to report to the control economic commissions.[64] The effort of the trade unions to limit the powers of lower control organs in relation to management, and to compensate this limitation by broadening their rights in matters of labour defence, did not find total expression in the final draft of the instruction on control commissions.[65] The tasks of the commissions were precisely defined and strictly limited to vigilance over the process of production and labour discipline. The decree on control commissions dropped the fixing of output norms and access to administrative documents and meetings, which had figured in the original project.

The final instructions stated that the control commissions should be elected by a general meeting of manual and clerical workers, to which they had to report not less than twice a month. In the largest enterprises the clerical workers had to be represented as such in the commissions. The commissions had the following duties: to ascertain the amounts of materials, equipment and labour necessary to the factory, and the amounts actually available; also the appropriate proportions of these inputs for full utilization of productive capacity; to ensure labour discipline; to check fulfilment of decision by superior economic agencies (such as *glavki*) on supply and delivery of goods; to prevent unauthorized transfer of equipment and materials; to seek the causes of declining labour productivity and measures to increase it; finally, to examine the possibility of conversion of productive activity and the necessary modifications. Later on, information on workers' control does not distinguish between control commissions and *fabzavkomy*, so that one cannot evaluate the impact that the congress' resolution had in practice. Nor is it possible to assess whether control commissions replaced factory committees or coexisted with them. The information available suggests, instead, that no precise connections between factory control organs and higher union organs were established, and that in some cases the control commissions did not submit any account of their activity.[66]

One of the party's arguments for limiting the sphere of competence of factory committees was the alleged restricted viewpoint of the organs of workers' control, by which was meant their lack of an overall appreciation of the country's economic problems and their obstinate defence of workers' immediate interests. This argument was partially true; but, of course, it dated back to long before the October Revolution, when the Bolsheviks had never thought of raising it. On the other hand, the allegation was not entirely justified. There is evidence that until late 1919, some factory committees performed managerial tasks successfully. In some regions factories were still active thanks to their workers' initiatives in securing raw materials. There were cases in which the factory committees assumed on their own the hard decision of dismissing part of the labour force. Lists were made of workers having other income besides their factory wage, in order to distinguish between those who could be dismissed and those who lived entirely by their job. In more than one case food supply was maintained by the efforts of the factory workers on land belonging to the enterprise.[67] In such activities factory committees went beyond the tasks reserved to them by the regulations issued by the All-Russian Council of Trade Unions in mid 1918.[68]

A major concern of the party leadership, in fact, was to check spontaneous confiscations, to curb demands for wage increases in enterprises depending on state financing and to reach agreement with former managerial staff so as to smooth the transition. To take an example on the wages question, when transport was nationalized, the Water Transport Workers' Trade Union demanded that management be concentrated in its hands. The workers expected a wage increase. This claim was rejected by Lenin, in a meeting of the Central Committee of the Party on 4 March 1918, on the ground that not the workers but Soviet power was responsible for management. Lenin warned that before granting sailors a wage increase one should decide to whom the ships belonged and, further, that if workers insisted on a wage increase despite the initial agreement on wage rates, he personally would raise the question of cancelling nationalization.[69]

After the Brest–Litovsk Treaty, Lenin spoke in even sharper tones on workers' claims. On 29 April 1918, he asserted the need for state capitalism in the phase of transition to socialism 'since state capitalism is something centralized, calculated, controlled and socialized'.[70] The challenge was directed against the left-wing communists, but was also

intended to show that spontaneous workers' initiatives could be harmful
to the solution of economic problems:

> I told every workers' delegation with which I had to deal when they came to me
> and complained that their factory was at a standstill: you would like your factory
> to be confiscated. Very well, we have blank forms for a decree ready, they can be
> signed in a minute. But tell us: have you learnt how to take over production and
> have you calculated what you will produce? Do you know the connection between
> what you are producing and the Russian and the international market?
> Whereupon it turns out that they have not yet learnt this; there has not been
> anything about it yet in Bolshevik pamphlets, and nothing is said about it in
> Menshevik pamphlets either.[71]

At the beginning of 1918 the Tanners' Union came to an agreement
with the All-Russian Association of Manufacturers and Factory Owners
of the Leather Industry, under which the tanneries were to work. The
government provided subsidies and the factories agreed to put their
output at the disposal of the state. The Central Committee for Leather
was composed two-thirds of workers and one-third of private manufacturers and bourgeois technical experts. Analogous agreements were
concluded in textiles, sugar and other branches of the food-processing
industry. Lenin praised these agreements.[72] This solution was considered
positive, since it entailed joint responsibility of workers and owners in
directing the *glavki*, and at the same time it deprived workers at the factory
level of most of the grounds for intervening in management and raising
claims against the higher administration. Another reason in favour of this
solution was that, with respect to nationalization, it implied a smaller
burden on the State Budget, since the government could intervene
through subsidies, without assuming complete financial responsibility.

The leadership was primarily concerned to limit workers' intervention
in management in large-scale industry, after nationalization.[73] One
instruction of the Baku *Sovnarkhoz* made explicit reference to the decree on
nationalization of the oil industry, signed by *Sovnarkom*, to stress that
'control' was intended to be *ex post* – i.e. any instruction by the central
administration had to be immediately and precisely fulfilled.[74] The
instruction to the factory committees for implementation of the decree on
nationalization of joint-stock companies stated that workers had to
participate directly in the protection of factory property and surveillance
of inventories, and that the right to decide individual and factory output
norms belonged to management.[75]

The merging of the factory committees with the trade unions was used
to confine their concern to labour relations, rather than to promote their
evolution to wider responsibilities. A conference of Textile Trade Union
factory committees in Moscow *Oblast* on 2 June 1918 decided that

minimum wages were to be tied to the output norm and that workers' courts should be organized in each factory and locality to promote labour discipline.[76] The Fourth Conference of Factory Committees in Moscow on 2 July 1918 declared that factory committees should not hesitate to take exceptional measures against any violation of labour discipline and that plundering, abuses and careless work must be resolutely fought.[77]

Nonetheless, the variety of experience in the area of workers' control that the Bolsheviks had inherited from 1917, and which developed amidst the disorganization following the October Revolution, could not easily be mastered by laws and instructions. Between March 1917 and August 1918, factory committees were set up at 4,398 Russian enterprises (excluding the Urals and the Donets Basin). Special control commissions functioned at another 2,371 enterprises.[78] The census of industry on 31 August 1918 shows that most of the factory committees and special organs of workers' control took part in management (see Table 3.1). This situation occurred independently of the directives from the centre. The Second All-Russian Congress of Trade Unions, in January 1919, where the Bolshevik representation was overwhelming, affirmed that the rights of workers in the matter of control were limited to surveillance of the pace of work and to the *ex post* supervision of management and production.[79] The congress imposed quite severe limitations on the powers of control commissions in nationalized enterprises. Their powers were limited to the

Table 3.1. *Participation in management by factory committees and special organs of workers' control, August 1918*

Enterprises by number of workers	Number of factory committees taking part in management	% of total factory committees	Number of special organs of workers' control taking part in management	% of the total number of special organs of workers' control
below 50	993	60.8	333	55.9
51–200	900	62.5	472	57.2
201–500	361	70.6	278	73.7
501–1,000	174	76.6	143	73.7
1,001–5,000	183	84.3	166	84.7
Above 5,000	23	100.0	21	95.4
Unknown	196	56.2	105	65.2
Total	2,830	64.3	1,518	64.0

Source: V.Z. Drobizhev, 'Sotsialisticheskoe obobshchestvlenie promyshlennosti v SSSR', *Voprosy Istorii*, 1964, no. 6, 55

right to collect data for the control department of the trade union concerned; and checking of the enterprise book-keeping and balances could be done only on approval of the control department.[80] For private enterprises, as distinct from nationalized ones, the decree on workers' control still applied.

The degree of workers' interference in management allowed in private enterprises by the decree on workers' control was mainly based on political considerations and on the fear that capitalists would sabotage the plan of the new government. From the economic point of view, indeed, it would have been contradictory to limit workers' control on the ground that workers had no adequate knowledge and experience, and to let it survive for private enterprises, which at the beginning of 1919 still constituted the greater part of the economy. The need for a political control *in loco*, through the organs of workers' control, explains why the field of competence of the factory committees was never, throughout war communism, clearly defined. According to Lozovskii, the final settlement of the question of workers' control was decided at the Third Congress of Trade Unions, held in April 1920, when it was resolved that the factory committee must definitely be fixed as the local nucleus of the trade unions, with similar functions, and must not interfere in management.[81] By April 1920 the civil war was practically over and the political function which the factory committees had performed *in loco* could finally be removed.

As long as the civil war lasted, there was no possibility of abolishing workers' control as such, even though from points of view other than those of mere political convenience this possibility was foreseen, as is indicated by rumours circulating in summer 1918.[82]

To prevent workers' control eluding central directives, the Bolsheviks had either to conquer the organs of workers' control, or to limit their autonomy by empowering parallel *state* organs to watch over them. Both solutions were sought.[83] In one case the section of the party attached to a factory demanded obligatory admission of two Bolsheviks into the factory committee on the ground that the leading party had to be represented in all democratic institutions. It is possible that similar demands were made in other factories. The number of Bolsheviks engaged in the civil war, however, did not leave much room for direct political control over workers' organs.

The leadership tried to circumvent the problem by establishing state control over business activity.

3.4 STATE CONTROL VERSUS WORKERS' CONTROL

The Commissariat of State Control, which had been set up in December 1917 as a consultative organ of *Sovnarkom* on financial questions, remained inactive until July 1918. In the summer of 1918 its central control board and local accounting control boards and commissions were formally completed.[84] The state control agencies were to supervise the accounts of industrial enterprises and check their book-keeping.[85]

Workers' control, which according to Lenin's project was supposed to fulfil the same tasks, had gone much further. The relations between the two institutions were not clear to most and were subject to various interpretations. In the government milieu emphasis fell on limitation of the autonomy of workers' control organs. The Commissariat of State Control proposed the combination of workers' control with state control.

The local *sovnarkhozy* disagreed. They argued that workers' control, as it worked out in practice, contained functions not of inspection but of management and, as such, it provided the eyes and ears of the *sovnarkhozy*. To merge workers' control with state control was considered inappropriate, since state control was responsible for keeping the activity of workers' organs within their proper limits.[86]

On the contrary, the argument in favour of merging the two organs of control was grounded on the need for a more highly centralized control independent of the local organs of Soviet power.[87]

In October 1918 a workers' control conference resolved to distinguish two aspects of control applicable both to nationalized and private factories: first, a practical (*fakticheskii*) control by workers through their elected organs (i.e. factory committees); second, an inspection (*dokumental'nyi*) control, exerted by the agents of the Commissariat of State Control.[88]

The question of the relations between workers' control and state control was also debated at a session of VSNKh. Following the increasing pace of nationalization, VSNKh and its *sovnarkhozy* had become directly involved in managerial functions. To this extent any form of administrative control which could hinder the normal speed of managerial decision-making was viewed with apprehension.

Agents of state control claimed overall control over the financial activity of enterprises with respect to the correctness, legality and regularity of their operations.[89] Representatives of VSNKh, who did not oppose the hypothesis of central control over the financial sides of entrepreneurial activity, claimed that VSNKh itself, being charged with the direction of industrial activity, was better suited to exert financial control as well. Lomov even proposed the abolition of state control as such.[90] VSNKh's proposal, however, turned out to be a device for removing the possibility of an independent organ exercising control over its own activity. This eventuality was firmly rejected by the representative of state control on the ground that, if financial control were given to VSNKh, the latter would itself remain uncontrolled.[91]

VSNKh members considered workers' control to be a lesser evil than state control. Centralization, which for the economic leaders was, rightly or wrongly, synonymous with efficiency and rapidity of decisions, required a minimum number of intermediate levels between management and execution. The directors of the production sections of VSNKh were afraid that the supervision exerted by a state organ over all phases of the process of decision-making would result in all sorts of delays and finally turn out to be only a bureaucratic device. The economic crisis favoured a solidarity of interests between the technocratic soul of VSNKh and factory workers, against state interference. The VSNKh leaders felt that there was room for a deeper involvement of workers' organizations in the matter of control at all levels, combined with more responsibility. Some of them, primarily concerned with establishing a single central direction, considered workers' control a deterrent against illicit activities; they underlined the need for an *ex post* control by workers coupled with technical and financial control from organs of the central administrations of industry.[92]

One point was common to the various proposals formulated by VSNKh members: preference for a solution which would avoid the interference of state bureaucracy in management, possibly through the utilization of people *in loco*.[93]

The fear of bureaucratic intermediaries was justified. Though by law the organs of state control should have been organs of revision, i.e. *ex post* inspection over industrial management, they, in fact, went beyond these tasks. Complaints can be found in the Press that transfers of money for purchase of raw materials or payments of wages had first to be submitted for approval. Furthermore, state control revealed itself to be unsuitable for enforcing the proper administration of public property, though this was the first reason for its institution. State control was accused of bearing the same deficiencies as the other Soviet institutions: a mostly incompetent staff, whose principal function turned out to be rubber stamping.[94] VSNKh, which supported giving these functions to the existing workers' organs, was, on its part, unable to provide adequate guidelines to enforce workers' control *ex post*. The divergences in the operation of workers' control in practice within the nationalized factories were so wide that a commission was established to produce a common scheme of instructions on workers' control. This commission never started work.

The Second Congress of *Sovnarkhozy*, which met at the end of 1918, when already the necessity of confronting problems of organization could not be separated from the effects of civil war on economic priorities, treated the question of workers' participation in management only indirectly, along with the pending question of the involvement of trade unions in the direction of industry. The burning question of workers' control was evaded by the congress.[95]

The impossibility of finding a final solution to the problem of embodying workers' control in an institutionalized form within the framework of public enterprise is a reflection of the confusion which characterized economic organization. This shows also as a consequence of the inadequacy of any model to encompass the plurality of experiences which the leadership was incapable of subjecting to its authority.

As late as August 1919, the metal workers' conference concluded that a duality of power characterized the relations between the administration and factory committees in state enterprises, and that the divergences between them, due to the antagonism between the overall perspective of an industry and the local syndicalist interests of workers, had not yet been solved.[96]

3.5 DECISION-MAKING: PROJECTS AND IMPLEMENTATION

Kritsman distinguished six stages in the process of the formation of Soviet managerial organs: (1), self-regulated workers' control before the October Revolution; (2), imposed workers' control after the revolution; (3), compulsory participation of capitalists in the organs of the state proletarian administration, until nationalization of the joint-stock companies; (4), obligatory retention (*prikreplenie*) of specialists at their posts in the enterprises, between the end of 1918 and the beginning of 1919, until the formation of the organs of workers' management; (5), collective workers' management; (6), one-man management.[97] This chronology, as in any temporal schematization, suffers from an excessive linearity; but it is useful to underline the basic steps through which decision-making went. Forms of management should be seen in the light of the political hypotheses prevalent at each stage. Initially, the Soviet government looked for collaboration with bourgeois specialists (a euphemism for capitalists, often used by Lenin) within the hypothesis of state capitalism. The chief and central committees (*glavki* and *tsentry*) in several important branches were reorganized by including in their boards representatives of other Soviet institutions. The problem of finding representatives of the working class capable of carrying out managerial tasks was made more urgent by the scarcity of educated people willing to offer their services to Soviet power. As soon as the problem of forcing some order into the economy was raised in connection with the administration of state enterprises, the Bolshevik leadership turned to the trade unions to find possible means of collaboration, and to sift out of them people suitable for management.

At the time of the First Congress of Trade Unions, in January 1918, the debate centered around the role which trade unions should have under Soviet power. Should they actively support Soviet economic policy or remain in a neutral or independent position? Indirectly, the question of 'stateization' (*ogosudarstvlenie*), which during war communism epitomized the Bolshevik effort to institutionalize trade unions and make them dependent on central power, was raised already at the time of the First Congress of Trade Unions. This question, from the institutional point of view, concerned the relations between trade unions and the Commissariat of Labour (*Narkomtrud*).[98] But, from the political and economic point of view, what mattered was the trade unions' acquiescence to central economic policy. The debate demonstrated that it would not be easy to gain the support of the unions for the government's economic policy by relying only on political slogans. The Russian trade unions, despite their recent formation and composite political extraction, strove for more autonomy and claimed for themselves the role of defenders of labour. This position precluded them from directly engaging in management. Administrative functions would have meant, as long as workers were not emancipated from subordination, sacrifice by the unions of their support of workers' economic interests, and their resignation to an ancillary role with respect to the government's goals and policies. This conern was expressed in particular by the Mensheviks, who at that time still had a broad following among unionized workers. For the Mensheviks, the autonomy of trade unions should have been maintained so long as the Soviet Revolution was considered as simply a bourgeois stage in the transition to socialism. In the Menshevik perspective, the October Revolution had not brought about such change as to justify renunciation of their views on the need for state control: a position which they had already expressed in July 1917 at the Third Conference of Trade Unions.[99] The Mensheviks saw in the trade unions a means to fight factory separatism, which was nourished by the organs of workers' control. For this purpose, too, control over industrial activity ought in their view to be the responsibility of state economic organs.[100]

Moving from different evaluation of the current stage, the Bolsheviks urged the trade unions to collaborate with government policy. The Bolsheviks considered the current stage as a transition to socialism. They deplored the neutrality of trade unions. Since the new government was considered as the expression of the dictatorship of the proletariat, any other organization aspiring to represent the working class must either actively support state power or be antagonistic to it and thus hinder the interests of the working class.[101] The Bolsheviks used the same argument in favour of merging factory committees into the trade union organization. The Left Socialist-Revolutionaries supported the Bolshevik claims. They even added a new emphasis. At the First Congress of Trade Unions, they maintained that the trade unions had to behave as state organs (*gosudarstvennye organizatsiia*).[102]

Participation of trade unions in decision-making was, for the Bolshevik leadership, a means to gain workers' support on economic policies which – at least immediately – could not offer any material benefits in exchange. Such responsibility in decision-making amounted to much less than workers' management.

The only support that the hypothesis of workers' management had among political groups was that of the anarcho-syndicalist faction. Maksimov defended management by factory committees on the ground that they were the spontaneous emanation of the working class. As such, they were acting under the immediate control of workers. The resolution of the anarcho-syndicalist group affirmed that only through the initiative of the working people could economic disruption be avoided. Maksimov and his group showed that they distrusted trade unions as potential leaders of economic management. The unions were not suited, in their view, to perform these tasks; they should instead work for the emancipation of the working class as a whole.[103] The anarcho-syndicalist position on the trade unions depended on the fact that most of the union leaders and members belonged to the existing political parties; a peculiarity of the Russian situation, which Maksimov had already deplored in August 1917: 'The unions tend to identify their interests with the interests of other parties'; they are 'cautious, inclined toward compromise, complacent, calling [themselves] militant, but in reality striving for class harmony'.[104]

Whether of Marxist extraction or not, however, the trade unions manifested from the First Congress a 'unionist' standpoint which did not coincide with any of the political lines represented at the congress. The resolution adopted by the congress rejected a position of neutrality, as a bourgeois idea, but also rejected institutionalization. The unions agreed 'to shoulder the main burden of organizing production and rehabilitating the country's shattered productive forces', and confirmed 'their energetic participation in all central bodies called upon to regulate output, and in the organization of workers' control' and in several other organizational tasks. But they refused 'statization' as such and formulated the possibility of an evolution in this sense only on conditional terms: 'As they develop, the trade unions should in the process of the present socialist revolution become organs of socialist power, and as such they should work in coordination with, and subordination to, other bodies in order to carry into effect the new principles.'[105] The Mensheviks interpreted the result of the congress in the sense that the trade unions had refused 'to become sections of VSNKh'.[106]

The leadership multiplied its efforts to involve trade unions in government economic policy when, in connection with the Brest–Litovsk negotiations, the economic organization seemed to be defined as state capitalism. Avoidance of labour conflicts was sought in the merger of trade union organs with the organs of the Labour Commissariat. Tomskii claimed that trade unions were assuming an overall state significance in that they were in a position to regulate the conditions of labour and production in the interests of the working class as a whole. In so doing, they were exerting an activity parallel to that of the Labour Commissariat, resulting in a useless duplication of work.[107] At the Fourth All-Russian Conference of Trade Unions (12–17 March 1918), where Tomskii's resolution on merging trade union organs with state labour organs was passed by a majority vote, the opposition to the Bolshevik line on the institutionalization of the trade unions was nonetheless still consistent. Maiskii warned that trade union relations with the Labour Commissariat could be friendly, neutral or antagonistic, depending on the character of the state labour policy, since as long as capitalism or state capitalism remained, owners remained too.[108] The opinion of the Mensheviks was shared by other groups. Lozovskii argued that, in spite of the modification of the social, territorial, economic and production bases of the country, the Soviet system was not yet a proletarian one. The state organs represented the interests of the whole population, that is, both of the proletariat and of the petty-bourgeoisie (by which the Marxists intended the peasantry). Therefore, Lozovskii argued, state organs could not be organs of the trade unions, which should remain autonomous and independent of state power in order to safeguard workers' interests.[109]

For the opposition, direct participation in state administration should be a result of the effective process of socialization. For the Bolsheviks, the former was a prerequisite for the latter. Though unable to defeat completely the trade unions' opposition to 'statization', the Bolsheviks' weight was decisive in forcing trade unions to adopt very strict regulations on labour discipline. The All-Russian Council of Trade Unions issued on 3 April 1918 regulations introducing piece-wages as a means of increasing labour productivity, and also regulations on sanctions, such as expulsion from the trade unions, on workers who refused to subject themselves to union discipline.[110] This decision happened to coincide with the sharp turn in economic organization that Lenin endeavoured to impose, first of all on the members of his own party. In the first version of the article 'On the Immediate Tasks', written at the end of March 1918, Lenin made it clear that he considered the period of meetings where the airing of questions prevailed over the business aspect to be over, and he added:

> Now has come the turning point when – without in any way ceasing to prepare the masses for participation in state and economic administration of all the affairs of society, and without in any way hindering the most detailed discussion of the new tasks (on the contrary, helping them in every way to carry out this discussion so that they independently think out and arrive at correct decisions) – we must at the very same time begin strictly to separate two categories of democratic functions: on the one hand, discussions and the airing of questions at public meetings, and, on the other hand, the establishment of strictest responsibility for executive functions and absolutely business-like, disciplined, voluntary fulfilment of the assignments and decrees necessary for the economic mechanism to function really like clockwork.[111]

At that time, Lenin did not contest the principle of election of the leading organs, but he stressed the need for one-man management (OMM):

> Neither railways nor transport, nor large-scale machinery and enterprises in general can function correctly without a single will linking the entire working personnel into an economic organ operating with the precision of clockwork..., when there is the slightest opportunity for it, responsible persons should be elected for one-man management in all sections of the economic organism as a whole.[112]

In the final version of this article, published on 28 April 1918 in *Pravda*, Lenin related the question of OMM to the specific tasks of the present moment and compared OMM to 'the mild leadership of a conductor of an orchestra'. Such an oddly poetical image was immediately corrected by the stress he put on the need for *'unquestioning subordination* to a single will' (Lenin's italics).[113]

Nevertheless, neither Lenin nor Trotskii, who shared his ideas on this point,[114] was able to defeat the principle of collegiality in decision-making in 1918.

The first decree on the management of nationalized enterprises in March 1918 established two directors at the head of each enterprise, one technical and the other administrative. Both directors were appointed by the central administrations of the corresponding branch. The principle of *appointment* of the directors was balanced by the *elective* principle which applied to a new organ – the economic and administrative council. This council deliberated on administrative questions, such as the budget estimates of the enterprise, the programme of work, internal regulations, solution of grievances, working conditions and 'everything else concerning the [internal] life of the enterprise'. Decisions of the council were binding on the administrative director, who could appeal against them, only after their application, to the commissar of the central administration for that branch. On questions of a technical nature the council had only a consultative vote. Supply and delivery of goods remained outside its competence. The economic and administrative council, however, did not reflect a syndicalist conception of management. Besides some representatives of workers, employees and engineers of the enterprise, the council included representatives of the trade unions, the local *sovnarkhozy*, the local soviets, workers' cooperatives, and the councils of peasants' deputies of the *raion* concerned. This composition weakened the impact of the factory workers on decision-making, without in turn providing a firm connection with the central administration of the corresponding branch. The workers' control organs remained in a subordinate position with respect to the council. Their statements and deliberations had to be submitted to the latter for examination. Moreover, the council had the right to lay off workers without notice for any period of time.[115]

The decree on management of nationalized enterprises reflected an interesting compromise between technocratic principles and general interests, expressed by the several productive groups represented in the economic and administrative council. However, the potential antagonisms between the management and the council jeopardized their equilibrium and firmness of decision-making. This fact was likely to lead to a predominance of one organ over the other. In case of conflict, there was no neutral organ to settle the dispute. Final decisions were taken by the central administration, the same which appointed the two directors.

VSNKh started appointing commissars to the factories where tensions and conflicts jeopardized the directives of the centre. The appointment of commissars chosen from union members was recommended by the All-Russian Central Executive Committee, as a form of political supervision over management.[116] The commissars had substantial powers, extending to dismissal of workers. Since the sphere of their autonomy was not regulated by law, their activity depended on the aims and conditions of the enterprise. The commissars' undefined powers provoked reactions among workers and political leaders, who accused them of military methods of management.[117] The wave of criticism was directed against Lenin's approach to state capitalism.

In 'The Immediate Tasks of the Soviet Government', Lenin stressed the need for coercion in the transition from capitalism to socialism and asserted that there was no contradiction between Soviet democracy and the exercise of dictatorial powers by individuals.[118] He ridiculed the 'mania for meetings'. Among the points of the six theses on the immediate tasks, which were approved unanimously by the Party Central Committee on 3 May 1918, particular significance was attached to measures for improving labour discipline and productivity; that is, piece-work, adoption of the Taylor system, and payment of wages according to productivity.[119] On OMM, however, the solution approved by the central committee was ambiguous and reflected the contrasting feelings of the Bolsheviks on this question. Agreement was reached on the anodyne assertion that unquestioning obedience during work to one-man decisions of Soviet directors was far from being guaranteed as yet, and that the reason for this was the anarchy of petty-bourgeois habits, feelings and sentiments.[120]

At the First Congress of *Sovnarkhozy*, the question of decision-making was subject to the precise criticism of the left wing and resulted in a new decree on management, which reaffirmed the collegiality principle. Osinskii, who had resigned his post as head of VSNKh after the signing of the Brest–Litovsk Treaty, criticized Lenin's thesis that state capitalism was a step towards socialism. The representative of the left wing maintained that so long as the proletariat still remained a class living on wages, the bourgeoisie was going to hold on to economic power. In his view, the proletariat was charged only formally with accounting, control and regulation, since practically all these functions remained con-centrated in the hands of the bourgeoisie, who remained in control of property and decision-making. Osinskii defended state socialism against state capitalism, meaning by the former the concentration of all leading functions in the hands of the proletariat. This approach was better developed in his work on 'Construction of Socialism', published in 1918. In this Osinskii wrote that the party on the morrow of the revolution did not have a clear idea of the meaning of workers' control, or any idea about what system ought to replace the old one. However, workers' control had a discriminatory meaning. Added to nationalization of the banks and large-scale industry, it represented an alternative to state control which belonged to the Menshevik programme. Before the revolution the essence of workers' control did not correspond to its form: formally, workers' control was not *kontrol'* but tutelage (*opeka*); substantively, it was not *kontrol'* but regulation (in the sense of greater authority than is indicated by *kontrol'*).[121] Osinskii proposed the institutionalization of the practice. He argued that after the revolution the essential question was how to organize management in order to strengthen the class victory and extend the leading role of the proletariat over production. Against Lenin's claims in favour of the participation of bourgeois experts in management,

Osinskii demanded their expulsion and the concentration of administrative direction in the factory-shop committees, with a broad participation of the masses. In no case, stressed Osinskii, should workers remain ignorant of the overall business situation of their own factory.[122]

By these arguments, the left wing affirmed the possibility of transforming workers' control into workers' management, which Lenin never considered immediately realizable.[123] The left-wing propositions, however, were based on a distinction between administration (*pravlenie*) and management (*upravlenie*), which considerably reduced the scope for decision-making in an entrepreneurial sense by the lower organs. Osinskii asserted that central and *oblast* organs ought to be competent for the general direction and the assignment of orders to the lower units, that is, they ought to carry out the 'administration'. The enterprise ought to perform 'managerial tasks', i.e. to fulfil assignments and perform technical tasks. The enterprises ought to receive from above financial and material funds, labour assignments, instructions and orders for delivery of output. Smirnov said that the task of the centre was to ascertain the productive capacity of each factory.[124] In effect, the left-wing communists were establishing the rudiments of central planning. Theirs was an alternative hypothesis of economic organization and a very different one from the programme of the anarcho-syndicalists and anarcho-communists, who rejected any form of centralized direction of the economy.

The anarcho-syndicalists had in mind a horizontal organization based on unionized workers carrying out production under the direction of their branch union. The trade unions should set the number of factories, their productivity, the inputs of labour and raw materials. They also should compute the total demand for the finished product. That is, trade unions were expected to perform the statistical and administrative functions which, at the First Congress of Trade Unions, the anarcho-syndicalists reserved to the upper organs of a federative system governed by factory committees.[125] The anarcho-communists conceived economic organization as functioning in the interests of the whole of society. They took into account the interdependence between agriculture and industry, and the interrelations among industrial branches. Free associations of people were supposed to provide the connection between sectors and branches, in order to realize a necessary element of competition.[126]

Though they did not have much support for their political programme,[127] the anarcho-syndicalists had some impact on the formulation of the new decree on management. Thanks to them, the resolution on election of experts for a maximum of one-third of the whole council was passed, rather than the alternative one, which proposed a system of appointment.[128] This was a sign of the isolation of the leadership on the very crucial question of management in mid 1918, and a pointer to the compromising and precarious nature that the regulations on management were to take. The commission, which was to draw up the final wording of the decree, accepted the amendments of the anarchists. But it incurred Lenin's opposition.[129] Through his influence, the resolution presented for final voting to the congress with the signatures of Lenin, Rykov and Veinberg modified the conclusions of the commission and contained a clause which left open the possibility of appointment.[130]

This controversy on management also involved the question of centralization and the meaning of it. For the delegates of the local *sovnarkhozy*, collegiality of decisions meant the possibility of local officials having representation on higher bodies. Against this claim, the supporters of strict centralization employed arguments based on practical as well as theoretical reasons. Central appointment of managers was justified by arguments based on economic crisis, immaturity of workers, local 'particularism'.[131] By the term 'particularism', the supporters of central appointment had essentially in mind local reactions against the shutting down of factories: a policy which the *glavki* claimed to be necessary for rational allocation of resources in a time of scarcity of raw materials.

Rykov, the president of VSNKh, objected to decentralized management on the grounds that nobody, neither the left-wing communists nor the anarcho-syndicalists, accepted the full principle of election. This was correct. The left-wing communists proposed that factory managements be elected by unionized workers.[132] The anarcho-syndicalists proposed that two-thirds of factory managements should be composed of representatives of unionized workers, and one-third of engineers, technicians and employees, all by election. This was a sign that nobody really believed the maturity of the Russian proletariat, as such, to be adequate for self-management. But there were also theoretical arguments against decentralized management. Lozovskii argued that the tendency of capitalism was towards centralization and that socialism had to carry this legacy forward.[133] Another argument was that if VSNKh was supposed to elaborate a single overall plan for all industrial branches, it had also to hold sufficient authority to carry it out at the level of factories.[134] Both arguments sounded rather abstract in the light of Russian reality.

The left-wing communists agreed on centralization of economic policy. But they disagreed on the centralization of its execution, arguing that socialism meant a broader mass participation in the direction of economic life.[135]

To the argument for VSNKh authority at factory level, two objections were raised: first, VSNKh did not have an adequate staff at its disposal to appoint an enormous number of local commissars, and experience had proved that the quality of the appointed people was rather poor.[136] As a second counter-argument, the anarcho-syndicalists observed that the role of the supreme council of the economy ought not necessarily to be an executive one. In their view, the central organ ought to coordinate and register local activities, that is, to perform statistical functions, while the connections between enterprises and the centre should be by way of reciprocal consultation.[137] For the left-wing communists, each organ should have defined functions, hierarchically ordered, so that the relations among organs would be defined by the limits of competence of each organ. Within its competence, each organ would be granted a high degree of autonomy and self-regulation. But they did not explain which sort of indicators should be used for the correct transmission of guidelines and for their application and verification.

The supporters of straightforward centralization in decision-making, that is, most of the Presidium of VSNKh, were apprehensive of autonomy for the lower units. They rejected the idea of a hierarchy based on the defined competence of each unit. This rejection implied that the only way for the centre to maintain control of the whole economic organism was a system of personal ties based on the political reliability of the appointed people. The system of commissars was supposed to guarantee the transmission of orders and surveillance over their execution as well. This system had no theoretical foundation, other than the fear that things might otherwise get out of control. It provided the appearance of a coordination in default of planning, of a technical means of communication and of an adequate system of sanctions and rewards. Appointment, of course, was the only principle suitable for such a framework.

The final resolution of the Congress of *Sovnarkhozy*, which became the new decree on management, was the result of a compromise between extreme centralization, i.e. central appointment of economic commissars, and extreme decentralization, i.e. collegiality and complete election of the managerial councils.[138] The separation between technical and administrative functions disappeared. Two-thirds of the factory management were to be appointed by the *oblast sovnarkhozy* or by VSNKh. Of this number, VSNKh had the right to grant the *oblast* or central trade unions the nomination of half of the candidates. The remaining third were to be elected by the trade union members in the enterprise. One-third of the whole number were to be experts.

The principle of election of the experts was rejected, but the principle of appointment was made less rigid, since experts could also be elected by the trade union members. Only in cases in which they did not do so was the principle of appointment from above to complete the quorum.

The discretionary powers granted to VSNKh with regard to letting trade unions nominate a third of the candidates reflected the suspicion of the composition of some trade unions, and it left the door open to political manipulation of the factory management councils. Owing to the views of the left-wing communists and the anarcho-syndicalists,[139] the right of the central administration to appoint a commissar to the lower units was limited to cases of necessity. Rights and duties of the factory-shop management were strictly specified.

The management council drew up the enterprise estimates, the production plan, the plan of development and re-equipment, and the plan of supply. Other tasks concerned drafting the internal regulations, calculating prime costs and wage rates; also the appointment of technicians and executives to the highest posts and definition of their tasks, surveillance of the execution of plans, and welfare. At certain dates, the management council had to present an account of its own activity and of the situation of the enterprise to the higher administration of nationalized enterprises, i.e. either to the *oblast sovnarkhoz* or to VSNKh. The council was in charge for a period of six months,[140] after which its membership could be changed.

The highest economic organs had the right to reject members of the administrative staff chosen by the managerial council and to appoint their own candidates in extraordinary cases. Members of the *oblast* administrations were elected by conferences of the factory-shop managements and *oblast* trade unions and approved by the Presidium of VSNKh. One delegate of the presidium was present in each *oblast* administration. The new decree on management was supposed to provide a part of the necessary institutional framework for further nationalizations, but at the time of its approval there was no presumption that the pace of nationalization would be a rapid one. A gradual approach to nationalization was the prevailing line, and its prerequisites were registration of existing enterprises and their inventories and balances, etc., which was expected to take some time. Rykov stressed that the information which VSNKh had required from each factory was quite modest and lacked precision. He concluded that the transition from capitalism to socialism, that is, to nationalization of industry, depended on how fast the preparatory work would go ('maybe one or two years or more'), depending on the available staff and means.[141] This whole plan was jeopardized by the decree on nationalization of large-scale industry and the civil war. The effort of the central organs to keep up with the number of nationalized enterprises began to fail increasingly. The lack of managerial staff became the most important impediment to a proper organization of industrial direction and to correct implementation of the decree on management.

The ambitious quota of managerial posts that VSNKh endeavoured to reserve for itself could only be met if no regard were paid to the specific competence of the appointees. Another complication was the lack of intermediate cadres. This was a legacy of Russian backwardness. The pre-war ratio between manual and white-collar workers was 10–15 : 1 in Russia versus 5–8 : 1 in Germany and the United States.[142] Centralization plus incompetence were likely to bring about the bureaucratization of economic life and to worsen relations with the provinces.

In the first half of 1918, the reasons for demanding the participation of trade unions in industrial management had to do primarily with the need for central control over wages and labour discipline. In the second half, some economists started looking to the trade unions as the only possible source of reliable intermediate cadres. Arskii, one of the best Soviet economists according to some contemporaries, asserted that it had become impossible to manage the economy from one centre and proposed a modification of the appointment system in favour of a broad elective system. Two-thirds of the management council should be elected by the trade unions of the corresponding branch and one-third by the factory workers. Arskii proposed that *glavki* and *tsentry*, which in the course of 1918 had acquired the status of production sections of VSNKh, should issue precise instructions and directives to their subordinate enterprises, but should leave supervision over them to the local *sovnarkhozy*.[143] He considered this system preferable to the practice of appointment by the *oblast sovnarkhozy* or by VSNKh of two-thirds of the managerial councils, since in spite of the possibility given by the decree on management to trade unions to nominate half of the centrally appointed members, direct central appointment had become prevalent, and had made insignificant the relations between trade unions and management.[144] The small participation of trade union members in management was evident also in the local *sovnarkhozy*. A VSNKh census in August 1918 revealed that only 1.7 per cent of members of the presidia of the *sovnarkhozy* (of an overall figure of 686 people) had formerly been officials of trade unions.[145]

However, not everyone shared the opinion that broader mass participation in management was suitable. On the one hand, civil war strengthened the sectarian spirit which already existed in Marxist ideology. Nogin expressed the fear of free elections in factories 'which deviate from the tasks of class policy'.[146] On the other hand, the trade unions were not ready to accept the responsibility of taking part in management. The principle of personal responsibility of the collegiate members was affirmed by the Second Congress of *Sovnarkhozy* in December 1918.[147] Another reason impeding participation of trade unions in management was presumably the policy of wage differentials through which the leadership tried to enlist the services of the specialists. Lozovskii argued that as long as there was a difference between a 3,000 rubles salary for a specialist and a 300 rubles wage for a worker, it was absurd to envisage the co-responsibility of trade unions in management. He defined Arskii's proposal as only a new way of demanding again the institutionalization of trade unions and said that this was out of the question.[148]

In fact, the resolution of the First Congress of Trade Unions, thanks to its ambiguity, could have favoured the interpretation that along with the process of socialization of the economy, the unions would accept new responsibilities and direct participation in state administrative life.[149] The nationalization drive, after June 1918, fed the expectations of the Bolshevik leadership in this sense. However, neither the extension of nationalization nor the spread of war at the end of 1918 affected the basic position of trade unions on the question of institutionalization.

Tsyperovitch said afterwards that the main object of the debate at the Second Congress of Trade Unions, 16–26 January 1919, was not the question of 'statization' of the trade unions, but that of its timing, thereby implying that a basic consensus existed on this goal.[150] However, this was not true for the whole congress, though it may have been for most Bolsheviks. In fact, the institutionalization of trade unions was not passed by the congress, though the Bolshevik representation had more than doubled in one year. The discussion about schedules was, in effect, used as a means to reject institutionalization at the very time that the political leadership desired it. If institutionalization had been put forward as a theoretical desideratum, the timing of its realization would not have mattered. But trade union 'statization' was urged for the highly practical purpose of consolidating power in a social and economic framework which was becoming dangerously hostile to the immediate targets of a war economy and its priorities. Unionized workers, however, did not always understand or did not always accept this message. At the Second Congress of the Textile Union, it was claimed that the best union officials had been absorbed by the top administrations, *Tsentrotekstil'* and *Glavtekstil'*, and that the time spent in such organizational work was detrimental to specific union activity.[151]

Among unionized workers there spread a fear that the gains made by labour – amidst the general economic disorganization following the February Revolution – and extended in the labour legislation after October 1917, could be lost as a consequence of the severe regulations on labour productivity and labour discipline enacted in the spring of 1918. The political context in 1919 reinforced these fears and justified the reluctance of union members to abandon the traditional trade union functions of the defence of labour in favour of a deeper involvement in the organization of the economy. Tomskii's assertion that strikes ought not to take place in Soviet Russia, where trade unions regulated wages and labour conditions and appointed the Labour Commissar,[152] were bound to raise suspicion about any further attempt to draw unions into state administration.[153]

Unionized railway and textile workers, mostly represented at the Second Congress of Trade Unions by the Social Democratic Internationalists, protested against the centralizing Bolshevik policy. They claimed that state organs, namely the *glavki* and *tsentry*, hindered the work of the control commissions; that state control, through its control–technical sections, created parallelism of functions and was a source of bureaucratic methods; and that the Soviet bureaucracy and the top managers made efforts to free themselves of control from below.[154] These criticisms echoed the concern, already expressed by the Second Moscow *Oblast* Congress of Nationalized Factory Managements in May 1918, that the reduction of the scope of workers' control would lead to a separation of working people from the administration, by transforming the latter into 'a special category of technical decision-making aristocracy'.[155] The policy of VSNKh had, indeed, favoured the appointment of technical experts at the highest posts. An informant of the British Information Service reported on 21 January 1919 that he was surprised to see how many members of the committees were former officers, factory directors and so forth.[156]

The Social Democratic Internationalists affirmed that trade unions could have a greater role in regulation and organization of production without being institutionalized. Other arguments against institutionalization were presented by Lozovskii. First, practice proved that as efforts were made to institutionalize trade unions, workers formed other unions. Second, the Russian trade unions were not yet ready to carry out the tasks they were supposed to perform because of their small size and the backwardness and disorganization of the working class. The Social Democratic Internationalists joined the Mensheviks in denouncing the pressures on trade unions, which derived from a too rapid pace of nationalization. They argued that, if there were not enough people to carry out major tasks in management, it was a mistake to get involved in the nationalization of small-scale commerce and industry.[157]

The arguments presented by the opposition influenced the conclusions of the Second Congress on the role of trade unions. The final resolution acknowledged that merging of trade union organs with the state was a goal which could not be realized in the then existing conditions. Merging needed preparation of the working masses for management with the help of the trade unions.[158] The resolution affirmed a principle, but failed to give guidelines for its realization. The absence of any indication as to practical steps for furthering trade union involvement in administration reveals that their defensive line prevailed over the Bolshevik stand on institutionalization. The congress declared that workers' control should not interfere in the general administration of the activity of state and collective institutions, but stressed the importance of workers' control taking part in hiring and firing, and in the correct application of wage tariffs.[159]

The chief aim – how to get the collaboration of trade unions with Soviet power and at the same time mass acquiescence in central policy – was, however, tenaciously pursued by the leadership. It was attained by means of a tortuous path. The congress accepted the principle of 'production' unions, meaning the 'unification of all trade unions of all manual and clerical workers of a given industrial branch independently of their functions' and justified this decision by the elimination of antagonisms, thanks to the revolution, between different categories of employed labour. This principle was used to demand the exclusion of all unions which were based on a national, religious or any other than a productive basis, from the All-Russian Trade Unions, which resulted, as the Mensheviks commented, in trade unions having to accept the communist platform.[160]

This discrimination made it possible to demand the trade unions' participation in the organization of production. The congress decided that the collegia of the directive sections and centres should be composed essentially of representatives of trade unions by agreement between the corresponding production unions and the All-Russian Council of Trade Unions on the one side, and the Presidium of VSNKh on the other.[161]

Within this framework it is not surprising (nor does it seem a syndicalist slip or a promise for the future[162]) that the economic section of the new Party Programme required the organizational apparatus of state industry to be based primarily on the trade unions and that, by their participation in industrial administration, the unions should finally concentrate in their hands all the administration of the entire national economy.[163] The party absorbed the trade unions in its programme for the transformation of society. The unions were not considered as autonomous bearers of legitimate interests of some social groups, but as organizations of 'producers' conceptually deprived of any reason for 'antagonism' to state decisions. They were expected to work for common goals, in spite of the persistence of distinctions among categories, differentiation of salaries and wages, and the application of labour discipline to those reluctant to conform.[164]

The impasse in which the Soviet leaders were caught in their effort to reorganize the economy was due to their effort to carry out a communist revolution by non-communist means. It was the bitter legacy of an unprepared revolution in an unprepared country. But it was also the consequence of political sectarianism which found in civil war a reflection as well as a fertile soil. As I. Deutscher has stigmatized it, a process took place in which the more confused the mutual relations between trade unions, VSNKh and the Labour Commissariat were, 'the more strongly did the Communist Party insist on its own supreme control over all these bodies'.[165] By the formation of party factions inside the trade unions, the Communist Party was able to enforce party discipline on its trade union members. The Eighth All-Russian Conference of the RKP, held in Moscow on 2–4 December 1919, adopted unanimously a resolution on party discipline which was to empty of its inner vitality and debate any institution of which party members had succeded in gaining control. A faction (*fraktsiia*) was supposed to be organized in all non-party congresses, meetings, organizations and institutions (soviets, executive committees, trade unions, communes, etc.) where not less than three members of the party were operating, in order to strengthen from all sides the party impact, to carry out its policy among non-party people and to exert party control over the working of the above-noted institutions and organizations. The factions, regardless of their importance, had to be fully subordinated to the party. In any question on which party organs had already taken a final decision, the faction was obliged to stick to it strictly and with no discussion. The party committee had the power to dismiss any member of the faction. Before discussing any question within a non-party organization, the faction had to discuss it at a meeting of communist members or simply within itself. At the general meetings of non-party organizations the party members were bound to vote unanimously according to whatever decision had been approved in the party faction. Infringements of this rule would incur disciplinary measures.[166] Together with rules on party discipline, an effort was made to conquer non-party institutions by affiliation to them.

Deliberate policy brought about a rapidly increasing union membership, as well as a Bolshevik presence (see Tables 3.2 and 3.3).

By the time of the Third All-Russian Congress of Trade Unions, 6–13 April 1920, political and economic power was formally concentrated in the hands of the Bolsheviks. They and their sympathizers formed 84 per cent of the congress (see Table 3.3). The Congress approved the theses passed by the Ninth Congress of the Communist Party and asked the

Table 3.2. *Trade union membership reported to conferences and congresses*

	According to trade union councils (1)[a]	According to departments and branches (2)
Third Conference (June 1917)	1,120,819	1,475,429
First Congress (January 1918)	1,888,353	2,632,000
Second Congress (January 1919)	2,037,700	3,638,812
Third Congress (April 1920)	3,980,435	4,326,000

[a] The difference between (1) and (2) is explained by the fact that not all categories entered the composition of Trade Union Councils.
Source: A Lozovsky, *Trade Unions in Soviet Russia: Their Development and Present Position*, Collection of Russian Trade Unions' Documents compiled by the ILP Information Committee, 1920, p. 38

presidium of the All-Russian council of Trade Unions to operate on the basis of these theses as unique directives.[167] The question of the most suitable form of management of the state enterprises, however, remained for the most part unresolved. Should the managerial councils be elected or appointed, or, indeed, replaced by one-man management (OMM)? Outspoken criticism of the system of appointment by VSNKh or the *oblast sovnarkhozy* revealed that in many cases it had ended up in clashes between workers and management boards or local *sovnarkhozy* on the one hand and the higher economic councils on the other.[168] This outcome had been foreseen by the left-wing communists when the composition of management had been discussed at the First Congress of *Sovnarkhozy*. At the Second Congress of *Sovnarkhozy* in December 1918, the effectiveness of collegiality as such was debated. Lenin stressed that collegiate bodies were necessary, but he also stated that collegiate management should not be allowed to become a hindrance to practical work. Anticipating the future departure from the principle of collegiality, Lenin pointed out that collective discussion was often detrimental to getting things done.[169] The VSNKh leadership moved away from the question of collegiality to that of appointment. If the problem was to make factory management responsive to central directives, the system of central appointment was preferable to the elective system. Nogin, a VSNKh leader, argued that if factory management was supposed to fulfil the tasks assigned by the central administration, it should be organized by the latter.[170]

Despite Lenin's argument, the congress maintained the principle of collegiality and stressed the personal responsibility of each collegiate member. Composition of the factory-shop management councils was

Table 3.3. *Political affiliation of trade union delegates*

	Total delegates	Mensheviks, **Right**-wing Socialist Revolutionaries and sympathizers	%	Bolsheviks and sympathizers	%
Third Conference (June 1917)	220	120	55.5	80	36.4
Democratic Convention (September 1917)	117	45	38.5	70	59.8
First Trade Union Congress (January 1919)	416	66	15.8	273	65.6
Second Trade Union Congress (January 1919)	748	29	3.8	449	60.0
Third Trade Union Congress (April 1920)	1129	48	4.2	949	84.0

Source: Lozovsky, pp. 30, 41. The percentages have been calculated on the basis of the absolute figures provided by Lozovsky, because the published percentage figures did not match the absolute numbers.

restricted to 3–5 people appointed by the group (*kust*) to which the factory belonged, or immediately by its central administration if a *kust* of enterprises had not yet been formed, in agreement with the corresponding trade unions. The council membership had to be approved by the central administration. No specification was made about the percentage of experts in the managerial councils. The term of office was extended to one year. The principle of appointment prevailed at every level. The administrative boards of *kusty* were to consist of 5–9 people appointed by the central administration. The board of the latter was to comprise 7–11 people, of whom not less than two were to be appointed by VSNKh, and the remainder by the trade union members of the enterprise and their trade union at a higher level. The board was to be subject to approval by VSNKh.[171] The final resolution took into account the pressures to include more union members in the boards of the central administrations, increased their composition to a maximum of thirteen people and added that these boards were to consist 'in the majority, of trade union members'.[172] In practice, however, the percentage of unionized members in these boards did not significantly increase.

A census taken in August 1919 on the social composition of managerial boards, conducted in fifty *glavki*, showed the following percentages of members according to their former occupations:

Table 3.4. *Social composition of management boards, August 1919 (%)*

Workers and full-time factory-committee members	Trade union officials	Higher administrative technicians	Medium-level administrative technicians	'State employees'	Other
20.2	3.1	29.6	22.6	10.5	14.0

Source: *Narodnoe Khoziaistvo*, 1919, nos. 7–8, pp. 46–7

The census also showed that VSNKh appointed 62 per cent of the qualified staff, the presidents of the central administrations and the members of their presidia.

Membership of the councils of the *glavki* was determined by the appointing institutions (see Table 3.5).

The census provided indirect evidence of the reluctance of trade union members to participate actively in management, though they did not abstain from participating in the appointment of managers, since they chose more than one-third of the managerial boards. Given the high

Table 3.5. *Membership of the councils of glavki by appointing institutions (% of total)*

VSNKh	Trade union	Factory committee	Congress or conference	Other	Unknown
37.6	35.2	9.1	8.0	4.5	5.6

Source: *Narodnoe Khoziaistvo*, 1919, nos. 7–8, p. 47

percentage of technicians in the managerial boards, it could be argued that the trade unions' contribution to the appointment of technicians might have been more important than their participation in the appointment of workers, although it no doubt accounted for a substantial part of the latter.

Preference for highly qualified people, and the lack of competent cadres from among the working class, resulted in a very modest representation of both the working class and the party in the highest administrative boards. Among members of the highest councils, only 4 per cent came from a working class milieu, 12 per cent were people of education lower than the average, and 10 per cent were members of the Communist Party or sympathizers.[173]

A higher representation of the working class could be found in the local *sovnarkhozy*, whose tasks in management were more limited. Workmen formed 44.5 per cent of the presidia of the district (*uezd* and *raion*) *sovnarkhozy* and 34.7 per cent of the provincial ones (*gubsovnarkhozy*), while clerical workers were 16.4 per cent and 11.6 per cent respectively; and technicians 14.1 per cent and 10.5 per cent respectively.[174]

Political control over members of the local *sovnarkhozy* was, however, significant. Fifty two per cent of *gubsovnarkhoz* presidium members and 43.1 per cent of *uezd sovnarkhoz* members were appointed by the executive committees of the local soviets (*ispolkomy*), and respectively 6 per cent and 10.1 per cent by the Communist Party directly. The plenum of the local *sovnarkhozy* appointed 10.2 per cent of the *gubsovnarkhoz* presidium and 13.5 per cent of the *uezds'*: trade unions and factory committees appointed 15.3 per cent and 9.4 per cent respectively. The local executive committee (*ispolkom*) appointed the president in 85 per cent of *gubsovnarkhozy* and 65.4 per cent of *uzed sovnarkhozy*.[175]

Trade union participation was poor even in local administrations: 31 per cent of the representatives appointed by trade unions did not belong to any union and 36.6 per cent belonged to the union of clerical workers.[176] Nor did membership of the councils last long enough to

Table 3.6. *Participants in management by category at various levels, 1920*

	Total	Workmen	%	Specialists	%	Clerical Workers	%
Presidia of VNSKh and *Gubsovnarkhozy*	187	107	57.2	22	11.8	58	31.0
Boards of chief administrations and of *glavki* and *tsentry*	184	48	26.0	72	39.0	64	35.0
Councils and one-man management of factory or shop	1,143	726	63.5	398	34.8	19	1.7
Total	1,614	881	58.0	492	33.0	141	9.0

Source: *8i Vserossiiskii S"ezd Sovetov Rabochikh, Krest'ianskikh, Krasnoarmeiskikh i Kazach'ikh Deputatov. 22–9 Dekabria*, Stenograficheskii otchet, 1920 g, Moscow, 1921, p. 14. The figures presumably represent sampling at each level.

produce that aquaintance with administration needed to transform workers' control gradually into workers' management: 20 per cent of the members remained at their posts for no more than 1–2 months.[177]

Differences in percentage composition of the local *sovnarkhozy* and the central administrations increased during the course of war communism. The higher concentration of specialists in the boards of the central bodies is evidence of another aspect of centralization, i.e. the convergence at the centre of the best human resources and the corresponding impoverishment of the provinces (see Table 3.6).

Workers did consistently take part in management at the factory-shop level, but this depended on necessity rather than on any deliberate effort to train workers in management. By law, the members of the factory-shop managements were personally responsible to the higher organs of administration, not to the assembly of factory workers. Even the training of workers in technical matters was a by-product of war. The resolution adopted by the Second All-Russian Congress of Trade Unions noted that the shortage of materials necessitated a reduction of hours worked and that the crisis should be used for the introduction of obligatory courses for the technical and cultural training of workers.[178]

Nonetheless, a new leading class had emerged, painfully, in a confused and non-uniform way: 58 per cent of managerial posts were occupied by workers (see Table 3.6). Did this fact provide evidence for the strong assertions which Lenin formulated on the morrow of the revolution, when the redemption of the working class from the yoke of capitalism seemed to be able to provide strength and hope for a new society?

> Very often the intellectuals give excellent advice and instruction, but they prove to be ridiculously, *absurdly* , shamefully, 'unhandy' and incapable of *carrying out* this advice and instruction, of exercising *practical control* over the translation of words into deeds.
>
> In this very respect it is utterly impossible to dispense with the help and the *leading role* of the practical organizers from among the 'people', from among the factory workers and working peasants.[179]

The Ninth Congress of the Communist Party, held in April 1920 in the midst of enthusiasm for the Red Army victories, sanctioned the end of the experience of the councils and promoted one-man management (OMM) as the most suitable form of management. The sharp debate which this aroused at the congress showed how much and how differently the protagonists of the revolution were marked by the bitter experience of war communism; how deeply the ideology of human redemption was affected; how much less heroic and more insidious would the further developments be as compared with the bold days of the struggle for power.

3.6 IDEOLOGY OF WAR COMMUNISM: ONE-MAN MANAGEMENT VERSUS MANAGERIAL COUNCILS

The organization of the army based on a rigid military hierarchy and strict obedience to orders brought positive achievements in the military field. By the time the Ninth Congress of the Party was held, the Bolsheviks were in control of the whole country and its basic resources, from the Donets Basin and the North Caucasus to the Baltic States, from the Ukraine to Turkestan.

In a country where disorganization and improvisation dominated at every level and economic disruption was dangerously increasing, the army was the only institution which could provide an organizational model for success. It is significant that Trotskii, the organizer of the Red Army, was the most tenacious supporter of OMM, and was the outstanding proponent at the congress for drastic changes in industrial management. The patient work of the Second Congress of *Sovnarkhozy*, in safeguarding the principle of collegiality and in concluding a workable agreement with the trade unions, fell to pieces under the attacks of the military imprint that civil war had stamped on ideology. Trotskii made no effort to temper the arguments against the principle of managerial councils.

Trotskii declared sternly that men are 'lazy animals' and that only a militarized labour organization employing coercion and discipline could circumvent laziness and stimulate all the energies necessary for increased output and technical progress.[180] His severity was elicited by the catastrophic situation in employment. In 1920 there were 687, 864 more vacancies than the number of people registered as able to work. The labour shortage, which concerned both skilled and unskilled labour,[181] accentuated the problem of raising labour productivity. Trotskii added that an elected council, composed of the best workers but lacking in technical competence, could not replace one single technician who, thanks to his training, knew how to do the job and should be left free to do it. Technicians, engineers and educated people as a whole, Trotskii said, were national capital which Soviet power had to exploit like any other means of production.[182] Trotskii did not single out new elements justifying this approach to management. He preferred to stress the continuity of his thought on this subject and recalled that in March 1918, when the Moscow city conference was held and there was no war, he had formulated identical arguments on the need to utilize qualified labour.

At that time, Lenin had shared Trotskii's views, as was recalled at the congress.[183] However, in 1918 the need to strengthen the support of industrial workers around the Bolshevik Party, and simultaneously to reinforce labour discipline, had led to the strategy of making the trade unions function as a buffer between party and workers, rather than implementing OMM – which would probably have provoked hostile reactions on the part of workers' organizations and would certainly have jeopardized the programme of institutionalizing the trade unions. In 1918 OMM sounded more like a threat to workers' organizations than a principle of industrial organization in the young republic of the 'councils'. At the Ninth Party Congress Smirnov attacked Lenin's arguments on OMM as doctrinal, since they had not been applied for two years and nobody had minded.[184] Tomskii recalled that the question of OMM had been confronted two years earlier, but Lenin himself had hesitated two and a half months before opting for one or the other alternative on management.[185]

In 1920 victory over the White Armies and suppression of the internal political opposition made the Bolshevik Party the unquestionable leader of economic reorganization, and enabled it to enforce labour discipline and control which in 1918 did not have a strong political context.

At the Ninth Party Congress Trotskii drastically asserted that experts ought not to be subordinated to councils knowing nothing in their field, and ridiculed participation in management as a school of management. 'The one who wants to learn', he said, 'goes to school, the one who ought to manage does the managing.'[186] In fact, Trotskii's assertion meant the disavowal of two years' experience in industrial management and, more than that, the negation of workers' natural capacity for organization, on which most of Lenin's hopes in the potential of workers' control had been based in 1917 and 1918.

Trotskii's attacks were mostly directed against the VSNKh leadership, whom he accused of inefficiency in industrial organization and of hypocrisy on the principles of management. He recalled that Rykov, the head of VSNKh, who had been in charge of the agency for supply to the army, *Chusosnabarm*, had been compelled to resort to OMM after the military defeats due to lack of munitions, though he was now claiming the merits of collegiate direction.[187]

Actually, VSNKh's leaders, Miliutin and Rykov, supported the collegiality principle as an expediency. Miliutin cited a number of cases where collegiality already existed in 1916 and was maintained, since it provided a suitable division of functions. Rykov stressed that specialists themselves demanded continuation of collegiality when it was impossible for one man to be in charge of labour supply, internal regulations, supply of materials and provisions.[188] Two months before the Ninth Congress, Lenin had declared that the question of collegiality had to be dealt with not in an abstract way, but empirically. 'Collegiality, as a basic type of management', he said, 'is something rudimentary, necessary to the first stage, when one begins to build. The example of the army shows that OMM does work. Collegiality, at the best, represents an enormous waste of energies and does not satisfy rapidity and responsibility of work.'[189] This curious rationalization of the Soviet experience, which Lenin elaborated at the Third Congress of *Sovnarkhozy* in January 1920, was employed both by Rykov and by Bukharin at the Party Congress, but in opposite claims. Rykov tried to convince the Party Congress that only when the differences between workers and specialists were levelled out and questions of supply, labour and wage tariffs became easier, would the alternative of OMM become realizable.[190] Bukharin, on the contrary, urged the adoption of OMM as a solution for economizing labour and the introduction of criteria of competence instead of criteria based on social origin.[191]

The attachment of VSNKh to collegiality was not due to the appeal exerted on the economists by democratic principles, but to the need for coordination between the centre and the periphery, which the composition of the councils could to some extent provide. The VSNKh leaders agreed that the number of council members ought to be reduced to a minimum, but collegiality was deemed necessary in so far as it made possible representation of the provinces at the highest economic levels. That is to say, collegiality was interpreted as a way to make up for workers' incomprehension of national economic necessities and to develop local economic initiative.[192] In other words, for VSNKh, collegiality was the most suitable form of management to make palatable the model of economic centralization. OMM would have been dangerous for political and economic reasons. On the one hand, it meant subordination of workers to technicians, who in most cases were former managers or owners. On the other hand, it was the ground either for workers' apathy or for labour conflicts. Moreover, in cases where one enterprise was subdivided into several factories or plants, OMM was likely to hinder local initiative, which in a situation of breakdown of transport and fuel scarcity was the only way to ensure a minimum of local activity.[193] According to this approach, the real alternative was to enforce the personal responsibility of each member of the managerial council.[194] This late insistence on enforcement of personal responsibility, which had already been approved by the Second Congress of *Sovnarkhozy* at the end of 1918, suggests that the resolution of that congress had not brought about effective changes in this field.

For the economic experts, the problem was to have the right people in the right posts: technicians should be appointed to technical posts and managerial decisions taken by councils of workers of the production branch to which the factory belonged.[195]

Thus, the whole defence of collegiality rested on the assumption that crucial decisions had to be taken at the centre and their implementation carried out below and locally, in such a way as to smooth over the sharp effects of centralization which could entail difficulties in labour relations. Collegiality made possible a system of personal ties and facilitated the several functions falling on management, such as food and raw materials procurement, which should have been granted by the central system of supply, but, in fact, were carried out by all kinds of expedients at the local level, owing to the inefficiency of the centralized system of distribution.

That VSNKh leaders were not eager to extend the scope of democratic management was clear to some of its critics. A member of the party imputed VSNKh's position on collegiality to its need for trade union support of 'any kind of bureaucratic aspirations'.[196] For VSNKh, collegiality was a surrogate for a workable system of interrelations in the domain of supply and labour rewards. It was hard, however, to defend collegiality on these grounds. Indeed, the councils refused to assume the whole responsibility for the direction of the enterprise without being protected by joint responsibility of the council members and by consensus of the factory workers. Thus, any initiatives carrying some personal responsibility were submitted to a factory meeting.[197] For analogous reasons specialists rejected OMM.[198] Unlike the VSNKh experts, Tomskii, the official spokesman of the trade unions, defended the principle of collegiality rather than its practice. Tomskii recalled that for two and a half years all the leaders, from Lenin to Bukharin, had been saying that workers should take part in the business of production, and that they ought to carry on management through their elected representatives. For the trade unions, the real problem to be handled was finding a way by which workers could do the managing. Tomskii affirmed that OMM should be rejected as a principle, though not necessarily as an isolated form of practice, and recalled that trade unions did not oppose some applications of OMM and that 51 per cent of the Petrograd factories were run in this way. But he added that the outcome was not always good, as in the cases of the railways and the Moscow Coal Basin. Tomskii rejected Bukharin's arguments for OMM by saying that, since the average number of council members attending was only three, one could not allege a waste of technical forces.[199]

The supporters of OMM presented the question under its technical aspects, but the core of their concern was to find out methods of direction which would enforce labour discipline on a working class composed mainly of former peasants. Trotskii maintained that the core of the problem was to compel workers to follow an organized plan, which they would not do if left free to choose.[200] If put in these terms, the discussion on management could not but involve principles and values. The revolution and the chaos which followed had liberated forces, aspirations and tensions which the new political philosophy of power was unable to control on the basis of the principles which it professed. When Tomskii affirmed that trade unions were against OMM as they had been before, under the Tsarist regime,[201] he expressed the hostility of workers to being reintegrated into an authoritarian economic organization which, under whatever banner, would mean a restoration of oppressive controls over labour and the adoption of heavy disciplinary measures. On the other hand, the trade unions were not ready to accept the consequence of the collegial system of management, as put forward by VSNKh, that is to say, the institutionalization of workers' organizations. The experience of war communism offered additional arguments against it. Tomskii, who one year before had supported the thesis of the merging of trade union bodies with state labour agencies, had been reconsidering since then. At the Party Congress in March 1920 he bitterly opposed those who still argued for institutionalization of trade unions. Polemically he asked his comrades to explain what institutionalization would mean if, together with it, the People's Commissariat of Labour were to remain in charge.[202] The practice of OMM in the military factories and its rationalization as a 'Soviet (*sic!*) principle were bound to raise the suspicion of trade unionists, whether of Bolshevik outlook or not, as to the real content of 'statization' of trade unions and its implications for labour.

The left-wing communists joined the trade unionists against OMM. Awareness that OMM was more than a technical device, and that crucial values were at stake, inspired most of their arguments against Trotskii's report. Osinskii stressed that Trotskii's project was but a 'blind copy' of military organization, while the principles of the 'soviets' had to be defended as such. Recalling his own experience at the head of the People's Commissariat for Food Procurement (*Narkomprod*), Osinskii maintained that a three-member council could work and that collegiality could be a necessary step towards broader mass participation in economic administration. He pointed out that technical and administrative councils existed also in the most advanced capitalist systems.[203] The left-wing communists feared that, once the principle of managerial councils was dropped, it would entail the collapse of the whole Soviet structure in the political domain too.[204] Why, argued Sapronov, a left-wing member of the party, if OMM was found to be good in factories, should it not work in the executive committees at the level of the *uezd*, province and central civil administration? What an odd meaning, he concluded, the dictatorship of the proletariat would acquire in that case!

Each group, for its own purposes, refused to assume responsibility for presenting workable alternatives to the current system of management, whose deficiencies were known to everybody. Thus, it fell upon senior leadership to propose and enforce an unpolitical line. Lenin and Trotskii had not hesitated to stress the consistency over time of their views on OMM since early 1918. Lenin had never made a point of councils as a method or goal, though he had let his focus upon workers' control be interpreted as support for managerial councils composed of workers. It was not hard, therefore, for Lenin to reject the ambiguity which he had allowed to continue on this point, when he considered it to be no longer politically necessary. Trotskii did not need such arguments. The prestige that the Red Army had acquired under his direction was a powerful argument in itself.

However, rather than stress the defence of a principle, the congress decided to shift the emphasis to the need for reliable experts at the head of economic institutions. This solution had already been prepared by the All-Russian Central Executive Committee, to which Trotskii's proposal on OMM had been submitted before being presented for discussion at the

Party Congress. The CEC mitigated the sharpest aspects of the draft.[205] Trotskii's original formulation: 'Congress considers it necessary to apply the principle of OMM at every link-point (*zveno*) of industrial management',[206] was modified in order to make it less rigid. The resolution as adopted stated that management ought to be 'competent, firm, energetic', from which the adoption of OMM was deduced. After the assertion that full and unconditional OMM should be adopted in shops and departments of factories, the resolution envisaged steps toward enactment of this rule at factory and higher levels up to the very highest. Various 'combinations' were proposed, 'keeping in mind that an unquestionable type of management had not yet been elaborated'. First, a 'director-administrator' from the 'real workers', of strong will and able to ensure the assistance of technical specialists, including an engineer as his assistant on the technical side; second, a technical specialist in charge, with a commissar from the 'real workers', having wide powers and overseeing everything; third, one or two 'real workers' as assistants to a specialist director, with powers to go into every aspect of management but without the right to stop an order by the director. There was a fourth possibility, which seemed a concession to the opposition. In cases of small and strictly cohesive councils, whose members were complementary and had already manifested their capacity to work together, the councils could be retained – by enhancing the rights of the chairman and increasing his responsibility for the council as a whole. The resolution invited the *sovnarkhozy* at all levels to reduce the numbers on their boards to a minimum and to enforce the personal responsibility of each member for his own work.[207] Each of the first three options had in common special authority for the 'real worker'. The Russian term *rabochii–professionalist* is unusual, and appears to indicate – together with qualities of character listed, such as ability to control and enforce – the 'new man' of the time, whether himself the director or supervising the director. The term was intended to denote a 'professional member of the working class' in some new sense which the context made clear enough.

Further publication of archive materials and additional evidence as to the composition of management would be needed to assess the actual importance of managerial councils at each level of economic organization and to reach a clearer appreciation of the issues really at stake when the leadership opted for OMM. Given the paucity of managerial cadres, which favoured the segmentation of management into several specific tasks (the reason adduced by VSNKh for continuing with collegiality), and the understandable reluctance of potential managers to assume full responsibility for management at a time when any deficiency could mean accusation of sabotage, it is reasonable to suppose that managerial councils were of some importance, though not necessarily very important in the crucial branches of the economy. Tomskii said that 49 per cent of Petrograd industry was collegially managed, but Kritsman reported that only 14 per cent of the central administrations were under collegial management.[208] Trotskii's resolution, therefore, was to have an actual impact on the future economic organization. There is certainly room for further studies on the changes involved.

The crucial change, however, the change which anticipated future developments, concerned not so much the number of people taking part in management as their qualifications. Though not explicitly, but clearly enough, the resolution demanded, in fact, that the choice of people for commanding posts would be based thereafter on their party affiliation.

3.7 OMM AND THE TRADE UNIONS IN THE NEW PHILOSOPHY OF POWER

The All-Russian Congress of Trade Unions, held in Moscow immediately after the Ninth Party Congress, was dominated by party-member delegates. The delegates with voting rights included 940 members of the party and sympathizers, 45 Mensheviks, 191 members of no party and 50 representatives of various parties.[209] Congress accepted the theses of the Ninth Party Congress and invited the Presidium of the Council of Trade Unions to adhere to them as the sole directives for its work.[210] The trade unions were asked to collaborate with VSNKh in preparing access of the most capable workers to management by the instruction and training of such workers, and their promotion – first to assistant management and then to management in small enterprises. The unions were invited to convince workers of the needs of production, to inform them about the role of the enterprise in the overall framework of the socialist economy, and to hold regular meetings to let them know past performance and forthcoming plans.[211] After the statement of principle that trade unions ought to participate not only in management but in the direction of economic life as a whole, the resolution listed trade unions' prerogatives in this field which, in effect, firmly circumscribed their scope for decision-making. Trade unions were allowed to have initiative for making proposals pertaining to economic policy, but were bound to observe the directives already taken by the party. More specifically, unions were to take part in all questions pertaining to labour conscription, in joint sessions with other economic organs, in order to elaborate the plan of transition from collegiality to OMM. A further point was that trade union bodies from the lower to the higher levels should take part in the organization of production, but should not interfere in the functioning of enterprises and in instructions of an administrative or economic character. Even the right of appointment of candidates to management in agreement with economic organs was circumscribed by the prescription that appointment should be proposed on the basis of 'practical experience, technical competence, firmness, organizational capacity and ability to get things done'.[212] In this way the umbilical cord that had been created between the party and the trade unions through the institution of the party cells[213] was reinforced at the very moment when the trade unions were firmly relegated to a subordinate role. Separation of functions provided the criteria for relations between organs. The local *sovnarkhozy* were asked not to interfere in the unions' activities. The unions had to reject any introduction of 'harmful parallelism in management and appropriation of functions outside their competence with regard to organs of management and the immediate regulation of industry'.[214]

Lozovskii's resolution on organizational work made it clear that trade unions ought to refuse parallelism also at the level of the central administrations and the factory units.[215]

After the adoption of OMM, the Bolshevik trade unionists retreated from the principle of institutionalization of trade unions, an aim which the Second Congress of Trade Unions had affirmed but postponed until the working class was ready for management. The trade unionists reaffirmed the importance of the specific function of workers' organizations within the traditional domain of their competence – the defence of labour interests. But little scope remained possible for independent trade unionism. When Lozovskii, one of the foremost spokesmen for trade union autonomy, claimed that the competence of trade unions and the Labour Commissariat lay in the improvement of welfare, he had to add labour discipline and productivity as equally valid aims.[216]

Statutory rules for factory committees were approved by the Third Congress of Trade Unions, which finally subordinated such organs to the unions. The first steps in this direction had already been taken by the First Congress, which decided the subordinate control commissions to the higher trade union organs. But, as already mentioned,[217] the application of these rules failed.

The final ruling on factory committees drastically reduced their functions. The resolution of the Third Congress stated that factory committees, acting as primary union organs, had no right to interfere with management and, being organs of the unions, their task was to implement union decisions concerning labour conditions and welfare. Their tasks were limited to:

(1) improving labour discipline and labour productivity by all means

contemplated in the union's regulations (propaganda for production, disciplinary courts, agitation, etc.). A 'culture and production' commission was envisaged to perform these tasks;

(2) settlement of conflicts with management, by taking initial decisions and passing on such information to higher union organs for final settlement;

(3) checking the activity of the wage tariff commission, with right of appeal against its decisions to higher union organs;

(4) inviting the mass of workers to participate in management, by providing periodic comments on management, outside working hours;

(5) selecting from among the workers specially capable people for specific tasks, in agreement with management.[218]

The capitulation of the trade unions to the party was attacked only by the Mensheviks. Their resolution, which got only thirty-three votes and was not included in the stenographic record of the congress, affirmed that the current economic policy of Soviet power, totally based on the tackling of economic tasks by coercion and bureaucratic and militaristic measures, was impairing the proletariat in large industry, thus making necessary the existence of strong and independent trade unions. The Mensheviks denounced the policy of 'statization' of the past two years, obligatory trade union membership, financial dependence of the unions on the state, and their executive functions tied to the plans of higher state organs, as causes of the transformation of trade unions into bureaucratic bodies. The Mensheviks warned that the programme of militarization of labour, which involved low productivity of compulsory labour and thus wasted energies and resources, deprived workers of any means of defending their interests, and eliminated trade unions from participation in management.[219]

These criticisms remained unheard. Bolshevik control over trade unions was reinforced by mechanical, obligatory membership in the unions, which was a characteristic of the war communist period,[220] though no trade union congress passed any resolution in this sense.

The resolution of the Fifth Conference of Trade Unions held in Moscow on 2–7 November, 1920, shows the extent to which trade unions accepted the function of 'transmission belts' for political orders. The conference, composed of 261 delegates, of whom 252 were party members, invited trade unions to teach their members to single out, in each department, shop and factory, deficiencies in the utilization of labour arising from incorrect use of equipment and unsatisfactory administrative work. Though trade unions were deprived of any specific power in decision-making, they were to find methods to combat red tape and poor organization. Not only premia, but also wages, should be strictly dependent on the degree of fulfilment of the production plan. Payment in kind, to which initially workers had resorted in order to protect wages affected heavily by inflation, was to become gradually 'a system of supplying workers depending on the level of labour productivity'.[221]

However, neither the programmes of the Third Congress of Trade Unions, nor the resolution adopted by the November Conference of Trade Unions, were implemented. Hostilities against Poland, and Wrangel, added new delays to the programme of economic reconstruction. But, as Rudzutak noted at the conference, another obstacle was 'internal weaknesses'.[222] On the other hand the resolution of the Moscow Conference, which had been inspired by the conclusions of the Third Congress, had not time to be implemented before steps towards the new economic policy were taken.[223]

At the Tenth Party Congress of March 1921, which anticipated a moderate liberalization of the economy, the main attacks on the communist policy on trade unions came from the 'workers' opposition', a group formed inside the party and finding some support in major industrial regions like Moscow and the Donets Basin, but having only a small representation at the congress.[224] The 'workers' opposition' demanded transfer of the entire economic administration to the trade unions, appealing to point 5 of the 1919 Party Programme; and they also demanded a larger role for the factory committees in production.[225] The 'workers' opposition' proposed that the appointment of candidates presented by trade unions to economic posts be binding on the economic authorities, and that the highest organs of economic administration be formed through elections at local, regional and national level. At the factory level, the factory committees should be in charge of management.[226] A motion proposed by Trotskii and Bukharin urged, instead, the complete 'statization' of trade unions,[227] without giving details. The focus was on the initial steps to be taken in this direction, i.e. gradual merging of VSNKh with the Presidium of the Central Council of Trade Unions, by the joint appointment to both organs of one-third to one-half of their respective members. Analogous measures were proposed for the lower levels of both organizations. Trade unions, however, were to remain in charge of wage regulations and labour conditions and were to operate as an arbitration body responsible to the government in the settlement of conflicts between management and workers.[228]

Lenin took an intermediate position. Against 'statization' he affirmed the need for trade unions as a 'link' between the vanguard and the masses, and as a 'reservoir' of state power. From the end of 1920, Lenin envisaged the dictatorship of the proletariat as an inflexible hierarchy since 'it cannot work without a number of "transmission belts" running from the vanguard to the mass of the advanced class, and from the latter to the mass of working people', i.e. the mass of peasants.[229]

Against the theses of the 'workers' opposition', Lenin said that Marxists had been combating syndicalism all over the world, that trade unions were schools of communism and administration, but that workers in touch with peasants were liable to fall for non-proletarian slogans. If trade unions were allowed to appoint and administer, added Lenin, 'it may sound very democratic and might help us to catch a few votes, but not for long. It will be fatal for the dictatorship of the proletariat.'[230]

At the Tenth Congress of the Party, Lenin got rid of Shliapnikov's proposal for an All-Russian Congress of Producers, by rejecting its principles and the social analysis on which it was based as non-communist. The 'workers' opposition 'maintained that the theoretical matrix of its theses could be found in Engels' *Origin of the Family, Private Property and the State*.[231] Lenin replied:

Engels speaks of a communist society which will have no classes, and will consist only of producers. Do we have classes? Yes, we do. Do we have class struggle? Yes, and a most furious one! To come in the midst of this furious class struggle and talk about an 'All-Russian Congress of Producers' – isn't that a syndicalist deviation, which must be emphatically and irrevocably condemned?[232]

What Lenin was above all concerned about was the predominance of party rule. The difference between Trotskii's and Lenin's positions was one of precept, not practice.[233] The party leadership was not at all willing to let trade unions conduct autonomous policies, as the demotion of Tomskii from his post in the Central Committee of Trade Unions manifested. The institution of party cells within the unions did the job. The overwhelming number of Bolshevik members in the trade unions, and the party discipline to which they were bound, were already a powerful means of directing the penetration of the party's will into labour organizations.[234] This was done all the time, according to Shliapnikov, who warned the congress that the factory-shop committees were becoming non-party organs because of this method.[235] Shliapnikov, however, criticized the method used to subject trade unions to party decisions, because such decisions meant the annihilation of workers' rights.[236] In fact, nobody within the party was against the view that trade unions ought to be schools of communism. Divergences concerned the implementation of this view. The 'workers' opposition', which included several members of the Metal Mining and Textile Unions, and some managers of heavy industry,[237] maintained that trade unions should be concerned with the factory or institution where their members worked and should concentrate on promoting the consciousness of producers within the production process itself. The 'workers' opposition' explained what it meant by 'school of communism':

> Promoting in the process of production and in its development the formation of a free producer, the Union must organize the work in such a way as to transform the worker from an appendix of a dead economic machine into a conscious creator of communism, on the basis of an efficient economic division of labour.[238]

These principles were quite ignored by Trotskii's and Bukharin's versions of the role of trade unions in a communist society. They affirmed the necessity of an organic incorporation of trade unions into the state administration of the 'workers' state', owing to the needs of a planned economy, where the concept of freedom of labour was to be reshaped as a function of overall proletarian tasks, i.e. of the general interests. Bukharin affirmed:

> Since these tasks (i.e. universal proletarian tasks) must be mastered at any price, it is understandable that, from the point of view of the proletariat, in the very name of actual effective and not fictitious freedom of the working class, an abolition of the so-called 'freedom to work' is required. For the latter no longer agrees with the regularly organized 'planned economy' and a corresponding division of labour powers. Consequently, the regime of compulsory labour and state distribution of labour in the dictatorship of the proletariat expresses a relatively high degree of organization of the entire apparatus and the stability of proletarian power on the whole.[239]

Bukharin's *Ekonomika* provided the theoretical framework for the Trotskii–Bukharin motion at the Tenth Congress of the Party:

> The unions ought in every way to encourage and train a new type of professional, energetic, creative producer, looking at economic life not from the viewpoint of distribution and consumption, but from the viewpoint of the rate of output, not through the eyes of a petitioner and a negotiator with the Soviet Power, but through the eyes of a master.[240]

Although basically agreeing with Bukharin's view on control over labour, Lenin continued to adhere to his realistic philosophy of power, which was absent in the idealistic programme of the 'workers' opposition' as well as in the rigid and too abstract approach of Trotskii and Bukharin. At the Tenth Party Congress Zinoviev, who joined Lenin's attempt to compromise on the trade union question, expressed the fear that the All-Russian Congress of Producers proposed by the 'workers' opposition' would be dominated by members of no party, Socialist-Revolutionaries and Mensheviks.[241] The preoccupation with strict control by the party over the unions was embodied in the resolution adopted by the congress on this subject:

> The Communist Party unconditionally leads the whole ideological aspect of the trade unions' work through its central and local organs... Appointment of the leading staff of the trade union movement is to be done under the control of the Party.[242]

Lenin's and Zinoviev's motion explained what the trade unions were then supposed to do, in order to help the state in the realization of a socialist society:

> The trade unions, as a school of communism, should attend to all sides of the everyday life of the working masses, gradually introducing large strata of working people into matters of state construction, always illuminating the way by the ideas of our programme, leading them from the individual to the collective [attitude], gradually lifting them from non-party positions to communism.[243]

Lenin's theory of trade unions as transmission belts of the party was reinforced by the adoption of the New Economic Policy, the alternative to war communism promoted by him and approved by the Tenth Congress of the Party. The moderate liberalization of the economy, OMM based on former bourgeois specialists and technicians, the desire for a rapid pace of economic reconstruction after the failure of expectations for a European revolution, were all reasons for political control over the basic institutions. Once this form of control had been imposed, institutionalization of the trade unions became unnecessary. Lenin did not hesitate to borrow from Maiskii the arguments against 'statization' which the Menshevik representative had expressed at the Fourth Conference of Trade Unions in 1918.[244] He agreed that defence of industrial and labour interests was not necessarily pursued by a state which was not only proletarian, but which also promoted the peasants' interests. Lenin also agreed on the danger of bureaucratization of the trade unions if they became state organs.[245] But these arguments were not employed to support even a limited autonomy of the trade unions. By the time of NEP the influence of the party on all elements of the administrative apparatus was strong enough to provide the political cohesion that the leadership considered necessary for its policy. The economy of war had already mortally wounded the councils (soviets) which alone could have nourished alternative programmes. By 1920, 86 per cent of the 2,051 enterprises of the first group, i.e. the centrally administered enterprises, were under OMM.[246]

Presenting the plan of electrification, Lenin, with his usual directness, announced at the end of 1920 the transition to a new phase of the short-lived republic of the councils:

This is the beginning of an epoch where there will be less and less politics and one will talk about politics less often and less long, and where engineers and agronomists will have more to say.[247]

Less emphatically, but with his flair for foreseeing future developments, Trotskii anticipated that 'the road to socialism lies through a period of the highest possible intensification of the principle of the state'.[248]

3.8 SUMMARY

Lack of Bolshevik managerial cadres and a number of factory committees operating at various levels of managerial activity were an uncomfortable legacy to the Bolshevik Government. They represented throughout war communism a constraint on any option in organization which compelled the leadership to cope with the problem of management from a political rather than a technical point of view. In this field legislation is but a poor guide for the understanding of what occurred in practice, while the debates within party and trade union congresses provided better indications for both the issues and the gap between principles and practice. The integration of the existing factory committees into the new economic organization was not an easy task. The understanding of what workers' control should mean was by no means univocal among the Bolsheviks themselves. Lenin was interested in their political role, though finding them unsuitable for management; some Bolsheviks at the factory level insisted on the essential and managerial role of factory committees; the top administrators, while glad to share their responsibilities with politically accepted labour representatives, tried to confine them to the *ex post* supervision of business, a role accepted by the trade unions themselves, reluctant to engage directly in management as long as wage labour remained.

Three decrees on management were issued between 1918 and 1920. All envisaged forms of management open to a certain degree to workers' participation. However, they also show that collegial management was kept as a second best among alternatives to one-man management, since sharing managerial responsibilities among people of low competence alleviated the burden of full management while allowing for a certain degree of political control.

In most factories working for military needs one-man management was adopted. The institution of political commissars helped the leadership to maintain its control over industry. This system proved to be more effective than any form of collective management. When, at the end of civil war, the organization of a 'peace economy' was debated the arguments in favour of one-man management were strengthened by experience. Although the time was not yet ripe for the abolition of managerial councils as such, the strength acquired by the Bolsheviks permitted a reconsideration of the question of management on firm political terms, preparing the way for the future selection of managers out of party ranks. While leaving some room for collective management, the last regulations on this matter approved in 1920 made obligatory, in practice, the inclusion of a party member in any managerial option.

NOTES

1 V.I. Lenin, *Collected Works,* 4th edn, 45 vols., London, 1964–70, vol. 27, pp. 90–1.
2 *Ibid.,* p. 90.
3 A.M. Pankratova, *Fabzavkomy i profsoiuzy v revoliutsii 1917 goda,* Moscow, 1927, p. 53.
4 A.G. Egorova, 'Profsoiuzy i fabzavkomy v period podgotovki i provedeniia Oktiabr'skoi Revoliutsii' in *Rabochii klass: vedushchaia sila Oktiabr'skoi Revoliutsii, Sbornik statei,* Moscow, 1976, p. 138.
5 Except the Baku Basin: *Commercial and Industrial Gazette,* 3 July 1917.
6 G.A. Trukhan, 'V.I. Lenin o gegemonii proletariata v Oktiabr'skoi Revoliutsii', in *V.I. Lenin ob istoricheskom opyte Velikogo Oktiabria,* Moscow, 1969, p. 69.
7 L.I. Mints, *Istoriia Velikogo Oktiabria,* Moscow, 1968, pp. 416–17.
8 *Ibid.,* pp. 155–6.
   Egorova, p. 151. Cf. Egorova, *Profsoiuzy i fabzavkomy v bor'be za pobedu Oktiabria (mart–oktiabr' 1917 g),* Moscow, 1960, pp. 14–15. The Mensheviks blamed the Bolsheviks for seeking support among the uneducated masses and provoking conflicts both between leaders and people and between unions and workers' committees: cf. F.I. Dan, *La politique économique et la situation de la classe ouvrière en Russie Soviétque,* Bruxelles, 1923, p. 70.
10 Lenin, 'Inevitable Catastrophe and Extravagant Promises', in *Collected Works,* vol. 24, p. 425 (published in *Pravda* on 29–30 May, 1917 g).
11 *Ibid.,* p. 420.
12 Lenin, *Collected Works,* vol. 26, 4th edn, Moscow, p. 107.
13 *Ibid.,* p. 110.
14 Reported by V.P. Miliutin, *Sovremennoe ekonomicheskoe razvitie Rossii i diktatura proletariata (1914–1918 gg),* Moscow, 1918, p. 23.
15 *Ibid.,* p. 16. Twenty-nine per cent of these enterprises belonged to the food-

processing industry, 16 per cent to the metal industry and about 10 per cent to the cotton industry.

16 P.I. Liashchenko, *Istorii narodnogo khoziaistva SSSR*, Gos. izd. politicheskoi literatury, 1948, vol. 2, p. 683.
17 P. Labry, *L'Industrie russe et la révolution*, Paris, 1919, pp. 95–7.
18 Cf. V.I. Grinevetskii, *Poslevoennye perspektivy Russkoi promyshlennosti*, Kharkov, 1919, p. 13.
19 S.G. Strumilin, *Zarabotnaia plata i proizvoditel'nost' truda v Russkoi promyshlennosti v 1913–1922 gg*, Moscow, 1923, p. 14.
20 L.S. Gaponenko, 'Rabochii klass v Oktiabr'skoi Revoliutsii' (nekotorye itogi issledovanii)', *Voprosy Istorii*, 1968, no. 1, 81.
21 Strumilin, p. 74.
22 Labry, pp. 95–6.
23 Cf. B. Ward, 'Wild Socialism in Russia: the Origin' (unpublished article), 1971, 13. Cf. the table on functions of *fabzavkomy* from a 1917 sample of 372 enterprises in V.I. Selitskii, *Massy v bor'be za rabochii kontrol'* (*mart–iiul' 1917 g*), Moscow, 1971, p. 195; cf. Also A. Pankratova (*Fabzavkomy Rossii v bor'be za sotsialisticheskuiu fabriku*, Moscow, 1923, p. 177), who, however, focuses in general on the political aspects of the *fabzavkomy*. The fact that factory committees on the ground rarely discussed political matters emerges also in the detailed analysis by S.A. Smith, *Red Petrograd: the Revolution in the Factories, 1917–1918*, Cambridge, 1983, p. 160, although the author emphasizes the politicization of such organs.
24 *The Bolsheviks and the October Revolution. Central Committee Minutes of the Russian Social-Democratic Labour Party* (*Bolsheviks*), August 1917–February 1918, London, 1974, p. 99.
25 Lenin, *Collected Works*, vol. 26, pp. 264–5. The draft was written on 8–9 November 1917.
26 *Ibid.*, p. 554n; according to V.S. Orlov, 'V.I. Lenin i sozdanie apparata pervogo v mire rabochego-krest'ianskogo pravitel'stva', *Voprosy Istorii*, 1963, no. 4, 21-2, the draft on workers' control was discussed by several workers' conferences and governmental agencies, such as the People's Commissariat for Labour, before being approved.
27 *Sobranie uzakonenii*, 1917–18, no. 3, art. 35.
28 Lenin, Collected Works, vol. 26, p. 555.
29 I. Deutscher, *Soviet Trade Unions: Their Place in Soviet Labour Policy*, London–New York, 1950, p. 14, defines the Leninist workers' control as 'a sort of dual control of employers and workers over industry, a condominium in which the workers were to train themselves for future exclusive management and in which they were progressively to widen the sphere of their responsibilities'.
30 *Novyi Luch*, no. 1, 24 November 1917, 3. Cf. also F. De Los Rios, *Mi viaje en la Russia Sovietista*, 2nd edn, Madrid, 1922, pp. 165–72 for the hint that Larin was against workers' committees and for trade unions because he condemned the particularism of the former and believed that the unions were more concerned for general interests.
31 *Novyi Luch*, no. 3, 26 November 1917, 1.
32 *Sobranie uzakonenii*, 1917–18, no. 3, art. 35, pars. 4 and 9.

33 Only three months before, the resolution of the Bolshevik Party on the economic situation signed by Miliutin and Stalin stated that the organs of workers' control should be composed of representatives of soviets, trade unions and *fabzavkomy*, as well as of technical and scientific cadres, and affirmed that workers' control was to develop gradually through a series of measures aimed at the full regulation (*regulirovanie*) of production. See *VKP (b) v rezoliutsiiakh i resheniiakh s"ezdov, konferentsii i plenumov Ts. K.*, 5th edn, Moscow, 1936, pp. 262–3. On Bolshevik and Menshevik arguments in favour of and against workers' control, see: P.H. Avrich, 'The Bolshevik Revolution and Workers' Control in Russian Industry', *Slavic Review*, vol. 22, no. 1, March 1963, 47–61.

34 Cf. J. Bunyan, *The Origin of Forced Labor in the Soviet State, 1917–1918*. Documents and Materials, Baltimore, 1967, p. 7 and pp. 4–7 for a translation into English of the Decree on Workers' Control.

35 Cf. I.A. Gladkov, *Natsionalizatsiia promyshlennosti v Rossii*, Moscow, 1954, pp. 18–20; N. Silantiev, *Rabochii kontrol' i sovnarkhozy*, Moscow, 1957, p. 3; L.E. Ankudinova, *Natsionalizatsiia promyshlennosti v SSSR (1917–1920)*, Moscow, 1963, p. 33.

36 See, for instance, the decree on nationalization of an electrical enterprise in *Uprochenie Sovetskoi Vlasti v Moskve i Moskovskoi Gubernii, Dokumenty i Materialy*, Moscow, 1958, n. 188.

37 Lenin, *Collected Works*, vol. 26, p. 468.

38 L. Trotsky, *The History of the Russian Revolution*, London, 1936, pp. 816–18. Trotsky dates back to July 1917, at the moment of the Sixth semi-clandestine Congress of the Party, Lenin's decision to shift from the slogan 'all power to the soviets' to 'power to the factory committees'.

39 *Sobranie uzakonenii*, 1917–18, no. 5, art. 83. The instructions on workers' control circulating after the First Trade Unions Congress in 1918 stressed that decisions in the economic field issued by VSNKh and other state regulatory organs were obligatory at all levels of workers' control: see B.F., *Rukovodstvo po rabochemu kontroliu*, izd. Soveta Rabochego Kontrolia Tsentral'noi Promyshlennoi Oblasti, Moscow, 1918, pp. 8–9.

40 I. Stepanov, *Ot rabochego kontrolia k rabochemu upravleniiu v promyshlennosti i zemledelii*, Moscow, 1918, pp. 239–40.

41 See e.g. C. Bettelheim, *Class Struggles in the USSR, First Period: 1917–1923*, Brighton, 1976, pp. 125–30.

42 Some Soviet literature attributes to the Mensheviks the attempt to transform the Leninist active (*rasporaditel'nyi*) control into an informational (*vosvedomitel'nyi*) control, through their influence in the economic section of the Moscow Soviet and in the Council of Trade Unions (see G.A. Trukhan, 'Rabochii klass i sotsialisticheskoe obobshchestvlenie promyshlennosti (1917–1918 gg)', in *Rabochii klass*, p. 204.

43 Deutscher, p. 18; F.I. Kaplan, *Bolshevik Ideology and the Ethics of Soviet Labour*, London, 1963, pp. 124–7; Avrich, 'The Bolshevik Revolution', 50–2, and *Rabochee dvizhenie v 1917 godu, podg. k pechati V.L. Meller i A.M. Pankratova*, Moscow, 1926, pp. 326–8, reproducing the instructions on implementation of workers' control issued by the All-Russian Council of Workers' Control and by the economic section of the Moscow Soviet on 25 November and

published in the *Izvestiia TsIK* on 13 December 1917. These instructions, which prepared the discussions on workers' control at the First Trade Unions Congress and were basically accepted by the congress, assigned to workers' control the tasks of accounting (*uchet*) and vigilance (*nabliudenie*) and made it clear that workers' control did *not* mean regulation and management by workers of a given enterprise (*v vedenie i upravlenie rabochikh dannogo predpriiatiia*), but by central regulating organs.

44 Reported by Bunyan, pp. 8–11.
45 Gladkov, *Natsionalizatsiia promyshlennosti*, p. 82.
46 Ankudinova, p. 34.
47 *Izvestiia*, no. 150, 18 July 1918, 6.
48 *Izvestiia*, no. 136, 3 July 1918, 7.
49 *Uprochenie Sovetskoi Vlasti*, p. 210.
50 *Izvestiia*, 12 September 1918, 6.
51 Gladkov, *Natsionalizatsiia promyshlennosti*, p. 83.
52 *Ibid.*, pp. 84–5, 86–7.
53 *Ibid.*, p. 97.
54 *A Collection of Reports on Bolshevism*, London, 1919, p. 65.
55 G. Lansbury, *What I Saw in Russia*, London, 1920, p. 79.
56 *Rabochii kontrol' i natsionalizatsiia promyshlennosti v Kostromskoi Gubernii. Sbornik dokumentov 1917–1918*, Kostroma, 1960, pp. 26, 107–8, 120–1.
57 *Ibid.*, p. 97.
58 Gladkov, *Natsionalizatsiia promyshlennosti*, p. 102.
59 E.G. Gimpel'son, 'Sotsial'no-politicheskie izmeneniia v sostave rabochego klassa v pervye gody Sovetskoi Vlasti', in *Rabochii klass*, p. 353. A. Lozovsky (*Trade Unions in Soviet Russia: Their Development and Present Position*, Collection of Russian Trade Unions' Documents compiled by the ILP Information Committee, 1920, p. 30) gave the figure of 416 for the total number of delegates at the congress.
60 *Putevoditel' po rezoliutsiiam Vserossiiskikh S''ezdov i Konferentsii Professional'nykh Soiuzov* (sos. Iu. Milonov), Moscow, 1924, p. 111.
61 *Ibid.*, p. 112.
62 *Ibid.*, p. 114.
63 *Ibid.*, p. 114.
64 *Ibid.*, p. 114.
65 *Sbornik dekretov i postanovlenii po narodnomu khoziaistvu*, 2 vols., Moscow, 1918–21, vol. 1, 1917–1918, pp. 172–3.
66 *Materialy po istorii SSSR*, vol. 3, Moscow, 1956, p. 290.
67 *Ibid.*, pp. 254–7, 264, 266.
68 See Lozovsky, p. 24, for these regulations.
69 Lenin, *Collected Works*, vol. 42, pp. 64–5, 506n.
70 Lenin, speech at the All-Russian Central Executive Committee, in *Collected Works*, vol. 27, p. 294.
71 *Ibid.*, p. 297.
72 Lenin, *Collected Works*, vol. 27, pp. 297–8 and 587n.
73 For nationalization as a better option for managing than workers' control, see Jay B. Sorenson, *The Life and Death of Soviet Trade Unionism, 1917–1928*,

New York, 1969, pp. 66–8.
74 *Sbornik dekretov i postanovlenii po narodnomu khoziaistvu,* vol. 1, p. 177.
75 *Ibid,* p. 232.
76 *Uprochenie Sovetskoi Vlasti,* document no. 213.
77 *Ibid.,* doc. no. 220.
78 V. Vinogradov, *Workers' Control over Production, Past and Present,* Moscow, 1973, p. 51.
79 *Rezoliutsii Vserossiiskikh Konferentsii i S''ezdov Profsoiuzov,* Petrograd, 1919, p. 192. The Bolsheviks had 449 delegates with the right to vote, against 29 Mensheviks, 42 representatives of other parties and 23 non-party delegates: cf. Gimpel'son, 'Sotsial'no-politicheskie izmeneniia v sostave rabochego klassa', p. 353.
80 *Ibid.,* p. 192.
81 Lozovsky, p. 25.
82 *Severnyi rabochii,* no. 344, 18 September 1918, reported in *Rabochii kontrol' . . . v Kostromskoi Gubernii,* pp. 127–9; and *Narodnoe Khoziaistvo,* 1919, nos. 1–2, p. 23.
83 *Rabochii kontrol' . . . v Kostromskoi Gubernii,* pp. 254–5. Cf. also F. Kaplan, *Russian Labor and the Bolshevik Party, 1917–1920,* Berkeley, 1965, where the thesis that the Bolsheviks created parallel institutions whenever they did not have full political control over the existing ones is well developed in an analysis of the relations between Russian labour and the party.
84 *Leninskaia sistema Partiino-Gosudarstvennogo Kontrolia i ego rol' v stroitel'stve sotsializma (1917–1932 gg),* Moscow, 1965, pp. 19–20.
85 *Sbornik dekretov i postanovlenii po narodnomu khoziaistvu,* vol. 1, pp. 333–5; *Dekrety sovetskoi vlasti,* Moscow, 1957, vol. 1, p. 80.
86 *Izvestiia,* no. 208, 25 September 1918, 5.
87 *Izvestiia,* no. 210, 27 September 1918, 5.
88 *Izvestiia,* no. 212, 1 October 1918, 6 and no. 220, 10 October 1918, 6.
89 *Narodnoe Khoziaistvo,* 1919, nos. 1–2, p. 34
90 *Ibid.,* pp. 35–6.
91 *Ibid.,* pp. 35–6.
92 *Ibid.,* pp. 33–6.
93 *Narodnoe Khoziaistvo,* 1919, no. 3, 66–70.
94 *Ekonomicheskaia Zhizn',* no. 281, 14 December 1919, 2; cf. also N.N. Rovinskii, *Finansovyi kontrol' v SSSR,* Moscow, 1947, pp. 14–16.
95 R. Arskii, 'Itogi S''ezda Sovnarkhozov', *Narodnoe Khoziaistvo,* 1919, nos. 1–2, p. 15.
96 *Narodnoe Khoziaistvo,* 1919, nos. 9–10, p. 51.
97 Kritsman, *Geroicheskii period Velikoi Russkoi Revoliutsii,* Moscow (no date, probably 1924), p. 96.
98 Deutscher, pp. 18–22. See F.I. Kaplan, *Bolshevik Ideology,* pp. 211–21, on the problem of the relationship between trade unions and the Commissariat of Labour, the former as representatives of the 'organized' proletariat, the latter as a state organ endowed with compulsory force.
99 *III Vserossiiskaia Konferentsiia Professional'nykh Soiuzov,* stenogr. otchet, Moscow, 1917, pp. 301–2.

100 *Putevoditel'*, p. 126.
101 *Ibid.*, pp. 91–2.
102 *Ibid.*, p. 94; see the resolution presented by Strazhevskii.
103 *Ibid.*, pp. 103, 128.
104 Quoted in P. Avrich, ed., *The Anarchists in the Revolution*, London, 1973, p. 73.
105 *Putevoditel'*, pp. 91–2; for an English translation see Deutscher, p. 23.
106 *Novyi Luch*, no. 22, 14 February 1918, p. 3.
107 *IV Vserossiiskaia Konferentsiia Professional'nykh Soiuzov, 12–17 Marta 1918 goda. Protokoly i materialy*, Moscow, 1923, pp. 25–6.
108 *Ibid.*, pp. 29–33.
109 *Ibid.*, pp. 37–9; Lozovskii proposed that local and provincial labour commissariats be elected by the trade unions and intervene in labour conflicts only after these had gone through trade union arbitration.
110 *Narodnoe Khoziaistvo*, 1918, no. 2, 38.
111 Lenin, *Collected Works*, vol. 27, pp. 210–11.
112 *Ibid.*, p. 212.
113 *Ibid.*, p. 269.
114 This is what Trotskii affirmed at the Ninth Congress of the RKP: *9i S"ezd Rossiiskoi Kommunisticheskoi Partii, 20 Marta-4 Aprelia 1920 g*, stenogr. Otchet, Moscow, 1920, p. 92.
115 *Sbornik dekretov i postanovlenii po narodnomu khoziaistvu*, vol. 1, pp. 311–15, and paragraph 15 of the decree.
116 This recommendation specified that the commissar was to be to the technical manager the same as the commissar attached to the regiment to its commander-in-chief (cf. U.S. Department of State, *Resolutions of the All Russian Council in the second week of March 1918*).
117 Iu. K. Avdakov and V.V. Borodin, *Proizvodstvennye ob"edineniia i ikh rol' v organizatsii upravleniia Sovetskoi Promyshlennosti*, Moscow 1973, pp. 8–9.
118 Lenin, *Collected Works*, vol. 27, p. 268.
119 *Ibid.*, vol. 27, p. 316.
120 *Ibid.*, pp. 316–17.
121 N. Osinskii, *Stroitel'stvo sotsializma*, Moscow, 1918, pp. 34–6.
122 *Ibid.*, p. 75.
123 Even in the unpublished pamphlet 'How to Organize Competition', written 6–9 January 1918, where Lenin sharply asserted that the prejudice that only the upper classes were capable of administering the state and organizing society had to be removed, he acknowledged that the advice and instruction of intellectuals and specialists could not be dispensed with: *Collected Works*, vol. 26, pp. 409–12.
124 *Trudy I Vserossiiskogo S"ezda Sovnarkhozov*, pp. 79, 343.
125 Cf. *Putevoditel'*, p. 129 and *Trudy I Vserossiiskogo S"ezda Sovnarkhozov*, p. 259. Cf. also S. Kanev, *Oktiabr'skaia Revoliutsiia i krakh anarkhizma*, Moscow, 1974, p. 237.
126 Kanev, pp. 237–40.
127 Out of 428 delegates at the First Congress of Trade Unions, the programme of the anarcho-syndicalists got only four votes: Kanev, p. 222.

128 *Trudy I Vserossiiskogo S"ezda Sovnarkhozov*, pp. 362–3.
129 Cf. F.V. Samokhvalov, *Sovety narodnogo khoziaistva v 1917–1932 gg*, Moscow, 1964, pp. 50–1.
130 *Trudy I Vserossiiskogo S"ezda Sovnarkhozov*, pp. 259–60.
131 *Ibid.*, pp. 358, 353.
132 *Ibid.*, pp. 354, 350.
133 *Ibid.*, pp. 150, 351.
134 *Ibid.*, pp. 150, 350, 355.
135 *Ibid.*, p. 343.
136 *Ibid.*, pp. 344–5.
137 *Ibid.*, p. 350.
138 Avdakov and Borodin, p. 11, interpret the new decree as a victory of the centralistic tendency. For the decree see *Sbornik dekretov i postanovlenii po narodnomu khoziaistvu*, pp. 315–19.
139 Cf. *Trudy I Vserossiiskogo S"ezda Sovnarkhozov*, pp. 89, 363.
140 This term was soon extended to a longer time span. The Kostroma provincial *sovnarkhoz* extended it to one year from 26 September 1918: *Rabochii kontrol' ... v Kostromskoi Gubernii*, p. 173.
141 *Trudy I Vserossiiskogo S"ezda Sovnarkhozov*, pp. 113–14.
142 Grinevetskii, pp. 151–2.
143 *Ekonomicheskaia Zhizn'*, no. 4, 12 November 1918, 1 and *Ekonomicheskaia Zhizn'*, no. 34, 17 December 1918, 1.
144 R. Arskii, *Regulirovanie promyshlennosti*, Moscow (no date, presumably 1918–19), p. 24.
145 Cf. V.Z. Drobizhev and A.B. Medvedev, *Iz istorii sovnarkhozov*, Moscow, 1964, p. 108.
146 *Trudy II Vserossiiskogo S"ezda Sovnarkhozov, 19–27 Dekabria 1918 g*, stenogr. otchet, Moscow, 1919, p. 261.
147 R. Arskii, 'Itogi s"ezda sovnarkhozov', *Narodnoe Khoziaistvo*, nos. 1–2, 1919, 13.
148 *Trudy II Vserossiiskogo S"ezda Sovnarkhozov*, p. 61; *Ekonomicheskaia Zhizn'*, no. 39, 22 December 1918, 1.
149 On this point see Deutscher, p. 23 and M. Dewar, *Labour Policy in the USSR, 1917–1928*, London–New York, Royal Institute of International Affairs, 1956, p. 34.
150 Cf. Introduction written by G. Tsyperovitch in *Rezoliutsii Vserossiiskikh Konferentsii i S"ezdov Profsoiuzov*, Petrograd, 1919, pp. xxiv–v.
151 *Ekonomicheskaia Zhizn'*, no. 19, 28 January 1919, 3.
152 Cf. Deutscher, p. 26.
153 At the Fourth Trade Union Conference in March 1918 Tomskii wanted to strengthen the unions' powers by merging their organs with those of the Labour Commissariat, saying that in this way the commissariat would become subordinated to the trade unions: *IV Vserossiiskaia Konferentsiia Professional'nykh Soiuzov, 12–17 Marta 1918, Protokoly i materialy*, Moscow, 1923, pp. 40–1.
154 *Putevoditel'*, pp. 194–5.

155 Drobizhev and Medvedev, p. 158.
156 *Parliamentary Papers on Bolshevism*, United Kingdom, 1919, p. 29.
157 *Putevoditel'*, pp. 160, 164–5.
158 *Rezoliutsii Vserossiiskikh Konferentsii i S''ezdov Profsoiuzov*, Petrograd 1919, pp. 101–2.
159 *Putevoditel'*, p. 169.
160 *Ibid.*, pp. 171, 175.
161 *Ibid.*, p. 197.
162 This comment is due to Deutscher, p. 29. For a criticism of it, see Dewar, p. 74.
163 *8i S''ezd RKP (b). 18–23 Marta 1919 g*, Moscow, 1933, pp. 392–3.
164 Such were the other points of the Party Programme: *ibid.*, pp. 392–94.
165 Deutscher, p. 31.
166 *VKP (b) v rezoliutsiiakh i resheniiakh s''ezdov konferentsii i plenumov Ts K*, 5th edn, Moscow, 1936, p. 330; Deutscher, pp. 31–2; according to P.A. Garvi, *Professional'nye soiuzy v Rossii v pervye gody revoliutsii (1917–21)*, New York, 1958, pp. 85–6, party members in the trade unions showed military-like discipline when faced with party decisions. From archive funds published by P.P. Grebennikov, 'Iz istorii borb'y kommunisticheskoi partii protiv pravogo opportunizma v profdvizhenii v period uprocheniia Sovetskoi Vlasti (noiabr' 1917 g–1918 g', in *Materialy mezhvuzovskoi nauchnoi konferentsii kafedr obshchestvennykh nauk*, Omsk 1917, p. 59) it appears that the Communist Party gave special importance to measures directed to strengthen the communist presence in the unions. Following instructions by the Central Committee of the Party issued on 18 May 1918, the local party organs introduced the obligation for all communists 'to carry out detailed work in the trade unions, in order to strengthen the influence of the RKP (b) in trade unions' councils and in *fabzavkomy*'.
167 *Putevoditel'*, p. 263; and 4i S''ezd RKP (b)', in *KPSS v rezoliutsiiakh i resheniiakh S''ezdov, konferentsii i plenumov TsK*, vol. 2., 1917–24, Moscow, 1970, pp. 164–9.
168 *Trudy II Vserossiiskogo S''ezda Sovnarkhozov*, pp. 238, 264; *Rabochii kontrol' v Novgorodskoi Gubernii v 1917–1921 gg*, Moscow, 1974, p. 102.
169 Lenin, *Collected Works*, vol. 28, p. 378.
170 *Trudy II Vserossiiskogo S''ezda Sovnarkhozov*, p. 259.
171 *Ibid.*, pp. 196–7. 'Thus any absurd result can be eliminated', said Miliutin to a foreign observer; cf. W.T. Goode, *Bolshevism at Work*, London, 1920, p. 30.
172 *Sbornik dekretov*, vol. 2, pp. 179–80.
173 Kritsman, p. 94.
174 *Narodnoe Khoziaistvo*, 1920, nos. 3–4, p. 65.
175 *Ibid.*, p. 65.
176 *Ibid.*, p. 68.
177 *Ibid.*, p. 64.
178 *Rezoliutsii Vserossiiskikh Konferentsii i S''ezdov Profsoiuzov*, Petrograd, 1919, p. 100.
179 Lenin, 'How to Organize Competition', in *Collected Works*, vol. 26 (written 6–9 January 1918, published in *Pravda*, no. 17, 20 January 1929).

180 *9i S"ezd RKP, 20 Marta-4 Aprelia 1920 g*, p. 79.
181 Cf. Dewar, p. 50.
182 *9i S"ezd RKP*, p. 92.
183 *Ibid.*, p. 131.
184 *Ibid.*, p. 133.
185 *Ibid.*, p. 136.
186 *Ibid.*, p. 94.
187 *Ibid.*, pp. 94, 91.
188 *Ibid.*, pp. 123, 112.
189 *Sovety narodnogo khoziaistva i planovye organy v tsentre i na mestakh (1917–1932).
Sbornik dokumentov*, Moscow, 1957, pp. 36–40.
190 *9i S"ezd RKP*, p. 112.
191 *Ibid.*, p. 117.
192 *Ekonomicheskaia Zhizn'*, no. 230, 18 October 1919, 1.
193 *Ibid.*, 1.
194 *Ekonomicheskaia Zhizn'*, no. 287, 21 December 1919, 1.
195 *Ekonomicheskaia Zhizn'*, no. 295, 31 December 1919, 1.
196 Kassior; cf., *9i S"ezd RKP*, p. 148.
197 Arskii, p. 26.
198 *9i S"ezd RKP*, p. 123.
199 *Ibid.*, pp. 138–41.
200 *Ibid.*, p. 80.
201 *Ibid.*, p. 141.
202 *Ibid.*, p. 140.
203 *Ibid.*, pp. 99–103.
204 *Ibid.*, p. 119.
205 This was recalled by Kamenev at the congress: *ibid.*, p. 141.
206 Reported by Tomskii at the congress, *ibid.*, p. 137.
207 *Ibid.*, pp. 182–93: the final form of Trotskii's resolution.
208 See p. 141 above.
209 *Putevoditel'*, p. 218. By that time the Internationalists had joined the Communist Party.
210 *Ibid.*, p. 263.
211 *Ibid.*, pp. 270–1.
212 *Ibid.*, pp. 276–8.
213 *Ibid.*, p. 222. This tie was confirmed by Tomskii, when he asserted that 'being formally non-party institutions... trade unions as a whole... unconditionally followed the highest leader of the proletarian revolution, the Communist Party'.
214 *Ibid.*, p. 222.
215 *Ibid.*, pp. 231–2.
216 *Ibid.*, p. 232.
217 See pp. 100–1 above.
218 *Putevoditel'*, p. 278.
219 *Ibid.*, pp. 280–4.
220 Ia. Fin, *Profdvizhenie SSSR*, Moscow, 1928, pp. 58–9.
221 *Putevoditel'*, p. 299.
222 *Ibid.*, p. 300.

223 *Ibid.*, p. 296.

224 Cf. on this point Bettelheim, pp. 395–404.

225 *10i S"ezd Rossiiskoi Kommunisticheskoi Partii, 8–16 Marta 1921 Goda*, stenogr. otchet, Moscow, 1921, p. 360: discussion in the session preceding the congress.

226 *Ibid.*, p. 213; Deutscher, pp. 46–7; A. Lozovsky, *Lenin and the Trade Union Movement*, Washington, T.U. Educational League, 1924, p. 23.

227 *10i S"ezd RKP*, pp. 351–60.

228 Deutscher, p. 45.

229 Lenin, 'The Trade Unions, the Present Situation and Trotsky's Mistakes', in *Collected Works*, vol. 32, pp. 20–1 (originally written on 30 December 1920).

230 Lenin, 'Report on the Role and Tasks of Trade Unions at the II All-Russian Congress of Miners', in *Collected Works*, vol. 32, pp. 61–2 (first published on 25 January 1921).

231 *10i S"ezd RKP*, p. 196.

232 Lenin, *Collected Works*, vol. 32, pp. 212–13.

233 Deutscher, p. 56.

234 *Ibid.*, pp. 56–7.

235 *10i S"ezd RKP*, pp. 212, 360.

236 *Ibid.*

237 *Ibid.*, p. 364.

238 *Ibid.*, p. 362.

239 Bukharin, p. 158.

240 *10i S"ezd RKP*, p. 355.

241 *Ibid.*, p. 190.

242 *KPSS v rezoliutsiiakh i resheniiakh*, vol. 2, 1917–24, Moscow, 1970, p. 232.

243 *10i S"ezd RKP*, p. 213.

244 See Maiskii's intervention at the *IV Vserossiiskaia Konferentsiia Professional'nykh Soiuzov*, pp. 29–33.

245 *10i S"ezd RKP*, pp. 207–8.

246 Kritsman, p. 201.

247 *8i Vserossiiskii S"ezd Sovetov, 22–29 Dekabria 1920 goda*, stenogr. otchet, Moscow, 1921, p. 28.

248 L. Trotsky, *Defence of Terrorism: Terrorism and Communism. A Reply to K. Kautsky.* London, 1921, p. 157.

4

Money and value

4.1 MONEY, BANKS AND FINANCIAL POLICY

Nationalization of the banking system proceeded much faster than that of industry and commerce. It was a firm point in the Bolshevik programme and a justifiable outcome of the ideology of socialism.

The growing importance of banks in Western industrial society was a theme that socialist literature had seized upon before the development of Marxism. In the early nineteenth century Saint-Simon already understood that banks were able to influence economic life. Through advancing capital to industry, banks had a direct influence on the volume of investment.[1] The Saint-Simonians developed this idea. They proposed the creation of a single central bank controlled by big industries and divided up into separate branches, in order to channel capital to the most efficient uses.[2] The technocratic approach of the Saint-Simonians to investment control may have exerted some influence on Lenin's approach to this question. Lenin decided to end his essay on imperialism by a critical reference to Saint-Simon's ingenuity.[3]

The unfortunate history of the French Republic further justified belief in the necessity of central control over banking. Centralization of credit in the hands of the state through a national bank was considered by the Communist Manifesto of 1848 to be the initial step towards centralization of all the means of production under state power.[4] Marx claimed that the French Bank had a crucial role in discrediting the republic when credit operations were suspended, and he suggested that the French Government should not have hindered financial bankruptcy. If the state, argued Marx, had refused financial support when people rushed to the banks, the financial aristocracy would have been swept away and the bourgeoisie would have understood the necessity of state control over banking policy.[5]

In 1910 the penetrating analysis of Hilferding added substantial new arguments for state control over business. Hilferding foresaw that the socializing function of finance capital would make it easier to overcome capitalism. After examining the whole encompassing role of finance capital in the economy, Hilferding concluded that the state would only have to take over finance capital in order to get control over the economy. To emphasize his conclusion, he pointed out that the expropriation of the six largest Berlin banks would be equivalent to state control over the most important branches of industry.[6]

Hilferding's approach to finance capitalism was very well known to the Russian Marxists. Bukharin made several references to it in his *Imperialism and World Economy*. This 'merging of banking capital with industry',[7] a notion by which Bukharin epitomized the core of Hilferding's analysis, was praised by Lenin and incorporated in the revision of the Party Programme in April 1917.[8] The national economy, argued Bukharin, was being transformed into a single combined enterprise by the processes of concentration and vertical centralization of production which accompanied the transformation of capital into finance capital, and this was 'the prerequisite for organized production on a higher non-capitalist level'. Banking acted as an organizer of industry. The greater the concentration of industry and banking, the stronger the organization of national production would be.[9]

Lenin's approach to finance capitalism was close to Bukharin's. In his essay on imperialism, Lenin did not hesitate to point out that the crucial aspect of the transformation of capitalism was the transition from the rule of capital as such to the rule of finance capital. From simple dealers in capital, banks had become powerful monopolists. Concentration of capital and centralization of banking policy were considered as evidence of a new phase of capitalism. Lenin added special emphasis on the power of banks over industry. Banks had precise information about specific businesses, which allowed them total freedom to choose individual recipients of credit, thus permitting the use of credit policy in such a way as to influence industrial profitability.[10]

The polemical arguments which Lenin used against the Provisional Government at the end of May 1917 show that his analysis was not confined to the realm of speculation. In a *Pravda* article on 'The Inevitable Catastrophe and Extravagant Promises', Lenin challenged the government to issue a one-stroke decree instructing 'councils and congresses of bank employees, both of individual banks and on a national scale, to work out immediately practical measures for amalgamating all banks and banking houses into a single State Bank, and exercising precise control over all banking operations, the results of such control being published forthwith'.[11] In 'The Tasks of the Proletariat in Our Revolution', written on behalf of the Bolshevik faction in April 1917,

Lenin demanded the 'nationalization of all banks, or at least the immediate establishment of the control of the Soviets of Workers' Deputies over them'.[12]

The Social Democratic Party, which had voted for 'state control over all banks and their amalgamation into a single bank' at the Seventh (April 1917) All-Russian Conference,[13] modified this request in favour of 'nationalization and centralization of banking operations' at the Sixth Party Congress (July–August 1917).[14]

Convinced of the inefficacy of the Provisional Government's policy of economic control, Lenin added new arguments for nationalization of the banks on the eve of the October Revolution. In 'The Impending Catastrophe and How to Combat It', he wrote:

It is utterly absurd to control and regulate deliveries of grain, or the production and distribution of goods generally, without controlling and regulating bank operations... Banks nowadays are so closely and intimately bound up with trade (in grain and everything else) and with industry, that without 'laying hands' on the banks nothing of any value, nothing 'revolutionary–democratic' can be accomplished.[15]

By an implicit reference to the power of information in the operation of the modern banking system, outlined in his essay on imperialism, Lenin affirmed that the meaning of nationalization was that:

the state put itself in a position to know where and how, whence and when, millions and billions of rubles flow... Only control over banking operations, provided they were concentrated in a single state bank, would make it possible, if certain other easily-practicable measures were adopted, to organize the effective collection of income tax in such a way as to really prevent the concealment of property and incomes...[16]

Lenin was optimistic about the technical feasibility of state control over finance capital. Two or three weeks were considered to be sufficient to carry out the unification of accountancy, which, according to Lenin, had already been prepared by the diffusion of bills, shares, bonds, and so on. Moderate optimism was also shown regarding the political feasibility of the nationalization of banks. Lenin argued that this measure would not hinder private ownership of capital, since savings would continue to belong to their owners as before. Moreover, part of the middle class, peasantry and small industrialists would benefit by the distribution of credit agencies over the country and by easy credit terms.[17]

When optimism failed to be supported by economic arguments, Lenin devised compulsory measures. Confiscation of property and imprisonment should be the fate of bank employees reluctant to collaborate with government policy.[18]

Lenin's assertion of the need for bank nationalization may be considered as valid evidence of the Bolshevik projects in this field, in spite of the peculiar events which prompted the schedules of nationalization.

The particular importance that the Bolsheviks attached to state control over banking depended not only on the development of Marxist analysis with regard to advanced capitalism, but had specific origins in the Russian situation, though Russian capitalism could not be called mature capitalism. Foreign investments accounted for a great deal of the Russian take-off. Though the highest quotas of foreign finance capital belonged to France and Britain – the allies of Russia in the First World War – the Bolsheviks could not ignore the fact that the implementation of a new social and economic policy, less respectful of foreign interests, would provoke financial retaliation. State control over banking was one of the means of reducing the impact of the reduction in foreign investment and could be justified by the considerable development of the Russian banking system.

On the eve of the First World War, the concentration of the banking system was no less evident in Russia than in more developed countries. Twelve of the fifty joint-stock banks held 80 per cent of the total banking capital. The share of foreign capital was conspicuous in the five most important banks with head offices in Petersburg. Sixty per cent of the stock of the Russian Asiatic Bank, which represented more than 17 per cent of the total assets of the joint-stock banks, were in the hands of French capitalists. One-third of the capital of the International Bank of Commerce, representing 10 per cent of the total assets of the joint-stock banks, belonged to German capitalists. The Russian Bank of Foreign Commerce, which controlled 30 per cent of the sugar industry and 20 per cent of the Urals metallurgical companies, was under the control of British capitalists. The Siberian Bank of Commerce, financing mines and industries of the East, was tied to French and British capital and participated in the operations of the Russian Asiatic Bank. The Azov–Don Commercial Bank was connected with German and French banks.[19]

The penetration of foreign capital was strictly related to the financing of the most important industrial branches, particularly in heavy industry. In the Ukraine and Russian Poland, the iron and steel industry was under the control of French and German capital. Foreign capital was dominant in key sectors, like locomotive construction, machine building and military industry. Iron mines depended on French banks, coal mines to a great extent on foreign capital, and electrical industries on German capital.[20] Foreign investment was conspicuous until 1917. In that year, the total capital of the Russian commercial banks amounted to 679.7

million rubles, 34.9 per cent of which was foreign capital. The role of the latter was particularly important in financing mining and the processing of raw materials. Of the total foreign capital, 54 per cent was invested in the mining and metal working industries.[21]

Banking was also concentrated territorially. The largest commercial banks had their head offices in St Petersburg and Moscow. Provincial banks held only 9 per cent of the total deposits of commercial banks.[22] This fact may have justified Lenin's idea that peripheral customers may have benefited from the nationalization of the banks and diffusion of credit agencies over the country.[23]

Other credit institutions had only a minor role in industrial financing. The Mutual Credit Companies were the most important for medium-term credit to small industries and commerce. In 1914 there were 1,108 of them over the country, with 595 million rubles' worth of deposits. They financed investments of 738 million rubles, that is to say, a sixth of total investment financed by commercial banks.[24]

The financial and territorial concentration of the Russian banking system facilitated rapid nationalization. The Bolsheviks turned their attention first of all to the large credit institutions. It can be maintained that the speed of nationalization was influenced by the opposition shown by the financial milieu to the new government and by the reluctance of the individual banks to comply with the government's directives on advances for wage payments to commercial and industrial enterprises.[25] There are, however, no significant indications that the Bolsheviks would not have undertaken nationalization if the financiers had not been so hostile to the government.

The first measure taken in money control was the occupation of the State Bank by the People's Commissar of Finance on 20 November 1917. The State Bank controlled money circulation and credit. Since 1897 it had been the only issuing bank.[26] Private banks deposited their reserves in the State Bank, from which they received cash. Commercial banks had reserves which amounted to 1,601.5 million rubles in the form of securities at the end of October 1917. The total stock of gold amounted to 1,260 million rubles when the State Bank was taken over by the Bolsheviks.[27]

A State Commissar was appointed to the State Bank after the Bank officials repeatedly refused to finance the current expenditure of the new government. On 27 December 1917, the largest commercial banks were occupied by troops. The immediate motivation for this decision may have been the refusal of the commercial banks to finance factories under workers' control.[28] Soon after the nationalization, two decrees were issued ordering the transfer of all banking operations to the State Bank and authorizing it to control all forms of deposits.[29] In January 1918 the nationalized banks started operating under new management. In February their capital was transferred to the State Bank and shares in them were annulled. Private funds were not confiscated, but their use was put under control.[30]

The Bolsheviks did not dare to apply 'workers' control' to banks, though the law contemplated this possibility. State control over money was used as a deterrent against any opposition by managers to the application of government measures. The Moscow Soviet instructed the Moscow commercial banks not to finance enterprises which did not apply workers' control, by threatening the freezing of the banks' reserves held at the State Bank.[31] When the Bolsheviks realized that nationalization of the State Bank did not bring about sufficient state control over money circulation, their interest turned to the private banks. The consequent drive towards overall nationalization of the banking system, before an alternative financial system had been set up, may be explained by the panic of the Bolsheviks in face of the unexpected financial autonomy manifested by the credit institutions. In fact, the private banks had tried to avoid the central control which the holding of their reserves at the State Bank could ensure. In November 1917 private bankers had made an agreement to issue cheques payable to the bearer in round sums, which could be used by the banks for their operations. The banks had succeeded in printing one million rubles in this form.[32]

Between December 1917 and April 1918 the Bolsheviks undertook a number of measures to put the incomes of capitalists under direct control, and to alleviate the financial burden of the State Treasury. Dividends on bank shares were abolished. Withdrawals of deposits placed in current accounts before 1918 were restricted. Foreign debts were cancelled, as was interest on domestic loans to former governments. All shares, bonds and interest-bearing notes were subject to obligatory registration. The government renounced the national debt, reimbursing only holdings of less than 10,000 rubles.[33]

The nationalization of the largest banks alone was probably meant to circumscribe and reduce the impact of the hostility of the financial milieu to the Bolshevik Government. But the access to credit thus provided did not help to improve the financial situation. In January 1918, the fear of losing control over money induced the Commissar of the State Bank to establish that no loans could be made available to anybody, unless approved by a committee composed of experts and Party members in the proportion of 1:2.[34] The nationalization of banks was not accompanied by precise instructions on financing or by the appointment of state officials sympathetic to the new government. Addressing the Central Executive Committee on 29 December 1917, Lenin asserted that

Soviet power had been forced to nationalize the banks because of their sabotage. He added that the decree on nationalization contained nothing but principles and that specialists in this field would be asked to collaborate only 'when we have the keys in our hands'. The draft decree on nationalization mentioned, in fact, that implementation of the law was to be supervised by mobile groups of inspectors from trade unions and other workers' organizations.[35] Nothing was said about new forms of financial organization.

In April 1918 the Bolsheviks tried to take a step back, in order to limit the negative consequences of the unprepared nationalization of the banks. The absence of Bolshevik cadres to fill voluntary or compulsory vacancies among the highest posts was the major obstacle to enforcing a new policy on finance. In the first version of 'The Immediate Tasks of the Soviet Government', written between 22 and 28 March 1918, Lenin spoke of the need to enlist in the service of Soviet power the former captains of industry, masters and exploiters, in the role of technical experts, managers, consultants and advisers, in view of the failure of prospects for revolution in advanced countries:

If the socialist revolution had won simultaneously throughout the world, or at least in a number of advanced countries... backward Russia would not have to wrestle with this problem on her own, as the advanced workers of the west-European countries would have come to her help and relieved her of most of the complexities involved in that most difficult of all tasks, arising in the period of transition to socialism, known as the organization task.[36]

In fact, not only the expectation of the German revolution, but also Lenin's hypothesis about the relative simplicity of nationalizing finance capital and its benefits, which he had asserted on the eve of the revolution, collapsed in a few months. Nationalization of the banks did not bring much order to the economy. Osinskii reported from the Donets Basin that the private enterprises which in Kerenskii's time had received all sorts of subsidies from the government had remained without money after nationalization of the banks, and workers' wages had not been paid since December 1917.[37] The leadership tried to come to an agreement with bank representatives, which was aimed at gaining the support of the former directors by allowing them the autonomous management of the nationalized credit institutions.[38] A foreign observer even reported that Lenin and Trotskii were favourable to the idea of denationalization of the banks, proposed by the Commissar of Finances, Gukovskii.[39] Whether grounded or not, rumours about denationalization of the banks provoked a reaction from VSNKh. Larin intervened at the VSNKh plenary session of 19–21 March 1918 to reply to Press statements about a project to denationalize the banks.[40] He stated that not only did the government not have such a project in mind, but that, on the contrary, it was determined to carry nationalization forward to its ultimate conclusion: the unification of all individual private banks, amalgamated with the State Bank in a single institution. The opposition of VSNKh to denationalization of the banks succeeded.

However, for some time Bolshevik control over the financial institutions did not bring about substantial changes in financial policy. Theoretically, the orthodox principles of budget equilibrium based on increased taxation and curtailment of public expenditure were not challenged, although the concern for more equity in fiscal policy justified the preference for direct income and property taxes rather than indirect levies. The abolition of all indirect levies and the introduction of a progressive income and property tax had been reaffirmed in the revision of the SDLP Programme of April 1917 as the basic condition for the democratization of the country.[41]

The Bolsheviks, in fact, tried to increase state revenues by enforcing direct taxation, but they did not succeed. In 1918, income taxes provided only 7.3 per cent of total revenue; revenue from total taxation was only 200 million rubles. On 30 October 1918, the government introduced an extraordinary income tax of ten billion rubles, by which it was planned to obtain about two-thirds of the estimated revenue. Indirect levies were not abolished; on the contrary, they were increased, from 5 per cent of the estimated budget revenue in 1918 to 8.9 per cent of the 1919 budget. In 1919, revenue from direct and indirect taxes increased to 1,628 million rubles, i.e. about 17 per cent of the effective state revenue.[42] Increasing state expenditure, both in the civil economic sectors and in the military sphere, could be matched only by issue of paper money.

The control of inflation encountered serious difficulties. The state deficit had already reached 81 per cent of total expenditure in 1917. The Bolsheviks faced with mixed feelings the problem of controlling price increases. Nationalized and confiscated factories, as well as military expenditure, were an increasing burden for the Treasury. From 27 December 1917 to 10 May 1918, VSNKh examined requests for funds (credits, advances and subsidies) for 922 million rubles.[43] On the other hand, price control on foodstuffs was accompanied by scarcity and price increases on the free market. Some steps towards financial discipline were undertaken on 16 February 1918, when a special commission was formed to curtail state expenditure.[44] This commission was attached to VSNKh and given the task of controlling money advances to any institution. No extraordinary credit was to be approved without its financial source being indicated. Tight financing made it harder for the existing economic institutions to carry on their business and made them resort to local expedients. On 21 February 1918, the Moscow Soviet approved the 'armouring' (*bronirovka*) of cash on hand for the most important economic institutions. When, six days later, all banks closed down for lack of cash, the soviet authorized monetary loans for extraordinary needs.[45] In the first quarter of 1918, 405 undertakings employing 200,000 workers closed down, owing to the stoppage of bank credit.[46] In the provinces, money hunger increased because of delays in dispatching means of payment. Since the use of the telegraph for this purpose was prohibited, money payments were authorized only by mail.[47] On 4 March 1918, Lenin confirmed the financial disorder at the Central Party Committee:

we are suffering from a money famine, we are short of currency notes, the Treasury cannot print all we need ... It is a rare week when I do not receive a complaint about money not being paid out...[48]

Table 4.1. *Money issue and price increase, November 1917–December 1918*

Years and months	Issue of all money tokens (million rubles)	Price increase (preceding month = 100)[a]	Issue as a percentage of the monetary mass existing on the first day of each month
1917			
November	5,717.6	151	29.2
December	2,355.2	134	9.3
1918			
January	1,913.3	129	6.9
February	1,455.8	122	4.9
March	2,956.3	131	9.5
April	4,290.6	132	12.6
May	2,477.2	122	6.5
June	2,968.5	125	7.3
July	2,683.0	114	6.1
August	2,279.1	92	4.9
September	2,851.5	100	5.9
October	2,770.2	111	5.4
November	3,074.9	125	5.7
December	3,955.6	121	5.9

Source: Z.V. Atlas, *Ocherki po istorii denezhnogo obrashcheniia v SSSR (1917–1925)*, Moscow, 1940, p. 30
[a]Budget index of the All-Russian Central Council of Trade Unions.

Money worries were decisive in slowing down the pace of national-ization after January 1918, and were taken into account by economic experts in the formulation of the cautious programme of industrial nationalization proposed by Miliutin at the First Congress of *Sovnarkhozy*.

The rate of issuing money slowed down between December 1917 and February 1918, increased in March and, after reaching a peak in April 1918, was drastically reduced in May 1918 (see Table 4.1).

In May 1918 the State Bank of Petrograd registered a credit balance (of 37.1 million rubles) for the first time since the October Revolution.[49]

At the First Congress of *Sovnarkhozy*, Gukovskii, who was at that time the People's Commissar of Finance, affirmed that the government's financial policy was based on the criterion of budget equilibrium and its goal was the convertibility of money into gold.[50] The price increases, in fact, were almost checked in August and September, possibly because of the fall in the rate of money issue after April 1918.[51] However, the problem of economic organization after Brest–Litovsk urged more complex measures of monetary policy than those designed merely to secure budget equilibrium. Other proposals were formulated against Gukovskii's line. Sokol'nikov rejected the policy of convertibility of the ruble. He agreed that the stock of gold should be increased, but only because gold could still be used as an international means of payment. Sokol'nikov argued that gold had ceased to be an internal means of exchange even in capitalist countries. In order to check inflation by reducing the amount of money in circulation, he proposed transforming the compulsory tax represented by inflation into an interest-bearing loan.[52]

One year before, the Provisional Government had aimed at financing government expenditure through a voluntary loan; but this project had ended in failure.[53] Sokolnikov devised an obligatory loan. This interest-bearing Red Loan would be formed by the compulsory deposit at the bank of a specific percentage of new money tokens, obtained by the obligatory conversion of old currency into new notes. Sokol'nikov rejected the idea of denationalizing the banks, on the ground that it would be likely to reintroduce the control of private banks over industry, as long as the means of production had not yet been nationalized. The only alternative, he argued, citing the example of Britain, was the institution of a single national banking system, based on a central issuing bank and several credit institutions dependent on it.[54] Nobody challenged Sokol'nikov's point that foreign banks should be allowed to operate in Soviet Russia. Most of the Soviet economic experts agreed that the financial system had to be restored before any alternative project in the financial domain could be undertaken.[55]

The Bolsheviks did not pay attention to proposals coming from other groups, which aimed to reduce the state deficit by resort to land property taxation. From the mere economic point of view, such proposals were sound. It was calculated that about forty billion rubles could be collected in this way.[56] Very likely, political considerations persuaded the leadership not to undertake what could be interpreted as an oppressive policy towards the peasants; though, very soon, the policy of grain surplus appropriation adopted by the People's Commissariat of Food Procurement (*Narkomprod*) brought about fiscal effects far greater by the end of war communism than the proposed land tax would have entailed.

In complete contrast to the rest of the congress, the left-wing opposition looked with some scepticism on the efforts inspired by the aim of reducing the budget deficit. Smirnov expressed the left-wing position on the financial question in the following terms:

In our opinion, the financial and monetary crisis may not be solved by the restoration of finance and money circulation, which lead back to a bourgeois system, but by liquidation of the monetary-financial system, leading toward the socialist organization of production.[57]

Tightening of credit was condemned as a source of economic disorganization. The left opposition criticized the work of the special commission of VSNKh responsible for examining the estimates of enterprises, which were necessary for the assignment of funds, for being punctilious and slow. It was alleged that only four estimates had been passed out of those from 300 nationalized enterprises.[58] Smirnov affirmed that several nationalized enterprises had been compelled to stop work because of the government's restrictive financial policy. The circulation of money, he argued, was out of control. The only way to deprive the bourgeoisie of its power was to speed up the process of nationalization and organization of production. Smirnov proposed adopting a policy of high industrial prices to extract money from the countryside (a proposal which the left wing would present again during NEP). He concluded that financial policy could be successful only if industry were socialized and organized in such a way as to make the countryside effectively dependent on the towns.[59] Each of the alternatives on financial policy had its own drawbacks. From the economic point of view, the proposal of pumping money out from the peasantry by taxing land was possibly the most efficient, but was likely to provoke strong reactions from the political point of view. The free use of land by the peasantry was the price that the Bolsheviks had to pay to get their support and the agreement of the Left Socialist-Revolutionaries on the other social and economic measures.

The alternative of the left wing of the party was politically feasible, although it entailed heavy economic losses in the short term. The arbitrary ratio between industrial and agricultural prices was based on the assumption that the state would be able to acquire full monopolistic powers in trade, determine the price ratio and enforce it on the population. The left-wing communists did not realize that such a disequilibrium system must affect agricultural supply. Even if the centre would have been able to fix the price ratio between industrial and agricultural prices for the whole country, other measures would have been needed, to force the peasants to produce and sell the necessary quantity of foodstuffs. The demand of the rural population for industrial goods was probably overestimated. Self-subsistence was still a strong tendency in the Russian peasantry, which the theoretical exercises of the leftist economists ignored and which heavily jeopardized the possibility of financial accumulation by central price policy.

On the other hand, a tight financial policy penalized industry and the proletarian strata, on whose support the Bolsheviks founded their power. Besides, the idea put forward by Sokol'nikov to make obligatory conversion of the old currency into Soviet currency required time and could not guarantee success. The political instability of the new government was likely to produce the effects of Gresham's law, rather than help to restore money circulation. In fact, what occurred in February 1919 when the Soviet government issued Soviet currency was that Soviet tokens gradually pushed the old currency out of circulation (see Table 4.2).

The First Congress of *Sovnarkhozy* avoided taking a precise stand on the financial question. Financial policy continued to be worked out until the autumn of 1918 partly according to restrictive criteria and partly according to expediency. It is possible that the refusal to increase the price

Table 4.2. *Percentage of different notes in circulation*

Years	Tsarist notes	Duma notes	Kerenskii notes	Soviet notes	Total
1918	15.3	52.4	32.3	—	100
1919	4.0	10.5	16.7	68.8	100
1920	0.11	0.75	0.18	98.96	100

Source: R.E. Vaisberg, *Den'gi i tseny* (*podpol'nyi rynok v period 'voennogo kommunizma'*), Moscow, 1925, pp. 136–7

of grain in April 1918[60] was also a consequence of the option for a restrictive monetary policy.

The lack of paper money was most acutely felt by the provinces. Lack of money was a powerful incentive to raise all sorts of local contributions (*kontributsii*) and to favour commodity exchange and naturalization of wages.[61] In April 1918, Osinskii reported to a VSNKh plenum that workers of the Donets Basin had started requisitioning bread grains and distributing foodstuffs within the factory by a system of bonuses. In Kharkov some metallurgical plants were exchanging their stocks of unused metal for coal. Iron was exchanged for bread grains, applying the pre-war price ratio between the two products. The financial crisis affected transport and increased scarcity. Railways refused to pay cash for coal from *Monotop*, the central administration responsible for coal distribution. In West Siberia coal could not be purchased except with cash.[62] The commercial relations between the Urals, where the iron and steel industry was concentrated, and the South, which provided iron, were seriously jeopardized by the disruption of transport, already affected by the curtailment of imports of engines and spare parts from Germany.

It was in this context that the idea of generalizing commodity exchange emerged. At the plenary session of VSNKh in April 1918, Larin said that efforts had been made to reduce state expenditure and the issue of paper money. But, he added, the transition to the organization of economic life required new measures: 'We have made up our minds to establish commodity exchange on new bases, as far as possible without paper money, preparing conditions for the time when money will only be an accounting unit.'[63] Between July and December 1918 several laws and regulations were issued to circumscribe the fiscal powers of the local soviets: their financial estimates were subject to approval by the centre, local taxation was restricted to specific sources, and local sections of the *Narkomfin* were attached to the local *ispolkomy*.[64] But taxation could not replace money issue.

The sharpening of military hostilities in the autumn of 1918 demanded the renewal of higher rates of issue. Together with the development of measures aimed at reducing money circulation within the state sector, the printing press continued to try to keep pace with the falling purchasing power of the ruble (see Table 4.3).

The paragraph on money in *The ABC of Communism* states with the force of a commandment: 'Communist society will know nothing about money.'[65] But it does not seem that this principle inspired Bolshevik measures in the monetary domain (though some 1920 rationalizations of the war communism experience may provide arguments against this

Table 4.3. *Circulation and issue of money (as at 1 January each year)*[a]

Years	Circulation in billions of old rubles	Circulation in millions of pre-war rubles	Issue in billions of old rubles	Issue in millions of pre-war rubles
1917	10.99	3,739.01	16.32	2,432.58
1918	27.31	1,315.64	23.95	535.26
1919	61.26	373.57	163.75	222.89
1920	225.02	92.98	943.58	122.01
1921	1,168.60	69.56	16,370.84	149.00

[a]By old rubles, the statistics mean the current value in the years from 1917 to 1921, before the 1921 monetary reform. By pre-war, 1913 is meant.
Source: *Sbornik statisticheskikh svedenii po Soiuzu SSR*, vol. 18, 1918–23, Moscow, 1924, p. 316

view). In 1918 efforts to control money circulation were made, though they ended in failure. At the end of that year, financing the war became a priority. Between September 1918 and May 1919 several decrees allowed local divisions of the State Bank to issue banknotes within certain limits and authorized the State Bank itself to issue as much money as was needed by the economy.[66] The plans for obligatory deposits by private people and institutions at the National Bank were not carried out.[67] The measures which Larin had proposed at the plenary session of VSNKh in April 1918 were adopted in August 1918. *Sovnarkom* approved the decree on accounting operations, which introduced the system of clearing balances within the state sector,[68] when VSNKh started implementing the 28 June decree on nationalization of large-scale industry, thereby necessitating greater state expenditure for financing industry. This measure, of course, had nothing to do with abolition of money as such. The realization of mutual transactions without the intermediary of money tokens was supposed to control money circulation. This system was extended to all institutions receiving their funds from the state during 1919–21. Money hunger tended to increase, together with the fall of the purchasing power of the ruble and increasing scarcity. Whether or not the system of clearing balances was helpful in reducing money circulation in production, there still remained the problem of money circulation in the consumer sector.

The Second Congress of *Sovnarkhozy* agreed that abolition of money was the final goal of socialist society, but – apart from the homage to principles – the economic experts recognized that, so long as adequate funds of foodstuffs and consumer goods had not yet been formed, complete naturalization of wages was impossible. While the economic experts thus implicitly admitted that money issue was a forced tax falling also on factory workers, *The ABC of Communism* attempted a rationalization of this policy consistent with ideology. Bukharin and Preobrazhenskii recognized that inflation had fiscal properties, but considered only its consequences in terms of class principles. They affirmed that inflation was a form of forced expropriation of the wealthy classes and a good substitute for taxation, helping the 'proletarian state to cope with the exceedingly difficult conditions now prevailing'. Their theoretical argument which was used to explain the continuing existence of money in the transitional phase between capitalism and communism was the exclusion of the agricultural sector and of small industry and trade from socialization:

Let us suppose that the resistance of the bourgeoisie has been overcome, and that those who formerly constituted the ruling class have now become workers. But the peasants still remain. They do not work for the general account of society. Every peasant will endeavour to sell his product to the State, to exchange it for the industrial products he sees for his own use. The peasant will remain a producer of commodities. That he may settle accounts with his neighbours and with the State, he will still need money; just as the State will need money in order to settle accounts with those members of society who have not yet become members of the general productive commune.[69]

Bukharin and Preobrazhenskii added that as long as Soviet power did not substitute a socialist system of distribution for private trade, money could not be abolished. The two economists showed themselves to be perfectly aware that the existence of money allowed 'freedom' of consumption;[70] but they did not seem to realize the importance of money even for supply at the industrial level. The experience of war communism shows that money issue continued at a high speed and that money transactions never ceased, in spite of the high degree of naturalization of the economy, not only because a national fund of consumer goods was not formed and state distribution of rations was not sufficient to feed the towns, but also because a centrally directed system of supply of raw materials and fuel was not achieved. While barter spontaneously took place among people on the black market, as a normal reaction to galloping inflation and scarcity, cash payments were still concluded between enterprises and institutions. The state institutions, which were supposed to make use of cheques rather than money tokens, did not apply the system of compensatory book-keeping (*putem oborotnykh bukhgalterskikh perechislenii*)

Table 4.4. *Budgetary revenue as proportion of expenditure, 1918–20*

| | Revenue as % of expenditure | | |
	Plan (budget)	Fulfilment	Revenue as % of 'true' expenditure[a]
Jan.–June 1918	16.2	15.3	5.2
July–Dec. 1918	9.5[b]	21.9	12.3
Jan.–June 1919	40.1	16.9	5.4
July–Dec. 1919	17.3	14.8	3.9
1920	13.1	—	—

[a]'True' expenditure = revenue fulfilment + currency issue. According to Davies, it is likely that the second column over-estimates the ratio of revenue to expenditure, and the third column under-estimates it, in view of the fact that not all revenue passed to the centre.
[b]The planned receipts from the Extraordinary Revolutionary Tax are excluded (since they were collected later). If they were included this figure would rise to 43.9.
Source: R.W. Davies, *Development of the Soviet Budgetary System*, Cambridge, 1958, p. 31.

systematically.[71] In 1919, direct (*priamy*)* expenditure amounted to 89 per cent of the total budget, while 'circular' (*oborotny*)[†] expenditure, which covered the clearing balances among departments, was only 11 per cent.[72] In June 1920, *Narkomfin* asserted that it was not possible to determine precisely how much of the state budget was involved in the system of compensatory (non-monetary) accounts, since there were not sufficient data. A guess was made that not more than one-half of the State Budget and not less than one-third of the expenditure were covered by non-monetary accounts.[73] 'Circular' non-monetary income was estimated at 8,750 million rubles, about 60 per cent of which came from supply of foodstuffs, that is, from the peasantry's obligatory delivery by quotas of agricultural products.[74] The estimated State Budget deficit increased from two-thirds of total expenditure in 1918 to more than four-fifths of it in 1920.[75] But current figures underestimated actual expenditure, which R.W. Davies has calculated taking into account also currency issue (see Table 4.4).

Priamye figures showed the effective budget revenue and expenditure.
† *Oborotnye* figures of the budget did not reflect real budgetary revenue and expenditure, but were only used to compute the movement of material values within the state economy, realized without any effective disbursement.

| | million rubles | | | % of total | | |
Revenue	1918	1919	1920	1918	1919	1920
Total revenue	15,580	48,959	159,604	100.0	100.0	100.0
1 Revenue from state enterprises, properties, land and forests	3,636	40,591	155,655	23.3	82.9	97.5
Including:						
industry	151	16,397	56,868	1.0	33.5	35.6
supply	—	18,105	51,104	—	37.0	32.0
transport and communications	1,952	3,175	22,522	12.5	6.5	14.1
forestry income	204	355	9,301	1.3	0.7	5.8
agriculture	2	697	8,175	0.01	1.4	5.1
foreign trade	—	—	4,800	—	—	3.0
obrok-type charges[a]	44	839	2,872	0.3	1.7	1.8
state sugar-processing	1,116	513	10	7.2	1.0	—
state alcohol-processing	150	260	3	1.0	0.5	—
2 Taxes, duties, excise	11,834	7,165	426	76.0	14.6	0.3
Including:						
extraordinary revolutionary tax	10,000	611	20	64.2	1.2	—
other direct taxes	735	1,972	1	4.7	4.0	—
excise and other duties	674	4,333	329	5.0	8.9	0.2
customs income	130	19	27	0.8	0.04	0.02
charges	296	230	49	1.9	0.5	0.03
3 Various revenues	110	1,203	3,523	0.7	2.5	2.2
Including:						
repayment of loans, etc.	53	393	2,811	0.3	0.8	1.8
Estimated deficit	31,126	166,443	1,055,555			
As a percentage of total expenditure	66.6	77.3	86.9			

[a] Charges for use of land and other natural resources, traditionally derived from peasant quit-rent, which comprised a substantial part of land rent in some areas, including the Ukraine, restored to Soviet rule in 1919.

Source: V.P. D'iachenko, *Sovetskie finansy v pervoi faze razvitiia sotsialisticheskogo gosudarstva*, Moscow, 1947, pp. 156–7.

Table 4.5. (*Contd.*)

Expenditure	million rubles			% of total		
	1918	1919	1920	1918	1919	1920
Total expenditure	46,706	215,402	1,215,159	100.0	100.0	100.0
1 Economic commissariats and institutions	22,239	111,941	725,166	47.6	52.0	59.7
Including:						
VSNKh	7,370	53,121	368,212	15.8	24.7	30.2
NK food	4,515	33,322	175,154	9.7	15.5	14.4
NK railways	8,743	19,018	90,543	18.7	8.8	7.5
NK post and telegraph	858	2,290	16,095	1.8	1.1	1.3
NK agriculture	641	3,109	63,011	1.4	1.4	5.2
2 Social-cultural NKs	6,236	42,807	269,716	13.4	19.9	22.2
Including:						
NK education	3,011	17,244	114,366	6.4	8.0	9.4
NK labour and social security	2,860	14,767	75,328	6.2	6.9	6.2
NK health	365	10,796	80,022	0.8	5.0	6.6
3 NKs and institutions for defence	15,267	41,340	137,842	32.7	19.2	11.4
4 Legislation, administration, courts and control	1,412	10,547	68,290	3.0	4.9	5.6
Including:						
NK internal affairs and Cheka	607	6,406	44,410	1.3	3.0	3.7
NK justice	345	919	5,450	0.7	0.4	0.4

State control – workers and						
peasants inspection	88	533	3,444	0.2	0.2	0.3
Central statistical administration	49	322	3,722	0.1	0.1	0.3
NK finance	254	1,711	8,621	0.5	0.8	0.7
5 Other expenditure	1,552	8,767	14,145	3.3	4.0	1.1
Including:						
Subsidies to local soviets						
and republics	625	1,276	2,500	1.3	0.5	0.2
Debt liquidation	402	125	25	0.9	0.1	—
Exchange of local money issue	—	—	500	—	—	0.04
For liberated areas	—	5,540	11,120	—	2.5	0.9
Payments to Germany	325	—	—	0.7	—	—
Interest on debts	—	1,626	—	—	0.8	—
Above-estimate expenditure	200	200	—	0.4	0.1	—

Table 4.6. *Rate of issue as a percentage of the monetary mass on the first of each month*

Month	1919	1920	1921
January	6.8	15.7	11.1
February	5.8	12.6	14.6
March	8.4	16.2	13.3
April	7.8	13.8	13.7
May	14.1	16.2	10.7
June	9.2[a]	13.6	
July	11.2	13.5	
August	12.3	12.2	
September	17.4	14.4	
October	14.8	15.8	
November	13.1	15.4	
December	16.9	17.4	

[a] In spring 1919, the printing press was not able to supply all the paper money needed by the state and the economy. Krestinskii, the head of the financial department, affirmed that at that time an acute financial crisis was experienced.[76]
Source: Atlas, p. 92

During 1918–20 four half-yearly and one yearly (in 1920) budgets were produced. Although the figures are not quite reliable, from their composition one may see the structural changes taking place in relation to the progressive 'stateization' of the economy (see Table 4.5).

The printing press worked ceaselessly. Money issue increased each month (see Table 4.6).

The apex of the monetary crisis was reached when steps had already been taken towards a new economic policy (see Table 4.7).

In July 1921, the real value of the paper money issued by the Treasury was three million rubles. This sum did not even cover the production costs of money tokens.[77]

One of the reasons for the overall nationalization of industry in November 1920 was the attempt to extend the system of non-monetary accounts to the sphere of small-scale and *kustar'* industry, which had been working under war communism on the system of cash payments. A decree of *Sovnarkom* in July 1920 did, in fact, extend the rules of non-monetary payments to contracts negotiated with private institutions.[78] However, law did not change habits and the motivations behind them. Although

Table 4.7. *Currency circulation, 1920–21 (million rubles)*[a]

Year and quarter	Currency circulation on first day of quarter (1)	Quarterly issue as % of currency circulation on first day of quarter (2)	Real value of (1) (gold rubles) = (1)/(5) (3)	Real value of new issue (Treasury index no.) (4)	Price index on first day of quarter (1913 = 1) (5)
1920 1st	225,015	51.4	93 ⎫	10	2,420
2nd	340,662	50.2	71 ⎬		4,470
3rd	511,816	45.6	63 ⎭	10	8,140
4th	745,158	56.8	77 ⎫		9,620
1921 1st	1,168,597	44.3	70 ⎬	6	16,800
2nd	1,686,684	39.2	47 ⎭		35,700
3rd	2,347,164	—	29	—	80,700

[a]Figures for real value of currency in circulation and the price index for 1921 given by different sources show some variation.
Source: Davies, p. 31

monetary transactions with private intermediaries were forbidden to state enterprises and institutions, they did take place in practice. Most of the money issue ended up in the pockets of private intermediaries.[79] The volume of money issued during war communism was evidence of the state's dependence on the remnants of the market economy, which played a not minor role in production and distribution, in spite of the efforts to centralize both.

Two factors have been singled out to characterize the policy and ideology of Soviet power in the field of monetary circulation between 1919 and 1920. Firstly, the unlimited increase, in relation to the effective requirements of the national economy, in the issue of money. Secondly, the lack of any measures aimed at fighting the harmful consequences of inflation. These two features have been emphasized to show that Soviet power was carrying out a regular process of money depreciation to achieve the aim of abolishing money.[80] *The ABC of Communism* asserted, indeed, that 'The gradual disappearance of money will likewise be promoted by the extensive issue of paper money by the State, in association with the great restriction in exchange of commodities dependent upon the disorganization of industry.'[81] It could also be noted that it was not only the Bolsheviks who had a positive assessment of the extension of the naturalization of the economy. In April 1920 the Party Programme of the Left Socialist—Revolutionaries, for example, supported 'the, widespread diffusion of non-monetary accounts through exchange of industrial goods against agricultural products carried out by cooperatives of consumers, and wage naturalization by the gradual conversion of monetary notes into savings-books, cheques, etc., giving all people the right to get consumer goods on the principle of egalitarian collectivism'.[82]

There are, however, reasonable doubts that the rationale of the monetary policy was, in fact, abolition of money. One may wonder whether, instead, the need to rationalize in communist terms the financial disorganization, which war made it impossible to cope with, had adversely affected the impartial evaluation of economic phenomena and had consequently deprived the authorities of the capacity to devise and implement alternative methods of control. Krestinskii, one of the Commissars of Finance, said later that, since the Brest–Litovsk peace, 'we thought that, after all, the period had begun in which monetary tokens would become unnecessary and it would be possible to get rid of them without any damage to the economy. From such a perspective originated our easy attitude towards money issue and our lack of concern to increase the value of the ruble'.[83] While Krestinskii offers an explanation for the Bolshevik superficial or dismissive approach to money, the reason *for* money issue must be looked for in the failure of their attempts to control production and distribution centrally, after the decision not to use market indicators. In other words, money issue was not aimed at reaching the point when the annihilation of the purchasing power of the rubles hoarded by the 'wealthy' would automatically ensure full control of the economy, but the other way round: the issue was needed to purchase goods and services which still remained outside government control in spite of its efforts. It was simply used to finance government expenditure, just as in so many other countries.

The quantity of money to be printed was in no way planned. The actual amount issued depended on the requests of individual departments, which produced their financial estimates taking into account market prices. This occurred in spite of the intentions of the central organs to enforce fixed prices. In these circumstances, it was *Narkomfin* itself which advised enterprises to assume a realistic attitude when they elaborated their financial estimates. In fact, though VSNKh's instruction to enterprises was to produce their estimates on the basis of centrally fixed prices, when these had been approved, and to refer to market prices only if fixed prices had not yet been determined, *Narkomfin* did take market prices into account. *Narkomfin*'s comment on VSNKh's instruction was that it was absurd, since 'it was no secret that not much could be bought at VSNKh prices'. Enterprises were, thus, invited to give their estimates as an average between free and fixed prices, considering these as upper and lower limits.[84]

The section of money and accounting of notes at *Narkomfin* worked as a *glavk*. It received orders from other institutions and, within the limit of the total monetary mass, it partially satisfied their requirements.[85] Printed money was never sufficient to satisfy the demand. In 1919 none of the People's Commissariats obtained the funds it demanded.[86] As one can see from the following table (Table 4.8), fulfilment fell far short of each Commissariat's estimates. Even the Commissariat of War was allocated only 37 per cent of its estimated expenditure.

From this point of view it would be hard to maintain that the money issued was abundant compared with demand. Figures show that demand was higher then actual expenditure, since a very large percentage of total allocations (67 per cent for the first half of 1919 and 72 per cent for the second half) remained unused. This could be the result of several factors, such as inflationary expectations inflating demand, precautionary reserves, shortage of goods or, as in the case of *Narkomprod* (which was assigned an insignificant sum as compared both with estimated requirements and with total allocations: the lowest one in absolute figures) the explicit option for a policy of expropriation of agricultural goods. One

Table 4.8. *Fulfilment of the State Budget for 1919*

	Estimate		million rubles Fulfilment		% Fulfilment	
	Jan.–June	July–Dec.	Jan.–June	July–Dec.	Jan.–June	July–Dec.
REVENUE						
Total revenue	20,350	28,610	2,266	4,038	11.1	14.1
1 From state enterprises and properties	15,600	24,991	596	992	3.8	4.0
Including:						
industry	6,256	10,140	46	253	0.7	2.5
transport and communications	1,257	1,920	146	562	11.6	29.3
forestry income	164	191	98	261	59.8	136.6
sugar	493	20	268	125	54.4	625.0
supply	6,500	11,605	—	42	—	0.3
2 Taxes, duties, excise	4,402	2,763	947	978	21.5	35.4
Including:						

extraordinary revolutionary tax	100	511	613	447	613.0	87.4
other direct taxes	1,632	340	88	58	5.4	17.1
sales taxes	2,555	1,776	191	341	7.5	19.2
charges	98	132	54	128	55.1	97.0
3 Other revenue	348	856	723	2,068	207.8	241.6
Including:						
repayment of loans, etc.	66	327	441	1,303	668.1	398.5
impost on enterprises for the non-mobilized	200	10	7	2	3.5	20.0
fines and other monetary penalties	59	50	3	10	5.1	20.0
various small and occasional revenues	19	460	271	748	1,426.3	162.6

[a]The January–June budget of 1919 was adopted only on 21 May 1919. The July–December 1919 budget was adopted, only formally, on 11 August 1921 (see Davies, p. 36).

Source: V.P. Diachenko, *Sovetskie finansy,* pp. 186–7, 188–9

Table 4.8. (*Contd.*)

	Estimate		Fulfilment		% Fulfilment	
EXPENDITURE						
Total expenditure	50,703	164,699	40,879	98,138	80.6	59.6
1 Economic NKs and institutions	26,177	85,093	4,140	6,071	15.8	7.1
Including:						
VSNKh and NK trade and industry	11,044	42,077	529	1,359	4.8	3.2
NKs: railways, water transport, post and telegraph	6,252	15,056	2,960	3,740	47.3	24.8
NK food	8,153	25,169	193	205	2.4	1.4
NK agriculture	526	2,583	430	680	81.7	26.3
2 Social–cultural NKs	7,456	35,351	2,553	6,735	34.2	19.1
Including:						
NK education	3,920	13,324	1,622	2,567	41.4	19.3
NK health	1,301	9,495	463	1,669	35.6	17.6
NK labour and social security	2,235	12,532	468	2,499	20.9	19.9
3 NKs defence	12,239	31,171	5,122	10,740	41.8	34.5
Including:						
NK war	11,718	26,368	4,536	9,573	38.7	36.3
NK fleet	521	1,803	586	1,167	112.5	64.7
4 Legislation, administration, courts and control	2,336	7,384	1,055	2,405	45.2	32.6
Including:						
NK internal affairs and Cheka	1,420	5,871	742	1,984	52.2	33.8
5 NK finance	467	3,159	364	710	77.9	22.5
6 Other expenditure	2,028	2,541	149	587	7.3	23.1
7 Unused credits on central expenditure account (People's Bank)	—	—	27,496	70,890	—	—

Table 4.9. *Percentage price increases in Moscow (1914–21)*

Annual average	1914–15	1915–16	1916–17	1917–18	1918–19	1919–20	1920–21
Consumer goods	31.8	53.4	118.0	2,122.4	1,221.4	1,461.0	579.0
Foodstuffs	33.2	53.0	176.2	3,299.1	1,564.8	1,312.1	668.7
Non-food goods	30.2	54.0	61.0	946.0	879.0	1,608.0	490.0
% average increase of money in circulation	130.0	77.2	94.6	236.0	132.0	410.0	362.0

Source: S.A. Pervushin, 'Vol'nye tseny i pokupatel'naia sila russkogo rublia v gody revoliutsiid (1917–1921)', *Denezhnoe obrashchenie i kredit*, vol. 1, Petrograd, 1922, p. 82

of the heads of the Commissariat of Finance affirmed at the beginning of 1920 that non-monetary balances had to be enforced, in spite of efforts of 'renegades' to avoid the law, because 'we have to consider that the printing press is not going to have the time to print what is needed'.[87] Furthermore, money issue was a quite expensive business and a hardly appropriate one to be used to attain the aims proclaimed by ideology. Between January 1920 and January 1921, the year in which Trotskii formulated the proposal of militarization of labour as a way of filling the growing number of vacancies, the number of people employed by the printing press increased from 11,260 to 13,616. Gold, on which the leadership had relied to carry out international purchases, was used to buy the dyes necessary for printing money.[88]

Another reason for questioning the validity of the alleged rationale of Soviet monetary policy is the relationship between money issue and the rate of price increases. The rate of issue always lagged behind the rate of money depreciation. This fact may suggest that the printing press was not used to lead the economy into galloping price inflation and so to a natural economy, but that, all things considered, price increases were determined in the first place by the fall in production, and in the second place by the high velocity of circulation of money, induced by inflation itself.

The data provided by Pervushin on price increases in Moscow, for which the time interval between issuing paper money and getting it into circulation was presumably the minimum (as compared with the provinces), indicate that a direct and exclusive relationship between money emission and price increases cannot be ascertained between 1917 and 1921.[89]

The comparison between prices of foodstuffs and prices of other consumer goods between 1919 and 1921, which shows a relatively higher increase of industrial prices between 1919 and 1920 and a relatively lower increase between 1920 and 1921 may, instead, suggest a relationship between prices and productivity. However, the use of a single price index to extend this conclusion to the whole of Russia would not be useful, since prices diverged consistently over the country and money issued did not reach different regions at the same time and regularly. A detailed study of the relationships between the dispatch of money to a locality and price increases in several regions[90] allows us, however, to extend Pervushin's conclusions to the rest of the territory under Bolshevik rule. Prices increased most in the regions, like Moscow, Petrograd, Ivanovo-Voznesensk, where there was a record decrease in the availability of the chief bread grains and livestock. The lowest price increases occurred in Penza, Saratov, Perm and Sverdlovsk, whose markets, in spite of the heavy losses due to war and revolution, were relatively better supplied. Yaroslavl, Kostroma, Smolensk, Vitebsk and Tver lie between these two extremes.[91] Regional price variations may be imputed to natural conditions and events related to civil war. Isolated moments of respite from war produced greater price uniformity, while prices rose significantly in consuming regions, like Petrograd, when they happened to be cut off from producing provinces. When the end of civil war made it easier to restore trade between regions, a general price increase was even registered in regions where price levels had previously been lower.[92] Observation of the relative price increase and the relative increase in the monetary mass for twelve regions shows that the two magnitudes may have influenced each other reciprocally at times. But the total average of the ratios between July 1919 and January 1921 precludes any conclusion about the positive impact of the monetary mass on price levels.[93]

Regardless of the rationalizations adduced in 1920 in favour of the ideological content of the monetary policy, the fact was that the Soviet government had to resort to money issue to finance war, and cover the budget deficit, as Krestinskii said at the Ninth Congress of Soviets.[94] Money depreciation particularly affected towns and provincial budgets and real wages. A report on the budgets of thirteen town councils revealed that town revenues at the beginning of 1920 were no higher than 0.2–6.0 per cent of total expenditure.[95] Before deciding to make public facilities free of charge, the government allowed the provinces to raise public charges. The municipalities tried also to increase local taxes. But taxation could not provide enough. National and municipal undertakings were exempted from taxation, and levies could not exceed a certain percentage of taxable income. In 1919 the local authorities charged levies amounting to 1,501 million rubles, of which they collected only 53.4 per cent. In 1920, levies were increased to about 3,000 million rubles, of which only 60 per cent was collected.[96] At the end of 1919 the Petrograd Council increased the local rates for transport, energy and gas by 80–100 per cent.[97]

The strict centralization of financial policy was the major hindrance to local soviets in disposing of local budgets. Central funds were turned over to municipalities casually and without a predetermined plan. In practice, local finance, in spite of *Narkomfin*'s claims for strict centralization, i.e. unification of state and local finance, continued to play an important role until 18 July 1920, when the principle of unification of the State Budget was adopted.[98] Scarcity of funds increased competition also among departments. In February 1920 a commission formed by the representatives of the economic commissariats proposed that, owing to scarcity of funds, other departments and local organs should not be financed at all, or should be financed indirectly from the financial surplus of the 'shock' departments, that is the departments of war, food procurement, communications, and VSNKh. A quarrel developed between *Narkomfin* and the other commissariats on the percentage of funds which *Narkomfin* ought to be left free to dispose of. *Narkomfin* proposed letting the commission dispose of 60 per cent of the funds, while the 'shock' commissariats claimed 75 per cent.[99] VSNKh demanded control over the financing of local industry. *Narkomfin* argued that the responsibility for distributing and controlling local funds ought to be devolved to the People's Commissariat for Internal Affairs[100] (which indicates the impact that civil war had on financial decisions). In June 1920 the Central Executive Committee opted for strict centralization. *Narkomfin* was confirmed as the only institution responsible for distribution of money, while the commission was allowed to survive as a consultative body. Iron-clad funds were limited to special cases; though the fact that they were not abolished may be interpreted as an acknowledgement that some departments still needed some financial autonomy.[101] The more rapid the fall of the purchasing power of the ruble, the stricter became central control over available money. In this context, solutions to reduce local deficits were not even looked for. As noted above, in July 1920 the All-Russian Central Executive Committee abolished the local budgets and introduced the Single National Budget System, inclusive of all local budgets.[102]

The policy of free public services started officially on 11 October 1920, when *Sovnarkom* abolished charges for telegraph, telephone and postal services for Soviet institutions.[103] This law was followed by two decrees concerning the free delivery of products, signed by *Sovnarkom* on 4 and 17 December 1920, which were to come into force on 1 January 1921.[104] The law specifically mentioned people and categories having the right to free products.[105] The use of a priority scale indicates that the law foresaw the impossibility of satisfying all categories, and did not attempt a general system of distribution. In 1921 free postal, telegraph and radio-telegraph services were extended to everybody.[106] Charges for fodder, books, journals, newspapers, etc. were abolished.[107] The free provision of cultural services was extended to everybody in March 1921, when the change of compulsory collection (*prodrazverstka*) into the system of a tax in kind had already started the new course of economic policy, but the monetary crisis had not yet been overcome. When eventually inflation was being seriously tackled, VSNKh announced – on 11 July 1921 – that the state would give nothing free of charge.[108]

Financial disorganization and inflation also played a prominent role in the trend towards the naturalization of wages. The theses of the Seventh Congress of the Party on Soviet power mentioned the aim of 'progressive equalization of wages and remuneration for all trades and categories', but not naturalization of wages. As already indicated, wage differentials increased during war communism, in spite of original intentions. From June 1918 until October 1920 several decrees were issued modifying the system of grades and categories as well as the wage rates.[109] In June 1918 the ratio between the highest and the lowest category was 3.4 : 1 (in rubles per month: 1,200 : 350). In February 1919 it increased to 5 : 1 (3,000 : 600 rubles). In April 1919 a ratio of 3.6 : 1 applied between the highest and the lowest of twenty-seven categories (excluding specialists). Taking into account, however, that specialists assigned to special duties could claim a 50 per cent increase on their basic earnings, the differential was 7.5 : 1. In September 1919 new regulations applying to thirty-five categories – but excluding specialists (who might have enjoyed special treatment) – brought the ratio up to 4 : 1 (4,800 : 1,200 rubles). In June 1920, a bonus system granting wage increases up to 200 per cent of the basic earnings, and the piece-work wages system, were intended to raise wage differentials even more. The question of wages in kind developed in parallel with the erosion of real wages caused by inflation. Isolated cases of remuneration in kind started as early as 1917.[110] By the end of 1918 the Metal Workers' Union was demanding partial or full wages in kind linked to productivity and skill.[111] In the Summer of 1919 the central committee of the Metal Workers' Union started negotiations with *Narkomprod* for the right to undertake commodity exchange with the countryside on the basis of a given percentage of output, as a partial naturalization of wages. Until 1920, naturalization of wages proceeded spontaneously and without a plan.[112]

The Second Congress of *Sovnarkhozy* had debated in December 1918 the question of wages in kind. It had resolved to state only some broad principles in this matter, rather than try to devise ways to implement a general policy of wage naturalization. Point 7 of Miliutin's resolution mentioned: 'the assignment of products and goods necessary to life, rather than monetary wages (or part of monetary wages) to industrial workers and workers of the communes and state farms, in view of the necessary transition to naturalization of wages'. However, concrete measures were deferred to the future, because of theoretical as well as practical impediments. The economists admitted that they were not able to evaluate goods by any monetary unit. Moreover, in the absence of a clear definition of the content of wages, it was acknowledged that naturalization would have caused confusion at the provincial level, when the question would have arisen as to which sort of commodities should be used and which methods adopted.[113]

A year later the president of *Glavtekstil'*, Nogin, acknowledged that the attempt to naturalize wages in the current economic situation had turned out to be a failure, owing to scarcity of commodities.[114] But great pressures for naturalization came from labour. Representatives of labour did not discuss the matter from the point of view of principles, but as a concrete issue to defend real wages. A conference of labour representatives on 9 October 1919 demanded the formation of a supply fund attached to the Wage Rates Bureau, supplied by contributions from the state and individual entrepreneurs to the tune of one thousand rubles per worker. This fund was supposed to finance direct purchase of goods by the trade unions, without going through central organization.[115] State advances, however, amounted to only 50 million rubles, a derisory sum to start any large-scale policy of wage naturalization.

When the practice of paying wages in kind was extended to several works in Moscow, the Moscow Soviet approved it formally in February 1920.[116] This initiative was a serious hindrance to central control over product distribution. On 2 March 1920 a special decree, inspired by VSNKh, prohibited enterprises and other institutions delivering to working people output above the general norm of consumption. The reason given for this interdiction was that such a practice jeopardized the overall pattern of supply and strengthened speculation.[117] The agreements that several departments and institutions had concluded with *Narmomprod*, allowing direct distribution of products in kind to their own workers, were declared illegal by *Sovnarkom* in mid 1920.[118] The practice of reward in kind had led to a widespread differentiation of real wages, outside central control, and without any relation to labour productivity.

The central decision to apply rewards in kind to those categories of

Table 4.10. *Razverstka and paper money issue*

	1918–19	1919–20	1920–21	1921–22
Razverstka in millions of gold rubles	127	253	480	244
Emission in millions of gold rubles	523	390	186	—
Total	650	643	668	244

Source: E. Preobrazhenskii, *Voprosy finansovoi politiki*, 1921, p. 6

work defined as 'shock work' because of their importance was aimed at linking remuneration to labour productivity. The decision to naturalize premiums applying to 'shock workers' was the consequence of scarcity of foodstuffs and other consumer goods. In addition to monetary wages, workers were assigned different and variable daily rations of foodstuffs.[119] The rations of the metal workers of a small town near Petrograd evaluated at market prices amounted to 13,000–15,000 rubles per month,[120] which was three or four times the highest level of monetary pay.

The way in which naturalization of wages developed and was used shows that it was a matter of expediency and became a means of adopting wage differentiation, in spite of the declarations of principle on wage levelling which inspired the first programmes of the Bolsheviks. Even in this field, war and extreme scarcity, rather than plans or goals, determined economic choices.

Learning by doing, however, determined subsequent choices and became confused with vague ideological goals.

By 1920 the considerable extent of centralization of distribution, the extensive spread of wages and premiums in kind, the application of *prodrazverstka* to an increasing number of products,[121] aroused hopes that the market economy was definitely perishing and preparing the way for communist society. In summer, financing was totally centralized. The most important items of local public expenditure were put on the State Budget.[122] Most of the budget income came from *razverstka* (obligatory delivery by quota). Preobrazhenskii calculated the following proportions between *razverstka* expressed in pre-war prices (gold rubles) and the gold equivalent of the paper money issue.

Preobrazhenskii concluded that if *razverstka* were fully realized in 1920 only 50–60 million gold rubles would be required to buy *kustar'* (handicraft) and other marketable products, and affirmed that the time for abolishing paper money was near.[123]

The belief that the age of money was over and that other methods had to be worked out for economic policy dictated the path taken by theoretical studies and economic measures during 1920 and 1921. Although by April 1920 the civil war was practically won and a programme of reconstruction of the country had started, there were no signs of the possibility of a return to orthodox financial policy aimed at restoring the value of the ruble. At the theoretical level, the economists worked on the project of substituting the *trudovaia edinitsa* (*tred*), a labour unit of account, for the ruble. In the economic field, steps were taken to construct a systematic framework which would include wages in kind.

4.2 PRICE AND VALUE: THEORY AND PRACTICE

The concentration of efforts around the problem of an alternative unit of value conditioned financial policy and favoured the continuation of forms of natural economy until and after the introduction of the new economic policy in the spring of 1921.

Forms of commodity exchange had been taking place since the October Revolution and had been determined, as has been shown, by necessity and by local initiative. Larin anticipated at the VSNKh plenary session in April 1918 that commodity exchange would be promoted by the economic organs and expanded to achieve the total disappearance of money.[124] Miliutin's theses approved by the First Congress of *Sovnarkhozy* confirmed the objective of centralization and concentration of the whole commodity apparatus in the hands of state and cooperative organizations, and the intention of arriving at the gradual liquidation of private trade. It was believed that the system of monopoly of foodstuffs and other consumer necessities would make it possible to establish natural exchange. For the time being, it was decided to keep fixed prices on all goods of prime necessity. The problem of price determination in the future was simplistically reduced to one of gradually increasing prices and maintaining proportions between them. Only Groman, at the congress, seemed aware that the problem of price determination in the absence of market relations was not an easy one. The alternatives, he argued, were two: either to adapt to the existing situation, fix a ceiling on money issue and collect money through indirect taxation, or let the issue of money expand until it was abolished, and fix prices. But, in this case, Groman asked, how do we fix prices?[125] The Bolshevik economic experts had no precise ideas about alternative laws of value.

To the extent that the economic situation urged some forms of price control on basic raw materials and foods, expediency could be said to have played a role. There was, however, from the beginning of Bolshevik price policy, a basic principle for price determination: to keep the level of industrial prices above the level of agricultural prices. This principle inspired both price policy and economic research. In the autumn of 1918, Rykov reported at a plenary session of VSNKh that industrial prices had been set by taking into account, not so much the utility of goods, as the organization of commodity exchange and the aim of alleviating the food procurement crisis. Prices were determined on the basis of the pre-war relation between one pud of grain and every other single product, with some corrections reflecting changes in the value of industrial products in relation to agricultural products. The coefficient of price inflation for industrial products was set higher than the coefficient for agricultural products and raw materials. Rykov cited the example of flax: the coefficient of price inflation for flax was taken as equal to 12, while the coefficient of price inflation for other industrial products was made equal to 20. The economic reason adduced was that the value of industrial products had increased more than the value of agricultural products.[126]

In reality, Rykov had no evidence to claim that the value of industrial products had become higher than that of other products. Pervushin's data on price increases in Moscow in 1917–18 and 1918–19 show, on the contrary, that the percentage price increase of agricultural staples was much higher in both years than the percentage price increase of industrial consumer goods.[127]

In revising prices, the price committee probably followed the same criteria as those adopted between March and September 1917, when fixed prices on industrial products were increased much more than fixed prices on agricultural products, though, even in the producing provinces, agricultural market prices rose significantly more than industrial market prices.[128] Military production orders benefited industry comparatively more than agriculture. After the Brest–Litovsk Treaty, however, price revision should not have been guided by the criteria of a war economy or, at least, not only by such criteria, since by then the Bolsheviks were undertaking a programme of reorganization for a peace economy.

The price committee not only applied arbitrary criteria of price determination, as compared with market values; it did not even take into account the change of price ratios within the industrial sector itself. The work of the price committee seems to have been inspired by the criterion which Smirnov presented in *Kommunist* in June 1918; i.e. it aimed to extract money from the countryside by depressing agricultural prices with respect to industrial prices.[129] This criterion, which, of course, had nothing to do with relative production costs in both sectors, was elaborated further by Fal'kner at the beginning of 1919.[130]

Fal'kner took it for granted that price ratios within the state industrial sector could be changed only in accordance with changes in wage rates. The major problem, according to him, was the determination of a correct price ratio between industrial and agricultural products. Internal price ratios could be derived by taking as the unit the price of one industrial commodity, say fabrics, based on production costs, and rye in agriculture. Fal'kner maintained that the price system should aim at neutralizing the self-subsistence tendency of the countryside. If the countryside were to be forced to give up its stocks of hoarded money, the coefficient of price increase of industrial products had to be set higher, Fal'kner argued, than the corresponding coefficient for agricultural products. For otherwise this monetary mass would reinforce the decentralization of private economy and destroy the controlled market, by shifting higher quantities of goods on to the illegal market. Fal'kner did not see that the policy he suggested contained an implicit contradiction. How could the countryside be forced to pay higher prices for goods, the surrogates for which could be obtained at lower costs? Fal'kner assumed that scarcity relations justified new price ratios favourable to industry. He stated, indeed, that this policy would correspond not only to political necessity, but to the law of economic proportionality. But his argument concerned only the supply side at the macroeconomic level, neglecting the demand side. If supply of industrial goods had shrunk more than supply of agricultural goods, it was also likely that demand for industrial goods had fallen, while demand for agricultural goods increased, not only from the army and town populations, but also from the countryside, where redistribution of property was improving the living conditions of the peasantry.

To restore economic proportionality between industrial and agricultural products, Fal'kner proposed to determine: firstly, the monetary mass in circulation; secondly, the quantity of commodities; thirdly, the (industrial) commodity surplus; and fourthly, the agricultural surplus available for exchange. To solve the first problem, Fal'kner proposed using a sample population of a given district, room being left for errors due to higher money circulation in towns as compared with provinces, where money arrived later. The second problem was to be solved by adding together town and countryside surpluses, computing the norm of reduction of commodity stocks in relation to pre-war data on productivity, and comparing it with consumers' budgets spent on commodity purchase. Commodity surplus was obtained by computing consumption of own output first; then decrease in output, from which the coefficient of price increase was derived, and finally demand in the countryside. Calculation of agricultural surplus should take into account normal harvests and marketed proportions.

Fal'kner's procedure was complicated and hardly realizable in times of civil war. From the theoretical point of view a definite obstacle to his approach was consumers' demand as independent of price-ratios, and to a certain extent, also of incomes. If demand was to be considered as the expression of 'objective' needs, which seems to have been the implicit assumption of this approach, 'objective criteria' for the computation of demand had to be sought.

Research in this direction was undertaken by Miliutin, who proposed dividing products into four groups. First, products for direct consumption; second, productive consumption; third, tools and means of production; and fourth, export products. The first step was to determine prices of consumer goods, respecting two constraints. Firstly, correct ratios between products had to be found and expressed in monetary terms. Secondly, the solution should satisfy the equilibrium of the monetary budget, for as long as money was still to be used as a means of exchange. To calculate demand, Miliutin proposed taking as a basis the average material budget of an average worker. Part of consumption would be expressed in calories, the remainder in physical units. Material budgets were to be converted into values by dividing monetary state expenditure (on wage and other purchases in the course of the year, i.e. the total money flowing back to the Treasury after distribution of products) by the entire population, to get the necessary amount of money belonging to each personal material budget. Then, product relations would be transformed into monetary relations by taking as a basis the percentage distribution of an average consumer money income among different products. Relative prices were determined by taking as a unit the yearly consumption of bread necessary to provide a norm of calories, by calculating the percentage of money income spent on it and carrying out the same calculation for other products coming into the average material budget. Prices of materials would be derived from the final goods prices, by computing their percentage proportions in the total composition of final goods. Prices of the means of production could then be determined on the basis of production costs. Only export prices should be based on world market prices, concluded Miliutin.[131]

Miliutin's model provided one of the first approaches to price determination independently of market laws. The model, however, was quite abstract. It assumed identical needs among individuals. Prices were, in reality, units of account, which guaranteed overall monetary equilibrium, by definition, but not equilibrium in the goods market.

Both Miliutin's and Fal'kner's approaches to price determination tackled the question from a static point of view. The problem, however, was not only to fix new price proportions for the time being, but to find eventually alternative indicators of value capable of internal dynamism.

Some experts seemed aware of the difficulty which this problem entailed. The system of state regulation of prices required firmly established relations between prices of consumer goods and labour prices on the one hand, and prices of raw and processed materials and production costs on the other hand. But 'even in theory', observed an expert, 'it does not seem possible to fix firmly all prices for labour, production costs, raw materials and so on, and in this way to put a stop to their increase in the subsequent period and hold them at that level'.[132]

What actually occurred was that the list of prices approved by the price committee in the first half of 1919 did not take into account production costs and was not subject to revision when the latter changed. Fixed prices were applied to 950 articles in the textile industry, 550 in the leather industry, 4,250 products in the metal industry and 1,500 products in the chemical industry. In August 1919 monetary wages were increased, taking into account some rough indexes of the cost of living based on free market prices, especially of food and heating.[133] But industrial prices were not revised.[134] Rather than modify the price list, it was preferred to approve extraordinary credits for state departments and institutions.[135] It is possible that industrial prices were no further increased because the Price Committee had started already investigating the possibility of using prices only as accounting units, rather than expressions of value. The rules established by the Price Committee for price determination in the summer of 1919 were in fact to meet the following requisites: fixing correct relations between products from the point of view of organization of distribution and state purchase as well as from the point of view of supply for production purposes; accounting of the activity of enterprises and industrial branches, reflected in the estimated costs and receipts; foreign trade; and maintenance of the state monetary budget as long as the monetary system remained.[136]

It is likely that the price policy adopted by VSNKh helped the fall in supply of some products, thus indirectly adding to inflationary pressures. Between 1917 and 1921 the area under flax cultivation shrank by 41 per cent in the central regions,[137] that is, the main regions for flax, demand for which started increasing following the loss of Turkestan, the major supplier of cotton. This was not independent of the level of the price for flax. Since February 1919, representatives of the 'flax section' had complained about a reduction in the flax cultivated area of 9–10 per cent, owing to the unfavourable relation between the prices of flax and grain.[138] Agents responsible for purchasing flax in Latvia reported that scascely any appreciable quantity could be bought there, though the harvest had been substantial, because of the low price fixed for flax. A price increase was also demanded by the wool section of *Tsentrotekstil*.[139]

Owing to such pressures, the wool price was increased in March 1919 by 60–70 per cent compared with the 1918 level.[140] Fixed prices, however, rapidly lost any meaning. In November 1919 the ratio between the fixed price of wool and the market price had already fallen to a sixth and the wool commissioners asked for a new price increase.[141]

Errors in price setting of agricultural raw materials may have affected the types of crops grown. Similar doubts had been manifested since mid 1919. It was suggested that price ratios between agricultural products ought to respect the original proportions, since otherwise peasants shifted from one product, say hemp, to another, say potatoes.[142]

By the end of 1919, however, no further efforts were made to raise prices in line with inflation. The system of *razverstka* was being extended to agricultural raw materials, which meant that coercion, rather than economic criteria, was chosen to deal with supply. Inflation and fixed prices made any budgetary financial system based on the value of the ruble impossible.

In 1920 some economic experts started working on the problem of finding a substitute for the monetary unit. The new approach had some precedents. In 1918 Shefler' proposed the elaboration of new criteria of value based on 'labour evaluation' (*otsenki truda*).[143] Shefler' gave some guidelines for defining a new price system. First, normal wages were to be consistent with a precise productivity norm and a normal level of labour still. Second, in order to define all elements adding up to the value of final products, the basic similarities of the production process ought to be singled out. Shefler' proposed subdividing production into aggregates, starting from the simplest stages and proceeding to the more complex ones, from production of raw materials to production of machinery. Each stage would contain the specifications for further processing of output. The classification of economic aggregates suggested by Shefler' was intended to provide the elements for establishing a definite proportion between labour value and price in the initial stages of production, in order to pass from 'the obsolete monetary system to a labour system, from gold currency to labour currency'.[144]

From the second half of 1919, some members of the staff of VSNKh started working out a project of transition to a labour unit as a measure of value. A special commission was formed in the spring of 1920 for this purpose.[145] The 'abolitionists' (of the monetary system) gained a certain importance at the end of 1920.

The immediate problem which attracted the abolitionists was to find a stable unit of value. The incomparability of monetary values even in the short term, owing to the excessive rate of inflation, obliged book-keepers to add several special items to the monetary budget, including forms of accounting in physical units. Length, weight and pieces were used to give some meaning to the budget. The coefficient of money depreciation could not help much, since regional price differences were large enough to make a single coefficient ambiguous and unsuitable for the purpose. Furthermore, several means of production had lost, during war communism, all market value.[146] Some economists tried to find accounting units with physical properties. There were even proposals to base money on salt or on cooperative funds.[147] Smit suggested the adoption of a *combined labour and energy unit*, obtained by computing all mechanical and thermal costs in units of energy. The use of a *combined* unit was proposed on the ground that – during the transition period to higher levels of growth – not all production branches were evenly equipped with mechanical power, and so two units of measures would be necessary: labour time and unit of consumed energy. Smit postponed to the era of overall mechanization the elaboration of a single physical accounting unit based on a constant ratio between labour time and energy spent in production. Klepikov, on the contrary, maintained that a single accounting unit based on energy could be used right away. He proposed to call this unit of energy *ened* – computed as the total energy expenditure of the complex labour and the thermo-mechanical energy necessary to obtain a given output. The value of one unit of output would then be the quantity of *ened* used for the extraction or production of one unit of output. Both economists followed the Bogdanov approach to value,[148] and were apparently unaware that the same unit of energy could produce different results in economic terms, and that 'energy' itself could be obtained by different sources and at different costs.

A more interesting attempt at devising an alternative economic model based on planning in physical units was made by Chaianov. Chaianov considered that the socialist economy was comparable to the patriarchal peasant economy, where the pater familias decides the needs, assigns the targets and distributes the proceeds. Given a target, expressed in physical units, the problem was: first, to compute the *normal* technical coefficients of production (which could be done on the basis of past records); second, to calculate the actual coefficients; third, to express these coefficients as indexes, by dividing each by the *norm*; fourth, to attribute eventually a 'weight' to each factor and then add them up to get a single coefficient characterizing the efficacity of the actual production. The tasks of the planner would be:

(1) to issue orders in terms of normative costs;
(2) to determine the *norm* of labour productivity;
(3) to give 'weights' to each factor of production.

Chaianov's approach was the closest to a model of non-monetary economy, and one of those which prepared the way to further studies on planning.[149]

Other approaches merely tried to replace the ruble as a unit of account with some unit based on labour, but without seriously tackling the problem of the allocation of resources in production and of equilibrium in distribution.

The commission formed by VSNKh suggested taking the average output of a normal day of simple labour, of an intensity normal for the given type of work, as the labour unit of account. The labour unit was called a *tred* (*trudovaia edinitsa*).[150] The aim was to establish a direct relation between the accounting unit and labour remuneration, in such a way as to obtain a means for socialist control over the quantity of labour and the quantity of consumption.[151] Strumilin put the problem in this way: 'as a unit of labour value I propose to take the value of the product of labour of a worker of the first [wage] tariff category fulfilling his output norm at 100 per cent.[152] Shmelev proposed taking as a unit of labour the normal workday of a worker of the first category of the wage structure, fulfilling his task at 100 per cent. In this approach, pre-war wages were used to find indexes which might make comparisons meaningful. The average pre-war prices were converted into *treds* by dividing them by the quantity of gold rubles corresponding to the labour unit. The value of the *tred* was the ratio between the cost of the product in gold rubles and the number of labour units of simple labour necessary to produce it. To transform complex labour into units of simple labour, Shmelev proposed compiling a standard nomenclature, based on tables giving the labour composition of each product.[153]

Strumilin proposed evaluating the social labour contained in the product of labour by selecting one product as a measure of value. The other products, representing materialized social labour, would be related to one another, through the product chosen as measure of value, and related to labour through this same product. Following this approach, socialist society would have ended up establishing values no differently from capitalist society, where the unit of measure was a single commodity, gold. The only variation would be that under socialism, state planning, rather than the market, would establish the value of the accounting unit. Strumilin stressed that the labour accounting unit did not exclude the possibility of utilizing a monetary unit for accounting operations, adding that, once the parity between the two units was determined, the current value of the labour unit would fluctuate together with the monetary unit. Strumilin concluded that the labour day could be made equivalent to the pre-war gold ruble.[154]

The efforts of the abolitionists, therefore, resulted in the creation of a new monetary unit, whatever its denomination might be. A satisfactory way to 'invent' a new measure of value was not found since, in any case, the economists had to resort to pre-war prices and relations to determine the new measure of value.

One specific aspect of the Soviet approach to price determination was the belief that prices could be manipulated in accordance with the state's aims. This attitude implied that no importance was attributed to the demand side. The assumption was, in fact, that the state would carry out distribution independently of market signals and according to objective norms. The corollary of central price determination was the concentration of supply in the hands of the state. But neither assumption was realized during war communism, in spite of efforts to concentrate monopolistic and monopsonistic powers at the centre. The state never gained control over commodity exchange. Natural price ratios developed in the different regions, subject to local conditions. Vaisberg described the underground panorama of war communism's impressive, but empty, economic organization in picturesque words:

Natural commodity-exchange did not develop spontaneously and on the basis of revolutionary laws, changing the process of paper-money circulation, but hatched out of the latter and organically grew on its senile shoulders. A new market was formed on the basis of non-monetary accounts. It dominated the countryside and started extending to relations between country and towns. From the localities, it reached the towns, particularly the *uezd* towns, bearing all sorts of products and equivalents.[155]

The debate at the Ninth Party Congress shows that most of the Bolsheviks grasped the meaning of the illegal market only in terms of speculation. Kamenev stated that only a minimal part of money went to Soviet institutions, while the greater part ended up in the pockets of speculators, and concluded that the struggle ought to be carried out against what he called *Sukharevka* capitalism, from the name of the largest illegal market in Moscow.[156]

While economists started working on a new unit of value based on labour, and some of them magnified the role of the printing press in crushing the bourgeois system,[157] market laws were currently determining the real price ratio between goods. Money was drawn out of the market thanks to commodity circulation, rather than money circulation, Vaisberg said later. Money tokens kept performing their usual function as means of exchange, on the basis of the new values determined by market exchange of commodities. When money surrogates existed, like cheques, notes, etc., they were used and were associated with specific commodities and storehouses. As the general equivalent of values, paper-money never disappeared.[158] The Bolsheviks committed the mistake of believing that the rapid depreciation of money would also entail the passage from individual commodity exchange to state product distribution. Preobrazhenskii affirmed that the increase in goods distributed by the state in place of marketable commodities was the struggle that *Narkomprod* was waging against *Sukharevka*. The breakdown of the capitalist monetary system, argued Preobrazhenskii, would occur in the period of the utilization of paper-money circulation, even before the total disappearance of marketable commodities and before the accumulation by the state of enough goods to meet the minimum wage requirements. But, he added, the breakdown of the capitalist system would coincide with the realization of the socialist society only if the latter held enough goods to allow naturalization of wages.[159] This approach was based on two assumptions, which needed more careful examination, if ideology had not produced a definite bias in their favour. Firstly, there was the belief that the Soviet system was ready to concentrate total supply and distribution in its hands and dispose efficiently of physical quantities without a price system reflecting to some extent relative scarcities and degrees of substitution between commodities. Secondly, there was the belief that state distribution would automatically entail the disappearance of market laws, for it would imply the disappearance of marketed commodities. If Soviet economists had explored more carefully what occurred in the illegal market, they would have seen not only peasants selling agricultural products, but also factory workers exchanging industrial products as well as ration cards, which carried a right to state quotas of goods. Even in the hard times of war communism, individual necessities and preferences which did not coincide with the central criteria of distribution of goods found loopholes in a model of social organization which was too abstract to reflect what millions of poor wretches preferred amongst what little was available.

'The New Economic Policy', said Vaisberg, who worked during NEP for Gosplan, 'did not fall from heaven, but grew out of the guilty soil and developed out of the "sins" of October against the capitalist system.'[160]

4.3 SUMMARY

The rapid nationalization of the banking system, which was one of the primary aims of the Bolsheviks, did not help central control over the economy, but on the contrary, was one of the causes of financial disorder. High rates of money issue and increasing inflation jeopardized the establishment of financial control, while fiscal policy – under the pressures and the constraints imposed by the revolution – could not help in restoring budget equilibrium. During war communism state expenditures were essentially financed by money issue. It does not seem true that the Bolshevik Government consciously pursued a policy of abolition of money, through high rates of depreciation. What the government desired was control of the market, not only on the side of supply – through nationalization of industry and requisition of stocks – but also by regulating demand. This was pursued through a policy of high price ratios between industrial and agricultural products, coupled with distribution of basic foodstuffs according to norms of consumption. But full control over supply and demand was never attained during war communism, while through the several loopholes of the state economy the illegal market continued to flourish.

Money continued to be used as a means of exchange and accumulation and the institutions kept registering their transactions in monetary units.

At a theoretical level, however, feverish work was undertaken to find alternative regulators of supply and distribution, based on 'objectively' determined values and norms. The problem of finding substitutes for the vanishing monetary unit was tackled by working on the only alternative which seemed compatible with a Marxist approach, that is, by trying to relate value to the only productive factor, according to the Marxian analysis, i.e. labour time. No workable conclusions could be reached during war communism. This approach to value, however, was not without its consequences for overall economic policy. It nourished, in fact, the prevailing climate of disregard for the possible use of monetary and fiscal policies, which had not a minor impact on the breakdown of the economy.

NOTES

1 G.D.H. Cole, *A History of Socialist Thought*, 5 vols., London, 1953–60, vol. 1, p. 43.
2 *Ibid*, p. 47.
3 V.I. Lenin, *Polnoe sobranie sochinenii*, 5th edn, 55 vols., Moscow, 1958–69, vol. 27, 1962, p. 426.
4 'Manifesto of the Communist Party', in K. Marx and F. Engels, *Selected Works*, London, 1958, p. 53.
5 K. Marx and F. Engels, *Collected Works*, London, 1978, vol. 10, pp. 59–60.
6 R. Hilferding, *Das Finanz Kapital, Marx Studien*, vol. 3, Vienna, 1923, pp. 472–74

7 N. Bukharin, *Imperialism and World Economy*, London, 1972, p. 70.

8 Lenin, *Polnoe sobranie sochinenii*, vol. 27, pp. 339–40; *Collected Works*, 4th edn, 45 vols., London, 1964–70, vol. 24, p. 496.

9 Bukharin, *Imperialism*, pp. 70–1, 73–4.

10 Lenin, *Polnoe sobranie sochinenii*, vol. 27, pp. 326–38.

11 V.I. Lenin, *Collected Works*, vol. 24, p. 426.

12 *Ibid.*, p. 74.

13 *Ibid.*, p. 311.

14 *VKP (b) v rezoliutsiiakh*, Moscow, 1941, vol. 1, p. 257.

15 Lenin, *Collected Works*, vol. 25, pp. 329–30.

16 *Ibid.*, pp. 330–1.

17 *Ibid.*, pp. 330–2.

18 *Ibid.*, pp. 331–2.

19 R. Portal, *La Russie industrielle de 1881 à 1927*, Paris, 1976, p. 145.

20 *Ibid.*, p. 146; the participation of Russian capital started increasing on the eve of the war in the textile industry and in the Urals. In the central regions, Russian financial capital participated together with foreign capital in industrial financing. Bukharin quoted the case of the Russian Metal Syndicate among the examples of 'gigantic international banking trusts' (*Imperialism*, pp. 58–60).

21 M.S. Atlas, *Natsionalizatsiia bankov v SSSR*, Moscow, 1948, pp. 9–10; P.V. Ol', *Inostrannye kapitaly v Rossii*, Petrograd, 1922, p. 8.

22 M.S. Atlas, p. 13.

23 Lenin, *Collected Works*, vol. 25, pp. 330–2.

24 M.S. Atlas, pp. 17–18, 22; other banks were: the deposit banks, which gradually became incorporated in the commercial banks; the State Nobility Bank and the State Peasantry Bank, which were mortgage credit institutions; and credit cooperatives, which financed purchase of livestock, land and agricultural implements.

25 E.H. Carr, *The Bolshevik Revolution, 1917–1923*, 3 vols., London, 1952, vol. 2, pp. 135–7.

26 *Ibid.*, p. 133.

27 Z.V. Atlas, *Ocherki po istorii denezhnogo obrashcheniia v SSSR (1917–1925)*, Moscow, 1940, pp. 16–18.

28 *Trudy I Vserossiiskogo S"ezda Sovnarkhozov*, p. 174. The cases of refusal of banks to finance factory committees were interpreted by the Bolsheviks as hostility to workers' control.

29 *Sobranie uzakonenii*, 1917–18, no. 10, arts. 150, 151; Carr, *The Bolshevik Revolution*, vol. 2, p. 137.

30 Carr, *The Bolshevik Revolution*, vol. 2, p. 137; Z.V. Atlas, p. 23; A.D. Gusakov, *Planirovanie denezhnogo obrashcheniia v SSSR*, Moscow, 1974, p. 18: the ceiling was 50 million rubles a week.

31 Z.V. Atlas, p. 82.

32 *Ibid.*, p. 20.

33 *Ibid.*, pp. 23–4; and *Sobranie uzakonenii*, 1917–18, no. 32, art. 420. By the cancellation of public debt, the state saved more than 400 million rubles of interest each year. See I.B. Berkhin, *Ekonomicheskaia politika Sovetskogo Gosudarstva v pervye gody Sovetskoi Vlasti*, Moscow, 1970, p. 53.

34 Gusakov, p. 19.
35 Lenin, *Collected Works*, vol. 26, pp. 389–90, 393–4.
36 Lenin, *Collected Works*, vol. 42, p. 78.
37 *Biulleten' VSNKh*, April 1918, no. 1, 37–9.
38 Carr, *The Bolshevik Revolution*, vol. 2, p. 137. See E. Epstein, *Les Banques de Commerce Russes*, Paris, 1925, pp. 96–105, and G.A. Kozlov, *Sovetskie den'gi*, Gosfinizdat, 1939, pp. 29–30. The conference on banking policy attached to the State Bank and formed in part by representatives of the private banks proposed separation of emission from the ordinary credit institutes. This and other proposals were initially agreed upon by the Soviet representatives.
39 J. Sadoul, *Notes sur la révolution bolchévique*, Paris, 1919, pp. 309–10.
40 *Biulleten' VSNKh*, April 1918, no. 1, 26
41 Lenin, *Collected Works*, vol. 24, p. 473. On fiscal policy of the Provisional Government and its implementation see R.W. Davies, *Development of the Soviet Budgetary System*, Cambridge, 1958, p. 9.
42 Carr, *The Bolshevik Revolution*, vol. 2, pp. 141–6, 245–52; V.P. D'iachenko, *Sovetskie finansy v pervoi faze razvitiia sotsialisticheskogo gosudarstva*, Moscow, 1947, pp. 186, 188 and G.L. Mar'iakin, *Ocherki istorii nalogov u naseleniia v SSSR*, Moscow, 1964, pp. 35, 36, 43. The revolutionary tax should have been collected by 15 December 1918, but only 2,288 million rubles were collected by the end of 1919 in depreciated money. I ignore the total value of the belongings which were confiscated, in default of payment: cf. Davies, p. 27, n7. Only on 3 February 1921 did the All-Russian Central Executive Committee decide to put an end to monetary levies: cf. *Finansy i kredit* (pod red. A.G. Kozlova), Leningrad, 1938, p. 84.
43 V.P. D'iachenko, *Istoriia finansov SSSR*, Moscow, 1978, pp. 45, 47.
44 *Sobranie uzakonenii*, 1918, no. 27, art. 349.
45 Z.V. Atlas, p. 26: the Moscow Oblast even started a collection of five rubles per person to form a foodstuffs fund.
46 *The Russian Almanac*, London, 1919, p. 111.
47 M.S. Atlas, pp. 81–2.
48 Lenin, *Collected Works*, vol. 42, p. 64.
49 Z.V. Atlas, p. 28.
50 *Trudy I Vserossiiskogo S"ezda Sovnarkhozov*, pp. 128–30.
51 D'iachenko, *Istoriia finansov SSSR*, p. 42.
52 *Trudy I Vserossiiskogo S"ezda Sovnarkhozov*, pp. 117–18.
53 Carr, *The Bolshevik Revolution*, vol. 2, pp. 140–1; Davies, p. 9 and N. Nordman *Peace Problems: Russia's Economics*, London, 1919, p. 92. The subscription of the war loan was approved by a resolution of the Soviet of Petrograd.
54 *Trudy I Vserossiiskogo S"ezda Sovnarkhozov*, pp. 120–1.
55 *Ibid.*, p. 423.
56 Z.V. Atlas, p. 32.
57 *Kommunist (organ gruppy levykh kommunistov)*, no. 4, June 1918, 5.
58 *Ibid.*, 15.
59 *Ibid.*, 5–6.
60 See pp. 356–8 below.
61 Local soviets had been authorized on the morrow of the revolution to use all

local taxes to meet their requirements, which they did, because of the institutional vacuum, necessity and also revolutionary ardour. *Narkomfin* was unable to restore central control over local finances: see Davies, pp. 17–19.

62 *Biulleten' VSNKh*, April 1918, no. 1, 39–40, 44.
63 *Ibid.*, 30.
64 Cf. Davies, pp. 19–20.
65 N. Bukharin and E. Preobrazhensky, *The ABC of Communism*, London, 1969, p. 389.
66 I.A. Iurkov, 'Finansovaia politika Sovetskogo Gosudarstva i tovarno-denezhnye otnosheniia v gody grazhdanskoi voiny (1918–1920 gg)', *Voprosy Istorii*, no. 10, 1980, 64–5.
67 *Denezhnoe obrashchenie i kredit*, vol. 1, Petrograd, 1922, p. 455.
68 *Sbornik dekretov*, vol. 2, pp. 195–6.
69 Bukharin and Preobrazhensky, *The ABC of Communism*, p. 390.
70 *Ibid.*, pp. 389–92.
71 *Denezhnoe obrashchenie*, p. 456.
72 Z.V. Atlas, p. 75. D'iachenko, however, suggests that fixed prices used in calculating the *oborotnyi* part of the budget might have artificially lowered its percentage in the overall budget (D'iachenko, *Sovetskie finansy*, p. 182).
73 *Izvestiia Narodnogo Komissariata Finansov*, nos. 10–11, 16 June 1920, 15.
74 *Ibid.*, 15.
75 Narkomfin, *K 8 S"ezdu Sovetov*, Moscow, 1920, 20 December 1920, pp. 18–19: by December 1920, the State Budget deficit was already 84.9 per cent of total expenditure.
76 *Izvestiia NKF*, no. 10, 7 November 1919, 3.
77 *Finansovaia politika Sovetskoi Vlasti na 10 let. Sbornik statei*, Moscow–Leningrad, 1928, p. 4.
78 *Sobranie uzakonenii*, 1920, no. 67, art. 305.
79 *Denezhnoe obrashchenie*, p. 483.
80 *Ibid.*, p. 465.
81 Bukharin and Preobrazhensky, *The ABC of Communism*, p. 391.
82 *Znamia*, no. 1(3), April 1920, 58–9.
83 Quoted by I.A. Iurkov, 'Finansovaia politika', *Voprosy Istorii*, 70.
84 *Izvestiia NKF*, nos. 13–14, 6 December 1919, 11.
85 Z.V. Atlas, pp. 70–1.
86 Narkomfin, '*K 8 S"ezdu Sovetov*', p. 23.
87 *Narodnoe Khoziaistvo*, 1920, nos. 1–2, p. 10.
88 Z.V. Atlas, p. 58.
89 *Denezhnoe obrashchenie*, p. 82.
90 R.E. Vaisberg, *Den'gi i tseny (podpol'nyi rynok v period 'voennogo kommunizma')*, Moscow, 1925.
91 *Ibid.*, pp. 60–3.
92 *Ibid.*, pp. 70–4, 154–5.
93 *Ibid.*, p. 161, Table 8.
94 N. Krestinskii, *Finansy i biudzhet: doklad na 9-om S"ezde Sovetov*, 1922, p. 5.
95 *Izvestiia NKF*, no. 4(20), 15 March 1920, 1.
96 NKF, *K 8 S"ezdu Sovetov*, p. 12.

97 *Izvestiia NKF*, nos. 5–6, 3 October 1919, 10.
98 See Davies, pp. 33–5 and the decree of VTsIK in *Izvestiia Narkomfin*, 1922, no. 10, 4.
99 Z.V. Atlas, p. 73.
100 *Izvestiia NKF*, no. 4(20), 14 March 1920, 2.
101 Z.V. Atlas, p. 73.
102 *Finansy i kredit SSSR* (pod red. Kozlova), p. 87.
103 *Sobranie uzakonenii*, 1920, no. 85, art. 422.
104 *Sobranie uzakonenii*, 1920, no. 93, art. 505, no. 99, art. 531.
105 In first place were all Moscow and Petrograd people having a right to rations: in second, working people from other areas having a right to rations; third, members of the families of Red soldiers, having 'Red Star' cards; fourth, the workers' supply fund under the control of the Central Committee for Workers' Supply.
106 *Sobranie uzakonenii*, 1921, no. 2, arts. 20 and 18.
107 *Sobranie uzakonenii*, 1921, no. 40, art. 211.
108 *Promyshlennost' v usloviiakh NEP*, Moscow, 1925, p. 25.
109 Cf. *Sobranie uzakonenii*, 1917–18, no. 48, art. 567; no. 75, art. 815; *Sobranie uzakonenii*, 1919, no. 5, art. 52; no. 15, art. 173; no. 15, art. 178; no. 41, art. 396; *Sobranie uzakonenii*, 1920, nos. 61–2, art. 276.
110 In October 1917 workers in a perfume factory had been rewarded with six funt of meat, six bottles of eau-de-Cologne, some pomade and perfume per month, and obtained twice as much the next year. At the end of 1918, workers in the provinces threatened to plunder factory products if they were not paid their wages. Workers in a mill were partly remunerated with flour until August 1919. *Glavtekstil'* autonomously started the policy of wage naturalization, by giving workers some arshins of fabric (*Izvestiia*, no. 8, 14 January 1920, 2; *Ekonomicheskaia Zhizn'*, no. 32, 14 December 1918, 4; *Izvestiia*, no. 183, 19 August 1919, 2; *Ekonomicheskaia Zhizn'*, no. 148, 9 July 1919, 2; *Narodnoe Khoziaistvo*, nos. 9–10, 1919, 49 and *Ekonomicheskaia Zhizn'*, no. 145, 5 July 1919, 1).
111 A.I. Gurevich, *Desiat'/let profdvizheniia SSSR*, Moscow, 1927, pp. 51–2.
112 Larin and Kritsman acknowledged that wages in kind were the necessary consequence of money depreciation: see their *Ocherk khoziaistvennoi zhizni i organizatsiia narodnogo khoziaistva Sovetskoi Rossii*, 1920, pp. 134–5.
113 *Trudy II Vserossiiskogo S"ezda Sovnarkhozov*, pp. 170, 171.
114 *Ekonomicheskaia Zhizn'*, no. 251, 9 November 1919, 1.
115 *Rabochaia Zhizn'*, no. 11, 26 October 1919, 2–3, 8–10.
116 *Izvestiia*, no. 30, 11 February 1920, 1.
117 *Sobranie uzakonenii*, 1920, no. 35, art. 166.
118 *Sobranie uzakonenii*, 1920, no. 84, art. 415.
119 British Parliamentary Papers, *Report of the Committee to Collect Information on Russia*, no. 1, 1921, p. 97; I.A. Gladkov, *Ocherki sovetskoi ekonomiki 1917–1920 gg*, Moscow, 1956.
120 British Parliamentary Papers, p. 97.
121 See Chapter 8 below.
122 G.Y. Sokolnykov *et al.*, *Soviet Policy in Public Finance 1917–1928*, Stanford, 1931, p. 136.

123 E. Preobrazhenskii, *Bumazhnye den'gi v epokhu proletarskoi diktatury*, 1920, p. 78.
124 *Biulleten' VSNKh*, April 1918, no. 1, 26–7.
125 *Trudy I Vserossiiskogo S"ezda Sovnarkhozov*, pp. 87, 434.
126 VSNKh, *Plenum, 14–23 sent. 1918 goda*, stenogr. otchet, Moscow, 1919, p. 14.
127 See p. 179 above.
128 *Ekonomika i politika tverdykh tsen. Sbornik statei*, Moscow, 1918, pp. 91–2.
129 See p. 163 above.
130 *Narodnoe Khoziaistvo*, 1919, no. 7, 17–20.
131 *Ibid.*, 11–13.
132 *Ekonomika i politika tverdykh tsen*, p. 93.
133 *Narodnoe Khoziaistvo*, 1919, no. 7, 12 and *Rabochaia Zhizn'*, no. 3, 13 July 1919, 14 and *Sobranie uzakonenii*, 1919, no. 41, art. 396.
134 *Narodnoe Khoziaistvo*, 1919, no. 5, 38.
135 *Sobranie uzakonenii*, 1919, no. 42, art. 413.
136 Cf. G.G. Bogomazov, *Marksizm-Leninizm i problemy tovarno-denezhnykh otnoshenii v period stroitel'stva sotsializma v SSSR*, Leningrad, 1974, p. 60.
137 Vaisberg, p. 62.
138 *Ekonomicheskaia Zhizn'*, no. 46, 28 February 1919, 3.
139 *Ekonomicheskaia Zhizn'*, no. 59, 18 March 1919, 3; *Ekonomicheskaia Zhizn'*, no. 67, 28 March 1919, p. 3.
140 *Ekonomicheskaia Zhizn'*, no. 74, 5 April 1919, 3.
141 *Ekonomicheskaia Zhizn'*, no. 251, 9 November 1919, 2.
142 *Ekonomicheskaia Zhizn'*, no. 86, 24 April 1919, 3.
143 M.E. Shefler, 'Zamena zolotoi valiuty – trudovoi', in *Ekonomika i politika tverdykh tsen*, pp. 94–101.
144 *Ibid.*, p. 101.
145 *Denezhnoe obrashchenie i kredit*, vol. 1, pp. 4, 458.
146 Z.V. Atlas, p. 104.
147 See one of the best accounts of this work in L.N. Iurovskii, *Denezhnaia Politika sovetskoi vlasti (1917–1927)* Moscow, 1928, pp. 88–117; see also I.A. Iurkov, 'Finansovaia politika Sovetskogo Gosudarstva', 69.
148 During war communism the best known book on political economy was A.A. Bogdanov's old *Short Course in Economic Science*, the first edition of which dated from 1897. Although criticized by Lenin for its non-Marxist philosophy (V.I. Lenin, *Polnoe Sobranie Sochinenii*, vol. 24, pp. 238–341), Bogdanov's approach identifying value with the physiological expenditure of energy in the labour process was attractive in so far as it offered an alternative in terms of physical accounting to market value bond on demand. On the influence of Bogdanov on young Soviet economists, see Bogomazov, pp. 29–30, 61.
149 For Strumilin's criticism of Chaianov, see Bogomazov, pp. 75–6. Planning in physical units is discussed further on pp. 314–18 below.
150 A.Z. Arnold, *Banks, Credit, and Money in Soviet Russia*, New York, 1937, pp. 107–8.
151 Z.V. Atlas, p. 105.
152 S.G. Strumilin, *Problemy ekonomiki truda*, Moscow, 1925, p. 217.
153 Arnold, pp. 108–9.
154 Z.V. Atlas, p. 106; Iurovskii, pp. 107–12.
155 Vaisberg, p. 110.

156 *RKP, 9i S"ezd*, p. 142.
157 Bukharin and Preobrazhensky, *The ABC of Communism*, pp. 391–2.
158 Vaisberg, pp. 121–3; see also N.I. Bazylev, *Stanovlenie ekonomicheskoi teorii Sotsializma v SSSR*, Minsk, 1975, pp. 121–2 on the permanent role played by the *chervonets* rubles, during war communism, as a measure of value for accumulation purposes.
159 E. Preobrazhenskii, *Bumazhnye den'gi*, pp. 34–5, 39, 83.
160 Vaisberg, p. 10.

5

Industrial administration

Several factors affected the process of forming Soviet economic institutions, the nature and function of which did not remain stable during war communism. Marxist ideology did not provide concrete guidance about economic organization, but it did provide a general hint about what had to be kept and what dropped on the path of economic development. This hint was not irrelevant in the selection of alternatives facing the leadership. There was no disagreement among Russian Marxists regarding the belief that socialism had to carry forward the latest achievements of capitalism. This peculiar form of determinism exerted an impact on the continuity of economic institutions and methods, which were the legacy of the Tsarist war economy to Soviet power. In a revolutionary process, however, continuity was inevitably challenged by change. Change was furthered by the outburst of social and individual demands, which the revolution heightened after the fall of the Tsarist regime, and by the conflicting interpretations given to the relative urgency of tackling immediate problems and to the choice of priorities.

Civil war and the foreign economic blockade added exogenous constraints limiting the possibility of a stable institutional framework, and jeopardized any consistent programme of economic reconstruction. These factors did not have equal and simultaneous effects on economic policy. They were, however, interwoven from the beginning to the end of the experience of war communism in such a way that the isolation of one single factor from the others would be misleading for an interpretation of the origin of the war communism experience as well as for an understanding of its non-linear evolution.

Legislation on economic organization proceeded in a spasmodic way and sometimes in a rather anarchic fashion. The complex of factors which affected the formation and evolution of Soviet institutions had a definite effect on the nature and development of the Supreme Council of the National Economy (VSNKh) too. Attempts to form an organ in charge of the coordination of the economy had some precedents in pre-revolutionary Russia. During the war, the Tsarist Government created a Chief Economic Committee to coordinate the various production branches. This organ was a sort of small council of economic ministries. It supervised the branch chief committees (*glavnye komitety*, known as *glavki*), which had been set up with the specific purpose of controlling the prices and distribution of a number of products related to military needs.[1] The Chief Economic Committee remained active until 17 November 1917.[2] Under the Provisional Government a more ambitious project was undertaken in the form of a general plan for organizing the national economy and labour, and for drawing up laws and general measures of an economic nature. For this purpose, an Economic Council was attached to the government in June 1917.[3] The Economic Council did not have much time to develop its activities. However, the expectations which led to its formation remained and probably affected the organization of VSNKh. A shrewd French observer stressed that VSNKh simply appropriated the proposals which were elaborated after the February Revolution and which began to be implemented by the Provisional Government.[4] The scope and aims of VSNKh, from its origin, suffered from the ambiguity deriving from the former existence of the economic committees, the Chief Economic Committee and the Economic Council. The Chief Economic Committee was abolished only four days after *Sovnarkom* instructed a group of experts to draw up a scheme for the organization of a supreme economic organ.[5] The formal continuity between these two organs, however, was not a sign of agreement among the leadership about the outlines of Soviet economic policy. The events from November 1917 onwards suggest, on the contrary, that divergences about economic policy and organization were deep and that misunderstandings about the aims, role and scope of the new economic institutions lasted through the short but eventful experience of war communism and added to the disorganization and instability.

Bukharin's original project saw VSNKh as a consultative organ, formed by unification of the organs of economic control inherited from the Provisional Government. Larin proposed the participation of entrepreneurs and technicians, representatives of the so-called collective organizations (factory committees, etc.) to make up one-third of the total membership.[6] The first president of VSNKh, Osinskii, presented it as an organ endowed only with consultative powers, whose function was confined to drawing up projects for centralization and coordination of economic institutions with political institutions.[7] All these approaches were akin to the project of instituting a consultative economic organ, which the Petrograd Soviet had formulated in May 1917, following the Menshevik view on this question.[8]

Divergences about VSNKh concerned its composition. Parties and factions attached much importance to the forthcoming role of VSNKh and endeavoured to enlarge as much as possible the representation of their constituencies. The Mensheviks, who at that time had a big following in the trade unions, demanded representation for the latter on VSNKh's board. The Left Socialist-Revolutionaries, whose constituency was in the countryside, claimed a fifty-fifty representation for the peasantry.[9] The future leaders of the left-wing communist faction, Smirnov and Osinskii, pursuing the aim of having in VSNKh a large forum for discussion, proposed that VSNKh should be attached to the Central Executive Committee rather than to *Sovnarkom*.[10]

Lenin had a personal view on the functions and scope of VSNKh. On 1 December, 1917, he affirmed at the Central Executive Committee that VSNKh ought to be for the economy what *Sovnarkom* was for politics, that is, an organ for the struggle against capitalists and owners, not a parliament.[11] On 23 December, 1917, *Sovnarkom* issued an instruction stating that VSNKh should immediately be transformed from an organ of discussion into an organ for the effective management of industry.[12] The instruction of *Sovnarkom* went against the letter of the decree which instituted VSNKh on 1 December, 1917. The decree established that VSNKh was in charge of the coordination of economic life, the coordination and unification of the activity of central and local regulating institutions (the fuel committee, the metal, transport and central foodstuffs committees and other relevant people's commissariats, for trade and industry, foodstuffs, agriculture, finances, war and the fleet, and so on). VSNKh was also in charge of the coordination and unification of the activity of the All-Russian Council of Workers' Control, whose formation had been announced by the Decree on Workers' Control, and of the corresponding activity of the factory shop and trade union organs of the working class. VSNKh was responsible for issuing directives to the local economic councils (*sovnarkhozy*). The economic sections of the local soviets were to be incorporated in the VSNKh structure, since the decree established that VSNKh decisions were to be made binding to them. All existing institutions for the regulation of economic life were subordinated to VSNKh, which had the right to reorganize them. The decree did not mention the composition of VSNKh, but stated that it should be determined by the All-Russian Council of Workers' Control, once the latter had been elected in accordance with the provisions of the Decree on Workers' Control. VSNKh was attached to *Sovnarkom*.[13] Regarding the rest, the decree kept silent. Nothing was said about the current management of VSNKh, about the future election rules and number of members of the council. No mention was made of sections and specific functions. VSNKh was formed with statutory powers, but without any specified organization. It was a sort of ministry without portfolio for economic affairs.

The organization of VSNKh developed pragmatically, to cope with immediate problems. The section of precious metals was formed when efforts were made to increase gold reserves to meet the sharp paper-money inflation. The demobilization section was formed on 15 January 1918, following the suspension of orders for military supplies and the consequent growth of unemployment. One after the other, the technical committee, the construction section, the state economy and banking section, were formed.[14] The section for public works was formed in connection with the problem of utilizing unemployed labour.[15] At the beginning of 1918, VSNKh's structure corresponded to the following scheme:[16]

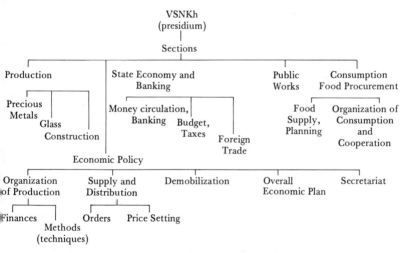

Fig. 5.1 The structure of VSNKh, beginning of 1918

From this scheme, one can see that VSNKh was organized in such a way as to be able to carry out government economic policy, rather than as an organ for industrial administration. The production sections were not formed immediately. In the course of 1918 there were formed sections for agriculture, industry, machine building, fibres, leather, food-processing, the paper and timber industry, and various other branches. But, as

Rykov, who was appointed president of VSNKh in 1918, revealed in September 1918, many of them remained on paper until May 1918,[17] that is, until the moment when a serious effort was made to prepare a plan of nationalization. After the First Congress of *Sovnarkhozy*, the sections of consumption and food supply, public work, commerce and banking disappeared from VSNKh's structure.[18] The Committee for Economic Policy, the only organ within VSNKh which could have carried forward a policy of preparation for planning, which since May 1918 had been subordinated to the presidium of VSNKh, was abolished on 1 November 1919.[19]

The original structure of VSNKh corresponded more to an inter-departmental committee for the economy, with the functions of coordinating and drafting economic plans, rather than to Lenin's idea of an economic bureau of a business nature, implementing the political directives in the economic field. VSNKh's production sections were charged with regulating individual branches of the economy and consequently with draft measures in the fields of competence of economic People's Commissariats. VSNKh, however, never had the time to work out a plan of coordination for the economy encompassing all economic activities, nor was it able to 'invent' methods for regulating branch production other than those practised by the chief committees (*glavki*) formed by the Tsarist Government. VSNKh's production sections started dealing with the distribution of raw materials to enterprises, working out norms of production and allotting orders to individual factories,[20] as the pre-revolutionary *glavki* had done.

Given the existing situation, where a number of economic organs had already been formed locally within the soviets or side by side with them, the efforts to coordinate the economic institutions were aimed at creating a network of area economic councils, *sovnarkhozy* (i.e. *sovety narodnogo khoziaistva*), depending on and conforming to VSNKh's structure.[21] Each *sovnarkhoz* was to be subdivided into fourteen production sections covering all branches of production. The number of the *sovnarkhoz* representatives was supposed to be fixed by the soviet of the same area.[22] The shape of the economic organization was spurious from its very beginning, since it was modelled under the impact of two different influences. On the one side, VSNKh's ambition to become the only organ responsible for economic problems, including finance, reflected the technocratic soul of the Menshevik cadres who had recently joined the Bolshevik Party. On the other side, the lack of an administrative apparatus, the existence of peripheral economic organs, the provinces' claims for decentralization, all made for a decentralized territorial organization, which some Bolsheviks were interpreting as the expression of Soviet democracy.

Reality forbade both souls of VSNKh to develop fully. The conflict between a desired but not achieved centralization and an effective but unwanted decentralization characterized the first communist experience in economic organization in Russia.

On 2 January 1918 VSNKh incorporated the existing commission for defence, which was in charge of financing war industry and appropriated its financial means. By the same decision VSNKh imposed its preliminary approval on financing of private enterprises by the State Bank, by the Ministry of Trade and Industry and by other state institutions.[23] According to E.H. Carr, VSNKh did not show an equivalent ability in getting control of the financial levers.[24] Carr also maintains that VSNKh would never have been able to function as an economic *Sovnarkom*, nor were the local *sovnarkhozy* able to compete with the political soviets. Therefore, the idea of economic soviets would never have been practicable.[25] Evidence is somewhat varied. On the one hand, it seems true that the *sovnarkhozy* represented a bureaucratic replication of VSNKh: their sections were not always justified by the local conditions and the administrative staff had no precise responsibilities.[26] On the other hand, however, one might reply to Carr's assertions by pointing out that events were also the results of former choices. The dissolution of the Constituent Assembly, the preference for centralized management both in industry and in the sphere of foodstuffs distribution, the distaste for market tools and incentives, the approach to economic problems from a voluntaristic rather than a technical point of view, all had an impact on the future institutional framework.

It could be argued that the *sovnarkhozy* were not allowed to develop because they represented the interests of a large and hardly manageable peripheral territory which could have hampered the implementation of central policy. At the same time, it would be hard to argue that they were not justified in the circumstances of war communism. In spite of the policy of economic centralization pursued by the leadership, the *sovnarkhozy* played an important role during the civil war, helping the local economy to survive and supply, though modestly, the needs of the local population and the army.

Differences of opinion on the role of VSNKh did not come into the open at the moment of its creation, since nobody had a definite economic plan. The actual activity of VSNKh at the beginning consisted in the approval of single acts of confiscation and nationalization undertaken by different institutions, and in reorganization of the existing central committees in the main industrial branches.

Economic guidelines were only sketched out at the Seventh Congress of the Party, in March 1918. At that time attention was still concentrated on the development of revolutionary tensions abroad, particularly in Germany. The prevailing line was that the Party Programme ought to be devised in such a way as to provide an incentive and an encouragement to the revolutionary forces fighting abroad, not only as a guideline for the Russian people.[27] Emphasis was laid on the goals of communist society, rather than on the means of reaching these goals. It was for this reason, according to Lenin, that the name of the Party was to be changed to 'Russian Communist Party', a denomination showing that the goal of formation of a communist society was not limited to the expropriation of means of production, nor to social accounting and control over production and distribution, but must include 'from each according to his ability, to each according to his needs'. Bukharin maintained that the lines of socialist construction had to be developed in broad detail in the Party Programme, rather than focusing on transitional features, although, he added, he was not opposed to the transitional system as Lenin conceived it.[28] Lenin opted for pragmatism. He insisted that a description of socialism could not be given, since 'what socialism will be like when its completed forms are arrived at – this we do not know, we cannot tell'; otherwise, he warned, the programme would lose its power of attraction, since 'it will be suspected that our Programme is only a fantasy'.[29]

The programme of the party was the result of a compromise between these two positions. A precise reference to organization was avoided, by putting forward some very popular aims and by stressing, thanks to Lenin's firmness on this point, the persistence of the state.[30] In spite of Lenin's insistence on caution and accuracy in drafting the Party Programme,[31] the economic theses were general and inspired by political preoccupations rather than by a clear vision of what had to be done immediately. At a time when efforts were still being made to find an arrangement with some capitalist groups for the direction of industry, when VSNKh was reluctant to undertake further nationalization, when polemics were starting with the left-wing communists on the utilization of bourgeois experts at high salaries, on the introduction of the Taylor system and piece-wages, on the needs for one-man management, in other words, when Lenin was pursuing his project of 'state capitalism', the Party Programme ignored reality. The economic theses mentioned the socialist organization of production 'on the scale of the whole state', management by workers' associations (trade unions, factory committees, etc.), planned organization of distribution, compulsory organization of the whole population in consumer and producer communes, immediate steps to the full realization of compulsory labour service, the complete concentration of banking in the hands of the state and of all financial operations of trade in the banks, standardization of accounting and control, the gradual reduction of the working day to six hours and the gradual equalization of all wages and salaries in all occupations and categories, and finally, systematic measures to replace individual domestic economy by public catering.[32]

The disparity between the pronouncements of the congress and what was going on outside proves that a broad consensus could be reached only on the most general principles. It was easier to reach agreement among the party members by focusing on the far-reaching goals of society than on the practical details of their implementation. Given this purpose, it would be misleading to check the consistency of further policies only with the directives set forth by the Party Programme.

The congress did not discuss the pace of transformation of the economic and social system, although everyone was aware that the timing and priorities of the transition period were not irrelevant to further evolution. The lack of a serious debate about the implications and content of a Soviet economic policy left the leadership unprepared in face of the anarchical developments in the economy and favoured the multiplication of individual projects, which often conflicted with one another. Political differences of opinion on the means to be used to attain immediate or future goals, which were concealed before the revolution by the enthusiastic consensus regarding distant aims, by common ideals and by all those motives which make it easier to formulate and carry out political opposition than to materialize it into positive proposals, became unavoidable when the problem of administration became real.

The tasks, structures and responsibilities of the new institutions, the relations among them, the formation and application of decision-making, implied different appreciations of the order of priority of the pending problems, within an ideological framework realistic enough to accept all sorts of exceptions but utopian enough to encourage all sorts of expectations. Constraints on change were appreciated to differing extents. Differences of opinion on the role and scope of the new institutions were bound to reflect not only political nuances, but also the individual cultural backgrounds of the people involved.

Decisions were often the result of untenable compromises. VSNKh was an example of this. Kritsman gave a good description of the contradictory impulses which accompanied its formation.

Being the most important economic organ, VSNKh suffered more than other institutions from the deficiencies of overall economic organization, from the amateur approach of most political leaders to economic problems. VSNKh embodied the aspirations of the most brilliant economists to realize a new economic order as an alternative to the existing one.[33]

The decree on nationalization of large-scale industry was a further element which forced VSNKh to undertake tasks other than those at which Kritsman hinted. The decree on nationalization of large-scale industry caught VSNKh unaware, disorientated its programmes and definitely destroyed its chances of becoming the leading economic agency of the country. The role which Lenin had intended to reserve for VSNKh since December 1917 became actual and was imposed upon the economic leaders against their will and their aspirations.

When *Sovnarkom* wished to revise the functions of VSNKh, Miliutin repeatedly refused to take part in such a revision. Disputes went so far that Lenin threatened to put VSNKh on a diet of bread and water if it refused to accept the leadership of *Sovnarkom*. Miliutin's sarcastic reply: 'water, maybe, but as for bread, that's a utopia',[34] reflected the critical opinion of VSNKh on the centralized scheme of food supply, which the leadership had been working out since March 1918, and which virtually ended in failure.

VSNKh started working on a draft resolution of its own, by which it would have assumed direct and autonomous control over all enterprises belonging to the republic, through its own organizations. The main points of the project, by which VSNKh claimed the status of the highest economic institution in the country, leadership of financial policy and control over all economic commissariats, were rejected by *Sovnarkom*, which decided to downgrade VSNKh by changing the verb 'to lead' (*vedat'*) in VSNKh's draft into 'to manage' (*upravliat'*). The importance of political control over VSNKh's work was affirmed through the inclusion of the Commissar of Internal Affairs in its presidium.[35] By virtue of its new statute approved on 13 August 1918,[36] VSNKh became an economic section of the Central Executive Committee and lost its power of initiative in the economic field. Its tasks were confined to implementation of the economic policy decided by the political organs, namely *Sovnarkom* and the Central Executive Committee. The regulation and organization of production remained the responsibility of VSNKh, but its financial powers were made less than those it had claimed for itself soon after its creation: that is, the right to finance any state institution and to take preliminary decisions on the financing of enterprises by the State Bank, the Ministry of Commerce and Industry or any other state institution. These claims for financial control responded to a hypothesis of central, indirect control over business, which could make VSNKh's programme of control over orders, agreements and contracts of delivery particularly effective, if one considers that together with these rights, VSNKh claimed also the right to appoint its representatives in the administration of the enterprises.[37]

The August statute put a stop to any possible evolution by VSNKh towards a model of indirect planning based on financial instruments as means of persuasion or as deterrents. VSNKh became a supervisory organ on technical financial aspects of the budget. Financing industry required the agreement of the Commissariats of Finance and State Control. VSNKh's dependence on the government was also guaranteed by *Sovnarkom*'s power to confirm the membership of its presidium. This consisted of nine people elected by a plenary session of sixty-nine, representing the All-Russian Central Executive Committee, the Association of Trade Unions and the All-Russian Council of Trade Unions, the economic commissariats, the Council of the Union of Workers' Cooperatives and the *oblast* economic councils (*obsovnarkhozy*).[38]

The formation in November 1918 of the Council of Workers' and Peasants' Defence (later called the Council of Labour and Defence, STO) has been interpreted as indicating that at that time VSNKh ceased to be the supreme economic organ.[39] The Council of Workers' and Peasants' Defence, in fact, was given broad powers in the economic sphere in connection with military requirements. This interpretation implies that war communism started in the autumn of 1918 as a response to military necessity. One may argue, however, that the fate of VSNKh had already been determined in August 1918 by the decision of *Sovnarkom* to curb its ambitions. The wave of nationalizations brought about by the June Decree necessarily confined VSNKh to current economic business; the reform of VSNKh's statute, following this, was the sign that the party leadership did not intend to grant excessive margins of freedom to an organ whose political orthodoxy was not certain. The members of VSNKh's Presidium were Communist Party members and sympathizers; but of the overall number of VSNKh staff in October 1918, totalling some 5,031 people, only 164 were party members and only 374 were considered as sympathizers.[40] Elements of war communism were already present in the spring of 1918, when the policy of class struggle was extended in the countryside to curb the peasants' unwillingness to deliver their grain surplus at derisory prices, and the leadership had already started employing a political filter in each crucial decision.

From the institutional point of view, the subordination of VSNKh to *Sovnarkom* represented a conservative choice with respect to the Leninist principle of the merging of legislative and executive functions on which the soviets were based, and it deprived the Soviet system of an institution capable of coordinating all economic measures in a very delicate phase of overall economic organization. The organization of the food supply, the agrarian transformation of the countryside and the policy pursued by the Commissariat of Finance, which were bound to affect industrial organization, did not have a common platform. The departmental subdivision of the administration according to the traditional division of ministries (translated into People's Commissariats) was bound to create competition between the different agencies, rather than cohesion and joint efforts in the regulation of the economy. The First Congress of *Sovnarkhozy* had already debated such themes. Together with the claim that VSNKh ought to maintain directive functions and draw up the guidelines of the country's economic policy, the congress maintained that the responsibilities of economic commissariats ought to be reduced, and even that a number of them ought to be abolished.[41] These claims were not curbed after the reform of the VSNKh statute.

In his book *The Construction of Socialism*, written after the First Congress of *Sovnarkhozy*, Osinskii maintained that the gradual liquidation of the Commissariat of Commerce and Industry, through the transfer of its bureau to the corresponding sections of VSNKh, and the cases in which local economic commissariats had been incorporated into a single organ, were necessary developments leading towards a single dominant economic centre.[42] Arguing against the departmentalization of the economy, Osinskii proposed that VSNKh should be a sort of small cabinet within *Sovnarkom*, entrusted with decision-making on the most important economic questions, like general legislation in the economic field, forms of economic management, finance, and distribution of the labour force. Against the danger of having an economic executive not responsible to the political institutions, Osinskii proposed that the economic cabinet, composed of 10–12 members, half being economic People's Commissars, should be responsible to the Congress of Soviets. Broad economic questions should be dealt with by a central bureau formed, in equal proportions, by representatives of *sovnarkhozy*, trade unions and commissars. The guidelines of economic policy should be formulated by the Congress of *Sovnarkhozy*. Osinskii wanted an operative role for his proposed central bureau and its organs, with considerable autonomy. The central formulation of economic policy was to be balanced by extensive participation of localities and unionized workers in the discussion of alternatives. At the same time, therefore, Osinskii demanded more powers for *sovnarkhozy* and for workers' management. The local *sovnarkhozy*, in Osinskii's approach, should be more concerned with local details, in order to leave the central economic body free for the most important decisions.[43]

The left wing of the party thus showed a clear concern for a single economic centre, but was also preoccupied by the internal political control of such an organ and by an external feedback on its policies. The economic experts wanted concentration of economic decisions into economic organs, *tout court*. Arskii desired all economic commissariats to be absorbed into the *sovnarkhozy*. He argued that the centralization of economic policy presumed that a single organ and its local sections should be responsible for economic decisions. In this framework the existence of the economic commissariats was considered an anachronism. Arskii pointed out Lenin's contradictory feelings about VSNKh. On the one hand, Lenin despised the theoretical formulation of economic models, which attracted the experts; on the other hand, he refused to provide VSNKh with the means to carry out the operative tasks which he assigned to it.[44]

Demand for the concentration of economic policy in the hands of VSNKh not only did not diminish after the creation of the Council of Workers' and Peasants' Defence, which was but a partial image of the small cabinet proposed by Osinskii, but actually increased. At the Second Congress of *Sovnarkhozy*, in December 1918, Larin interpreted the feelings of the whole economic presidium of VSNKh when he imputed the lack of an overall economic policy to the existence of a number of economic commissariats, each one carrying on its own policy. If the isolation of the economy demanded a rational division of resources, Larin argued, a single plan was needed and all economic commissariats ought to be subordinated to VSNKh. Rykov added that VSNKh could not do its job well if the whole distributive system was in the hands of the People's Commissariat of Food Procurement (*Narkomprod*). It was a nonsense, said Rykov, to fix prices, if *Narkomprod* was unable to collect the mass of raw materials and semi-manufactured products necessary to industry. VSNKh claimed full responsibility for distributing industrial products, and authority over *Narkomprod*. This claim was shared by Lozovskii, who proposed transforming the economic commissariats for food procurement, finance and industry into sections of VSNKh and completely subordinating local *sovnarkhozy* to the centre.[45]

The editorial in the first number of the VSNKh economic organ, *Ekonomicheskaia Zhizn'*, stressed that the transformation of VSNKh into an operative organ ordered by Lenin never gained the agreement of the economic experts.[46] Larin commented ironically on the functions assigned to VSNKh, which 'has turned out to be a college of industrial managers which carries out daily operations without deciding on general economic questions. If it is necessary to buy raw materials, it does so; if it is necessary to take a decision for Ivanovo-Voznesensk, it makes a plea.'[47]

The bureaucratism and inefficiency of VSNKh's organization partially derived from its position in the administrative hierarchy, which exposed it to friction with the other commissariats. After the reform of August 1918, VSNKh retained a very broad scope of action concerning the regulation and organization of production, but was not considered as a commissariat with full rights or a consultative board, but rather a technical and implementational organ. The other commissariats refused to accept VSNKh's directives until they had been checked and approved by *Sovnarkom*.[48] On the other hand, VSNKh could not claim the authority which could have been derived from the composition of its plenary session, since that body, which was supposed to meet once a month, did not do so. Military operations favoured dispersion of the cadres and lack of communications. Plenary sessions were made almost impossible. Increasing isolation of the presidium became unavoidable, deprived it of the authority necessary to balance the extending influence of other economic commissariats in *Sovnarkom* and, finally, sharpened the drive towards centralization and verticalism.

During war communism VSNKh reinforced its internal structure and developed several production sections, which were the outcome of its transformation into the department of industry. The production sections developed along the line of central administrations. In December 1920 the production sections of VSNKh were as follows:

sections incharge of *glavki* and *tsentry*. The Chemical Section included eighteen *glavki* and four special divisions. The Metal Section included five *glavki* and a number of central administrations in given industrial regions, GOMZA, GOMOMEZ, the Association of the Largest Metal Enterprises of Moscow, the Central Direction of Heavy Industry Works in South Russia, the *raion* management of the Urals enterprises. The Mining Council included seven *glavki*. The section of food-processing had five *glavki* and two production divisions. The Electrotechnical Section had two production associations, *Elektrotrest* and *Elektrosil'*;

sections having no *glavki*, e.g. the Printing Section;
Central Administrations directly under VSNKh: *Glavtekstil'*, *Glavodezhda* (garments), *Glavkozh* (leather), *Glavles* (timber), *Glavtorf* (peat);
mixed sections: the Committee of State Construction with six 'managements', the Transport-Materials Section, the Central Section of Communications, the Chief Administration of Agriculture and *glavkustprom* (for handicraft industry).[49]

VSNKh also had functional sections. These included sections and commissions entrusted with drawing up production plans and estimates for the central administrations subordinated to VSNKh, the plan of supply and the plan of distribution of industrial products. The functional sections comprised:

the Central Committee for Production. This committee started operating in February 1920, working on methods to calculate production-technical coefficients for some products, to prepare the way for some forms of central planning;

    the Committee for Utilization. This committee was formed in 1918 and took over the functions of the Central Committee for Production in the summer of 1920, after being provided with a technical apparatus;

    the Financial-Economic Section and the Estimates Committee;

    the Financial-Accounting Section, which began to operate in June 1919;

    the Council of Supply and Distribution, which operated from September 1920. It distributed raw and auxiliary materials to enterprises for further processing;

    the Scientific–Technical Committee;

    the Price Committee;

    the Section of Industrial Statistics;

    the 'Section of Other Towns', responsible for relations with the local *sovnarkhozy*;

    the Juridical Section.[50]

The strains exerted by war on economic resources and the impossibility of using market signals to direct investments and production compelled VSNKh to make some efforts towards planning. The Committee for Utilization, which made up lists of the available products for distribution, issued orders for their specific allocation and computed terms and percentages for fulfilment of these orders. These functions nourished some economists' hopes that, after the end of hostilities, VSNKh might rescue the old programme which was at the origin of its formation and develop into a central planning organ. But at the end of the war, relations between VSNKh and *Sovnarkom* had deteriorated to such an extent that the plan of reconstruction was worked out without the participation of VSNKh. The most comprehensive and impressive scheme of VSNKh provided by Miliutin in 1920 and including all its sections and committees, even the organs which never became active or rapidly exhausted their functions, is by itself evidence of the immense gap which had widened in two years between projects and immediate tasks, goals and available means, planning and feasibility (see Fig. 5.2).

The Eighth All-Russian Congress of Soviets, held from 22 to 29 December 1920, agreed to empower STO (Council of Labour and Defence) 'to establish the economic plan for the RSFSR and present it for approval to the All-Russian Executive Committee, to lead the work of the

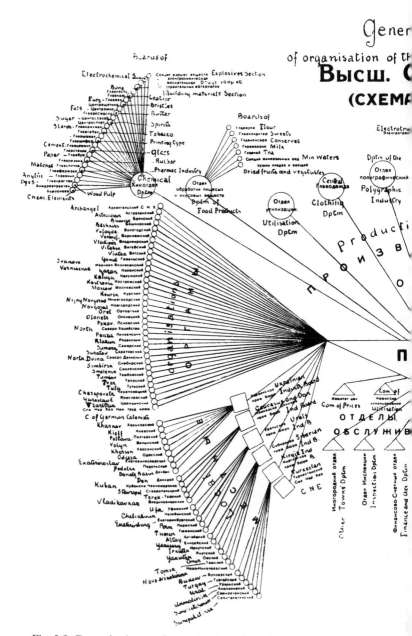

Fig. 5.2 General scheme of organization of the Supreme Council of National
Economy (from *The Russian Economist*, January 1921, vol. 1, no. 2, facing p. 332

national economic commission according to this plan and supervise its implementation'.[51] VSNKh was mentioned only as one of the central bodies having the right to membership in STO on an equal footing with the People's Commissariats of War, Labour, Communications and Transport, Agriculture, Food Procurement, Workers' and Peasants' Inspection, and the All-Russian Central Council of Trade Unions.

The reasons for VSNKh's downgrading have to be sought in the activities of its institutions and in the phenomenon of *glavkism*.

5.2 THE ORIGIN OF GLAVKISM

From its origin, VSNKh incorporated the several existing chief committees (*glavki*), which had been created during the war in the most important fields connected with war economy. This had been suggested by Bukharin, when the economists of the party met to discuss the role and functions of VSNKh,[52] but was in any case almost inevitable.

The Tsarist *glavki* fixed prices within their own branches. The application of uniform rules was aided by the policy of cartelization which had been taking place between 1907 and 1909 in several branches of the main industries. During the war chief committees were formed for fuel, metals, leather and textiles. Through these committees the government controlled prices, the distribution of raw materials and fuel, and the allocation of orders. Among the duties assigned to these committees were the fixing of maximum prices permissible for raw and semi-manufactured materials and manufactured goods; determination of productive capacity; distribution of raw materials among factories; purchase of raw materials, if necessary, and their distribution to factories; and other supervisory tasks.[53] Gradually control was extended from manufacturing industries to the raw materials industries and to distribution centres.

The existence of such economic organs, which already allowed some forms of state control over industry, provided a ready-made institutional framework for futher policies of coordination and control. The *glavki* were incorporated into VSNKh, as such. For those who wanted VSNKh to become a centre of research and originator of economic guidelines, the *glavki* represented in VSNKh's structure a spurious element which was likely to distort its policy, evolution and specific goals.

VSNKh's production sections often sprang out of former *glavki*, by the absorption of their technical staff and finances. Such was the origin of the Fuel Section, which originated from the Special Committee for Fuel formed by the Tsarist Government in August 1915. Together with the belongings of the former committees, VSNKh absorbed their methods and evolutionary tendencies. Examples of such a development may be found in the origin of the Central Committee for Tea, and by the transformation of *Prodameta* and *Krovlia*, two distribution syndicates, into state organs for the sale of cast iron.[54]

The utilization of existing economic structures was not only a transitional necessity or an economic device in the preparation of new methods and new organizations. It also conformed to the conscious effort to strengthen the elements of market control implicit in the structure of the *glavki*, inasmuch as these latter were interpreted as the latest forms of capitalist organization.[55] The creation of trusts and unions of enterprises was a major point of Lenin's programme. The whole idea of state capitalism rested on the organization of trustified industry controlled by the state, but essentially operating by capitalist methods. The industrial administrative organization by branches under the supervision of *glavki* corresponded to what Osinskii defined as the approach of left-wing Mensheviks, when he emphasized the fundamental principle of such an organization as the significant independence of *glavki* from VSNKh and an inverse relationship between *glavk* power and the power of VSNKh's sections.[56]

The Second Congress of *Sovnarkhozy* confirmed the structure of VSNKh as based on production sections supervising branch industrial activity. It also sanctioned the increasing power of the *glavki*, by assigning to *glavki* and *tsentry* (central committees, with similar functions) 'the rights of production sections of VSNKh'.[57] *Sovnarkom* having by that time decreed the operative role of VSNKh in industry, *glavki* and *tsentry* turned out to be the natural organs for the regulation and management of industry. The conspicuous role and the great deal of autonomy which these organs enjoyed during war communism justify the opinion that war communism did not quite accomplish real centralization.[58] They also justify the hypothesis that VSNKh was not able to formulate a consistent central economic policy and implement it. One of the arguments used to justify centralization was the need to avoid wasting resources, by carrying out a policy of supply according to national priorities. The evolution of the Fuel Section of VSNKh is, however, indicative of the forces which counteracted this programme and demanded other solutions. Together with material and labour belonging to the Special Committee for Fuel, the Fuel Section also inherited its business divisions, responsible for the regulation of individual branches of the fuel industry, such as coal, oil, peat, and charcoal. The great autonomy which those divisions already enjoyed under the Provisional Government affected their behaviour even after the formation of the Fuel Section. The individual divisions operated independently of one another as regards fuel supply and delivery. Corresponding *glavki* sprang out of them and were incorporated by the

Fuel Section: *Glavneft'* (oil), *Glavugol'* (coal), *Glavtorf* (peat) and *Glavles* (timber). The Fuel Section tended to lose its own function, and this jeopardized the possibility of a rapid substitution of one sort of fuel for another,[59] which would have been required by discontinuous military control over the supplying regions. The loss of the Donets Basin and the separation from Ural sources of coal stimulated VSNKh to undertake an effort of coordination. In the autumn of 1918 the Fuel Section was liquidated. To counteract the independent policies of *glavki* in fuel distribution, VSNKh decided to separate the organization of production from the administration of distribution. In December 1918 a chief committee for fuel (*Glavtop*) was organized. It included representatives of the fuel production organs, the Railways Commissariat, the War Commissariat and the central organs of the most important industries.[60] *Glavtop* was made responsible for drawing up the overall plan for distributing fuel among national sectors – railways, the fleet, industry, and the population – and for the overall estimation of fuel demand.[61] These measures, however, did not improve the administration of fuel delivery. *Glavugol'*, which since July 1918 had been in charge of regulating, financing, and formulating a programme of nationalization in the coal industry, in practice limited its activity to assisting production, in terms of supplying means of production, and consumer goods to coal workers, through a rather complicated procedure.[62] *Glavneft'*, entrusted since 20 June 1918 with nationalization of the oil companies and management of the oil industry, could not develop its activity in this field, because of the occupation first by the Turks and then by British troops in mid September of the Baku Basin, which supplied three-quarters of total oil output. Other sources of oil, in the Groznii Basin, could not be exploited despite control by Soviet troops, because transport was cut, and after February 1919, because of enemy occupation. Conceived initially as a production organ, *Glavneft'* began to operate only in 1919 as a distributive organ, in charge of oil stocks and oil price fixing.[63] Only *Glavleskom*, in charge of wood fuel, a poor but very important surrogate for other fuels in war communism, kept functions in the organization of production, retaining overall responsibility for distribution. The interdepartmental council of *Glavtop*, which should have met periodically to ensure coordination at the distributive level, did not meet at all.[64] Thus, *Glavtop* became a supplementary organ for the receipt and transfer of orders and was not able to provide a flexible distribution of substitution products, when contingent reasons prevented the use of planned resources. The individual *glavki* remained in charge of distribution, though, as has been shown, they often could not seriously carry out a plan of delivery.

The proliferation of organs, whose tasks became rapidly obsolete in a fast-moving situation, and the lack of coordination among them, increased the length of delivery and bureaucratism in supply. The permanence of the former staff in several *glavki* was a further element of bureaucratization, in so far as it necessitated forms of control over decision-making. Hence VSNKh gave its own direct representatives the right of veto in the decisions of the several *glavki* operating under the Chemical Section.[65]

The fuel crisis of 1919 prompted the idea of a commission with plenipotentiary powers. This proposal, however, was rejected and a special commission was formed consisting of representatives of the fuel-producing *glavki* and *Glavtop*. *Glavtop* was defined as the supreme organ of fuel policy in the republic and the sole organ in charge of distribution and delivery of fuel and control over its rational utilization. Leading experts were appointed and sections were formed for timber, coal, oil and transport, plus a number of functional sections. During the summer of 1919, *Glavtop* carried out an inventory of stocks of timber, peat, charcoal, through enquiries, reports and inspections. Special agents were appointed to verify the exact needs of the local economy. Some principles of priority in fuel distribution were worked out. The fuel commission worked jointly with the interdepartmental committee which represented the relevant *glavki* and *tsentry* and large industrial unions. To fix some priorities the Committee for Utilization broke down industry into categories and groups. A statistical section collected information on industrial consumption. When the growing importance of wood fuel was understood, STO decided to concentrate into *Glavtop* the supervision of all wood fuel purchase operations, to build up a national stock. A system of premiums was introduced to speed up timber collection. In October premiums were increased twice.[66] By that time the improvement of communications and transport, due to the military situation on the Eastern front, allowed some steps to be taken towards an effective concentration of distribution. By a decision of VSNKh's Presidium, a single transport agency was formed by joining together all competing agencies in this field, in order to concentrate the dispatch of all types of fuel on behalf of *Glavtop*. In February 1920 a plan of fuel dispatch was worked out, taking into account, first of all, the quantity of wood fuel needed by the railways. With the collaboration of the Railways Commissariat, the number of wagons necessary for the transport of various types of fuel was calculated. Demand was calculated by taking into account, first, the requirements of Moscow and Petrograd, and then those of other consumers.[67] Some improvements were registered in the collection of timber. While the percentage fulfilment of the first plan of timber collection in the well-endowed region of the North was only 19 per cent of the original target, amounting to almost two million cubic sazhens (1 sazhen = 2.134 metres),[68] the second wood fuel campaign of 1919–20 was 79 per cent fulfilled.[69] In the first nine months of 1919 1,124,000 cub. sazh. of wood were collected and 439,000 dispatched. In the first nine months of 1920, 1,579,700 cub. sazh. were collected and 662,400 were dispatched from the forests.[70] But the collection of timber was far from being concentrated in the wood administration of VSNKh. The following data on participation in wood fuel collection show that a significant part was undertaken outside the organization of *Glavleskom*, in the first six months of 1920.[71]

Table 5.1. *Fulfilment of targets for wood fuel collection, January–June 1920*

	% of general target	% fulfilment of own target
Gubleskomy (provincial timber committees)	41.5	95.0
Railway committees	24.0	91.0
Military organs	16.0	60.0
Glavki and *tsentry*	14.0	52.0
Other agencies	4.0	30.0

The success of the railway committees was attributed to incentives in the form of higher wages, supply of feed for horses and consumer goods for timber collectors. This was considered by the VSNKh organs as unfair competition, probably because the other agencies did not have items for material incentives and were obliged to rely on compulsory labour for timber collection. The relative success of the railway committees, however, could also be explained by the fact that the railways had formed a network of contacts with wood fuel agents during the First World War[72] and they probably kept these contacts after the revolution. The improvement of timber fuel collection in 1920, however, was not sufficient to meet overall demand, taking into account the dramatic fall in production of other fuels. *Ekonomicheskaia Zhizn'* reported in November 1920 that the supply of fuel, calculated as units of wood fuel, had been 9,497,000 cub. sazh. in 1918 and 7,155,000 in 1919.[73] Factories provided wood fuel for themselves.

The increase of peat production was significant, but was due to a more than proportional increase in machinery and labour. In 1919 the number of enterprises under *Glavtorf* (the central administration of peat) rose from 170 to 205, the number of machines from 832 to 881 and the work force from 49,000 to 57,860, compared to 1918. Output increased from 57.7

million puds to 67 million. Average productivity decreased.[74] The distribution of coal should have occurred only through the coal section of *Glavtop*, according to monthly plans of orders, consumer demand, industrial consumption norms worked out by the technical section, and capacity of the furnaces. But even in this field an effective centralization did not take place, owing to the precariousness of communications. Until the beginning of 1920 *Glavtop* did not have local agents in the Urals, and *Glavugol'* remained in charge of the distribution of Urals coal. There is evidence that *Glavtop* achieved an effective concentration only in the policy of distribution of oil, petrol and kerosene.[75] But oil represented only a small percentage of total consumption of fuel and, furthermore, its main sources in 1919 were cut off from the centre. The output of oil in January 1920 was 18,200,000 puds, and in October 1920 only 10,800,000 puds. The Baku oilfields were finally captured by the Bolsheviks at the end of April 1920, but in three months, from June to August 1920, the number of (working) wells fell from 1,518 to 845 and the number of workers by 2,000, owing to the difficulty in food supply.[76]

In this situation, *Glavtop* should have centralized the supply of the existing stocks of fuel, but it did not succeed in this task. People responsible for fuel distribution complained that superior organs took decisions often opposite to *Glavtop*'s, thereby nullifying its planning effort. The lack of a deliberate connection between productive *glavki* and *Glavtop* jeopardized the possibility of working out meaningful plans of distribution, inasmuch as *Glavtop* ignored the quantity of output which could be produced, collected and dispatched. The individual sections of *Glavtop*, on the other hand, were not sufficiently in touch with each other and distribution remained fragmented. The weakness of the local apparatus did not make it possible to gather reliable figures on local stocks.[77]

An analogous fragmentation of decisions occurred in other fields. During war communism the *glavk* system developed into *glavkism*, i.e. a proliferation of central authorities for each branch of production, rather than evolving towards a centralized system of supply and distribution.

Recalling the formation of the *glavki*, Larin emphasized the innovating role of VSNKh, thus involuntarily starting the epic distortion of post-revolutionary records: 'I established a certain number of *glavki* in an "anarchic way", by simply publishing in the Official Journal the decision to set them up with my own signature ... A great number of other *glavki* were, afterwards, set up by Rykov, with my agreement and at my invitation ... without consulting any of the three existing legislative authorities.'[78] Larin's statement was misleading for two reasons. Firstly, because concealment of the pre-revolutionary origin of *glavki* tended to confuse any analysis of the behaviour of such organs, which would have been more accurate if their connection with the liberal economy had been acknowledged.[79] Secondly, because the formation of Soviet *glavki* did not respond to an immediate necessity of imposing central control over all industrial activities, which would have justified their 'anarchical' development, but to a conscious effort to continue and reinforce the policy of control over distribution, by which the Bolshevik leadership believed an end could be put to concealment of stocks and to speculation. As long as stocks of finished products and semi-manufactured goods lasted, more or less until mid 1919, the activity of *glavki* and *tsentry* consisted in the collection of materials and distribution of products, as did the Tsarist committees'. The latter coordinated the activity of the factories working for military needs. Their tasks were not clearly defined at once, but took shape during the world war. Likewise, the Soviet *glavki* and *tsentry* did not have a pre-defined sphere of competence, but a sphere 'anarchically defined by scattered decrees'.[80]

Continuity between Tsarist and Soviet institutions, however, should not conceal some innovations. *Tsentrotekstil'*, which was formed by the unification of existing committees for cotton, yarn, cloth, flax and jute, had the right of approving and changing past instructions, of accounting and distributing raw materials, semi-manufactured goods and fabrics, like the former committees. Its autonomy, however, was much larger. *Tsentrotekstil'* had powers in production and financing,[81] and rights of requisition of materials, and confiscation and sequestration of enterprises. Only the Presidium of VSNKh had the right to change or abrogate any resolution of *Tsentrotekstil'*. The rights of this organ included even the requisition of private enterprises supplying raw materials, equipment and auxiliary materials to the textile industry.[82]

Ekonomicheskaia Zhizn' affirmed that *Tsentrotekstil'* had been a managerial organ since the second half of 1918,[83] though the Second Congress of *Sovnarkhozy* in December 1918 had decided that the *glavki* and *tsentry* were only organs of supply and distribution.[84] In fact, the effective autonomy of the *glavki* was great and it was displayed when conditions were favourable. The technical section of *Tsentrotekstil'*, for instance, was competent in all concerning the technical side of productive activity. It formulated proposals about new investments and new production processes and was supposed to evaluate their efficiency. It also proposed new products and norms for repair and construction. Its board was to be convened not less than twice a month.[85] Earlier researches were continued into the possibility of substituting flax for cotton and on their combined use, which gave satisfactory results when, Russia being cut off from the cotton territory of Turkestan, the production of flax which exceeded normal domestic needs was found to cost no more to produce than cotton fabrics.[86] If rights in matters of production sometimes remained on paper, the reason was civil war, which obstructed a consistent policy for production and made a policy for distributing existing stocks urgent. Intervention of the *glavki* and *tsentry* in production occurred, however, in a peculiar way: by shutting down factories, by transferring machines and equipment from one factory to another, by making an autonomous policy for provision of raw materials and setting their prices, often in agreement with the suppliers. In so doing, the *glavki* did not follow a central plan. Their initiatives could spring only from a one-sided outlook, which in many cases jeopardized central coordination.

VSNKh, which had to bear the burden of Tsarist legacies, started to see in the *glavk* system the possibility of forcing on the economy an industrial organization by branches, capable of providing the vertical connections on which centralization could be based. Some of the most authoritative leaders of VSNKh affirmed that the regional organization, on which the system of *sovnarkhozy* was based, was the result of an anarchical system leading to greater industrial disorganization.[87] In war communism, *glavkism* was seen as an alternative to the *sovnarkhozy*. This alternative began to involve the best energies of the country in tacit polemics, sometimes with the political power.

The most vigorous accusation against the *glavk* system came from the left-wing communists. Osinskii had singled out the danger of their unlimited autonomy since 1918. He believed that this autonomy could hinder the efforts to establish effective centralization and planned direction of the economy and lead to bureaucratic centralism. Long before the revision of economic organization, which started with Trotskii's denunciation of *glavkism* at the Ninth Congress of the Party, Osinskii affirmed that horizontal connections were needed as much as vertical ones, and that proletarian socialism ought to be based on the transfer of a number of decisions from above to below and on mass participation in management.[88] This criticism, however, remained unheard in a political context dominated by other preoccupations and in an economic context which was unable rapidly to replace the existing forms of organization by new forms.

Foreign intervention and the aggravation of civil war in the autumn of 1918 gave rise to a climate of emergency which undermined the importance of a challenge to *glavkism* as such, for the *glavki* acquired additional strength from the losses of territory where raw materials were concentrated. At this time Russia was cut off from international economic relations. The loss of the Urals and the Baku Basin made the provision of ferrous metals and fuel critical. Of the remaining coalfields under Soviet control, the Moscow Basin produced very little (around 2 per cent of total coal output in 1916), of poor quality.[89] In these fields, labour productivity fell in 1918 to 48 per cent below the 1916 level.[90] The coalfields in the Moscow Region supplied in nine months of 1918 only 2 per cent of the total industrial fuel consumption of the same region.[91] Supply to the metallurgical industry using Urals ferrous metals was limited to 4 per cent of the normal supply of iron.[92] The textile industry, where the scarcity of fuel was less injurious since peat and wood fuel could be used, was hindered by the interruption of transport with Turkestan, which together with Bokhara and Khiva supplied eight-ninths of the pre-war cotton yield.[93]

In this situation, the need for central control over existing stocks added a concrete rationale to the *glavk* system and to the theoretical motivations for *glavkism* pronounced by Larin and Kritsman before the worsening of the economic and political situation. One may still wonder, however, whether the instability of power, the challenge of the class struggle to efficiency, the mobility of frontiers, the defectiveness and irregularity of the transport system, were, in that situation, elements which conflicted with the *glavk* structure, its hierarchy and the political bureaucratism which it entailed.

5.3 GLAVKI AND TSENTRY: THE VERTICAL ECONOMIC ORGANIZATION

Chief and central committees provided an institutional framework for all industrial enterprises of a given branch, to assist them in the provision of raw materials and, at the same time, exert control over output. In a sense, such a framework was well adapted to Lenin's aim of overall accounting and control over stocks and inventories. Initially, *glavki* and *tsentry* were conceived as organs for the regulation of the corresponding branch of production. Subsequently, they became direct managerial organs.[94]

The identification of a *glavk* with a single branch of production implied the automatic inclusion of any enterprise of the branch, even a new one, into the *glavk*. These organs, therefore, covered both nationalized and non-nationalized enterprises. *Tsentrotekstil'*, for instance, had the right to control the productive activity of *kustar'* and small industry and to form amalgamations, if this met the needs of the textile industry.[95]

The power of the *glavki* was such that Kritsman defined them as autonomous organizations with unlimited rights within the confines of their branch. Or in other words, in an expression indicative of the preference for such forms of organization, as 'centres of proletarian dictatorship in a given branch of the national economy'.[96] Osinskii, on the contrary, focusing on the composition of management, attributed to the *glavki* the role of state capitalistic organizations.[97] In spite of a different understanding of the political implications of these organs, however, both economists acknowledged their economic importance.

In the original scheme of economic organization, *glavki* and *tsentry* occupied an intermediate position between the production sections of VSNKh and the enterprises:

VSNKh
(Presidium)
production sections
glavki and *tsentry*
enterprises

The production sections were supposed to coordinate the overall activity of an individual branch, by issuing general guidelines concerning the allocation of investments and development of new production, as well as being in change of financing.

When the original model fell to pieces, because of *Sovnarkom* pressure to transform VSNKh into a high managerial board, and because of the exogenous effects of war, *glavki* and *tsentry* were elevated to the status of production sections, which in some cases dissolved into the corresponding *glavki* or *tsentry*.[98]

During war communism, depreciation of capital was not paid for, nor were current repairs made: active plants renewed their capital equipment at the expense of inactive plants.[99] This fact enhanced the importance of the *glavki* and *tsentry*, since they reviewed all the enterprises in their branch and were able to decide which to shut down, in order to transfer their equipment to the active ones. *Glavki* and *tsentry* made widespread use of the right to close down, which in the context of war communism organization was equivalent to allocating resources at a microeconomic level. Whilst the production sections officially remained alive, they were not, in fact, separated from the *glavki*. For instance, the Board of the Chemical Section was formed by the presidents of the individual *glavki* comprising the main branches of this indusrty, who presented their estimates to the board for approval.[100]

During war communism, the effective hierarchy was as follows:

VSNKh
(Presidium)
Glavki and production sections on equal footing
enterprises

In some branches, where a policy of unionization was carried forward, the hierarchy respected the following order:

VSNKh
(Presidium)
glavki and production sections on equal footing
unions (trusts, and *kusty*)
enterprises

In the absence of an overall organizational framework, *glavki* and *tsentry* behaved like industrial conglomerates. They endeavoured to extend their scope and activity at the expense of other economic institutions, such as the *sovnarkhozy*, or reciprocally to invade each other's branches. VSNKh's Presidium was alleged not to coordinate their activities. Kaktyn, a member of the Northern Region *Sovnarkhoz*, commented: '[*Glavki*] quietly do their business apart from the centre, without letting it know about their life, goals, tasks... [they] only get from the centre instructions and working capital [*operatsionnyi fond*], that's all.'[101]

Financing, which by law was under VSNKh's control, via its Estimate and Anticipation Commission,[102] was gradually concentrated into the *glavki*. Their indirect responsibility in this field, i.e. collection and coordination of the enterprises' estimates,[103] evolved into direct financing.

In so far as stocks of finished and semi-manufactured products made supply and redistribution possible, the activity of the *glavki* remained confined to registration of enterprises' inventories and to removal of their stocks, according to lists of orders. In branches where the provision of raw materials could not be directly controlled, such as agriculture and forestry, *glavki* carried out a lively purchase activity, so long as market relations allowed. Before the introduction of *prodrazverstka* and *razverstka* of the agricultural raw materials, in fact, prices were a matter of bargaining between central agents and local producers. *Tsentrotekstil'* negotiated directly with producers the terms of purchase for flax, cotton, hemp, etc.[104] In 1919 the lack of a good system of supply to replace the market was particularly felt in the provision of raw and auxiliary materials. The interests of the enterprises clashed against the policy of centralization of all sorts of fuel, which entailed bureaucratic delays in distribution. The enterprises claimed autonomy in procurement. A conference of representatives of textile enterprises urged the Chief Peat Committee on 6 March 1919 to let enterprises with a production process based on peat make autonomous purchases, by their own methods, and claimed the right to purchase wood fuel directly, through their own purchasing organs.[105] The inefficiency of the centralized policy of supply of auxiliary materials was felt not only by branches of lesser military importance, but by all industrial branches. The factory managements of GOMZA, for example, claimed the right to the direct exploitation of forests and sent a petition for it to VSNKh, to the Chief Timber Committee and to the Central Fuel Administration (*Glavtop*).[106] In March 1920 only 20 per cent of the raw materials received by GOMZA were supplied centrally.[107]

When the system of *razverstka*, i.e. obligatory delivery by quota, was extended to raw materials,[108] the *glavki* had a principal role in determining prices and the scale of the distribution quotas which applied to producers.[109] In this field, the overlap with the parallel activity of *Narkomprod* was not an insignificant source of interdepartmental conflict. In some cases the central committees adopted an economic viewpoint, which was not appreciated by a *Narkomprod* more inclined to military methods. *Tsentrotekstil'* formed its local flax bureaux, which applied price differentiation according to the quantity delivered: four million puds of flax were paid 100 million rubles, five million puds were paid 150 million rubles, and so forth on an increasing scale.[110] This policy was not appreciated by the organs of *Narkomprod*. The second conference of the food procurement organs agreed that uniform methods had to be adopted for the collection of consumer agricultural products and raw materials, and that only the local organs of *Narkomprod* should be entrusted with *razverstka*.[111] However, pragmatism prevailed in practice and procurement of raw materials remained under the competence of the *glavki* for a long time. Only in June 1920 did *Sovnarkom* try to put an end to the ambiguous situation prevailing in the collection of agricultural raw materials by declaring that state purchase of the principal sorts, such as hemp, flax, wool, leather, silk and oil seeds, was to be transferred to *Narkomprod*. The connection with industry was ensured by the inclusion of one representative of VSNKh with a casting vote in each local organ of *Narkomprod*.[112] The interests of the *glavki* were, however, safeguarded. The funds provided by VSNKh were tied to each individual item and could not be transferred to other products by decision of *Narkomprod*. The system of premiums was maintained, and in some cases extended to individual rewards.[113] This compromise settled an interdepartmental conflict between two central organs and therefore worked in favour of centralization and against the efforts of local *sovnarkhozy* to regain control over the provision of raw materials in opposition to the policy of the *glavki*.[114]

The *glavki* were also able to maintain their control over the stocks and use them in transactions forbidden by law. Although the law on payment by clearing balances should have allowed central control over transactions of the state sector, Rykov stated at the plenary session of VSNKh in

September 1918 that commodities were transferred from state producing organs to state consuming organs through 'the speculators of nationalized enterprises'.[115] It is likely that this practice continued. In February 1921, *Pravda* reported that a certain amount of goods were concealed from inspection and control in state warehouses, and that figures concerning outgoing materials were often exaggerated. Goods were delivered to private enterprises as a result of falsification.[116] By these activities, the enterprises were able to gain an extra source of financing, independent of the legal one, which was a powerful incentive for the maintenance of interdepartmental monetary transactions, despite efforts made by VSNKh to implement the clearing system.

5.4 THE CENTRAL ADMINISTRATIONS (GLAVNYE PRAVLENIIA)

With the extension of nationalization the problem of management of state enterprises added new tasks, which required the formation of new organs. Savel'ev, one of the promoters of VSNKh, was in favour of transforming *glavki* and *tsentry* into managerial organs subordinated to the production sections of VSNKh, which carried out a unifying function within each main branch. Savel'ev argued, at the end of 1918 when war had already added new reasons for centralization, that *glavki* and *tsentry* as such should not exist.[117] This idea was at the origin of the central administrations (*glavnye pravleniia*).[118] These administrations, however, were formed within the existing *glavki*, or parallel with them, and not as substitutes for them. In some cases the transition from the *glavk* as a regulatory organ to the *glavnoe pravlenie* as a managerial organ was quite clear. On 25 January 1919, VSNKh decided 'to transform the chief committee (*glavk*) for tobacco, owing to the nationalization of all tobacco companies... into the central administration (*glavnoe pravlenie*) of nationalized enterprises... and to entrust the latter with the organization of tobacco production on condition that it used the best-equipped enterprises and closed down small factories'.[119] In other cases, a *glavk* coexisted with a central administration in the same branch, as, for instance, in textiles, *Glavtekstil'* and *Tsentrotekstil'*. One main difference was in the composition of the central boards. *Glavki* and *tsentry* were directed by councils of 30–50 people, who elected a smaller presidium (or board). The central administration had no plenary council and was directed by a board of people appointed by VSNKh in agreement with the trade unions.[120] Many of the subsections of the production sections of VSNKh were transformed into central administrations of the nationalized enterprises.[121] Another difference concerned the enterprises' status. The central administrations were presumed to be directly concerned with the nationalized enterprises and to control their business activities closely, while *glavki* and *tsentry* were to control private enterprises. But this distinction was not always clear, owing to the inclusion of nationalized enterprises in several *glavki* as well. There was perhaps another reason for the formation of central administrations in several branches: the need for direct central management of those factories and plants which VSNKh considered to be the most efficient and where raw materials and labour could be concentrated and output more closely controlled. VSNKh tried to include experts and technicians on the boards of the central administrations. A commission was formed of representatives of the Presidium of VSNKh and representatives of the Central Council of Trade Unions to examine candidacies. The list of candidates was then submitted for approval of the presidium.[122]

When *Glavtekstil'* was formed, seven people were appointed to its board by VSNKh in agreement with the trade union of the textile workers, and technicians were appointed at the head of each subsection.[123] The creation of *Glavtekstil'* was decided after an inspection of *Tsentrotekstil'* ordered by *Sovnarkom*. This inspection led to the conclusion that the administration of *Tsentrotekstil'* had contributed to increasing disorganization and that a single autonomous management was needed, a sort of trust, to manage the practical business of the chief committee for the textile industry.[124] By the initial statute of *Tsentrotekstil'* its presidium was to be formed by eleven people, nine of whom were elected by the council and consisted of two-thirds workers and one-third technicians, plus one person appointed by VSNKh and one by the All-Russian Trade Union of Textile Industries.[125] When *Glavtekstil'* was formed, a representative of it was introduced into the *Tsentrotekstil'* Presidium.[126] In this case the central administration was given higher authority than the central committee of the same branch. But in branches where the large number of enterprises did not justify the formation of a single managerial board, *glavki* and *tsentry* remained the prevalent institutional form of administration.[127]

Some authors distinguish the role of the central administrations from that of the *glavki* by focusing on the managerial activity of the former and on the regulatory activity of the latter.[128] This difference was probably the reason for the creation of the central administration as a new organ. However, in practice, the actual work of the two organs was such that it is not possible to draw a clear distinction between them. The statute which Savel'ev proposed to draw up for all *glavki* was never worked out. In effect, the *glavki* were not confined to the role of mere procurement organizations, and the central administrations, on the other hand, sometimes had the function of regulating an entire industrial branch.[129] In addition, decisions regarding closure, transfer of capital equipment, distribution of financial funds and price setting, were currently taken by both *glavki* and *tsentry* during war communism, in the way that the specific managerial functions of the central administrations were supposed to do. At the end of 1920, VSNKh claimed to have eighteen *glavki* and thirty-four central administrations in its organization;[130] but Kritsman reported fifty-two central administrations only, without making any distinction among them:[131] a pointer to the levelling of functions which occurred in practice.

5.5 SHORTCOMINGS OF GLAVKISM

Enterprises depended on their own *glavk* for financing and supply of raw materials. This system, however, was never fully implemented. Several *glavki* did not know the true number of enterprises in their branch.[132] This was likely to occur because private enterprises tried not to be included in the *glavk* system, since they could be shut down and their stocks and equipment transferred against their will; and because a significant number of undertakings went on working under protection of the local *sovnarkhozy*. The fluctuations in territories under Soviet control constituted, of course, another obstacle to accurate record-keeping by *glavki*.

Efforts to centralize orders for production were made, but they did not succeed. VSNKh formed a central orders committee, which should have functioned as the intermediary between producers and consumers. Orders from customers ought to have been presented to this VSNKh committee, which in turn was responsible for passing them on to the corresponding production sections and *glavki*.[133] This procedure should have made possible central control over the destination and use of state financing and eventually the drawing up of a list of priorities. The central orders committee of VSNKh, however, was unable to cope with these enormous tasks.[134] A similar endeavour did not have more success at the level of the Northern Region *Sovnarkhoz*. *Severozakaz*, the department of orders of this *sovnarkhoz*, was established to decide which factory could best fulfil each order, and to fix prices, deadlines and other terms of delivery by preparatory negotiations with the executants. After conclusion of an agreement, the contract was to be registered in the Journal of Orders and become mandatory. In practice, however, *Severozakaz* became a registration bureau, while the whole work of negotiation went to the production sections of the *sovnarkhoz* and their respective orders divisions.[135]

Purchase orders were to be received by production sections and *glavki*, which transferred them to enterprises for execution, according to their own appreciation of priorities.[136] But in some cases, enterprises endeavoured to find less bureaucratic channels. For raw materials, either they directly contacted the distribution organs, rather than applying first to their own *glavk*, as in the case of ferrous materials with *Prodrasmet* (the organ in charge of their distribution), or they resorted to the illegal market, as in the case of wood fuel.[137]

The support furnished to *glavki* by the various functional sections of VSNKh which dealt with coordination in the financial and productive fields was of a bureaucratic nature and did not help to speed up execution.[138] The comparative efficiency of factories remaining outside the *glavki* sphere increased. At the end of 1919 Miliutin complained that in Moscow 65 per cent of orders fell to the factories of the city *sovnarkhoz* (*gorsovnarkhoz*) and only 35 per cent to those of *glavki* and *tsentry*.[139] The most evident shortcoming of the *glavk* structure was that it did not ensure central allocation of resources and central distribution of output, in accordance with any priority ranking. The *glavki* were quite independent of each other and released their products according to their own criteria. Thus, complementary materials were provided to the factories in arbitrary proportions: in some places they accumulated, whereas in others there was a shortage.[140] Moreover, the length of the procedure needed to release the products increased scarcity at given moments, since products remained stored until the centre issued the purchase order on behalf of a centrally defined customer.[141] Unused stocks coexisted with acute scarcity. The centre was unable to determine the correct proportions among necessary materials and eventually to enforce implementation of the orders for their total quantity. The gap between theory and practice was significant. In theory, enterprises belonging to the *glavk* system lost the right to decide what to produce and consequently were supposed to be relieved of the obligation of selling. On this theoretical framework was based the system of non-monetary clearing balances. The enterprises were to get the necessary materials and means without cash payment, and were to deliver their products to the distributive organs of the *sovnarkhozy* or the central administrations without compensation.[142] Clearing balances were, therefore, consistent with the assumption that enterprises were not autonomous units and need not keep money reserves for production purposes in addition to working capital for payment of wages. Enterprises would possibly have been willing to renounce their autonomy if a coherent system of orders, supply and incentives had been replacing market regulators in a satisfactory way. This did not occur in practice, and enterprises strove to keep some margins of autonomy. They started hiding stocks of products and semi-finished materials for the purpose of illegal trade.[143] In some cases, only part of output was delivered to the competent organs. For the remainder, no book-keeping was done. State control organs frequently reported cases of discrepancies between reported and real stocks.[144] Underestimation of inventories reached in some branches even 80 per cent of total value.[145]

Irregular, unsystematic and insufficient financing by *Narkomfin*, together with a random supply of raw materials and fuel,[146] compelled the production organs to increase their reserves and stocks of finished products, which they eventually used to fill out the meagre wage fund, anticipating the system of payment in kind, or to obtain raw materials. *Tsentrotekstil'* was reported to have exchanged ten wagons of manufactured products for wool, with the approval of VSNKh.[147] Clearing by money or by values in kind took place in spite of the law.[148] Though, on the one hand, these forms of illegal behaviour hindered accounting and plans by the central authorities, on the other hand they may have helped the economy to reduce the severity of the inconsistencies and conflicts that the abrupt changes in economic organization were bound to produce.

5.6 FINANCING INDUSTRY

According to VSNKh's own decision on financing, VSNKh itself had the right of financing any state institution and the right of taking preliminary decisions on financing private enterprises, whether this was to be done by the State Bank, the People's Commissar of Trade and Industry, or other public institutions. Points 7 and 9 of the decree made it clear that VSNKh's financial power was intended as a form of control over private business. VSNKh had, indeed, the power to modify orders, agreements and contracts of delivery and to appoint commissars in the administrations and managements of the financed enterprises with powers of control over them.[149] After nationalization of the banks, *Sovnarkom* attached a commission to the National Bank for the examination and approval of monetary advances to industry. This commission included representatives of the All-Russian Central Executive Committee, VSNKh, the All-Russian Central Council of Trade Unions, and representatives of other People's Commissariats. Local commissions were attached to the local branches of the National Bank.[150] This initiative was an early pointer to the fact that the political power did not intend renouncing its privileges in the financial domain in favour of an organ whose political credentials were still uncertain.

The leadership of the party, however, did not have precise ideas about alternative forms of financing. Projects in this field were related to individual views on industrial organization. In the course of the negotiations with the Meshchersky group a project was elaborated for forming special banks of production. These banks were to finance major branches of production (a grain bank, a metal bank, a textiles bank, and so forth). Half the shares would be held by the state and half by private interests in the industry.[151] This project was related to the possibility, which was ventured at that time, of partially compensating the shareholders of the nationalized factories by converting their shares into state bonds or by letting shareholders keep a certain quota of the shares of the newly organized trusts.[152]

This approach to financing industry and to industrial organization found consistent opposition among some financial leaders of VSNKh and among the left. The fear that, by this operation, private banks would regain control over industry doomed such projects. In 1918 enterprises continued to be financed by a system of advances on commercial papers.[153] To obtain finance the enterprise had to apply to the *glavk* to which it belonged, by producing its provisional estimates. If the *glavk* had not yet been formed, the certification of approval of the estimates had to be produced by the *oblast sovnarkhoz*. The tight financial situation did not enable money to be advanced for more than a two-month estimate, as Larin affirmed at the plenary session of VSNKh in April 1918.[154] As a norm, monetary advances covered 75 per cent of the value of inventories. The enterprise had a current account, through which it settled its payments.[155] In May 1918 VSNKh was given the right to approve money advances out of the State Treasury for nationalized and confiscated enterprises. Two billion rubles were assigned to VSNKh for this purpose. But a further decree specified that each single expenditure out of this VSNKh fund was subject to the approval of *Sovnarkom*.[156]

The question of industrial financing was debated at the First Congress of *Sovnarkhozy*, which tried to define the guidelines of policy in this field, to remove it from the uncertainty and randomness of government decisions. Sokol'nikov proposed that a special fund of two and a half or three billion rubles be assigned to VSNKh,[157] in order to speed up industrial financing. Owing to the increasing social and political tensions of summer 1918, *Sovnarkom* became even more reluctant than before to extend VSNKh's powers. As indicated above, in August 1918 the draft project prepared by VSNKh experts concerning its reorganization, which in the financial field assigned to it the direction of financial policy at the national level, was rejected by *Sovnarkom*. But VSNKh did not intend to renounce easily what it considered its necessary prerogatives. On 29 August 1918, an instruction of VSNKh reaffirmed its rights in the financial domain. VSNKh stated that its Financial-Economic Section was responsible for preliminary examination of all policy in this sphere, for preliminary examination of the estimates of all sections, *glavki* and *tsentry* and other institutions and enterprises, as well as for the preliminary examination of the estimates of the other People's Commissariats according to law and regulations, and finally, for the preliminary evaluation of all questions concerning industrial financing in the form of loans, credits, etc. This instruction claimed also competence for decisions concerning the amount and the terms of industrial financing to private industry.[158]

The features of what should be financial control in the new economic framework were discussed again in October 1918. The representatives of the Commissariat for State Control maintained that they were to check not only book-keeping and industrial financial activity, but also the correctness, legitimacy and regularity of the whole activity of an enterprise. Their arguments suggest that even VSNKh's financial operations were to be checked by state control.[159] The government's approach to financial control, however, was not shared by the Second Congress of *Sovnarkhozy* which, in December 1918, supported VSNKh's claims in industrial financing. It was Larin who for the first time presented the features of a 'state command economy' and the role of financing in it. Enterprises did not need rewards or payments, since they were to receive from above the necessary means, such as metals, fuel, and funds for wage payments and small expenditures. The financial problem was, therefore, reduced to one of having correct procedures of accounting and book-keeping. Depreciation and insurance allowances were to be assigned by the state. The current book-keeping of material and monetary flows was to be carried out by the *sovnarkhozy*. VSNKh was to be credited with the state's funds deposited at the National Bank. The bank was to be transformed into an accounting bureau (*kassa*), for the mere implementation of VSNKh's decisions on the allocation of finance. A distinction was drawn between investment decisions at the macroeconomic level and criteria for assignment of funds to each production unit. The allocation of investments by branches was to be determined by VSNKh. The criteria for assignment of enterprise finance to individual units were to be worked out by the production sections, with the power to approve an enterprise's estimates. Representatives of the People's Commissariats of Finance and of State Control would assist the productive sections in this task.[160]

In such a framework the transactions between enterprises need not be carried out in money tokens, but through a system of clearing balances on the basis of credit accounts opened by the state financial organs, after approval of the estimates submitted by the enterprises. It was assumed that enterprises would need cash only for wage payments and purchase of materials which had not yet been put under state control. A *Sovnarkom* decree of August 1918 on accounting operations had, in fact, allowed Soviet institutions to clear mutual payments through the system of clearing balances. Mutual payments and transfer of funds were to be simply registered as a budgetary transfer from the customer's to the seller's budget. The National Bank, which kept the current accounts, was authorized to turn over to the customer a receipt concerning the new balance of his budget and to inform at the same time the seller of the new entry into his budget.[161] Payments in cash were authorized only for purchases below five thousand rubles. The August 1918 decree sought to prevent higher payments disguised as separate small purchase of raw materials, if nationalized industry was unable to meet the demand, or if notice of the agreement had not been received by the customer within three days of the presentation of the request. Money contracts and the address of the supplier were to be reported to the corresponding financial organs of the local soviets. The decree on non-monetary clearing balances had, however, met several objections, particularly in the provinces. Representatives of the provinces at the Second Congress of *Sovnarkhozy* manifested irritation at the slowness of the financial procedure attached to the advance of state funds and to the dispatch of money. Some delegates reported that provincial enterprises had been left without any source of finance, and that wage payments were delayed for 5–6 months.[162] Not always did the Soviet delegates realize that the disorganization was mainly due to the too hasty nationalization of banking. In addition to the big banks, relatively small credit institutions had been suppressed, without thought of satisfactory alternatives. The provincial and city cooperatives were abolished on 17 May 1918, and the mutual credit cooperatives on 10 October 1918. Soon after, foreign banks and city public banks were liquidated, and the Moscow National Bank was nationalized.[163] A provincial delegate reminded the congress that private production needed to be financed too.[164] But the claims of the provinces remained unheard. Among central representatives, only Gukovskii expressed doubt as to the rules on which the 'command economy' was to operate and develop: 'We say that enterprises must act upon orders, without payments. The question is: what if they do not do it?' He maintained that *Narkomfin* should be responsible for deciding whom to satisfy and whom not, in relation to general financial policy. He added that not only should the production estimates be checked, but also the correspondence to them of actual output.[165] Gukovskii's proposals, however, were too strict to be practicable. The directors of the central administrations agreed to the principle of central control of financing, because they believed that this would shorten the financial procedures and would ensure a better control of output. The concentration of financial turnover within VSNKh was argued also on the ground that private enterprises too were obliged to produce upon orders, according to state requirements. And, even when they supplied local markets, they should be compelled to apply for state financing according to normal procedures, that is, by producing their production programme for approval to the competent organ (i.e. *glavk*, central administration or *tsentr*).[166]

The Second Congress of *Sovnarkhozy* opted for centralization of industrial financing under the control of VSNKh. The resolution on the question of financing contained the principles and criteria which were to be implemented, in the main, during war communism. The congress agreed that the socialist reconstruction of economic life necessarily required renouncing the former capitalist-private relations in production, that is, market relations, and abolishing, in due course, the active role of money in business decision-making. Financing was to be subordinated to the requirements of production plans. Separate criteria were required for nationalized industry. The only source of funds for state enterprises was to be the system of monetary advances upon the presentation of estimates. Advances and loans were to depend upon the decisions of VSNKh and its organs. The congress agreed that enterprises' output was to be turned over to the corresponding sections of VSNKh, or, in certain cases, to local organs, without material payment. The principle of the unification of the State Budget inspired the rule that state enterprises were to be exonerated from paying state and local taxes as well as social insurance. Book-keeping of output value in the revenues of the State Budget was, therefore, to include social costs, including defence, social insurance, education and transport (i.e. prices were to incorporate a sort of turnover tax covering non-productive costs).[167] Direct contacts between enterprises were allowed only as an exception to the rule, in cases and scope to be decided by the Presidium of VSNKh.

Strict centralization was also to be applied to the transactions of the commissariats. The congress decided that the funds for production and for purchase of products required by other Soviet institutions were to be turned over directly to VSNKh's organs in charge of the specific economic activity. Conversely, the state institutions were relieved from paying for the commodities delivered to them by VSNKh's organs. The state institutions were authorized to dispose of state funds on their own only when the production sections or *glavki* of VSNKh were unable to provide the necessary commodities.[168]

Throughout 1918 the National Bank had been the third source of industrial financing, after the State Treasury and VSNKh. State enterprises obtained from the Bank advances for purchase of fuel and raw materials.[169] The Second Congress of *Sovnarkhozy* decided to suppress the functions of credit, which the National Bank had kept until then. The National Bank was defined as 'the auxiliary executive apparatus of VSNKh for accounting'. Its functions were limited to checking the appropriate destination of the funds as approved by the financial-economic section of VSNKh. Allocation of finance was to be decided by the VSNKh Presidium and its sections.[170]

On 17 May 1918, it had been established that a condition for the assignment of state advances was central approval of the enterprise's estimates, but no specific guidelines on how to apply for state financing had been worked out. On 3 December 1918, VSNKh established some general rules. Nationalized enterprises were required to produce detailed estimates concerning: (1), expenditure for management and technical direction, including salaries of the executive and technical staff and payments to members of workers' organizations, factory-committee inspection and control commissions; (2), production costs (wages, raw materials and current repairs) with the additional requirement that wages had to be reported together with the list of wage tariffs, and raw materials had to be computed both in fixed and market prices; (3), capital depreciation of plant and equipment; (4), social insurance, and wage percentage quotas for the unemployment fund; (5), debts.[171] Though detailed, the rules still allowed the enterprise to transfer funds supplied under a given head to another one, subject only to State Control being informed of the change, and provided that in no case could funds be transferred to the wage fund.

Financing depended on the approval by the central administration or *glavk* of the enterprise's estimated expenditures for wages, raw materials, fuel and other costs. The role of the local *sovnarkhozy* in financing was severely limited. Their own financial sections were to be the intermediaries between industrial financing assigned from the centre to local enterprises and the enterprises themselves. This was intended as a safeguard against the discretion of the *glavki* in industrial financing, which some local representatives considered excessive. The local *sovnarkhozy*, however, had no real power in financing. The assignment of financial means to them was made dependent on the branch production plans of the corresponding sections of VSNKh. Enterprises had the right to a two-month advance for immediate and seasonal needs, independently and before the approval of their estimates.[172] Concrete steps towards the inclusion of most of industry into a State Budget system of financing were taken soon after the Second Congress of *Sovnarkhozy*. On 23 January 1919, the system of clearing balances was extended from the 'accounting operations between Soviet institutions and Soviet enterprises' to 'enterprises under the inspection or control of Soviet organizations'.[173] The decree specified that Soviet institutions were not authorized to demand payment for products and materials delivered to the above organs, thereby formally including most of industry in the state system of supply. Direct contacts with private firms were restricted to cases when it was impossible to obtain supply from the state sector. The distinction was made between nationalized enterprises having a right to state financing from the budget on production of their estimates or to advances upon approval of figures (and therefore their output value would be registered as state revenue) and other enterprises, which were entitled to get state funds only to clear the difference between the value of input and output. Other qualifications to the system of State Budget financing of industry, on the lines of the resolution voted by the Congress of *Sovnarkhozy*, were translated into law in March 1919,[174] though with additional emphasis on political control over the destination of funds. The March Decree established that the only source of financing for state industry was to be the State Budget and that any monetary revenue accruing to enterprises had to be paid into the State Budget, under the head referring to that particular enterprise or branch. The Decree on Financing of March 1919 established the participation of representatives of *Narkomfin* and State Control in the procedures of examination and approval of industrial estimates along with the production sections and the *glavki* of VSNKh. The *Narkomfin* and State Control commissars were authorized to raise their objections against specific estimates, though they were not allowed to question the provisional budget as a whole. In the event of disagreement, the question was to be discussed again by a joint meeting of representatives of the People's Commissariats and VSNKh. If agreement had not been reached at this stage, the question was to be taken to *Sovnarkom*, which had to decide upon it. In the mean time, the estimates which had been agreed upon and approved followed their regular course. The decree allowed *glavki* and production sections to receive their funds from the VSNKh Presidium and to finance directly the unions of enterprises; that is, to by-pass, in this case, the control of the local *sovnarkhozy*. The *raion* and *gubsovnarkhozy* were allowed to administer the funds of the individual provincial enterprises subject to the administration of VSNKh's production sections or *glavki*. The National Bank remained, but only for verification of the observance of financial laws.[175] For this purpose, the organs which had approved the estimates were to report to the bank a compendium of the production plans, including quantity and value of the expected output at the end of the budgetary period; and the enterprises were to report periodically to the bank the quantity and value of their output.

The cumbersome procedure of central control over the destination of state financial means was bound to produce either excessive delays in the assignment of funds or, simply, lack of financial vigilance[*] as a partial alleviation of red tape. The March decree allowed enterprises to produce only a compendium of general expenditure on wages and salaries, raw materials, fuel and other costs.

After the March decree, VSNKh's budget included advances, 'operational' funds and 'circular' funds. VSNKh's money advances were computed from the total estimates produced by enterprises and organs of VSNKh. After examination by a budgetary commission attached to *Narkomfin*, if approved, the total monetary advances of VSNKh were included in the national budget and presented to *Sovnarkom* and the All-Russian Central Executive Committee for final approval.[176] The 'operational' fund was like a buffer financial section allowing VSNKh to satisfy extraordinary demands for financing. Osinskii drew a parallel between the operational fund in the Soviet model and the financial banking funds of the capitalist economy.[177] However, the operational fund was formed for the purpose of having 'excess reserves' in order to face the contingencies of highly imperfect financial programming. The operational fund was computed from information given by sections and *glavki* on industrial financial requirements as a whole. Precise indications as to the specific destination of the funds, which the law demanded for financing upon estimates, were not required. The difference between the fund of monetary advances upon estimates and the operational fund consisted in the fact that the latter was presented for approval to the budgetary commission of *Narkomfin* at any time and amounted, therefore, to extra-budgetary financing.[178]

The 'circular' fund was a special fund for advances up to 20 per cent of the enterprise's yearly estimates. It was defined as circular because the money was supposed to be refunded to the fund when the enterprise reimbursed the advances received on account of its total budget. Though this fund was not very large, the financial experts considered it quite important in the years of war communism, since it helped to make credit procedures easier.[179] Estimates were hardly likely to be realistic in the financial field, with the inflation and the general instability due to war. The estimated budget of VSNKh in the first half of 1919 was as follows:[180]

(1) Fund for advances upon estimates: 3,798 million rubles;
(2) Operational fund: 5,162 million rubles;
(3) Circular fund (20 per cent of 1 + 2):   1,792 million rubles.

---

[*] *Narkomprod* and various other departments did not pay their revenue into the State Budget but kept it or left it in the localities with their local agencies.

Table 5.2. *Total financing of industry in 1918 and 1919, according to different sources of financing (million rubles)*

	Upon estimates	%	Upon special paragraph[a]	%	Out of the fund[b]	%	Total
1918	2,274	43.0	2,784	52.6	229	4.4	5,287
1st half	14	1.8	745	98.2			759
2nd half	2,261	49.6	2,038	45.4	230	5.0	4,529
1919	23,936	46.8	18,478	36.0	8,766	17.2	50,982
1st half	6,834	43.2	6,331	40.0	2,644	16.8	15,899
2nd half	16,902	48.0	12,147	34.5	6,122	17.5	35,173

[a]The financial-accounting section of VSNKh mentioned as the second source of financing industry a 'special' paragraph under which were probably registered the definite yearly total operational funds.
[b]Probably refers to circular funds.
Source: T.T. Syromolotov (VSNKh), *Finansirovanie natsional'-promyshlennosti po VSNKh v 1919*, Moscow, 1921, p. 18

But financing upon estimates, which presumed the workability of a central financial plan, based on correct and regular production estimates, on rapid procedures for examination, approval and releasing of funds, and on the correct destination of the assigned funds, could not but be an unattainable aim in the years of war communism. The figures presented by the financial-accounting section of VSNKh for the years 1918 and 1919 show that financing upon estimates never reached more than 50 per cent of total financing.

The relative weight of the different sources of financing, and the discrepancy between draft budget and final expenditure, are evidence of the enormous obstacles which the attempts to enforce planned central control over financing encountered. The experts of VSNKh admitted that a uniform financial discipline did not exist and imputed this to, among other things, inexperience of the managerial cadres and to delays in the presentation and approval of the enterprises' estimates. Lack of cadres was felt acutely: 42.5 per cent of the *glavki* had less than one clerical worker per ten workers.[181] but delays were mainly due to the very nature of financial rules. Institutional lags characterized the handing over of the estimates as well as their approval. In the first half of 1919 only 38.2 per cent of the estimates were presented on schedule while more than

26 per cent were presented from three to six months late. In the second half of 1919, 36.8 per cent of the estimates were produced on schedule and about 20 per cent with delays of three to six months. The financial-accounting section of VSNKh focused mainly on 'the injurious bureaucratism' of the financial departments, *Narkomfin* and Workers' and Peasants' Inspection (the organ which replaced State Control). It was shown as evidence of this that 58 per cent of the estimates in the first half of 1919 and 60 per cent in the second half needed from one to thirty days to be approved; the remainder were approved with delays ranging from one to eight months.[182] To those accustomed to present-day bureaucratic lags, VSNKh's figures might not appear surprising. They were, however, observed with suspicion and astonishment by the promoters of the bureaucratic management of industry when they realized that it did not work with the efficacy and flexibility that they expected from the rationale of centralization. A series of severe rules on financial inspection, on the other hand, did not necessarily bring about the increasing concern for accurate estimates that they were supposed to enforce. The rigidity of the procedures was in striking contrast with the effective implementation of the financial rules. *Glavki* and *tsentry* were required to produce quarterly accounts of their expenditure, subdivided according to the nomenclature of the approved estimates of the past quarter. After March 1919 the relative autonomy enjoyed by *glavki* as to the allocation of the funds disappeared. A circular of VSNKh on 25 March 1919 informed enterprises that funds pertaining to a given section or to a specific destination could not be allotted to other destinations without informing the Presidium of VSNKh. The latter was to petition *Sovnarkom* for authorization to transfer the assigned fund from the original destination or section to another without producing supplementary estimates.[183] The instructions of VSNKh were intended to force enterprise managements to formulate their drafts with higher accuracy and to exert at the same time stricter control over the use of state funds. But several factors worked against financial planning. On the one hand, it occurred that financial funds were sometimes insufficient, simply because, as has been said, *glavki* were not aware of the effective number of the enterprises belonging to their branch,[184] a fact that fluctuations in territories under Soviet rule explained in part. The objective lack of accuracy in the presentation of the branch estimates for approval compelled the financial authorities to make their own forecasts, which, due to bureaucratic inertia, ended up in the allotment of funds according to estimates and output figures pertaining to the former period.[185] On the other hand, the current rate of inflation was by itself a formidable obstacle to correct assessment of financial requirements.[186]

Financial waste as well as excess demand for financing characterized industrial financing during war communism. *Narkomfin* calculated that between 15 and 80 per cent of the accredited funds were not used.[187] In the first half of 1919, 17 per cent of the organizational funds were not used by the *glavki*. In the same period, 12 per cent of the operational funds remained unused.[188] At the same time, VSNKh failed in its attempt to obtain circular funds up to 50–60 per cent of total estimates.[189] The financial-accounting section of VSNKh produced the following figures on utilization of the accredited funds by forty-five *glavki* (see Table 5.3).

Non-utilization by the twenty *glavki* in the chemical industry was between 69 per cent and zero. The highest percentages of non-utilization occurred in the branches concerned with wood working, alcohol and cement; the lowest ones in leather, tobacco and paper.[190]

In some branches the non-utilization of funds depended on the lack of raw materials and metals. *Prodrasmet*, the central administration for the supply of metals, used in 1919 only 37 per cent of the allotted funds, and GOMZA, which had been accredited more than half the total funds going to the metal industry, used 88 per cent of them.[191] A major cause of the financial disorganization was the uncertainty caused by war and the changing number of production units falling under Soviet rule. The textile industry, which in 1919 had been assigned the substantial sum of 17,951,161 thousand rubles, actually received only 35 per cent of this, i.e. 6,186,964 thousand rubles. The metal and electrotechnical industry, on the contrary, were effectively assigned more than they had been originally accredited.[192] But, in general, financing was heavily curtailed as compared with estimates based on inflationary expectations, and not very accurate. Some of the most important factories were accredited between 25 per cent and 66 per cent of the requested funds. In the first half of 1920 the financial section of the Petrograd *Sovnarkhoz* reduced by 32 per cent the estimates produced by the enterprises. In the third quarter of the year the estimates were cut by 51 per cent.[193] Further nationalizations and an extension of the territory under Soviet control at the beginning of 1920 made it necessary to increase VSNKh's share of the national budget. In 1918 the estimated VSNKh expenditure was 15 per cent of the total expenditure in the national budget, in 1919 it was 24.7 per cent, and in 1920, 30.2 per cent. But total allocations to VSNKh's budget for 1919 were about 3.5 per cent of its estimates.[194] Through the system of non-monetary clearing balances *Narkomfin* tried to check the rate of increase of money in circulation and enforce correct book-keeping. What occurred in practice was additional red tape to get the authorization to spend the accredited funds, and increasing efforts to be granted a special status allowing the use of money. To be authorized to spend the accredited

Table 5.3. *Utilization of funds by forty-five 'glavki', 1919*

Branches	Glavki reporting information	Allocated funds (thousand rubles)	Utilized funds (thousand rubles)	Non-utilized funds as % of allocated funds
Oil industry	1	161,333	96,464	41
Electrical	1	1,076,547	737,752	32
Food-processing	7	705,638	606,998	15
Metal working	7	2,900,690	2,579,153	14
Minerals	5	477,010	432,503	10
Coal	1	570,896	515,653	10
Chemicals	20	9,396,329	8,377,935	10
Peat	1	141,233	130,223	8
Wood	1	14,912,116	14,038,108	7
Textiles	1	6,186,964	6,141,407	1
Total	45	36,588,756	33,557,196	7

Source: VSNKh (Syromolotov), p. 21

funds, several steps were needed. Firstly, the customer presented the purchase certificate accompanied by the relevant demand for payment to the section of financing. Secondly, the section in charge of estimated credits at the given institution registered the corresponding transfer on the customer's account and issued against this an authorization of delivery, which allowed the supplier to release the purchased commodity. Thirdly, the seller had to present the purchase document to the section of financing, which then registered the transfer of *money* to the seller's budget.[195] *Narkomfin* received several petitions to make the system of non-monetary payments less rigid, but the fear that otherwise speculation would be enhanced[196] induced the financial authorities to stick even more strictly to the existing financial rules. Not to renounce principles meant, however, to make use of exceptions. Amendments to the law on non-monetary clearing balances were allowed in special cases. Only some institutions – the Central Fuel Administration, agencies of the Commissariat of Transport collecting wood fuel, and the agencies of the War Commissariat, were allowed to buy with cash in hand.[197] The 'war organization', in fact, was based on a system of exceptions to the general rules limiting the autonomy of the civil institutions. The Extraordinary Commission for Army Supply (*Chrezkomsnabarm*) was allowed to by-pass the financial rules concerning the composition of estimates.[198] The system of 'armouring' (strictly reserving the use of) money allowed some central institutions to be relatively autonomous of the policy of *Narkomfin* on financing. The armouring of money had started in 1918, when agencies of the National Bank found it impossible to convert cheques and bills into money tokens, because of the lack of currency notes. In these circumstances, departments which had the right to be granted state funds or to deposit their funds at the bank demanded and were accorded a guarantee of the 'return' of their rights and deposits. This meant the 'armouring' of their monetary competences in their own favour, since the bank was bound to meet depositors' claims at any moment. The War Commissariat made extensive use of the armouring of money. Other departments claimed the same privileges. It became customary to claim the armouring of the funds assigned by the centre, to protect them from the claims of other commissariats.[199] Enterprises made efforts to accumulate their own reserve funds.[200] *Narkomfin* tried to fix stricter rules for direct monetary contracts. To reduce the scope for simulation, monetary transactions required production of the identification card of the dealer to the credit agencies, and the payment to be made in the presence of a representative of the state organs of financial inspection. Monetary transactions outside the state sector were allowed only if nationalized factories were unable to meet the requirements.[201] For this purpose VSNKh was asked to prepare a list of products and machinery which could be bought in the market.[202]

Civil war was a powerful incentive to reinforce by any means state control over transactions with private dealers who could be hostile to the Bolshevik Government. Non-monetary clearing balances were supposed to keep control, but the economic system as a whole was not prepared to operate on such a basis. During the war the institutionalization of exceptions to financial rules allowed the necessary flexibility in military supply. The end of civil war should have induced a thoughtful re-examination of the financial system. On the contrary, the massive expropriation of the means of production and wealth, the relative 'success' of *razverstka*, labour conscription in some fields implying the obligation to feed workers, reinforced the idea that the basic institutions of central supply and distribution should be maintained. Thus the system of non-monetary centrally controlled transactions should be extended as a first step towards the transition from a partially monetary national budget into a non-monetary budget.[203] In July 1920 the All-Russian Central Executive Committee decided that 'the system of armourd money practised until now is abolished and is allowed to survive only in extraordinary cases'.[204] In the same month, *Sovnarkom* passed a decree which introduced additional rigidities in the operations of purchase. This decree confirmed the principle of settlement of transactions through non-monetary accounts. All purchases in the free market were abolished, except those specifically authorized. Only specially entrusted institutions were allowed to sign contracts of purchase from private individuals. Negotiations with private dealers were subordinated to the presentation of their terms to the Workers' and Peasants' Inspection, which was required to take a decision within seven days, and in some cases within three days. The decree limited the number of exceptions. However, their scope increased. A note specified that Soviet institutions and other agencies which were authorized to deal directly with producers could make cash payment without limit.[205] On the other hand, the end of the civil war left room for more generous financing, given the existing regulations. In the second half of 1920, advances for production expenditure for the time span January–June 1921 were extended to cover six months. The new financial law acknowledged that several departments were not able to finance their production costs before their estimates had been approved, and that the provinces had to resort to illegal devices in order to obtain the necessary funds. The provincial financial sections were authorized to make the advances bearing in mind preceding allocations between items as well as additional funds available in the current year. Because of inflation a modification of estimates was allowed up to 25 per cent without special authority, and up to 50 per cent under authority of

Narkomfin and Workers' and Peasants' Inspection. Greater modifications required *Sovnarkom* authorization.[206]

By the end of war communism, the state had firm overall financial control over the economy.[207] On 28 February 1921, it was established that the estimates of all local sections and enterprises directly subordinated to VSNKh and its central administrations were to be turned over to the corresponding administrations.[208] Soon after, the March 1919 decree on the financing of state enterprises was confirmed and extended to 'all enterprises and operations of VSNKh inseparably related to the industrial activity of VSNKh'.[209] This decision was not only the natural consequence of the nationalization of the whole of industry, which had been decided in November 1920, but also the institutionalization of current practice in this field. In spite of *Narkomfin*'s instructions, during war communism the *glavki* had continued submitting to the competent commissions for financial affairs also the estimates of enterprises which had fallen under the control of the local economic organs for whatever reason, independently of a decision on nationalization.[210]

During war communism, nationalized industry went on working thanks to state subsidies. The economic disruption caused a rapid enlargement of the deficit of the industrial sector, which Preobrazhenskii estimated at one-quarter of the total budget deficit, producing the following figures:[211]

Table 5.4. *Revenues and expenditure of the nationalized factories (millions of rubles and percentage of budget)*

	Revenues	%	Expenditure	%
1918	12,000	0.1	4,924	10.6
1919	14,676	30.0	48,596	22.5
1920	52,631	33.1	337,238	27.8

By the end of 1920, no industrial branch was able to finance itself. The only source of net state revenue was agriculture.

5.7 REGROUPING OF ENTERPRISES

With the increasing pace of nationalization, the number of enterprises directly and not only formally dependent on the *glavki* increased. This required the formation of lower and intermediate organs of management. Trusts and *kusty* (groupings) of homogeneous production or productive cycles were formed. The formation of unions of enterprises followed empirical criteria rather than technical or productive principles. Soviet trusts were unions of industrial enterprises (which could be vertical or horizontal) belonging to a given industrial branch and subject to the immediate direction of a general administration, with a single budget and a single plan of supply and distribution.[212] *Kusty* were formed in particular locations to counteract centrifugal forces by connecting horizontally industrial units which were scattered and not easy to control from a single centre. *Kusty* had their own budget and book-keeping.[213] They were, however, strictly dependent on orders from the *glavk* or *tsentr* to which they belonged. Initially, *kusty* were formed among the best-equipped enterprises of a single branch. The Moscow *kust* for fine-linen and half-wool fabrics united fifteen factories, with an average fixed capital of 1,200 thousand rubles (as compared with an average of 650 thousand rubles of fixed capital in the enterprises excluded from the June decree on nationalization).[214] The *kust* administrations had the power to transfer technical personnel and materials between factories.[215]

The formation of unions of enterprises was entended to complete the organization based on the *glavk* system, i.e. vertical organization, by facilitating concentration of management, and objectively worked against the possibility of organizing territorial complexes of interdependent units of production, even when the geographical situation would have justified it. At times the pressures of some *glavki* on the VSNKh Presidium were so powerful as to bring about the liquidation of self-sufficient economic districts, in order to obtain the inclusion of some enterprises in their corresponding branch organizations.[216]

Eighty per cent of all unions were formed between October 1918 and July 1919, when there were major efforts to implement centralized management.[217] By January 1920 1,449 enterprises employing 669,205 workers had been united in trusts.[218] VSNKh reported at the Eighth Congress of Soviets that about half the mines were unionized. In other branches the percentage was lower, but equally impressive: about one-quarter of the metal and chemical industry and something more than one-third of the nationalized metal-processing enterprises.[219] VSNKh was mainly concerned with large-scale industry, but unionization went further in some branches. In November 1919, 80 per cent of the enterprises controlled by *Tsentrotekstil'* were united into *kusty*. Unions, however, did not always strengthen the power of the central administrations; in some cases they reinforced the solidarity of interests of the local units against central management. Among the factors promoting centrifugal tendencies were deficiencies in the central system of supply of raw materials and fuel, inadequate information about central plans, and lack of autonomy in crucial managerial decisions. The *kust* administrations of Ivanovo-Voznesensk province rejected direction by *Glavtekstil'* and claimed their own autonomy within the provincial territory.[220] The largest metallurgical works of Tula and Tambov, which should have been directly supplied by *Prodrasmet*, the organ in charge of the distribution of metals, complained that instead of metal they received 'papers' giving the right to metal supply according to the norm. They were able to keep going, it was said, thanks to output under control of the local *sovnarkhozy*, which supplied not only the *glavki* but also the Commissariat of Railways and other organs.[221] Some *kusty* claimed the right to purchase peat on their own behalf adducing the incapacity of their own *glavk* to perform this function.[222] The shortcomings of the central administrations and *glavki* increased together with the number of enterprises under their control. While individual shoemakers were able to find leather, the Committee for Leather, *Glavkozh*, was unable to supply its own factories. Textile factories depending on *Tsentrotekstil'* were not given price lists on time and were then compelled to keep unsold stocks of finished products.[223]

The deficiencies of the *glavk* system of supply was felt even at the level of shock works, i.e. those with high priority, working essentially for the army. The economic units had to compete against one another to capture materials, thus leading to a system where it was not priority criteria but 'the dexterity of their agents, amounting to virtuosity', which counted.[224] At the end of 1919, an authoritative article inspired by military interests[225] intervened in the question of economic organization with strong criticism of the VSNKh apparatus. Excessive departmentalization and the lack of coordination among economic units were seen as causes inducing each institution to obtain necessary inputs by its own efforts. The *glavki* were accused of lacking the speed and responsiveness to orders essential in war. Anticipating Trotskii's criticism of *glavkism* made at the Tenth Party Congress, the article demanded the abolition of superfluous sections, and the simplification of methods of financing and disposal of funds.

In the literature on war communism, *glavkism* has been widely interpreted as a rational system for distributing resources in wartime. This view has not been seriously challenged. There is, however, more than one reason for arguing that *glavkism* was not the best system for collecting and distributing resources, regulating industry and being the intermediary of financing in wartime; nor was it just a product of war. The Soviet economists saw in the Tsarist *glavki* not an extraordinary organization for price regulation and military supply based on a few precise operational criteria, but a permanent skeleton of the future 'command economy'. To Marxists, centralization was equal to coordination, and decentralization to anarchy. Independently of war, centralized direction and management represented for the leadership the choice for progress against reaction.[226] The Bolsheviks interpreted the antagonism between the provinces and the centre in terms of parochialism and separatism, rather than as a spontaneous manifestation of self-defence of local economic interests against the policy of despoliation of local resources and disruption of the local economy carried out by the central committees and administrations without planning and without the means to implement a serious policy of distribution of resources according to criteria of priority. The transformation of VSNKh into a high managerial board deprived the Soviet system of the only organ which might have formulated the guidelines of a planned economy and unified at the centre the vertical organization based on the *glavki*. The specific interest of each *glavk* in its own branch of production was conducive to friction and antagonism between *glavki* and worked objectively against the rapid fulfilment of priorities that war required. War industry was put under a special regime and the army found in the local *sovnarkhozy* better support for military supplies than the one provided by *glavki* and central administrations. In March 1920, when the special importance of transport for all economic operations had definitely been assessed, GOMZA (the Amalgamated State Engineering and Machine Building Works), producing rolling stock and spare parts, was unable to get from *glavki* and *tsentry* more than 13 per cent of the total supply of the materials it needed. The remainder was obtained independently of the *glavk* system.[227]

Requisition and confiscation of resources, largely undertaken by the *glavki*, worked against any possible territorial network of complementary industries which might have been more efficient in reducing delays resulting from central financing, central ordering, central supply and delivery. The peculiarity of civil war, as compared with national wars, was that frontiers were utterly movable and transport depended on all sorts of uncertainties. Several homogeneous territorial organizations would have provided immediate alternatives to the loss of a territory and would have helped to compensate through local resources the loss of regions traditionally supplying raw materials, thus reducing the impact of transport disruption and avoiding losses due to idle stocks. If *glavki* and *tsentry* (and central administrations) had been limited to a regrouping of large enterprises of national importance, leaving medium-sized and small-scale industries under the responsibility of the local *sovnarkhozy*, the system of central supply of materials and funds would have been more profitable to the operations of a few key sectors. But this was not the programme of the heads of the central bodies. The idea was that each *glavk* was to become the centre of gravity for its own production branch and that the local *sovnarkhozy* had no place in this system, being only temporary organizations within the boundaries of the *oblast* in so far as *glavki* and *tsentry* were not yet capable of ensuring industrial management.[228] That is to say, the managers of the central bodies interpreted the local economy not as an organization of production activities, but as a reservoir of stocks, on which the centre wished to have a privileged claim. Control over output, more than management, was what mattered. From this point of view, the question of efficiency was only a secondary one. The operations of the Soviet *glavki* reflected a bureaucratic approach to economic direction rather than a managerial one or, in words close to that time, they were inspired by distribution rather than by production criteria. It was this approach that led VSNKh to create even a special section designed to coordinate small and handicraft industry, *Glavkustprom*, in order to incorporate the output of small producers into its own system. This approach explains also why the *glavki* were eager to extend their control over an increasing number of enterprises (and their output), once enterprises under their control did not work according to expectations or former stocks had been exhausted. For the same reasons, the leadership of VSNKh did not want a stable line of demarcation between the organization of *glavki* and the system of *sovnarkhozy*. Though spurious with respect to the ideal of vertical economic organization based on central administrations, they provided the necessary buffer section of the economy. To it faults could be imputed when the *glavk* apparatus was accused of inefficiency; from it output could be extorted to make up for bad outcomes in the centralized sphere.

5.8 THE LOCAL ORGANS OF THE GLAVKI

Glavki and *tsentry* carried out their activity in the provinces through their local agencies and through the *kust* administrations which united into a single management the scattered and small production units. The local ramifications spread across the borders of the *oblast, raion, gubernia* and *uezd* administrative divisions. In some cases a *kust* was formed of units belonging to different administrative divisions. The form and scope of the local organs depended on the characteristics of individual *glavki* and *tsentry*.

The Chief Committee for Coal, *Glavugol'*, formed an *oblast* administration for the Moscow Coal Basin and six *raion* managements which acted as local organs of the *oblast* administration. The administration had functions of management and technical, financial and administrative organization.[229] It directed the activity of all nationalized enterprises in the region and was in charge of exploring new sources of coal. The same system was later applied to the Donets Basin, where in addition sixty *kusty* were organized for the small mines.[230] The local managements had also representatives of the central administration. The *raion* oil committees were formed by one representative of the Chief Committee for Naphtha, *Glavneft'*, two representatives of the local *sovnarkhozy* and two of the local trade unions.[231]

When the size of an industrial agglomeration was such as to justify particular attention, independent administrations for fuel were formed locally. Such was the case of Petrograd, which was independent of the centre for fuel supply.[232]

Production programmes and financing of the *raion* managements were worked out by the higher administration of the *glavk*. The Second Congress of *Sovnarkhozy* agreed to incorporate the local organs of the *glavki* into the *sovnarkhoz* organization, whilst leaving them directly dependent on the centre for financing and direction.[233] This decision was not quite effective. The Chief Timber Committee, *Glavleskom*, maintained its local plenipotentiaries and developed a parallel series of provincial committees, with the same rights as sections of the corresponding *sovnarkhozy*. The *glavki* refused direct management only in cases where distance made links with the centre impossible. Such was the case of a *raion* timber committee in Siberia, the rights of which included the computation of overall local demand, the plan of distribution for timber and wood products, regulation of relations with other institutions, and supervision of distribution. *Kusty* and trusts came under its direct control.[234]

The agents of the *glavki* were so highly empowered that in Soviet terminology they were known as plenipotentiaries. Their powers included the formation and organization of factory managements, approval of internal regulations and instructions, orders concerning quantity and quality of output, registration of local resources and labour forces, and the formation of *kusty* which they thought necessary for any sort of output.[235] In some cases local agents were responsible for the allocation of finance, as in the paper industry,[236] and for purchase prices, as in the local leather committees.[237]

Tsentrotekstil' was a special case in the *glavk* system where forms of collaboration with local economic councils were sought. Since many local *sovnarkhozy* had their own textile sections, the *raion* committee of *Tsentrotekstil'*, which supplied raw materials and fuel to non-nationalized factories,[238] were combined with the local sections in the main industrial centres. The *sovnarkhozy* disposed of the assigned funds with absolute autonomy.[239] This collaboration gave good results in the collection of wool[240] However, when *Glavtekstil'* was formed the parallel existence of

the two highest organs of administration created problems. The conspicuous number of private enterprises in this branch, the single section of
supply of raw materials for all enterprises,[241] and the uncertain limits of
responsibility between the two organs, favoured a climate of suspicion
and competition in the highest administrations and put *Glavtekstil'* in a
less advantageous position since supply was practically in the hands of
Tsentrotekstil'. The latter had its local agents and control of the central
fund. In some cases, *Tsentrotekstil'* obtained raw materials by handing
over fabrics and tried to adjust prices to the market situation.[242] However,
when cases of advances on commercial documents of fictitious enterprises
were discovered,[243] VSNKh tried to reduce the power of *Tsentrotekstil'*,
whose commercial behaviour was already suspect. This organ could not
be disbanded since its connections with local producers of raw materials
were considered to be essential for supply. Therefore, the *raiontekstili* were
transformed into *kusty* and the latter were subordinated to *Glavtekstil'*,
while the local *raion* purchasing agencies were transformed into *Gubtekstil'*
(provincial) committees.[244] The aim was to reinforce centralized administration, whilst at the same time keeping *Tsentrotekstil'* as an organ of
supply of raw materials. *Gubtekstili* remained dependent on *Tsentrotekstil'*,
but extended their intervention in production. All non-nationalized large
and medium enterprises and small producers of the province, including
kustar' activity, were put under their charge. The *gubtekstili* were made
responsible for the assignment of production orders and their fulfilment.
They had also to approve estimates for submission to *Tsentrotekstil'*, and
issue finance when authorized by *Tsentrotekstil'*. The *gubtekstili* had
current accounts at the State Bank branches. By the creation of such
organs, the centre put an end to the possible participation of local
sovnarkhozy in the management of non-nationalized industry. The local
sovnarkhozy were only granted the right to appeal against the decisions of
Gubtekstil', but the grievance could not delay implementations of the
decision.[245]

A different form of local organization was provided by the organs of the
Metal Section of VSNKh. This section did not develop a local network
through the hierarchy of the *sovnarkhozy*, but formed a special apparatus
independent of the local councils and their production sections.
Production unions were formed nonetheless, respecting the territorial
borders of the *oblast* and the *raion* and the district administrations for the
direct management of the largest enterprises in the Urals.[246] The organization of metal supply was particularly inefficient. Visiting peti-
tioners for metals at the centre numbered as many as 800 people a day.
In September 1919 VSNKh decided to allow the *raimetals* to turn 60 per
cent of their stocks of metals over to local *sovnarkhozy* without going

through the central body.[247] The local organs of the Metal Sections, *raimetals*, were also charged to supply *kustar'* undertakings, when their importance grew so much as to justify state financial assistance.[248] This reform was an anticipatory admission of the inefficiency of central supply as such, and disclosed new perspectives which, at the end of the war communism experience, led to a serious questioning of *glavkism*.

5.9 THE HORIZONTAL ECONOMIC ORGANIZATION: THE SOVNARKHOZY

The system of *glavki* was developed as an alternative to the territorial ramification of economic regulatory centres consisting in a network of local councils called *sovnarkhozy* (*sovety narodnogo khoziaistva*), distributed in accordance with the former administrative divisions. The superimposition of the *glavki*, organized on a branch principle, upon the territorial economic organization, was a conflicting element, which from the beginning showed itself to be inconsistent with the forms of economic organization based on the political-administrative principle of the soviets. The *sovnarkhozy* developed soon after the October Revolution by a combination of spontaneity and necessity. The local soviets, in the vacuum of power which followed the revolution, started forming economic sections to cope with closures, temporary problems of management and economic disorganization in general. The first economic section of a local soviet was formed in November 1917 in the province of Kostroma. The most important industrial centres, like Petrograd, Nizhni-Novgorod, Saratov, Ekaterinburg, Ivanovo-Voznesensk and some others belonging to the Northern Region, formed their economic sections during December 1917.[249] These economic organs, which in part resulted from the abdication of private initiative in face of social unrest, and in part were an expression of the will of the emerging classes to extend their power in economic affairs, were interpreted by some Bolsheviks as the natural translation of the Soviet political system into the economic field. The decree of 23 December 1917 institutionalized the existing economic sections and councils by including them in VSNKh's framework, which connected the periphery with the centre by way of production sections endowed with regulatory powers in specific industrial fields.[250] The decisions of VSNKh became obligatory on all existing institutions operating in the economic field.[251] One of the first problems to arise between centre and localities concerned expropriation of industry. The *sovnarkhozy* often expropriated private enterprises under the pressure of local workers and with no concern for their national importance. This was an important reason for limiting their rights in this field. But, aside from these concerns, the leadership tried to make rules which would check as rapidly as possible any autonomistic tendency of the periphery. An example of this effort was VSNKh's project to form a Central Section of Orders (*Tsentrozakaz*), so as to make sure that the nationalized factories would accept only production orders issued by *Tsentrozakaz* and its *raion* agencies. According to this project, the *sovnarkhozy* were to receive orders from the centre and turn them over to local enterprises for execution. VSNKh established that the *sovnarkhozy* could autonomously distribute orders only in exceptional cases and after having informed VSNKh of such an initiative.[252] This project was never implemented. It was, however, not only a sign of VSNKh's inability to formulate a planned system of economic organization in practicable terms, but also a premonition of the gap between the goal of formulating economic policy in unifying terms and the means available for implementation.

Taking for granted the existence of the local *sovnarkhozy* and their irreplaceable functions of local economic control, at least for the time being, the leadership endeavoured to find means to make them consistent with the project of a new economic organization in which voluntaristic economic criteria should prevail over traditional ways. Throughout the second half of 1918, the economic experts discussed the problem of reshaping the former administrative divisions according to the principle of industrial and economic weight (*tiagotenie*, which indicates gravitational pull) of the production units.[253] This question was also mentioned at the Second Congress of *Sovnarkhozy*, but nothing was decided. Military emergency and the proliferation of the *glavki* concentrated attention on other problems. The *sovnarkhozy* developed along the inherited administrative divisions and on the basis of the structure of VSNKh, i.e. with productive sections. The hierarchy was expressed in terms of supervision and control of the higher organs over the lower ones:

V (*vysshii* = supreme) SNKh
oblast SNKh
gubernia SNKh
uezd SNKh

Central control of banking and financing was considered to be sufficient for effective control of the local economic activity. But, in reality, the scheme was not so neat and owed much to contingent features. In April 1918 there were sixty economic sections and local *sovnarkhozy* spread over the country.[254] In some cases these organs had been formed, independently of central instructions, by workers' committees, with their own criteria.[255] In certain cases workers' membership was quite consistent. The *raion* (*oblast*) Petrograd *Sovnarkhoz* was formed by the Central Council of Factory Committees of Petrograd in February 1918 and inherited its apparatus.[256] The Ivanovo-Voznesensk *gubsovnarkhoz* worked in close contact with control commissions and trade unions, whose representatives participated in the boards of its production sections.[257]

Norms for the composition and competence of the *sovnarkhozy* were issued only after the Second Congress of *Sovnarkhozy*, but did not contribute to greater uniformity. A plenary committee had to elect the presidium and was to consist of not more than twenty-eight members: ten representing provincial and town soviets, one for each section (agriculture, consumption, finance and labour) of the soviet, no more than five for local trade unions, five for large nationalized enterprises and four for cooperatives. In practice, however, the norms for membership were not strictly implemented. Many *sovnarkhozy* considered the plenary committee superfluous and let the presidium take decisions.[258] The Tambov *gubsovnarkhoz* worked until November 1918 without trade union representatives, who were replaced by members of the Communist Party.[259] By 1919 the plenary committee had been activated only by 71.4 per cent of the *gubsovnarkhozy* and 51 per cent of the *uezd sovnarkhozy*. The following figures – though not necessarily accurate (the sum is well under 100 per cent) – may nevertheless serve as an indication of how membership was distributed. The membership of the *uezd sovnarkhozy* was even less respectful of the norms. The representatives either of trade unions or factory committees, to whom should have been granted 15.6 per cent of the total membership, got 24.7 per cent, and members having no right to representation constituted 15.5 per cent.[260] Adapting to their own reality, the *uezd sovnarkhozy* accepted membership of the *volost* (small rural district) and village organizations, of *kustari* and their associations, which were excluded by the law.

Table 5.5. *Distribution of the membership in the gubsovnarkhozy, 1919*

Representatives of provincial and town soviets	24.2%
Production sections of economic councils	21.7%
Trade unions	19.0%
Sections of local soviets	12.9%
Other	less than 10.0%
Members having no right to representation	5.4%

Source: *Narodnoe Khoziaistvo*, 1919, nos. 9–10, pp. 105–9

The norms on *raion* and local *sovnarkhozy* conferred on them the rights of local organs of VSNKh, acting under the general control of the corresponding local soviets.[261] The *sovnarkhozy* were responsible for coordinating and directing the activity of the lower organs of workers' control and their interrelations, for directing nationalized enterprises under the control of VSNKh, for adjusting supply and demand in the means of production, for verifying local resources and for establishing plans and distribution of labour forces, raw materials, fuel and consumer goods. To carry out their tasks, the *sovnarkhozy* were divided into production sections, following the structure of VSNKh. Each section was subdivided into four sub-sections – for management, supply and distribution, labour, and statistics.

These organizational norms were aimed at transforming the existing economic organs into auxiliary organs of VSNKh, taking into account the functions already performed by most of them and trying to reorder them into a system which bore the image rather than the reality of decentralization. The parallel formation of the *glavki* and the first decree on management of nationalized enterprises were concrete signs that the policy pursued by the leadership from early 1918 was one of centralization.[262] Centralization received a further impulse after the Brest–Litovsk Treaty. Osinskii, Bukharin and Smirnov left the Presidium of VSNKh, in which Larin and Miliutin became the most prominent members. The influence of Larin, who was well acquainted with the German war organization, was crucial in shaping the policy of industrial concentration. Another reason for centralization became the economic losses due to the treaty: e.g. 70 per cent of iron and steel output and 90 per cent of sugar.[263]

At the First Congress of *Sovnarkhozy*, in May 1918, VSNKh leaders stressed that the immediate aim was abolition of all intermediate steps between VSNKh and nationalized enterprises. The congress laid down the hierarchy of the *sovnarkhozy*. The presidium of each *sovnarkhoz* was to be approved by the higher *sovnarkhoz*. The most important economic council after VSNKh was to be the *oblast sovnarkhoz*. *Oblast sovnarkhozy* were to guide and direct the activity of the local *sovnarkhozy* and economic sections. They kept the right of requisition, sequestration and confiscation in so far as such decisions would not interfere with the overall plan of regulation and supply. Grievances were to be settled by VSNKh in not more than one week. Instructions issued by *oblast sovnarkhozy* were obligatory for the local economic councils, all other institutions and managements.[264] The resolution voted by the congress lacked precise indications about the responsibilities of each economic council before the higher council and about each council's tasks. The *oblast sovnarkhozy* were to be formed by representatives of the trade unions, *oblast* soviets and *gubsovnarkhozy*. Representatives of factory committees, cooperatives and factory managements were not given the right to membership. The *oblast sovnarkhozy* were responsible for coordination of the economy of their territory, distribution of orders from the centre to individual enterprises, supply of the means of production and the setting of prices and wage rates.[265] But this organization had no time to be set fully in motion over the whole country. Some activities began to be performed only in the regions of Moscow and Petrograd. The Moscow *Raion* Economic Committee was cleansed of members of the 'bourgeoisie' and of other parties and was transformed by the Second Economic Congress of the Moscow *Oblast*, held from 20 to 25 May 1918, into the Moscow *Oblast Sovnarkhoz*.[266] Twenty-two sections were created, of which only five were production sections. Its governing body was a plenary committee, a presidium of seven people being responsible for current business.[267]

Among other economic councils at the regional level, the Petrograd *Sovnarkhoz* was one of the most active. The Central Council of Factory Committees which had formed it became a technical organ for control over factory activity and had equal rights with other sections.[268] The Petrograd Plant Conference (*Petrogradskoe zavodskoe soveshchanie*), a pre-revolutionary organ, was transformed into a section for financing and management, concentrating in its hands various functions of economic regulation, such as distribution of orders to enterprises, advances, etc.[269] During war communism this region enjoyed a relative autonomy with respect to the centre. All Petrograd unions of enterprises, which formally were supposed to be under the direct control of VSNKh, were in fact directed by the Petrograd *sovnarkhoz*.[270]

Other *oblast sovnarkhozy*, however, had no time to organize their administration and perform the tasks assigned to them. The Second Congress of *Sovnarkhozy*, held in December 1918, when the country had already lost much of its territory in military operations, decided to abolish the *oblast sovnarkhozy*. The decision was justified by the fact that 'their presence complicated the whole system of economic interrelations and affected the further process of planned centralization'.[271] The uncertain borders of the national economy ravaged by war may have influenced the decision. But this was not the only reason for it. In fact, those *sovnarkhozy* which were most exposed to the impact of war were allowed to survive – in the Urals, the Northern Region and the West. The abolition of the *oblast sovnarkhozy* depended also on the fact that the Second Congress, in spite of the increasing involvement of the country in war, approved new administrative divisions, based on the principle of 'gravitation' by which it was intended to take into account economic criteria in territorial administration. *Raiony* were to replace *oblasty*, which were considered out of date, and unite more small provinces, or part of a province, with their surroundings.[272] But the congress did not go further than to affirm the principle, since nothing was done to implement the new administrative divisions. The decision of the congress was implemented only in its negative implications: i.e. abolition of the *oblast sovnarkhozy*, like the Moscow economic council, the administration of which was considered to be a duplicate of the Moscow *Gubernia Sovnarkhoz* and VSNKh, and thus unnecessary. All tasks which were formerly assigned to the *oblast sovnarkhoz* in connection with the regulation and management of industry were assumed by *glavki* and *tsentry*.

The regions in which the *oblast sovnarkhozy* were maintained were not accessible to *glavk* local agencies or, as in the case of Petrograd, were politically strong enough to impose their will over that of the centre.[273] To circumvent the law on the financing of industry, which centralized state funds, the *oblast sovnarkhoz* of the Northern Region drew off money from the funds earned by selling finished products, which were supposed to be paid to the Treasury.[274] It was only in February 1920 that the *oblast sovnarkhoz* of the Northern Region was suppressed and transformed into a *gubernia sovnarkhoz*, after a harsh dispute with VSNKh on the handling of financial funds.[275]

The limited size of the territory under Soviet control for most of war communism, and the impossibility of organizing *raion sovnarkhozy*, were the reasons for which the *gubernia sovnarkhozy*, that is the provincial economic councils, became the highest territorial economic authority. By virtue of the hierarchy approved in May 1918, the *gubsovnarkhozy* were to be subordinated to the *oblast sovnarkhozy*. After the abolition of the latter, the *gubsovnarkhozy* became more directly connected with VSNKh. The Presidium of VSNKh appointed the presidents of the production sections, whose councils were appointed by the presidium of the local *sovnarkhoz* and approved by VSNKh.[276] The plenary committee was to include five representatives, appointed respectively by the provincial soviet, by the town soviet, by the local association of trade unions, the large nationalized enterprises and their unions, plus representatives of the economic sections of the soviets, of the production sections and of the cooperatives. The plenary committee was to elect a presidium of 3–7 people, subject to the approval of the executive committee and VSNKh. The presidium was to remain in office for six months and single members could be recalled by a decision passed by the plenary committee.[277] But rules on election were seldom applied. A census showed that during war communism the plenary committee appointed only 10.2 per cent of the presidia, and that in 52 per cent of cases the presidium was directly appointed by the local executive committee.[278] It was the presidium's function to direct the general work of the *sovnarkhoz*, and to implement decisions of VSNKh and of its organs as well as the decisions of congresses of *sovnarkhozy* and of the plenary committee. *Gubsovnarkhozy* became executive organs of VSNKh for the regulation and organization of the national economy of a given territory, within the limits of the decisions and directives of VSNKh and the All-Russian Congress of *Sovnarkhozy*.

Following the logic of *glavkism*, VSNKh tried to direct the energies of the *sovnarkhozy* toward the requirements of central policy. Efforts were made to delimit the relative autonomy of the provinces, by reinforcing hierarchical ties rather than by defining precise spheres of responsibility. The whole question of *gubsovnarkhozy* was handled at the Second Congress of *Sovnarkhozy* from the point of view of their interrelations with *glavki* and *tsentry*, rather than as an autonomous problem of territorial and administrative organization. The VSNKh leaders demanded more freedom, initiative and independence for the *glavki* and criticized the separatism of the *sovnarkhozy*. The latter were alleged to be refusing collaboration with central policy, on the pretext that 'you are not us', as soon as an enterprise had been 'trustified', i.e. put under the authority of a central administration. Besides objecting to *glavki* on the ground that they were residuals of Kerenskii's time, *sovnarkhoz* delegates considered local economic organs essential for procurement of raw materials and criticized the failure of *glavki* in this field.[279] These arguments had some weight in the final decision of the congress about the competence of different economic organs in the crucial fields. Centralization had an impact on the spirit of the decision, but could not affect the means of implementing it, since the congress was aware that the centre had no capacity to manage the whole economy. Solutions were sought in compromises. The resolution on management affirmed that local *sovnarkhozy* had no right to interfere in the activity of conglomerate enterprises and local factory management, or in regulations of the central administrations which were applied to their subordinate units. In this field, the *sovnarkhozy* were left with watchdog functions over the property of enterprises and, in case of conflict, had to address their grievances to the central administration of VSNKh itself.[280] The *sovnarkhozy*, however, were recognized as having some rights regarding the local economy. The *gubsovnarkhozy* were granted the right that individual enterprises could not be taken away from their responsibility without a decision of the Presidium of VSNKh. Also, they could requisition and confiscate raw materials, and products and equipment of purely local importance (*chistomestnoe znachenie*), after informing VSNKh.[281] *Glavki* and *tsentry* were obliged to attach their sections to local *sovnarkhozy*. Settlement of the most crucial matter of dispute, the collection of raw materials and fuels, is indicative of the fact that the centre was unable to substitute its own agents for the activity of the *sovnarkhozy* in respect of supply. The *gubsovnarkhozy* were allowed to carry out, upon VSNKh's instructions, the purchase and state collection of raw materials and fuels within the limits of their territory. VSNKh kept the right to delegate its own representatives to the organization in charge of such activity, and he had to proceed according to VSNKh's instructions.[282] Incorporation of local agencies of the *glavki* and *tsentry* into the organization of the *sovnarkhozy*, which meant respecting the rules on the composition of sections established for the *sovnarkhozy*, did not grant officially any special advantage for the *sovnarkhozy*, since the local organs of *glavki* and *tsentry* were obliged to 'unconditionally execute orders, circulars and anything else coming from the centre'. However, the *sovnarkhozy* were at least informed about the decisions of the centre regarding local undertakings. The crucial way to limit the autonomy of the *sovnarkhozy* was found in financing. The *gubsovnarkhozy* had no right to collect taxes on factory raw materials, semi-finished or finished products, and financial funds for operational and organizational costs were received upon the approval of VSNKh. On questions of local importance, the *gubsovnarkhozy* were allowed to issue obligatory decisions within the limits of the general directives and decisions of VSNKh. Petitions to VSNKh for nationalization had to be accompanied by detailed data on the financial and technical situation of the enterprise and detailed reasons for expropriation. Extensive responsibilities remained only in the sphere of relations with the peasantry, since *sovnarkhozy* dealt with the collection of agricultural raw materials and helped the local agents of *Narkomprod* to distribute consumer goods among the population. The *sovnarkhozy*, however, could not dispose of the output of the state farms, which they were in charge of, except upon *Narkomprod*'s directives.[283]

In practice, the resolution of the Second Congress of *Sovnarkhozy* did not work. An effective way of making the *sovnarkhozy* participate in the formulation of central policy and understand central decisions was not found. On the other hand, the central administrations did not feel themselves subject to any precise rules or responsibilities. On the contrary, the incorporation of their local organs into the *sovnarkhozy* provided the possibility of conditioning their policy. In the autumn of 1919, VSNKh had to issue an instruction in which it was 'categorically established that sections, *glavki* and *tsentry* of VSNKh had no right at all to enter the formation of the composition of the *gubsovnarkhoz* of any province.'[284]

From their own side, the *gubsovnarkhozy* tried to conquer in practice the autonomy which they were denied officially. They resorted to expediency to keep working, in spite of the cumbersome rules on financing. Delays in dispatch of financial funds were as long as half a year,[285] and drastically reduced the real value of their budgets, owing to the galloping inflation. Besides the effects of delays on the value of money, the *sovnarkhozy* did not receive much out of the total budget of VSNKh, as compared with *glavki* and *tsentry*. In 1919 the latter got more than 51 per cent of the total budget, whilst the *sovnarkhozy* were assigned only about 12 per cent.[286] Thus, some *sovnarkhozy* refused to turn over payments received from industries to the national budget.[287] Others reserved for themselves a quota of the sale value of products produced by nationalized factories, which should have been written into the budget of the *glavk*.[288] If some central decisions were circumvented by illegal devices, others could not always be correctly implemented in spite of the good will of the *sovnarkhozy* themselves. The coexistence of productive and functional sections, whose competence was not precisely defined, and the overlapping of one section with another, often jeopardized implementation of central guidelines.[289] Only at the end of 1919 did VSNKh resolve to work out a detailed list of the specific functions of *gubsovnarkhozy*, following the instructions of the Second Congress of *Sovnarkhozy*. The *gubsovnarkhozy* were made responsible for:

(1) unification and guidance of the activity of the provincial industrial organs, regulation of their interrelations, formulation of instructions;
(2) formulation of production programmes and corresponding estimates for the provincial enterprises and their realization;
(3) regulation and control of the activity of the administrations, both of public and private enterprises under their responsibility;
(4) technical organization of production, organization of shop management both of individual enterprises and their unions;
(5) assignment of advances upon estimates and loans;
(6) verification of consumption of fuel, raw materials, production equipment, labour and other factors related to the regular functioning of industry within the provincial territory;
(7) collection, accounting and distribution according to central plans of the means of production listed in point 6;
(8) distribution of orders among enterprises in the provincial territory;
(9) issue of obligatory instructions for all institutions and enterprises of the province, related to fulfilment of the targets set by the centre;
(10) accounting of all local operations and output.[290]

Gubsovnarkhozy were still excluded from participating in the formulation of central policy, but there were signs of a tendency towards separation of the functions of administration and management, which had been at the time of the First Congress of *Sovnarkhozy* one of the points made by the left-wing communists. The actual functions assigned to the local *sovnarkhozy* amounted to an admission that they were essential, that central policy could not be enforced locally without them.

Recent Soviet literature has pointed out the significance of the *sovnarkhozy* in war communism, in spite of the choice of *glavkism* made by the leadership.[291] The same literature, however, does not question the validity of the choice of *glavkism* as a synonym for 'centralization'. One may wonder, instead, whether the *sovnarkhozy* were able to expand and survive despite the hostility of *glavkism*, and whether *glavkism* itself came under attack before the end of the war communism experience precisely because the territorial economic organization had shown itself to be more suitable and flexible than the vertical administrations, especially in the contingencies of war. The importance of the *sovnarkhozy* grew with the increasing significance of medium, small and handicraft industry for military supply. Being more in touch with local possibilities and needs, the *sovnarkhozy* better realized which activities and operations ought to be supported.

An important role in keeping alive small industry was played by the *uezd sovnarkhozy*. Within the boundaries of districts these *sovnarkhozy* inherited the functions of the former *zemstvos*.[292] The *zemstvos* had been created in 1864 as institutions of local government outside the urban areas. Before the war, their activities ranged from education to public health, welfare, agronomic and economic measures, veterinary services, roads and administration generally. On the eve of the First World War the total budgets of municipalities and *zemstvos* equalled one-fifth of the State Budget.[293] During the war, the range of their activities increased. The union of *zemstvos*, through their appropriations and voluntary contributions, helped the army. Their services were not only limited to hospital care, but concerned also transport and repair workshops. Funds were obtained through taxation levied on rural strata, who, however, had only indirect electoral rights. During the war *zemstvo* appropriations reached more than 32 million rubles, a considerable sum which allowed them to start supplying fabrics and other items. Raw materials were purchased on the basis of monopsony and were assigned to local factories and craft industries for processing. Some *zemstvos* also requisitioned cattle and foodstuffs.[294]

After the revolution, the *uezd sovnarkhozy* tried to keep alive former initiatives. Twenty-one *uezd sovnarkhozy* were formed between January and April 1918 and eighty-three from May to November 1918.[295] Representatives of the *uezd sovnarkhozy* took part at the First Congress of

Sovnarkhozy on the same footing as other representatives. An unusually large number of sections were developed, which is indicative of their multifarious activity. Together with sections for agriculture and municipal services, other divisions were organized for rural housing, electricity, telephones, urban housing, etc. The *uezd sovnarkhozy* intervened also in the sphere of production.[296]

A survey of VSNKh on the composition of the *sovnarkhozy* showed that in 1919 about 51 per cent of the *uezd sovnarkhozy* included in the survey had a plenary committee, which on average numbered sixteen people. Those which had no plenary committee were directed by a presidium consisting of representatives of the executive committee of the local soviet, sections of the soviet and members of the Communist Party. The composition of the plenary committee, when it existed, reflected local realities instead of central rules. The survey considered that the plenary committee should be formed by representatives of the local executive committees (31.3 per cent of total membership), of the trade unions (15.6 per cent), and of cooperatives (12.5 per cent). Facts were different. Local executive committees provided 7.5 per cent, factory committees 3.4 per cent and cooperatives 6.9 per cent. Trade unions were over-represented at 21.3 per cent, while an important share was reserved for representatives of *volost* agricultural organizations, *kustari* and their associations, say 15.5 per cent, to whom the law granted no right of membership.[297] Depending on the functions actually performed, some *uezd sovnarkhozy* employed up to 200 persons, but on average the staff numbered between forty and sixty.[298] The *uezd sovnarkhozy* did not survive war communism. VSNKh tried initially to limit their competence and finally decided to abolish them. An ostensible reason for this was their excessive staff and the number of useless sections. But these were a consequence of deliberate policies. On one side, the *uezd sovnarkhozy*, which in some cases immediately took care of a number of local economic activities, were accused of duplicating functions only when higher *sovnarkhozy* came on the scene. On the other side, cases of 'parallelism' increased together with the pervasive operations of central bodies. It was reported that an *oblast sovnarkhoz* refused to finance the collection of timber made by the *uezd* since this was considered to be the responsibility of the *gubsovnarkhoz*. The same *oblast sovnarkhoz* accused the mining section of being a duplication of the chemical section and claimed that the printing section was unnecessary.[299] But local activities went on for some time. When hindered by financial rules, the *uezd sovnarkhozy* started financing themselves by borrowing from other departments and by levying taxes on production. Municipalization of local undertakings also became a source of funds.[300] The Second Congress of *Sovnarkhozy* confined the *uezd sovnarkhozy* to municipal questions. They were transformed into 'regulatory organs of the municipal economy', by which they lost the right to participate in *sovnarkhoz* congresses.[301] VSNKh tried to replace the *uezd sovnarkhozy* by other economic organizations covering a wider territory: the *okruzhnye sovnarkhozy*, whose competence was to be extended over a territory 'not smaller than that of the *uezd* having homogeneous economic characteristics. The *okruzhnye sovnarkhozy* should have been directly subordinated to the *gubsovnarkhozy*.[302] Like the *raion sovnarkhozy*, which also belonged to projects of late 1918 based on the principle of 'economic gravitation', the *okruzhnye sovnarkhozy* were conceived in such a way as to provide suitable bases for the local activity of *glavki* and *tsentry*. The existing administrative divisions, in fact, often jeopardized the policy of provision of raw materials, which was the principal task of several central administrations, since the borders of the provinces and districts often did not coincide with economic regions. The *raisovnarkhozy* which were formed had mostly distributive functions.[303] The *okruzhnye sovnarkhozy* probably did not become a reality. Neither institution was taken into account by the VSNKh survey on *sovnarkhozy* between 1919 and 1920.

Though the *uezd sovnarkhozy* should have been confined to public services, they went far beyond. They participated in the collection of raw materials, and helped small and craft industry working for local needs and for the army. Some *uezd sovnarkhozy* distributed kerosene, milk, and meat to the population. The struggle for survival nourished ingenuity. Cases were reported of steps being taken for mechanizing the collection of wood fuel.[304] Associations were promoted among artisans producing agricultural tools, bricks and lime. Repair shops were organized. In most cases, the activity of *kustari*, which was important for the supply of consumer goods to the army, was able to develop thanks to the local *sovnarkhozy*. The relative success of these initiatives favoured good relations between military headquarters and the local organizations, while such success embittered relations with the central administrations. The enterprises of the Novgorod province, which had been turning over to the army a substantial number of pumps and other tools in 1919, underwent a catastrophic decrease in production when they were taken under the direction of *glavki*.[305] Ingenuity was shown also in the choice of production techniques. Some local *sovnarkhozy* prohibited high fuel consumption techniques and promoted better local production methods. Raising steam from peat, for instance, was dropped in favour of wood furnaces.[306]

During war communism the main source of conflict between the centre and the local *sovnarkhozy* was the disposal of raw materials. The *gubsovnarkhozy* were allowed to confiscate and requisition only raw materials of local importance. But this right was inevitably to be questioned. Doubts about this decision were already raised at the Second Congress of *Sovnarkhozy*.[307] Acute scarcity made it hard to define anything available as 'locally' important, that is, uninteresting to the centre. Conversely, everything within the reach of provinces and districts became utterly essential to the local economy. Against the theory and practice of centrally decided closures, motivated by the state of the equipment and/or lack of stocks of raw materials,[308] the local *sovnarkhozy* endeavoured to keep their own reserves of fuel and raw materials in order to maintain a minimum level of local economic activity. Most of the accusations of separatism concerned this practice, which, of course, was competing against the central plans of supply. VSNKh directives were not respected in several ways. Removal of equipment and plant in accordance with directives of the central administrations was resisted.[309] Sometimes vehicles already loaded, particularly in the case of wood fuel, were not allowed to move over the borders of the province. In other instances, only a minimum quota was turned over to the local agencies of *glavki* and *tsentry*.[310]

War acted as a catalyser on the potential frictions that necessarily opposed the system of *glavki* to the system of *sovnarkhozy*, since scarcity increased the arrogance of the central administrations along with their bureaucratic power as well as the hostility of the provinces against central directives, which they often did not understand and which harmed their immediate interests. But the antagonism between *glavki* and *sovnarkhozy* existed independently of war, and may be seen as an interesting premonition of the nature of the tensions which, after decades of economic experience, still keep alive the Soviet debate over the efficacy of the ministerial (*glavk*) system versus the territorial (*sovnarkhoz*) system.

5.10 THE ANTAGONISM BETWEEN GLAVKI AND SOVNARKHOZY

The antagonism which opposed the provinces to the centre during war communism was to a great extent an expression of the unfitness of the *glavki* to carry out a policy of planned centralization. This required coordination at the centre of supply and distribution according to alternative criteria with respect to market signals. But VSNKh had neither the capacity nor the means to formulate a central plan. The vertical system based on the *glavki*, in effect, lacked a head. Besides, VSNKh lacked a very important element for enforcing *glavkism* on public opinion: it lacked consensus. Suspicion about the membership of *glavki* and *tsentry* was echoed even at the Congress of *Sovnarkhozy* in the autumn of 1918 by some Bolshevik delegates. Molotov observed that 57 per cent of the members of these bodies belonged to the upper classes.[311] The participation of bourgeois specialists in the direction of economic policy had been sought in spring 1918, following Lenin's belief that their services could be obtained, though at higher salaries. Civil war could only increase distrust of the highest administrative officials. Conversely, war made more reliable the local *sovnarkhozy*, in which party representation was higher, though average education was much lower.[312] Around the end of 1918 the reasons for conflict between *glavki* and *sovnarkhozy* were broadly discussed in a political framework already dominated by military preoccupations. Positive and negative features of both organizations were evaluated from several aspects. Efficacy, mass participation in management and objective constraints were taken into account.

On the one hand, it was argued that decentralization, through *sovnarkhozy*, had been the outcome of the revolution. It had promoted local initiative and management. The importance of the *sovnarkhozy* was connected with the possibility of having correct information about regional economic life, useful advice and valuable directives concerning specific enterprises.[313]

On the other hand, it was maintained that without systematic centralization anarchy would prevail. Central administrations were supposed to be more suitable for the direction and distribution of output. Some economists found it obvious that 'all activities and operations tending to centralization are correct since they help the creation of a planned centralized economy and, through it, the creation of socialism'.[314]

Arskii proposed what seemed an equitable solution to the problem of 'who controls whom', within a centralized system. *Sovnarkhozy* were to be strictly subordinated to decisions of the *glavki* and *tsentry*, whose directive boards were to be formed by representatives of the trade unions and workers' organizations of the provinces elected *in loco*, Against the Manichean attitude of left-wing communists towards bourgeois economic experts, Arskii commented that no matter what its orgin, 'power corrupts, especially the uncontrolled power which is in charge of the distribution of materials resources to individual people or groups'.[315]

In September 1918 the All-Russian Central Executive Committee declared Russia a war fortress. The Second Congress of *Sovnarkhozy*, which met two months later, however, did not evince a military point of view in discussing economic organization, even if the atmosphere may have been influenced by alarming news about military losses. The arguments for or against alternative forms of economic organization rested primarily on theoretical speculations and on recent, at times, personal, experience.[316]

The supporters of strict centralization affirmed that *glavki* and *sovnarkhozy* were incompatible. Life had proved, argued Rudzutak, that a choice must be made between two alternative organizations: either *glavki*, i.e. industrial commissariats, or local *sovnarkhozy*, on the lines of a new administrative division. According to Lomov, local *sovnarkhozy* should have been suppressed if it was true that nationalization required centralization, since they could not have real control over *glavki*, but only paper control. Veinberg affirmed that the production principle on which *glavki* were formed was not reconcilable with the territorial principle. Larin observed that factories working on homogeneous products ought to be unified and managed by single administrations, since it was inconceivable to return to the former system. Kaktyn maintained that *glavki* had exhausted their distributive function, which had been taken over by *Narkomprod*, and they ought to become production administrations under the sole direction of VSNKh. In his role as representative of the *obsovnarkhoz* of the Northern Region, Kaktyn stressed the dependence of *glavki* on the VSNKh production sections. Miliutin concluded that *glavki* needed freedom, independence and initiative.

Nonetheless, no one was ready to demand the abolition of *sovnarkhozy*. Differences of opinion about the functions which *sovnarkhozy* could perform within a system dominated by industrial commissariats, as Rudzutak had defined the *glavki*, hint at the gulf between the abstraction of the principles on centralization and its reality. Veinberg believed that state purchase and distribution of raw materials were to remain under the competence of *glavki*, while *sovnarkhozy* had to carry out the management of enterprises of local importance and the distribution of output. Vice versa, Rudzutak conceived that *sovnarkhozy* ought to carry out state purchasing and the supply of raw materials in place of *Narkomprod*. Larin said that *sovnarkhozy* were to assist *glavki*, by supplying fuel and raw materials in accordance with central plans, but that their specific functions ought to be concerned with the sphere of public utilities, formerly provided by *zemstvos*. Not unwilling to dream about the future, Larin added that *sovnarkhozy* should extend their scope to such fields as public canteens, public baths and other collective facilities 'which would totally change the life of the people by pulling them out of the domestic economy'. *Sovnarkhozy* had not yet done anything in this field, complained Larin, since they had been busy with the management of factory-shops. The time had come to start changing living conditions which in the mean time had even worsened. Even Larin, however, had to admit that the *sovnarkhozy* had also to perform managerial functions, until central administrations were formed. Moved by feelings which dated back to the years of militancy in the trade union movement, Nogin underlined the political role of the *sovnarkhozy* with respect to *glavki*, which had to be translated into vigilance and control over the formal aspects of the latter's activity.

Against the centralistic drive expressed by the VSNKh leaders, provincial delegates offered their own evidence. Examples were produced of the inactivity of *glavki* in preparatory work for nationalization and management of factories, which, *per contra*, had been done by *sovnarkhozy* using their own financial means. Some state purchases of raw materials by *glavki* were wasted because they had no collaboration from other *glavki*, which were supposed to provide the means of using them. Waste of time was alleged to be the effect of strict compliance with the principle of vertical administration. Evidence was given of semi-finished products being transferred to other provinces for further processing, while local factories operating in the field were shut down. Examples were cited to show that in some cases *sovnarkhozy* had proved to be more far-sighted than the centre. The purchase of flax was undertaken by a local *sovnarkhoz* in substitution for cotton, before guidelines in this direction had been issued by the agents of *Tsentrotekstil'*. Arguments reversing the logic of centralization went thus: there was a lot of talk about scarcity of raw materials, while small factories and mills were stuffed with them in some provinces: what's better, to let work go on, or to make plans? Though simplistic, this argument vigorously expressed feelings in the provinces about the inefficacy of the *glavk* system and the waste which was visible locally. The provincial representatives reached the conclusion that it would have been better to let *sovnarkhozy* manage the economy and the centre watch over them. The challenge was not accepted by VSNKh. On the contrary, the arguments of the provinces were used to demand a more precise hierarchy between the existing institutions and central control over crucial appointments.

Arskii's proposal to gain local support for central policies by a system of election to central boards, and extension of responsibility for central choices to local trade unions and *sovnarkhozy*, through the election of the managers, remained isolated. Following Miliutin's propositions, the congress affirmed that *sovnarkhozy* were necessary in the transition period and that they had to comply with central directives, decisions and plans. Transformation of the local agencies of *glavki* into sections of *sovnarkhozy*, responsible to the centre, was but a defective surrogate for Arskii's suggestions about management, since crucial decisions were devolved to the appointees of the central boards, without regard to local consequences and local support.

Pressure to limit the autonomy of *glavki* and *tsentry* began to increase in 1919. The industrial centres were the most reluctant to conform to central policy. The Kostroma provincial *sovnarkhoz* congress affirmed that 'specialists' from the centre hindered the activity of the local executive committee and deprived the presidium of the *sovnarkhoz* of any initiative in the economic field.[317] The *sovnarkhoz* of the Northern Region claimed that the local inspection organs of VSNKh should be transformed into executive organs of the local *sovnarkhoz*.[318] The *sovnarkhozy* challenged not only VSNKh's policy, but also the central directives of the party. The economic resolution of the Eighth Congress of the Party, in fact, approved the principles on which the *glavk* system was based. The Communist Party shared the idea that maximum centralization of production ought to be achieved by carrying forward unification by single branches and groups of branches and concentration of production in large industrial unions, strictly bound to the fulfilment of economic commands.[319] *The ABC of Communism* considered it advantageous to restrict production to the best-equipped undertakings, rather than to waste energies fruitlessly by relying on inefficient and badly equipped enterprises.[320] The further admission that some of the largest works had been closed down, owing to scarcity of raw materials and fuel, did not induce the economists of the party to question the validity of concentration, although in Russia at that time impediments due to lack of transport jeopardized the whole idea of convergence of all productive activities in a few centres. Disorganization was imputed to the lack of 'material things', rather than to 'the lack of organization, properly speaking'.[321]

The local *sovnarkhozy*, on the contrary, questioned the system whose failures they were experiencing day after day. The absence of an overall financial system and plan, the lack of money tokens, and the inefficiency of central financing seriously jeopardized local activity. The Second Congress of *Sovnarkhozy* of the Northern Region in February 1919 demanded greater autonomy in the disposal of financial funds and in control over private industry. The congress established that the local economy should depend on local regulations and financing.[322] In fact, funds should have been assigned to the productive sections of the *sovnarkhozy* and then distributed according to production plans.[323] But, to speed up times of dispatch, *Narkomfin* invited *glavki* and *tsentry* to finance their own enterprises directly. In response to the resentment expressed by the local *sovnarkhoz* about such procedures, VSNKh made the short comment that evidently *glavki* and *tsentry* did not conform to its own instructions on financing.[324] Time was lost trying to find an agreement between the major interested institutions. A special northern conference consisting of the *oblast sovnarkhoz* of the Northern Region, *gubsovnarkhozy* of that area and the local offices of the *glavki*, was convened in spring 1919 to discuss this question, but no agreement was reached. The *gubsovnarkhozy* demanded that an end be put to the formation of local agencies of the *glavki* and claimed the right to participate in the examination of the estimates of production plans submitted by *raion* administrations of the *glavki*. VSNKh tried to find a compromise which would partially satisfy local claims and safeguard the authority of the centre. A proposal was made to distinguish 'trustified' from 'non-trustified' enterprises and let the local *sovnarkhozy* be in charge of financial funds and production plans of non-unionized enterprises.[325] The question was not settled and opposite claims continued throughout 1919. The process of forming trusts and *kusty* was still going on, thus making meaningless the separation between the realm of the central economy and the realm of the local economy. By the formation of *kusty*, *glavki* and *tsentry* were able to put even small enterprises under their own control. The *gubsovnarkhozy* at this point claimed the right to have at least their own representatives on the *kust* administrations, with the right of veto.[326] The *oblast sovnarkhoz* of the Northern Region reported cases of mismanagement of state funds by dishonest managers having caused stoppage of industrial activity and, in order to avoid repetition of such cases, insisted on the request that 'without exception, all financing of enterprises of the Northern Region should go through the financial-accounting section of the *sovnarkhoz*'.[327]

The claims of the provinces found a positive echo in the party leadership. At the Seventh All-Russian Congress of Soviets, from 5 to 9 December 1919, Lenin affirmed that questions concerning the economy had to be examined from the aspect of practical experience, rather than from considerations of principle. In opposition to the president of VSNKh, Rykov, and to Sereda, the People's Commissar of Agriculture, who both defended the principle of centralization in economic organization, Lenin presented the evidence produced by the provinces and confirmed by Trotskii and some other People's Commissars about the possibility of employing people *in loco* for management:

Since the comrades from the localities assure us (and comrade Trotskii and many people's commissars confirm it) that in recent times in the gubernias and to a considerable extent, in the *uezd*, functionaries of a higher type have appeared (I am constantly hearing such an assertion from comrades arriving here from the provinces and from comrade Kalinin who has visited many places) we shall have to take them into consideration and ask ourselves whether the matter of centralism is rightly understood in the present instance.[328]

The possibility of devolving some functions to the provinces was examined also by Lomov. Lomov agreed with Lenin that a number of functions, primarily the purchase of all sorts of raw materials, should be transferred to the localities. In this field, Lomov admitted, the centre had displayed a great deal of conservatism and routine thinking, while, he added, the provinces had already found ways of rationing raw materials, a measure which had not yet been decided upon at the centre.[329]

Though reluctant to modify its views on centralization, the leadership of VSNKh resolved to adhere to Lenin's invitation and to comply with the guidelines of the Seventh Congress of Soviets on limitation of the autonomy of the *glavki*. A draft resolution was worked out and was submitted for approval to the All-Russian Central Executive Committee. The draft concerned the division of enterprises into three groups. Enterprises of national importance were to be directly subordinated to the central administrations or to the existing production sections of VSNKh. Enterprises of lesser importance, but not quite of local significance, were included in the second group. Their plans of production were to be subordinated to central directives while the organization was to be left under the supervision of the local *sovnarkhoz*. A third group of enterprises was to remain under the exclusive direction of the local *sovnarkhoz*, which would draw up their plans of production.[330]

The resolution of the All-Russian Central Executive Committee on the division of enterprises into three groups, while allowing some decentralization in management, tried to fix rigid rules in financing, in order to keep even local enterprises under central control. The first group of enterprises was to be financed directly from the centre. The central administrations were to formulate their plans of supply and execute them. The *gubsovnarkhozy* were explicitly refused orders to enterprises of the first group. These enterprises could supply local social needs, such as repair, electricity, etc., making efforts, in such cases, to be paid in agricultural products. Local orders were to go through the sections of the local *sovnarkhoz* and to be accepted only if they did not jeopardize the fulfilment of central orders. The central administrations were to be informed about such an initiative within three days. The second group of enterprises were to be financed through the control organs of the *gubsovnarkhozy* and their estimates were to be presented directly to the *gubsovnarkhozy* and the central organs of VSNKh. The plan of supply of raw materials was decided by the centre and the *gubsovnarkhozy* had to implement it. The output of the enterprises of the second group was accounted for and subject to the decision of the corresponding central administrations of VSNKh. The presidium of the *gubsovnarkhoz* was made responsible for fulfilment of the orders. The third group of enterprises was financed through a special fund formed for this purpose, which was put under the responsibility of VSNKh. The *gubsovnarkhozy* had the right to spend money out of this fund only after presentation of their financial estimates. The means of production were distributed on the basis of central norms. The *gubsovnarkhozy* were made free to distribute only the quota of means which they had been assigned. The output of the third group of enterprises was to satisfy, firstly, the needs of the given province and secondly, the needs of the centre or other provinces. But the norms of distribution were decided by the centre. The provincial output programmes were to be elaborated by the *gubsovnarkhozy* and approved by the provincial executive committees.[331]

Compilation of the list of enterprises belonging to each group took some time. Rykov recalled at the Eighth Congress of Soviets (22–9 December 1920) that commissions had been formed to draw up a detailed list of enterprises belonging to the three groups. Their work had been submitted to *Sovnarkom*. Another commission, consisting of representatives of VSNKh and of the Moscow Soviet had been appointed by *Sovnarkom* to check the work done. The Presidium of the Central Executive Committee had approved the list only at the end of April 1920.[332] By his detailed report on the work done, Rykov hoped to convince the assembly that a broad consensus had been reached on the division of enterprises. But it was not so. By the middle of 1920 the whole system of *glavki* was under discussion and sharp criticism. The left-wing communists affirmed that the centralized economic structure based on the *glavki* was negative as such. It was negative not because of the bad state of transport and communications, but because it elevated 'a Chinese wall' against local workers, thus compromising the workability of the whole system. It was on these grounds that the left wing of the party proposed the transfer of local industry to local management as well as the continuation of collegial direction. Trotskii called the policy of VSNKh 'glavkocracy' and accused VSNKh, the trust of trusts, of continuing to work out plans whose percentage rate of fulfilment was so insignificant as not to deserve the name.[333] Sapronov proposed to transfer to management of the corresponding sections of the *gubsovnarkhozy* all the enterprises of the first group, including local (*raion*) organs of the *glavki*, but not large-scale metallurgical, machine building and electric equipment works, mines and oil wells. Political and technical organs should participate in this transfer. Sapronov said that the commission entrusted with this task should consist of representatives of VSNKh, provincial executive committees, *gubsovnarkhozy* and provincial councils of the trade unions. *Glavki* and *tsentry* should be reorganized in such a way as to become organs charged with the regulation and direction of the tasks of the *gubsovnarkhozy* in accordance with a single economic plan.[334]

However, for the party leadership the question of economic organization was tightly interwoven with the consolidation of power, and the technical aspects of the problem were not given an appropriate importance.

Unwilling to allow latitude to the autonomistic tendencies of the provinces, afraid of provoking local tensions soon after the end of the civil war, aware of the drawbacks of *glavkism*, but scared of the unforeseeable outcome of decentralization, the leadership decided to concentrate the tasks of economic reconstruction in the hands of the higher organs of the state. At the Ninth Party Congress, Trotskii put forward the idea of an overall economic plan of reconstruction based on heavy industry and transport. Lenin affirmed before the Eighth Congress of Soviets that the coordination of all plans of production necessary for constructing a single economic plan was to be carried out by the Council of Labour and Defence.[335] Zinoviev stressed that the work of the local sections of the *glavki* and *tsentry* should be directly guided by the local soviets.[336] Even Larin, the promoter of the *glavk* system, agreed that it was time to abolish VSNKh, which he called the Soviet hydra with its several tentacles of interdepartmental committees, and to assign to the Council of Labour and Defence the task of economic reconstruction according to a central plan.

The approach of major party leaders to the economic policy of reconstruction was definitely influenced by the experience of civil war.

The isolation as well as the importance of the party leadership increased as a consequence of civil war and its successful conclusion. Though *glavkism* incurred the criticism of party members, the need for political control over economic activity was not questioned, but, on the contrary, was the alternative form of 'centralization' which the party leadership proposed in place of technical centralization. In 1918 the idea of economic centralization reflected the technocratic inclination of the economic experts of the party, nourished by German experience and culture. But the *glavk* system in Russia did not work. The logic of distribution prevailed over the logic of production. Confronted with production problems, the central managers needed the collaboration of local organs, which they could not obtain both because of reciprocal suspicion and because of the lack of an efficient system of information, communications and transport. But the failure of *glavkism* did not bring about a reconsideration of the problems of economic organization from a more liberal point of view. On the contrary, the ideology of centralization was reinforced. The idea of an overall economic plan originated in the realm of political concerns, rather than through a serious search for new levers and methods of economic direction. Rykov and Miliutin were hostile to the idea of planning amidst the widespread destruction and disruption of the means of communication caused by war, and in the absence of adequate statistics.[337] In 1920, however, under the slogan of planning, the party leadership advocated the need to militarize the economy, under political control. The 'military Soviet culture', which Osinskii passionately accused of being the antithesis of 'Soviet civil culture', definitely prevailed at the Ninth Party Congress, leaving durable legacies on the Soviet interpretation of democratic centralism in all fields.

The VSNKh resolution on the division of enterprises into three groups was enforced after the Ninth Party Congress, which affirmed the need to keep and develop vertical centralism by reinforcing managerial direction. In November 1920, out of the 6,908 enterprises subject to this division, 2,374, i.e. 35 per cent, remained under the direct management of VSNKh; 3,450 (50 per cent) were transferred to the second group; and 15 per cent were turned over to the *gubsovnarkhozy*.[338] This solution did not encounter total support either by local organs or by central administrations. On the one hand, it was proposed to abolish entirely the first group and to transfer all enterprises to the local provincial executive committees. On the other hand, VSNKh defended the principle of forming trusts, as the basis of economic organization. This implied continuation of the activity of *glavki* in the provinces and the possibility of revision of the established groups in favour of the centre. A more authoritative commission, which had been formed to settle disagreements,[339] decided to transfer a higher number of enterprises to the provinces than in the originally proposed division.[340] But the final solution could not be sought in different arithmetical arrangements, in the absence of objective criteria for separating industry of national importance from local economy. Thus, it was not surprising that in February 1921 VSNKh confirmed that *Glavtorf* had the right to dispossess, as and when it wished, any other institution of any undertaking in the industry.[341] Nor was it odd that VSNKh's Presidium claimed the right to decide which kind of products of *kustar'* industry were to belong to the competence of *glavki* and which to the competence of *Glavkustprom*, the central administration in charge of issuing regulations for craft industry.

The division of industry into three groups, which could have been a satisfactory solution to the problem of central control over key sectors, if accompanied by adequate legislation on reciprocal duties and financial reform and if accepted as a stable framework for future policies, was instead but a fragile compromise with the provinces over the destination of national resources. The militarization of the economy which Trotskii's plan of reconstruction entailed was likely to favour extension of the policy of appropriation over consumer goods, that is over *kustar'* output. The progressive naturalization of the economy, i.e. increase of barter as compared with money transactions, implied central control over 'wage goods', mainly produced by small and craft industry, as a form of financial control over wages and labour productivity. At the end of the war communism experience, centralization was becoming a necessity.

An article in *Izvestiia* on 5 March 1921, the day of the Kronstadt revolt, claimed that only *Glavkustprom* had the right to regulate the economy of craft industry. A number of examples were reported to accuse the *sovnarkhozy* of turning a deaf ear to central orders to transfer *kustar'* undertakings to *Glavkustprom*. The article anticipated the decision of the Tenth Party Congress. Small undertakings were to be taken away from *gubsovnarkhozy* and concentrated under *Glavkustprom*. Management was to be centralized over the whole national territory and be subject to appointment by VSNKh, *Narkomzem* and the *oblast* trade unions. *Gubsovnarkhozy* were to be left in charge of 'control', in the sense of inspection and audit, only.[342] Such developments show the extent to which the leadership, long after the end of the war, remained imprisoned within the constraints of an economic model which, to a great extent, had been the result of expediency and misconception about the real possibility of mastering economic laws.

Vainshtein's very careful investigation of the industrial division into three groups concluded that, in spite of the decision of the Eighth Congress of Soviets, the number of enterprises remaining under central control was very high: 2,516 enterprises, plus 25 territorial mineral complexes embracing 350 industrial units, altogether employing 975,173 workers; say about 50 per cent of the total industrial labour force[343] (see Table 5.6). Enterprises were subdivided in each group according to their size. The largest remained in the first group.

In some cases the nature of output determined inclusion in the first group. When the chemical section, for instance, carried out the division of enterprises, the sugar and rubber industries were left, as a whole, under central administrations.[344] Coordination with the provinces was ensured by the setting-up of provincial economic conferences (*gubkhozsoveshchaniia*), approved by the Eighth Congress of Soviets.

The provincial economic conferences were attached to the provincial economic committees and formed from the members of the executive committee appointed for economic affairs. The new organs were entrusted with coordination of the activity of local organs of the economic people's commissariats (VSNKh, *Narkomzem*, *Narkomprod*, *Narkomtrud*, *Narkomfin*). Measures to decentralize auxiliary supply to enterprises were to be taken, by instructing the *gubsovnarkhozy* to supply the enterprises of all three large groups the necessary materials, within the limits of the overall state supply plan. VSNKh was to remain in charge of the formulation and realization of production programmes for all spheres of

Table 5.6. *Compendium of enterprises and workers according to production branches and groups of management in March–May 1921 for the RSFSR*

Branches	First group		Second and third groups		Total		Per cent of total	
	Enter-prises	Workers	Enter-prises	Workers	Enter-prises	Workers	Enter-prises	Workers
Mineral and materials processings	85	31,590	1,844	51,012	1,929	82,602	7.5	4.2
Mining	25	36,805	219	20,673	25,219	57,378	2.2	2.9
Metal and electrical	179	228,791	3,472	141,745	3,651	370,536	14.1	18.9
Wood working	156	10,637	2,336	106,756	2,492	117,393	9.6	6.0
Chemical	148	41,248	2,080	82,729	2,228	123,977	8.6	6.4
Agricultural processing	730	41,196	6,635	176,822	7,365	218,018	28.4	11.1
Organic materials processing	60	13,954	2,265	115,454	2,325	129,408	8.9	6.6
Textiles	459	334,650	3,207	194,554	3,666	529,205	14.1	27.0
Paper and printing	72	21,815	749	52,048	821	73,863	3.2	3.7
Coal and peat	594	190,925	218	45,053	812	235,978	3.1	12.0
Oil and other	33	23,562	37	693	70	24,255	0.2	1.2
Total (excluding *raiony*)[a]	2,516	975,173	23,062	987,440	25,578	1,962,613	100.0	100.0

[a] *Raiony* = territorial industrial complexes
Source: Narodnoe Khoziaistvo, March 1922, 55

the national economy, computation and approval of production programmes and plans of supply and the overall direction of industry. *Glavki* and *tsentry* were to be reorganized into organs of direction, for the working out of tasks, regulations and supervision over the activity of *gubsovnarkhozy* according to the overall economic plan. Management of enterprises was devolved to *gubsovnarkhozy*. The principle was agreed upon that VSNKh was to remain in direct control over the enterprises already subject to trustification.[345]

As compared with the original draft,[346] the final version of the resolution on provincial economic conferences shows the precise intention of the congress to limit VSNKh's functions in economic policy. The right of the VSNKh presidium to decide the transfer of enterprises from one group to another was abolished, as well as the legally binding nature of VSNKh directives, decisions and instructions. The Eighth Congress of Soviets accepted the continuing process of naturalization of the economy. It was decided to form local supply funds, consisting of stocks of raw and semi-manufactured materials, fuels, auxiliary materials and equipment, foodstuffs and other consumer goods used for rewards in kind to workers and employees. For this purpose, the *gubsovnarkhozy* were assigned a quota of resources out of the overall state fund, local output and state purchase. This decision was motivated by the need to give the *gubsovnarkhozy* the possibility of displaying more initiative and autonomy in industrial development as well as by the need to do away with red tape and avoid intermediation in the field of supply to enterprises and institutions. Decisions on quotas and composition of supply funds were to be taken jointly by VSNKh and *Narkomprod* and agreed on by other commissariats.[347]

However, a precise idea as to the future relations between the centre and the provinces was not yet developed in 1920. The fear of autonomistic tendencies of large territorial units seems to have been prevalent in the decisions taken about *oblast* economic organizations. The Second Congress of *Sovnarkhozy* at the end of 1918 had discussed the creation of new economic industrial regions on the basis of the economic gravitation of productive activities. Civil war had prevented any action in this field. In 1920, when Russian territory had been brought fully under Soviet control, the question of the formation of *oblast* organs was discussed again, but in the light of two years' experience in management and central administration of national resources. This experience suggested two things: firstly, the need to rely on local administrators for the exploitation of local resources; secondly, the need to control from the centre the destination of mining and metallurgical output. The Ninth Party Congress decided to form economic *oblasti* fully empowered 'to implement the plans established by the centre' and to coordinate the administrative work of the *gubsovnarkhozy* and *raion* administration.[348] VSNKh formed *oblast* industrial boards, the *prombureaux*, which started operating through the local organs of *glavki* and production sections. The *prombureaux* were developed according to the scheme on which the central machinery of VSNKh was based. Their sections were also subordinated to VSNKh through the *glavk* system.[349] The party resolution stressed that local officials should be appointed on the basis of their 'exemplary' behaviour and for their capacity to appreciate the 'overall point of view' in the performance of their duties.[350]

Nonetheless, some autonomistic tendencies developed. The local sections of the central administrations were incorporated into the organization of the *prombureaux* and were subordinated to their boards. When this occurred, VSNKh intervened by reshaping the local *prombureaux*. In the Urals, new production sections were formed for the most important branches. *Raion* administrations of the coal industry were linked with the local coal section, which was subordinated both to the board of the *prombureau* and to the central administration for coal of VSNKh. The double subordination, which had been experienced also by the local sections of the *glavki*, once they had been included in the *gubsovnarkhozy*, was, as in this case, a formal compromise. *Glavugol'*, VSNKh's central administration for coal, kept the right of appointing *raion* administrators and technicians, of shutting down local undertakings temporarily or permanently, and of approving the enterprises' production plans. The local coal sections were entrusted only with coordination of the programmes of production in the coal industry with other programmes, checking fulfilment, and vigilance regarding the rational utilization of resources.[351]

As long as war communism lasted and was not subject to an overall re-examination, that is, until spring 1921, a fair solution to the problem of coordination between the vertical hierarchy and the territorial organization was not found. But even after 1921, the ideology of *glavkism*, which to a great extent was the expression of a belief in the possibility of managing the economy from above, according to a faith in some special power of the leadership, remained and nourished the spirit of the Soviet model of planning.

5.11 SUMMARY

The evolution of VSNKh reflects the contradictory claims which characterized the organization of the Soviet economy from its origin.

Unplanned events forced the technocratically orientated leadership of VSNKh to renounce, unwillingly, its aim to be the only supervisory organ of the national economy, and to concentrate on the regulation of the rapidly increasing sphere of nationalized industry. Productive sections and functional committees were formed in response to emerging necessity. Former regulatory organs, such as *glavki* and *tsentry*, were incorporated into VSNKh, not only in a mere constitutional sense, but also as institutions working according to their own rationale. Their vertical structure, which was considered suitable for centralization, was a powerful obstacle, during war communism, to the strengthening of the *sovnarkhozy*, which were allowed to survive only as a buffer section of the economy supervising local small-scale industry and handicrafts. The experience of war communism shows, however, that centralization was far from being reached, and that through their effective control over raw materials and local activities, the *sovnarkhozy* maintained a much more important role in the organization of production than the rationale of central control would have admitted.

The conflicts inherent in the unbalanced combination of a vertical structure (*glavki*) with a horizontal one (*sovnarkhozy*) remained unsettled even after the 1920 industrial reorganization, following which the enterprises were divided into three groups according to their national importance. War communism shows that the leadership never agreed on, and was unable to come to terms with, the problem of the most suitable organization for central control. Lack of reliable cadres in the crucial posts was a major reason for this, together with the manifest inefficiency of the existing central administrations.

The civil organization was manifestly unable to convert rapidly to the military priorities. The reasons for economic centralization advanced by VSNKh did not coincide with, and did not respond to, the requisites of a war economy. The nucleus of activities directly connected with war developed autonomously from VSNKh and was often in conflict with it.

The poor achievements of the centralized economy, as compared with the local economy, added further reasons for the downgrading of VSNKh to mere managerial functions at the very time when the debate on planning started, a debate which resulted in the formation of *Gosplan* as the future centre for the elaboration of planning.

The criticism of *glavkism*, once the civil war was ended, however, was not able to defeat the strenuous effort of VSNKh to keep as many enterprises as possible under central control, about one third of the total number, which, therefore, remained the stable nucleus and the theatre for the trials and errors of future planning.

NOTES

1 P.V. Volobuev, *Ekonomicheskaia politika Vremennogo Pravitel'stva*, Moscow, 1962, p. 139.
2 A.V. Venediktov, Organizatsiia gosudarstvennoi promyshlennosti v SSSR, vol. 1, Moscow, 1957, p. 258.
3 *Sobranie uzakonenii*, 1917, no. 82, art. 1015.
4 P. Labry, *L'Industrie russe et la révolution*, Paris, 1919, pp. 156–7.
5 *Ekonomicheskaia Zhizn'*, no. 1, 6 November 1919, 2; the experts were Obolenskii (Osinskii), Smirnov, and Savel'ev. When the first two were given other responsibilities, the matter passed to Savel'ev and Bukharin.
6 A.A. Voronetskaia, 'Organizatsiia VSNKh...', *Istoricheskie Zapiski*, 1953, no. 43, 7.
7 M. Philips Price, *My Reminiscences of the Russian Revolution*, London, 1921, p. 213.
8 Volobuev, p. 137.
9 Venediktov, p. 259.
10 E.D. Kozochkina, *Iz istorii organizatsii upravleniia promyshlennosti*, Moscow, 1964, p. 24.
11 V.I. Lenin, *Polnoe sobranie sochinenii*, 5th edn, vol. 35, Moscow, 1962, p. 134. Lenin wanted Bukharin as the president of VSNKh, but the Central Committee of the Party on 12 December 1917 decided to appoint Bukharin to the editorial board of *Pravda*. See *The Bolsheviks and the October Revolution, Central Committee Minutes of the Russian Social-Democratic Labour Party (bolsheviks), August 1917–February 1918*, London, 1974.
12 D.A. Baevskii, *Rabochii klass v pervye gody Sovetskoi Vlasti (1917–1921 gg)*, Moscow, 1974, p. 28.
13 *Sobranie uzakonenii*, 1917–1918, no. 5, art. 83.
14 Labry, p. 143.
15 The initiative came from the second Moscow *raion* economic congress, which proposed organization of collective work, 'not as a question of philanthropy, but in the framework of economic policy as a whole'. Like VSNKh's committee for public works, other committees were planned at the level of the *sovnarkhozy*: see *Uprochenie Sovetskoi Vlasti v Moskve i Moskovskoi Gubernii, Dokumenty i Materialy*, Moscow, 1958, document no. 212.
16 V.Z. Drobizhev and A.B. Medvedev, *Iz istorii sovnarkhozov*, Moscow, 1964, pp. 94–95.
17 *Narodnoe Khoziaistvo*, 1918, no. 12, 26.
18 Iu. K. Avdakov, *Organizatsionno-khoziaistvennaia deiatel'nost' VSNKh v pervye gody Sovetskoi Vlasti (1917–1921 gg)*, Moscow, 1971, p. 110.
19 *Narodnoe Khoziaistvo*, 1918, no. 12, 26, and *Narodnoe Khoziaistvo*, 1920 nos. 1–2, p. 35.
20 *Narodnoe Khoziaistvo*, 1918, no. 12, 25.
21 This decision was taken at the first public meeting of VSNKh and issued as a decree of 5 January 1918 (*Sobranie uzakonenii*, 1917–18, no. 13, art. 196). For an appraisal of the meeting see Philips Price, pp. 213–15.
22 *Sobranie uzakonenii*, 1917–18, no. 13, art. 196.
23 *Sobranie uzakonenii*, 1917–18, no. 11, art. 167.

24 E.II. Carr, *The Bolshevik Revolution, 1917–1923*, 3 vols., London, 1952, vol. 2, pp. 77–8.
25 *Ibid.*, p. 77.
26 Avdakov, p. 76.
27 Cf. Lenin's speech at the *7i S"ezd Rossiiskoi Kommunisticheskoi Partii, 6–8 marta 1918 goda, sten. otchet*, Moscow, 1923, pp. 165–6.
28 *Ibid.*, p. 173.
29 V.I. Lenin, 'Speech against Bukharin's Amendment to the Resolution of the Party Programme', 8 March, in *Collected Works*, 4th edn, 45 vols; London, 1964–70, vol. 27, p. 147.
30 Bukharin had proposed that the programme should mention the withering away of the state, while the resolution affirmed 'Transition *through* the Soviet State to the gradual abolition of the state...', *ibid.*, p. 156.
31 *Ibid.*, p. 148.
32 *7i S"ezd RKP*, pp. 207–8.
33 L. Kristman's essay in *Oktiabr'skii perevorot i diktatura proletariata, sbornik statei*, Moscow, 1919, p. 62.
34 Drobizhev and Medvedev, *Iz istorii sovnarkhozov*, p. 96.
35 *Sbornik dekretov*, vol. 1, p. 8; F.V. Samokhvalov, *Sovety Narodnogo Khoziaistva v 1917–1932 gg*, Moscow, 1964, pp. 60–2.
36 *Sbornik dekretov*, vol. 1, p. 8.
37 See p. 231 and cf. *Sobranie uzakonenii*, 1917–18, no. 11, arts. 167, 172, 174.
38 During 1919–20, the plenary session did not meet. Power was entrusted to the presidium (Venediktov, pp. 500–1).
39 F.V. Samokhvalov, *Sovety Narodnogo Khoziaistva v 1917–1923*, Moscow, 1926, p. 62.
40 G.A. Trukhan, 'Rabochii klass i sotsialisticheskoe obobshchestvlenie promyshlennosti (1917–1919 gg)', in *Rabochii klass: vedushchaia sila Oktiabr'skoi Revoliutsii, Sbornik statei*, Moscow, 1976, p. 211.
41 *Trudy I Vserossiiskogo S"ezda Sovnarkhozov*, pp. 99, 105, 107, 109.
42 N. Osinskii, *Stroitel'stvo sotsializma*, Moscow, 1918, pp. 64–5.
43 *Ibid.*, pp. 65–74.
44 *Ekonomicheskaia Zhizn'*, no. 37, 20 December 1918, 1.
45 *Trudy II Vserossiiskogo S"ezda Sovnarkhozov*, pp. 18, 47, 61–2.
46 *Ekonomicheskaia Zhizn'*, no. 1, 6 November 1918, 1.
47 *Ekonomicheskaia Zhizn'*, no. 38, 21 December 1918, 1.
48 Osinskii, p. 63.
49 Venediktov, p. 501.
50 *Narodnoe Khoziaistvo*, December 1920, 28, 30; Venediktov, p. 502. According to Miliutin, the Committee of Production, the Committee for Utilization, the Financial Economic Section and the Accounting Section, together with the Section of Other Towns, were supposed to work out the economic plan of the current year and be responsible for its general direction (cf. V.P. Miliutin, *Narodnoe Khoziaistvo Sovetskoi Rossii*, Izd. VSNKh, Moscow, 1920, p. 9).
51 *Sobranie uzakonenii*, 1921, no. 1, art. 2.
52 See pp. 203–4 above.
53 S. Zagorsky, *State Control of Industry in Russia during the War*, New Haven, 1928, pp. 97–8, 145–9.

54 G. Tsyperovitch, *Sindikaty i tresty, v dorevoliutsionnoi Rossii i SSSR*, Leningrad, 1927, pp. 400–1.
55 Cf. *VSNKh: Plenum*, 14–23 sent., 1918 goda, Moscow 1919, p. 88.
56 Osinskii, pp. 133–4.
57 *Trudy II Vserossiiskogo S"ezda Sovnarkhozov*, p. 413; *Narodnoe Khoziaistvo*, 1919, no. 3, 70–1; M. Dobb, *Soviet Economic Development after 1917*, London, 1951, pp. 106–24: on the initial distinction between *glavki* and *tsentry* according to rules of appointment of management, which was then made uniform.
58 Cf. Ia. S. Rozenfel'd, *Promyshlennaia politika SSSR*, Moscow, 1926, p. 127.
59 L. Kritsman, *Edinyi khoziaistvennyi plan i komissiia ispol'zovaniia*, 1921, pp. 12–13.
60 *Narodnoe Khoziaistvo*, 1920, nos. 1–2, p. 13.
61 *Narodnoe Khoziaistvo*, 1919, no. 3, 51; Tsyperovitch, p. 401.
62 For access to transport, Glavugol' went through VSNKh's Presidium, the Extraordinary Commission for Army Supply, and STO. Only after approval by STO could Glavugol' contact the Commissariat of Communications and be granted the right to secure goods wagons. *Narodnoe Khoziaistvo*, 1919, no. 3, 47.
63 *Ibid.*, 50–1.
64 *Narodnoe Khoziaistvo*, 1920, nos. 1–2, p. 13.
65 *Narodnoe Khoziaistvo*, 1919, no. 4, 32.
66 *Narodnoe Khoziaistvo*, 1920, nos. 1–2, p. 14.
67 *Narodnoe Khoziaistvo*, 1920, nos. 3–4, pp. 18–19.
68 *Ibid.*, p. 53.
69 *Narodnoe Khoziaistvo*, nos. 15–16, August 1920, 31–2.
70 *The Russian Economist*, vol. 1, September 1920–January 1921, London, 1921, 359.
71 *Narodnoe Khoziaistvo*, nos. 15–16, August 1920, 31–2.
72 *Narodnoe Khoziaistvo*, 1920, nos. 1–2, p. 12.
73 Cf. *The Russian Economist*, vol. 1, 358–9.
74 *Statisticheskii Ezhegodnik 1918–1920 gg*, vyp. 2, Moscow, 1922, p. 222.
75 *Narodnoe Khoziaistvo*, 1920, nos. 1–2, p. 15.
76 *The Russian Economist*, vol. 1, 359–61.
77 *Narodnoe Khoziaistvo*, 1920, nos. 1–2, p. 16.
78 *Izvestiia*, no. 206, 1918, 1.
79 As did Kaktyn, for instance: *Narodnoe Khoziaistvo*, 1919, no. 4, 17.
80 *Izvestiia*, no. 206, 1918, 1.
81 Zagorsky, pp. 293–6, 309–11.
82 *Sbornik dekretov*, vol. 1, pp. 113–16, 123–6.
83 *Ekonomicheskaia Zhizn'*, no. 18, 26 January 1919, 4.
84 *Trudy II Vserossiiskogo S"ezda Sovnarkhozov*, p. 413.
85 *Sbornik dekretov*, vol. 1, pp. 135–6.
86 *Ekonomicheskaia Zhizn'*, no. 16, 26 November 1918, 3; no. 42, 26 December 1918, 3 and no. 231, 17 October 1919, 2.
87 Cf. Kritsman's intervention at VSNKh's plenary session in September 1918, in *Narodnoe Khoziaistvo*, 1918, no. 12, 26.
88 Osinskii, pp. 135–6.
89 W.H. Beable, *Commercial Russia*, London 1918, p. 245.
90 *Statisticheskii Ezhegodnik 1918–1920*, p. 219.

91 *Narodnoe Khoziaistvo*, 1919, no. 4, 47.
92 *Narodnoe Khoziaistvo*, 1919, nos. 1–2, p. 16.
93 J.M. Goldstein, *Russia: her Economic Past and Future*, New York, Russian Information Bureau, 1919, p. 75.
94 *Narodnoe Khoziaistvo*, 1919, no. 4, 16.
95 *Sbornik dekretov*, vol. 1, pp. 123–6.
96 *Oktiabr'ski i perevorot*, p. 64.
97 Osinskii, p. 135.
98 *Narodnoe Khoziaistvo*, 1919, no. 4, 16.
99 Rozenfel'd, p. 386.
100 VSNKh, *Plenum*, September 1918, p. 94.
101 *Narodnoe Khoziaistvo*, 1919, no. 3, 17.
102 VSNKh, *Plenum*, p. 119.
103 *Sobranie uzakonenii*, 1918, no. 29, art. 397; no. 37, art. 490.
104 *Ekonomicheskaia Zhizn'*, no. 26, 7 December 1918, 4.
105 *Narodnoe Khoziaistvo*, 1919, no. 4, 42.
106 *Izvestiia*, no. 41, 22 February 1919, 4.
107 *The Russian Economist*, vol. 1, p. 104.
108 By gradual decisions: *Sobranie uzakonenii*, 1919, no. 10, art. 112; 1920, no. 19, art. 102.
109 *Sobranie uzakonenii*, 1919, no. 17, art. 190.
110 *Sobranie uzakonenii*, 1919, no. 41, art. 387. This system was also applied to the obligatory delivery of hemp: *Sobranie uzakonenii*, 1920, no. 19, art. 102.
111 *Prodovol'stvennaia politika v syete obshchego khoziaistva stroitel'stva Sovetskoi Vlasti*, Sbornik materialov, Moscow, 1920, p. 240.
112 *Sobranie uzakonenii*, 1920, no. 57, art. 260.
113 *Ibid.*
114 *Pravda*, no. 22, 1 February 1920, 1.
115 VSNKh, *Plenum*, p. 116.
116 *Pravda*, 4 February 1921, 1.
117 *Ekonomicheskaia Zhizn'*, no. 34, 17 December 1918, 1.
118 Cf. Lomov's speech at the Second Congress of *Sovnarkhozy*, *Ekonomicheskaia Zhizn'*, no. 37, 20 December 1918, 2.
119 *Narodnoe Khoziaistvo*, 1919, no. 4, 55.
120 Avdakov, p. 117; *Oktiabr'skii perevorot*, p. 66.
121 Avdakov, pp. 114–16.
122 *Narodnoe Khoziaistvo*, 1920, nos. 1–2, p. 33.
123 *Ekonomicheskaia Zhizn'*, no. 11, 20 November 1918, 2.
124 *Ekonomicheskaia Zhizn'*, no. 32, 12 February 1919, 4. Cf. also B. Sokoloff, *Les Bolchéviks jugés par eux-mêmes. Documents des Soviets de 1919*, Paris, 1919, pp. 25–7.
125 *Sbornik dekretov*, vol. 1, pp. 113–16.
126 *Ekonomicheskaia Zhizn'*, no. 42, 23 February 1919, 3.
127 *Oktiabr'skii perevorot*, p. 66.
128 Avdakov, pp. 115–16.
129 *Ekonomicheskaia Zhizn'*, no. 34, 17 December 1918, 1, on Savelev's proposal; and *Sobranie uzakonenii*, 1918, no. 96, art. 962 and no. 97, art. 994 on the functions of some central administrations.
130 Avdakov, pp. 114–16.

131 L. Kritsman, *Geroicheskii period Velikoi Russkoi Revoliutsii*, Moscow (no date, probably 1924), p. 101.

132 VSNKh, *Plenum*, p. 74; *Ekonomicheskaia Zhizn'*, no. 146, 6 July 1919, 3.

133 *Narodnoe Khoziaistvo*, 1918, no. 4, 63.

134 See Rykov's report at the plenary session of VSNKh, in September 1918: VSNKh, *Plenum*, pp. 77, 113.

135 Venediktov, p. 383.

136 *Ekonomicheskaia Zhizn'*, no. 43, 27 December 1918.

137 *Izvestiia*, no. 67, 28 March 1919, 3; Kritsman, *Geroicheskii period*, p. 136.

138 In order to obtain a spare part, a factory had to send a delegate to the Procurement Section of the highest economic council of Moscow or Petrograd, which was to grant approval of the purchase. Having obtained the purchase certificate, the delegate was to deliver it to the Machine Section of the corresponding economic council, which on the basis of the order issued a further purchase certificate for the specific factory producing the spare part. In some cases the approval of VSNKh was needed before delivery. For examples of this procedure see A. Akselrod, *L'Oeuvre économique des Soviets*, Paris, 1920, pp. 77–105.

139 *Ekonomicheskaia Zhizn'*, no. 269, 30 November 1919, 1.

140 Kritsman, *Edinyi plan*, pp. 53–58.

141 VSNKh, *Plenum*, pp. 83–4.

142 *Trudy II Vserossiiskogo S''ezda Sovnarkhozov*, pp. 266–70.

143 *Ekonomicheskaia Zhizn'*, no. 10, 19 November 1918, 3; no. 14, 23 November 1918, 1.

144 *Ekonomicheskaia Zhizn'*, no. 12, 21 November 1918, 3; no. 41, 25 December 1918, 3; no. 27, 6 February 1919, 3; no. 231, 17 October 1919, 2; no. 232, 18 October 1919, 2; *Narodnoe Khoziaistvo*, 1919, no. 7, 78.

145 *Ekonomicheskaia Zhizn'*, no. 14, 23 November 1918, 1.

146 This was a source of interdepartmental conflicts and bureaucratism. *Glavtekstil'* had to send a petition to the People's Commissariat for Transport to get approval for and assignment of transport freights (*Ekonomicheskaia Zhizn'*, no. 3, 4 January 1919, 3). *Glavki* and *tsentry* were reported to compete with each other for transport necessary to carry their own supplies of wood fuel, owing to the inability of *Glavleskom* to ensure dispatch of the collected wood fuel (*Ekonomicheskaia Zhizn'*, 24 December 1919, 1).

147 *Ekonomicheskaia Zhizn'*, no. 151, 12 July 1919, 2.

148 Cf. Iu. K. Avdakov and V.V. Borodin, *Proizvodstvennye ob''edineniia i ikh rol' v organizatsii upravleniia sovetskoi promyshlennosti*, Moscow, 1913, p. 32.

149 *Sobranie uzakonenii*, 1917–18, no. 11, art. 167.

150 *Sobranie uzakonenii*, 1917–18, no. 24, art. 332.

151 Carr, *The Bolshevik Revolution*, vol. 2, p. 253.

152 Cf. *Oktiabr'skii perevorot*, p. 88.

153 On 25 March 1918, *Sovnarkom* charged the committee of economic policy of VSNKh with examination and elaboration of financial estimates of sequestered and nationalized factories, which were afterwards to be presented for approval to *Sovnarkom*: *Sobranie uzakonenii*, 1917–18, no. 30, art. 396.

154 *Biulleten' VSNKh*, April 1918, 31.

155 *Ekonomicheskaia Zhizn'*, no. 55, 12 March 1919, 31.
156 Osinskii, *Stroitel'stvo sotsializma*, p. 69; *Sobranie uzakonenii*, 1917–18, no. 36, art. 477.
157 *Trudy I Vserossiiskogo S"ezda Sovnarkhozov*, pp. 122, 126.
158 *Sbornik dekretov*, vol. 1, pp. 891–2.
159 *Narodnoe Khoziaistvo*, 1919, nos. 1–2, 34–6.
160 *Trudy II Vserossiiskogo S"ezda Sovnarkhozov*, pp. 266–70.
161 *Sbornik dekretov*, vol. 2, pp. 195–6.
162 *Trudy II Vserossiiskogo S"ezda Sovnarkhozov*, pp. 272, 274, 276.
163 NKF, *K 8 S"ezdu Sovetov*, p. 3; see also V.V. Kabanov, 'Natsionalizatsiia Moskovskogo Narodnogo Banka', *Voprosy Istorii*, 1970, no. 4, 207–10, on the particular events which led to the nationalization of this bank.
164 *Trudy II Vserossiiskogo S"ezda Sovnarkhozov*, p. 276.
165 *Ibid.*, pp. 279–80.
166 *Ibid.*, p. 282.
167 This decision was probably aimed at ending the interference of *Narkomfin* in price determination, which should have been assigned to VSNKh only, in such a way that the fiscal department dealing with indirect taxes would become a section for the accounting of total industrial output: cf. M. Al'skii, *Nashi finansy za vremiia grazhdanskoi voiny i NEPa*, Moscow, 1925, p. 63. In 1919 mark-ups (*nachisleniia*) were applied on prices of textiles and leather goods, paper and sewing machines (R.W. Davies, *Development of the Soviet Budgetary System*, Cambridge, 1958, p. 22 and n1).
168 *Trudy II Vserossiiskogo S"ezda Sovnarkhozov*, pp. 396–9.
169 M.S. Atlas, *Natsionalizatsiia bankov v SSSR*, Moscow, 1948, pp. 149, 151.
170 *Trudy II Vserossiiskogo S"ezda Sovnarkhozov*, p. 399.
171 *Izvestiia NKF*, nos. 1–2, 1 September 1919, 2.
172 *Trudy II Vserossiiskogo S"ezda Sovnarkhozov*, pp. 399–400.
173 *Sobranie uzakonenii*, 1919, no. 2, art. 12.
174 *Sobranie uzakonenii*, 1919, nos. 10–11, art. 107; also *Sbornik dekretov*, vol. 2, pp. 187–9.
175 The National Bank was suppressed on 25 January 1920, on the ground that it was 'useless': *Izvestiia*, no. 16 (863), 25 January 1920, 2.
176 *Ekonomicheskaia Zhizn'*, no. 259, 19 November 1919, 1.
177 Osinskii, *Stroitel'stvo Sotsializma*, p. 69.
178 *Ekonomicheskaia Zhizn'*, no. 259, 19 November 1919, 1; the operational fund of the first half on 1919, which had been estimated at 5,162 million rubles, was then raised to 14,000 million rubles.
179 *Ibid.*
180 *Ibid.*
181 T.T. Syromolotov (VSNKh), *Finansirovanie natsional'-promyshlennosti po VSNKh v 1919*, Moscow, 1921, p. 33. Figures refer to January 1920.
182 *Ibid.*, pp. 19–20.
183 *Sbornik dekretov*, vol. 2, pp. 193–4.
184 *Izavestiia*, no. 61, 21 March 1919, 4.
185 *Izvestiia NKF*, nos. 1–2, September 1919, 12–14.
186 On the loss of the purchasing power of the ruble see: L.N. Iurovskii, *Denezhnaia politika Sovetskoi Vlasti (1917–1927)*, Moscow, 1928, p. 72. Prices

increased by 300 per cent in the first half of 1919 and 269 per cent in the second half.

187 *Izvestiia NKF*, nos. 1–2, September 1919, 17–18.

188 *Ekonomicheskaia Zhizn'*, no. 229, 14 October 1919, 1.

189 *Ekonomicheskaia Zhizn'*, no. 259, 19 November 1919, 1.

190 T.T. Syromolotov (VSNKh), p. 21.

191 *Ibid.*, p. 22.

192 *Ibid.*, p. 20.

193 *Natsionalizatsiia promyshlennosti i organizatsiia sotsialisticheskogo proizvodstva v Petrograde 1917–1920 gg. Dokumenty i materialy*, vol. 1, Leningrad, 1958, pp. 381–2.

194 Cf. V.P. Diachenko, *Sovetskie finansy v pervoi faze razvitiia sotsialisticheskogo gosudarstva*, Moscow, 1947, p. 187.

195 *Natsionalizatsiia... v Petrograde*, pp. 376–7.

196 *Izvestiia NKF*, nos. 1–2, September 1919, 11.

197 *Ibid.*, p. 12.

198 *Sobranie uzakonenii*, 1919, no. 42, art. 42 (22 August).

199 Z.V. Atlas, *Ocherki po istorii denezhnogo obrashcheniia v SSSR (1917–1925)*, Moscow, 1940, pp. 70–3.

200 *Natsionalizatsiia... v Petrograde*, p. 384.

201 *Izvestiia NKF*, no. 10, 7 November 1919, 26–7.

202 *Izvestiia NKF*, nos. 1–2, September 1919, 11.

203 *Izvestiia NKF*, nos. 10–11, 16 June 1920.

204 *Izvestiia NKF*, nos. 12–13, July 1920, 1.

205 *Sobranie uzakonenii*, 1920, no. 67, art. 305.

206 *Sobranie uzakonenii*, 1920, no. 88, art. 448.

207 By 27 January 1920, even the 20,000 small local credit institutions and loan cooperative organizations which during war communism had been performing some functions in the trade of agricultural products were merged together and put under the joint control of *Narkomprod, Narkomzem*, state control and VSNKh: see L. Pasvolsky, *The Economics of Communism*, London, 1921, p. 57.

208 *Sobranie uzakonenii*, 1921, no. 16, art. 102.

209 *Sobranie uzakonenii*, 1921, no. 21, art. 128.

210 *Izvestiia NKF*, nos. 13–14, 6 December 1919, 12.

211 E. Preobrazhenskii, *Bumazhnye den'gi v epokhu proletarskoi diktatury*, 1920, pp. 51, 59.

212 *Narodnoe Khoziaistvo*, 1920, nos. 9–10, p. 11.

213 *Ekonomicheskaia Zhizn'*, no. 11, 20 November 1918, 3.

214 *Ekonomicheskaia Zhizn'*, no. 10, 16 January 1919, 3.

215 *Ekonomicheskaia Zhizn'*, no. 55, 14 March 1919, 3.

216 Avdakov and Borodin, pp. 16–17.

217 *Narodnoe Khoziaistvo*, 1920, nos. 9–10, p. 12.

218 *Narodnoe Khoziaistvo*, March 1922, 56.

219 Avdakov and Borodin, p. 16.

220 *Ibid.*, p. 21.

221 *Narodnoe Khoziaistvo*, 1919, nos. 9–10, p. 3.

222 *Ekonomicheskaia Zhizn'*, no. 55, 12 March 1919, 3.

223 *Ekonomicheskaia Zhizn'*, no. 28, 10 December 1918, 1.
224 *Biulleten' Moskovskogo Soveta Narodnogo Khoziaistva*, 30 January 1921, no. 1, 4.
225 *Ekonomicheskaia Zhizn'*, no. 250, 7 November 1919, 22.
226 VSNKh, *Plenum*, p. 90.
227 See pp. 228–9 above.
228 *Narodnoe Khoziaistvo*, 1919, nos. 9–10, 12–13.
229 Venediktov, p. 521.
230 Avdakov, pp. 121–2.
231 *Narodnoe Khoziaistvo*, 1919, no. 3, p. 51.
232 Avdakov, p. 123.
233 *Trudy II Vserossiiskogo S"ezda Sovnarkhozov*, p. 197.
234 Avdakov, pp. 125–6.
235 *Ekonomicheskaia Zhizn'*, 13 July 1920, 2.
236 *Sobranie uzakonenii*, 1920, no. 68, art. 309.
237 *Sobranie uzakonenii*, 1919, no. 3, art. 41.
238 *Rabochii kontrol' i natsionalizatsiia promyshlennosti v Kostromskoi gubernii, Sbornik documentov 1917–1918*, Kostroma, 1960, pp. 191, 185
239 *Ekonomicheskaia Zhizn'*, no. 67, 28 March 1919, 3.
240 *Ekonomicheskaia Zhizn'*, no. 2, 3 January 1919, 5.
241 *Ekonomicheskaia Zhizn'*, no. 24, 2 February 1919, 3.
242 *Ekonomicheskaia Zhizn'*, no. 67, 28 March 1919, 3.
243 *Ekonomicheskaia Zhizn'*, no. 43, 25 February 1919, 3.
244 *Ekonomicheskaia Zhizn'*, no. 56, 14 March 1919, 3.
245 *Sbornik dekretov*, vol. 2, pp. 66–8.
246 Avdakov and Borodin, p. 17.
247 *Narodnoe Khoziaistvo*, 1919, nos. 9–10, 3–4.
248 Avdakov, p. 132.
249 *Narodnoe Khoziaistvo*, 1918, no. 2, 25–6. On similar functions performed in practice by local sections of the soviets, organs of workers' control and *sovnarkhozy*, cf. also: *God Proletarskoi Diktatury*, Nizhni-Novgorod, 1918.
250 *Sovety narodnogo khoziaistva i planovye organy v tsentre i na mestakh (1917–1932)*, Moscow, 1957, p. 63.
251 *Sobranie uzakonenii*, 1917–18, no. 5, art. 83.
252 Venediktov, p. 382.
253 *Ekonomicheskaia Zhizn'*, no. 3, 10 November 1918, 1.
254 *Narodnoe Khoziaistvo*, 1918, no. 2, 25–6.
255 *Izvestiia Moskovskogo Oblastnogo Soveta Narodnogo Khoziaistva*, no. 3, October 1918, 44–5.
256 *Narodnoe Khoziaistvo*, 1918, no. 11, 8–9.
257 Baevskii, *Rabochii klass*, p. 31.
258 *Narodnoe Khoziaistvo*, 1919, nos. 9–10, p. 105.
259 *Narodnoe Khoziaistvo*, 1919, nos. 1–2, pp. 52–3.
260 *Narodnoe Khoziaistvo*, 1919, nos. 9–10, pp. 105–9.
261 *Sobranie uzakonenii*, 1918, no. 13, art. 196.
262 *Narodnoe Khoziaistvo*, 1918, no. 11, 18; Carr, *The Bolshevik Revolution*, vol. 2, pp. 80–1. *Glavkozh* (the Leather Committee) was formed in January 1918. Between January and March 1918 *Glavbum* (the Paper Committee),

Glavsakhar (the Sugar Committee), *Tsentrochai* (the Tea Committee) and *Tsentrotekstil'* were formed.

263 *Trudy I Vserossiiskogo S"ezda Sovnarkhozov*, p. 15.
264 *Sbornik dekretov*, vol. 1, pp. 9–10.
265 *Ibid.*, pp. 315–19.
266 Avdakov, p. 37.
267 *Ibid.*, p. 38.
268 *Ibid.*, pp. 38, 41–4; *Natsionalizatsiia ... v Petrograde*, vol. 1, doc. 193.
269 *Novyi put'*, 1918, no. 1, 12.
270 Venediktov, p. 526.
271 *Narodnoe Khoziaistvo*, 1919, no. 3, 71–3.
272 Avdakov, pp. 22–3.
273 R. Arskii (VSNKh), *Regulirovanie promyshlennosti*, (no date, presumably 1918–19), p. 21.
274 *Narodnoe Khoziaistvo*, 1919, nos. 9–10, p. 91; *Natsionalizatsiia ... v Petrograde*, p. 374.
275 Cf. *Natsionalizatsiia ... v Petrograde*, pp. 374–5, 377–8.
276 *Narodnoe Khoziaistvo*, 1919, no. 3, 71–5.
277 *Ibid.*, pp. 71–5.
278 *Narodnoe Khoziaistvo*, 1920, nos. 3–4, p. 65.
279 *Trudy II Vserossiiskogo S"ezda Sovnarkhozov*, pp. 226, 237, 231–2, 248, for the delegates' arguments for or against the autonomy of the *sovnarkhozy*.
280 *Ibid.*, p. 197.
281 *Narodnoe Khoziaistvo*, 1919, no. 3, 71.
282 *Ibid.*, 72.
283 *Ibid.*, 271–2.
284 Avdakov, pp. 63–4.
285 *Ekonomicheskaia Zhizn'*, no. 286, 20 December 1919, 1.
286 T.T. Syromolotov (VSNKh), p. 8.
287 *Narodnoe Khoziaistvo*, 1919, nos. 9–10, p. 91 and *Natsionalizatsiia ... v Petrograde*, p. 374.
288 *Rabochii kontrol' ... v Kostromskoi Gubernii*, p. 201.
289 Drobizhev and Medvedev, pp. 88–90, 92.
290 *Ekonomicheskaia Zhizn'*, no. 219, 2 October 1919 and *Sbornik dekretov*, vol. 2, p. 738.
291 Avdakov, pp. 16–18.
292 The word *zemstvo* derives from the Russian word *zemlya*, land, and was traditionally associated with the local organizations of social groups like the landed gentry and farmers.
293 Cf. T.J. Polner, *Russian Local Government during the War and the Union of Zemstvos*, New Haven, 1930, pp. 37, 77; and N. De Basily, *Russia under Soviet Rule*, London, 1938, p. 20.
294 A. Belevsky and B. Voronoff, *Les Organisations publiques et leur rôle pendant la guerre*, Paris, 1917, pp. 3–21, 26, 101; N. Karabtschevsky, *La Révolution et la Russie*, Paris, 1921, p. 193.
295 Drobizhev and Medvedev, p. 69.
296 See Appendix, to Chapter 2 on *kustar'* industry, pp. 77–87, and Avdakov, p. 77.
297 *Narodnoe Khoziaistvo*, 1919, nos. 9–10, pp. 107–8.

298 Avdakov, p. 77.
299 *Ibid.*, p. 76.
300 *Narodnoe Khoziaistvo*, 1919, nos. 1–2, 53–4.
301 Avdakov, p. 101.
302 *Trudy II Vserossiiskogo S"ezda Sovnarkhozov*, p. 190.
303 Avdakov, pp. 78–9.
304 *Ekonomicheskaia Zhizn'*, no. 18, 26 January 1919, 5; *Narodnoe Khoziaistvo*, 1919, no. 7, 86; *Narodnoe Khoziaistvo*, 1919, no. 4, 88–9.
305 *Rabochii kontrol' i natsionalizatsiia promyshlennosti Novgorodskoi Gubernii v 1917–1921 gg*, Moscow, 1974, pp. 35–6.
306 *Ekonomicheskaia Zhizn'*, no. 225, 9 October 1919, 4.
307 *Trudy II Vserossiiskogo S"ezda Sovnarkhozov*, p. 190.
308 *Narodnoe Khoziaistvo*, 1918, no. 12, 30–1.
309 *Ekonomicheskaia Zhizn'*, no. 4, 12 November 1918, 1.
310 *Trudy II Vserossiiskogo S"ezda Sovnarkhozov*, p. 226; *Ekonomicheskaia Zhizn'*, no. 225, 9 October 1919, 1 and Avdakov, p. 21; *Ekonomicheskaia Zhizn'*, no. 225, 9 October 1919, 4.
311 *Trudy II Vserossiiskogo S"ezda Sovnarkhozov*, p. 213.
312 Drobizhev and Medvedev, p. 109, give the following distribution by educational levels of the members of presidiums of the *sovnarkhozy*: no education at all: 2.4 per cent; elementary: 55.6 per cent; incomplete secondary: 15.2 per cent; secondary: 11.3 per cent; secondary with a qualification: 10.0 per cent; higher: 5.5 per cent.
313 *Ekonomicheskaia Zhizn'*, no. 3, 10 November 1918, 1; no. 4, 12 November 1918, 1.
314 *Ekonomicheskaia Zhizn'*, no. 3, 10 November 1918, 1; no. 32, 14 December 1918, 1.
315 *Ekonomicheskaia Zhizn'*, no. 4, 12 November 1918, 1.
316 *Trudy II Vserossiiskogo S"ezda Sovnarkhozov*, pp. 218–51 for the debate on economic organization.
317 *Ekonomicheskaia Zhizn'*, no. 225, 9 October 1919, 4.
318 *Ekonomicheskaia Zhizn'*, no. 226, 10 October 1919, 1.
319 *8i S"ezd RKP(b). 18–13 Marta, 1919 g*, Moscow, 1933, p. 392.
320 N. Bukharin and E. Preobrazhenskii, *The ABC of Communism*, London, 1969, p. 323.
321 *Ibid.*
322 *Natsionalizatsiia ... v Petrograde*, vol. 2, p. 365.
323 *Trudy II Vserossiiskogo S"ezda Sovnarkhozov*, p. 403.
324 *Natsionalizatsiia ... v Petrograde*, p. 365.
325 *Narodnoe Khoziaistvo*, 1919, no. 5, 44.
326 *Narodnoe Khoziaistvo*, 1919, no. 6, 84.
327 *Natsionalizatsiia ... v Petrograde*, p. 379.
328 Lenin, *Collected Works*, vol. 30, pp. 246–7.
329 *Ekonomicheskaia Zhizn'*, no. 286, 20 December 1919, 1.
330 *Sobranie uzakonenii*, 1920, no. 9, art. 55.
331 *Izvestiia*, no. 29, 10 February 1920, 1.
332 *8i Vserossiiskii S"ezd Sovetov Rabochikh, Krest'ianskikh, Krasnoarmeiskikh i Kazach'ikh Deputatov. 22–9 Dekabria 1920 g*, sten. otchet, Moscow, 1921, p. 106.
333 *9i S"ezd RKP*, pp. 79, 119–21.

334 *Ezhednevnyi Biulleten' VIII S"ezda Sovetov*, no. 1, 21 December 1920, 4–5.
335 *9i S"ezd RKP*, pp. 26–7, 79–81.
336 *Ezhednevnyi Biulleten'*, 2–3.
337 *9i S"ezd RKP*, pp. 112, 123.
338 Kritsman, *Geroicheskii period*, p. 102.
339 *8i Vserossiiskii S"ezd Sovetov*, p. 106.
340 Venediktov, pp. 440–1.
341 *Izvestiia*, no. 24, 4 February 1921, 4.
342 *Izvestiia*, no. 49, 5 March 1921, 1.
343 *Narodnoe Khoziaistvo*, March 1922, 55.
344 *Izvestiia*, no. 49, 5 March 1921, 4.
345 *8i Vserossiiskii S"ezd Sovetov*, pp. 186–7.
346 *Ezhednevnyi Biulleten'*, no. 2, 8.
347 *8i Vserossiiskii S"ezd Sovetov*, p. 187.
348 *9i S"ezd RKP*, p. 185.
349 Avdakov, p. 54.
350 *9i S"ezd RKP*, p. 186.
351 Avdakov, pp. 54–5.

6

Planning

In considering the origins of the idea of planning, it may be noted at the outset that war communism was not a planning system, but a system of economic centralization. The idea of planning took shape within it as a natural outcome of a tendency towards full central control. As far as intellectual sources of the idea of planning are concerned, the Marxian analysis of capitalism is more easily seen as an ideological rather than a theoretical source.

Marx's works did not suggest much about the mechanism which would govern economic relations in a socialist system. Some hints, however, may be derived from the perspective which the Marxian analysis opened with regard to the functioning of competitive capitalism and the perverse effects of competition on the production and distribution of values. The Marxian analysis focused on the anarchy of the competitive market, the inevitability of economic crises within this mode of production and the waste of resources which they entailed. Conversely, Marx attributed to the socialist society a capacity for foresight and initiative in promoting future developments that the market economy would not have, or would 'necessarily' ignore. Marx's excursions into future socialist societies were marginal, accidental and scarcely suited to further elaboration. They may, however, have influenced proselytes in their search for certainties as milestones on the dark road to socialism.

Das Kapital offered few suggestions as to the possible organization of a socialist society. Marx underlines the importance of accounting as 'control and ideal synthesis of a process', which capitalism needed more than did a society of craftsmen, and socialism more than capitalism. The increasing importance of accounting in modern societies was attributed by Marx to the process of concentration, which he presumed would continue under socialism and thanks to which accounting costs would become relatively lower.[1] Marx assumed that only the abolition of capitalism would make it possible as a matter of principle to shorten the working day and limit it to 'necessary labour', i.e. to the working time necessary for the maintenance and reproduction of the labour force. But, he added, two constraints to effective reduction of working time would persist under socialism: first, increasing standards of living for the workers; second, the imperative of accumulation. Marx stressed that the absolute limit to further reductions of the working day should coincide with the general obligation to work.[2]

Marx distinguished decisions concerning production from decisions concerning distribution. What he called the 'social product of a communist society' was formed by two elements: the social means of production and social distribution. Distribution, according to the first volume of *Das Kapital*, would depend on the particular nature of the social organization of production and on the corresponding historical stage of development of the producers. If distribution occurred according to each individual's labour time, said Marx, labour time would have a double function. Firstly, its distribution, socially determined *according to a plan* (my italics), would define the exact proportion between different functions in work and different needs. Secondly, labour time would be the measure of the individual's participation in the distribution of the social product.[3] Marx assumed here the working of 'central planning' for the allocation of labour to various functions depending on the demand for final products. That the socialist society should have planning capacities was also presumed in relation to the problem of overhead capital investment having a long gestation period. Marx was convinced that one of the causes of economic crisis was the incapacity of the competitive market economy to foresee the consequences of long periods of capital immobilization. He explored the consequences of this in terms of consumption of raw materials, means of subsistence and fixed capital during a time span in which no corresponding output would be generated, thus inducing pressures on supply, price increase, artificial profit gains and, finally, economic crisis. The crisis would occur at the end of the process of immobilization of resources, when new output flows would start competing with the existing one.[4] Marx hinted at the anarchical developments of the competitive economy also in the case of its being limited to simple reproduction. In this case, reserves would also be needed to confront different sizes of capital depreciation. Different life spans of capital, said Marx, require proportional reserves. Competitive society, he argued, would fall into anarchy. Under socialism, on the contrary, the creation of reserves would be facilitated by society's control over the means of production.[5]

Marx explained in the second volume of *Das Kapital* why monetary capital has to disappear in the communist society and, together with it, all the 'disguised transactions' which it entails. He argued that the communist society calculated in advance how much labour, production means and subsistence means it might allocate, without damage, in branches such as railway construction, which do not provide for a year or more either means of production or subsistence means or use values, but on the contrary use them up, taking them out of the total annual output.[6] In such a case, producers would be given coupons enabling them to draw out of social consumption reserves the quantities which corresponded to their working time. These coupons would not circulate; they would not be money.[7]

From these hints at the possible working of the communist society, one may see that Marx believed in its capacity to channel resources into different fields, in order to satisfy demand, and check in advance the effects of the pressure on supply of frozen means of production and subsistence, by providing an adequate accumulation of reserves. That is, he believed in the 'planning' capacity of the communist society, in the sense of a capacity for foresight. His hints do not seem to imply that he believed in the stimulating force of planning on development. The capacity of communism to determine economic growth was based on the mere presumption that society would be able to avoid the disequilibria of capitalist development, thanks to ownership of the means of production, which would imply by itself the disappearance of 'competition'. The fact that Marx believed in the necessity of 'central control' over the allocation of resources seems to be confirmed by his criticism of the Gotha programme, which the two major workers' parties of Germany had agreed upon in 1875. His criticisms were aimed at pointing out what, even under socialist rule, should be considered necessary economic constraints: he emphasized the need to set aside from the total social product *before distribution* (my italics) the necessary quota for depreciation and net investment and for a reserve fund against contingencies. According to Marx, such deductions were 'an economic necessity' and their magnitude should be computed by way of 'the available means and forces, and partly by calculation of probabilities'.[8] Marx distinguished between economic deduction and social deductions. The latter, too, should be set aside before distribution of the social product. Social deductions were considered to be the general costs of administration outside the production sector, collective consumption (schools, health, etc.), and funds for those unable to work.[9]

The fact that Marx underlined that decisions on allocation of resources for productive as well as collective utilization ought to be taken before distribution – a norm which he opposed to the Gotha Programme's norm of distribution of the 'undiminished proceeds of labour' with equal right to all members of society – may be interpreted as an argument in favour of some sort of central planning. By his proposal, in fact, he rejected the hypothesis that socialism would leave the individual producers free to determine the proportion of their own income to devote to investment. Marx, however, had no idea of how society as a whole would determine the equilibrium level of national income or the rate of growth. He seems to have realized that even forecasting would be subject to real limitations, owing to available techniques and means.

Kautsky's development of Marx's ideas and his stress on concentration and planning counteracting the flaws of market anarchy[10] as well as his enthusiasm for the revolutionary potential of industrialization itself – carrying on the heritage left by Engels' *AntiDüring*[11] – had probably a stronger impact on Marxists than did Marx's teaching itself. Karl Ballod, the German socialist economist, tried to work out how the German economy could be regulated under socialism. His writings on *The State of the Future*, which were known in Russia, thanks to several translations between 1903 and 1906, concerned the working of specific institutions and provided details on how to improve efficiency and increase product per caput.[12] According to Ballod, production should have been concentrated in enterprises with lower input–output ratios and small-scale producers should have been eliminated following the adoption of modern technologies and the diffusion of electric power. Land was to be nationalized and partitioned into state farms. The peasants were to be granted the use of small plots and the property of their houses, and were to make to the state obligatory deliveries of foodstuffs, which were to be rationed to the town population. Ballod has been defined as a 'planner without theory',[13] because he did not work out a general methodology of planning and was mainly concerned with details rather than with the functioning of the economy as an organic whole. Another major shortcoming of his approach was his reference to empirical German statistics to derive the lowest input–output economic units – which made them dependent on former price ratios – to extrapolate future equilibria, without grasping the relevance of price determination in a planned economy. Nonetheless, the fact that Ballod's works were well known in Russia and praised by some of the leading economists[14] suggests that he may have exerted an influence on the early approach to planning. Assessment of this influence, however, requires examination in detail of the parallels between Ballod's hypotheses and the works of the Menshevik economists who first advanced planning projects under the Provisional Government. It is probably here that the influence should be sought, rather than in the specific institutions and rules on which war communism was based. The degree of improvisation which characterized the whole experience does not make it possible to detect a straightforward influence of the German professor on economic policy. On the one hand, war itself was conducive to a mental attitude regardless of ideology, receptive to measures not normally favoured by supporters of market-oriented policies. Not only Groman, who was a Menshevik, but also Stepanov, who was a cadet minister of the Provisional Government, shared the opinion that the government should issue planning guidelines and take investment decisions in the period of reconstruction, both fearing the economic chaos which would result from private investment decisions.[15] On the other hand, the Bolsheviks did not seem much concerned about technicalities and were attracted by the possibility of political control over the economy, rather than by the specific criteria on which economic control should be based.[16] *The ABC of Communism*, written by Bukharin and Preobrazhenskii, discussed the characteristics of the communist mode of production in terms of a few axiomatic points. Firstly, communism should be an organized society 'freed from the anarchy of production, competition among individual managers and from war and crisis'. Secondly, communism meant a classless society. Thirdly, 'factories, workshops, mines and other production institutions will all be subdivisions, as it were, of one vast people's workshop which will embrace the entire national economy of production'. The drafters of this programme added that it was obvious that 'so comprehensive an organization presupposes a general plan of production... and that everything must be precisely correlated'. The variables subject to planning were: allocation of labour and resources, investment, and the quantity and quality of output.[17] Planning was to be centralized. Osinskii also stressed the need for 'a single, centralized, global accounting'. Central control over commodity circulation was considered from three angles: central distribution of industrial products for personal consumption, central supply of the means of production, and central organization of exchange between town and countryside. The centre should plan production and distribution and the 'mutual adjustment' of production and supply to industrial and final demand.[18] Osinskii, thus posed the problem of equilibrium between demand and supply, but did not explore what criteria should be applied in default of a market mechanism. For the young Bolsheviks of the left, centralized planning was a goal, not an expedient. Osinskii wrote in 'The Construction of Socialism' that only a developed 'state socialism, i.e. a centralized system of socialized production, monopolized product distribution and planned utilization of labour' would ensure the construction of socialism.[19]

Osinskii tried to depict the characteristics of the socialist society, following the traditional Marxist tenets, under the principal aspect of monopoly of the means of production. Basic features of the socialist economy were considered to be those pertaining to the ownership of all means of production by working people as a whole. The socialist economy, argued Osinskii, was like a large enterprise directed by a single centre on the basis of an overall, consciously elaborated, plan. The task of the socialist economy, Osinskii explained, at a time when the experiment of war communism was in progress, was the full, efficient utilization of social productive forces for the satisfaction of the needs of working people. The market was abolished. Products ceased to be commodities, in the sense of possessing market value. Money withered away. 'Commodity [in the sense merely of goods] exchange becomes a conscious and planned distribution: the transfer of products among factories supplying to each other materials for further processing, and the transfer of products from factories to final consumers.' Consumer goods appropriation was not to be determined by the purchasing power of the buyer. Osinskii affirmed that each member of the working community had the right to satisfy his needs out of the social product which he had helped to generate.[20] Nonetheless, in spite of the ardour with they were presented, these propositions remained in the realm of goals and probably would not have gone further if experience had not provided concrete arguments in favour of planning.

All the countries involved in the First World War to some extent renounced the market mechanism of allocation and distribution of resources and adhered to some form of centrally controlled economy in order to pursue their vast military endeavours. For people who were ready to learn from attempts at a command economy, Germany was a source of information on planning which could not be found in the literature on economic analysis or economic theory. By 1917 Rathenau was already questioning the validity of competition as the economic framework of reconstruction. 'New principles' generated by the economy of war were seen as the foundations of a new economic system. Rathenau focused on the tragic consequences of war in terms of destruction of wealth, state indebtedness, unemployment, and moral and material poverty, and he foresaw a need for central coordination instead of competition:

All energies spent in protection and distribution of national means, in defence against foreign products and protection of our products, or primarily and finally aimed at making it possible for our national economy to intensify production of higher economic importance at the expense of products of lesser or only apparent utility, may be directed only by a single will of an organized and rational production and be moved out of the free play of price formation and individual utility.[21]

The German economy of war attracted also the attention of some of the future protagonists of the Soviet Revolution. Larin reported enthusiastically from his German experience that Germany had offered to the world an example of central direction of the economy comparable to one single machine working according to a plan, and that such an experience, in spite of the question of power, had a theoretical interest and a social and scientific value.[22] Bukharin was also impressed by the process of concentration and centralization furthered by war and by the progressive formation of state capitalism as an economic system alternative to the market economy. Bukharin stressed the role of direct state intervention in the economy. The forms of intervention were state monopolies, mixed enterprises, state control over private production, obligatory delivery of products, public distribution, state warehouses of raw materials, fuel and foodstuff, and state financing. These measures were accompanied by increasing fiscal pressure and were tending towards monopoly. In *Imperialism and World Economy*, Bukharin affirmed that, to the extent to which capitalism would remain, the future would belong to economic forms close to state capitalism.[23]

Lenin agreed with Bukharin and went even further. After the February Revolution, Lenin expressed the opinion that obligatory associations, i.e. the obligatory formation of unions of enterprises controlled by the state, which capitalism had produced in Germany, could be implemented in Russia under the dictatorship of the proletariat.[24] What Lenin had in mind were very likely the *Berufsverbände* and the *Gewerbsverbände*, to which Rathenau referred when he mentioned the formation of an economic system working according to a single will. Rathenau considered the *Berufsverbände* as economic unions of enterprises based on vertical concentration and the *Gewerbsverbände* as groups of enterprises working in the same field, that is as horizontal unions. The purpose of unionization was to limit the defects of the market. As Rathenau put it, the union had union life, eyes, ears, sense, will and responsibility. The immediate advantages were seen, so far as production was concerned, in the possibility of control over sales and profits and in the particular relation which unions should have with the state. Concentration and centralization of production were interpreted by Rathenau not as mere monopoly measures, but as vehicles towards further coordination and subordination to a superior 'will', as prerequisites for planning, though Rathenau did not mention that explicitly. It is possible that the future builders of Soviet society had been attracted by this sort of connection between production unions and the state. On the one hand, the concentration of production reduced the extension of market commodity exchange. On the other hand, the unions' importance would be higher than that of mere monopoly or trusts in the extent to which, as Rathenau said, the state favoured the concentration process, by allowing the unions to accept or refuse new associates, and by granting them the right of monopoly on the sale of commodities produced domestically or imported, and other rights, concerning the purchase, closure and transformation of enterprises. It is indicative of the influence that such a programme may have exerted on some Bolshevik leaders that Rathenau had defined the rights of such unions as virtually sovereign, and that Kritsman later mentioned the unlimited rights of the *glavki* within the confines of their branch.[25]

Rathenau was concerned that the state might be excluded from control, once the unions had been formed. He therefore envisaged governmental participation in the administration of the unions, with rights of inspection and intervention into all questions except labour.[26] Those Bolsheviks who, like Kritsman, believed in the identification of the *glavki* with the proletarian dictatorship were free from analogous concerns.

6.2 THE PATH TO SOVIET PLANNING

Throughout 1918 the Bolsheviks endeavoured to build the structures of a concentrated and centralized economic system, striving to do away with the autonomy of production units, to reduce market outlets and to maximize the power of central management. Centralization was stimulated not only by scarcity, but also by the conscious drive to eliminate market competition.[27] In this sense, one may say that the economic experts worked for planning, though nobody had a precise idea of how, through which indicators and mechanisms, central directives would be implemented.

The first plans concerned infrastructures and the location of industry, and were the continuation of works already undertaken before the revolution. After Brest–Litovsk, Lenin charged the Academy of Sciences with forming a commission of experts for the elaboration of a plan concerning the reorganization of industry and the economic reconstruction of Russia. Lenin's principal concern was to explore the possibility of reaching self-sufficiency of industrial output, given the current situation, that is, given the loss of the Ukraine and the territories occupied by the Germans. Considerable financial help was given to the Academy's Commission for the Study of Russian Natural Productive Forces. Lenin recommended that the plan should include the rational distribution of industry, taking into account the following: proximity of raw materials; low labour intensity at all stages of production; rational merging and concentration of industry in a few big enterprises; the utilization of domestic raw materials; and electrification of industry and transport.[28]

VSNKh started exploring the possibilities of increasing the output of coal by developing the Kuznets Basin of Western Siberia and linking it by rail to the Urals. Larin reported to the April Plenum of VSNKh that in five years 300 million puds of coking coal would be dispatched to the Urals. It was also calculated that about 1,700 kilometres of track were sufficient to connect the existing railways with the coal basin. The rails should be supplied by industries of the Donets Basin.[29] Another project concerned the electrification of the Petrograd Region, through the exploitation of local water power. This project was to supply alternative types of energy to the industrial centre in order to keep it working in face of the shortage of coal from traditional sources. A more ambitious project concerned the irrigation of Turkestan's cotton fields, to ensure a regular cotton supply to Moscow's industries. The highly concentrated Russian textile industry depended on imports for about 48 per cent of its cotton supply before the war.[30] The project was to obtain the necessary domestic supply from Turkestan within two or three years.[31]

All these projects were halted by the civil war. They are, however, interesting in order to understand the point of view from which the economic experts and part of the party leadership evaluated the problems of economic reconstruction immediately following the Brest–Litovsk Treaty. The government was then ready to undertake a revision of the existing economic framework, by concentrating on the development of local resources. Miliutin informed a VSNKh Plenary Committee in March 1918 about a project to reconvert the military industry of Petrograd to civil industry for production of agricultural machinery,[32] which Russia had traditionally imported from the West. In May 1918 VSNKh presented at the Congress of *Sovnarkhozy* a plan for the complete utilization of Russian natural resources and for the development of the transport and energy sectors. The president of the Committee of Public Works, which had been entrusted with the elaboration of the plan, maintained the necessity of concentrating into a single organ all tasks of national importance in this field, since the several commissariats among which the matter had been fragmented up to then had obstructed due consideration of both the domestic and the international policy of the government.[33]

The outbreak of civil war induced some economic organs to elaborate concrete projects for the coordination of production programmes. In June 1918 the Metal Section elaborated the first production programme for the Petrograd works, through a group of technicians of the railway construction plant. All factories were to provide information about the activity of the preceding months in a brief schedule. On the basis of such information, the corresponding bureau of the Metal Section decided the input–output programme for each factory. When reasonable doubts were raised about the correctness of information supplied, the section sent one of its representatives to investigate on the spot.[34] The production programme covered a two months period, but it was not fulfilled. The failure was ascribed to tensions derived from an inadequate food supply and to the temporary closure of some plants.[35]

The first experiment in elaborating an overall economic plan concerning all economic activities was undertaken by the Northern Region. On 14 July 1918, the First Congress of *Sovnarkhozy* of the Northern Region approved a resolution on the organization of production. This 'economic plan' set out a list of priorities. Firstly, the organization of railway and water transport. Secondly, agricultural machinery. Thirdly, industrial products for exchange with agricultural products. Fourthly, various machinery. Lastly, production for export. This plan was approved when the political situation had already changed and prevented any serious steps for its implementation. The plan had been formulated in the context of the demobilization of military industry, which followed Brest–Litovsk. The main constraints of the plan were considered to be scarcity of raw materials and fuel as well as tendencies towards separatism, which were ascribed to the rural population of the agricultural regions. These constraints were considered sufficient grounds for the utmost centralization of management, utilization of local resources and concentration of production. In fact, the Northern Region claimed centralization of decision-making at the regional level, which from the national point of view turned out to be a claim for regional autonomy in economic decisions.[36]

In the autumn of 1918 the debate on centralization indirectly touched on the principles of planning, though planning itself remained more an aspiration than a concrete economic policy. The arguments for centralization stressed that productive activity was impossible and bound to end in anarchy if it was not accompanied by systematic (*planomernoi*) centralization.[37] Though most of the people who participated in the debate were aware that Russia was a backward country and that this fact hindered a programme of centralization of management, the idea that centralization was a correct goal since it helped the creation of a planned economy, which was considered a synonym for socialism,[38] prevailed over the arguments of opponents of such a policy. For its supporters, centralization meant primarily planned supply of raw materials and planned distribution of products from the centre. They believed, however, that this could be ensured by the *glavk* system. The counterarguments that only *oblast* unions had up to then succeeded in working out production programmes and that the proliferation of *glavki* was going against the goal of coordination[39] continued to attract little support. Miliutin affirmed at the Second Congress of *Sovnarkhozy* that national-ization of industry was almost complete, that economic management had been centralized around VSNKh and the local *sovnarkhozy*, and that significant steps toward implementation of the overall accounting of raw materials and finished products stocked in the Soviet warehouses had been made. All these facts, argued Miliutin, made the formulation and implementation of a 'single economic plan' possible in 1919. However, what Miliutin defined as a plan was only a series of economic measures for promoting the activity of nationalized industry. He mentioned the formation of trusts and *kusty*, increased productivity through the establishment of norms of obligatory output in agreement with trade unions, the organization of socialist emulation and, finally, the so-called plan of supply of fuel and raw materials.[40] Rykov explained that supply of metals to industry was on the basis of plans worked out by the industrial branches. All plans were put together at the centre and demand was satisfied in accordance with national importance. He noted that military requirements were met totally. Secondly, supply had to satisfy the demand for wagons, for the munitions industry and for agricultural machinery production. But, Rykov informed the congress, a revision of the initial plans had been imposed by lack of fuel and metals. As to the wagons, the plan had been limited to repair, the average share of 'sick' wagons and engines having reached about 40–50 per cent of the existing stocks.[41] In truth, during 1918 and 1919 there could not be any single economic plan in the sense of 'a gigantic statistical bureau based on exact calculation for the purpose of distributing labour power and instruments of labour',[42] since VSNKh had not sufficient information about the existing production units under its control, nor did it have control over enough economic levers. Control over inventories, essential in wartime, was in the hands of the *glavki*, but their pervasive activity of requisitioning materials and products, closing enterprises and concentrating materials and means in undertakings employing modern techniques did not necessarily aid the best utilization of resources according to central criteria. Modern techniques, in fact, were highly dependent on energy and specific sorts of fuel, which could not be provided in sufficient quantities. In default of increased production, the *glavki* extended their control over still more enterprises. By the end of 1918 it was clear to many that nationalization was going beyond the programmes of June 1918. Lozovskii spoke against nationalization of small commerce and industry, on the grounds that it hindered the concentration of efforts on organizing the principal industrial branches and supply of the necessary equipment and materials to them.[43] Rykov's reply reflected the embarrassment of VSNKh's leadership in explaining to the congress of economic representatives economic measures which, as Lozovskii complained, were bound to increase economic disorder rather than contribute to planning. Rykov said that nationalization was necessary to obviate transfer of goods abroad by merchants. He added that the sale of fabrics had been monopolized by the state for this purpose, since attempts had been made to transfer them to the Ukraine on behalf of foreign subjects.[44] These measures, however, jeopardized VSNKh's price policy, because of the odd solution which had been found for distribution. VSNKh's experts were not wrong when they complained that the autonomy of the economic commissariats hindered the formulation of a single national plan. VSNKh's leadership was particularly offended by the method which *Sovnarkom* adopted in November 1918 for the distribution of consumer goods and finished products. The decree on trade monopoly, in fact, devolved decisions on distribution to *Narkomprod*. Its decisions in this field, however, were biased by the criteria of collective commodity exchange, which prevailed in the policy of foodstuffs procurement.[45] The stocking of industrial products in state warehouses was likely to increase scarcity and exert a perverse effect on prices. Rykov feared that, if VSNKh was not going to distribute adequate quantities, price determination would lose any meaning and wages would have to be set in relation to free market prices. The first steps towards a policy of central planning of distribution, however, were undertaken in connection with the establishment of a trade monopoly.

6.3 THE COMMITTEE FOR UTILIZATION

A decree on supply of 21 November 1918 created the Committee for Utilization. This Committee was to compute the overall demand for products and the quantity available for supply.[46] The committee started working only in the Spring of 1919, when the situation of emergency created by war had become extreme. The party then announced a maximum unification of all economic activity through a nationwide plan, centralization and concentration of production, and the rational and economic utilization of all material resources.[47] During 1919 and 1920 the number of products examined by the committee increased substantially and the committee was endowed with a technical staff of 200 people and 15 bureaux, each one dealing with specific products, carrying out what Kritsman called the preparatory work for the single economic plan.[48] The development of the Committee for Utilization coincided with the progressive awareness of some VSNKh leaders that *Sovnarkom* would never be persuaded to abolish the economic commissariats and devolve their functions to VSNKh, a solution which most of the VSNKh leaders considered essential for work on central planning. The decree on supply stated that the plan of utilization had to establish: firstly, allocation of output to exports, reserves, industrial use and distribution to the population; secondly, factory, wholesale and retail price determination; thirdly, the plan of distribution of all products earmarked for distribution to the population.[49] Kritsman affirmed that one of the reasons for the slow development of the plan of utilization was inadequate awareness of its importance on the part of Soviet organs. Whether this misunderstanding about the meaning of the plan of utilization was real or not, it must be admitted that the tasks assigned to the Committee for Utilization were impressive, as compared with the people and means available, and that military requirements conditioned the timing and content of decisions in all fields. Yet, in December 1918, the Committee for Utilization prepared the plans of utilization for nineteen products, most of which were destined by *Narkomprod* for consumption (fish, meat, oats, hay, sugar, salt, etc.). The plans did not concern total quantities, but only norms of consumption. In 1919 the committee started examining material estimates of the most important consumers. In the first half of that year, the committee approved seventy-one material estimates; in the second half, ninety-two. In the whole year, forty-four plans of utilization were elaborated. In 1920, 117 material estimates were approved for the first ten months and 55 plans of utilization were worked out. The overall number of products distributed according to the plans reached 325, taking into account the assortment for each product category.[50] By 1920 most processed food and some other items for personal use were included in the plans of utilization. Kritsman reported that the central administrations of textiles, leather, furs, porcelain, rubber, sugar, tobacco, matches, confectionery, paper, animal fats, soap, tea, salt, starch and garments released their products only in accordance with the plans of utilization worked out by VSNKh's Committee.[51]

The plans of utilization partitioned the output of products among the population and industry in physical units. For instance, the plan of utilization of cotton and flax approved in August 1920 was computed in millions of arshins (1 arshin = 28 inches) (see Table 6.1).[52]

The examples of plans of utilization presented by Kritsman show that these plans extended to three months. They concerned stocks of products and current output for the planning period. Possible surrogates were also taken into account. Tables were worked out to convert the planned quantities for distribution of the principal products into available

Table 6.1 *Plan of utilization of cotton and flax, August 1920 (million arshins)*

Glavodezhda (garment administration):	265
for war equipment	185
for workers of *glavki* and production sections	30
for children	35
Glavleskom (chief timber committee):	
as premiums for timber collection	17
Narkomprod	256
special allocation for liberated regions	30
for commodity exchange with the peasantry	80
for development of technical cultures	80
VSNKh: for production and technical utilization by industry	25

surrogates. Four categories of demand were taken into account. Firstly, the requirements of the army, fleet and workers of the militarized factories. Secondly, the demand of *Narkomprod* for special categories of workers in agreement with the Central Council of Trade Unions. Thirdly, the demand of other commissariats. Fourthly, the demand of the central industrial administrations and *glavki*. Reserves were planned for unforeseen needs of a technical nature.[53]

It is scarcely credible that the utilization plans rested on solid foundations. Percentages of fulfilment varied from a minimum of 38 per cent to a maximum of 425 per cent, depending on the type of product.[54]

In 1920 the Committee for Utilization worked out a list of 150 central supplying and consuming organs, which included commissariats, large sections of commissariats, *glavki* and *gubsovnarkhozy*. The central supplying organs were either direct producers or purchasing institutions, which were supposed to work on the basis of the utilization plans. Among consumers, only central organs properly registered had the right to immediate supply of products and materials from state funds and on the basis of the plan. Other consumers needed to go through the central organs in order to obtain commodities.[55] Delivery procedures were as follows: the Committee for Utilization communicated the order for delivery to the *glavk* or *tsentr* charged with the administration of the branch. The *glavk* or *tsentr* assigned the order to a factory for a given quantity within forty-eight hours. The factory was expected to fulfil the order in a maximum of ten days. If the order could not be fulfilled within this period, the factory was allowed ten more days to deliver the assigned output. If the order was not fulfilled by then, the factory administration was to inform the *glavk* of the reasons and the *glavk* had forty-eight hours to assign the order to another factory.[56] When delivery orders concerned consumer goods used for special rewards, like premiums for the collection and dispatch of wood fuel,[57] the Committee for Utilization established the value equivalents in terms of puds, arshins, and other physical units.

Efforts were made to reduce to a minimum the information necessary to establish the plans of supply. Information concerned output, profitability, reserves and expected supply. Two sections were formed for the elaboration of information concerning both central supplying and central consuming organs. The *gubsovnarkhozy* were not taken into account. Supply was calculated with the help of the Central Technical Committee for Production, which established production programmes. Demand was computed, taking into account the effective utilization of capacity and the technical coefficients of production.[58] For example, supply of spun cotton and flax to the central administration for industrial clothing was calculated taking into account the number of workers, shifts and machines. Demand for this clothing was calculated by the trade unions, which provided estimates of requirements, distinguishing workers by branches.

The Committee for Utilization did not always accept as reliable the information provided by other organs. At times the Central Technical Committee for Production was urged to increase the production programmes of some branches. The efforts to gain full control over supply clashed with the irregularity of provision of agricultural materials, transport failures and non-fulfilment of production programmes. Variations of the territory under Soviet control were a further source of difficulty for the elaboration of correct estimates, particularly regarding the distribution of consumer goods. The Committee for Utilization met periodically with *Narkomprod* and the Central Administration for Army Supply, in order to consider province tables of rural and urban population by workers' occupation. The policy of wages in kind which was furthered in 1920 compelled the Committee for Utilization to start verifying also available supplies for special categories of workers, such as railwaymen or builders. This was a sensitive matter. Some departments did not accept the decisions of the Committee for Utilization on distribution of products for wages in kind and claimed the intervention of *Sovnarkom*, whose approval was needed in order to implement the decisions of the committee.[59]

By the summer of 1920, the Committee for Utilization had in part succeeded in applying to utilization of products criteria of 'destination' instead of demand criteria. For consumer goods, the committee used the tables of equivalents, in order to allow some flexibility in payment in kind. The approach to distribution from the point of view of the character of needs was a very important achievement on the path towards planning. This approach promoted a production standpoint on distribution, and it affirmed central decision-making in supply as against the policy of distribution carried out by the *glavki*, which in the course of war communism had hindered a serious policy of assortment reduction and the achievement of rapid substitution between surrogates.

6.4 THE DEBATE ON PLANNING

At the end of 1920 the conclusion of hostilities nourished the hopes of economists that the major obstacles to the formation of central planning organs with real powers had been overcome, and that effective programming supply and distribution could be undertaken. The debate among economists was influenced to a great extent by awareness that *glavkism* had led to waste and disorganization and had hindered effective centralization. The economists agreed that any planning endeavour had first to confront the problem of central supply. They agreed that in Soviet Russia planning was not only possible, but also inevitable, and that the prerequisites for a single integrated economic plan were already present. Such prerequisites were seen as having an economic and technical nature as well as a socio-political one. Unions of enterprises on the principle of like output and unification of all trusts under VSNKh were considered technical prerequisites. Nationalization, and the utilization of some existing structural elements for the construction of a new system, were considered as prerequisites of a socio-political nature. Some economists believed that planning could also be based on a new revolutionary cultural foundation through the general and vocational education of the masses.[60]

The debate on planning was started by an article written for *Izvestiia* by Larin, in December 1920. Larin had already intervened against the leadership of VSNKh, which was reluctant to accept the idea of a single economic plan put forward by Trotskii on the eve of the Eighth Congress of Soviets. Opening the discussion on the organization of distribution, Larin tried to convince the leadership that the logic of distribution which had dominated economic policy during the past two years had to be transformed into a logic inspired by production criteria. Larin criticized the existing system, in which some of the finished products were distributed by the Committee for Utilization and some by the supply organs of VSNKh's production sections, for instance *Prodrasmet* for metals, *Khimsnabzheniia* for chemical products, and *Stroimotdel* for building materials, under the coordination of a Council of Supply and Distribution attached to the VSNKh Presidium.

Larin affirmed that distribution had to be separated from production and concentrated in a single organ. Three sources of inefficiency in the current system of allocation of products among industrial consumers were identified. Firstly, a *glavk* allocated any goods produced in its branch, though the products of the branch did not necessarily have to be substitutes of one another. Secondly, this system of allocation of products caused a significant under-utilization of existing resources, since allocation was arbitrary and did not observe the constraints of complementarities between products in such a way that scarce supply of one product entailed idleness of a complementary one. Thirdly, Larin accused this system of enhancing the incompetence of the central supply organs, which did not need to know the objective actual requirements of their customers. Requirements, complained Larin, were satisfied mechanically to a certain percentage of demand without attention being paid to their objective consistency. A consequence of this was the deliberate exaggeration of production plans on the part of the enterprises. Casual fulfilment of production plans was the outcome of lack of coordination of supply. Larin concluded that such casualness would end only if the whole matter were concentrated under the Committee for Utilization, which would take into account in its work the manifested 'coefficients of exaggeration'.[61]

The head of the Supply Section of the Chemical Branch replied to Larin's observations, trying to bring the question of distribution back to empirical grounds. He attributed the incomplete realization of the plans for distribution to general disorganization, and maintained that, even though they were well prepared, the utilization plans were not implemented because local materials were not correctly computed; quantity, quality and assortment of output did not correspond to the assumptions of the plan-makers. Contrary to Larin's opinion, he affirmed that production organs should not be separated from distribution organs, since they helped to determine the existing local stocks and the exact proportions between resources used in production and the expected output. Concentration of distribution under the Committee for Utilization was of no help for correct allocation of resources in so far as the branches of production were under the control of different organs. He warned that Larin's project would produce 'fussing around' every time each type or aspect of demand had to be dealt with. To avoid this, he affirmed that the simultaneous distribution of the necessary products and the connection between production and distribution plans should be the task of the VSNKh Council of Supply and Distribution. This council approved the plans, which were made up under its general instructions by the corresponding distributive organs of VSNKh, and coordinated the planned assignments of various materials and products, trying to avoid the formation of idle stocks. The Committee for Utilization had gone beyond its original tasks. From an organ entrusted with planning the broad allocation of resources between principal consumers, like the army, the economy, the population and foreign commerce, as a framework for the work of the special distributive organs, the Committee for Utilization was accused of having become 'a universal storehouse which released units of all possible materials and products to meet the various demands from all possible consumers, by signing papers'.[62]

A conciliatory proposal was made by D.N. Shapiro, who suggested distinguishing products for final consumption from products for industrial use, by assigning the distribution of the former to the Committee for Utilization and of the latter to VSNKh's Council of Supply and Distribution. He argued that the Committee for Utilization had released products up to then without knowing what had been released by other organs, and that distribution had been carried out by the mechanical subdivision of the existing stocks, just as other distributive organs had done. Shapiro affirmed that over-estimation of requirements and under-evaluation of reserves were residuals of the capitalist mentality, rather than effects of the distribution mechanism. Supply was defined as 'the natural conclusion of the planning work and the material incarnation of the utilization plans'. Coordination between the sphere of consumer goods and the sphere of industrial, single as well as mixed, products was to be ensured by a commission formed by representatives of both organs, which should be subordinated to the Council of Labour and Defence, with functions of supervision and direction. Shapiro considered that procedures for delivery should remain the same as before. Orders were to be examined by the highest production sections, like the metal or the chemical section, and were to be sent forward to the distribution organs for each sort of product attached to the production sections, which had to implement the orders according to the instructions of the Council of Supply and Distribution. Shapiro affirmed that the solution of the distribution problem had to be sought within a decentralized framework. In the phase of realization, plans should be sent forward to the Councils of Supply and Distribution at the regional level, which should fulfil the orders through the provincial distributive organs and organize delivery to consumers.[63]

Kritsman had no difficulty in replying to his colleagues' criticism, which showed, he argued, how little certain managers appreciated the fact that reasonable alternatives had to be found to market laws of distribution if the market was to be suppressed. Kritsman pointed out that the absence of the market made a crucial difference between the distribution systems of socialism and capitalism. He recalled that war had already introduced some novelties in the forms of distribution, and stressed that the question of distribution as such did not exist in the capitalist system and that this was, therefore, a new economic problem to be dealt with in new ways. Kritsman emphasized the economic facets of the problem: the need to take into account complementarity and substitution between products, both in industrial utilization and in final consumption. He argued that evidence of past performance in these fields showed that certain distribution organs did not respect production complementarities, and challenged the mental habit which induced the heads of VSNKh departments to consider distribution as the mere allocation of stocks of products among people. Kritsman explained that distribution was not to be considered as mere supply of goods to people. He argued that the idea that *Narkomprod* had to be the central organ of distribution was based on a misunderstanding of the rationale of distribution. *Narkomprod* was to be considered only a central organ for supply, one amongst others such as the People's Commissariat for Post and Telegraph. Distribution was not a function to be assigned to any of the existing commissariats. Kritsman emphasized that the crux of the matter was 'who is going to decide how much iron, for instance, is to be allocated to locomotives, how much to ploughs and how much to knives, spoons and forks'. Even bread grains could not be considered only as goods for mass consumption. The real question was decision-making on the allocation of output among different uses.[64]

Kritsman had the merit of pointing out that the crucial question behind distribution, in the absence of market mechanisms, was the division of the national product between consumption and investment, and that this question could not be left to the individual commissariat's discretion. This question, of course, was of primary importance for planning.

Nonetheless, the proposal that the Committee for Utilization should fix the proportions between consumption and investment, and allocate investment to each branch, was optimistic about the real possibility of control over output flows and the capacity to calculate effective (that is, disaggregated) technical coefficients of production. Centralized planning seemed out of reach in late 1920. On the other hand, *Sovnarkom* was orientated towards a moderate decentralization in the field of supply, after the excessive and wasteful centralization of wartime. On 2 December 1920, a decree was passed concerning the formation of Councils of Supply and Distribution attached to the *Oblast* Bureaux of VSNKh. These councils, *obsnaby*, were composed of two appointees from the VSNKh Central Council of Supply and Distribution and a president. The *obsnaby* had the right of representation on the *oblast* bureaux. Their tasks concerned the accounting of stocks and output of materials and equipment in the *oblast*, and computation of demand for such products in relation to production programmes. The *obsnaby* examined and approved planned estimates for such products and worked out the *oblast* plan of supply and distribution, which was to be approved by the Central Council of Supply and Distribution of VSNKh.[65] This initiative, of course, automatically reduced the role of the Committee for Utilization.

Another limitation of Larin's and Kritsman's proposal was their technocratic bias, which tended to assume that the allocation of the national product between consumption and investment could be treated as a mere technical question which affected political decisions only incidentally. This was not the leadership's approach. The leadership did not intend to renounce political control over economic priorities, the rate of development, and demand. This was made clear at the Ninth Congress of the Party, which approved Trotskii's plan of reconstruction. The initiative on planning, in fact, was attributed to the Council of Labour and Defence. Trotskii's plan was based on criteria of priorities, which were not to be devolved to the discretion of technicians. Food procurement, raw material and fuel supply and machine building were subordinated to the improvement of the transport system. Last in priorities were consumer goods. Trotskii declared to the congress: 'In the immediate future, we must direct our work towards the production of the means of production.'[66] The Council of Labour and Defence was entrusted by the Eighth Congress of Soviets with 'the formulation of a unified economic plan, guidance of the work of the economic commissariats on the basis of the plan, verification of [its] fulfilment and, eventually, modification of the plan itself'.[67] The concentration of planning activity under the 'small *Sovnarkom*' (the inner cabinet) was supported by Lenin, who recalled that the Council of Labour and Defence had been working until then without any statute and that the time had come to convert it into a body for the closer coordination of economic policy. Lenin discarded a project which proposed demarcation of competence between *Sovnarkom* and the Council of Labour and Defence, alleging that this would have entailed 'numerous codifiers' and the utilization of 'reams of paper' and invited the Congress of Soviets to attach the council to *Sovnarkom*, as a commission of it, in order to avoid frictions and accelerate implementation.[68] But Lenin was still thinking in terms of single plans. He praised Trotskii's plan for transport, known as Order no. 1042, because it concerned a specific sector and entailed strict coordination of the plans of other branches related to this sector.[69] Lenin did not well understand the problems of planning as an alternative to the market economy, that is, as a global alternative hypothesis of economic policy, such as was presented by Larin and Kritsman. When the economists demanded that the principles of economic policy should be defined, since, afterwards, 'their implementation would have to follow',[70] Lenin accused them of scholasticism. On 22 February 1921, in *Pravda*, Lenin declared that Kritsman's arguments amounted to 'empty talk and word-spinning'.[71] Lenin was convinced that 'a complete, integrated real plan is a bureaucratic utopia'; this is what he wrote to Krzhizhanovskii, the head of the plan for electrification (GOELRO), on 19 February 1921, accusing Miliutin of writing nonsense about planning.[72] Larin's partici-pation in the General Planning Commission, approved by *Sovnarkom* on 22 February, was viewed by Lenin with concern.[73]

At the same time, Lenin invited the technicians who had been taking part in the preparation of GOELRO to start working on economic *current* plans (Lenin's italics), first of all for fuel and secondly for grain.[74]

Lenin's fear that the economists would lose time by concentrating on theory instead of working on concrete problems prevented him from appreciating the current elaboration of planning criteria as one of the first original contributions of the short war communism experience in the economic field. He complained that there was on the part of the economists 'the emptiest drawing up of theses' and a concoction of plans and slogans, in place of 'painstaking and thoughtful study of practical experience'.[75] According to Lenin, the only serious work on the subject was GOELRO, the plan for electrification of the RSFSR published in December 1920 and distributed to participants of the Eighth Congress of Soviets.[76] GOELRO was considered to be the first detailed plan in Soviet history.[77] The All-Russian Central Executive Committee approved the project at the beginning of February 1920, as the first step towards a nationwide state economic plan on scientific lines.[78] The VSNKh Presidium formed a Commission for Electrification on 21 February. At the end of April GOELRO was already issuing its first bulletin, which contained the programme of work, the list of commissions entrusted with specific assignments and the people charged with them. By the time of the Eighth Congress of Soviets, GOELRO had already worked out the plan for electrification covering ten years. Lenin was fascinated by this plan. It concerned not only the construction of electric power stations, but also the estimates of fuel supplies, water power and manpower required, and forecasts of the rate of development of agriculture, transport and industry over ten years.

Implementation of the plan for electrification, however, presupposed the implementation of several economic plans. That is, it implied determination of the allocation of the national product between con-sumption and investment, and calculation of the yields from units of investment, which, in turn, required an overall national plan, definition of priorities, and concentration of economic resources. Lenin became aware of the importance of these questions only some months later. On 14 May 1921, he complained that there was scarcely any evidence of the operation of an integrated state economic plan, and that the prevalent tendency was the revival of everything, of all branches of the national economy without distinction, including enterprises inherited from capitalism.[79] The dependence of the whole economy on the food situation induced Lenin to propose that variants of the plan should be made, depending on the expected food surplus and fuel supply and the possibility of increasing them, taking into account the size of grain reserves. Lenin suggested giving priority to industry. Shortage of fuel and food dictated the concentration of production in a few large factories. 'After industry', he concluded, 'from which the building industry must be singled out, comes transport (perhaps this should be put before industry?) and electrification as a distinct item. And so forth.' In a postscript, Lenin demanded that special attention be paid to industries producing goods which could be exchanged for grain.[80] But in this way everything was to be given priority! Lenin was unable to come to terms with planning. The low productivity of agriculture had become in the mean time the conditioning element of any planning effort. The introduction of the New Economic Policy was also a result of the incapacity of the leadership to define reasonable priorities for reconstruction. In the course of 1921, the interest in planning was diluted and deferred. At the Ninth Congress of Soviets, no mention was made of the integrated economic plan.[81]

6.5 THE WORK ON ECONOMIC CRITERIA OTHER THAN VALUE

Economic policy between 1918 and 1921 was not shaped by planning criteria, but it contributed to the formation of an appropriate mental outlook for planning and to the first attempts to adopt economic criteria suitable for the evaluation of economic activity independently of market prices. Trotskii affirmed at the Party Congress in 1920 that Russia had to advance towards socialism at high rates, just as Russian capitalism had advanced more rapidly than other capitalisms. On this the economists of VSNKh agreed,[82] in spite of the initial polemics about planning. The experience of a non-market economy had brought about some interesting attempts to devise suitable criteria to measure efficiency by way of physical units. The principal motivation was galloping inflation, which, together with the instability of relative scarcities, had made fixed prices totally unsuitable for the computation of economic results. But there were also ideological motivations. Some economists affirmed that under capitalism profit was the only means to assess the efficiency of the undertaking, since owners had no interest in value added or in the volume of output, whereas under socialism it was quite the contrary: 'We are not interested in the realization of surplus-value or in dividends, but in real output: the higher the output volume of each individual factory, the higher will be the total quantity of socially available commodities... [and] the more advantageous will be factory work to society.'[83]

The problem of evaluating economic activity in the absence of meaningful prices had been explored at the industrial level since 1919. In June 1918 the Section of Metal Works of Petrograd elaborated the first production programme for thirteen factories, subdivided by quarter. At the end of July 1918, the section started elaborating the second production programme, which covered 50–60 works and workshops for six months. The enterprises were expected to produce the maximum output given the stocks of raw materials and fuel at their disposal.[84] It was in this context that the problem of assessing the efficiency of the works engaged in the production plan emerged.

The Metal Section of the *sovnarkhoz* of the Northern Region elaborated a system to check comparative efficiency, given different percentages of used capacity.[85] The coefficient of success k was calculated as the ratio between the percentage of fulfilment of the production plan P and the percentage of planned labour and fuel supply O_{fl}:

$$k = P/O_{fl}, \quad \text{for } O_{fl} = RT$$

where R = % labour supply
and T = % fuel supply

The percentage of supply was taken as the relation between actual supply and needed supply. Given:

$$k = P/RT$$

if P, R, T were equal to 100 per cent, k would be equal to 1, i.e. success would be normal. If R or T were nil and P higher than zero, k would tend to infinity. A coefficient of success higher than 1 corresponded to success above the norm; vice versa, k lower than one corresponded to an unsatisfactory outcome.

This expression embodied a weakness which the authors did not ignore. Taking R_f as actual supply of labour and R_p as needed labour supply, $R = R_f/R_p$. Taking T_f as actual stocks of fuel and T_p as needed stocks, $T = T_f/T_p$. The coefficient of success could be expressed:

$$k = P(T_p \cdot R_p)/(T_f \cdot R_f) = P(1/RT)$$

The new expression showed that k would be the higher, the lower the target P, since wanted labour and fuel supply were always higher than actual supply. It was considered, in fact, that such an index of success induced enterprises to set lower targets, in order to show a high degree of fulfilment. And conversely, it led to overevaluation of needed supply of labour and fuel. Nonetheless, this index was used in the military industry. In the first half of 1919 the coefficient of success was 0.75. In the second half of the same year it was 0.89:

	P	R	T	k
First half of 1919	50%	57%	83%	0.75
Second half of 1919	42%	64.5%	34.7%	0.89

These results were interpreted as an approximation to a correct index of success. When the coefficient of success was judged to be too high, it was corrected by correcting the estimates for R or T. The factor which was supposed to have been under-estimated was assumed equal to the wanted supply. Taking the same percentage of fulfilment of the plan as given, resources were considered to have been used efficiently if k was still higher than 1.[86]

The coefficient of success was also used in industrial comparisons. If factories equally endowed with production factors showed different performances, the cause of relative inefficiency was sought in other fields, such as labour time, food rations and bonuses in kind.[87]

Alternative methods of economic accounting were studied also at the centre, which anticipated somewhat future work on material balances. Under the sponsorship of the People's Commissariat of Agriculture, Vainshtein worked out a system of accounting on the basis of technical coefficients, starting from the view that the financial book-keeping of state enterprises was useless because fixed prices were based partly on consideration of general economic policy rather than on costs and partly on pre-war price ratios. The rapid depreciation of the ruble between the beginning and the end of the production process, observed Vainshtein, had made financial book-keeping meaningless in private undertakings too.[88] Vainshtein's aims were: firstly, to define an accounting unit; secondly, to define the meaning of potential productivity and the coefficient of utilization; thirdly, to divide expenditure into constant and variable expenditure, and fourthly, to define the meaning of the value of a unit of useful labour.

The accounting unit was interpreted in terms of 'useful' labour as opposed to 'auxiliary' labour. Vainshtein explained that useful labour was the labour applied to machinery production, while auxiliary labour could be labour spent in repair or farming. He also distinguished between 'useful' and 'operatively useful' or 'effective' labour.[89]

Potential productivity was considered the productivity of enterprises in normal conditions, that is, working with no extraordinary disruption. The coefficient of utilization was computed as the ratio between labour currently employed and labour which the enterprise could absorb potentially.[90] Expenditure was divided into constant expenditure, if it was related to potential productivity, and variable expenditure, if it was related to current productivity. Further subdivisions were taken into account in relation to the labour time. Heating costs, for instance, were considered a variable quota of constant expenditure.[91]

Vainshtein rejected the unit of transformed (processed) raw materials as a unit of accounting on the ground that this unit would require resort to other coefficients. It may occur, he explained, that expenditure for material resources and labour per pud of raw materials increases while it diminishes per unit of output, if output increases even a little. Two other approaches were considered: the unit of useful labour, i.e. the working day, and the unit of output, which was equivalent to a unit of 'effective' (actually, useful) labour. Vainshtein proposed that material costs be computed per unit of output by the following expression:

$$x = A/n + B/n + C/n + G/n + D/n + E/n$$
$$= ak_1/n + bk_2/n + ck_3/n = gk_4/n + D/n + E/n$$

where x = the value of the output unit

n = number of output units

A = value of raw and auxiliary materials

B = cost of fuel

C = supplementary expenditure (repair, etc.)

G = reward for labour

D = general expenditure (administration, laboratory)

E = depreciation in rubles

k_1, k_2, k_3, k_4 = values of a unit of raw materials, fuel, auxiliary materials, and day's labour

a, b, c, g = quantity of the corresponding units spent for output

Vainshtein pointed out the usefulness of the technical coefficients, a, b, c and g, in a non-monetary budget. The magnitude of the technical coefficients and their deviation from the norm were to show whether management was rational and correct. Vainshtein believed that the technical coefficients could be determined a priori, but suggested that they should be empirically calculated in the current situation. Showing little sympathy for taut planning, Vainshtein suggested calculation of the norm as the modal value, except in the case of radically asymmetric data, where a combination of simple average and modal value would be suitable. The simple arithmetic average and the mean were considered unsuitable, since they could happen to include unreal chance magnitudes.[92]

The introduction of NEP and the gradual restoration of the market attracted the economists' attention towards other problems. But the theoretical work pursued in the years of war communism was probably not lost. It certainly contributed towards the climate of confidence which accompanied the introduction of the first Soviet plans. Much more was done than has been surveyed here, and when the relevant materials become available they will merit serious studies. On the basis of the limited evidence which has been presented, however, one may affirm that the work done by the economic experts under war communism contributed to the creation of a new approach towards economic management and opened the way to later imaginative efforts to correct and improve, if not to replace, the existing economic models and their institutions.

6.6 SUMMARY

Some ideological foundation for planning can be found in both Marx and Kautsky. Both focused on the potential of the foresight and initiative of a non-market communist society, where investment decisions would be centralized. But neither of them went further into the technical details which should have produced a higher level of efficiency in a centrally planned economy. From this point of view, Ballod's well known essay on the 'state of the future' may have provided more specific suggestions, especially to those economists, who, under the leadership of Groman, undertook the first steps for the elaboration of a national plan under the Provisional Government. One should not forget, however, that the Bolsheviks were attracted, as the works of Bukharin, Preobrazhenskii and Osinskii show, more by the hypothesis of centralization as such than by the technicalities it involved. It is possible that the main propositions related in any way to a planned organization would have remained in the realm of goals for a long time, if war had not provided concrete examples of economic control from above and scarcity of resources during civil war had not imposed the problem of priority.

War communism cannot be considered a centrally planned economy in any meaningful sense. But it operated in an ideological and constrained framework which was conducive to experiments in planning. At both the macro- and micro-economic levels an impressive amount of work was done – at present only partially known – to replace market indicators with physical indicators, which, it is reasonable to assume, were positive legacies for future work on planning.

When the debate on planning started, the civil war economic experience was practically over. This experience had provided, however, a fertile soil for the imagination of alternatives and trials of new economic regulators. Even more important, it had helped to pose the correct questions as to the need for, and feasibility of, alternative evaluations of efficiency, which were bound to force the imagination to confront concrete problems, the solution of which would later require much more patient and serious work than the initial revolutionary enthusiasm had foreseen.

NOTES

1 K. Marx, *Capital*, 3 vols., Moscow, 1957, vol. 2, p. 135.
2 *Ibid.*, vol. 1, p. 530.
3 *Ibid.*, vol. 1, pp. 78–9.
4 *Ibid.*, vol. 2, pp. 315–16.
5 *Ibid.*, vol. 2, p. 466–9.
6 *Ibid.*, vol. 2, p. 315.
7 *Ibid.*, vol. 2, p. 358.
8 K. Marx, *Critique of the Gotha Program*, New York, 1966, p. 7.
9 *Ibid.*
10 See pp. 30–1 above.
11 See: F. Engels, *AntiDüring*, 2nd edn Rome, 1971, pp. 285–304.
12 K. Ballod, *Der Zukunftstaat*, 2nd edn, Stoccarda, 1919. Six different translations were published in Russian from the first edition of 1898 during 1903–6. The second edition was written in 1918 and contained a revision of the original data. (Cf. L. Smolinskii, 'Pianificazione senza teoria, 1917–1967', *L'Est, Rivista trimestrale, CESES*, 1971, no. 3, 76, from which the main lines of Ballod's essay have been here reproduced.)
13 Smolinskii, *cit.*, 79.
14 Working on GOERLO, Krzhizhanovskii hinted at the need for an economic plan based on interbranch relations, following the model proposed by Ballod for Germany (G.M. Krzhizhanovskii, *Izbrannoe*, Moscow, 1957, pp. 46, 66.). Popov, the head of the Central Statistical Administration in the early twenties, affirmed even that the planning methodology of Ballod was broadly applied during war communism (P.I. Popov, (ed.), *Balans narodnogo khoziaistva SSSR v 1923–24 goda*, Moscow, 1926, p. 20), exaggerating the role of 'planners' on the far from planned economy of war communism.
15 Cf. Smolinskii, 60–1.
16 See pp. 31–9 above.
17 N. Bukharin and E. Preobrazhenskii, *The ABC of Communism*, London, 1969, pp. 113–14.

18 Cf. N. Osinskii's article in *Oktiabr'skii perevorot i diktatura proletariata. Sbornik statei*, Moscow, 1919, p. 81.
19 N. Osinskii, *Stroitel'stvo sotsializma*, Moscow, 1918, p. 38.
20 Osinskii, *Oktiabr'skii perevorot*, pp. 77–8.
21 W. Rathenau, *L'economia nuova*, Turin, 1976, p. 44.
22 Cf. E.H. Carr, *The Bolshevik Revolution, 1917–1923*, 3 vols., London, 1952, vol. 2, p. 361.
23 N. Bukharin, *Imperialism and World Economy*, London, 1972, pp. 149–51, 156.
24 V.I. Lenin, *Sochineniia*, 3rd edn, Moscow, 1924–37, vol. 21, pp. 261–2.
25 Rathenau, pp. 45–7. See also Chapter 4 for Kritsman's excerpts.
26 Rathenau, p. 48.
27 It was with pride that Miliutin wrote in June 1920 that 'all enterprises and all industrial branches are considered like a single large enterprise. Instead of competition, instead of struggle, Soviet Power with determination implements the principle of the unity (*edinstva*) of the national economy in the economic field' (V.P. Miliutin, *Narodnoe khoziaistvo Sovetskoi Rossii*, 1920, p. 8).
28 Cf. Carr, *The Bolshevik Revolution*, vol. 2, pp. 363–5 and V.I. Lenin, *Collected Works*, 4th edn., 45 vols., London, 1964–70, vol. 27, p. 589n and pp. 320–1.
29 *Biulleten' VSNKh*, no. 1, 1918, 27.
30 V.I. Grinevetskii, *Poslevoennye perspektivy Russkoi promyshlennosti*, Kharkov, 1919, p. 102.
31 *Biulleten' VSNKh*, no. 1, 1918, 27.
32 *Ibid.*, p. 21.
33 *Trudy I Vserossiikogo S''ezda Sovnarkhozov*, pp. 180–1.
34 *Natsionalizatsiia promyshlennosti i organizatsiia sotsialisticheskogo proizvodstva v Petrograde (1917–1920 gg). Dokumenty i materialy*, vol. 2, Leningrad, 1960, pp. 44–6.
35 *Ibid.*, p. 46.
36 *Ibid.*, pp. 36–8.
37 *Ekonomicheskaia Zhizn'*, no. 3, 10 November 1918, 1.
38 *Ekonomicheskaia Zhizn'*, no. 32, 14 December 1918, 1.
39 *Ekonomicheskaia Zhizn'*, no. 25, 6 December 1918, 2.
40 *Trudy II Vserossiiskogo S''ezda Sovnarkhozov*, pp. 15–16.
41 *Ekonomicheskaia Zhizn'*, no. 39, 22 December 1918, 2.
42 A. Bogdanov, *A Short Course of Economic Science*, London, 1925, p. 383.
43 *Ekonomicheskaia Zhizn'*, no. 39, 22 December 1918, 2.
44 *Ibid.*
45 On collective commodity exchange, see pp. 341–9.
46 *Izvestiia*, 24 November 1918, 1.
47 *8i S''ezd RKP(b). 18–23 Marta 1919 g*, Moscow, 1933, p. 392.
48 L. Kritsman, *Edinyi khoziaistvennyi plan i komissiia ispol'zovaniia*, 1921, p. 15.
49 *Izvestiia*, 24 November 1918, 1.
50 Kritsman, *Edinyi khoziaistvennyi plan*, pp. 15–17.
51 *Ibid.*
52 I.A. Gladkov, *Voprosy planirovaniia Sovetskogo khoziaistva v 1918–1919*, Moscow, 1951, pp. 81–2.
53 Kritsman, *Edinyi khoziaistvennyi plan*, pp. 37–43.
54 *Ibid.*, pp. 44–5.

55 *Ibid.*, p. 24.
56 *Ibid.*, pp. 16 8.
57 *Ibid.*, pp. 49–50.
58 *Ibid.*, p. 24.
59 *Izvestiia*, no. 234, 19 October 1919, 4.
60 *Narodnoe Khoziaistvo*, 1920, nos. 15–16, p. 2.
61 *Izvestiia*, 10 December 1920, no. 278, 2.
62 Cf. S. Grishechko-Klimov's article in *Ekonomicheskaia Zhizn'*, reproduced in Kritsman, *Edinyi khoziaistvennyi plan*, pp. 59–63.
63 *Ibid.*, pp. 71–5.
64 *Ibid.*, pp. 76–7.
65 *Sobranie uzakonenii*, 1920, no. 93, art. 508.
66 *9i S"ezd RKP(b)*, pp. 82–3.
67 *Sobranie uzakonenii*, 1921, no. 1, art. 2.
68 V.I. Lenin, *Collected Works*, vol. 31, pp. 510–13.
69 *Ibid.*, p. 513.
70 *Narodnoe Khoziaistvo*, 1920, nos. 15–16, 3.
71 Lenin, *Collected Works*, vol. 32, p. 137.
72 Lenin, *Collected Works*, vol. 35, p. 475.
73 *Ibid.*, pp. 476–7.
74 *Ibid.*, pp. 480–1.
75 Lenin, *Collected Works*, vol. 32, p. 137.
76 *Ibid.*, p. 137.
77 But much work had been done before the revolution, and use was made of it. For a detailed comparison between GOERLO and preceding works – embodying planning criteria – conducted by Grinevetskii, see: L. Smolinskii, 'Grinevetsky e l'industrializzazione Sovietica', *L'Est, Rivista trimestrale, CESES*, 1968, no. 4, 95–117.
78 Lenin, *Collected Works*, vol. 32, pp. 138–9.
79 *Ibid.*, pp. 371–2.
80 *Ibid.*, pp. 371–3.
81 Cf. Carr, *The Bolshevik Revolution*, vol. 2, pp. 780–1.
82 *Narodnoe Khoziaistvo*, 1920, nos. 15–16, 5–6.
83 A.P. Serebrovskii, *Upravlenie zavodskimi predpriiatiiami*, 2nd edn; Moscow, 1919, pp. 27–8.
84 *Narodnoe Khoziaistvo*, 1918, nos. 6–7, pp. 11, 17.
85 *Natsionalizatsiia ... v Petrograde*, vol. 2, pp. 114–17.
86 *Ibid.*, p. 119.
87 *Ibid.*, p. 123.
88 A. Vainshtein, *Metody bezdenezhnogo ucheta khoziaistvennykh predpriiatii*, Nar. Kom. Zemledeliia, 1921, pp. 73–93.
89 *Ibid.*, p. 81.
90 *Ibid.*, p. 81.
91 *Ibid.*, p. 81.
92 *Ibid.*, p. 82.

7

Food procurement

During the First World War, a series of measures were undertaken by the Tsarist government to control the market in cereals and raw materials. The peculiar location of industry in Russia made the problem of food supply harder than in other countries. The producing regions formed a semicircle around the largest areas of consumption in the north, north-west, west and centre of the country. The largest consuming regions absorbed a yearly average of about 241 million puds* of the principal cereals – wheat, rye, oats and barley, which were provided by other regions. The largest industrial centres belonged to the consuming regions.[1] The producing belt included the Ukraine, Novorossiisk, and the Central Agricultural Regions from the south-west to the south-east of Russia. The south-western, Ukrainian and south-eastern regions produced the four principal cereals and dispatched a total of 228 million puds of rye and wheat, plus 30 million puds of barley.[2]

The transport system suffered from chronic shortages of rolling stocks, low capacity of the lines and uneven geographical distribution of the railway network. As compared with other countries, pre-war Tsarist Russia revealed its backwardness in this field. Russia had a tenth of the length of German railway lines per 100 sq. km. and about an eighth of the French. Total Russian railway capacity was less than half the German and about a third of the French. The maximum capacity of the lines east of Petrograd–Moscow–Kharkov–Sevastopol was only a third of that in the western part of the country.[3]

During the war military shipments running from the East to the West rapidly congested eastern transport and traffic from the South to the North was blocked. Food supplies coming from the eastern and southern

*1 pud is equivalent to 16.38 kg.

regions could hardly reach western and central consuming regions. Moreover, by January 1917, 16.8 per cent of the locomotives needed repair.[4]

In 1915 the Tsarist Government formed a special commission for foodstuffs with extensive rights of price regulation.[5] The commission fixed local price rates for agricultural goods and decided to reduce exports.

The government, however, had a hard time enforcing price control. Although a moderate price increase was allowed in the autumn of 1916, the food procurement agents in several cases negotiated local prices above governmental ceilings.[6] On 29 November 1916, an order from the Minister of Agriculture introduced *razverstka*, that is, the requisitioning from producers of a pre-established quota of cereals. Provincial quotas were to be computed on the basis of the harvest, stocks in hand, and consumption of the province. Further subdivisions of the obligatory quotas were planned at the level of the *uezd*, *volost*, village and individual farmers.[7]

The planned *razverstka* for 1917 was about 772 million puds of various grains, a quantity which was not much below net marketing in pre-war years according to the lowest estimates of pre-war grain output.[8] The target was ambitious, but no special machinery to carry it out at the local level was set up.[9] There are no complete figures on the achievements of *razverstka*. At the end of the collection year an enquiry by the Provisional Government revealed that no more than 100 million puds were collected over 2,070 *volosti*. Since food procurement agents and military organs resolved in some cases to buy foodstuffs at market prices, the total figure of collected grains during the agricultural year 1916–1917 (excluding the Ukraine and Turkestan), reported as being 393,089,000 puds, i.e. about half of the planned *razverstka*,[10] cannot be considered solely a result of the new method of collection. In 1917 the situation in the industrial centres was already becoming critical. The urban population had risen from 22 million before the war to 28 million in 1916.[11] According to Soviet sources, between December 1916 and February 1917 only 14–16 per cent of total demand for foodstuffs was met.[12] Other factors, besides the congestion of the transport system, jeopardized food procurement. Normal trading in foodstuffs was seriously affected by expectation of price increases, the corruption of state commissioners responsible for grain purchase, military impediments to transport and the accumulation of grain at the railways.[13] Market prices began to reflect the separation of the markets and the distress of the towns. In December 1915 the price of wheat flour was 2.63 rubles per pud in Kiev and 3.48 in Moscow. A pud of oats cost four rubles in Moscow and forty kopeks in Akmolinsk, in the Steppe Region.[14] In Russia the average increase in the price of foodstuffs for the first two years of the war was about 114 per cent, as compared with the corresponding increase of 50–70 per cent in Britain.[15]

In the second half of 1916 the central industrial regions received only 36.8 per cent of the planned provisions. Moscow received only 35.5 per cent.[16] Food procurement became a crucial issue for the Provisional Government also. In March 1917 it established the state monopoly of grain and introduced fixed prices for cereals. The law established that cereals were to be kept at the disposal of the government and were subject to state purchase, except those quotas which were estimated as necessary for consumption and for the economic requirements of the farm household.[17] The consumption norms were worked out taking into account the size of the cultivated area, the size of the household, the number of hired peasants paid in kind and the number of livestock. Speculation was to be punished by requisitioning stocks at half the ordinary price. The law, however, admitted the assistance of private organization of food procurement, paid on a commission basis. Some forms of compulsory requisition were applied in May 1917, but as a rule, the Provisional Government preferred to increase purchase prices.[18] Until the October Revolution, market rules virtually prevailed. The state purchase price policy of the Provisional Government seems to have taken into account regional differences, fixing higher prices in regions such as Petrograd and Moscow, where demand was higher, and lower prices in the food supply provinces (see Table 7.1). The state purchase of cereals and fodder increased from a total of 305 million puds in 1914–15 to 502 million in 1915–16 and 508,125,000 puds in 1916–17.[19]

Together with the policy of fixed purchase prices for grain and norms on requisition, which were dictated by the war, the Provisional Government undertook some steps for the implementation of far more ambitious and all-encompassing plans concerning agriculture and trade. The goal of greater marketable output, the reduction of which was generally ascribed to the fall of landlords' cultivated area, which before the war had provided 70 per cent of the marketed output,[20] was aimed at in two ways. On the one hand, it was sought by a policy directed to improve the productivity of peasants' farms. Assistance to farms was planned in terms of provision of seeds, implements and other means of production. On the other hand, it was sought by a far-ranging scheme of state commodity exchange, which was to induce peasants to sell foodstuffs in exchange for industrial products at price ratios established by the government. The latter approach may have been furthered by food commissioners' reports indicating that peasants held their stocks because of the lack of industrial products on the market,[21] although it is also likely that these reports were exaggerated to conceal the inefficiency and

Table 7.1   *State purchase prices for 1 pud of rye and rye flour (kopeks)*

Provinces	5 October 1917 (rye)	14 October 1918 (rye flour)	12 March 1919 (rye)	12 March 1919 (rye flour)
Akmolinsk	410	1675		
Vitebsk	540	2200	2540	2840
Vladimir	570	2300	2620	2920
Voronezh	486	1950	2360	2660
Viatka	470	1900	2290	2590
Kostroma	580	2350	2680	2980
Moscow	570	2300	2620	2920
Nizhnii Novgorod	565	2300	2620	2920
Orel	506	2050	2470	2770
Orenburg	500	2025	2400	2700
Penza	486	1950	2350	2650
Perm	470	1900	2290	2590
Petrograd	600	2425	2730	3030
Riazan	506	2050	2430	2730
Samara	460	1925	2320	2620
Saratov	486	1950	2350	2650
Simbirsk	486	1950	2350	2650
Smolensk	530	2175	2510	2810
Tambov	486	1950	2350	2650
Ufa	470	1900	2290	2590
Yaroslavl	500	2325	2680	2980

Source: Sbornik Postanovlenii i rasporiazhenii obshchikh i mestnykh (reguliruiushchikh prodovol'stvennoe delo v Moskve), vyp. 1 (Izd. po 1-e ianvaria 1918), Moscow, 1918, pp. 78–80, 120–3 and Sistematicheskii Sbornik dekretov i rasporiazhenii Pravitel'stva po prodovol'stvennomu delu, 2 (January–September 1919), Novgorod, 1920, pp. 619–37; also Izvestiia, no. 55, 12 March 1919.

corruption, elsewhere denounced, of the food procurement state agents. At any rate, specific sections of the Ministry for Foodstuffs were charged with computing the demand for agricultural machinery, metals and other goods, and with establishing selling prices. A ministerial fund formed through state purchase was to be provided for distribution to the rural population of such prime necessities as metal, metal products, leather, leather goods, fabrics and kerosene.[22] To begin with, a sum as large as four milliard rubles seems to have been assigned to state purchase of grain.[23] At the same time, the existing local foodstuffs committees were re-organized at the *oblast* and provincial level, allowing for a broader participation of *zemstvos*, cooperatives, soviets of workers' deputies and private organizations. The broad reshuffling of the food procurement policy and administration, carried out by the Provisional Government, which some observers blamed for both the waste of money it entailed and the incompetence of the newly appointed officials,[24] was a legacy which no doubt conditioned the Bolshevik approach to food procurement and commodity exchange, to an extent that will be revealed only by the publication of pertinent documentation and serious research into the atmosphere of the 'imagination in power' after March 1917.

7.2 FOOD PROCUREMENT AFTER THE OCTOBER REVOLUTION

The Soviet People's Commissariat for Food Procurement (*Narkomprod*) absorbed both the former administrative divisions in charge of the distribution of agricultural machinery and tools and the former attitude to the question of food supply. Large stocks of agricultural tools passed under its control. Thanks to that the Northern and Moscow *Oblast* foodstuffs committees were able to start some forms of commodity exchange, using their stocks of machines, in barter for agricultural products.[25]

Centrally controlled commodity exchange found a favourable ideological framework in the Bolshevik milieu. *Narkomprod* was made responsible not only for supply of foodstuffs to the population and the army, but also for the procurement of agricultural tools, seeds, metals and other industrial products for mass consumption, following the example of the former ministry. The Bolshevik approach to food procurement, however, had some peculiarities of its own, to some extent related to new aspects of the food crisis, arising not only from the change in power itself but also to the ideology of the new leadership.

Reports to the All-Russian TsIK in November 1917 indicated that foodstuffs were insufficient not only for Moscow and Petrograd, but also in other provinces, such as Kostroma, Vladimir and Smolensk. Available foodstuffs were calculated as sufficient to meet no more than a quarter of demand.[26] On 29 December 1917, food procurement officials declared that *Narkomprod* was preparing to dispatch 120 wagons of manufactures to the food-producing provinces in exchange for grain.[27] At the same time, one of the first decrees of the Bolshevik Government granted to the local municipalities the right to take control of the foodstuff freights formerly dispatched to special institutions and persons with the right to supply themselves independently of the local authorities, and to distribute the foodstuffs through their own food agencies.[28] This opened the door to anarchy and arbitrary decision-making. Later, a former official of *Narkomprod* affirmed that this decree was the prelude to the May decree on food dictatorship which gave extraordinary powers to the Commissar for Food Procurement.[29] The decree anticipated, in fact, the Bolshevik approach to food procurement which would prevail later, although the Bolsheviks were divided on the question of more drastic measures in this field. The need for central coordination of the several organs concerned in one way or another with the provision of foodstuffs – the state organs, the former ministry, the railways – was generally agreed upon. But, while some Bolsheviks urged the confiscation of foodstuffs as means of tackling speculation, others observed that there could not be any more dealings with the peasants if such measures were implemented.[30]

Towards the end of the year, the food situation appeared to improve. Shlikhter affirmed, on behalf of *Narkomprod*, that things were settling down in spite of active counter-revolutionary sabotage, that a colossal quantity of grain existed in Russia and that bread rations could be increased immediately.[31] The short-lived optimism was probably due to the over-estimation of the peasants' willingness to sell grain at fixed prices in the situation of growing inflation and rising farm consumption, as well as to over-estimation of their need for industrial products. The land reform of November 1917 induced a flow of people to the countryside to take part in the distribution of land. By the spring of 1918 it was calculated that about two million had returned to the countryside.[32] But this was not the only factor affecting the net marketability of grain. The redistribution of land holdings promoted by the land reform was apparently carried out as a general rule on a *per mouth* basis as distinct from *per pair of hands* (i.e. according to consumption norms instead of labour norms). Some sources present coefficients of distribution reflecting this conception: coefficients were set at 1.0 for men, for women at 0.8, for young people at 0.75, for boys at 0.6 and for babies at 0.5.[33] Comparisons between the samples of farms presented by different sources seem to confirm that a remarkable reduction of the size of farms took place in 1918, although we do not have figures for that year, and the debate is still open as to the actual degree of land equalization occuring after the revolution. Knipovich's figures show 59.1 per cent of households having less than four desiatins in 1916 and 74.0 per cent in 1919 (see Table 7.2). Other figures for 1917 and 1919 give respectively 57.6 per cent and 72.2 per cent of the households having less than four desiatins.[34]

This reduction occurred at the expense of wealthier peasants, as well as voluntarily, because some of the largest households decided to turn over a part of their land to the older sons and their families so as to take full advantage of the free provision of timber out of state forests or former landlords' woods.[35] Most of the small farms were in the North and the Central Industrial regions,[36] that is, those most affected by the food crisis.

Table 7.2. *Distribution of households according to size of farms, 1916–19*
(per cent)

	No. of households	Landless	Less than 4 desiatins	4–8 desiatins	more than 8 desiatins
1916	6,034,114	11.4	59.1	21.6	7.9
1919	6,119,616	6.5	74.0	16.6	3.1

Source: B. Knipovich, 'Napravlenie i itogi agrarnoi politiki 1917–1920', *O zemle*, vyp. 1, 1921, 23–5

Table 7.3. *Distribution of farms according to number of working horses and cows, 1917–19 (per cent)*

	working horses		cows	
	none	4 or more	none	4 or more
1917	28.7	1.2	17.9	3.1
1919	25.1	0.7	15.7	1.0

Source: Knipovich, p. 25

Egalitarian criteria seem to have prevailed also in the redistribution of working animals and cattle. (See Table 7.3).

According to Knipovich's figures, the number of farms having one horse increased from 43.8 per cent to 79.3 per cent between 1917 and 1919.[37] It is likely that the improved situation of the average farm increased its potential for self-sufficiency. The traditional handicraft skills of the peasantry helped to make it less dependent on industrial products[38] and, therefore, added to the factors promoting a reduction of the marketable surplus at current prices. Moreover, the narrowing of purchase price differentials between consuming and producing regions, carried out by the Bolsheviks' policy (see Table 7.1) added new incoherence in the already difficult food situation. The state purchase price for rye in Samara was 76.6 per cent of that in Petrograd in 1917, 79.4 per cent in 1918 and 84.9 per cent in 1919. It increased by 31.8 per cent between 1917 and 1918 and by 20.5 per cent between 1918 and 1919, while the purchase prices in Petrograd increased by 30.4 per cent and 12 per cent respectively.

Less inclined to adopt the moderately reformistic although imaginatively bold approach to food procurement which characterized the

Provisional Government's policy when confronted with immediate, and probably unforeseen, difficulties, the Bolshevik Government opted for coercive measures, on which ideology exerted an influence which deserves some consideration.

7.3 IDEOLOGY AND FOOD PROCUREMENT POLICY

The political framework which conditioned Bolshevik food procurement policy was class struggle. The small group of people who took power in the autumn of 1917 fully realized that the decisive factor for consolidation of the new regime was support of the urban proletariat.

Social tensions, which a less dramatic economic situation could have helped to smooth out gradually, became burning issues when scarcity of goods and hunger, owing to the economic isolation of the country, sharpened the division between towns and countryside and emphasized the proletariat's expectations of politically governed economic changes. When confronted with difficulties of all sorts, workers' delegations from the industrial centres applied directly to Lenin – as the peasants used to apply to the Tsar – as to a charismatic leader capable of enforcing immediate decisions on the Soviet institutions.[39] The resentment of the industrial working class at speculative withholding of grain from the market increased since the peasantry seemed to improve its standard of living considerably, thanks to the process of land distribution, whereas urban life deteriorated progressively because of the scarcity of food. In the months of agitation which followed the seizure of power, it seemed that only the peasants had really benefited from the 'proletarian' revolution. This resentment found a fertile soil in the ideological background of the leadership, who were inclined to interpret the food crisis mainly in terms of speculation and kulak greed rather than as a more complex phenomenon, depending on the general economic disorganization, particularly of transport, as well as on the prevalence of small-scale farming, a feature which only some Soviet economists emphasized.[40]

The Bolshevik leadership concentrated all its energies in trying to solve economic and social problems which former governments had left unresolved. But, like the former governments, the Soviet leadership could not find a workable compromise between opposing interests, and was unable to put forward a coherent alternative economic policy. Marxism provided too schematic a framework for the very complex social reality confronting the new power. Since it concerned a developed capitalist system, it could not offer positive indications for a basically rural country like Russia.[41] In 1914, the urban population of the entire territory later to become the Soviet Union was estimated to be only 24.7 million while the rural population accounted for the remaining 114.6 million.

The socio-economic determinism of Marx's analysis was the basis of the
ideology and policy of all European parties of the Marxist creed, which
derived from this analysis the leading and exclusive role of the proletariat
in political change as well as the subordinate position of other social strata
to the Marxian scheme of social change.[42] Lenin's theory of the vanguard
party provided a most important addition. Following this theory a
threefold goal was pursued and attained. Firstly, the contradiction
between the charismatic role of the proletariat and its incompetence in
crucial leading posts[43] was made irrelevant, since the *party* would be the
living consciousness of the proletariat.[44] Secondly, the social composition
of the leadership would not necessarily have to reflect the class whose
interests it claimed to interpret and promote. Thirdly, the leadership,
which by definition was the trustee of the political creed, was legitimized
in adopting policies which might oppose the immediate interests and
aspirations of the masses so long as the general aims required them. By
and large the role attributed to the proletariat by Marxism and the
nature of the Bolshevik Party exerted an indirect influence on the range of
policies towards the peasantry that the leadership was willing to adopt.
Essentially made up of intellectuals and others totally deprived of contact
with the rural population,[45] the party leadership tended to minimize the
role of the latter in the social transformation and, conversely, to emphasize its importance as a mass to manoeuvre. It was not accidental that
the Bolshevik Party had no peasant constituency. Unlike the *Narodniki*
(populists, from *narod* = people), who were persuaded that the peasantry
were the key to Russian social development,[46] the Russian Marxists
adhered to the Western European belief in social progress along the
industrial pattern.[47] The *Narodniki* attached such importance to Russian
tradition and history as to believe that Russia would not necessarily have
to follow the Western path of capitalism. The Russian Marxists, who
owed much to the teaching and leadership of Plekhanov, believed that
Russia was undergoing the changes which had been experienced in
Western Europe. They emphasized the role of the new classes, the
proletariat and the bourgeoisie, as instruments of the transformation of
the precapitalist Russia. Conversely, the role of those strata which in the
Marxian analysis were bound to disappear, such as small producers and
farmers, both included under the name of petty-bourgeoisie, was
minimized. Isaac Deutscher remarks how this 'strictly' or even exclusively proletarian attitude, so distrustful of the peasantry, was
characteristic of the entire Russian Social Democratic Party.[48] Until the
beginning of the twentieth century, Lenin also basically adhered to this
approach. Like other Marxists, he expected the proletarianization of the

Russian peasantry and the widening of the cleavage between a minority of capitalist farmers and a majority of 'proletarianized' peasants.[49] From the political point of view, this meant that relations with the peasantry were to be governed by efforts to awake the peasants' consciousness.[50]

Within the Marxist movement different assessments of the strategy for power emerged in the early 1900s, following the appearance of a liberal movement and the outburst of peasants' revolts. The signal of the formation of a liberal–moderate party was the appearance of the journal *Osvobozhdenie* (*Emancipation*), published in 1902 by a small liberal group led by Struve, Bulgakov and Tugan Baranovskii. The liberals estimated that Russia was ready for peaceful reforms and that the *zemstvos* could become the nucleus of local democracy in Russian society.[51] The gathering of liberals around a political organ sharpened divergences between the Menshevik and the Bolshevik wings of the Social Democratic Party. The Mensheviks emphasized the possibility of tactical collaboration between bourgeois and proletarian movements and envisioned support of the bourgeois revolution by proletarian elements. Conversely, Lenin feared that this alliance could turn against the interests of the proletariat. *Osvobozhdenie*, as a matter of fact, had a very moderate stand on elections, whose consequences were considered dangerously unpredictable if classes 'unaccustomed to political life' were to participate in them.[52] The events of 1905 further promoted an alternative strategy to power, based on the support of the peasantry.[53] What distinguished that of 1905 from other revolts was the combination of peasants' insurrection with the use of strikes and barricades by the working class in Moscow. This premature test of a possible alliance between the proletariat and the peasantry, however, did not infringe the dogma of the leading role of the proletariat. Lenin was always firm on that point. His comment on the second draft of Plekhanov's project for the Social Democratic Party Programme was that there existed a greater possibility for attracting small producers into the ranks of the party than was the case in the West. But, added Lenin, this was only a possibility, not an actuality, and the proletariat as a class was still to be distinguished from the rest of the population.[54] While focusing on the opportunity for an alliance with the peasantry, Lenin put further emphasis on the need for the hegemony of the proletariat. The suspicion remained that once the peasants had achieved their goals, above all, that of becoming independent smaller producers, they would turn against the proletariat in its striving for socialism. In the 1906 revision of the Agrarian Programme of the Party, Lenin affirmed: 'We shall support the peasants' movement to its end, but we must remember that this movement is that of a class other than the one which may and will accomplish the socialist overturn.'[55] The peasants' movement had to be supported 'without losing sight of the inclination for property of the peasant-owner, an inclination which will manifest itself as soon as the process of revolution takes off.'[56] This point was shared by Trotskii, who with his usual emphasis predicted that the peasantry would betray the revolution as soon as it had satisfied its own interests.[57] The difference between Trotskii and Lenin at that time was not a matter of strategy but of tactics. Neither of them wanted the transitional phase of compromise between antagonistic interests to last. But Trotskii concluded that the dictatorship of the proletariat and the peasantry had to be converted rapidly into proletarian dictatorship, while Lenin hoped that the revolutionary movement could be reinforced by attracting into it the most disinherited strata of the peasantry. The peasants' committees mentioned by Lenin in 1905[58] were much on the lines of the rural poor committees, *kombedy*, whose formation was promoted by the Bolshevik leadership in the spring of 1918.

For Lenin the peasantry was not to be a partner, but a follower subject to surveillance. The Marxist ideology entitled the proletariat to pursue its interests in the revolutionary struggle, but it did not provide scope for the aspirations of the peasants. The Russian peasants were eager for land. They probably did not care whether land distribution would be the result of socialization, municipalization or nationalization, which were matters of dispute between populists, Social-Revolutionaries and Marxist factions.[59] Lenin, on the other hand, focused on the form of expropriation of land. He believed that the nationalization of land was necessary, because it meant the prevalence of state interests (with the special significance that this would have in a socialist country) over the interests of the peasantry as a class. Theoretical arguments were borrowed from Marx himself. Marx had focused on the distinction between differential and absolute rent. While differential rent would not disappear with nationalization, since it depended on the differential fertility of the land, absolute rent would be abolished. The advantage of nationalization would be twofold, according to Lenin. Differential rent would become state rent, i.e. national income, and prices in agriculture would be lowered, the decrease being equal to the absolute rent. Following Marx, Lenin believed that the peasants had no interest in investing in land, since investment benefited the landlords alone.[60] This argument, however, applied also to state ownership, if the payment of rent had to remain; but Lenin did not pursue the question. He rather stressed that money spent on the buying and selling of landed properties was lost as potential investment, and therefore private property was detrimental to growth.[61] These arguments were developed when the main hypothesis was still that of a transition to a 'state' capitalist system, as a stage preceding the socialist revolution.

Lenin added a specific personal contribution in support of national-ization as an alternative to municipalization, which other members of the party, like Plekhanov and Larin, defended. Lenin maintained firstly that municipalization did not abolish absolute rent – and therefore higher prices; and, secondly, that municipalization circumscribed the class struggle and substituted particular claims for general ones.[62] When, after the 1905 Revolution, Plekhanov observed that municipalization was a more democratic system than nationalization, which strengthened state power,[63] Lenin replied that the capitalist state was centralized and that only a centralized peasants' movement could fight against centrali-zation.[64] His preference for nationalization was also based on the belief that it was better suited to the introduction of modern farming and increased productivity of the land. Lenin did not believe that the springs of technical progress could reach the backward and ignorant Russian peasants without the intervention of the government. But above all, public intervention was to profit the working class. Thus he did not share Larin's opinion that in the Russian case the payment of rent to the local municipalities was to the benefit of economic growth.[65] Following Kautsky, Lenin believed that large agricultural estates were necessarily far more efficient than small farms. The apparent efficiency of small farms, conversely, except for the case of specialized cultures, was explained by the under-consumption of the farmers.[66] At the First Congress of Peasants' Deputies held in Petrograd between May and June 1917, at which the Socialist-Revolutionaries were strongly represented, Lenin warned the peasants that land distribution would not help them to overcome the difficulties stemming from the uneven distribution of implements, animals and financial means. At the congress Lenin put forward his April Theses on nationalization of land and the conversion of large estates into model farms – which had been finally accepted by the Bolshevik Party (though with some dissent)[67] – and tried to convince his audience that the interests of agricultural labourers would be better served if independent local organizations of agricultural labourers got control of the land, and if common cultivation of land with the best machinery and under the guidance of scientifically trained agronomists were undertaken. 'We cannot continue farming in the old way', he affirmed to the peasants' representatives. 'If we continue as before on our small isolated farms, albeit as free citizens on free soil, we are still faced with imminent ruin.'[68] Lenin's dramatic vision of the future was certainly exaggerated, since given the great backwardness of Russian agriculture, even modest financial help and technical improvement may still have resulted in productivity increase; however, his position had some validity in so far as there were then no clear signs that such financial aid would be forthcoming. At any rate, Lenin's radical standing on the agrarian question and his criticism of land partitioning in accordance with the traditional labour or subsistence standards did not find much support.[69] The lack of peasant support, however, did not induce Lenin to reconsider his too rigid ideological tenets. On the contrary, he chose to put even greater emphasis on the radicalization of the social struggle. His April Theses of 1917 revealed the potential for compulsion which remained in the ideology, despite the attention paid to the peasantry as a re- volutionary force. Carrying to extremes the thesis of the polarization of the Russian peasantry, Lenin focused on the political importance of the process by which poor farmers were often turned into wage labourers. In his view, hired peasants, seasonal workers and the rural poor (semi- proletarian elements) were to join the industrial proletariat against capitalism because their antagonists, the middle and wealthy peasants, were in fact capitalists – as he did not hesitate to call them.[70]

Belief in the polarization of the peasant society had become part of the Russian approach to society and agriculture, 'not only', as Shanin put it, 'in the normative, but also in the cognitive sense'.[71] The Marxists, who were convinced that such would be the course of history, emphasized the social polarization expected from the Tsarist land reform and, conversely, under-estimated the complicated interactions of social, economic and cultural factors in the process of change, which much reduced the significance of polarization.

The situation of the peasantry had undergone significant changes since 1906. The area of land cultivated by the peasants doubled between 1892 and 1911. According to the data provided by Oganovskii and Kondrat'ev, covering forty-seven provinces of European Russia, in 1892 the peasants worked on their own land consisting of 16,252,000 desiatins; in 1905, they had 24,747,000 desiatins and in 1911, 30,439,000 desiatins, while the nobility then had 43,205,000 desiatins, which represented half of landlords' ownership in 1862.[72] Between 1911 and 1915 492,479 peasant farms bought land through the Peasant Bank. On the basis of a sample, covering forty-seven provinces, Oganovskii and Chaianov calculated that from 1906 to 1910 the gentry had lost 6,563,300 desiatins, while 5,617,000 desiatins went into the hands of the peasantry (including *kazaki*, settlers, and other rural citizens). Four-fifths of the purchased land was black-earth land. Most of the acquired plots ranged from 10 to 50 desiatins, but the tendency was towards smaller properties, say 9 or 10 desiatins.[73] The census of 1916 indicated that over a total sown area in forty-nine provinces covering 71,430,800 desiatins, 15,482,202 peasant farms (*krest'ianskie khoziaistva*) worked 63,743,900 desiatins of land, although peasants did not necessarily own this land. If the Caucasus and

Siberia were included, the figure would be increased to 7,686,900 desiatins.[74] By 1913, about half the land belonging to the nobility at the time of the emancipation had been sold, mainly to peasants, and half of the remainder had been rented out, again to the peasants. In 1914 to 1915, only about ten per cent of the land sown in Russia belonged to the estates. The nobility owned only 5 per cent of the livestocks.[75]

Peasant type farms were by 1916 the dominant form of land tenure, and not many of the other properties remained to be distributed to the peasantry to satisfy its hunger for land. Oganovskii pointed out on the basis of data provided by the Peasant Bank, which financed the peasant purchase of land, that after 1906 peasants had started buying land from other peasants, instead of from the gentry as before. Who was buying land? Stolypin aimed to strengthen the better-off peasants, to increase the productivity of land and to consolidate around the central power the support of a new agrarian class. But some estimates indicated that Russia was becoming a country of small farming. Most of the buyers were reported to be landless peasants and small farmers. Oganovskii estimated that between 1906 and 1912 16.3 per cent of the purchasers of land were landless peasants, 68.4 per cent were households with not more than nine desiatins, and 13.3 per cent had more than nine desiatins.[76] The small size of the peasant farms could also be derived from data on horse ownership. Considering that in Russia at least one horse was necessary for farming and two in the heaviest soils, and estimating that in 1912 36.5 per cent of the farms had no horses, 40.4 per cent had one or two and only 1.9 had four or more, Jasny concluded that the Russian countryside was characterized not so much by the riches of relatively few (as the Marxists believed), but by the great poverty of the mass.[77] His comment derives from an implicit comparison with countries more advanced in agricultural development. It might be argued, however, that some improvements in the peasants' well-being had taken place since 1905. Although precise data are not available, it can be concluded that between 1900 and 1913 (both years of good harvest) agricultural output increased more than the population. This was the result too of more extensive cultivation.[78]

The productivity per desiatin remained much below other countries, according to all the available estimates.[79] This explained the peasants' traditional hunger for land as well as what has been called the multidirectional dynamism of the peasant society and the peculiar aspects of its mobility,[80] which were ignored by the too schematic Marxist approach of the time.

When Lenin put forward the idea of alliance with the rural poor, he probably over-estimated their number. According to Lenin, in 1905 80.6

per cent of the Russian peasantry were poor, 7.7 per cent were middle peasants and 11.5 per cent were wealthy peasants (or capitalist farmers).[81] But the average size of a poor peasants' holding was estimated to be as high as seven desiatins. If Lenin had applied his 1905 criteria for defining peasant poverty to the relevant figures of the census of 1917 he would have come to the conclusion that the pauperization of the peasantry was overwhelming (see Table 7.4).

Increasing polarization – although not to the extent foreseen by Lenin – was also shown by studies based on the budgets of sample peasant households carried out by some *zemstvos*.[82] But dynamic studies which traced back the individual histories of peasant households and analysed them statistically showed that the relative uniformity and continuity of the peasant society hid a strong centripetal mobility in relation to median wealth, i.e. the rise of the poorer households and the descent of the wealthier ones.[83] Not all Russian Marxists were well acquainted with sophisticated techniques which could be, and were, used in such investigations. If they became concerned with measurements of relative wealth based on land holding and similar critieria, it was not only because such measures were relatively easier and available, but also because of their a priori adherence to the polarization thesis. If, on the other hand, evidence for polarization had been sought in the number of wage labourers in agriculture, it would have been rather weak. In 1917 there was only 1.4 million of them.[84]

Other elements which should have been taken into account if polarization processes alone had not been sought belonged to the specific culture of the peasant society, where levelling mechanisms concerned not only the practice of land redistribution, but a common way of living. Accidents such as bad harvests, famine, plague, and animal diseases, as well as the state taxation system, were seen as evil to all and enhanced the feelings of a common fate and mutual aid. The neglect of these elements and the confusion which was introduced into the otherwise clear concept of a rural proletariat by replacing Marxian qualifications with spurious and arbitrary indices of poverty led to a systematic under-estimation of the internal cohesiveness of the peasant communities, which turned out to be the source of political mistakes as to both the estimated consensus and the government's ability to control the peasantry. In the summer of 1917, when the peasantry claimed the distribution of the remaining land belonging to other strata, such as the gentry, the state and the church, and basically still adhered to the old redivision principles, Lenin stressed in *Pravda* that the Bolshevik position expressed and voted by the Party Congress in 1906 had to be maintained and translated into action. However odd it may sound, Lenin thought that the time had come to set

Table 7.4. *Size of peasant holdings (desiatins)*

Year of census	0	1	1–2	2–4	4–6	6–8	8–10	10–13	13–16	16–19	19–22	22–50
1917	11.49	10.34	18.4	29	14.6	7.34	3.82	2.68	1.6	0.55	0.29	0.14

Source: Ekonomicheskoe rassloenie krest'ianstva v 1917–1919 gg, Trudy TsSU, vol. 6, vyp. 3, Moscow, 1922, p. 20. The census covered the provinces of the Northern, Central Industrial and Central Agricultural Regions, the Middle and Lower Volga Regions, the regions of the Urals and Belorussia. Overall, it covered twenty-five provinces and 10 per cent of the total farm households.

up a rural workers' union which would start fighting against the wealthy peasants as well as against the 'equalized' land tenure. The party proposition read (Lenin's quote):

The Party should in *all* eventualities, and whatever the situation, with regard to democratic agrarian reforms, consider it as its tasks to steadfastly strive for an *independent class* organization of the *rural proletariat* and explain to it the irreconcilable antithesis between its interests and the interests of the peasant bourgeoisie, to warn it against illusions about the smallholding system, which can never, as long as commodity production exists, do away with the poverty of the masses, and lastly, to point to the need for a complete socialist revolution as the only means of abolishing all poverty and exploitation.'[85]

There is no sign that Lenin changed his ideas about the antagonistic character of the interests of the proletariat, including what he considered to be a rural proletariat, and the interests of the peasants in disposing on their own of the produce of the land, of the whole land – which was in fact a common goal of the peasantry as such. His attitude to this question may be considered as a red thread that, in spite of occasional alliances such as that with the Left Socialist-Revolutionaries on the morrow of the revolution[86], marked the continuity of the Bolshevik strategy towards the peasantry both before and after the Bolshevik Revolution.

7.4 COLLECTIVE COMMODITY EXCHANGE AS A MEANS OF FOOD PROCUREMENT: PRACTICE AND THEORY

In the first months of Soviet rule, food procurement was left to the spontaneous initiative of workers' organizations and local soviets. The local food procurement organs were directly subordinated to local soviets. Amidst the institutional breakdown which followed the revolution, workers' delegations started negotiating with the grain producing centres to get agricultural products in exchange for industrial goods. The initiative was taken by the largest industrial centres. On 9–10 December 1917, the Moscow Provincial Congress of Soviets came to an agreement with the Kolomna Soviet to obtain some goods wagons. Instructions were given to take an inventory of all stocks of manufactured and other industrial products, in order to set up a general plan for food procurement by way of exchange of industrial commodities for agricultural produce.[87] In February 1918, a delegation of workers and members of the procurement organs was sent to Eastern Russia to negotiate an exchange of goods wagons loaded with industrial commodities for grain.[88] A month later a delegation of Putilov workers left for Omsk with twenty-three goods wagons loaded mostly with agricultural tools, while agents of the

Petrograd Administration were sent to the provinces to negotiate the barter of manufactures for potatoes.[89] Some cases were reported of peasants' delegations trying to meet representatives of the industrial regions to negotiate the terms of trade.[90] But the pressure to re-establish town–countryside relations came essentially from the industrial centres.

Commodity exchange in place of money exchange was helped by the temporary disposal of stocks of industrial products by workers' committees, and by the financial crisis. The allegation that peasants refused money exchange because of the rapid depreciation of money cannot be accepted as a general rule which explains commodity exchange in all circumstances. In 1916, when the rate of inflation was not as high as in 1917, the foodstuffs agents of Kharkov province reported that peasants refused to deliver rye irrespective of its price, because of money depreciation.[91] But this was not true everywhere. Other reports emphasized the perverse effects of the official exchange ratio between industrial and agricultural prices or expectations of price increase.[92] Until late 1918 newspapers reported that peasants not only accepted monetary transactions, but in some cases even solicited them.[93] In December 1918 *Narkomprod* officials were sent to the Ukraine to buy cereals and for this purpose were endowed with 'large sums of money'.[94]

Lack of rubles at least as much as money depreciation became an incentive to barter in 1918. In April 1918, the Soviet Commissar for Finance, Gukovskii, observed that currency demand had multiplied many times as a result of the absence of any substitute for the financial and banking system, which had been destroyed by the Soviet Government, and as a result of the cost of nationalization.[95]

In Soviet literature, the allegation that peasants refused money does not take into account the effects of the price policy on food supply. Petitions for authorization to apply market prices, in order to collect more grain and other foodstuffs, were made until at least the end of 1919. In July 1918 the *uezd* soviet of Tambov declared that it was possible to buy grain at market prices.[96] An increase in the fixed price of grain was urged by the *uezd* soviet of Moscow.[97] At the Second Congress of *Sovnarkhozy*, in the autumn of 1918, Briukhanov, who was in charge of food procurement for the Moscow province, affirmed that the crucial question was to find satisfactory price ratios and declared that the August price increase was not sufficient.[98] The foodstuffs division of the Moscow Soviet claimed at the beginning of 1919 that *Narkomprod*'s prices for meat, raw agricultural materials and potatoes did not cover production costs and that they should be increased.[99] Similar charges were raised by local procurement agencies responsible for the purchase of non-monopoly products, i.e. those products whose prices were centrally fixed but whose purchase could be carried out independently of the state purchase organization.[100] In some cases local soviets decided independently to raise purchase prices above those centrally fixed.[101] The local procurement agents of the Samara province seized military funds to purchase grain, alleging that grain provisions were being jeopardized by lack of money.[102] The disagreements regarding price policy reached the highest authorities and continued until November 1919. In March 1919 the Council of Workers' Cooperatives claimed at the joint meeting of *Narkomprod, Narkomzem* and VSNKh that only price increases could act as an incentive to increase output.[103] Newspapers reported that peasants did not refuse to sell their stocks of raw materials, wool and leather when the price offered was satisfactory for local conditions.[104] In November 1919 the Moscow foodstuffs division estimated that potatoes could be bought in some provinces, if *Narkomprod* had authorized a price increase which took into account transportation and production costs.[105]

During 1919 and 1920 the economic situation was barely controllable by mere economic measures, and resort to administrative measures became inevitable. But in 1917 to 1918, recourse to ordinary economic tools might still have had an impact on the food crisis. Thus, it is a legitimate question to wonder why compulsory methods prevailed in food procurement from the very beginning. One reason derives from the nature of the Bolshevik Revolution itself. The banking system was destroyed before an alternative credit mechinery had been set up. The fear that money could be used to finance counter-revolution was one of the reasons for reducing the rate of issue in the spring of 1918.[106] The State Bank was not authorized to release funds to workers' committees, which in several cases performed managerial functions. In this situation factory workers started using commodity stocks as a means of exchange.[107] The centralization of the financial system did much to reduce the local capacity to negotiate the terms of trade with local producers.[108] At times soviets advertised the municipal selling of manufactured goods for cash in hand or grain.[109] Dispersed and autonomous commodity exchange had started before any central decision in this sense had been formulated. When the problem of coordinating several dispersed initiatives arose, the government, incapable of finding an immediate solution to the financial crisis, chose to put commodity exchange under state control and to bend it to a central policy of food procurement.

In March 1918 a three-month advance of 1,160 million rubles was assigned to *Narkomprod* for establishing commodity exchange with the countryside. *Narkomprod* was also granted the right of monopolistic purchase of the commodities destined for exchange.[110] Central policies were based on the concern that independent food procurement contributed to the exhaustion of the national stock of commodities, on the assumption that independent purchase prevented the enforcement of a fixed purchase price for grain,[111] and on the possibility of obtaining bank credit on easy terms from nationalized banks for *Narkomprod*'s purchases of industrial commodities to be exchanged for grain. Credit would be paid back after the sale of the collected foodstuffs.[112] In order to work, this plan had to be based on central price control, that is, a price ratio favourable to industrial commodities had to be imposed if food ration prices were to be lower than market prices and if credit received could be paid back. The question of a price ratio 'correct' for that purpose was behind the whole project of commodities purchased and the value of food rations sold was not to be covered by the state budget; it had to be covered by larger quantities of foodstuffs obtained in exchange or, in other words, by lower food unit prices, as compared to industrial prices. This approach, which was presented by Miliutin at the conference of food procurement committees at the end of January 1918, was probably VSNKh's approach to food procurement, reflecting the work done previously in this direction by the Economic Council under the Provisional Government.[113] To carry out this project, there should have been full state price control over final products and distribution. That was far from being realized or feasible. Nonetheless it was with this aim that people in charge of food procurement were confronting their tasks. A Council of Supply composed of fifteen Bolsheviks, eleven Left Socialist-Revolutionaries and maximalists and three non-faction members was charged to work out the details of this plan.[114] But the direction in which food procurement was going to move, under options more acceptable to the Bolsheviks, was better expressed by Lomov in an article published in *Pravda* on 10 February 1918.[115] Lomov recalled that before the revolution several food committees had already solved the problem of getting foodstuffs by sending commodities for exchange, and that this practice had spread even more afterwards. But he criticized the complications of this previous commodity exchange. As he saw it, buying grain required too many operations and too much money. Firstly, the food committee bought *products* from the factories for *money*, then it sent them to the food organs of the localities, which in turn bought *foodstuffs* with *money*, dispatching them back to the centre, where again they were sold for *money*. The operation, said Lomov, could be expressed as $M - C - M - C - M$ (M = money, C = commodities), whereas it would have been much simpler if direct commodity exchange had taken place between food committees and localities, i.e. $C - C$. Lomov did not advocate the abolition of money, merely shorter circulation. The reason for this was that – given differences in wealth among peasants – poor peasants were compelled to sell their grain at low prices, while wealthy peasants could wait, keeping their stocks to sell them later at higher prices. They gained more, they obtained more commodities and they were even able to speculate with them, selling them at higher prices to the needy. Lomov concluded by citing the Saratov case, where the *volost* collected both commodities and grain, according to the capacity of the suppliers, and delivered them according to the need of each person. He concluded that the realization of such a plan on an overall national scale raised major difficulties, but it could be achieved with power in the hands of proletarians and semi-proletarians.

The initial plan of *Narkomprod* was much more limited than Miliutin's or Lomov's projects, though it was inspired by their philosophy. It concerned 200.3 million arshins of fabrics to a total value of 401.2 million rubles. The fabrics were to be distributed among regions in relation to their capacity for food supply. Thus West Siberia and the Urals, which were relatively less populated, were planned to receive proportionately more fabrics. The following table outlines the plan of supply:

Table 7.5. *Planned distribution of fabrics by regions, 1918*

	Population (million)	Fabrics (million arshins)	Value in rubles (million)
West Siberia and South Urals	11.1	55.5	111.0
Kuban, North Caucasus and Tavria province	13.1	46.3	92.6
Ufa, Voronezh, Kursk, Orel, Tambov provinces	16.0	53.2	106.4
Perm, Viatka, Kazan provinces	10.1	14.8	29.6
Ural *oblast*, Kaluga, Penza, Riazan, Tula, Smolensk	10.8	10.5	21.6
South-East and Lower Volga Region	13.1	10.0	20.0
Central Regions	10.2	5.0	10.0
Northern Regions	5.9	5.0	10.0

Source: Orlov, *Prodovol'stvennaia rabota Sovetskoi Vlasti*, Moscow, 1918, p. 225.

Fabrics, garments, processed leather, boots, matches, tobacco, tea and a number of other products were transferred to *Narkomprod* to be exchanged for grain and other foodstuffs in accordance with centrally established rules and terms of trade.[116] Industrial prices were to be determined on the basis of factory price plus a mark-up for administrative costs. A fixed price was established for grain. The sale value would be certified by a receipt granting an equivalent amount of industrial products. *Narkomprod* was obliged to deliver the commodities within a month and for a value corresponding to at least a quarter of the value of the collected grain.[117]

The ratio of exchange between an arshin of fabric and a pud of cereals was set at 1 : 5. The *Narkomprod* officials estimated that the stock of manufactures controlled by *Tsentrotekstil'*, if used only for commodity exchange, would have been enough to collect the greater part of the last harvest until the new harvest was in.[118] The funds assigned to *Narkomprod* were determined by the limited capacity of the existing transport facilities and were linked to the list of commodities and their corresponding prices. This operation, which in its commercial aspect appeared as a mere transaction on delayed payments, had, however, a peculiarity which reflected ideological and political motivations: the application of class principles in exchange, as Sviderskii, one of the head officials of *Narkomprod*, described it.[119] The assignment of a fund for exchange to *Narkomprod* was immediately followed by the decree on commodity exchange of 2 April 1918. It was decided that commodity exchange should not operate on an individual basis, but according to collective responsibility, as the Tsarist fiscal system operated at the *mir* level. The industrial products were to be distributed among *volosti* in proportion to the overall delivery of grain, and were to be delivered to the *volost* population in equal proportions. The law categorically forbade commodities being delivered directly to single farmers. The rural poor were to be included in the organization of commodity exchange, in order to participate in the distribution of commodities. The April Decree stated also that Soviet power had the right to take measures designed to extract from the gentry the highest possible quantity of money and the right to take possession of all state means involved in commodity exchange.[120] An instruction of *Narkomprod* reiterated, soon after publication of the decree, the principle of *collective* commodity exchange.[121]

In the mean time, anarchy prevailed. *Glavki, tsentry* and food procurement *uezd* organizations were continuing their own policies of food procurement. Finished products which should have been under *Narkomprod*'s control, like matches, soap and tobacco, were sold directly by the central administrations, or were delivered by the factory-shop committees to whoever paid for them. *Tsentrotkan'*, which was made responsible for the collection of cotton fabrics, could control only 10 per cent of the sales.[122] Steps towards the registration and control of fabrics, essentially with the aim of limiting foreign trade, had already been taken by the Provisional Government.[123] In June 1918 the value of the stock of manufactures was calculated to be 700–800 million rubles and the current monthly output equal to 400–500 million rubles. *Narkomprod* urged *Sovnarkom* to release the funds necessary to buy all existing stocks of cotton fabrics and their current output. On 29 June 1918, *Sovnarkom* approved the decree on state purchase and distribution of cotton fabrics and assigned to *Narkomprod* one billion rubles for this purpose. A council for the distribution of fabrics was formed and charged with planning this activity. The right of purchase was limited to the Purchasing Bureau of *Tsentrotekstil'*. Free sale of fabrics was forbidden.[124] The operation of monopoly purchase, however, required more time than the heads of *Narkomprod* probably anticipated. To dispose of the entire marketable quantity, other administrations, such as the central union of cooperatives and the Moscow food procurement committee, were allowed to take part. Precious time was lost in trying to organize the whole business. In summer, when the harvest was at hand, the government decided to speed up the timing of the entire operation, without caring any further for commercial fairness. *Tsentrotekstil'*'s Purchasing Bureau was accused of employing antiquated methods of economic policy and practice. The heads of *Tsentrotekstil'* affirmed that 'they had no intention of wasting one billion rubles for the purchase of fabrics, when fabrics could be put under the control of the republic by means of registering the stocks'. Following this declaration, the Purchasing Bureau was suppressed and the whole operation was transferred to the *Tsentrotekstil'* board itself. On 23 July 1918, a decree obliged all textile mills to deliver all their stocks of fabrics to *Tsentrotekstil'* against payment on their current account. However, the effective dispatch of fabrics fell much short of the planned figures, in spite of the monopoly right established by the decree. Instead of 524 million rubles' worth of fabrics, only 221.3 million rubles' worth were dispatched from November 1917 to September 1918, mainly to Moscow (127 loaded wagons), Siberia (131), and the Northern Caucasus (140), while other provinces like Riazan and Smolensk received only two wagons each.[125] As for other products, the distribution did not reach even the 20 per cent of the whole quantity assigned to *Narkomprod*.[126]

Collective commodity exchange was not easy to implement. There were deficiencies in its organization, including plunderings and requisitions by armed groups.[127] The criteria of distribution were questionable. Frumkin, one of the head officials of *Narkomprod*, affirmed that products were allocated to those who produced least and delivered even less.[128] This outcome, indeed, was not independent of the principle of *collective* commodity exchange, i.e. of the application of egalitarianism in distribution, which was then considered a class principle. If the industrial products had been enough for everybody, the application of this principle to people accustomed to the fairly egalitarian way of living in the *mir* would not necessarily have produced resentment and refusal to deliver foodstuffs. But scarcity of industrial products, and privilege in distribution to non-producers of grain, were not good means to increase grain collection.

The marginal role that *actual* collective commodity exchange had in the first year of the central policy of food procurement does not mean, however, that its rationale was indifferent to the whole policy of collection and distribution, which was then taking place as an alternative to market rules.

The events which led to the centralization of food procurement over the whole population in the hands of a governmental body were of various kinds, as mentioned above: independent use of industrial products by factory committees, lack of financial means, fear of counter-revolutionary movements, social pressure, and so on. The leadership did not have a predetermined plan of food procurement. However, this does not mean that the Soviet policy of food procurement did not have any coherence. The policy was, indeed, inspired by a *model* of exchange, which some Soviet economists considered an alternative to market exchange. Orlov's *Prodovol'stvennaia rabota Sovetskoi Vlasti*, written in 1918,[129] while the system of exchange – distribution on the national level was taking shape, is a decisive source for understanding what alternatives were then taken into consideration and why they were discarded. 'The system of products-exchange, which we endeavoured to realize', Orlov explained, 'is as simple as justice itself: each citizen has the right to demand from the state his own produce, which has a general use value and which is necessary to him, as a citizen, for subsistence. Products delivered to him and released by him are priced according to universal prices based on the social average labour unit.'[130] The pillars on which this economic policy was based were two: VSNKh, responsible for the control of *production* (helped by the People's Commissariats for Trade and Agriculture), and *Narkomprod*, responsible for *distribution* of output (together with *glavki* and *tsentry*).[131] Relying on these organs, the leadership consciously endeavoured to put the market under control.

In the spring of 1918 the market could not be suppressed altogether. But there were definite efforts to limit and circumscribe market operations and to extend the policy of distribution from the centre by granting monopsonistic rights to central administrations and discriminating among people and institutions authorized to trade. On 27 May 1918, the Council of Supply, formed by representatives of *Narkomprod*, VSNKh, and the Commissariats of Trade and Industry, Communications, and

Agriculture, was attached to *Narkomprod*. The tasks of the council concerned the elaboration of all plans of distribution and state purchase. This council was crucial in the reorganization of *Narkomprod*,[132] which aimed at the unification into a single organ of the supply of all essential consumer goods, the distribution of these commodities on a state level, and finally the nationalization of trade. State distribution instead of market distributing raised some problems when pricing rules had to be decided. The fixing of the ratio between industrial and agricultural prices was examined by Soviet economists from the point of view of political opportunity as well as from an economic standpoint. Each alternative had its drawbacks. Fixed prices established in 1916 and 1917 did not correspond any longer to production costs, transport costs and pro-fitability. Though the crucial problem was to find a 'correct' price ratio between industrial and agricultural products, the absolute level of prices did also matter. If industrial prices were taken as given and agricultural prices were increased, labour prices, i.e. wages, should have been increased. This would have jeopardized, according to Soviet economists, the industrial price policy as well as the state financial policy concerning industry, i.e. it would have created difficulties for the State Budget. If foodstuffs prices and labour prices had been allowed to rise (Orlov assumed a fifty times increase), the monetary system would have been totally wrecked. If, on the other hand, foodstuffs prices had remained constant and all other prices had been correspondingly lowered, the peasantry would not have understood the intention of this decision (which, in addition, would have needed some time to be implemented).[133] In May 1918, the joint session of the procurement organs of the Moscow and Northern *raion* soviets proposed another alternative. Rather than changing the price ratio in favour of agricultural products, which market criteria would have imposed, the session proposed to enforce an arbitrary price ratio, by concentrating monopsonistic power of grain purchase and monopolistic power of industrial goods sale into the hands of the state. It was argued, consequently, that if the grain monopoly did not work, the prices of all industrial products of prime necessity should be raised. This was considered to be feasible inasmuch as industrial supply was monopolized.[134]

An increase of industrial prices, however, was compatible neither with market trends nor with political preoccupations. The drawbacks of each alternative suggested a compromise. Taking labour prices as constant, it was proposed to raise food prices four times and industrial prices ten to twelve times. It was thought that the state monopoly of industrial goods would make grain price control more acceptable to the peasantry, though some *Narkomprod* officials had no illusion about total consensus. This solution, because of its compromising nature, appealed to Lenin, who in the summer of 1918 was much less confident in the 'economic' solution of the class struggle in the countryside[135] than he was in April 1918. On 2 August 1918, he urged *Narkomprod* to opt for increasing the price of grain instead of lowering industrial prices, to increase grain supply and 'to help us to neutralize as many peasants as possible in the civil war'.[136] The decree authorizing the increase in the purchase price of grain was passed at about the same time as the decree on obligatory commodity exchange for the grain-producing regions.[137] This decree was presented as a development of the April decree on commodity exchange. In August 1918 the political and military situation had much worsened. The counter-revolution already controlled three-quarters of the territory of the country. The leadership, which relied heavily upon the economic respite granted by the good harvest of the summer of 1918 (it was hoped to harvest 1,246 million puds of grain in twenty provinces of the Soviet Republic),[138] concentrated on strengthening control over the grain surplus which remained available. These facts probably had an impact on the timing of the decree on obligatory commodity exchange, though they were not determinant for the basic points of economic policy. By August 1918 the possibility of using monopolized goods for exchange had already materialized. *Narkomprod* officials did, indeed, consider that sugar, salt and tea (already under total state control) could be used as a means to force the peasants to accept state terms of trade.[139] On the other hand, Miliutin had announced since May 1918, at the congress of *sovnarkhozy*, that economic policy was orientated towards gradual liquidation of free trade and that a prerequisite for this was state monopoly of consumer goods and fixed prices for all of them.[140] Trade control was one of the firm points of Bolshevik economic policy, on which the agreement was broad. The disagreements eventually concerned timing. Osinskii's request to enforce state monopoly on 'all products capable of extracting agricultural foodstuffs from the countryside', like coal, oil, metal products, transport, construction, building materials, machines, molasses, and fabrics, was not considered to be realizable in May, but its logic was not challenged.[141] On 3 June 1918, a resolution of the Moscow Congress of Soviets affirmed that the food procurement question was very closely linked with the question of organization of national production, with workers' control, and with monopolistic price ratios, and that this justified the direct concern of the Soviets, not only that of the food procurement organs, in such affairs.[142] When the extension of civil war in the countryside urged rapid decisions, the approach of the left wing of the party gained support and was taken as the basis for policy measures. At the Fifth Congress of Soviets Tsiurupa, the Commissar for Food Procurement, affirmed that fixed prices had to be established for all industrial products and that this fact implied the ownership by the state of all products which the state intended to supply to the people.[143]

The August decree on obligatory commodity exchange was concerned only with certain agricultural regions, specifically designated for food collection. In these regions, free trade in manufactures and in all other non-agricultural goods was abolished. Purchase of these products was made dependent on delivery of grain. Only the poor sections of the non-rural population were allowed to buy industrial products with money. The state monopoly of trade in industrial products was to be used to sell these products only in exchange for grain up to 85 per cent of their value. The remainder was to be paid in money. The trade monopoly concerned all intermediate organs, agricultural cooperatives, state, collective and private institutions. Industrial products were to be sold at factory prices plus a mark-up on the value at the level of the provincial procurement organs, and a further 5 per cent mark-up on the value at the level of the *uezd* organs, to cover distribution costs. As has been shown, however, industrial prices were to be raised much above agricultural prices with the aim of extracting by this means a greater quantity of agricultural products. State monopoly rights were used to determine from the centre the quantity which should reach the provinces, according to the importance of the regions from the point of view of grain output and taking into account the size of the local population.

Two other steps towards comprehensive state commodity exchange were realized during the winter of 1918–19. On 21 November 1918, *Sovnarkom* introduced state monopoly for a number of items of personal consumption and household use. The decree on the organization of supply was worked out jointly by VSNKh and *Narkomprod*. It included clothing, processed foodstuffs, matches, heating oil, lubricating oil, candles, nails, agricultural machinery and tools.[144] Nationalized factories and other enterprises under VSNKh's control were obliged to deliver their manufactured goods to *Narkomprod*, going through the *glavk* system and on the basis of *utilization plans* worked out by an interdepartmental commission formed by representatives of VSNKh, *Narkomprod* and the People's Commissar of Industry and Trade.[145] All matters of supply to the public of monopoly and non-monopoly products of industrial and handicraft production were entrusted to the special administration for supply of *Narkomprod, Glavprodukt*. The decree on state supply concerned only a specific list of products. But it also introduced, as a general principle, that goods destined for personal consumption and household use should be distributed 'with the aim of replacing private trade and in order to supply the population systematically with all products from soviet and cooperative distribution points'. *Glavprodukt* was also assigned the task of organizing purchasing regulation centres for various groups of products, the manufacture and purchase of which did not come under state monopoly. Products were to be paid for by *Glavprodukt* and its organs within two weeks of notification to the factories of the purchase order for a given quantity of output. The decree on state monopoly did not mention state commodity exchange. However, it was closely related to it. A circular from *Glavprodukt* to all its local organs specifically instructed that the commodity fund was to be used primarily for exchange for foodstuffs.[146] The rules of distribution according to class principles were reaffirmed as a matter of necessity. *Glavprodukt* explained that the stock of commodities was not sufficient to reward individual suppliers of grain and that the delivery of huge quantities of commodities to wealthy peasants would have met opposition from broad peasant strata. The appeal to necessity, however, was probably intended to provide a quick explanation to the localities for something which locally was considered unfair. Reports did indeed affirm that distribution of industrial products on a communal basis was better implemented when it was carried out by central organs and that local organs endeavoured, against the spirit of the law, to draw up tables defining commodity equivalents, in order to have definite ratios between goods and objective ratios for the realization of commodity exchange.[147] At the centre, instead, the rationalization of state commodity exchange was ascribed to ideological tenets, which influenced the elaboration of future policies. In 1919 Frumkin, one of the head officials of *Narkomprod*, completed Osinskii's theorizing of state monopoly as an alternative to the market as such. Frumkin asserted that monopoly ought gradually to include all products, since 'products which remained totally or in part at the disposal of producers, above self-consumption, fed the living juices of the dying capitalist system by offering support to private trade circulation and speculation'.[148]

On 5 August 1919, obligatory commodity exchange was extended to the whole country and to include raw materials and wood fuel.[149] As one year before, the enforcement of overall state commodity exchange was made to coincide with the new harvest. By that time, central control over production and stocks of industrial commodities, and the regime of obligatory delivery of agricultural produce, provided firm grounds for the belief that the pillars of the non-market economy cherished by all Marxists had already been erected and that only determination – meaning struggle against remnants of the market – would be needed to achieve total separation between distribution and production – the ultimate goal of the communist society.

7.5 TRADE CONTROL, FOOD PROCUREMENT AND THE USE OF COERCION. FOOD DETACHMENTS AND COMMITTEES OF THE RURAL POOR (KOMBEDY)

The account of the main theoretical steps which were at the basis of the policy of state control of trade, and industrial and agricultural prices (in Marxist terminology collective commodity exchange), should not obscure the disordered, disruptive and harmful process of actual trade control, which preceded, accompanied and often conditioned the entire policy of food procurement.

Measures against free trade and speculation, ending in broad rights to requisition stocks of goods, which prepared the way for the general scheme of *prodrazverstka* (obligatory delivery by quotas of foodstuffs), had been undertaken by the government and by the local soviets since they had started dealing with food procurement. Earlier policies against trade and speculation have not yet been given the attention they deserve. This is both because they were not greatly reflected in the Press, which was then rapidly falling under Bolshevik control, and because relevant documentary material and the sources contained in Soviet archives still remain largely unpublished. But information provided by the Bolshevik Press itself is sufficient, for our purpose, to disclose the disruptive nature of the struggle against concealment of foodstuffs systematically carried out by those soviets under Bolshevik control,[150] with the sometimes honest, but certainly naive, belief that discovery of hidden stocks and the punishment of the 'speculators' would improve the availability of food. Requisitioning of foodstuffs was sometimes carried out upon information by the house committees; sections and squads against speculation inspected not only stores and shops, but also private houses.[151] But the vigorous assault on 'speculation' really started when Trotskii was appointed Extraordinary Commissar for the protection of railways carrying foodstuffs. On 17 February 1918 Trotskii issued an order to all local soviets, railways committees and patrols 'to fight *meshochichestvo* ('bagman' trade) disorganizing transport and food procurement'. Punishments ranged from confiscation of foodstuffs to killing on the spot.[152] Two days later railwaymen were ordered not to let 'bagmen' get into the trains. On 22 February, *Pravda* announced that trade in foodstuffs outside the Petrograd *uezd* needed the authorization of the *volost*.[153] Next day, Trotskii established control by the Petrograd Food Board over all railway stocks and shipments of food to Petrograd, in order to distribute them to the population. All shops were required to give account of their stocks in forty-eight hours.[154] Measures heralded as the fight against the food crisis also included food requisition detachments frightening the kulaks in Siberia to persuade them to deliver their stocks.[155] In the meantime the *raion* food procurement boards were ordered to send their money back to the Petrograd Board, to produce daily accounts of their budgets and to keep fixed prices under the threat of court trial.[156]

The measures against private trade did not spare small shops, such as butchers' shops, bakeries and other food shops. The Bolshevik Soviet of Tula announced the municipalization of all local butchers' shops from January 1918.[157] The idea that concentration of bread-baking would be appropriate in large towns was well publicized in *Pravda* from the beginning of 1918. Its supporters maintained that not only would concentration of baking allow workers' control over bread, but it would also be more efficient and aid the resolution of the current food crisis.[158] Isolated criticisms of the proposals as not feasible disappeared from the Press at the end of February, when debate was restricted to radical programmes. On 20 February, the Moscow Food Council announced the shutting down of 500 small bakeries and the concentration of baking in a few large ones.[159] On 15 March, the Moscow Soviet authorized the local food committee to sequester all bakeries, butchers' and other shops 'selling products which could be exchanged for grain' and to requisition and confiscate such products if the food committee's orders had not been fulfilled and no account of the rationed products had been produced.[160] The Petrograd Food Board, which was often accused of being inefficient by the Bolshevik papers, was more reluctant to undertake radical steps. On 20 March, this board asked the soviet to suspend the mobilization of bakers, to make it possible to deliver the existing stocks of flour, but on 1 April it resolved to open its own municipal bakeries.[161] Local soviets competed with the large centres in fighting *meshochnichestvo* and re-quisitioning foodstuffs and livestock. The cases of Ufa, Vladimir, Riazan, Saratov, and Tula were reported by the Press,[162] but these were not isolated and provoked reactions which were detrimental, in the end, to all. At the end of March, horse meat, which could not be sold to unwilling customers, filled the towns' cold stores. In April civil war was already stirring up in Tula, Riazan, Penza, Saratov and Kineshma (in the Moscow province) and in the Urals.[163] Much more should be done to explore and analyse correctly the initial experience of trade and food control. But it is unlikely that new evidence may change or attenuate the influence of the early Bolshevik policies on the rapid worsening of the availability of food. The development of the food situation in the large industrial centres in the early months may be followed through the available data on prices, rations and stocks of foodstuffs. Monthly prices were computed for some basic foodstuffs in Moscow by the Commissariat for Labour and scattered figures on stocks and rations in Petrograd were published in *Pravda*.

Prices for vegetable oil, fresh and salted fish, and cucumbers were

Table 7.6. *Market prices for foodstuffs in Moscow, 1918 (kopeks)*

Items	Unit	January	February	March	April	May	June
Rye flour	pud	6,000	10,000	12,500	18,000	20,000	25,000
Rye bread	funt	200	250	300	450	525	600
Groats	funt	250	284	—	—	—	712
Vegetable oil	funt	500	362	474.5	467	419.5	434
Potatoes	funt	60	—	—	86	137	166
Sauerkraut	funt	27	27	29	29	30	44
Pickled cucumbers	10	67	61	69	62	375	378
Onions	funt	70	70	90	103	166	320
Fresh fish	funt	219	277	297	282	369	470
Salted fish	funt	135	190.5	239	179	247	328
Smoked roach	funt	—	—	—	—	48	48
Salted herrings	1	73	109	126	126	133	142
Beef	funt	287	355	385.5	403	531	591
Boiled sausages	funt	375	443	513	529	696	845
Fat	funt	700	669	675	750	826	1,041
Milk	bottle	120	135	120	140	145	153
Butter	funt	1,000	1,080	1,241	1,400	1,270	1,406
Eggs	10	—	—	—	250	760	875
Sugar	funt	—	800	—	—	—	—
Honey	funt	—	—	—	800	1,166	1,467
Raisins	funt	—	825	800	—	1,131	1421
Salt	funt	—	—	—	—	12	11

Source: Statistika Truda, nos. 1–4, 1918, 44–5

decreasing between March and April 1918. At the meeting of food procurement committees of the Northern *Oblast* on 28 April 1918, the head of the Petrograd Province Food Procurement Committee, Shilov, announced that there was no scarcity of fish and fat in the province and that the April ration of meat was increased thanks to shipments from Siberia. April prices for cabbage, herrings, beef and sausages in Moscow were no more than 10 per cent above the March level (see Table 7.6). Potatoes, a substitute for bread, which were 43 per cent more expensive than in January, cost one-fifth of the price of bread.

Flour and bread prices deserve specific consideration, because they were subject to the regime of state monopoly. The figures produced by *Narkomtrud* concerned the average worker's basic staples, i.e. among grains, rye and not wheat, which was traditionally exported. This fact may explain the divergence in price trends of flour and bread between January and March. Flour increased in price by 66 per cent between January and February and by 25 per cent between February and March, while bread prices increased by 25 per cent and 20 per cent respectively. In two months the price of flour more than doubled, while that of bread increased by 50 per cent. Only in April and even more so in May was the rate of increase of bread prices higher than that of flour prices. It is possible that in the first months of 1918 stocks of wheat originally intended for export were being used on the domestic market, thus helping to moderate the increase in bread prices. Limited figures on stocks of various grains in Petrograd show higher stocks of wheat as compared with rye and other grains.[164] There are no figures on total stocks of grains each month that could help to determine the primary cause of the sharp increase of bread price in April. Policies were based on the strong belief that grain was, in fact, available. Groman said on 28 April that 116 million puds remained to be collected.[165] Information was published on large amounts of grain stocked in individual provinces but not sent to large cities. Information on the number of trains and wagons loaded with foodstuffs was also published, but it would be difficult to ascertain whether these shipments actually arrived. Requirements were also variable, since thousands of people left the towns.[166] An indication of the evolution of the food crisis vigorously denounced by the Bolsheviks during the winter and spring months may be derived from the relatively regular accounts of shipments and stocks produced by the Petrograd Food Board and published in *Pravda*.[167] (See Table 7.7). According to officials in charge of food procurement, the monthly norm for Petrograd was 250 wagons (1 wagon = 1,000 puds) of grains for a daily ration of 1/4 funt of bread per person.[168]

Additional information which may fill out the incomplete figures on stocks for January and February may be derived from the evaluations of

Table 7.7. *Stocks, shipments and food rations in Petrograd*

Months / Days	Stocks (Number of wagons (w) or puds (p))	Shipments No. of wagons (w) or puds (p)	Bread rations (funt)	Fat Oil (funt)	Meat (funt)
2 January	—	121 w	$\frac{1}{4} + \frac{1}{4}$ s[a]		
27	—	58 w	$\frac{1}{4} + \frac{1}{4}$ s		
30–1	—	68 w	$\frac{1}{4} + \frac{1}{4}$ s		
1 February	—	78,800 p	$\frac{1}{4} + \frac{1}{4}$ s		
3	—	—	$\frac{1}{4} + \frac{1}{4}$ s		
4	—	—	$\frac{1}{2} + \frac{1}{2}$ s	$\frac{1}{4}$	$\frac{1}{4}$
5	—	84 w (plus 109 other types of foodstuff)	—		
6	—	360 w foodstuffs	—		
9	—	—	$\frac{3}{4} + \frac{3}{4}$ s		
10	—	—	$\frac{3}{4} + \frac{3}{4}$ s		
14	—	—	$\frac{1}{2}$ groats		$\frac{1}{2}$
16	—	63 w	$2\frac{1}{2}$ groats		
19	—	—	$\frac{1}{4} + \frac{1}{4}$ s		
23	—	23 w (+ 57,800 puds potatoes and 25,000 puds meat)			
20 February	—	5 w (plus other foodstuffs)	—		
3 March	—	80 w	$\frac{1}{4} + \frac{1}{4}$ s	1	
5	78 w	—	$\frac{1}{4} + \frac{1}{4}$ s	1	
9	—	—	(plus 1 funt flour)		
12	—	—	—		
19	—	several w	$\frac{3}{4} + \frac{3}{4}$		
20	199,173 p foodstuffs	440 w foodstuffs	—		
1–15	—	427,685 puds (wheat, rye, flour)			
21	224,613 p 116,703 p groats	—	—		

Date					
28	—	—			2 eggs
30	—	—			¼
31	—	—			
11 April	206,908 p	43,717 puds		—	
23	53,760 p + 110,650 p groats	27,307		—	
8 May	31,688 p + 34,137 p groats	—	$\frac{1}{4} + \frac{1}{4}$ s	(for 1 May)	
9	35,924 p + 34,728 p groats	—	—		
10	43,683 p + 38,383 p groats	—	—		
11	33,045 + 41,699 p groats	—	—		
13	45,000 p + 28,000 p groats	—	$\frac{1}{8} + \frac{1}{8} + \frac{1}{2}$ f potatoes		
16 May	120,641 p (probably including oats) + 25,556 groats	—	$\frac{1}{4} + \frac{1}{4}$		
17	99,121 p	—	—		
18	35,672 p + 22,715 groats	—	—		
20	72,695 p (probably including oats) + 15,621	—	—		
24	30,000 p + 13,500 p groats	— (May)	—		
29	51,970 p + 17,285 p groats	(26	$\frac{1}{8} + \frac{1}{8} + \frac{1}{4} + \frac{1}{4}$ f vegetables + $\frac{1}{4}$ f groats for children		
30	33,453 p + 18,261 p groats	—	$\frac{1}{2}$ only to workers		
31	24,263 + 17,999 p groats	—	—		
3 June	38,682 p + 20,000 p groats	— (June)	$\frac{1}{4}$ funt butter for 1 June ration coupon: 1 funt, 1 funt meat, 1 funt fish		
4	35,169 p + 29,135 p groats	—	—		
6	27,846 p + 43,582 p groats	(13	—		
20	24,433 p + 51,884 p groats	—	$\frac{1}{4}$ funt bread + $\frac{1}{4}$ funt potatoes		

a S = supplementary ration

Source: Compiled from *Pravda*, various issues, January–June 1918

the food situation provided by the Petrograd Food Board. On 1 February, the situation was considered satisfactory, but the board thought it necessary to keep stocks for thirty to thirty-five days, to be ready to face worsening shipments in April and May, because of the thaw and mud jeopardizing shipments by road.[169] Summing up the shipments of wagons from 2 January until the end of February and considering only bread grains, one gets 495,800 puds, which was about the two months' supply considered to be necessary for Petrograd at the 1/4 funt daily norm per person. The shipments in the first two weeks of March were sufficient for about fifty days. Stocks of grain on 22 March were sufficient for about forty-five days and on 11 April for about twenty-five days. On 23 April, the stocks were still sufficient for twenty days. The stocks started falling from May, but they never fell below the quantity necessary for about one week.

A daily norm of 1/4 funt was quite low. At the end of February, prices for rationed bread were increased, because of the increasing cost of milling and rising wages. One funt of rye bread cost 25 kopeks (a tenth of the market price) and one funt of wheat bread 29 kopeks. Minimum wages ranged from 10 rubles a day for electro-technical workers to 22 rubles for metal workers of the machine tool industry, according to data published by *Narkomtrud* for the seven-month period beginning October 1917.[170] Nonetheless, the possibility existed of getting extra food from the free market, where, as has been shown above, for Moscow, the price increase for some staples was not excessive until April.

When the officials of food procurement met on 28 April 1918, there was no agreement on the causes of the food crisis or on the most suitable means to alleviate it until the new harvest. On 10 April, Briukhanov had declared at the All-Russian TSIK that Siberia could have dispatched to the Central Regions 150 million puds of cereals if the transport situation had permitted; but the railway lines were so bad that only five million were received. The moderate improvement made possible by water transport towards the end of March was neutralized by the loss of the Ukraine and the Southern Caucasus, which compelled the government to change the original plans and try to get more from the East.[171] Shipments were often plundered.[172] Improvised organization also contributed to the situation. The food procurement agents of West Siberia declared that the plans for provision for the current month had not been received and that 300 wagons of manufactured goods were lying at Omsk for lack of an assortment list and commercial receipts.[173] The producing provinces demanded immediate payment for their grain, but the local food procurement organs had had their hands tied since Trotskii's order on the concentration of financial means. Lack of money and inadequate organization were considered by many to be the principal reasons for the falling shipments not only of grain, but also of other foodstuffs, such as fish, of which there was plenty at the ports – but it was not shipped.[174] Groman, who was a strong supporter of a central plan of purchase and exchange of grain with commodities, was convinced that nothing could be done without a network of cooperatives and local agents.[175] On the one hand, however, local shops and stores were shut down or hindered in their activity, and on the other, the Bolsheviks were systematically dismantling the existing cooperatives, mainly controlled by Mensheviks and Socialist-Revolutionaries.[176] Allegations began to circulate that foodstuffs organs were not coping well because they were directed by members of the upper classes, while opponents of the Bolshevik policy at the All-Russian TsIK, protesting against the dispersal of non-Bolshevik soviets, were refused the right to speak.[177]

The idea of centralizing the whole business of feeding the urban population into a single organ received increasing support among Bolshevik leaders, but there was no agreement on how, and how far, food procurement should be carried out. There were different views on the appropriate purchase price and the scope of state monopoly. Some food procurement officials held that, side by side with a continued nationwide policy of food procurement, market trade should be authorized, while others maintained that free trade had led to a lamentable situation. It was mainly among the ex-Mensheviks that flexible policies received better consideration. Rykov, who had been in charge of food procurement in the provinces of Tula, Orel, Tambov, Volga and Kharkov, claimed that it was unrealistic to stick to a purchase price of grain fixed in August 1917, and that better results would be achieved if prices were free to fluctuate according to local conditions.[178] His view was shared by other officials, even among food procurement organs of the Northern *Oblast*, where the food situation was considered worse than anywhere else. According to many, stocks existing in the provinces could be obtained if the purchase price were increased. Others affirmed that state monopoly should be limited to grain and groats and that it should be abolished for foodstuffs such as eggs and oil.[179] Not terror, but organization was needed, said a Moscow official, adding that food procurement banks should be organized on a commercial basis, in order to draw out private savings.[180] Food rations were low but they were tolerable as long as other channels were open. They became a crucial issue when *meshochnichestvo* was suppressed, according to a food procurement official at the Petrograd 28 April meeting.[181] A protest of the Putilov workers was calmed on 12 May only by authorizing the free carriage of $1\frac{1}{2}$ pud of foodstuffs. On the same day, the Petrograd Soviet, which was discussing the food crisis, still agreed that

abolition of trade together with the formation of workers' food detachments was the only solution.[182]

It was in this context that the so-called class rations were introduced. In
order to increase the rations of industrial workers, the number of people
having a right to supplementary rations was reduced from 800,000 to
150,000.[183] After this decision figures on non-workers' rations were
seldom published. *Narkomprod*'s commissars worked under the pressure of
industrial unrest, rising unemployment, especially in demobilized industry, and the fear that anti-Bolshevik slogans could find increasing
support if there were no immediate improvement in food supply.
Although the existing institutions could not cope well with procurement
of the basic foodstuffs, it was advocated that state monopoly should be
extended to cover all foodstuffs.[184] Plans were made for supplies to the
towns until the new harvest, the necessary amount sufficient for one and a
half months having been calculated at 52 million puds. Tsiurupa claimed
that the 'rural bourgeoisie' would not deliver grain in exchange for
money, since it had enough money and did not need more.[185] Tsiurupa
produced figures on the available stock of grain, which according to
Narkomprod remained from previous harvests. The overall surplus available in Russia was estimated to be about the same as the amount of
razverstka in 1917.[186] The 52 million puds needed for the current months
for the urban population equalled the surplus of the Central Agricultural
Regions. Among the grain-producing provinces, Tsiurupa specified
Voronezh, Tula, Orel, Tambov, and Kursk.[187] Forecasts for the future
were gloomy. The May plan was to collect 36 million puds (comprising
25.7 million for the urban population, 5.5 million for the railways, and
5.935 for the army), but it was not expected that fulfilment would be
higher than 15–16 per cent. The programme of *Narkomprod* was to keep
fixed prices (that is, the August 1917 prices), to select a price ratio
between industrial and agricultural products favourable to the former,
and lastly – assuming that commodity exchange based on the artificial
price ratio would not work immediately – to organize the rural poor and
armed food detachments in their support against the rural 'bourgeoisie'.
The local food procurement agents were accused of weakness. A
forthcoming turn in the policy of food procurement was announced, in
connection with which agreements were made with the Commissar for
Internal Affairs and the Commissar of Justice. These agreements were
going to transform the *Narkomprod* organization and its tasks. The policy
of requisition of grain at fixed prices was considered to be temporary, i.e. to
last only until the new harvest. Wider plans for the future were
contemplated instead – a combination of the policy of food collection
with the policy of distribution of all consumer goods to the population,

through the intermediary of the Council of Supply – in order to provide basic consumption to people at fixed prices 'for their rational and correct distribution'.[188]

Tsiurupa's immediate plans met some opposition among other procurement organs. On 10 May the joint session of the Northern *Oblast* Food Procurement Board and the Moscow Food Procurement Committee, directed respectively by Groman and Shefler', passed a resolution against *Narkomprod*'s policy. The armed expropriation of cereals, normal as a means of obtaining foodstuffs, was considered as useless and seen as hindering effective methods of purchase. The resolution proposed, instead, commodity exchange on the basis of general price control, change of the state purchase agencies and the introduction of cooperatives and private trade, as well as authorization to change fixed prices within certain limits.[189] In view of the fact that between November 1917 and April 1818 the average monthly increase of prices was about 33 per cent, and that in town markets food prices were increasing at an accelerating rate, keeping the August 1917 prices for grain made no economic sense.[190]

Some food procurement agents were afraid of the possible consequences of the use of troops.[191] But none of the arguments advanced against the proposals of *Narkomprod* discouraged the government from exhorting people to bring the 'class struggle' to the countryside as a means of solving the food crisis. Lenin introduced some changes in the original draft proposals of *Narkomprod*, emphasizing the emergency nature of the policy measures and the need for severe sanctions against grain holders who should be declared *enemies of the people*.[192] On 13 May 1918, the All-Russian Central Executive Committee approved the decree conferring extraordinary powers on *Narkomprod*, thereafter known as the 'food dictatorship'. This important decree read as follows:

A ruinous process of disintegration of the food procurement of the country – the heavy legacy of a four-year war – continues to extend and aggravate the existing distress.

While the consuming provinces are starving, great stocks of cereals, including the 1916 harvest and the 1917 harvest which has not yet been threshed, lie, as habitually, in the producing provinces. These stocks are in the hands of the rural kulaks and wealthy people, in the hands of the rural bourgeoisie. Replete and satisfied, having accumulated an enormous mass of money earned in the years of war, this rural bourgeoisie remains deaf and unresponsive in the face of the moanings of starving workers and poor peasants; it refuses to dispatch cereals to the state station points with the aim of forcing the state to increase again and again the price of cereals, while at the same time it sells for its own benefit cereals in the provinces at fabulous prices to speculators and bagmen.

The obstinacy of the greedy kulaks and wealthy peasants must be brought to an end. The food procurement experience of the last years has shown that the failure to apply fixed prices on cereals and a grain monopoly facilitates the feeding of a small group of our capitalists by making food inaccessible to several millions of toiling people and exposing them to the inevitability of death by starvation.

The reply to the violence of grain holders upon the rural poor must be violence upon the bourgeoisie.

Not one single pud of grain must remain in the hands of the grain holders, except the quantity needed for sowing and subsistence of the household until the next harvest.

And it is necessary to implement all this immediately, especially after the occupation of the Ukraine by the Germans, as we must content ourselves with the resources of cereals which are barely sufficient for sowing and survival.

Taking into account this situation and considering that only by rigorous accounting and even distribution of all grain stocks of Russia is it possible to get out of the food provision crisis, the All-Russian Executive Central Committee has decreed:

(1) By keeping firmly the grain monopoly and fixed prices and also carrying out a merciless struggle against grain speculators and bagmen, to compel each grain holder to declare the surrender of all surpluses, except the quantity needed for consumption on established norms until the next harvest, in one week after the notification of this decree in each *volost*. The rules applying to the orders [of delivery] will be defined by the local food procurement organs of *Narkomprod*.

(2) To invite all toiling people and propertyless peasants to unite immediately in a merciless struggle against the kulaks.

(3) To declare enemies of the nation all people having surpluses of grain and not handing them over to the station points and even dissipating the stocks of cereals for their own home brew instead of delivering them to the collecting stations; to bring them before the Revolutionary Courts, put them in jail for not less than ten years, confiscate all their belongings, banish them out of the *obshchina* and condemn the holders of home brew to forced labour in public works.

(4) In the case of discovery of any surplus of grain which had not been declared for delivery, according to point 1, grain will be requisitioned without payment, and half of the value which was due at fixed prices for the undeclared surplus will be paid to the people who took part in discovering the surpluses, after they have been in fact received in the collecting stations, and the other half to the Agricultural Community. Information about discovery of surpluses has to be reported to the local food procurement organs.

Considering also that the struggle against the food procurement crisis requires the adoption of rapid and decisive measures, that the most fruitful realization of such measures requires in turn the centralization of all decisions on food matters into a single institution, and that such an institution is the People's Commissariat of Food Procurement, the All-Russian Central Executive Committee has decreed – for the purpose of a more successful struggle against the food crisis – to attribute to the People's Commissar of Food Procurement the following powers:

(1) To issue obligatory decisions on food procurement matters, exceeding the normal limits of competence of the People's Commissar of Food Procurement.

(2) To abrogate instructions of local food procurement organs and institutions contradicting plans and activity of the People's Commissar of Food Procurement.
(3) To solicit from institutions and organizations of all departments the undiscussed and immediate fulfilment of the commissar's decisions on food procurement matters.
(4) To make use of armed troops in the case of resistance to requisition of grain and other foodstuffs.
(5) To dismiss or reorganize the food procurement organs in the localities if they oppose the People's Commissariat of Food Procurement's decisions.
(6) To discharge, dismiss, take before the Revolutionary Court, and submit to arrest appointees and employees of all departments and social organizations, if they interfere in a disruptive way with the commissariat's decisions.
(7) To transfer the present powers, except the right to arrest of point 6, to other people and institutions in the localities upon authorization of the People's Commissariat of Food Procurement.
(8) All measures of the People's Commissars of Food Procurement related by their nature to the People's Commissariat of Transport and to VSNKh are implemented upon agreement with the corresponding departments.
(9) All instructions and decisions of the People's Commissariat of Food Procurement, issued on account of the present powers, are examined by its collegium which has the right – without interrupting their execution – to appeal against them before the Soviet of People's Commissars.
(10) The present decree comes into life from the day of its signing and will be notified by telegraph.

> (Signed)
> Chairman of VsTsIK: Sverdlov
> Chairman of Sovnarkom: Lenin
> Secretary of VsTsIK: Avanesov

The wording of the decree sounded like a declaration of war against peasants with any surplus of grain above strict personal needs. Party members in the Moscow *Oblast* were informed that the decree on food dictatorship was of the utmost importance and had to be read by each member.[193]

The Socialist-Revolutionaries characterized the food policy of the government as murderous.[194] The Mensheviks observed that the centralization of the policy of distribution was bound to be inefficient and undermine the social unity of the countryside.[195] The Mensheviks' criticism was not without foundations. One of the chief aims of the food procurement policy was the suppression of intermediate private dealers and other trade organizations between supply and distribution. The decree of 27 May 1918 established that *Narkomprod* was entrusted with the supply to the population of all consumer necessities, the distribution of such goods all over the country, and preparation of the nationalization of trade in such products. The same decree entrusted the local organs of *Narkomprod* with forming special detachments of 'conscious people' for the organization of the 'working peasantry' against the *kulachestva*, or kulaks' revolts.[196] On 1 June, *Sovnarkom* approved a decree prohibiting 'independent purchases' which were hindering the revolution.[197] On 24 May the food procurement council of Petrograd declared a monopoly on all products of prime necessity.[198] No attention was then paid to the fact that centralization of the policy of distribution would need a complex apparatus of state organs and rules, which would necessarily cause lengthy procedures and bureaucratism. A spirit of crusade animated the leadership. Lenin was a good interpreter of this spirit. Speaking to the Central Executive Committee of the Moscow Soviet and to the trade unions on 4 June 1918, he stressed the moral character of the measures chosen to fight hunger:

When we see the united workers and the mass of poor peasants, who were about to organize against the rich and the profiteers, against the people to whom intellectuals like Groman and Cherevanin are wittingly or unwittingly preaching profiteers' slogans, when these workers, led astray, advocate the free sale of grain wagons, we say that this means helping the kulak out of a hole. That path we shall never take ... We need detachments of agitators from among the workers ... they must sanctify and legitimize our food war, our war against the kulaks, our war against disorders ...[199]

Presented in this form, the appeal to class struggle found a broad response among the representatives of the working class. A joint assembly of the plenary session of the Moscow Soviet, the All-Russian Council of Trade Unions and the Moscow Council of Trade Unions, the representatives of the factory-shop committees and of the *raion* soviets, voted a resolution which affirmed that hunger was helping the power of proprietors and capitalists, that there was enough bread for all in Russia and that it had to be distributed under control (*planomerno*) and, finally, that the policy of food dictatorship undertaken by the Soviet power was correct, since it meant merciless struggle against the enemies of the nation – the kulaks, speculators, and pillagers.[200] The Bolshevik crusade against grain holders had, in fact, been anticipated by some local soviets. Detachments had been formed since the beginning of 1918 for the protection of trains and requisition of foodstuffs. In the winter of 1918 local soviets in the provinces of Penza and Saratov authorized the formation of armed detachments for requisition of foodstuffs from the kulaks.[201] On 15 February 1918, one of the commissars of *Narkomprod* assigned to the southern regions informed Lenin by telegraph that millions of puds of cereals could be collected if their confiscation were decreed and armed detachments sent for this

purpose.[202] During late April and early May some special detachments
for the requisition of cereals and control over the railways were formed at
localities in the province of Moscow and armed detachments of about 200
people were established in Tambov province. The formation of detachments was approved by the Petrograd Soviet on 12 May and the first
detachment left on 23 May.[203] After publication of the decree on food
dictatorship, pronouncements in favour of strong measures to solve the
food crisis increased. The Tambov food procurement sections invited the
volost soviets to requisition grain from the kulaks mercilessly, if necessary
with recourse to arrest and execution of whoever hindered it.[204] Following
the reorganization of *Narkomprod*, which included special attention to
food detachments having, *inter alia*, the task of 'organizing the labouring
peasantry against the kulaks',[205] on 4 June 1918 the Moscow Committee
of the Party laid down the criteria for formation of food detachments. The
detachments were to be formed under the control of the party committees
and the factory-shop units. Politically conscious comrades recommended
by the Moscow Party Committee or by the Central Committee were to be
put at the head of the detachments, which should also include good
agitators and a sufficient quantity of political literature. Groups of
reliable comrades in proper ranks should be ready to fight against the
'hooligans', but they would not be considered Red Army detachments.
The food detachments were supposed to make contact with the local
soviets and party organizations immediately after their arrival. The
Moscow instruction tried to focus on the voluntary nature and the moral
standing of the detachments. Their members would be elected or
approved by the general assembly of workers in the factory and would
continue to receive their wages. They were forbidden to dispatch any food
parcels to their home.[206]

The existing food organizations working under *Narkomprod* for the
collection of grain (for instance in Penza, Tsaritsin, Voronezh, Samara)
turned out to be unsuitable for the military tasks which the new policy
entailed. In some cases they even rose against central directives.[207] Lack of
support from outside parties and groups compelled the Bolshevik Party to
rely mainly on its own members and on conscription rules. Compulsion
soon prevailed over the voluntary enlistment.

At the end of May, Lenin informed Tsiurupa that the struggle for grain
requisitioning was going to be carried out in agreement with the
Commissariat for Military Affairs.[208] On 10 June 1918, the local military
authorities of Moscow specified that food armies had to be formed of
workers and poor peasants recognizing Soviet power, and that volunteers
should have the appropriate certification of the party, of the soviet and
other organizations supporting Soviet Power. Members of the armies,

whose ages should range between eighteen and forty, were required to sign a declaration that they would serve in the ranks of the army as long as it lasted.[209] On 11 June the Moscow Soviet decreed that 1 per cent of the factory workers had to join the food detachments, and appointed four commissars for such a purpose with unlimited powers and responsible only to the soviet.[210] On the same day, the Moscow Committee of the Party decided that each party organization ought to concentrate on food procurements not less than 5 per cent of its members and that the rules of formation of food detachments had to be applied over all Russia. As if preparing for a military conflict, the Bolsheviks strengthened their command positions. Two more members of the Moscow Party Committee were appointed at the head of *Narkomprod* together with Tsiurupa.[211] Bulletins on the formation and operation of food detachments in the provinces started hammering the party call and echoed from the pages of *Pravda*.[212] By 13 June 2,000 people from Moscow had reached the food armies operating in the countryside.[213] This figure was not very high, but it was accompanied by feverish slogans of class struggle, which may have frightened the peasants quite as much as the food armies themselves. On that day, the Moscow Soviet issued an appeal to the population claiming that the defence of the grain monopoly was equivalent to the defence of socialism and the revolution. Emphasis was put on the loss of the Ukraine, the Don grain and coal regions, and the Caucasus grain region to the enemy and the fact that the same was occurring in Siberia, where the Czechs had revolted against Soviet power. People were invited to defend the stability of fixed prices and to join food detachments, for the purpose of restoring the circulation of cereals through commodity exchange organized and supported by the rural poor.[214] In some provinces the opposition began to find support against Bolshevik policy. Revolts were reported in Saratov, Simbirsk and Penza.[215] Slogans called for convocation of the Constituent Assembly.[216] On 14 June a state of war was declared in Tambov.[217] The organization of the Red Army proceeded in parallel with the formation of food detachments. Factories which were reported as adhering to Bolshevik policy emphasized the nature of the struggle for bread – 'the march of armed proletarian detachments'. The factory-shop committees, meeting in Moscow on 28 June, approved Lenin's policy of unity with the rural poor, and the participation of workers in the food armies.[218] Unemployment may have helped enlistment into the food armies. Food soldiers were paid 150 rubles a month plus some payment in kind.[219] Food armies increased in size rapidly, though probably not sufficiently for their tasks. According to the Chief Administration of the Food Army there were 2,863 recruits on 30 June; 9,189 on 15 July and 11,030 on 30 July.

Half of these people were workers from Petrograd.[220] On the other hand, the hopes that the rural poor would join spontaneously the struggle against the kulaks – should there be any left at that time – were not fulfilled, and the authorities had no alternative but to resort to force.

The duties of the food detachments were not confined to collection of foodstuffs and protection of stored goods, and to the struggle against speculation and the bagmen; they were also entrusted with organizing the rural poor. The peasants had to be convened by the chief committee of the detachment and were supposed to declare how much cereals, potatoes and groats they had, and to deliver these products to the nearest collecting station in exchange for manufactures and other necessities. If the peasants refused to comply with these directives, the committee had to convene the rural poor, learn from them where the cereals were hidden, requisition them together with agricultural implements and deliver part of what was requisitioned to the land committee formed by the rural poor for further distribution to the population. Each person was allocated not more than one pud of food a month until the new harvest. Consumption norms were fixed for livestock: $1\frac{1}{4}$ puds of fodder a month for horses, 35 funt for cattle, 20 funt for small and medium-sized meat animals and 10 funt for calves.[221]

Measures to win the support of the rural poor had been seriously considered in enacting the decree on food dictatorship. Before the publication of the decree, an article in *Pravda* headed 'Fighting Hunger' affirmed that one million puds of cereals was available south of Moscow, that getting this was not the task of food procurement but the task of the class struggle, and that total support to the Soviet food dictatorship should be given by 'the rural poor who are as needy as the city poor'.[222] The campaign to organize the rural poor started immediately after publication of the decree. The Bolsheviks tried to get the support of the Left Socialist-Revolutionaries. The latter understood how difficult it would be to define the rural poor in the real circumstances of Russia, and therefore how large would be the scope for arbitrariness in the policy of grain collection and commodity distribution.

In spite of their disagreement on the overall approach to food procurement, the Left Socialist-Revolutionaries tried to persuade the Bolsheviks to change 'rural poor' into 'labouring peasant', thus making a distinction between peasants working land on their own and peasants hiring wage labour, instead of that between peasants having surpluses and peasants not having surpluses. For some time it looked as if the Bolsheviks had no major objections to this proposal. On their behalf Sverdlov affirmed that the current policy was necessary 'to spread in the countryside that same war we have been conducting in the towns' in order to crush the kulaks' opposition, and that there were requests to deprive of electoral rights peasants who hired labour – in which context the term 'rural poor' was to be changed to 'labouring peasantry'.[223] But the resolution on class struggle in the countryside adopted by the All-Russian TsIK did not leave much room for misunderstandings if 'The All-Russian TsIK, after examination of the question of the tasks of soviets in the countryside, considers it necessary to point out with extreme urgency the unity of the *labouring peasantry* against the *rural bourgeoisie*. All local soviets must start immediately and carry out energetically the work of illustrating the contradiction of interests between the *rural poor* and the *kulak elements, arming all the rural poor* and establishing their dictatorship.'[224] On 11 June the decree on the organization of the rural poor was approved. Rural poor committees were to be formed by the local soviets and put under the immediate direction of *Narkomprod*. Kulaks and 'other wealthy people having grain and other food surpluses' were deprived of electoral rights. No mention was made of 'labouring peasantry'.[225] The Left Socialist-Revolutionaries voted against on the grounds that the rights of the local soviets would be hindered and that entire categories of people would be excluded from political representation.[226] The Bolshevik leadership, at that time, was quite aware that the *labouring peasantry*, largely represented in the countryside by the Left Socialist-Revolutionary party, would be excluded from participation in the soviets and discriminated against in distribution. A leading article published in *Pravda* denied any qualification to labouring peasants as potential allies of the Soviet power. The argument was that labouring peasants were a more or less powerful group gravitating economically, socially and politically around the bourgeoisie and that their political nature could not be defined since 'it liked in socialism everything that was advantageous to it, but did not like to give up its surplus'.[227] The juxtaposition of labouring peasants and rural bourgeoisie indicates that the Bolsheviks were ready to cease to distinguish between the labouring peasants and the kulaks whenever it suited their purpose. Who had the surplus of grain? The Bolsheviks offered only a tautological definition. Tsiurupa stressed that 'one should not forget for a minute that the major part of the surplus is now held only by wealthy peasants, by kulaks'.[228] Remaining perplexities about the opportunity of an alliance with the rural poor rather than with the labouring peasantry were written off by the All-Russian Conference of Factory-Shop Committees and Trade Unions, which voted for the resolution proposed by Lenin on the union with the rural poor and fixed a grain price, but rejected an amendment tending to substitute labouring peasantry for rural poor in the wording of the resolution.[229]

Under the banner of the union with the rural poor, the leadership undertook two tasks: firstly, disbandment of the peasants' soviets in which Bolshevik representation was low or nil, and secondly, the formation of political organs subordinated to central policy and thus willing to implement a policy opposing the interests of the mass of the peasants. This operation was not a minor one, since even in the soviets where the Bolsheviks had a majority, potential opposition was high, in the name of non-party deputies. Data for 504 *volosti* of the Northern Region concerning elections between December 1917 and May 1918 give the following percentages of a total of 16,553 elected deputies.[230]

Bolsheviks	18.0%
Sympathizers	11.0%
Left Socialist-Revolutionaries	3.5%
Sympathizers	2.3%
Other	1.1%
Non-party	64.1%

Other regional data on elections between March and August 1918 show that the Bolsheviks were losing power not only in favour of the Left Socialist-Revolutionaries and other small parties hostile to the Brest–Litovsk Treaty, but also in favour of non-party people.[231] The formation of rural poor committees was carried out by food detachments, local party cells, and the Red Army. Soviet literature now agrees that in a number of cases without the help of armed representatives of industrial centres, poor peasants could not be mustered.[232]

The First Army organized 140 rural poor committees (*kombedy*). The Third Army formed thirty *kombedy*.[233] There are no complete data on the formation of *kombedy* by food detachments. Available figures suggest, however, that the role of the latter was significant. The Moscow and Petrograd food detachments organized 1,550 village and 215 *volost* rural poor committees in the province of Penza, where they helped to crush local revolts.[234] In Novgorod province they formed 4,500 rural poor committees. In the province of Simbirsk the majority of *kombedy* were organized by food detachments.[235] In some cases, factories formed what were still called *kombedy*, as may be inferred from a resolution of the Moscow provincial rural poor committees on 12 September 1918, which declared that *kombedy* should not be formed in the factories and that where they had been formed they should be abolished.[236]

The mass of *kombedy* in some regions, like the Middle Volga, Samara and Simbirsk provinces, were organized between June and September 1918. At the end of 1918 they began to operate on a very large scale. By November 1918, 122,000 rural poor committees were active in thirty-three provinces of the RSFSR.[237]

The responsibility of the *kombedy* in food procurement concerned the registration and gathering up of stocks of cereals, distribution to the local population from the collected stocks and other items, including agricultural equipment, under the control of *Narkomprod*. The rules were that the requisitioned grain surpluses were to be used first to satisfy local needs. The remainder had to be delivered to the local organs of *Narkomprod*. People who discovered hidden stocks were rewarded with half the payment for delivery of that quantity of grain to the collecting stations.[238] But their political role was also significant. After the organization of the *kombedy*, the village committees were re-elected and cleansed of elements other than rural poor. The operation was carried out in such a way that 'without changing the name of village committees', as an instruction put it, 'all power would be transferred to the rural poor'.[239] Clashes became frequent. Figures reported by *Pravda* on local fights did not hide cases in which small groups of rural poor encountered the hostility of the great majority.[240] Other documents indicate that civil war was in some cases the direct consequence of the formation of *kombedy*, which in some regions met the active opposition of the peasants.[241] Classification being left to the discretion of the rural poor, any peasant could become a kulak. Spiridonova accused the Bolsheviks of making use of the peasants rather than listening to them.[242] But the Bolsheviks did not care for peasants' arguments, as long as they felt able to curb their resistance. The question of the middle peasants arose only when an increasing number of revolts associated with food procurement policies started ravaging the country.[243] The impact of the *kombedy* should be evaluated in each case in order to assess their actual role in the rural 'class struggle'. A very large number of the documents available on the rural poor committees confirm their role in food procurement. In the province of Tambov, one of those most ravaged by revolts, 90 per cent of them calculated food surpluses and 53 per cent carried out some forms of requisition.[244] But they created more problems than they helped to solve. On the one hand, as Orlov pointed out, their power – and thus their number – was inversely proportional to the actual possibility of their procuring grain. They were weak in the producing regions, where they were needed for food procurement, and strong in the consuming regions, where they were of little help in solving the food crisis.[245] On the other hand, central directives were not always interpreted in accordance with state interests. Rural poor committees often decided to requisition agricultural products, buildings, timber, and even to abolish trade, without central guidelines.[246] In spite of the intention of the leadership, for whom the rural poor committees were a politically subordinate institution, these organs tended to act on their own initiative.

The *kombedy* were no small burden for the State Budget. *Narkomprod* evaluated their cost at about six and a half million rubles a month. But this estimate concerned only the State Budget. As they started replacing the elected soviets, the rural poor committees started competing in tax collection with central organs, in order to finance their activity and staff. Taxes and contributions in kind and in money were levied on the local population, falling sometimes even on people with a right to subsidies.[247] These levies often turned out to be a harassment above and beyond the obligation of grain delivery to the state. To finance book-keeping, the rural poor committees of a *volost* of Bogorodsk *uezd* in the Moscow province levied 200 rubles on each 'kulak'.[248] In other cases, taxes on land, and excise levies on requisitioned foodstuffs, were used to pay the salaries of *kombedy* members.[249] The fiscal powers of the *kombedy* did probably exceed what was tolerable both in fiscal capacity and politically. The Moscow provincial soviet of the rural poor committees formally condemned the practice of levying money upon land sales, speculators, grain holders and all counter-revolutionaries, and affirmed that the application of monetary levies remained 'the first and indivisible right' of the *uezd* executive committee, not of the *kombedy*, who were required only to inform on people's fiscal capacity.[250]

The large degree of autonomy which indirectly derived from the possibility of dissolving the local soviets and assuming their functions reinforced the power of the *kombedy* and may have stimulated efforts to organize them at higher levels. Provincial soviets of *kombedy* were organized and efforts were even made to organize an All-Russian Council of rural poor committees.[251] The Bolshevik leadership, which did not dislike anarchy as long as it could be utilized to get rid of opposition, was alarmed when forms of organization emerged outside their central directives.[252] The mechanism of class struggle in the countryside, which the leadership had believed to be under control, revealed setbacks rather soon, but it was not easy to revise this strategy quickly. Lenin tried to do so. Whereas in July 1918 the fact that the Kazan food procurement council (led by Socialist-Revolutionaries) had autonomously increased the price of grain had induced Lenin to demand its replacement,[253] at the end of the same month he was already trying to propose to the party another image of the rural population and differentiation. Speaking at the TsIK on 29 July, Lenin affirmed that 'middle peasants, who have no grain surpluses, who have consumed them long ago and who did not go in for profiteering', were on the side of the poor peasants and against the kulaks.[254] This hint to middle peasants, though accompanied by strict qualifications, was the first sign that the Soviet power was looking for a more flexible approach to the whole foodstuffs question, to avoid adding to the sparks of civil war in the countryside. Revolts had occurred increasingly in the provinces of Saratov, Simbirsk, Penza, Yaroslavl, Vitebsk, Smolensk, Tula and Nizhni-Novgorod.[255] Preobrazhenskii reported in *Pravda* from the Urals some details on the struggle there between 'rural poor' and 'kulaks', in which the rural poor were crushing the kulaks with levies, expropriation of seed, implements and cattle, and re-allotment of land. 'The struggle of the peasant strata against upper [strata] acquired at once a violent character', commented Preobrazhenskii, 'and, in any case, burning counter-revolutionary material in the countryside was abundantly accumulated.' Adding that the Muslims, who were accustomed to let land, had been hindered by such actions, Preobrazhenskii concluded that even poor strata had started demonstrating against Soviet power.[256]

Lenin noted at the TsIK 'the wave of revolts sweeping Russia' as a sign of the sharpening of class struggle over the food crisis. He urged *Narkomprod* to increase the price of grain and to introduce other forms of grain collection, such as tax in kind and free carriage of one and a half puds of grain.[257]

Between 6 and 8 August a number of decrees embodied Lenin's directives. The services of workers' organizations were enlisted in grain collection (half of the amount collected being granted to the factories and institutions to which they belonged). Obligatory commodity exchange was accompanied by an increase of the price of grain.[258] On 23 August *Sovnarkom* authorized free carriage of one and a half puds of grain per consumer to workers of the consuming provinces.[259] On 16 August 1918, Lenin sent a telegram to all provincial soviets and rural poor committees which stressed that the tasks of the latter were to fight the kulaks and that 'between the kulaks, who are a small minority, and the poor and semi-proletarians, there is the section of middle peasants', adding that any measure against them must be stopped and condemned.[260] The policy of agreement with the middle peasants announced by Lenin with the trebling of grain prices in August was immediately followed by an authoritative editorial in *Pravda*, signed by Lenin and Tsiurupa, which warned provincial soviets and local organs of *Narkomprod* against using rural poor committees as a means to fight middle peasants, who – the editorial stressed – were entitled as well as poor peasants to take part in the distribution of industrial products.[261]

Revolt against Soviet power by the same *muzhiki* who had fought for it in October 1917 was the analytical appraisal made by Stalin (while carrying out food procurement in Ufa)[262] of the situation determined by the strategy of class struggle chosen by the leadership in the spring of 1918. The support that the Bolsheviks had been able to gain among the peasantry thanks to the decree on land was rapidly dissipated. Data on the composition of 100 *uezd* soviets elected between April and August 1918, compared with their membership in March 1918, show a significant loss of support: the Bolshevik representation fell from 66 per cent to 44.8 per cent while Left Socialist-Revolutionaries and non-party representatives increased respectively from 18.9 per cent to 23.1 per cent and from 9.3 per cent to 27.1 per cent.[263]

But it was not easy to obtain the agreement of the whole party on a milder strategy towards the peasantry and, in general, on a new approach to the food procurement question. On the one hand, the Communist Party was still composed predominantly of workers' representatives (56.9 per cent), with peasants' representatives amounting to only 14.5 per cent.[264] On the other hand, the attempt to balance some concessions to the peasantry, like the increase in the price of grain, with the authorization of free carriage for a limited quantity of foodstuffs, encountered the opposition of those food procurement officials who believed that only state commodity exchange, based on state fixed price ratios, could provide an alternative to market distribution. On 10 October 1918, the authorization for free carriage was withdrawn, under the pressure of leading *Narkomprod* officials,[265] in spite of the influential opposition of the Petrograd Bolshevik leaders Kamenev and Zinoviev, who argued for some scope for market deals.[266] The discordance of opinions was important enough to push the leadership to call an Extraordinary Congress of Soviets in November 1918, the Sixth, to debate the controversial issue of the rural poor committees and their economic–political role.[267]

The provinces where the rural poor committees were used by the Bolsheviks to get rid of the existing peasant soviets sent their representatives to the congress, to demand a strengthening of their power. The leadership paid verbal homage to the role they had performed, but announced new elections in the countryside.[268] Though the congress did not mention the future disbandment of the *kombedy*, this was the decision taken by the Central Executive Committee, which translated the conclusions of the congress into a resolution. The disbandment of the *kombedy* should have followed the formation of the new local peasant soviets.[269] The formal ambiguity which characterized the decisions of the Sixth Congress of Soviets left room for different interpretations of the role of the *kombedy*, depending on the local balance of power.

After the Sixth Congress several instructions on local elections confirmed that the *kombedy* were to keep on working either as auxiliary organs of *Narkomprod*, or as unions of labouring peasants, or as political organs in all respects. The Tula provincial executive committee declared that the *kombedy* had to be considered as class vocational organizations.[270] A congress of the *kombedy* of the Union of Communes of the Northern *Oblast* affirmed that, after the elections, there was to remain only one soviet, that of the rural poor, to which only poor males and females had electoral rights.[271] In the Moscow *Oblast* it was agreed to dissolve the *uezd kombedy*, but not all *kombedy*, since they were still supposed to fulfil the functions attributed to them by the June decree.[272] The common feature seems to have been the effort to keep the newly elected organs under the control of the Communist Party. The directives of a local executive committee in the province of Tula were that the president of the electoral commission should be the president of the *volost* or village party committee or a member of it, and that all members were to be communists or – in default of that – members of *kombedy*.[273]

The need for the re-establishment of central control was reflected in financial rules as well. Several resolutions mentioned that the income of the new village soviets would have come to them down the administrative hierarchy.[274] In some cases, extraordinary commissions annulled all the decisions formally made by the rural poor committees.[275]

Together with the reshaping of the political organs in the countryside, the leadership tried to limit the discretionary powers of the localities and food procurement organs in the extraction of the surplus, and to introduce the criteria of taxation of rural income, as a means to control income distribution in kind. A draft of a tax in kind was presented to the All-Russian Central Executive Committee on 30 October 1918. General and practical reasons were adduced for this law. Firstly, the *uezd* soviets had already resorted to forms of taxes in kind instead of monetary levies, and decided that in order to rule out arbitrariness, central guidelines were necessary. The local institutions themselves demanded that the extraction of the surplus should be defined in such a way as not to differ from an ordinary financial levy. Secondly, it was argued that, in order to stop the process of price increase of grain, methods other than monetary levies which had been abolished by the constitution were necessary to compel the countryside to share fiscal duties towards the state. The tax in kind was still aimed at the extraction of a surplus, after calculation of the farm's consumption for personal and productive uses. However, it was admitted that an accurate individual check of fiscal capacity would be impossible. For this reason, it was proposed to exact the levy on the basis of sown area, and the number of livestock, taking into account the productivity of land. The tax was calculated in such a way as to free 40 per cent of the peasants from the levy and apply progressive rates depending on the size of holding. The norms of harvest yield were reduced and the norms of consumption raised. On this basis, the average farm household, considered as having 5–6 desiatins of arable land (13.5–16.2 acres), and six members of the family, should have handed over to the central fund 14–15 puds. A forecast was made of receipt of 200 million puds of cereals, through fiscal means, i.e. more or less the demand of the consuming regions under Soviet power.[276]

The tax in kind was not implemented. In January 1919 the system of *prodrazverstka* institutionalized the forced requisition of agricultural products. The Bolshevik leadership did not have time to repair the errors of the spring of 1918. The tragic impasse to which Soviet power was driven by its previous policies was once again to bring about the need for harsher measures.

7.6 REASONS FOR THE SELECTED ALTERNATIVE AND FORMS OF OPPOSITION

The Bolshevik policy of food procurement marked the beginning of war communism, that is, of that period which was characterized by a set of institutions aiming at central control over production and distribution, according to criteria and principles inspired by the nature of the class struggle and the ideology supporting it. If one appraises the tremendous importance of the decree on the extraordinary powers of *Narkomprod* within a context in which market exchange was considered equivalent to profiteering and speculation was morally condemned, but not yet replaceable by other economic instruments, Medvedev's thesis that other policies, of the future NEP type, might have spared a long ruinous civil conflict may hold true.[277] The early literature on war communism already pointed out that some of its characteristics were evident in the summer of 1918 when new organizations were formed in the industrial field and forms of expropriation of the grain surplus were adopted.[278] The course of events during April and May 1918 may justify seeing an even earlier beginning to war communism. Emphasis on the economic and military necessity of expropriation of agricultural produce provided the rationalization for the war communist policies only later, when it seemed necessary to justify the abandonment of this method as a whole. Lenin himself was the first to underline the military nature of the economic organization, when he decided that it had to be changed.[279] Subsequent historiography, particularly in the Stalin period, stressed the emergency nature of this period by placing its origin between the autumn of 1918 and the winter of 1919, coincident with the abolition of free commerce and the organization of *prodrazverstka*, as well as with the alliance with the middle peasants, expressed in the formation of the Council of Workers' and Peasants' Defence on 21 November 1918.[280] The intervention of foreign armies and the expansion of the civil war certainly prevented a serious re-examination of the policies adopted in the spring of 1918 and favoured consolidation of compulsion as well as the authoritarian approach towards economic problems. However, the foundations of such an approach were laid down in the 'Jacobin' phase of the revolution. It was then that *collective* commodity exchange was proposed as an alternative to the market and that the forced requisition of grain through the establishment of a paramilitary organization was considered a good alternative to other economic measures.

Was there any alternative to the Bolshevik policy? Untried possibilities, of course, do not provide factual evidence. But they are not irrelevant, if one does question the rationale of the ultimate choice. The Bolshevik leadership was not unaware that other policies could be tried. It was known that other countries during war, like France and Britain, had privileged state financing of the difference between procurement prices and distribution prices of foodstuffs.[281] It was not ignored, either, that the problem of getting money back from the countryside could be tackled by fiscal measures. On 23 May 1918, an article in *Izvestiia* underlined the existence of differential rent under socialism, and suggested a state tax on it to increase state revenues, which otherwise would be built on paper and would spur on the disorganization of the economy.[282] Other proposals were made, such as sale of industrial bonds to the peasantry at attractive interest rates and including all sorts of premiums, such as the lottery principle, 'relying on the primitive psychology of money fetishism'.[283] An increase in the price of grain was demanded by more than one Bolshevik in the spring of 1918.[284] It could not be true, at least everywhere, that paper money was refused, if *Narkomprod* officials themselves complained that grain could not be purchased at the fixed price because of the effect on price of workers' organizations privately purchasing foodstuffs from peasants. If it were true, why would Lenin urge an increase in the price of grain in August 1918, as a means to increase supply?[285] As a matter of fact, the policy undertaken then was based on a rough evaluation of the relative costs of the alternatives, as well as on political assessments. State financing – it was argued – was suitable only if it did not last too long and if it was considered a prerequisite for the restoration of economic life. Financing the purchase of grain by fiscal means was not considered feasible, since it was taken for granted that the fiscal capacity of the 'speculators of grain' could not be ascertained because trade would go underground as soon as fiscal measures were enforced. And finally, the strongest argument was that an increase in the purchase price of grain to sixty rubles per pud, as the opposition demanded, and fixing the selling price at forty rubles, would mean a loss of 660 million rubles per month, i.e. about eight billion per year. This sum was considered much higher than the cost of sending food detachments to the countryside, i.e. twenty to thirty thousand people eating one funt of bread a day each.[286] There is no evidence that deeper studies of the comparative costs of alternative policies were undertaken, but the considerations set out above are indicative of the confidence that the leadership initially had in the suitability of compulsory extraction of the surplus from an economic standpoint, a standpoint which did not take into account indirect costs, such as losses in the productivity of workers engaged in such expeditions, losses due to corruption, plunder and revolts, and worst of all, loss of political support. Some further considerations may be advanced in support of the thesis that the Bolshevik food procurement policy was not the only available choice. Firstly, the Bolsheviks exaggerated the importance of the food crisis in winter time, as figures on stocks, rations and prices for Moscow and Petrograd seem to indicate. The townspeople's life was hard, but it became harder as market channels began to disappear. Secondly, the struggle against both the shopkeepers and the cooperatives (the former because they held the stocks, and so could be easily accused of speculation, and the latter because they followed the Menshevik approach of 'neutrality')[287] aggravated daily provisions.[288] Thirdly, the dispatch of food could be expected to improve in May and June, with the improved possibility of navigation and road transport. Fourthly, the problem of feeding the town was immediate and short term, i.e. until the new harvest. The cost of this operation was not necessarily as high as Orlov suggested: if limited to one and a half months (which was the period taken into consideration by the food procurement officials) it amounted to about one billion rubles, i.e. less than what had been assigned to *Narkomprod* in March 1918[289] for commodity exchange for three months. Fifthly, substitutes should have been considered; potatoes were available from spring onwards, as well as other foodstuffs growing during April and May.

Was the Bolshevik policy at least fruitful, in terms of immediate needs? The answer is uncertain. Contemporary reports underlined that the first food procurement campaign ended in failure.[290] The state purchase prices fixed in October 1917 were maintained until August 1918, i.e. for the whole agricultural year. Forecasts of obtaining 250 million puds of grain proved utterly unreal. In the food campaign of 1917–18, including five provinces of Siberia and Kirgizia, the collection reached 47,520,000 puds of grain. When Tsiurupa presented the new Bolshevik policy before the Central Executive Committee in May 1918, he mentioned that 34 million puds of the available surplus had already been collected.[291] Therefore, from May until August 1918 only 13 million puds were collected over all Russia, while plans for monthly collection were for about 36 million puds.[292]

Some improvements were obtained in Petrograd. In mid July, the bread ration had increased to half a funt a day. However, this result is also uncertain, since the population was then divided into four categories (the fourth receiving a quarter of the ration of the first category); the increase of the upper rations was achieved at the expense of the lowest.[293] In any case, overall results were not impressive. Sviderskii affirmed that by July, most of the cereals centrally distributed in Petrograd and Moscow were obtained by requisition, but this amounted to little more than two million puds.[294] It was then argued that if 8,000 food detachment workers had collected two million puds, 80,000 would be necessary to collect the whole surplus.[295] Such an army, however, would have cost ten times more and caused more social and economic damage. This consideration probably made itself felt when the decision was taken in August 1918 to treble the price of grain.[296]

At the same time, owing to a very good harvest, the market price for grain fell considerably,[297] and may have preluded easier procurement and more flexible policies.

The May scheme of collective commodity exchange, however, added further frictions. It was calculated that in the first food procurement campaign four million rubles' worth of commodities (at current fixed prices) were sent to the grain-producing provinces. But this figure does not correspond to what the peasants received.

The commodities often remained far from the villages and were not distributed. In May 1918 *Izvestiia* reported that peasants in some regions were ready to give grain in exchange for kerosene, oil, salt, sugar and manufactures, if only those products had been dispatched to the villages as well as to the large centres.[298] Another fault was that the policy of commodity exchange was governed essentially by criteria of distribution, even when the delivery of agricultural equipment was concerned. These commodities should have been supplied on the basis of plans of distribution worked out together by *Narkomprod*, *Narkomzem* and VSNKh.[299] *Narkomzem* should have computed the demand and *Narkomprod* should have implemented the actual delivery through its local organs. In practice, however, *Narkomprod* decided on the distribution of equipment on the basis of the requirements expressed by its local organs, independently of other commissariats. At times, agricultural equipment was conveyed to the grain-producing regions and there stored in central warehouses, from which it never reached the *uezd* and *volost* farms.[300] The inefficiency of the system of distribution of agricultural implements was also revealed indirectly by the fact that agricultural organizations started dealing on their own with factories producing such equipment, and the *kustar'* production of sickles, ploughs and other agricultural tools received an indirect impetus.[301] Rather than making the countryside more dependent on the towns for industrial products, the system of collective commodity exchange favoured the separation of the agricultural economy into a sort of autarchical enclave. On the other hand, the system of regressive rewards which was implied in collective exchange hindered productivity and favoured the reduction of the sown area. When the autumn sowing campaign was completed, reports from some areas revealed a reduction of 30–50 per cent in sowing.[302]

The criteria used to calculate the farms' consumption norms, above which the surplus should have been extracted, may also have affected productivity. At the beginning, when a central policy had not yet been elaborated, consumption norms were set locally, by peasants' congress or local soviets.[303] When *Narkomprod* established central norms, the needs of reproduction and the development of agricultural output were probably under-estimated. The norm of grain consumption per person was set initially at twelve puds per year; if the household produced substitutes for grain, like potatoes, the norm was reduced. If the stock of potatoes was estimated at not less than eighteen puds per person, the consumption norm of grain was reduced to nine puds.[304] Briukhanov, one of *Narkomprod*'s commissars, commented that the norm was below the needs of the peasants, which were estimated at around sixteen to eighteen puds of grain.[305] The criteria of distribution which prevailed in setting the norms of consumption for people were also adopted for livestock. The calculation of such norms took into account the 'objective needs' of the farm household, rather than the actual number of livestock. The consumption norms applying to cows were based on the size of the household: one cow for five people, three for twelve people. Fodder consumption norms were limited to two horses if the farm acreage was below ten desiatins, three horses for up to seventeen desiatins, four horses for up to twenty-four desiatins. The permitted surplus above the farm's consumption was five puds of grain.[306] The policy of *Narkomprod* was charged with causing shortages of milk, butter, meat and livestock in general when the congress of *sovnarkhozy* met in the autumn of 1918.[307]

The waste brought about in agriculture by the sudden and unprepared centralization of distribution was not compensated for by comparable advantage to the towns. Like VSNKh's policy in the industrial field, the policy of *Narkomprod* was characterized by a disparity between aims and effective means available to implement central control.

When *Narkomprod* took the first steps towards centralization of foodstuffs policy, three arguments were used to justify the exclusion of free trade. Firstly, it was alleged that competition among buyers pushed up prices and hindered the state purchase of cereals and fodder. Secondly, it was said that the scarcity of transport imposed centralization under a single directorate, in order to prevent the overloading of wagons by a considerable number of private dealers, each one carrying his own food for sale.[308] Last, but not least, was the need to ensure a fair distribution of products of prime necessity without privileges for centres more endowed with materials and means of exchange, like Moscow and Petrograd.[309]

The prerequisite for the abolition of private competition in purchase, however, was a successful central policy of distribution. But this in turn was hindered by the same factors, such as transport shortages, which had caused the separation of markets since 1917,[310] as well as by delays caused by other factors of a bureaucratic nature. The Bolshevik policy of distribution was characterized by central efforts to enforce monopoly rules in supply and distribution and peripheral reactions tending to circumvent central rulings. The largest industrial centres often manifested their disagreement with too rigid rules on trade. The Petrograd *sovnarkom* allowed the private carriage of products coming under the regulations on state trade monopoly.[331] The Moscow *Oblast* Congress of Soviets allowed the *uezd* soviets and foodstuffs committees to undertake independent purchases, after fulfilment of general *razverstka* targets.[312] The authorization to workers of the private carriage of limited quantities of foodstuffs issued by *Sovnarkom* on 23 August allowed Moscow to increase the town's provisions at a moment when – in spite of the good harvest – central distribution was utterly insufficient.[313] But, when other industrial centres like Tula, Voronezh, Penza and Saratov also started implementing the central decree authorizing limited private trade, *Narkomprod*, fearing collapse of the barely adjusted central policy, urged the suppression of all authorizations.[314] Reactions to *Narkomprod*'s policy from industrial workers were strong. Textile workers wanted their own stores to be established for local trading of manufactured goods in exchange for grain.[315] The workers of the textile factories of the Moscow *Oblast* wanted extension of the authorization for a limited carriage of grain to the whole *oblast* and authorization to carry out commodity exchange on their own, using their stocks of fabrics.[316] When the formation of workers' food detachments was allowed, to speed up the collection of grain, the textile workers demanded that half of the collected grain be handed over to the detachments and the other half to factory workers rather than to the common fund of the food section of the Moscow Soviet.[317] Lack of coordination in food procurement was also reflected in local political decisions. The Moscow Soviet invited the procurement agencies to buy the maximum quantity of potatoes on the free market before the enforcement of a ceiling on their price.[318]

The highly politically conscious staff of *Narkomprod* criticized the government's measures aimed at easing private food procurement. They claimed that it was contradictory and, in fact, impossible to requisition the grain surplus if forms of private trade were authorized.[319] *Narkomprod* calculated the number of bagmen (*meshochniki*) at one million, and that 95 per cent of those who in the summer of 1918 went to the city were peasants from the producing regions.[320] In September 1918 almost 4.5 million puds of grain were apparently dispatched to the capital by individuals and private organizations.[321] By that time, however, civil war had already spread over the country. Local anti-Bolshevik cossack governments had emerged in several areas of the South and South-East. Southern Russia was under the control of the White Volunteer Army. Social-Revolutionaries and cossacks were organizing the opposition in the East. In the summer of 1918, Kolchak's units, advancing from Siberia, took Perm in the Urals and almost reached the Volga. Fighting back the several counter-revolutionary movements, the Bolsheviks took advantage, for some time, of the fact that they were not coordinated under a single military command and did not agree on a common policy. A stronger menace to Soviet power seemed, however, to materialize in the summer of 1918, when the Supreme War Council of the Allied and Associated Powers, although with hesitation and lack of firm anti-Bolshevik concentration of forces, finally resolved on intervention both in Siberia and in the North.[322]

The organization of counter-revolution and the menace of the Allied Intervention reinforced *Narkomprod*'s political and economic approach to food procurement, in so far as the provinces falling under enemy control were the most important for grain production. The small chance of restoring limited private trade in 1918 did not survive the spread of opposition.

7.7 SUMMARY

During the First World War the lack of food supply in some of the most important industrial centres was due primarily to the failure of the transport system. The Provisional Government decreed a grain monopoly and appointed new officials for food procurement who started work on a plan of foodstuffs – commodity exchange, based on estimated quotas of grain to be delivered by each province, net of the estimated rural self-consumption. The Bolshevik Government policy inherited the plans and staff of the former food procurement organs. Its food policy cannot be understood without considering the disruptive measures against trade carried out by the local soviets and the punitive, rather than economic, approach which inspired them. The taking over of factories and requisitioning of stocks of manufactured goods provided the material basis for a policy of collective commodity exchange. This policy was based on a high fixed price ratio between industrial and agricultural products and on the obligation placed on the peasant community to deliver their grain surplus in exchange for industrial goods, to be distributed in proportion not to individual grain delivery but to the village delivery. The government encouraged the formation of food-detachments and rural poor committees to ensure the implementation of this policy. This was considered a 'cheaper' method of procurement than increasing the price of grain. It was also used as a means of winning over those sections of the rural population who gained through politically controlled redistribution of implements, cattle and consumer goods.

The policy of food procurement was based on a wrong evaluation of the relative wealth of the peasant households after the redistribution of land. The means used reflected the lack of understanding of the cohesiveness of the peasantry. There was no time to amend the disruptive socio-political effects of this policy when the leadership became aware of its consequences.

NOTES

1 The consuming regions included the following provinces: Arkhangel, Olonets-Vologda, Novgorod, Petersburg, Pskov, Vitebsk, Mogilev, Minsk, Chernigov (in the northern and western areas), Smolensk, Tver, Yaroslavl, Kostroma, Nizhni-Novgorod, Vladimir, Moscow, Kaluga (in the central industrial areas); Perm and Astrakhan (respectively in the Urals and Lower Volga).

2 Only 27.1 million puds of rye and wheat were dispatched from West Siberia (Tomsk and Tobolsk) and from the steppe regions. The central agricultural producing areas (Penza, Tambov, Riazan, Tula, Orel, Kursk) produced mainly rye and oats. See S.S. Demostenov, 'Food prices and the Market in Foodstuffs', in *Food Supply in Russia during World War*, ed. P. Struve, New Haven, 1930, pp. 386–9.

3 NKP, *Prodovol'stvennyi transport, Sbornik materialov i zametok k VIII S"ezdu Sovetov*, Moscow, 1920, p. 3; Demostenov, 'Food Prices', p. 393.

4 NKP, *Prodovol'stvennyi transport*, p. 3.

5 A.L. Sidorov, *Ekonomicheskoe polozhenie Rossii v gody pervoi mirovoi voiny*, Moscow, 1973, p. 480.

6 *Ibid.*, pp. 482–5.

7 K.I. Zaitsev, 'Organization and Policy', in *Food Supply in Russia during World War*, ed. P. Struve, New Haven, 1930, pp. 89–90.

8 Various estimates for grain forage balances and net marketing have been produced in the course of time. According to the minimum estimates, pre-war net marketing was 920 million puds. According to the maximum estimates it reached 1,178 million puds. For a detailed analysis and conclusions on the reliability of grain output data, see: S.G. Wheatcroft, 'The Reliability of Russian Prewar Grain Output Statistics', *Soviet Studies*, April 1974, no. 2, 178–80.

9 Zaitsev, 'Organization and Policy', pp. 95–6.

10 See p. 406 below. This figure also included fodder grain.

11 N.J. Astrov, 'The Municipal Government and the All Russian Union of Towns', *The War and the Russian Government*, New Haven, 1929, p. 273.

12 Sidorov, pp. 495–6.

13 Astrov, pp. 274, 291–2.

14 T.J. Polner, *Russian Local Government during the War and the Union of Zemstvos*, New Haven, 1930, p. 178, *Piat' let vlasti Sovetov*, Moscow, 1922, p. 368.

15 Astrov, p. 271.

16 Sidorov, p. 488.

17 Zaitsev, 'Organization and Policy', p. 99; *Sistematicheskii Sbornik dekretov i rasporiazhenii Pravitel'stva po prodovol'stvennomu delu*, vol. 1 (October 1917–January 1919), Moscow, 1919, pp. 205–8.

18 *Piat' let vlasti Sovetov*, Moscow, 1922, pp. 213–14.

19 Sidorov, p. 480: *Piat' let vlasti Sovetov*, p. 377; these figures include the Ukraine and Turkestan.

20 Iu. Larin, 'Ocherk khoziaistvennogo razvitiia, *Prodovol'stvennaia politika v svete obshchego khoziaistvennogo stroitel'stva Sovetskoi Vlasti, Sbornik materialov*, p. 62, and P. Popov, *Proizvodstvo khleba v RSFSR i federiriushchikhsia s neiu respublikakh (khlebnaia produktsiia)*, 1921, p. 20, who estimated on the basis of the 1916 census that landlords' arable land represented 7.2 per cent of peasants'.

21 Demostenov, 'Food Prices', p. 428. But rural craftsmen provided most of the tools and consumer goods needed by peasant households (agricultural tools and knives, furniture, hardware, fabrics, boots, etc.). This was particularly true for Central Russia: Cf. N. Anavieroff, *Lo sviluppo della Russia sotto il governo bolscevico*, Rome, 1921, pp. 21–4.

22 *Sistematicheskii Sbornik*, pp. 16–18, 18–25. In the summer of 1917 the Provisional Government approved the draft of a law empowering the Ministry for Foodstuffs to register all industrial products held by producers and traders, to issue orders on them (if necessary having the force of law) and to distribute them among the population. Cf. also: N. Orlov, *Prodovol'stvennaia rabota Sovetskoi Vlasti*, Moscow, 1918, pp. 12–13.

23 Hans von Eckardt, *Russia*, London, 1932, p. 339.

24 Cf. N. Nordman, *Peace Problems: Russia's Economics*, London, 1919, p. 88, and *Oktiabr'skii perevorot i diktatura proletariata. Sbornik statei*, Moscow, 1919.

25 'Mery po obespecheniiu sel'skogo khoziaistva sredstvami proizvodstva', pod red. M. Sheflera, *Narkomfin*, vyp. 3, 1920, 19–22.

26 *Protokoly zasedanii Vserossiiskogo Tsentral'nogo Ispolnitel'nogo Komiteta Sovetov*

Rabochikh i Soldatskikh Deputatov, Moscow, 1919, Protokol no. 9, pp. 47–8 and M.I. Davydov, *Bor'ba za khleb*, Moscow, 1971, p. 20: in October 1917 the reserves of fodder for the Northern Front of Petrograd were sufficient for two and a half days, while less than 5 per cent of the loaded wagons were able to reach the war district.

27 *Protokoly zasedanii VsTsIK Sovetov*, Protokol no. 24, p. 192.

28 *Sobranie uzakonenii*, 1917–18, no., 1 art. 6.

29 Cf. A.G. Shlikhter's memoirs in *Khleb i Revoliutsiia. Prodovol'stvennaia politika Kommunisticheskoi Partii i Sovetskogo Pravitel'stva v 1917–1922 goda*, Moscow, 1978, pp. 25–6.

30 *Protokoly zasedanii VsTsIK Sovetov*, Protokol no. 9, pp. 47–8; the protagonists in this case were Lunacharskii and Derzhinskii.

31 *Ibid.*, Protokol no. 24 (29 dekabria 1917 goda), pp. 191–2.

32 Iu. Larin, 'Ocherk khoziaistvennogo razvitiia Sovetskoi Rossii', p. 71. According to one author eight million people moved from town to countryside between 1917 and 1920: see S.N. Prokopovitch, *Ocherki khoziaistva Sovetskoi Rossii*, Berlin, 1923, p. 70.

33 B. Knipovich, 'Napravlenie i itogi agrarnoi politiki 1917–20', *O zemle*, vyp. 1, 1921, 23–5.

34 *Ekonomicheskoe rassloenie krest'ianstva v 1917–1919 gg Trudy TsSU*, vol. 6, vyp. 3, Moscow, 1922, Tables, pp. 10–11 and T. Shanin, *The Awkard Class*, Oxford, 1972, p. 53.

35 Larin, 'Ocherk khoziaistvennogo razvitiia', p. 63.

36 Shanin, p. 55.

37 Knipovich, 'Napravlenie', 25. *Ekonomicheskoe rassloenie*, estimated that 47.62 per cent of peasant households had one horse in 1917 and 60.15 per cent in 1919.

38 Cf. Shanin, pp. 32–6.

39 For an example see *V.I. Lenin: vo glave velikogo stroitel'stva*, Moscow, 1960, pp. 223–6.

40 Larin, 'Ocherk khoziaistvennogo razvitiia', pp. 62–5.

41 Cf. S. Prokopovich, *Storia economica dell'Urss*, Turin, 1957, p. 41.

42 The origin of this theory may be traced back to Lenin's remarks on the first draft of the programme of the RSDLP, at the beginning of 1900: see V.I. Lenin, 'Zamechaniia na pervyi proekt programmy Plekhanova' and 'Proekt Programmy Rossiiskoi Sotsial Demokraticheskoi Rabochei Partii', *Polnoe sobranie sochinenii*, 5th ed., vol. 6, Moscow, 1959, pp. 195–202, 205.

43 As Lenin put it: 'Workers have to work in the factory as if on a chain gang and neither time nor possibility remains for them to become socialists', *Polnoe sobranie sochinenii*, 5th edn, 55 vols., 1958–69, vol. 4, p. 384.

44 In Berdiaev's terms one could say that Lenin negated the empirical reality of the proletariat: see N. Berdiaev, *Les Sources et le sens du Communisme russe*, Paris, 1951, pp. 207–10.

45 Before 1917 peasant communist cells did not exist. In 1917 they numbered only 203. Only after the Bolshevik seizure of power did the number of peasants in the party start increasing: in 1918 16,700 peasants belonged to the Communist Party, i.e. 14.5 per cent of its total membership (*Vserossiiskaia*

perepis' chlenov RKP v 1922g, vyp. 4, Moscow, 1923, 35, 37).

46 For the history of the development and ideas of the populists see F. Venturi, *Il populismo russo*, 2 vols., Turin, 1952.

47 A detailed and deep analysis of the evolution of Russian Marxism is to be found in L.H. Haimson, *The Russian Marxists and the Origins of Bolshevism*, Cambridge, Mass, 1955; on Lenin's contribution, see A.G. Meyer, *Leninism*, Cambridge, Mass., 1957.

48 I. Deutscher, *The Unfinished Revolution. Russia 1917–1967*, London, 1967, p. 17.

49 Lenin, 'Development of Capitalism in Russia', in *Polnoe sobranie sochinenii*, vol. 3, pp. 164–80.

50 From the Marxist standpoint, industrial strikes between 1893 and 1895 were understood as the expected signal of the revolutionary potential of the working class, while the peasants' revolts against landlords, which often assumed a very brutal character, were not interpreted as a sign of any revolutionary consciousness among the peasantry; cf. L. Volin, *A Century of Russian Agriculture*, Cambridge, Mass., 1970, pp. 94–5.

51 See Haimson, pp. 152–62 on the origin of the liberal party and its influence on the Marxist movements.

52 *Ibid.*, p. 153.

53 Cf. Meyer, p. 123.

54 V.I. Lenin 'Dopolnitel'nye zamechaniia na Komissionnyi Proekt', in *Sochineniia*, 3rd edn, Moscow, 1924–37, vol. 59, p. 59.

55 Lenin, *Polnoe sobranie sochinenii*, vol. 2, p. 265.

56 Lenin, *Sochineniia*, vol. 9, pp. 356–7. For a thorough analysis of Lenin's position on the peasants, see C. de Crisenoy, *Lénine face aux Moujiks*, Paris, 1978.

57 Cf. Meyer, p. 142.

58 Lenin, *Sochineniia*, vol. 9, pp. 336–61.

59 Several parties supported – on general lines – the programme of land distribution: the Peasants' Union, Zemlia i Volia, the Narodniki, the Socialist-Revolutionaries, the Union of Maximalist Social Revolutionaries and all factions of the Russian Social Democratic Party. See G. Demorgny, *Les Partis politiques de la Révolution Russe*, Paris, 1919, pp. 94–163.

60 Lenin, *Polnoe sobranie sochinenii*, vol. 16, pp. 274–7, 295. For Marx's approach to the theory of absolute rent and its influence on investment, see K. Marx, *Capital*, 3 vols., Moscow, 1957, vol. 3, ch. 45, pp. 730–3.

61 Lenin, *Polnoe sobranie sochinenii*, vol. 16, pp. 293–4, 341, 365. The reasons for Lenin's approach to nationalization of land from the socialist point of view are explored by B. Moore, Jr, *Soviet Politics: The Dilemma of Power*, New York, 1965, p. 78.

62 Lenin, *Polnoe sobranie sochinenii*, vol. 12, p. 365; vol. 13, p. 29; vol. 16, p. 342; Lenin was afraid that municipalization would aid communal land property (see vol. 16, p. 309).

63 B.D. Wolfe, *Three Who Made a Revolution*, New York, 1964, p. 366, suggests that Plekhanov was afraid that land nationalization would mean the

restoration of the age-old servile Asiatic tradition.

64 Lenin, *Polnoe sobranie sochinenii*, vol. 16, pp. 313, 316–17.

65 *Ibid.*, p. 342.

66 Lenin, *Polnoe sobranie sochinenii*, vol. 4, pp. 110, 122–3.

67 Cf. R.G. Wesson, *Soviet Communes*, New Brunswick, 1963, p. 38.

68 V.I. Lenin, *Collected Works*, 4th edn, 45 vols., London, 1964–70, vol. 24, p. 503.

69 At the First Congress of Peasants' Soviets Lenin obtained only 20 votes against Kerensky's 804 and Chernov's 820: see L. Trotsky, *The History of the Russian Revolution*, London, 1936, p. 871.

70 Lenin, *Sochineniia*, vol. 31, pp. 165–6.

71 Cf. Shanin, p. 1 and pp. 46–74 for an analytical discussion on data and arguments in favour of and against polarization.

72 N.D. Kondrat'ev and N.P. Oganovskii, *Sel'skoe khoziaistvo Rosii v XX veke, Sbornik statistiko-ekonomicheskikh svedenii za 1901–1922 gg*, Moscow, 1923, pp. 60–1.

73 *Statisticheskii spravochnik po agrarnomu voprosu*, vyp. 1, Moscow, 1917, pp. 14–15.

74 *Statisticheskii spravochnik*, p. 11; Popov, *Proizvodstvo khleba*, pp. 27–8.

75 Cf. Shanin, p. 20 and *Sovetskoe krest'ianstvo (kratkii ocherk istorii, 1917–1919)*, pod red. V.P. Danilova, M.P. Kima, N.V. Tropkina, Moscow, 1970, p. 16. In 1916, 14 per cent of the land of the *obshchina* was turned to private ownership.

76 N.P. Oganovskii, *Individualizatsiia zemledeliia v Rossii i ee posledstviia*, Moscow, 1917, pp. 30, 51.

77 N. Jasny, *The Socialized Agriculture of the USSR. Plans and Performance*, Stanford, 1949, pp. 147–9.

78 On the controversial issue of pre-war data for agricultural output S.G. Wheatcroft concludes that the truth probably lies somewhere in the middle between the lowest figures and the very high figures estimated in 1925 by *Gosplan* (a 19 per cent difference), that is, between 4,130 million puds (estimated by the Commissariat for Agriculture) and 5,690 million puds for gross output of grain forage (estimated by *Gosplan* in 1925–6); see Wheatcroft, 178–80. Indirect evidence for increasing agricultural output in the pre-war years may be derived from the falling price ratio between agricultural products and industrial goods during a stage of industrial growth: cf. A. Gerschenkron, 'The Rate of Industrial Growth in Russia Since 1885', *Journal of Economic History*, vol. 7, Supplement, 1947, 154. According to Kondrat'ev and Oganovskii, pp. 102–7, the cultivated area increased between 1900 and 1913 by more than four million desiatins in the black lands and by about twelve million throughout the territory of the future RSFSR, i.e. from 74,757,000 to 86,432,000 desiatins. *Sbornik statisticheskikh svedenii po Soiuzu SSR, 1918–23*, Moscow, 1924, pp. 130–1, estimated an average yearly gross output for cereals excluding fodder equal to 2,739,822,000 puds for RSFSR. For comments on the reliability of data, cf. also Iu. A. Poliakov, *Perekhod k NEPu i Sovetskoe krest'ianstvo*, Moscow, 1967, p. 63.

79 The productivity per desiatin estimated by Popov (*Proizvodstvo khleba*, p. 5) was less than half that of Germany.

	Russia	Germany
	(puds per desiatin)	
Wheat	45.0	142.4
Rye	52.2	117.2
Barley	55.0	136.4
Oats	51.0	125.8
Potatoes	477.0	899.0

Popov's figures for the average yearly total output of cereals between 1909 and 1913 were the lowest: 3,079 million puds versus 3,850,200 million puds estimated in *Sbornik statisticheskikh svedenii, 1918–23*, pp. 130–1, but the difference – though very high – was not such as to reduce significantly the comparatively poor performance of Russia.

80 Cf. Shanin, pp. 81–121.

81 Lenin, *Polnoe sobranie sochinenii*, vol. 16, pp. 202–3.

82 Budget studies also showed a positive correlation between the household's wealth, the number of its members and the number of horses, which seems to contradict the common belief that poor households had more children. According to a sample investigation in seven *volosti* of European Russia, in 1913 the so-called *zazhitochnye* (well-to-do) peasant households had 7.21 members on average, the middle peasants 5.86 and the poor peasants 4.37. Other studies indicated that wealth per head was also higher among the wealthiest: cf. S.G. Strumilin, *Ocherki ekonomicheskoi istorii Rossii i SSSR*, Moscow, 1966, p. 218 and Shanin, pp. 63–70 on several examples of budget studies and comments on their validity.

83 See Shanin, pp. 71–80.

84 Cf. Larin, 'Ocherk khoziaistvennogo razvitiia Sovetskoi Rossii', p. 66.

85 Lenin, *Collected Works*, vol. 25, pp. 122–3.

86 The publication of the minutes of the Central Committee of the Bolshevik Party in the stormy days preceding the October Revolution seems to confirm the thesis of Lenin's radicalism in his struggle for power as opposed to the conciliatory line supported by other party members (Kamenev, Miliutin, Riazanov, Zinoviev, Shliapnikov) and the specific impact that the latter's resignation from leading posts after the seizure of power had on Lenin's final compromise allowing the Left Socialist-Revolutionaries to join the government: see *The Bolsheviks and the October Revolution, Central Committee Minutes of the Russian Social-Democratic Labour Party (bolsheviks). August 1917–February 1918*, London, 1974, pp. 128–43 and R.V. Daniels, *Red October. The Bolshevik Revolution of 1917*, New York, 1967, pp. 210–12.

87 *Uprochenie Sovetskoi Vlasti v Moskve i Moskovskoi Gubernii, Dokumenty i materialy*, Moscow, 1958, pp. 302–3, 307, 362.

88 *Pravda*, 9 March 1918, 3.

89 *Pravda*, 20 March 1918, 3.

90 Davydov, *Bor'ba za khleb*, p. 64.

91 Demostenov, 'Food Prices', p. 423.

92 Zaitsev, 'Organization and Policy', pp. 95–6.

93 *Pravda*, no. 66, 7 April 1918, 3; no. 69, 11 April 1918, 3; no. 70, 12 April 1918, 3; no. 72, 14 April 1918, 3; no. 73, 16 April 1918, 3; no. 206, 25 September 1918, 3; no. 203, September, 1918, 2.

94 *Protokoly zasedanii VsTsIK Sovetov*, Protokol no. 24, p. 192.

95 *Pravda*, no. 75, 19 April 1918, 2.

96 *Materialy po istorii Sovetskogo stroitel'stva: Sovety v epokhu voennogo kommunizma. Sbornik dokumentov*, 1928, p. 389.

97 *Ibid.*, p. 391.

98 *Trudy II Vserossiiskogo S''ezda Sovnarkhozov*, p. 122; on grain prices see below, pp. 346–8.

99 *Izvestiia*, no. 8, 14 January 1919, 4.

100 *Izvestiia*, no. 16, 24 January 1919, 3.

101 *Izvestiia*, no. 18, 26 January 1919, 4.

102 *Krasnyi Arkhiv*, vol. 4, p. 42.

103 *Izvestiia*, no. 49, 4 March 1919, 3.

104 *Izvestiia*, no. 61, 21 March 1919, 5.

105 *Izvestiia*, no. 222, 5 October 1919, 3.

106 This preoccupation was actual not only in the spring of 1918 (see *Pravda*, no. 75, 19 April 1918, 2), but also later, when civil war spread all over Russia. On 14 August 1919, the People's Commissar for Food Procurement prohibited dispatch of currency notes at the front to cooperative organizations and local procurement organs, for fear that money could be confiscated by Denikin's troops; see *Sistematicheskii Sbornik dekretov i rasporiazhenii po prodovol'stvennomu delu*, Moscow, 1919, vol. 2, p. 920.

107 *Oktiabr'skii perevorot*, pp. 85–7. Cf. on workers' commodity exchange A. Antoshkin, 'Rabochii Trekhgornoi manufaktury v 1917 g', *Istoriia proletariata SSSR*, no. 8, 1931, 74; *Rabochii dvizhenie v 1917 godu, podg. k pechati V.L. Meller i A.M. Pankratova*, Moscow–Leningrad, 1926, pp. 312–38; A. Kovalenko, 'Bor'ba fabrichno-zavodskikh komitetov Petrograda za rabochii kontrol' nad proizvodstvom', *Istoricheskie Zapiski*, vol. 61, 1957, 75–7.

108 Credits were assigned by the central government only for predetermined expenditure on the basis of half-year estimates. Although the practice of monthly, quarterly and half-yearly reviews of the estimated budget allowances made a certain adjustment to price inflation possible, the local soviets had no money to carry out a ready policy of food procurement (*Sobranie uzakonenii*, 1918, no. 51, p. 582; G.Y. Sokolnykov *et al., Soviet Policy in Public Finance, 1917–28*, Stanford, 1931, pp. 123–4).

109 *Pravda*, no. 50, 20 March 1918, 3; no. 51, 4 March 1918, 3; no. 63, 4 April 1918, 3.

110 *Pravda*, no. 59, 30 March 1918, 4.

111 N. Orlov, *Prodovol'stvennaia rabota Sovetskoi Vlasti*, Moscow, 1918, p. 183.

112 *Pravda*, no. 56, 27 March 1918, 1.

113 *Pravda*, no. 17, 5 February 1918, 2. The Bolsheviks were not accustomed to refer to former work when they presented their own projects. Specific studies on the drawing up and implementation of projects by the Provisional Government may fill this gap in our knowledge in the future. But the fact that several former high officials and experts, especially among the Menshevik

cadres, remained at their posts or were even promoted to higher posts after the Bolshevik Revolution may well support the view that in the field of food procurement, which was already a great problem in 1917, much work had already been done. It is interesting to note that Groman, who was one of the promoters of the economic council of the Provisional Government, was in charge of food procurement in the Northern *Oblast*, and at the meeting of food procurement committees held on 28 April 1918 produced the only project of commodity exchange containing figures and details on organization (see *Protokoly zasedanii pervogo s''ezda prodovol'stvennogo komiteta severnoi oblasti*. Izd. Severnoi oblastnoi prodovol'stvennoi upravy. Moscow, 1918, pp. 33–4; and N. Jasny, *Soviet Economists of the Twenties*, Cambridge, 1972, pp. 92–101).

114 *Pravda*, no. 18, 6 February 1918, 4.
115 *Pravda*, no. 22, 10 February 1918, 2.
116 *Sobranie uzakonenii*, 1918, no. 30, art. 398 and *Sistematicheskii Sbornik*, vol. 1, pp. 148–9.
117 *Sistematicheskii Sbornik*, vol. 1, pp. 149–50.
118 Orlov, pp. 182–3.
119 A. Sviderskii, *Tri goda borb'y s golodom*, Moscow, 1920, pp. 8–9.
120 *Sistematicheskii Sbornik*, vol. 1, p. 149.
121 *Ibid.*, pp. 149–50.
122 Orlov, pp. 209, 224, 226.
123 See the regulations issued by the Commissar for the City of Moscow from August 1917 onwards in *Sbornik postanovlenii i rasporiazhenii obshchikh i mestnykh (reguliruiushchikh prodovol'stvennoe delo v Moskve)*, vyp. 1 (Izd. po 1-e Ianvaria 1918 g), Moscow, 1918 (under the heading Moskovskii Gorodskoi Prodovol'stvennyi Komitet SRD), pp. 274–80.
124 *Sobranie uzakonenii*, 1918, no. 48, art. 566.
125 Orlov, pp. 230 and 239, and *Izvestiia*, no. 154.
126 Cf. M. Frumkin, *Chetyre goda prodovol'stvennoi raboty. Stat'i i ochetnye materialy*, Moscow, 1922, p. 69.
127 *Khleb i revoliutsiia*, p. 90 and Orlov, p. 350.
128 M. Frumkin, *Chetyre goda*, p. 69.
129 Orlov was one of the head officials of *Narkomprod* at that time, sharing the views of the Left Socialist-Revolutionaries on political issues.
130 Orlov, pp. 351–2.
131 *Ibid.*, pp. 58–9.
132 *Dekrety Sovetskoi Vlasti*, vol. 2, Moscow, 1959, pp. 307–12.
133 Orlov, pp. 78–81.
134 *Uprochenie Sovetskoi Vlasti*, p. 313.
135 See below, pp. 358–71, on the strategy of class struggle in the countryside, based on rural poor committees and food detachments.
136 Lenin, *Collected Works*, vol. 28, pp. 45–6.
137 *Sistematicheskii Sbornik*, pp. 151–2.
138 S.A. Sokolov, *Revoliutsiia i khleb. Iz istorii Sovetskoi prodovol'stvennoi politiki v 1917–1918*, Saratov 1967, p. 43.
139 A. Sviderskii, 'Prodovol'stvennaia politika Sovetskoi Vlasti', in *Prodo-*

vol'stvennaia politika v svete obshchego khoziaistva stroitel'stva Sovetskoi Vlasti, *Sbornik materialov,* Moscow, 1920, p. 160.

140 *Trudy II Vserossiiskogo S"ezda Sovnarkhozov,* pp. 87–9.

141 *Ibid.*

142 *Uprochenie Sovetskoi Vlasti,* p. 318.

143 *Pravda,* no. 141, 10 July 1918, 3.

144 *Sobranie uzakonenii,* 1917–18, no. 83, art. 879, and *Sistematicheskii Sbornik,* vol. 1, p. 202.

145 On the Committee for Utilization see pp. 304–8 above.

146 *Sistematicheskii Sbornik,* vol. 2, pp. 163–5.

147 *Izvestiia,* no. 1, 1919, 3; *Sistematicheskii Sbornik,* vol. 2, p. 165.

148 M. Frumkin, 'Razverstka, kak osnovnoi metod gosudarstvennoi zagotovki', in *Prodovol'stvennaia politika v svete,* p. 267.

149 *Sistematicheskii Sbornik,* vol. 1, pp. 158–9.

150 See *Pravda,* no. 223, 6 January 1918, 3 on municipalization of local butchers in Tula; *Pravda,* no. 233, 27 January 1918, 4 on requisition of all grain stocks by a local soviet (Saratov Province) with the use of armed troops; *Provda,* no. 13, 31 January 1918, 3, on the instructions issued by the Petrograd Soviet on the inspections of buildings and requisitioning of foodstuffs and all commodities which might be used for speculative purposes; *Pravda,* no. 14, 1 February 1918, 4 on the requisitioning of foodstuffs and other commodities by the Sections for Struggle against Speculation in provinces where the soviets were controlled by Bolsheviks and Socialist-Revolutionaries; *Pravda,* no. 23, 12 February 1918, 1, on requisitioning of goods carried by *meshochnichestvo*; *Pravda,* no. 25, 14 February 1918, 2 on the *Sovnarkom* decree signed by Lenin, instituting an Extraordinary Commission for the Protection of the Railways, instructed to carry out police tasks and to prevent non-authorized transportation of goods.

151 See *Pravda,* no. 13, 31 January 1918, 3; *Pravda,* no. 16, 3 February 1918, 3, for statements that inspections should be carried out only in those houses where the probability of finding goods was well founded; see *Pravda,* no. 22, 10 February 1918, 4, for very small quantities of requisitioned foodstuffs (i.e., ten funts of meat or twenty funts of potatoes).

152 *Pravda,* no. 28, 17 February 1918, 1.

153 *Pravda,* no. 29, 19 February 1918, 3 and no. 32, 22 February, 3.

154 *Pravda,* no. 33, 23 February 1918, 1.

155 *Pravda,* no. 37, 28 February 1918, 3.

156 *Pravda,* no. 39, 2 March 1918, 1.

157 *Pravda,* no. 223, 6 January 1918, 3.

158 *Pravda,* no. 17 (244), 5 February 1918, 1; no. 19, 7 February, 1; no. 20, 8 February, 1 published an article signed by Mikhelson against concentration of baking; *Pravda,* no. 24, 13 February 1918, 1; no. 25, 14 February, 4 announced that all bakeries and shops for bread supply would come gradually under soviet control and that bread delivery would be concentrated in a few places.

159 *Pravda,* no. 30, 20 February 1918, 2.

160 *Uprochenie Sovetskoi Vlasti,* pp. 309–11.

161 *Pravda,* no. 53, 20 March 1918, 3.

162 *Pravda*, no. 52, 19 March 1918, 4; no. 54, 21 March, 4; no. 44, 8 March, 4.
163 *Pravda*, no. 53, 20 March 1918, 3; for clashes between 'wealthy bourgeoisie' and 'merchants' and rural poor and the Red Army, see *Pravda*, no. 65, 3 April 1918, 2; on kulaks abolishing the local soviet (Kineshma) and establishing a *golodnyi* (hungry) soviet, see *Pravda*, no. 70, 9 April 1918, 4; on the reshaping of the local soviet (Penza) including the poorest people and excluding 'kulaks, merchants and other bourgeois elements', see *Pravda*, no. 70, 9 April 1918, 4; on kulaks rising against the soviet in Saratov, see *Pravda*, no. 69, 8 April 1918, 4; on kulaks coming with wives and children to the session of the local *uezd* soviet (Kizhkina, Moscow *uezd*) dominated by 'rural poor' and claiming elections according to the old rules (*po staromu staroste*), see *Pravda*, no. 83, 25 April 1918, 4.
164 On 2 January 1918, for instance, Petrograd received eighty wagons of wheat and twenty-three of rye. The same proportion remained even later, although absolute quantities of both types of grain reported each day were diminishing.
165 *Protokoly zasedanii*, pp. 33–4.
166 The Petrograd Food Board announced on 17 May 1918 that since April the number of ration cards had diminished from 1,925,825 to 1,851,616 (*Pravda*, no. 99, 17 May 1918, 3).
167 Figures based on the accounts provided by the Petrograd Food Board can be taken only as an indication of monthly trends, but the important missing elements are the actual stocks remaining from 1917.
168 Cf. Shilov's report at the First Congress of Food Procurement Committees in the Northern *Oblast*, *Protokoly zasedanii*, p. 11.
169 *Pravda*, no. 14, 1 February 1918, 4.
170 *Pravda*, no. 37, 28 February 1918, 3 and *Statistika Truda*, nos. 4–5, 1918, 46 (figures on wages from October 1917 to August 1918).
171 *Pravda*, no. 68, 10 April 1918, 3; no. 71, 19 April, 2. The estimated monthly requirements were thirty million puds.
172 *Protokoly zasedanii*, pp. 11, 13.
173 *Pravda*, no. 73, 16 April 1918, 3.
174 *Protokoly zasedanii*, pp. 12, 36.
175 *Ibid.*, p. 34.
176 Cf. V.I. Miliutin, 'Problema raspredeleniia i potrebleniia', *Za piat' let* (*1917–1922*), *Sbornik Ts.K.R.K.P.*, Moscow: 1922, p. 311.
177 *Uprochenie Sovetskoi Vlasti*, pp. 311–12; C. Duval, 'Yakov M. Sverdlov and the All-Russian Central Executive Committee of Soviets (VTsIK). A study in Bolshevik Consolidation of Power, October 1917–July 1918', *Soviet Studies*, vol. 31, no. 1, 1979, 13–14.
178 *Pravda*, no. 84, 30 April 1918, 3; *Izvestiia*, no. 86 (350), 30 April 1918, 3; at the end of March 1918 local soviets, particularly in the Viatka Province, abolished the grain monopoly and allowed free purchase of grain: Z. Atlas, 'Iz razvitiia istorii tovaroobmena mezhdu gorodom i derevnei (1918–1921 gg)', *Voprosy ekonomiki*, 1967, no. 9, 78. Biographical information of Rykov in *Autobiografie dei Bolscevichi* (a cura di G. Haupt and J.J. Marie), Rome 1971, p. 84.
179 *Protokoly zasedanii*, pp. 14–15, 23, 27, 38, 39 on reports by Kostin (from

Vologda province), Galevich (also from Vologda), Vladimirov (Petrograd), and other reports from the provinces of Poltava, Tavria, and Novgorod.

180 *Ibid.*, Cf. Lopatin's report, p. 36.
181 Vladimirov, *Ibid.*, p. 27.
182 *Pravda*, no. 93, 10 May 1918, 2 and no. 95, 12 May 1918, 1, 2.
183 Cf. *Pravda*, no. 71, 19 April 1918, 3 on the decision by the Petrograd Food Board to deliver foodstuffs only to needy people; no. 95, 12 May 1918, 3, on the question of two supplementary rations for manual workers; no. 108, 28 May 1918, 2, announcing as a victory of the proletariat the establishment of priority in food rations for 150,000 manual workers.
184 Cf. Semenov's Report in *Protokoly zasedanii*, pp. 40–1.
185 *Izvestiia*, no. 93 (357), 12 May 1918, 4; and Sviderskii's Report in *Protokoly zasedanii*, pp. 42–3.
186 *Pravda*, no. 90, 11 May 1918, 2; the available surplus after deduction of Novorossiia, the Ukraine and the South-Western regions (outside Soviet control) was calculated to be 331 million puds, of which 34 million had already been used up. The *overall* surplus from the 1917 harvest was 881.9 million puds of which 322.5 were for sowing and fodder. Thus 559.4 million puds remained available.
187 *Ibid.* The overall demand was computed at 321 million puds, including Central Regions, 98 million (31 per cent), non-Black Earth Regions, 73 million (23 per cent), other Middle and Western Volga regions, 91 million (28 per cent), and Turkestan, Southern Caucasus and other regions 59 million. Overall supply was computed at about 850 million puds, 516 million of which were to be supplied by Novorossiia, the Ukraine and Southern and Western Regions (outside Soviet control), 131 million by the Northern Caucasus (16 per cent), 130 million by Siberia and the Steppe region (15 per cent), 52 million by the Central Agricultural Regions, and 18 million by other provinces. Tsiurupa also mentioned surpluses of past years' harvests (particularly in Samara, Tomsk and Ufa) which could still be collected.
188 *Ibid.* The council of supply had been attached to *Narkomprod* after its reorganization in May 1918.
189 Iu. K. Strizhkov, *Prodovol'stvennye otriady v gody grazhdanskoi voiny i inostrannoi interventsii 1917–1921*, Moscow, 1973, p. 59 from archive documents.
190 Cf. Z.V. Atlas, 'Iz razvitiia istorii', p. 30, and *Denezhnoe obrashchenie i kredit*, vol. 1, Petrograd, 1922, p. 94.
191 Cf. *Pravda*, no. 84, 30 April 1918, 3 and *Protokoly zasedanii*, pp. 38–9.
192 Lenin, *Collected Works*, vol. 27, pp. 356–7.
193 *Pravda*, no. 93, 15 May 1918, 1; also *Sobranie uzakonenii*, 1918, no. 35, art. 468.
194 Davydov, p. 78.
195 *Pravda*, no. 105, 29 May 1918, 2.
196 *Dekrety Sovetskoi Vlasti*, vol. 2, 1959, pp. 107–12.
197 *Ibid.*, vol. 2, p. 380.
198 *Pravda*, no. 101, 24 May 1918, 2.
199 Lenin, *Collected Works*, vol. 27, pp. 431, 435.
200 *Uprochenie Sovetskoi Vlasti*, pp. 320–1.
201 P.G. Sumerin, *Kombedy v Penzenskoi Gubernii*, Penza, 1960, p. 10. For other cases of local formation of requisition detachments see A.S. Umnov, *Grazhdanskaia voina i srednee krest'ianstvo (1918–1920 gg)*, Moscow, 1959, p. 39;

S.S. Khesin, *Matrosy revoliutsii, uchastie voennykh moriakov v bor'be za uprochenie Sovetskoi Vlasti (Oktiabr' 1917–Marta 1918)*, Moscow, 1958, pp. 74 5; *Bol'shevistskie voenno-revoliutsionnye komitety*, Moscow, 1958, p. 156; N.I. Podoviskii, *God 1917*, Moscow, 1958, pp. 184–5; M.N. Potekhin, *Pervyi Sovet proletarskoi diktatury*, Leningrad, 1966, p. 271.

202 Strizhkov, p. 48.
203 *Uprochenie Sovetskoi Vlasti*, p. 312; *Bor'ba rabochikh i krest'ian pod rukovodstvom Bol'shevistskoi Partii za ustanovlenie Sovetskoi Vlasti v Tambovskoi Gubernii (1917–1918 gg)*, *sbornik dokumentov*, Tambov, 1957, Document no. 101, p. 139. *Pravda*, no. 95, 12 May 1918, 2, and no. 106, 25 May 1918, 1.
204 *Bor'ba ... v Tambovskoi gubernii*, Document no. 105, pp. 142–3.
205 *Dekrety Sovetskoi Vlasti*, vol. 2, p. 310.
206 *Uprochenie Sovetskoi Vlasti*, pp. 319–20.
207 Strizhkov, pp. 72–3.
208 Lenin, *Collected Works*, vol. 44, pp. 95–6.
209 *Uprochenie Sovetskoi Vlasti*, p. 324.
210 *Ibid.*
211 *Ibid.*, p. 325.
212 *Pravda*, no. 112, 6 June 1918, 3; no. 113, 7 June 1918, 1; no. 116, 11 June 1918, 2; no. 118, 13 June, 3; no. 127, 25 June 1918, 3.
213 *Pravda*, 13 June 1918, 3.
214 *Uprochenie Sovetskoi Vlasti*, pp. 326–9.
215 *Pravda*, no. 100, 23 May 1918, 3; no. 102, 25 May 1918, 2; no. 110, 4 June, 1918, p. 2; no. 118, 13 June 1918, p. 2.
216 *Bor'ba ... v Tambovskoi Gubernii*, Document no. 125, pp. 169–70.
217 *Uprochenie Sovetskoi Vlasti*, p. 332; *Pravda*, no. 116, 11 June 1918, 2.
218 *Uprochenie Sovetskoi Vlasti*, pp. 335–6. Lenin, 'Report on the Current Situation' (27 June 1918), in *Collected Works*, vol. 27, pp. 459–77, 491.
219 *Pravda*, no. 106, 25 May 1918, 1.
220 Strizhkov, p. 83; also M. Dobrotvor, 'Moskovskie rabochie v prodotriadakh', *Bor'ba Klassov*, 1934, nos. 7–8, p. 154; and A. Berkevich, 'Petrogradskii proletariat v bor'be za khleb v gody voennogo kommunizma', *Bor'ba Klassov*, 1935, nos. 7–8, p. 178.
221 *Uprochenie Sovetskoi Vlasti*, p. 341.
222 *Pravda*, no. 92, 14 May 1918, 1.
223 *Pravda*, no. 99, 22 May 1918, 2.
224 *Ibid.*, my italics.
225 *Pravda*, no. 118, 13 June 1918, 2.
226 *Ibid.*
227 *Pravda*, nos. 123–4, 21–2 June 1918, 1.
228 *Pravda*, no. 127, 25 June 1918, 3.
229 *Pravda*, no. 135, 4 July 1918, 2
230 *Sovetskoe krest'ianstvo*, p. 43.
231 M. Spirin, *Klassy i partii v grazhdanskoi voine v Rossii*, Moscow, 1968, p. 175.
232 Strizhkov, p. 93.
233 A.S. Kon'kova, *Bor'ba Kommunisticheskoi Partii za soiuz rabochego klassa s bedneishim krest'ianstvom v 1917–1918*, Moscow, 1974, p. 139.
234 Umnov, p. 54; Kon'kova, p. 140.

235 Strizhkov, p. 94.
236 *Komitety derevenskoi bednoty Moskovskoi oblasti. Sbornik materialov i dokumentov*, ed. A.V. Shestakov, Moscow, 1938, pp. 201–2.
237 Kon'kova, p. 137, and *Sovetskoe krestianstvo*, p. 55.
238 *Pravda*, no. 119, 15 June 1918, 3; no. 127, 25 June, 1918, 2; 12 July 1918, 4.
239 *Materialy po istorii Sovestkogo stroitel'stva. Sovety v epokhu voennogo kommunizma, Sbornik dokumentov*, Part 1, 1928, p. 331.
240 *Pravda*, no. 133, 2 July 1918, 2.
241 *Pravda*, no. 144, 13 July 1918, 2; Strizhkov, p. 93; and L.M. Orekhova, 'Pokhod rabochikh v derevne v 1918 g', *Voprosy Istorii KPSS*, 1958, no. 1, 129.
242 *5i Vserossiiskii S"ezd Sovetov Rabochikh, Krest'ianskikh, Soldatskikh i Kazach'ikh Deputatov. 4–10 Iulia, 1918 g*, Sten otchet, Moscow, 1918, p. 57.
243 Between July and October 1918, 108 peasant revolts broke out in the most important provinces for food collection (*Sovetskoe krest'ianstvo*, p. 58). See also n. 255.
244 Cf. *Komitety bednoty. Sbornik materialov*, Moscow–Leningrad, 1933, vol. 1, p. 26, on the basis of archive materials relating to the Tambov, Penza and Ivanovo-Voznesensk provinces.
245 Orlov, p. 377.
246 *Materialy po istorii Sovetskogo stroitel'stva: Sovety v epokhu voennogo kommunizma, Sbornik dokumentov*, Part 1, 1928, pp. 349, 355, 385, 396.
247 *Komitety derevenskoi bednoty Moskovskoi oblasti. Sbornik materialov i dokumentov*, pp. 172–3, 180–1, 212, 241, 252, 285.
248 *Ibid.*, p. 285.
249 *Ibid.*, p. 212.
250 *Ibid.*, p. 338.
251 For the Moscow Provincial Soviet of Rural Poor Committees see *ibid.*, p. 338; also E. Medvedev, *Krest'ianstvo Srednego Povolzheia v Oktiabr'skoi Revoliutsii*, Kuibyshev, 1970, pp. 271–2.
252 *Sovety v epokhu voennogo kommunizma*, p. 374.
253 *Khleb i Revoliutsiia*, pp. 69–70.
254 Lenin, *Collected Works*, vol. 28, p. 27, (also in *Polnoe sobranie sochinenii*, vol. 37, p. 11).
255 See n. 219; also *Pravda*, no. 126, 23 June 1918, which reported fights between kulaks and food procurement militia; *Leninskii sbornik*, vol. 18, p. 201 containing Lenin's order to the local executive committees of Penza and Orel to expropriate all surpluses of cereals and to put down the kulaks' revolt; *Pravda*, no. 137, 6 July 1918, 3 for news on the 'tragic' revolt of Yaroslavl; *Pravda*, no. 147, 17 July 1918, 3 on news of revolts in Vitebsk and Smolensk and Tula provinces; *Pravda*, no. 150, 20 July 1918, 3 reporting Moscow detachments crushing revolts in Tula and the ensuing of penalties in kind and money; *Pravda*, no. 156, 27 July 1918, reporting the liquidation of a kulak revolt in Nizhni-Novgorod; *Pravda*, no. 156, 27 July 1918, again on revolts in Vitebsk, Nizhni-Novgorod, Novopansk (*Pravda*, no. 158, 30 July 1918); and finally *Pravda*, no. 159, 31 July 1918, reporting several interventions of the Extraordinary Commission (Cheka) in the struggle against 'speculation'.

256 *Pravda*, no. 135, 4 July 1918, 1.
257 Lenin, *Collected Works*, vol. 28, p. 27; and 'Theses on the Food Question', in *Collected Works*, vol. 28, pp. 45–6.
258 These decrees were published in *Izvestiia* on 6 and 8 August 1918; see also *Sobranie uzakonenii*, 1918, no. 57, arts. 633, 635.
259 Davydov, p. 97; on 5 September a similar decision was taken by the Soviet of Petrograd. The law authorized free carriage until 1 October 1918 (*Sobranie uzakonenii*, 1918, no. 64, art. 707).
260 Lenin, *Collected Works*, vol. 28, p. 59.
261 *Pravda*, no. 175, 18 August 1918, 1. On prices see Table 7.1.
262 Stalin, 'Letter to Lenin' of 4 August 1918, in J.V. Stalin, *Works*, vol. 4, Moscow, 1953, pp. 125–6.
263 Spirin, p. 174.
264 Poliakov, p. 178; also E. Gimpel'son, 'Sotsial'no-politicheskie izmeneniia v sostave rabochego klassa v pervye gody Sovetskoi Vlasti', in *Rabochii klass: vedushchaia sila Oktiabr'skoi Revoliutsii, Sbornik statei*, Moscow, 1976, p. 250.
265 Davydov, p. 99; A.A. Nelidov, *N.K.P. RSFSR i ego mestnye organy v period ustanovleniia i provedeniia v zhizn' prodovol'stvennoi diktatury (leto–osen' 1918)*, Trudy Moskovskogo gos-istoriko-arkhivnogo instituta, vol. 19, 1965, 41.
266 S.A. Sokolov, *Revoliutsiia i khleb*, p. 81.
267 Critical observers from the Left Socialist-Revolutionary Party pointed out that the congress had been concerned to disband the rural poor committees, but also noted that by that time the Communist Party was representing mainly the lumpen-proletariat (a fact that by itself would make it hard to revise the policy toward the peasantry); see *Teoriia i Praktika Sovetskogo Stroia – Respublika Sovetov*, vyp. 1, Berlin–Milan, 1920, pp. 19–20.
268 *6i Vserossiiskii Chrezvychainyi S''ezd Sovetov Rabochikh, Krest'ianskikh, Kazach'ikh i Krasnoarmeiskikh Deputatov*, stenogr. otchet, Moscow, 1919, pp. 97–175.
269 *Sobranie uzakonenii*, 1917–18, no. 86, art. 901.
270 *Komitety... Moskovskoi oblasti*, pp. 340–1.
271 *1i S''ezd Komitetov Derevenskoi Bednoty Soiuza Kommun Severnoi Oblasti, 3–9 Noiabria, 1918g*, Petrograd, 1918, pp. 11–14.
272 *Komitety...Moskovskoi oblasti*, p. 184.
273 *Ibid.*, p. 116.
274 *1i S''ezd Komitetov...Kommun Severnoi Oblasti*, pp. 11–12 and *Komitety... Moskovskoi oblasti*, p. 338.
275 E.g. the Bogorodinsk *uezd* rural poor committee in the province of Tula, which had been quite active in the confiscation of foodstuffs and horses and the taxation of local kulaks in the summer of 1918 (*Komitety... Moskovskoi oblasti*, pp. 281–302).
276 *Protokoly zasedanii*, 8 zasedanie (5-go soiuza), 30 October 1918, pp. 278–82; *Sobranie uzakonenii*, 1917–18, no. 82, art. 864, and nos. 91–2, art. 928.
277 R. Medvedev, *Dopo la Rivoluzione*, Rome, 1972, pp. 137–8.
278 L. Kritsman, *Geroicheskii period Velikoi Russkoi Revoliutsii*, p. 31.
279 Lenin, *Collected Works*, vol. 32, p. 320.
280 Cf. A. Lomakin, 'Ob osnovnykh etapakh istorii SSSR (1917–1934)', *Vestnik kommunisticheskoi akademii*, 1934, nos. 5–6, pp. 80–91.

281 Orlov, p. 81.
282 *Izvestiia*, no. 102 (366), 23 May 1918, 2.
283 Orlov, p. 394; *Pravda*, no. 112, 6 June 1918, 3.
284 Besides Rykov, Larin also urged a change in the principles of food procurement, but *Sovnarkom* rejected this proposal on 4 June 1918 (*Khleb i Revoliutsiia*, p. 140).
285 See p. 370 above.
286 Cf. Orlov, pp. 82–3.
287 Cf. *Za piat'let*, p. 311.
288 More than once Petrograd rations were not increased after shipments of foodstuffs 'owing to technical reasons': cf. *Pravda*, no. 92, 9 May 1918, 3 and no. 87, 30 April 1918, 3.
289 See p. 340 above.
290 *Piat'let vlasti Sovetov*, p. 377; also Larin, 'Ocherk', p. 73; and cf. A. Sviderskii, 'Prodovol'stvennaia politika', p. 162.
291 *Narodnoe Khoziaistvo*, 1918, nos. 8–9, p. 2.
292 *Ibid.*
293 Davydov, p. 185; *Pravda*, no. 145, 14 July 1918, 3. Petrograd was the first industrial centre to apply 'class rations' (on 1 July 1918); on 27 July 1918, *Narkomprod* introduced class rationing in all towns. These rules were implemented in Moscow from 1 September and in all other towns from 1 October 1918.
294 *Pravda*, no. 154, 25 July 1918, 2.
295 *Pravda*, no. 155, 26 July 1918, 1.
296 While the opposition proposed sixty rubles and Lenin thirty rubles: see Orlov, p. 82; Lenin, *Collected Works*, vol. 28, pp. 45–6; and *Izvestiia*, 8 August 1918, 1.
297 In the province of Vitebsk the price of one pud of cereals fell in three days from 240 rubles to 170 and in one week to 90 rubles (*Pravda*, no. 150, 20 July 1918, 4). Cases were even reported where the monopoly price was above market price: cf. *Pravda*, no. 191, 7 September 1918, 3.
298 Larin, 'Ocherk', p. 73; Orlov, p. 239; Iu. Larin and L. Kritsman, *Ocherk khoziaistvennoi zhizni i organizatsiia narodnogo khoziaistva Sovetskoi Rossii*, Moscow, 1920, p. 20; *Izvestiia*, no. 95 (359), 15 May 1918, 1.
299 *Sobranie uzakonenii*, 1918, no. 34, art. 447.
300 *Vestnik Sel'skogo Khoziaistva*, 1919, nos. 27–30, pp. 11, 14.
301 See pp. 78–9 on the *kustar'* economy.
302 Cf. E.G. Gimpel'son, *Velikii Oktiabr' i stanovlenie Sovetskoi sistemy upravleniia narodnym khoziaistvom (Noiabr' 1917–1920 gg)*, Moscow, 1977, pp. 127–8; though it must be remembered that statistics on land must be evaluated with great caution.
303 *Pravda*, no. 60, 31 March 1918, 4; 10 April 1918, 2; no. 79, 24 April 1918, 4.
304 *Krasnyi Arkhiv*, vol. 6, 1939, 30.
305 *Trudy II Vserossiiskogo S"ezda Sovnarkhozov*, p. 120.
306 *Krasnyi Arkhiv*, vol. 6, 1939, 30.
307 *Trudy II Vserossiiskogo S"ezda Sovnarkhozov*, pp. 105, 124.
308 *Pravda*, no. 184, 30 August 1918, 3.
309 *Pravda*, no. 270, 12 December 1918, 3.

310 The balance between requested and obtained freights for foodstuffs was as follows:

1918	Requested	Obtained	%
August	1,297	157	12.1
September	1,643	411	25.0
October	2,019	698	34.6
November	2,090	507	29.3
December	1,452	420	28.9

Source: NKP, *Prodovol'stvennyi transport, sbornik materialov i zametok k VIII S"ezdu Sovetov*, Moscow, 1920, p. 6.

311 *Pravda*, no. 93, 15 May 1918, 3.
312 *Uprochenie Sovetskoi Vlasti*, pp. 318–19.
313 *Pravda*, no. 181, 25 August, 1918, 3.
314 *Pravda*, no. 199, 17 September 1918, 3.
315 *Pravda*, no. 200, 18 September 1918, 3–4.
316 *Pravda*, no. 204, 22 September 1918, 4.
317 *Ibid.* and *Pravda*, no. 176, 20 August 1918, 3.
318 *Pravda*, no. 183, 28 August 1918, 3.
319 *Pravda*, no. 184, 30 August 1918, 3.
320 *Izvestiia NKP*, 1918, nos. 24–5, pp. 22–3; Kritsman, *Geroicheskii period*, p. 135. *Narkomprod* calculated that 1,345,611 people were involved in black market activities.
321 *Izvestiia NKP*, 1918, p. 23.
322 N. Riasanovsky, *A History of Russia*, 2nd edn, Oxford, 1969, pp. 531–4 and J.D. Clarkson, *A History of Russia*, 2nd edn, New York, 1969, pp. 524–6.

8

Prodrazverstka

8.1 MILITARY EMERGENCY AND SMYCHKA

At the beginning of September Trotskii urged concentration of supply policy and pooling of national resources in the service of defence.[1] Following his declaration that the Soviet Republic should become a war fortress, the Central Executive Committee prescribed a military regime of food procurement corresponding to the country's situation.[2] At the end of 1918 the territory under Soviet rule was one-eleventh of that covered by the Brest–Litovsk Treaty.[3] This loss included Siberia, which according to *Narkomprod*'s plans was to compensate for the loss of the Ukraine as a source of grain provisions.[4]

At the beginning of 1919 the army's monthly consumption of cereals was calculated at 6.5 million puds.[5] The collected surplus in the grain-producing provinces which throughout war communism were to remain under Soviet rule had been only 24,488,000 puds of cereals in the food campaign of 1917–18.[6] War added new impetus to centralization and provided the official justification for increasing and intensifying control measures.

Military emergency was to sublimate the drive to requisition foodstuffs, adding patriotic overtones to the struggle for the survival of the revolutionary government. The Bolshevik leadership understood that foreign intervention could give its power the legitimation that its own policy had been unable to secure. The tasks of defence were assigned to the Council of Workers' and Peasants' Defence, with the purpose of stressing the unity of the labouring people against the enemy and the formal halt to discrimination between the rural poor and other sections of the peasantry. An interesting question is whether the Bolsheviks succeeded, under the pressure of their need for peasants' military and economic support in the struggle against the Allied Intervention, in establishing an effective alliance with the peasantry, which could prelude its political rehabilitation and the establishment of new relations between

396

town and countryside. Soviet historiography has usually considered the *smychka* (alliance) with the peasantry as a consequence of success in the policy of neutralization of this class, which was allegedly achieved in the summer of 1918.[7] This interpretation is based on Lenin's rationalization of the 1918 Bolshevik strategy at the Eighth Congress of the Party in March 1919, which approved it. But in fact, in the summer of 1918, the Bolsheviks had succeeded in 'neutralizing' the Socialist-Revolutionaries who controlled the peasants' committees rather than the peasants themselves. The expulsion of the most challenging party representatives of the peasants' interests from the political organs were not only unsuccessful in gaining peasant support for the Bolshevik cause, but alienated most of it.[8] From July until the end of 1918, 129 revolts were counted in the European part of Russia. The reversal of the policy towards the peasantry desired by Lenin was an extreme attempt to remedy errors due to a too radical analysis of the social composition of the countryside, when civil war was already ravaging the country. But it was not accompanied by an ideological revision and could hardly have been understood by the middle peasants. One of them wrote in *Izvestiia* that Lenin wanted to help the peasantry, but Trotskii, who had formed his army with non-peasant elements, strove to extract from the middle peasants all their grain stocks, which amounted to no more than 2–5 puds per household.[9] The Sixth Congress of the Soviets, in November 1918, was meant to abolish the rural poor committee, and restore the peasant soviets which had been relieved of their functions during the summer and autumn of 1918. The alliance with the marginal sections of the rural population, which had been useful in getting rid of the Socialist-Revolutionaries, started alarming the leadership when it felt the need for wider acceptance of its power. The peasants had suddenly become the social force on which the fate of the revolution depended. At the same time, however, the Bolsheviks suspected that the forced extraction of the surplus necessary to finance the war could definitely alienate the support of the countryside for the Bolshevik Government, especially if the peasants had been promised or granted by other rulers the rights in relation to land which they had obtained under the Bolsheviks. Thus the need for political control over the peasantry became even more urgent than it had been under the pressure of the food units in the winter and spring of 1918. In this context, the resolution of the Sixth Congress of the Soviets on the disbandment of the rural poor committees by way of new elections in the countryside was not fully acceptable; nor was it going to be backed by an open acknowledgement of the mistakes made in food policy, which might have facilitated a firm alliance between workers and peasants. Therefore the true content of the *smychka* remained ambiguous and differences of opinion on how to deal with the peasantry remained as sharp as they were in the spring of 1918. While Larin ascribed the peasants' revolts to *Narkomprod*,[10] the officials of *Narkomprod* found in the sharpness of the military conflict the most propitious climate to enforce a regime of food delivery by quotas, *prodrazverstka*, which incorporated the principle of both collective commodity exchange and class conflict in the extraction of the surplus. From this point of view the rural poor committees could hardly have been dispensed with. It was in this context that on 4 December 1918 a party conference in Samara town agreed that one of the most urgent tasks was the dictatorship of the rural poor over the kulaks. As late as the end of 1919 a large number of rural poor committees still remained operative in the most important provinces:[11]

2,227 in the province of Saratov
2,274 in the province of Kazan
2,227 in the province of Penza
2,126 in the province of Perm
1,950 in the province of Simbirsk
more than 2,000 in the province of Samara

In several provinces exclusion of the middle peasants from the local soviets continued and was justified by their economic standing or by their political views.[12] When organs representing political positions other than Bolshevik remained, they were firstly deprived of their functions by strengthening parallel party organizations and then abolished on the ground that they were superfluous.[13]

If military emergency could be used to justify central policies of food procurement in 1919, more efforts could have been made to obtain the peasants' acceptance of Soviet power by revising the discriminatory criteria which separated the *bad* from the *good* peasant, and the kulak from the marginal elements.[14] Even in this respect, corrections were slow, difficult and hard to enforce. When the need to broaden the social agreement to power arose, Lenin promptly produced figures showing the majority to be on the side of Soviet power. His draft on the tax in kind, which was not implemented, suggested considering 40 per cent of the peasantry as rural poor and 20 per cent as middle peasants, exempting the former from the levy and applying only a moderate levy on the latter.[15] This approach was prompted by tactical considerations, but did not offer objective criteria for the levy, either. The fact that the party members to whom implementation of the policy towards middle peasants was assigned had no serious guidelines to follow is shown by the very measures which Lenin and Trotskii put forward in March 1919 for the defence of the middle peasants, such as reduction of delivery quotas, amnesty and the formation of a central commission for the *defence* (Lenin's italics) of middle peasants,[16] or instructions not to hinder middle peasants by inconsiderate seizure.[17] When Lenin decided to stake his whole authority on the question of the alliance with the middle peasantry, he came closer to the concept of labouring peasantry which the Bolsheviks had rejected in March 1918. Middle peasants became the ones who did not exploit the labour of others and did not live from other people's labour, who did not take advantage of other people's labour and who lived directly from their own.[18]

Though this effort to find a place for the middle peasantry in the Marxist ideological framework was a sign of higher political realism, it did not offer protection against arbitrariness in the requisition of grain, nor did it allow for a more flexible attitude to the peasants' own interests as an incentive to higher productivity.[19]

From the ideological point of view, even after the March 1919 Party Congress, the middle peasants remained a *class that vacillates* (Lenin's italics) between the antagonistic goals of the two souls of that class – of the property owner and of the working man.[20] But if the peasant could not find a moral status within the ideology of the regime, what law or instruction could prevent him from harassment and the accusation of being a profiteer? While condemning the province party of Nizhni-Novgorod for having issued instructions aiming at placing the burden of taxation on the *middle element of the peasants generally* (Lenin's italics), Lenin himself recognized that in the present situation the problem of exactly defining the attitude to the middle peasant was insoluble, if it had to be solved immediately and all at once.[21]

8.2 THE PRODRAZVERSTKA

The regime of *prodrazverstka*, obligatory delivery of foodstuffs by quota, was officially introduced in January 1919. It became the foundation of food procurement and lasted until March 1921. The reasons mentioned by the decree for the introduction of this regime of food procurement were the army's urgent requirements and implementation of the decree on the state monopoly of cereals as well as of the decree on the tax in kind. This system was, indeed, conceived as a sort of progressive levy in kind upon agricultural produce. But it was also meant to deprive the peasants of their right to any surplus over their own consumption. The decree on *prodrazverstka* affirmed the principle of the prevalence of the state's needs over individual needs. In this sense, it seemed to reverse the logic of the former surplus collection.[22] Rather than fixing the population's consumption norms in agricultural areas, the administration fixed the state consumption norm, that is, the overall state requirement of cereals to be exacted from producers, whatever the latter's consumption needs. This meant that the foundation of the state purchase of foodstuffs was considered to be the central distribution of the agricultural output to all people and not only to the army or the needy. In other words, the decree on *prodrazverstka* formalized the principles justifying the abolition of the market, though, in fact, the market was tolerated because an alternative machinery of distribution for all products could not yet fully replace it. The burden of the economic loss was to fall primarily on the wealthy peasants, but the village community, as a whole, was made responsible for implementation of the plan of delivery. The orders for obligatory delivery were sent to each province based on estimates of its sown area, harvest, population and numbers of livestock. The provincial organs were further entrusted to subdivide the delivery requirements at the lower administrative levels – *uezd*, *volost* and village. The obligatory quotas were due on predetermined schedules and at fixed prices.[23] Purchase prices were differentiated according to province, but the trend was towards a flattening of price ratios, by limiting price increases in the grain-consuming provinces (see Table 7.1 above). The local administration was supposed to apply *prodrazverstka* according to its own estimates of the relative wealth of each peasant group. The mutual responsibility for the delivery of the whole amount to the state organs resembled the operation of the Tsarist tax system in relation to the *mir*. Since the village as a whole was responsible for the overall delivery, the higher the quota falling on the wealthier, the lower would be the quota to be paid by lower strata. This was the assumption of those mainly responsible for the state procurement policy.[24] But it is also understandable that, to the extent to which the whole village was the tax payer, the whole village was interested in lowering the norm of extraction. This fostered efforts to conceal the true figures on average harvest, on the cultivated area, the kind of crops and quantity of livestock, as were allegedly made in 1918, when the local food procurement organs were entrusted with calculating each individual surplus. In practice, peasants resorted to many expedients to hide the threshed quantity. Diverting attention from the best fields, threshing with strong bows in order to disperse grain all around, and simple theft of grain, were reported by the food procurement organs. One of their official summarized the peasants' reaction to *prodrazverstka* in these words: 'All right – go on distributing your quotas; we'll do what we want.'[25] For this reason, the central computation of the 'fiscal' capacity in kind of the rural population was preferred to local data. The amount of the delivery in some cases was fixed on the basis of past records on ten-year periods of provincial import–export of grain.[26] The food procurement plan for

Table 8.1. *Planned grain deliveries, 1918–19 and 1919–20*

Provinces	1918–19 (thousand puds)	1919–20 (thousand puds)
Voronezh	18,000	22,350
Viatka	45,186	13,700
Kazan	10,777	18,400
Kursk	15,900	15,050
Orel	13,792	12,300[a] + 5,400 Perm
Penza	11,468	7,700
Riazan	4,760	7,050
Samara	50,000	46,650 + 15,400, Pokrovsk
Saratov	31,467	38,200 + 8,500 from German communes
Simbirsk	11,988	11,650
Tambov	32,290	31,100[a]
Tula	11,741	6,500[a]
Ufa	960	36,500
Total	258,331	296,450

[a]In October 1919 the province of Orel was occupied by the enemy. So was the southern territory of Tula province. Six out of the eight *volosti* of Tambov fell under control of the Whites.
Source: *Izvestiia NKP*, 1919, nos. 17–20, p. 7; and Iu. Strizhkov, *Prodovol'stvennye otriady v gody grazhdanskoi voiny i inostrannoi interventsii, 1917–1921*, Moscow, 1973 (from archive documents), p. 165.

1918–19 and 1919–20 computed an overall demand for grain equal to about 250 million puds, which were to be delivered by the provinces shown in Table 8.1.

Fulfilment in 1918–19 fell short of plans. According to data reported in *Vtoroi god borb'y s golodom*, which differ slightly from the above data as to provincial quotas, the percentage of fulfilment was 38.4 per cent, distributed among provinces as shown in Table 8.2.

In spite of the results, the law on *prodrazverstka* represented an enormous effort in organizing a state market in cereals, as compared with the rough policy of requisition carried out in 1918. There was, indeed, a continuity between 1918 and further policies for the appropriation of the surplus. *Narkomprod*'s instructions, in fact, stressed that *prodrazverstka* did not apply to farms without grain surplus and that the responsibility for collection fell upon the president of the *volost* soviet and the president of the rural poor committee.[27] This should have implied formal respect for the norms of consumption and enforcement of the policy of class struggle only in the form of the expropriation of the wealthiest. But the law on *prodrazverstka*

Table 8.2. *Fulfilment of the 1918–19 plan for grain deliveries*

	planned (thousand puds)	collected (thousand puds)	% fulfilment
Voronezh	15,500	4,869	31.4
Viatka	30,500	7,544	24.7
Kazan	13,500	8,251	61.1
Kursk	17,000	4,286	25.2
Orel	14,100	7,725	54.8
Penza	11,600	3,260	28.1
Riazan	5,000	3,075	61.5
Samara	60,000	22,997	38.3
Saratov	31,100	13,762	44.3
Simbirsk	12,000	4,689	39.1
Tambov	36,000	14,235	39.5
Tula	13,800	5,287	38.3
Total	260,100[a]	99,980	38.4

[a]Plus 8,167,000 puds from other provinces (Orenburg, Perm, Ufa, Ural *Oblast*).
Source: Quoted by M.I. Davydov, *Bor'ba za khleb*, Moscow, 1971, p. 154

went further, since it stressed the principle of state requirements over that of class privileges to the extent that *all* producers could be called to contribute, if necessary, to fulfil the state quota. This difference was important since it entailed the possibility of grain requisition beyond the estimated surplus of each single producer.

A rebate was allowed, for 30 per cent of the obligatory quota, if state requirements were considered fulfilled some months before the expiry of the collection deadline. The initial assignments could be modified in predetermined proportions by substitution of other products.[28]

Formally, *prodrazverstka* still respected the principle of collective commodity exchange. Individual producers received a receipt for the quotas delivered. All receipts were collected by the local consumers' cooperatives which all producers had to join, providing the basis for the community right to the acquisition of a corresponding quantity of industrial commodities. The local cooperatives kept the accounts of local transactions. The delivery of agricultural products was reported on the debit side and the value of the products received in exchange on the credit side.[29] Commodities were to be released by the cooperative centres, or by the agencies of *Narkomprod* or their respective distribution centres, in proportion to the amount of agricultural produce collected. *Narkomprod*'s officials estimated that for the 1918–19 agricultural campaign two billion rubles' worth of commodities were released to the peasants in exchange for 1.7 billion of grain.[30] Two-thirds in value of all products were textiles.[31] Other state monopoly products for exchange included salt, sugar, matches, tobacco, kerosene, glass, boots and other leather articles, galoshes, soap, tools, implements and metal articles. The price ratio was that established centrally by the state. In the original plans, four milliard rubles of industrial commodities should have been dispatched to the producing provinces, to obtain 216 million puds of cereals (at fixed prices for both). Commodities which were dispatched and not released, because of 'evident lack of correspondence between state purchase and supply to peasants of industrial products', remained for collective commodity exchange in the next food campaign of 1919–20, when the decree on obligatory commodity exchange was extended to the entire country.[32] Collective commodity exchange was still supposed to favour proletarian and semi-proletarian elements, who shared in distribution independently of their own contribution to the supply of grain. The leadership tried to enforce the principle 'from each according to his ability, to each according to his needs' and obtain local agreement to it,[33] in some cases by imposing complete respect for the law, first of all, on political representatives and communist cells. An instruction of the Military Bureau to the detachments put particular emphasis on the fact that *prodrazverstka* should be fulfilled 100 per cent by members of the *volost* and agricultural soviets and by party members.[34]

The application of collective commodity exchange, however, as well as the implementation of *prodrazverstka*, encountered practical difficulties. On the one hand, neither was well understood. The peasants sometimes tried to elude collective commodity exchange, and local soviets endeavoured to find objective equivalents for commodity exchange,[35] i.e. local price ratios between industrial commodities and foodstuffs supplied. Only one example concerning distribution in one *volost* is available (see Tables 8.3 and 8.4).

The criteria followed in this case indicate that products for personal consumption were distributed in such a way as to level down more or less the remuneration per desiatin, that is, distribution bore a certain relation to supply; though landless peasants and peasants having no delivery quota were not excluded from distribution. On the other hand, a regressive system of remuneration operated in relation to farm households and desiatins for farm implements, which was likely to stimulate intensive cultivation and penalize large farms, except the few collective farms.[36] Scarcity of industrial commodities made it impossible to satisfy all farms. Only one out of three farms in the above example received some agricultural equipment, the distribution of which favoured collective farms. Only one farm out of twelve received other agricultural tools. The

Table 8.3. *Distribution of products for personal use, 1919*

	Fabrics (arshins)		Salt (funts)		Boots (pairs)	
	Hh.	Des.	Hh.	Des.	Hh.	Des.
Landless peasants	2.5	1.5	1.8	1.07		
Individual owners	6.8	1.4	4.9	1.01	0.07	0.015
among whom						
with no delivery	4.6	1.4	3.3	1.03		
for less than 50 puds	5.9	1.4	4.1	1.00	0.03	0.007
for 50–100 puds	7.2	1.4	5.3	1.00	0.04	0.026
above 100 puds	9.2	1.4	6.8	1.04	0.06	0.009

Hh. = per household
Des. = per desiatin
Source: Prodovol'stvennaia politika v svete obshchego khoziaistva stroitel'stva Sovetskoi Vlasti. Sbornik materialov. Moscow, 1920, p. 188.

Table 8.4. *Distribution of industrial products for productive use, 1919*

	Nails, horseshoes, etc. (pieces)		Agricultural equipment (pieces)		Tools and metal goods (locks, hammers, etc.)	
	Hh.	Des.	Hh.	Des.	Hh.	Des.
Landless peasants	—	—	—	—	—	—
Individual owners	0.61	0.13	0.35	0.07	0.08	0.016
among whom						
with no delivery	—	—	—	—	—	—
for less than 50 puds	0.82	0.20	0.40	0.10	0.10	0.024
for 50–100 puds	0.50	0.09	0.33	0.06	0.07	0.013
above 100 puds	0.45	0.07	0.36	0.06	0.06	0.08
Collective farms	—	—	8.6	0.10	—	—

Source: Prodovol'stvennaia politika, p. 188

distribution of agricultural equipment and tools to farms of comparatively small dimensions was possibly related to the process of land distribution and the need to provide new farmers with some means of production. From October 1918 to June 1919 it was calculated that supply fell very much short of demand, except for small agricultural tools, which were generally produced by handicraftsmen. The organs of the Commissariat for Agriculture calculated the following figures:

Table 8.5. *The satisfaction of demand for agricultural equipment and tools,*
October 1918–June 1919

	Demand (thousand pieces)	Supply (%)
Ploughs	569	18.0
Cultivators	247	7.0
Seeding machines	31	3.0
Scythes	3,000	12.0
Mowing machines and horse rakes	46	6.5
Sickles	1,000	32.0
Grain-harvesting machines	37	13.0
Threshing machines	37	3.0
Grain-cleaning machines	77	4.0
Straw-cutters and root-cutting machines	32	6.0

Source: *Vestnik Sel'skogo Khoziaistva*, 1919, nos. 27–30, p. 14

Table 8.6. *Norms of distribution of fabrics during ten months of 1919*

	Cotton	Wool (arshins)	Flax	Silk	Coarse fabric (rolls)
Workers	20	1.0	4.0	0.35	4.0
Other urban population	10	0.5	0.5	0.25	2.0
Rural population	9	0.1	0.33	0.10	1.25

Source: N. Osinskii, 'Glavnyi nedostatok nashei razverstki', *Prodovol'stvennaia politika*, p. 232

Larin calculated that each year, out of the industrial products dispatched by *Narkomprod*, two-thirds went to peasants and a third to others.[37]

During 1919 and 1920, about 12,000 wagon-loads of industrial commodities were dispatched to the provinces.[38] The food procurement organs distributed among the population 228 million arshins of fabrics, 2.5 million puds of salt, one million puds of kerosene and about one million puds of sugar.[39] By that time, however, *Narkomprod* officials themselves admitted that the norm of distribution of fabrics to the rural population was 'a starvation norm giving to the countryside only the possibility of mending holes'.[40] The norms of distribution favoured workers as opposed to the rural population (see Table 8.6).

Because of the exhaustion of commodities, collective commodity exchange became an empty formula. In 1920 only 20 per cent of the value established for obligatory delivery was paid in commodities, according to official figures,[41] which took into account only aggregate flows reaching the provincial centres, not necessarily the agricultural villages. In default of means of exchange, compulsion prevailed. In the autumn of 1919, Tsiurupa declared to a congress of provincial food procurement organs that the fundamental method of work in this field was coercion, which he concisely summarized in a revealing sentence: 'If you do not give up what you are asked to, you will be fought by all means, including the expropriation of your farm.'[42] If an entire village community refused to comply with central orders, the food detachments were instructed to divide the population into groups of not more than fifty farm households and compel them to fulfil their obligation of *prodrazverstka*. In the event of hostile behaviour, the militia of the Republic would have to intervene.[43]

On the other hand, it was not easy to enforce the principles of 'class' distribution of the burden of *razverstka* in order to get the support of 'some' peasants against the surplus owners. *Razverstka* ended up in general discontent, in so far as it was not successful in discriminating among peasants according to their capacity to contribute in kind; and the norms of distribution objectively favoured the urban population which aroused among the peasants envy of townspeople, who were apparently getting the lion's share.[44] While instructions stressed that poor peasants and those middle peasants who owned no more than 3–4 desiatins for a six-member household must be freed from the obligation to deliver cereals,[45] some food procurement organs were informed that *razverstka* was falling on poor and middle peasants rather than on the 'rich peasants'.[46] Osinskii complained that when *razverstka* was decided upon by agricultural committees or soviets, it was treated as a poll tax (capitation) or as a charge per desiatin rather than per *cultivated* desiatin.[47] However, both the instructions and comments of the left wing of the party, which led to policy of *Narkomprod*, disregarded the objective criteria for a fair *razverstka* in the Russian case, where small peasant holdings had already become the prevalent type of rural farm. In 1919 74 per cent of farms had less than four desiatins, in 1920 75.9 per cent, and in 1922 86.4.[48]

The reduction in the average size of farm was itself an impediment to the policy of expropriation of the agricultural surplus exclusively or mainly limited to rich peasants. The percentage of farms with four to ten desiatins fell from 25.2 in 1917 to 20.8 in 1920, and those with more than ten desiatins from 3.7 to 3.3.[49] During the civil war, the burden of *razverstka* falling upon the peasantry became increasingly high. Table 8.7 gives only the *razverstka* of cereals and fodder. But food procurement greatly enlarged its scope after 1917. As in various countries during the First World War,[50] appropriation which began with grain was extended

Table 8.7. *Food procurement of bread grains, groats, and fodder between 1916 and 1922 (excluding the Ukraine and Turkestan)* (*thousand puds*)

Provinces	1916–17	1917–18	1918–19	1919–20	1920–1	1921–2
Producing provinces constantly taking part in food procurement	126,635	24,488	72,483	102,290	65,684	7,765
Producing provinces not constantly taking part in food procurement	79,663	—	32,438	61,487	66,271	40,224
Consuming provinces not constantly taking part in food procurement	6,279	808	1,936	14,643	25,088	48,959
Total	212,578	26,489	106,858	178,421	158,044	96,948
Siberia[a]	25,419	9,497	—	32,038	59,674	38,549
Kirgizia (except Orenburg province)	13,697	11,533	1,063	2,046	5,273	6,471
Northern Caucasus	71,393	—	—	—	60,942	7,712
Total	393,089	47,520	107,922	212,507	283,934	149,681

[a]In Siberia, three provinces took part in state purchase in 1916–17; five provinces in 1917–18; all provinces in 1919–20 onwards.
Source: *Piat' let vlasti Sovetov*, Moscow, 1922, p. 377

to other products. The peculiarity of the Soviet Republic was a conscious effort to prepare the way to a non-market economy lasting even after the war. Thus the regime of *razverstka* included raw materials, though an immediate aim was, as in other countries, to limit diversification of production by which producers tried to evade partly the burden of expropriation. After having submitted all cereals and fodder, meat, potatoes and some vegetables to *prodrazverstka*, *Narkomprod* started fixing obligatory quotas for oil seeds, eggs, hemp, beef cattle, honey and horses.[51] By 1920 *razverstka* already included thirty products, though for some of them free trade was still allowed in what remained after the obligatory delivery.[52] Potatoes, which for the 1918–19 food campaign should have been collected by state organs at fixed prices, were in fact sold to workers' organizations at market prices for the first part of the year, and then submitted to *razverstka* at fixed prices differentiated according to regions and quality.[53] The restriction on freedom to decide crops was accompanied in March 1920 by a prohibition on trade of cattle and meat across provincial frontiers, and on sale of cattle without *Narkomprod* approval.[54]

Taking into account all items subject to *razverstka*, including raw materials, Vainshtein calculated the amount of *razverstka* in pre-war rubles as a percentage of farms' conventional income, for 1920–1 (see Table 8.8).

Table 8.8. *1920–1 razverstka value for households of various fiscal capacities*

Arable land per household	A Income per household in prewar rubles	B *Razverstka* + Confiscation + Taxes	B As% of conventional net income from land
Consuming provinces			
1–2 desiatins	404.2	17.43	8.2
2.01–4 des.	526.5	32.20	11.6
4.01–6 des.	714.2	83.86	20.3
6.01–8 des.	683.2	44.11	11.5
above 8.01 des.	647.3	93.69	30.4
Producing provinces			
1–2 desiatins	312.1	76.47	34.8
2.01–4 des.	339.7	30.05	13.8
4.01–6 des.	418.8	55.62	20.5
6.01–8 des.	505.7	61.67	18.0
above 8.01 des.	712.6	142.71	34.5

Source: A. Vainshtein, *Oblozhenie i platezhi krest'ianstva*, Moscow, 1924, p. 71.

	Total income value Aᵃ	Income value of land B	Conventional net income C	Prodr-azverstka D	Confis-cations E	Money taxes F	D + E + F G	G as % of C
Consuming provinces								
1 Moscow	631.0	596.7	425.5	10.1	—	0.4	10.5	2.5
2 Vladimir	402.7	362.3	256.0	26.4	7.7	0.43	34.2	13.4
3 Ivanovo-Voznesensk	455.3	402.6	278.0	15.3	—	0.1	15.3	5.5
4 Novgorod North	515.0	475.6	283.2	35.5	7.0	0.04	42.7	15.1
5 Dvinsk	524.8	447.3	265.3	27.5	2.1	0.1	29.7	11.2
6 Petrograd	885.1	858.2	600.0	104.1	4.8	0.02	108.9	18.2
7 Pskov	549.8	524.1	325.5	40.6	7.7	0.01	48.2	14.8
Average per five provinces	505.8	456.9	301.6	23.0	3.4	—	26.5	9.5
Average per seven provinces	566.3	523.8	347.6	37.1	4.2	0.1	41.4	11.5
Producing provinces								
8 Ufa	288.1	242.6	186.7	41.4	3.3	2.9	47.6	25.5
9 Orel	420.0	416.1	348.0	66.1	8.5	—	74.6	22.3
10 German Commune	440.7	435.5	337.8	131.1	34.4	—	165.5	49.1
11 Tula	391.0	373.5	308.8	78.9	—	3.3	82.2	26.5
12 Kursk	539.4	487.0	423.3	38.7	2.9	—	41.6	9.8
13 Riazan	404.0	370.5	252.6	21.3	2.9	0.4	24.6	9.3
14 Penza	563.2	522.0	408.7	43.4	2.4	0.3	46.1	11.3
Average per five provinces	415.8	390.9	320.8	71.2	9.8	1.3	83.3	26.7
Average per seven provinces	435.2	406.7	323.6	60.1	7.8	1.0	68.9	22.1

ᵃA is the value of agricultural and artisan income plus other incomes, except loans and debt redemption. B includes produce of owned land and income from sale of cattle. C is equal to B less expenditure for seeds and fodder. Other agricultural costs are not taken into account.

Source: Vainshtein, Supplement to Table 4

Table 8.10. *Direct and indirect levies as a percentage of conventional income*

1912	10.8% of 650–70	rubles conventional income
1918–19	16.7% of 289	rubles conventional income
1920–1	26.1% of 307	rubles conventional income

Source: Vainshtein, pp. 71–2

Vainshtein showed that the total sum extracted from peasants through the regime of *razverstka* was more than twice that of foodstuffs only.[55]

Criteria of fiscal capacity did not quite hold: in the producing provinces small farms of no more than two desiatins happened to pay in absolute figures a third more than farms of up to six desiatins and in percentage terms more than all other farms (see Table 8.8).

The average *prodrazverstka* was also fairly independent of regional income distribution, though it was generally higher in the producing provinces (see Table 8.9). Moreover, if one takes into account the findings of Strumilin's 1922–3 investigation of a sample of seven *volosti* in different provinces of European Russia,[56] one realizes that *prodrazverstka* – contrary to the initial hypothesis that state monopoly of industrial goods was to improve the marketability of agricultural output – had the precise effect of reducing the 'socialization' of agriculture, since in 1920 the number of families participating in the sale and purchase of food decreased by 5 per cent as compared with 1917, while the number of peasant households only selling food decreased by 75.3 per cent.

If one considers that the estimated conventional net income in 1912 was on average about 650–70 rubles, one can see that this figure was halved, while bearing an increased fiscal burden (see Table 8.10). Not much was left for investment.

On the other hand, during the civil war collective farming, from which the leadership hoped to increase productivity and ease the policy of surplus appropriation, was quite limited, and ineffective for this aim. The insignificant proportion of state or collective tenure of land as compared with peasant farms does not justify a specific analysis of their role in the framework of the war communist economy. However, it may be of some interest to show under what specific circumstances both *sovkhozy* and forms of *kolkhozy* developed in the first years of Soviet power.

8.3 THE SOVKHOZY: AN EXPEDIENT FOR SURVIVAL

In the spring of 1919 *Narkomprod* succeeded in supplying 45 per cent of total consumption to the urban population, but in January 1920 only 36 per cent.[57] Though the efforts to organize distribution were impressive, results fell short of requirements. Sharp criticism of the food procurement policy came especially from the industrial milieu. At the Second Congress of *Sovnarkhozy*, Larin proposed an analysis of the failure of food procurement. A new policy of land tenure was a possible way out of the impasse of the low productivity of peasants' farms and their hostility to change. In October 1918 *Sovnarkom* had decided to transfer to the control of *Narkomzem* estates with marketable crops, livestock and processing facilities for agricultural products as well as large estates using progressive farming methods.[58] Larin reminded the economic representatives that during wartime Germany and Austria had let the workers in large factories take over some private estates, cultivate them and make use of their produce. Larin suggested that such a policy would prevent the fragmentation of large estates into small properties and would help to rescue workers from dependence on the peasantry. The inherent assumption of *Narkomprod*'s policy seemed to be that the state could and should expropriate the surplus from the kulaks, but, Larin objected, they amounted to no more than 1–3 per cent of the peasantry before the revolution and had probably disappeared altogether after it. From these premises Larin tried to convince the assembly that the solution to food procurement lay in associations, state farming and cooperative farming.[59]

Though the congress rejected the theoretical and political implications of Larin's criticism of *Narkomprod* policy, and approved centralization of food procurement, it accepted the idea that allocation of estates to workers for their own use would be helpful in solving current problems, and adopted a resolution on the organization of collective and state farms.[60] On 15 February 1919, *Sovnarkom* approved the allocation of unused land to factories, trade unions, city soviets, and other urban institutions and agencies for the purpose of growing food for their own staff.[61] The spontaneous development of vegetable gardens by workers in the localities was institutionalized and expanded. Following this decision, *Narkomzem* promoted some measures to enhance the productivity of the *sovkhozy* (state farms). Machines and implements were distributed among the provincial sections, which were supposed to supply first of all the *sovkhozy* and the farms of the industrial enterprises, and then collective farms and machine leasing stations.[62] During 1919 and 1920 several state farms came into being under the control of factory workers. The financial means were provided by VSNKh, with the proviso that 80 per cent of the output would remain with the workers and 20 per cent be turned over to *Narkomprod*.[63] Visitors to the RSFSR reported that almost all important factories had their own agricultural plots.[64] In some cases, plots were huge. The ammunition workers of Tula received 5,000 desiatins (13,500

Table 8.11. *The growth of the sovkhoz system, 1918–21*

1918	3,101
1919	3,547
1920	4,392
1921	4,316

Source: *O zemle*, vyp. 1, 1921, 32

Table 8.12. *Distribution of sovkhozy by size, 1920 (per cent of total farms)*

up to 9 desiatins	0.3
10–24 des.	2.3
25–49 des.	6.2
50–99 des.	10.5
100–49 des.	13.0
150–99 des.	11.5
more than 200 des.	57.0

Source: *O zemle*, vyp. 1, 34
(The figures as given total 100.8%.)

acres) for collective use from their *uezd*.[65] Some areas were for timber collection. Workers' organizations, trade unions, *artels* and house committees were assigned forest tracts for autonomous provision of timber. Potatoes and vegetables in remarkable quantities were apparently produced by Moscow citizens on public land.[66] In default of any census, the development of municipal land agriculture can be demonstrated by the fact that this kind of farming did not diminish during war communism, despite an urban population decline of 35 per cent.[67] The number of *sovkhozy* increased (see Table 8.11).

In 1920 3,635 *sovkhozy* over thirty-nine provinces covered an area of 1,399,365 desiatins (3,778,285 acres), with 53,574 workers, 6,541 clerks, 30,000 horses and 36,000 head of cattle.[68] The *sovkhozy* were generally large. More than 80 per cent had over 100 desiatins (270 acres) (see Table 8.12).

About 14 per cent of this area was allotted to the chief administrations of VSNKh, which exploited about half of it, or approximately 215,800 acres, for the needs of the workers employed in their enterprises.[69] In July 1920 there were 900 *sovkhozy* under VSNKh belonging to industrial enterprises and unions.[70] VSNKh created a special section, *Glavzemkhoz*, to regulate this activity. The allocation of plots to enterprises was decided by a committee composed of representatives of trade unions and *Narkomzem*.[71] The relative industrial importance of the chief administrations may have been a factor in deciding the proportions of allotments: GOMZA received 36 per cent of the total area; *Tsentrotekstil'* and *Glavbum* together got 16 per cent.[72]

Some industrial administrations, like those for sugar, tobacco, starch, tea and pharmaceuticals, were given land to grow their own raw materials. The sugar administration set up 218 sugar-beet farms.[73]

The development of the *sovkhoz* among the industrial workers, in spite of its contingent origin, gave rise to some naive hopes concerning alternative forms of land exploitation. In 1919 (from incomplete data) the *sovkhozy* produced seven million puds of cereals.[74] A year after his intervention at the Second Congress of *Sovnarkhozy*, Larin declared that industrial farming would attract the village proletarian and the poorest elements of the countryside, whose collaboration with the industrial workers was bound to speed up class differentiation in the countryside and simultaneously introduce scientific methods in agriculture.[75]

Larin's belief in the capacity of industrial workers to modernize agriculture did not have empirical support. Such assertions by Larin and others contained a great deal of naivety and belief in the charismatic virtues of the proletariat, and may have justified some scholars' picture of the visionary attitude of the Bolshevik leadership. However, rationalizations stemming from ideology should be distinguished from concrete reasons giving rise to definite policies. Under the cover of the *sovkhozy*, farming by industrial workers was primarily an expedient to allow the proletariat in large urban centres to keep on working under conditions which would have been otherwise intolerable by any ordinary standard. The idea of industrial farming stemmed from the concrete evidence that the machinery of *Narkomprod* was 'expensive, bulky and unskilful' and likely to arouse the peasants' reactions. The search for an alternative was justified both by the black market prices and by the state of transport. The peasant background of many factory workers may have suggested that agricultural work was not beyond their capacity, and that industrial training provided a favourable background for understanding what modern techniques were available. Furthermore, a *sovkhoz* was closely connected with its enterprise, which had a common interest in its maximum productivity, since the produce went to the factory foodstuff fund.[76] To industrial workers surrounded by passive and sometimes hostile peasants, the quest for self-sufficiency was not a strange idea. Within this context, farming by industrial workers may be considered as one of the crippled, decentralized forms by which the urban population compensated for the major faults of inefficient central distribution and carried on its daily struggle for survival.

8.4 COLLECTIVE FARMING: AN ALTERNATIVE ROAD TO SOCIALISM

Other forms of collectively organized farming developed under war communism as alternatives to individual farming. Like other Bolshevik economic institutions, the agrarian collectives had their origin in both ideology and economic necessity.

Marx and Engels had favoured cooperatives in agriculture, though in general they did not pay much attention to the agrarian question. For both of them, the state was the proper owner of land, but this would also allow communal or cooperative forms of land tenure.[77] Kautsky believed that the formation of cooperatives as well as state farms would increase productivity.[78] Lenin agreed on this point. In 1903, focusing on the fact that the peasant cooperatives would deliver to cooperatives of workers grain and other foodstuffs, while receiving from them machinery, livestock and fertilizers, Lenin underlined that in this way the cooperatives would not work for the market and would enjoy the benefits of productivity increases, which would enable them to improve work and machinery.[79] As indicated above, Lenin's stand on the agrarian question was deeply influenced by his admiration for the most developed forms of farming in capitalist countries, which he identified with large farms using modern techniques and capable of high productivity. From 1905, Lenin defended state ownership of land as a means of promoting economic development.[80] The state was to fix common rules of exploitation and prohibit subleasing as a crippling form of restoration of private property.[81] The promulgation of the decree on land which authorized the distribution of land according to local rules was accompanied by a comment suggesting that Lenin had not given up his hopes of reshaping the agrarian question: the peasants would understand by themselves that property based on equal sharing was not the best form of land organization.[82]

Though individual cases show that there was some concern for the development of the idea of socialist farming by proletarian and semi-proletarian elements of the countryside among local Bolshevik cadres,[83] the leadership basically ignored the problem of land tenure until the food crisis and the policy of class struggle in the countryside urgently required alternatives. Until June 1918 the local soviets still under the influence of the Socialist-Revolutionaries implemented the land decree, along the lines of distribution of land traditionally followed by the Russian *mir*.

Under the system of the *mir*, each member had the right to a plot on a uniform basis, and it was thereafter cultivated separately. Pastures, meadows and hay-cutting were in common. But there was no joint or cooperative farming of the *mir* as a unit. The peasant household was free to decide the kind of crops to be grown, the implements and tools used in its own domain, and disposed of its products on the free market.[84] According to several direct reports from different areas, after the revolution peasants distributed land 'equally, arithmetically' according to the old division system.[85]

In the first months of the revolution collective farming was almost nonexistent. It was given some impetus after the demobilization of soldiers, who appealed to the government for aid in joining together and forming communes.[86] In June 1918 the government expressed the intention of promoting collective farming 'for the purpose of transition to a socialist economy' and promised preferential treatment for land allotment to collective and cooperative farming.[87] The model charter approved by *Narkomzem* in August 1918 set out the principles of the agricultural communes; a preference was manifested for communes rather than 'profit-seeking *artels*' (though the latter were admitted as well as the communes under the competence of the Division of Collective Agriculture of the Commissariat at the end of 1918).[88] A commune consisted in the common ownership of land, means of production, livestock and implements. Only articles of personal use were considered to be private property. Work was to be performed according to capacity and rewarded according to needs and to the economic condition of the commune. Use of hired labour was forbidden. The agricultural surplus, after the consumption of the commune itself, was to be delivered for collective use to local food organs of the Soviet government in exchange for commodities, and the excess of monopoly products to the corresponding foodstuffs organs. To limit the possibility of the communes taking autonomous decisions aimed at satisfying the needs of their members rather than for productive social purposes, the law provided that land had to be repaid in kind, that is, in agricultural produce, and farming methods and techniques were to follow government instructions.[89] This charter probably reflected the Left Socialist-Revolutionaries' opinions, widely represented in *Narkomzem*.[90] But the events of the Summer of 1918 enlarged the support for collective tenure also among the Bolsheviks. The failure of food procurement was attributed to individual profit-seeking peasants. Collective farming seemed to provide a solution to the dichotomy between town and countryside. On 8 November 1918, at a meeting of the rural poor committees, Lenin affirmed that land division was not sufficient and that the way out was to be sought in collective land

tenure: 'communes, cooperative cultivation, association of peasants...
[are] the means of improving farming, of economical utilization of
resources, and combating the kulaks' parasitism and human
exploitation'.[91]

The new law on land of 15 February 1918 focused on the principle of
state ownership of land and on the aim of achieving a unified system of
socialist agriculture by means of state (soviet) farms, communes and
cooperatives. The law had the Bolshevik imprint. State farms (*sovkhozy*)
were given preference, in so far as they best corresponded to the criteria of
a state capitalist development of agriculture, and belonged to the whole
nation rather than as collectives to private people. Besides ideology,
however, as has been shown above, the *sovkhozy*, which were assimilated to
farming by industrial workers, arose for practical reasons. Collective
farms (*kolkhozy*) appeared as a second best, a device for converting the
peasants' small property mentality and milieu into a communist attitude.

Both alternatives represented an innovation. It would be wrong to
believe that the experience of the *mir* was conducive to collective farming
rather than to state farming. In fact, under the *mir* system the farm
household owned and could do what it liked with necessary implements,
cattle, etc., as well as the produce of its own work. Common obligations
concerned mainly the unpleasant side of the *mir*, such as the joint tax
liability of the members towards the state. From this point of view, then,
the road to collectivism was no less hard in Russia than in Western
countries. Collective farming included a number of forms of land tenure,
some of which could find historical roots. Side by side with the communes,
based on the full socialization of the means of production as well as of
agricultural produce, existed the *artels* (associations), a name which in
origin applied to a large variety of cooperative undertakings existing in all
spheres and in all times.[92] The agricultural *artels* socialized the means of
production, but their members disposed freely of their individual quota of
output, which was determined according to the quantity of labour.
Another form of collective farming developed from people pooling in
common their implements and carrying out common tillage, whilst
remaining individual owners of their own land allotment and disposing
freely of the produce of their own plot.[93] Incentives to collective farming
were to be provided by state supply of agricultural implements, working
animals and seeds.[94] But during war communism these were scarce and
the *sovkhozy* were privileged in supply as compared with the *kolkhozy*. In
several cases the communes got neither implements nor cattle and some of
them denounced the 'unsympathetic' attitude of the agricultural sections
and foodstuffs organs towards them.[95] At the end of 1919 Kalinin – one of
the few Bolshevik leaders of peasant origin – while praising the commune

for leading more rapidly than did individual land ownership to socialism, advocated better coordination of the communes with central policy by pooling their budgets together with that of the government.[96] This proposal suggests that the Bolsheviks never gave up hopes of converting the existing collectives into state farms, that is into centrally directed farms whose output would be directly disposed of by state organs.[97]

The development of collective farming from 1918 to 1921 seems to show that the forms of collective exploitation of land which most authentically responded to communistic ideals were less appealing to the peasantry than were forms of land tenure which granted a direct link between individual labour and reward. However, figures are not complete, for communes were registered only if they had something to do with the state, either because they supplied foodstuffs or because they distributed products. At the end of 1921, Knipovich estimated a total of 15,121 collective farms (communes, *artels*, and other types) throughout Russia, with 931,404 people and 1,133,326 desiatins of land, i.e. about 75 desiatins per farm and 1.2 per person.[98] Some data on the distribution of collective-farming by types are given by other sources:

Table 8.13. *Distribution of collective farming, 1918–20*

Year	Communes	*Artels*	Other collectives
1918	975	604	
1919	1,961	3,606	
1920	2,117	8,581	946

Source: *Agrarnaia Politika Sovetskoi Vlasti (1917–18): Dokumenty i Materialy*, Moscow, 1954

The average land per person was higher for the *artel*, at 22 desiatins, than for the commune, at 2 desiatins, and than the average individual farm.[99]

The peasants opposed the use of allotted land for the institution of collective farms, sometimes with violence.[100] In particular privileges in terms of land distribution and implements were not well understood, especially when the latter were not sufficient to put the whole land under cultivation, as was sometimes the case.[101]

Collective farming under war communism responded to an ideal not fully shared by the Bolsheviks, but which appealed to some idealistic revolutionaries seeking the immediate realization of communistic goals. The Bolsheviks were more interested in the possibility of increasing the agricultural surplus requisitioned by the state by favouring forms of land tenure open to state control, than in the alternative way of living that the communes might have represented for some. At the end of 1920 it became clear that collective farming could not be defended from a productive point of view. The technical improvement expected from it did not occur.[102] On the other hand, the war communist environment was not the most favourable, from the point of view of the actual opportunities, experience and methods. The implementation of an alternative model of human society based on the combination of personal responsibility and collective concern might have produced a way out of individualism and isolation only if the support of experience, technical expertise and financial assistance had been able to provide the social and economic environment needed to convert ideals gradually into practical programmes and realizable targets. The communes did not appeal to a peasantry which was just emancipating itself from centuries of oppression and misfortune, and which jealously defended its newly won rights to private tenure. Under war communism the experience of collective farming was abortive.

Nonetheless, the increasing number of *artels* may suggest that this form of associationism could have been a possible transitional form towards higher forms of emancipation and productive organization as compared with small farming in independent units. The egalitarian spirit, which proved to be so vigorous in land division after the revolution, could have been rescued and channelled into higher forms of collective organization – given determination, time, material and moral assistance and tolerance. But, once again, power proved to be incapable of mastering environment and schedules.

8.5 CENTRAL DISTRIBUTION AND PROLETARIAN ANARCHY

The organization of state distribution took shape gradually in 1919, when local organs of *Narkomprod* and a network of cooperatives were formed to replace private trade. The following scheme illustrates institutions and connections between central organs and local units in the field of distribution (see Fig. 8.1).

Major tasks were assigned to *Prodraspred* (abbreviation of *Otdel obshchego Raspredeleniia*, Section of General Distribution) in the localities. In each territory such sections were to compute the size of the population and the demand for foodstuffs by the given province, size of the industry and population, to survey the execution of *Narkomprod*'s orders concerning both provisions to and shipments from the province of foodstuffs, and to enforce the implementation of the principle of a uniform class *paiok* throughout the country. The *Prodraspred*'s subsection for distribution (ration) of foodstuffs to industrial workers was to check the number of

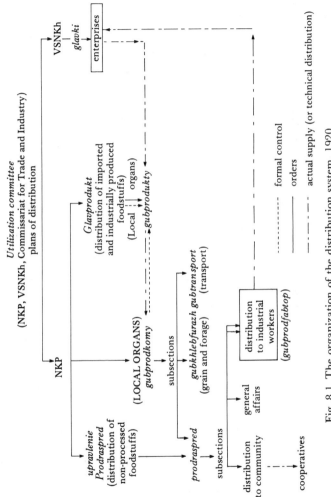

Fig. 8.1 The organization of the distribution system, 1920

workers, the plans of foodstuffs for workers produced by local industry, and the distribution of food, forage, perishable goods, vegetables and other products assigned by the centre between industrial workers and the other sections of the local working population. The section for distribution of the community was to count the number of children, sick people and other special groups of citizens and to organize collective nutrition for children. The section for general affairs coordinated the work of other sections and dealt with the processing of statistics, collection of information about actual stocks at each station point and the organization of their shipment. The shipment itself was arranged by the section for transport.[103] *Narkomprod*'s plans for territorial distribution to the population were obligatory for *glavki*, which were not allowed to deliver to local organs (*gubprodukty*) any output above planned quantities.[104] The *glavki* could only decide which enterprise was actually to implement *Narkomprod*'s order. *Gubprodukty* were fully independent of *gubprodkomy* (local committees of food procurement) from the financial point of view, but their activities were under their formal control. *Gubprodukty* received orders only from *Narkomprod* through *Glavprodukt*. These organs represented the connection between industry, foodstuffs and distribution. Their powers were broad. They could requisition or confiscate wholesale and commercial stocks of products and nationalize the corresponding firms and retail stores with the approval of the local *ispolkomy*. Their aim was to suppress private trade completely and to replace it with Soviet and cooperative bodies which would take into account the available resources and distribute goods exclusively in accordance with the need of each category of citizens as determined by central organs. The *gubprodukty* handed over to the local organs of *Narkomprod*, *gubprodkomy* or *uezdprod-komy*, whenever these were formed, the planned quantities, upon payment on current account. Credit was granted only for two weeks.[105] Once in the possession of the *gub-* or *uezdprodkomy*, foodstuffs and other consumer goods were rationed out to the population through local cooperatives, which performed only technical tasks.

For the purpose of distribution the population was divided into six categories: (1), workers performing physical work; (2), clerical workers; (3), members of workers' families; (4), other citizens; (5), army and fleet; (6), rural inhabitants. The division of the population into categories was decided by the Utilization Committee and could be modified only by it, upon approval of VSNKh and *Narkomprod*. On 15 December 1918, the number of workers performing physical work as estimated by the Utilization Committee was 1 million people, who together with their families added up to 3,200,000 people. In forty-two provinces the total number of citizens and rural inhabitants was estimated to be

14,600,000.[106] So much for laws, regulations and instructions; how did state distribution work in practice? It was hard to enforce central norms and class rations in the localities. The *gubprodkomy* did not always respect orders from the centre.[107] Local pressures for higher norms of distribution were not resisted.[108] But, above all, state distribution was unable to replace private trade, in default of both adequate organization and sufficient supply. The recurrent authorizations of private carriage of foodstuffs issued by the *Sovnarkom* reflected the incapacity of the state distribution system even to satisfy industrial workers. People survived thanks to *polutorapudnichestvo* (authorization to carry half a pud of foodstuff) and because of *otpustnichestvo* ('let it go', or tolerance of illegal trade). When, in the winter of 1920–1, these two channels became insignificant, famine spread all over the country.

Central distribution never succeeded in providing more than 50 per cent of the subsistence demand of the towns. The black market continued to provide a large part of consumer necessities. Even the introduction of class rationing (*paiok*), which started in Petrograd and was then extended to Moscow and other towns, was not sufficient to grant regular rations to the highest ration classes. In January 1919 Petrograd had thirty-three sorts of ration cards, for bread, potatoes, tobacco, cotton and flax fabrics, boots, soap, milk, butter, etc. Owing probably to the high mobility of the urban population, the cards were issued each month and their number oscillated widely.[109] Non-monopoly products were subject to price ceilings, but could be purchased by private organizations. In January 1919 there were 4,000 such organizations carrying out independent food procurement, upon authorization of the Military Food Bureau of Moscow, an organ representative of both the state and trade unions. In Samara province alone 225 representatives of various institutions, encompassing some 850,000 people, were involved in trading non-monopoly products.[110] At the beginning of 1919, under the pressure of *Narkomprod*, pursuing a centralized policy of food procurement, the Military Food Bureau stopped giving authorizations of purchase.[111] *Narkomprod*'s aim was to attract workers of the autonomous organizations into its food detachments, by granting to them half of the collected foodstuffs.[112] But pressures for free trade were never totally defeated. The irregularity of supply much reduced the efficiency of food procurement from the point of view of people living in towns. Rations were low. The average for bread per day was estimated at 300 grams, but sometimes even rations for the upper category were insignificant. The basic monthly *paiok* of factory workers, the first class in distribution, was supposed to be 25 funt of bread, half a funt of sugar, half a funt of salt, four funt of meat or fish, half a funt of oil, and one-quarter funt of coffee substitutes.[113] But during war communism these rations varied greatly, as the data on the average daily wage in kind and in money worked out by Strumilin show (see Table 8.14).

In March 1919 the Moscow Soviet again authorized the Moscow workers' organizations to process autonomously an amount of food equivalent to 20 funt of food products per person.[114] This step, which was

Table 8.14. *Real average daily wage (money and paiok), excluding the value of uniforms and rent, in actual rubles*

Year and Month	Money	Paiok	Money	Paiok
	(Petrograd)		(Moscow)	
1918				
January	7.70	1.37		
February	4.67	2.19		
March	5.74	2.13		
April	4.15	1.94		
May	2.76	1.41		
June	2.28	1.32		
July	2.74	1.47		
August	2.38	1.80		
September	2.61	0.98		
October	3.46	2.06		
November	3.30	1.58		
December	2.28	1.43		
1919				
January	2.39	2.46		
February	1.76	1.74		
March	1.28	2.07		
April	1.73	4.10		
May	1.43	3.66		
June	1.13	2.34		
July	0.82	2.67		
August	1.00	2.54		
September	1.90	3.48		
October	0.95	3.41	1.22	
November	0.74	1.85	0.60	
December	0.65	4.96	0.56	
1920				
January	0.53	2.01	0.44	1.98
February	0.49	2.78	0.42	2.07
March	0.52	3.84	0.52	1.98
April	0.47	2.88	0.43	3.06
May	0.46	2.31	0.41	2.52

June	0.52	2.20	0.45	2.24
July	0.46	3.08	0.54	1.50
August	0.44	2.52	0.63	2.33
September	0.53	2.57	0.59	1.38
October	0.53	1.80	0.71	1.43
November	0.50	3.74	0.61	2.25
December	0.46	1.32	0.38	1.83
1921				
January	0.35	1.90	0.27	2.30
February	0.20	3.98	0.22	2.81
March	0.22	4.11	0.23	2.99
April	0.25	3.66	0.23	2.46
May	0.30	2.84	0.22	2.30
June	0.28	3.03	0.28	1.88

Source: S.G. Strumilin, *Zarabotnaia plata i proizvoditel'nost' truda v Russkoi promyshlennosti v 1914–1922 gg*, Moscow, 1923, p. 76, Suppl. no. 6.

equivalent to an authorization of free trade, provoked a reaction in *Narkomprod*, which withheld purchase credits for non-monopoly goods, with the aim of reducing the purchasing power of the independent food procurement agencies.[115] The challenge, represented by what Kritsman later defined as *proletarian anarchy*, to the efforts of centralization stubbornly pursued by the government never ceased. Indeed, workers demanded an extension of their rights in this field.[116] In turn, the commissars of food procurement claimed that workers' organizations did not respect fixed prices and rules on authorization of purchase of non-monopoly products.[117] Products were requisitioned; clashes between people and the food inspectors were frequent. The Commissar of Internal Affairs had to intervene in this question, by officially condemning cases of harassment and illegal requisition of personal provisions by the militia.[118] The black market kept working and was systematically identified by the authorities as the cause of the failure of central distribution, rather than its result.

The black market was kept going by products and ration cards. On the one side, there were products which escaped *prodrazverstka*, and on the other, goods belonging to people, that part of wages and rations which was paid in kind.[119] Higher rations of industrial consumer goods for workers might also have helped the black market.[120] Corruption grew in the midst of misery. Of the four hundred thousand cards circulating in Moscow, many were forged. In 1920 the town population of the RSFSR, except Turkestan, amounted to some 12.3 million, whereas the number of ration cards reached almost 22 million, excluding the rural population.[121] Someone calculated that by selling ration cards, which were not always honoured, people were able to get back 30–40 per cent of their value in terms of commodities.[122]

The inefficiency of central distribution compelled the central organs to select a number of people from the highest category group for guaranteed regular supply. From 15 November 1919, some categories of workers were granted the *armouring* of their food rations. In the course of one year, however, the number of people with the right to such reserved rations more than doubled: from 642,000 in December 1919 to 1.5 million in October 1920.[123] The problem of supplying regularly an increasing number of people was aggravated by the introduction of a system of premiums in kind on 8 June 1920, with the aim of increasing the productivity of labour.[124] The number of people who enjoyed the premiums, some 750,000, suggests that this system rapidly became a means of increasing normal rations. When the problem of increasing productivity by raising ration norms was added to the problem of feeding citizens, *Narkomprod* increased its efforts to extend the range of products subject to *prodrazverstka* and, conversely, to abolish the free market entirely. The plan of state distribution in 1920–1 included 37,520,300 people, of whom 8,481,300 were industrial workers, their families and *kustari*; 4,767,000 were transport workers and their families; 1,808,000 were families of Red Army members; 570,000 were people receiving canteen food; and the rest were urban civilian population,[125] not falling into any of the above categories.

Figures elaborated by the central statistical organs on the calories consumed by people in the countryside and in towns show that a redistribution of material wealth took place. Although these figures include also calories obtained from market operations, they are still indicative of an improvement for the urban population of the consuming provinces as compared with other strata.

Table 8.15. *Calories consumed by the urban and rural population, 1919–21*

	Rural population			Urban population		
	(calories per capita per day)					
	1919–20 Jan. Feb.	1920–1 Nov. Dec.	1921 Feb.	1919 Mar. Apr.	1920 Oct.	1921 Apr.
Consuming provinces	3,365	3,331	3,229	1,966	2,847	2,498
Producing provinces	2,881	3,139	2,760	2,737	2,586	2,243

Source: *Sbornik statisticheskikh svedenii po Soiuzu SSR 1918–1923*, Moscow, 1924, pp. 380–1, 396–7

The figures indeed seem suspiciously high, for both the rural and urban population, when compared with the occasional published accounts on daily rations. One fact, however, emerges: that the *entire* population of the producing provinces substantially reduced its calory consumption from 1919 to 1921, while the comparative increase in consumption by the urban population in the consuming provinces does not seem large enough to explain the high loss of all other categories. Furthermore, the averages conceal differences in consumption within each category. Other figures show that calories per day of landless peasants in the consuming regions were 2,598 and in the producing regions 2,821 at the end of 1920, i.e. below those of the urban population in the corresponding period.[126]

Central food procurement entailed waste. The rural population suffered great losses, whilst the urban population did not receive the whole expropriated surplus. In the 1918–19 campaign, only 65 per cent of the cereals collected were dispatched from Saratov, 18 per cent from Tula, 12 per cent from Riazan, 10 per cent from Ufa and 8 per cent from Orenburg.[127] Much depended on transport. The orders of dispatch issued by the provincial food procurement organs were fulfilled by the railways only to 25 per cent in 1918 and 43 per cent in 1919. Even in October 1920, after the end of the war, orders could not be fulfilled by more than 70 per cent.[128] Whilst the producing provinces which had sustained the maximum effort in food provisions should have been relieved from further burdens, the remote regions could not be reached because of lack of fuel, disruption of train services, and banditism. This situation should have warned the leadership not to go further in the direction of trade monopoly. But the ideological tenets which ascribed most of the failures to the market's operation and behaviour prevented a serious analysis of the defects of Soviet organization compared with the ambitious aims of its proponents.

8.6 APPRAISAL OF THE RESULTS AND CONSEQUENCES OF PRODRAZVERSTKA

If account is taken only of those provinces which procured food continuously throughout the period,[129] then the policy of *Narkomprod* seems to have been less successful than former policies. Higher procurement figures for the consuming provinces were due to the fact that a larger number of such provinces participated in state purchase from 1919–20 onwards. As a whole, *Narkomprod* was never able to achieve the amount of food procurement attained in 1916–17.[130]

Different estimates of pre-war output, of course, condition estimates of the relative magnitude of actual losses incurred under war communism.

Figures have often been corrected upwards or downwards according not only to methodological assumptions, but also to the political biases (or instructions) of officials or scholars, as Wheatcroft's study has shown.[131] The purpose of my work is not to provide definite answers to statistical dilemmas, but to discern the general trends which made war communism a unique experiment in economic organization and the reasons why that experiment was abandoned. Attention will, therefore, be paid to the original contemporary estimates on output, sowings, productivity, etc., which helped to shape current policy, although they are not exempt from reservations as to the method employed for their derivation. Indeed, GOSPLAN in the mid twenties considered that it led to underestimation of the actual output. But some later, corrected figures are also proposed, in so far as they provide additional information which helps to explain why not everybody agreed with Lenin's decision to renounce war communism. Both are useful for determining general trends. To the usual reasons for reservations as to the correctness of the available statistics on agriculture (figures may vary considerably, depending on, for example, whether municipal land and personal plots are included or not), the following should be added: harvest figures are questionable because under *razverstka* peasants tried to conceal the true harvest; scattered yields or yields from new tillages were not always included; and information collected by volunteers, local institutions or *volost* soviets was often either inadequate or intentionally biased.[132]

It is unquestionable, however, that output as compared to any estimate of pre-war output fell considerably owing both to the reduction of sowing and to the decrease in productivity. The reduction of the crop area was significant. The contemporary estimates of this reduction were large. In 1924 the Central Statistical Administration (TsSU) estimated that between 1916 and 1921 the sown area in the RSFSR was reduced by 35 per cent, in the Moscow Industrial Region by 21 per cent, in the Central Agricultural Regions by 32 per cent, and in the Ukraine by 10 per cent. The statistics bring out also the annual differences in sowing during the war years (see Table 8.16).

These statistics did not take into account municipalized land and national estates: thus they did not include grasslands, meadows, etc.[133] More detailed figures are to be found in Popov's *Proizvodstvo khleba v RSFSR i federiruiushchikhsia s neiu respublikakh* of 1921 which, however, do not allow a proper comparison between Soviet and other territories, since the figures for the Ukraine are calculated on the basis of the application of an arbitrary coefficient of reduction of sown area and those for Siberia also contain some arbitrary coefficients of reduction, although in neither case was statistical evidence of reduced sowings available (see Table 8.17).[134]

Table 8.16. *Sown area, 1909 22 (thousand desiatins)*

	Year	Average sown area
RSFSR	1909–13	63,488.4
	1916	60,416.5
	1917	60,185.0
	1920	46,237.8
	1921	41,563.0
	1922	35,954.5
Ukraine	1909–13	19,641.2
	1916	18,614.4
	1917	19,245.0
	1920	16,721.0
	1921	16,721.4
	1922	13,343.1
Moscow Industrial Region	1909–13	4,393.0
	1916	3,463.6
	1917	3,397.2
	1920	2,630.7
	1921	2,744.2
	1922	3,103.8
Central Agricultural Regions	1909–13	12,840.8
	1916	12,159.5
	1917	12,345.0
	1920	8,647.9
	1921	8,301.2
	1922	8,973.1

Source: *Sbornik statisticheskikh svedenii*, pp. 122–3

Two main findings emerge from these contemporary estimates: findings which remain valid even when later statistical data are used. Firstly, the sown area decreased more in the provinces involved in military operations than in other provinces (in the producing provinces by 19.8 per cent and 11.6 per cent respectively and in the consuming provinces by 37.5 per cent and 22.4 per cent respectively). Secondly, the area devoted to hay and crops for industrial use (e.g. cotton) decreased more than that used for other crops. The 1924 estimates by TsSU of the relatively larger decrease in sown areas in the Central Agricultural Regions were confirmed by Timoshenko, who later stated that the crop area fell relatively more in the territory under Soviet rule (by 14.5 per cent in the grain deficiency area and by 25.7 per cent in the grain surplus area of European Russia), whether it was affected or not by war, than in the Ukraine (− 3.6 per cent) or in Siberia (− 1.8 per cent), between 1916 and 1921.[135]

Table 8.17. *Sown area, 1916 and 1920 (thousand desiatins)*

Regions	Year	Food grain	Fodder	Potatoes	Hay	Technical crops	Total
1 Producing regions	1916	20,196.9	8,331.8	865.6	504.3	933.4	30,832.0
	1920	15,059.1	6,381.6	529.0	63.0	477.2	22,509.9
1920 as % of	1916	74.6	76.6	61.1	12.5	51.1	73.0
2 Consuming regions	1916	5,114.9	3,472.6	852.9	650.1	924.9	11,015.4
	1920	4,539.3	2,176.8	578.2	192.8	379.9	7,867.0
1920 as % of	1916	88.7	62.7	77.8	29.7	41.1	71.4
3 South-East	1916	6,355.4	2,776.4	270.4	93.2	494.4	9,989.8
	1920	4,986.2	1,806.6	233.4	40.9	229.1	7,296.2
1920 as % of	1916	78.5	65.1	86.3	43.9	46.3	73.0
4 Siberia	1916	7,263.0	2,744.9	161.3	40.4	205.0	10,414.6
	1920	6,726.5	2,314.7	154.7	7.5	171.6	9,375.0
1920 as % of	1916	92.6	83.4	95.9	18.6	83.7	90.0
5 Ukraine	1916	10,525.9	6,555.8	726.1	507.0	705.4	19,020.2
	1920	8,148.9	4,621.5	583.3	73.8	492.8	13,920.3
1920 as % of	1916	77.4	70.5	80.3	14.6	69.9	73.0
Total	1916	49,456.1	23,881.5	2,876.3	1,795.0	3,263.1	81,272.0
	1920	39,460.0	17,301.2	2,078.6	378.0	1,750.6	60,968.4
1920 as % of	1916	79.8	72.4	72.3	21.1	53.6	75.0

Source: P. Popov, *Proizvodstvo khleba v RSFSR i federiruiushchikhsia s neiu respublikakh (khlebnaia produktsiia)*, 1921, p. 28

In 1924 TsSU estimated that in 1920 the USSR's sown area was 75.7 per cent of the area sown during the 1904–13 period. Krzhizhanovskii, whom Lenin commissioned to work out the plan of electrification and who was appointed first head of GOSPLAN in 1922, provided much higher figures for both 1913 and 1920.[136] According to these, the total sown area was 109.0 million desiatins in 1913; 99.0 million in 1917; 97.0 in 1918; 85.0 in 1919; 93.0 in 1920 and 83.0 in 1921–2. It is possible, as Wheatcroft has suggested, that the 30 per cent upward correction to the estimates provided by TsSU was to stress the feasibility of the plan of reconstruction and modernization, worked out by GOSPLAN. The GOSPLAN figures, however, confirmed the basic trend towards a remarkable decrease in the sown area (ranging from 15 per cent to 24 per cent in the crucial years of war communism) as compared to 1913.

Data relating to total sown area in the USSR before 17 September 1939 published in present day Soviet literature and regarded as better grounded[137] indicate 105.0 million hectares (96.1 million desiatins), i.e. about 16 per cent above Popov's estimates, sown area in 1913 (in comparable territories) and 94.4 million hectares (approximately 86.0 million desiatins) grain sown area. According to these estimates, the grain sown area would have fallen to 87.0 ha (79.6 million desiatins) in 1920 and to 70.8 million ha (about 64.5 million desiatins) in 1921.[138] These figures show a lower relative decrease (about 8 per cent) in cultivation compared with the earlier estimates of 1918–20 and indicate that in 1921 the grain sown area declined relatively more (− 25 per cent) than the total cultivated area (which was estimated to be 97.2 million ha in 1920 and 90.3 million ha in 1921). The area under technical crops, as has already emerged from Popov's estimates, decreased relatively more than that for other types of cultivation (see Table 8.18).

The above figures show also that the only crops whose area increased were those, such as potatoes and sunflower, which had a higher yield per labour input than other crops,[139] and were usable as foodstuffs that peasants could trade until mid 1919 outside *razverstka*.

Table 8.18. *Sown area, 1913 and 1920 (thousand hectares)*

Years	Cotton	Flax	Hemp	Sun-flower	Sugar-beet	Potatoes
1913	688.0	1,398.0	645.0	968.2	648.7	3,063.6
1920	97.8	884.5	446.1	1,347.1	195.7	3,727.9

Source: *Sotsialisticheskoe stroitel'stvo SSSR*, Moscow, 1934, pp. 176–7

If *prodrazverstka* is to be considered as one of the factors that affected total output and productivity, then data on the regional variations of the food grain area are more important than the aggregate figures (see Table 8.19).

The estimates given by Oganovskii and Kondrat'ev in 1923 show that the food grain area of the Lower Volga was reduced much more than that of the Middle Volga area, although both were major battlefields. But while the former area remained under Soviet control between 1918 and 1920, the latter underwent changes of rule. The decrease in the sown area since 1917 was higher in the grain-producing provinces of European Russia and lower in others – that is it affected more those regions which produced a marketable surplus. In the Northern Regions, where the cultivated land was less significant, the percentage of all grains increased, although in absolute terms the sown area decreased. A relatively lower decline since 1917 occurred in the Central Industrial Regions, including Moscow, Ivanovo-Voznesensk, Rybinsk, Yaroslavl and Kaluga, but as a whole, the Central Regions where *prodrazverstka* was systematically carried out show a sharp reduction in the sown area. The largest fall took place in the north-eastern regions of Kostroma, Viatka, Perm and Petrograd, and in the western regions of Vitebsk, Gomel, Briansk and Smolensk, where sowings of sunflower also decreased. The decline in the sown area was quite high in Ufa and significant in the Middle Volga Region[140] (see Table 8.19).

According to Popov, the fall in output depended not only on the reduction of sown area, but also on the productivity fall due to the distribution of land into small plots and the introduction of the backward three-field system of culture, which yielded less. Even when weather conditions affecting harvest are taken into account, the fall in productivity per desiatin of cultivated land indicates that output fell more than sown area. In 1920 the output of winter rye was about 60 per cent and that of wheat 43 per cent of 1917 levels. Comparing the same area, Popov estimated that the output of cereals in 1920 was 29.9 per cent and fodder 31 per cent below the average 1909–13 harvests.[141]

On the basis of archive data, Poliakov has worked out estimates of land productivity and obtained harvest figures which may be considered close enough to the data of TsSU's 1924 estimates to suggest that relative values may hold.[142] TsSU has provided since 1959 new data on productivity per ha, on total harvest and total deliveries of grain in pre-revolutionary Russia. But these corrections of which only the yield data are presented have shown an increase of productivity per ha in 1921 which is probably only the arithmetical consequence of keeping former estimates for the sown area, since it is hardly credible that productivity

Table 8.19. *Sown area by regions in 1901–5, 1911 and 1921, excluding fodder, hay, beet, and some minor crops (thousand desiatins; figures in brackets are percentage of 1913 figures)*

Years	South-west Ukraine	Central Russia	Middle Volga	Novorossiisk	Lower Volga	Total Black Earth
1901–5	9,985.1 (95.9)	10,610.1 (97.5)	9,956.5 (91.4)	13,556.2 (88.2)	4,306.8 (81.7)	48,414.7 (91)
1917	8,935.2 (85.8)	10,516.8 (96.6)	10,437.1 (95.8)	13,385.1 (87.1)	4,317.8 (81.9)	47,592.0 (90)
1921	8,496.2 (81.6)	5,811.1 (53.4)	6,789.7 (62.3)	9,052.3 (58.9)	2,075.1 (39.4)	32,224.4 (61)

Years	Belorussia	Lake District[a]	Central Industrial Regions	Northern Regions	Urals Region	Total non-Black Earth
1901–5	3,640.3 (95.9)	1,786.0 (102.8)	4,169.6 (104.6)	706.4 (96.7)	5,088.2 (92.2)	15,390.5 (97.6)
1917	3,370.2 (88.8)	1,632.4 (93.9)	3,154.0 (79.1)	636.7 (87.3)	4,713.9 (85.4)	13,507.2 (85.6)
1921	2,396.2 (63.1)	1,134.1 (65.3)	2,099.4 (51.7)	471.4 (64.6)	3,467.8 (62.8)	9,529.0 (60.4)

Years	Total European Russia
1901–5	63,805.2 (93.0)
1917	61,099.2 (80.1)
1921	41,753.4 (60.9)

Years	Northern Caucasus	Siberia	Steppe Region	Asiatic Russia	Total RSFSR
1901–5	4,682.2 (65.7)	3,401.1 (55.5)	2,867.9 (62.4)	10,951.8 (61.3)	74,757.0 (86.5)
1917 (1916)	5,422.8 (76.2)	6,753.3 (100.2)	5,777.5 (125.8)	17,953.6 (100.6)	79,052.8 (91.5)
1921	3,198.2 (44.9)	4,910.7 (80.1)	3,355.5 (73.1)	11,464.4 (64.3)	53,217.8 (61.6)

[a] Territory around lakes Ladoga and Onega in the North-West.

Source: *Sel'skoe khoziaistvo Rossii v XX veke. Sbornik statistiko-ekonomicheskikh svedenii za 1901–1922 gg*, pod red. N.P. Oganovskogo i N.D. Kondrat'eva, Moscow, 1923

Table 8.20. *Output and gross yield of grain in USSR (in pre-17 September 1939 borders)*

Years	Productivity per ha in quintals	Gross yield in million quintals	% of previous year's output
1913	8.1	765.0	
1909–13 (average per year)	6.9	651.8	
1917	6.4	545.6	
1918	6.0	495.3	90.7
1919	6.2	504.5	102.0
1920	5.7	451.9	89.5
1921	7.6	362.6	80.3

Source: V.P. Danilov, *Sovetskaia dokolkhoznaia derevniia Naselenie, zemlepol'zovanie, khoziaistvo*), Moscow, 1977, p. 284

would have increased in the very bad harvest year of 1921 (see Table 8.20).

The fact that the fall in productivity affected the grains such as wheat which were traditionally exported more than the poorer quality grains such as barley, oats and millet, may be an indication that institutional factors, such as the policy of foreign trade and the system of requisitioning the whole surplus, induced peasants to discontinue the growing of marketable crops and to concentrate on crops designed for farm consumption. Thus the area on which rye, millet, buckwheat and maize were grown was increased.[143] The fall in oats production was connected with the reduced numbers – and possibly the redistribution – of horses (see Table 8.21).

Spring wheat which in 1909–13 accounted for 23.7 per cent of total sown area fell by 4.3 points, whereas winter rye increased its share by 4.5 points (see Table 8.22). The only crops whose yield increased or did not decrease much after 1917 were millet and maize, which could have been used also to feed poultry.

The price ratio between different grains may also have had an influence on the change of crops. Rye was not only used as the peasants' principal staple food, but also as a means of exchange. An economic reason for extending the cultivation of rye may be found in the favourable price ratio between products of secondary necessity, like wheat, potatoes and meat on the one hand and rye on the other. The relative prices of the former products decreased during 1917 to 1921 as compared with the price of rye flour in 1917, whose market value was kept high by demand.[144]

Table 8.21. *Share of sown area of particular cereals, 1917–21 (% of total sown area)*

Years	Winter rye	Spring rye	Winter wheat	Spring wheat	Barley	Oats	Millet	Buckwheat	Maize
1917	26.6	0.9	9.3	23.2	12.3	19.9	3.9	2.4	1.5
1919	29.7	1.4	8.3	20.2	9.6	18.4	5.1	4.7	2.8
1920	27.9	0.9	7.9	23.6	10.9	17.3	6.6	2.7	2.2
1921	31.1	0.7	8.4	19.4	11.3	16.2	7.4	2.8	2.7

Source: Iu. A. Poliakov, *Perekhod k NEPu i Sovetskoe krest'ianstvo*, Moscow, 1967, p. 68

Table 8.22. *Gross yield of principal cereals (thousand puds)*

Crop	1909–13	1917	1920	1921	1921 as % of 1917
Winter rye	1,123,526	931,791	556,723	612,271	65.7
Spring rye	18,177	18,021	13,286	9,256	51.3
Winter wheat	311,727	396,377	171,364	114,916	28.9
Spring wheat	824,091	637,723	361,067	225,413	35.3
Barley	516,174	932,013	287,489	158,505	17.0
Buckwheat	61,748	68,449	53,543	56,005	81.8
Millet	143,316	113,825	136,150	123,614	108.6
Maize	56,894	75,456	70,719	70,674	93.6
Oats	794,391	674,488	430,266	318,480	47.2

Source: *Sbornik statisticheskikh svedenii*, p. 131

The system of *prodrazverstka*, which destroyed any incentive to increase the surplus, may provide an explanation for the larger fall of productivity per desiatin of winter rye in the Black Earth Regions as compared with the more favourable trends in non-Black Earth regions between 1918 and 1920, since the former were grain surplus regions (see Table 8.23).

However, other factors, such as war, weather and migration, to mention only the most important, should be taken into account in comparing the productivity of different regions, to distinguish as much as possible between occasional and institutional influences. The chronology of the shifts of military fronts (see Fig. 8.2) provides the basis for a crude distinction between grain-producing provinces of the Black Earth Region which remained under Soviet rule during 1918–20, such as Penza, Riazan, Tula, Saratov and Tambov, and those provinces, such as Simbirsk, Samara, Orel and Ufa, which were the main battlefields and underwent military and political changes.

The Orel province was under Bolshevik rule in 1918 and again in 1920, but not in 1919. Samara and Simbirsk shared a common fate, as the balance of power turned in favour of one or the other party. They were conquered by the Czechoslovaks in the summer of 1918 (27 July–9 September) and remained under Bolshevik control in 1919 and 1920. As can be seen from Table 8.24, output per desiatin was higher in 1918 than in 1919.

Samara suffered greater losses of productivity than Simbirsk in 1919 as well as in 1920, although their contiguity suggests that there would not have been major climatic differences. It may be suggested, however, that since Samara was more important strategically than Simbirsk because of the Samara–Ufa railwayline, the greater concentration of the army in

Table 8.23. *Harvest of cereals per desiatin between 1918 and 1920 in RSFSR (puds)*

Provinces[a]	Winter rye			Winter wheat			Summer rye			Summer wheat		
	1918	1919	1920	1918	1919	1920	1918	1919	1920	1918	1919	1920
Non-Black Earth	43.9	41.7	44.2	50.2	43.0	43.5	30.5	30.2	32.1	30.7	32.2	32.9
Black Earth	41.1	33.2	25.0	44.6	26.1	20.2	29.9	35.1	24.0	33.7	31.8	24.6

[a]The following provinces were included in non-Black Earth land: Arkhangel, Briansk, Vitebsk, Vladimir, Vologda, Viatka, Gomel, Ivanovo-Voznesensk, Kaluga, Korel, Kostroma, Moscow, Nizhni-Novgorod, Olonets, Perm, Petrograd, Pskov, North Dvinsk, Smolensk, Tver, Cherepovets, Yaroslavl.
The Black Earth provinces were: Astrakhan, Bkhiv Republic, Voronezh, Don Region, Ekaterinburg, Komsk, Kalousk *Oblast*, Marsk *Oblast*, German Volga *Oblast*, Orel, Penza, Riazan, Samara, Saratov, Simbirsk, Tambov, Tatar Republic, Tula, Ufa, Tsaritsin, Cheliabinsk, Chuvash *Oblast*.
Source: Statisticheskii Ezhegodnik (1918–1920 gg), vol. 8, issue 1, pp. 244–6

Fig. 8.2 The borders of the Soviet Union during war communism

Table 8.24. *Output per desiatin of rye in the most important food-providing provinces of the Black Earth Region, 1918 20 (puds)*

Provinces	1918	1919	1919 as a percentage of 1918	1920	1920 as a percentage of 1919	1920 as a percentage of 1918
Orel	42.9	36.5	85.0	14.4	39.4	33.5
Penza	54.9	26.1	47.5	25.0	95.7	45.5
Riazan	42.9	46.3	108.0	37.6	81.2	87.6
Simbirsk	73.4	62.9	85.7	32.0	50.8	43.5
Tula	42.0	29.8	71.5	30.8	103.0	73.3
Samara	58.0	28.2	48.6	13.1	46.4	22.6
Saratov	43.2	22.5	52.1	19.5	86.6	45.1
Tambov	37.0	42.0	113.0	23.0	54.7	62.2
Ufa	62.0	35.0	56.4	29.3	83.7	47.2

Source: *Statisticheskii Ezhegodnik*, p. 247.

the province led to its rapid spoliation. The same explanation may apply to the Orel province, which was crossed by north–south railways. The railways, however, were important also for the transport of foodstuffs, so that *prodrazverstka* might have had more devastating effects there than elsewhere. It may be concluded that while productivity dropped everywhere the decrease was much higher in those provinces which were within the zones of military combat (about 67 per cent between 1918 and 1920 on average) than in the provinces under Soviet rule (about 37 per cent). It would thus appear that institutional factors exerted a general negative influence on productivity, and that military factors, while not decisive, served to depress productivity levels further. Riazan and Tambov, the only provinces under constant Soviet rule where an increase in productivity was registered between 1918 and 1919, had very low output per desiatin in 1918, as compared with the average output, despite the fact that 1918 was a good harvest year. They were also among the provinces which resisted 1918 requisitions with revolts and killing of livestock, which were likely to lower productivity earlier than in other provinces. Only further specific and detailed studies for each province, however, can be expected to clarify what has been proposed here only as a hypothesis based on limited data from various sources.

According to the conventional approach of economic experts of the time, the fall in marketed grain could be attributed to the reduction of the average size of peasants' farms.[145] The process of land redivision which occurred between 1917 and 1921 may have influenced the total surplus available. By 1920, 73.7 per cent of the peasant households had plots

Table 8.25. Distribution of farms by desiatins of cultivated land, RSFSR, 1920 (% of total number of farms (14,267,300))

	No sowing	1 des.	1.1–2	2.1–3	3.1–4	4.1–6	6.1–8	8.1–10	10.1–13	13.1	16.1–19	19.1–22	22.1–25	more than 25
1920	8.1	16.5	22.5	17.0	11.8	12.8	5.4	2.6	1.6	0.8	0.4	0.2	0.1	0.2
1922	6.7	24.3	27.7	17.8	10.2	8.8	2.9	1.1	0.5	0.2	0.1	—	—	—

Moscow Industrial Region

	No sowing	1 des.	1.1–2	2.1–3	3.1–4	4.1–6	6.1–8	8.1–10
1920	7.8	29.7	34.4	16.8	6.9	3.6	0.7	0.1
1922	5.7	28.2	35.7	18.2	7.4	3.9	0.7	0.2

Central Agricultural Regions [b]

	No sowing	1 des.	1.1–2	2.1–3	3.1–4	4.1–6	6.1–8	8.1–10	10.1–13	13.1–16
1920	3.0	12.4	23.2	21.9	16.2	15.8	5.1	1.6	0.6	0.2
1922	3.4	15.2	23.6	20.3	14.7	15.4	5.2	1.6	0.5	0.1

[a]Data are based on selected materials of a 10 per cent agricultural census (covering from 6 to 14 per cent of farms in each province).
[b]In the Central Agricultural Regions, where land was more abundant, the average size of farms was somewhat higher.
Source: Sbornik statisticheskikh svedenii, pp. 116–17

ranging from one to four desiatins (see Table 8.25). This fact, however, should be considered in connection with the changes in the number of livestock, and thus with the requisition and redistribution of working animals. Given the size of farms and the lack of incentive to produce for sale, farmers kept only those animals essential for working their farms (see Table 8.26).

The proportion of small farms was much higher than average in the Moscow Industrial region (Vladimir, Ivanovo-Voznesensk, Kostroma, Moscow, Nizhni-Novgorod, Rybinsk, Tver, Yaroslavl).

The number of sheep fell by 40 per cent and that of calves by 58 per cent between 1916 and 1921 (see Table 8.26). Marketed meat and fat fell to half the 1916 level.[146] While during the world war the proportion of young horses increased, as compared with working horses, during the civil war they decreased significantly.[147]

Amongst the cattle, cows decreased significantly less than working animals. All working animals (mainly horses plus oxen) decreased from 51.7 million head in 1916 (USSR area as before 17 September 1939) to 43.7 million in 1921.[148] Comparisons between the years of the world war and the years of revolution suggest that economic policy exerted a definite impact on the falling number and composition of livestock. Cows fell relatively less than other animals (from 22,154,000 head in 1916 to 20,083,000 in 1921) not only because milk and butter could be sold on the black market,[149] but also because they were necessary to the farm household consumption, particularly when large farms split into small ones belonging to former members of the family.

The effect of *prodrazverstka* on livestock may also be observed in the relatively greater fall in the number of smaller animals – sheep, pigs and others – which were more exposed to the obligatory delivery by quota, as compared with horses and cattle. Gordeev recalls that people simply ate their pigs, which decreased in number by 37 per cent in regions affected by war, by 39 per cent in regions slightly affected by war, and by 56 per cent in other regions.[150] This fact confirms that peasants started reducing

Table 8.26. *Livestock in RSFSR (thousand head)*

	Horses	Sheep	Cattle	Total
1916	25,535.1	71,500.2	41,628.8	156,146.4
1920	20,002.2	40,018.2	31,013.5	102,394.4
1921	17,915.0	36,634.8	28,725.4	94,392.1

Source: Sbornik statisticheskikh svedenii, pp. 136–7

Table 8.27. *Number of livestock as compared with 1916 (%)*

	1916	1920	1921
USSR	100	72	68
RSFSR	100	68	63
Central Agricultural Region	100	57	54
Moscow Industrial Region	100	84	92

Source: *Sbornik statisticheskikh svedenii*, pp. 136–9

their draught animals, as they did with cultivated land, to a 'consumption' level, rather than trying to increase production. Working animals and cows decreased more slowly than sown area while other animals decreased more rapidly. The fall was more significant in the RSFSR than in the USSR as a whole, and very large in the Central Agricultural Regions as compared with the Moscow Industrial Regions (see Table 8.27).

The fact that working animals decreased less rapidly than sown area does not necessarily indicate a higher capital intensiveness of farming enhancing the productivity of land. These animals were subject to a significant redistribution among peasant households. Between 1917 and 1920, the number of farms having no working animals decreased in the Central Regions. The prevalence of the 'consumption' dimension may be observed from the significant reduction of farms having no cows and in the high percentage of farms having a maximum of one or two horses or cows (see Tables 8.28 and 8.29).

Prodrazverstka and the redistribution of land, livestock and equipment combined to reinforce the structure of the small peasant economy working substantially for its own consumption and living primarily on its own resources. The backwardness of Russian agriculture as compared with other European countries became more marked. Supply of agricultural machinery – owing to the conversion of the heavy and metal-working industries to military needs and to replacing imports – fell sharply. Other factors, such as the policy of distribution of agricultural machines by *Narkomprod* and the reduction of the size of farms, may explain the greater recourse to the traditional ploughs, the proportion of which in the total available equipment increased significantly between 1917 and 1921.[151] Only in March 1920 did *Sovnarkom* decide to transfer the stock of agricultural implements and machines to the control of *Narkomzem*.[152]

In an appraisal of the results of the food procurement policy, the benefits to the army of such a policy should not be neglected. The army

Table 8.28. *Average and relative magnitudes on the basis of the agricultural censuses of 1917, 1920 and 1922*[a]

Area	Year	Desiatins of		Working horses for 100 farms	Cows per 100 farms	% of farms having		
		Average no. of people per farm	land per head of live-stock			no arable land	no working animals	no cows
USSR	1917	6.1	2.8	133.3	20.1	16.8	29.4	24.0
	1920	5.5	2.8	106.2	21.1	8.4	28.5	18.3
RSFSR	1917	6.1	2.8	139.1	21.1	15.9	27.0	21.7
	1920	5.6	2.7	109.6	21.7	8.1	27.1	16.4
	1922	5.4	2.7	80.0	18.9	6.7	37.5	23.6
Belorussian SSR	1917	6.3	2.7	116.3	25.2	10.0	16.2	9.6
	1922	5.5	2.5	84.0	25.6	5.4	22.2	7.9
Moscow Industrial Region	1917	5.9	3.1	79.5	17.3	17.0	36.6	21.2
	1920	5.4	2.3	69.3	19.5	7.8	35.7	17.8
	1922	5.3	2.6	64.8	18.7	5.7	37.0	19.2
Central Agricultural Region[b]	1917	6.8	3.9	104.7	13.1	11.3	33.5	21.8
	1920	6.1	3.5	75.2	14.2	3.0	31.5	18.7
	1922	5.7	4.3	62.9	13.7	0.3	42.2	27.7

[a]The year 1922 was one of famine.
[b]The Central Agricultural Regions include Briansk, Voronezh, Kaluga, Kursk, Orel, Penza, Riazan, Tambov, and Tula.
Source: Sbornik statistitcheskikh svedenii, p. 107

Table 8.29. *Distribution of peasant farms according to working horses and cows (%, from data of 10 per cent of the 1922 agricultural census)*

Area	Year	No. of farms	without horse	with 1 horse	with 2 horses	with 3 horses	4 and more	without cows	with 1 cow	with 2 cows	with 3 cows	4 and more
RSFSR	1920	1,032,351	27.1	50.9	14.2	4.1	3.7	16.4	59.9	17.7	3.9	2.1
	1922	1,019,576	37.5	49.0	10.1	2.1	1.3	23.6	59.3	14.2	2.2	0.7
Moscow Industrial Region	1920	148,608	35.7	61.9	2.3	0.1	—	17.8	64.5	16.4	1.2	0.1
	1922	153,761	37.0	61.1	1.9	—	—	19.2	64.2	15.4	1.1	0.1
Central Agricultural Regions	1920	272,920	31.5	59.5	8.2	0.7	0.1	18.7	75.6	5.4	0.3	—
	1922	282,517	42.2	52.1	5.4	0.3	—	27.7	67.2	4.8	0.3	—

Source: Sbornik statisticheskikh svedenii, pp. 116–17

was the principal beneficiary of the central policy of distribution,[153] but there is no evidence that the policy had its origins in the need to supply the armed forces. Indeed, the supply to the army depended not only on *Narkomprod*'s deliveries: it had its own organs of supply. For some time the relations between these organs and the *Narkomprod* agencies remained rather tense. *Narkomprod* tenaciously pursued its policy of centralization of supply, following the state commodity exchange scheme, while the army demanded the immediate satisfaction of its privileged needs. The 'civil' organization of *Narkomprod* was found to be unsuited to military needs. In September 1918 the army formed the Central Commission for the regulation of Food Procurement Supply to the Army (*Tsekomprodarm*). On 29 December 1918, the Council of Labour and Defence issued instructions for the formation of its local organs. These organs, *oprodkomy*, should have been auxiliary agencies with control and assistance functions only, taking for granted the functions of supply performed by the *Narkomprod* agencies. But they soon evolved into food procurement organs and started working on autonomous bases. Both the army and *Narkomprod* agencies strove to extend their competence independently of one another. The Central Commission was transformed into an administration of *Narkomprod*, but this represented only an apparent success for the latter. The local organs of army supply refused to obey the instructions of the civil procurement agencies and carried out directly procurement of foodstuffs.[154]

The work of the *oprodkomy* was of great value in general not merely at the front, as in the Caucasus where they procured from 70 per cent to 97 per cent of the total military provisions. At the Second Congress of Food Supply on 29 June 1920, Briukhanov mentioned that the army food supply organs had collected, by that date, 27 million puds of grain, that is about 15 per cent of the total state purchase.[155] The Army also organized military farms which yielded a fair amount of vegetables and other crops. Three million puds of vegetables – half a year's consumption for the army – were autonomously produced. In addition the army procured by itself hay, of which 6.5 million puds were harvested in 1920, and milling.[156] Processed cereals in excess of the army's consumption were dispatched to the central regions. Instead of following the central policy of concentration of supply, the army also decided – taking into account the state of transport – whether to dispatch raw materials elsewhere or to process them *in situ*.[157]

There are no complete data on the total amount of foodstuffs that the army was able to procure through its own organs during war communism making difficult a proper comparative evaluation of the achievements of *Narkomprod* and army supply. However, it is plausible that the flexibility of the military organization helped considerably to compensate for the shortcomings of the *Narkomprod* organization, which was not adequate for military emergency requiring mobile units and rapid changes of programme.

Was there any alternative to *prodrazverstka* in the years of civil war? The answer could be yes, if one considers that isolated efforts to change the method of appropriating the agricultural surplus were made, and that the debate about the possibility of changing this method to some form of taxation in kind had already started at the beginning of 1920.

In March 1919 Shlikhter, the plenipotentiary in charge of foodstuffs procurement in the Ukraine when the region was under Soviet rule, affirmed that the procurement policy there was being changed not only because of exogenous constraints, but also because of what had happened in Moscow. In the Ukraine only the most important foodstuffs – bread grains, salt, sugar and tea – were put under the regime of state monopoly. Other foodstuffs could be sold in the free market. Instead of the full nationalization of commerce, a sort of tax in kind on all commodities was applied. The state appropriated 30 per cent of the registered commodities, to be used as a partial means of exchange for products badly needed by the centre.[158]

The comparatively smaller reduction of the Ukrainian crop area could suggest that alternative policies would have been less harmful to Soviet agriculture. But, given the intermittent nature of Soviet rule in the Ukraine, such a hypothesis requires more detailed assessment. There remains, however, the importance of efforts by some Soviet officials and members of the party to find alternative solutions – during war communism – to a policy which only later would the literature justify on the basis of military emergency. The deficiencies of *prodrazverstka* were not ignored by those members of the party who had the opportunity to verify *in loco* the damage it caused in terms of waste and political consequences.

In February 1920, after his experience in the Urals, Trotskii proposed to the Central Committee of the Party the replacement of *prodrazverstka* by a tax in kind based on output, and abolition of the system of collective exchange in favour of commodity exchange on an individual basis.[159] At that time, however, his was an isolated voice. The military section of *Narkomprod* was drafting improvements in the utilization of armed troops, in order to get 'better results' with 'smaller inputs'. It was planned to send troops to the most resistant *uezd* or *volost* or 'violent' village and to operate in such a way as to give a warning not only to the particular locality but also to adjacent areas. The plan included systematic support for the food procurement organs from troops. The political message that initially all members of the food detachments were supposed to propagate in the countryside, together with the policy of collection of the surplus, was to be reserved to detachments of workers acting as vanguard patrols and agitators to help avoid clashes, and 'true educational forces of the military units themselves'.[160] On 28 April 1920 – after adopting the system of premiums in kind in industry – *Sovnarkom* approved the use of army units under the orders of *Narkomprod* in support of the food procurement organs with the goal of carrying out the obligatory extraction of the surplus.[161] Workers' detachments which originally had been authorized by *Narkomprod* to carry out independent purchases were not considered suitable as military forces.[162] Better results were apparently expected by such measures as 'confiscation of the belongings and removal to concentration camps of those peasants who refused threshing or delivery of the obligatory quota'.[163]

It was only at the Food Procurement Congress taking place between June and July 1920, on the eve of the new harvest, that the question of the efficacy of the tax in kind was rescued and proposed for discussion by some food procurement officials. Furthermore, the president of the Moscow section of agricultural activity spoke in support of the tax in kind.[164] Nonetheless, the policy of the harsh hand prevailed once again over milder policies. Indeed, *Narkomprod* policy received further refinements along the lines of the state monopoly of the agricultural surplus. For the heads of *Narkomprod prodrazverstka* was to become the method of implementation of state monopoly. The All-Russian Food Procurement Congress approved Frumkin's theses, which identified the specific characteristics of distribution based on *prodrazverstka*: (1), abolition of sale and purchase of the most important products; (2), implementation of *prodrazverstka* according to class principles; (3), gradual inclusion of all agricultural products starting with raw materials; (4), application of *prodrazverstka* to the whole year, in order not to leave 'any free surplus'; (5), if the surplus happened to be higher than *prodrazverstka*, 'in no case' should it be allowed 'either free sale or supplementary *razverstka* to meet export quotas, but the produce should be appropriated in order to be redistributed among the rural poor'.[165]

In the summer of 1920, information that the harvest would be lower than in the previous year prompted new arguments for the supporters of continuation and refinement of *Narkomprod*'s policy as well as renewed appeals for change. While Larin proposed doubling the purchase price of grain from 50 rubles to 100 rubles a pud, which he expected to produce a 10 per cent increase in grain collection, Preobrazhenskii observed that peasants were already selling their grain on the black market at fifty to a hundred times the official price.[166] Only by making the peasants able to rely on getting salt, kerosene and manufactures at centrally fixed prices – stressed Preobrazhenskii – could bread supply be relied on. The policy criteria suggested by him (much the same as those which inspired the beginning of collective commodity exchange in April 1918) were incorporated in the new plan of *razverstka* for 1920–1. The target was the collection of 456 million puds of grain, 168,950,000 of which should come from the producing provinces and 110,000,000 from Siberia. The new programme emphasized that class principles were to be applied and that deliveries could be made throughout the year rather than, as before, on fixed schedules.[167] Information about a bad harvest coming to the centre, however, increased the concern of the food procurement commissars for more specific measures directed to counteract both the arguments of the supporters of milder policies and efforts by the peasants to avoid the burden of *prodrazverstka*. In this context, Osinskii started elaborating the lines of a project of state regulation of private agriculture. He assumed that no rural poor still existed in the countryside, which was typified at the time by the mass of middle peasants, that large masses of peasants had increased their wealth owing to local black markets, and that *prodrazverstka* had acted as an incentive to reduce the sown area to the size demanded by a moderate farm consumption. The bad harvest, according to Osinskii, was the product of bad or negligent work, the evidence of which was to be observed in different yields from similar agricultural areas. Moreover, he observed, peasants tried to avoid their state obligations, by changing crops and selling horses, and also attempted to avoid state labour conscription. Osinskii, therefore, proposed to spur on the transition to the socialist transformation of the countryside by strengthening the *sovkhozy* on the one hand and by prescribing centrally the crops and farming methods of individual peasants on the other. For this purpose Osinskii demanded labour conscription, the accounting and mobilization of all people, horses and inventories, their allocation according to state targets and plans, and finally new rules on the rotation of fields, considering the individual strips as forming a collective fund worked in common. This form of organization, according to Osinskii, would still allow the individual imputation of the product and incentives, and individual property in livestock and inventories – which would, however, remain subject to registration and state obligation.[168]

The arguments for increasing coercion were also based on alleged evidence from some localities proving the advantages of such a policy. In *Kak nado rabotat'* (*How to Work*) Osinskii stressed that the system of administrative repression should lead the way to a system of court repression, if the peasantry was to be convinced that *razverstka* was a state law, opposition to which would have judicial consequences.[169] While other people intervened in the debate by pointing out the perverse consequences of the policy of collective commodity exchange penalizing the peasantry and pushing it to economic autarky,[170] Osinskii cited the example of Tula *uezd* committees for the sowing campaign which were successful in speeding up the sowing, and concluded that food detachments were necessary to organize and regulate agriculture.[171] With polemics and arguments stressing the danger of the future reduction of agricultural output, Osinskii maintained that figures were often biased by local organs interested in showing lower results.[172] But he was the first to maintain that *prodrazverstka* led to reduced sowings, which was why he proposed that seeds should be made a state monopoly and be concentrated into a state fund 'in order to put an end to decreasing harvests'.[173] In the course of the polemics which opposed the supporters of the tax in kind to *Narkomprod*, Osinskii used political, practical and theoretical arguments. First, he claimed that the introduction of the tax in kind would open the way to a 'kulak' economy. Second, he elaborated the lines of an alternative state policy in agriculture, aiming at central planning of output. Not only the quantity but also the quality of seeds should be planned, i.e. not only the ploughed land, but also the crops. This meant the state monopolizing the quantity of seed needed for 'the full utilization of land and means of production'. Planning would become a state law, representing for peasants an obligation subject to strict control.[174] Osinskii observed that direct sowing to *Narkomprod*'s orders had been successful in the provinces of Ivanovo, Tambov, Tula, North Dvinsk, Penza, Ekaterinburg, etc., indicating that practice had already preceded theory and proved to be advantageous.[175] Some forms of state intervention, in fact, had already taken place in the central provinces in the autumn of 1920. After the fulfilment of *prodrazverstka*, *Narkomprod* imposed the so-called internal redistribution of stocks and livestock, following monthly norms for each farm.[176]

If necessity was one of the arguments for supporting compulsory state planning in agriculture – Osinskii observed that a commodity fund justifying the use of economic incentives[177] did not exist – still the major objection to change of policy was the fear that even a moderate liberalization might reverse the course towards socialism into one back to capitalism.[178]

Arguments against Osinskii's theses on planning in agriculture were that compulsion did no good, and that economic incentives would do better.[179] Additional arguments were put forward at the Eighth Congress of Soviets in December 1920 by other parties. The Mensheviks focused on the dangerous consequences of the reduction of the crop area and livestock, and advocated freedom for peasants to dispose of their produce, after fulfilling their obligation to the state, by free trade or at prices fixed in agreement with the state.[180] The Socialist-Revolutionaries proposed diminishing the amount of requisitions and letting the peasants dispose of the remainder for their own consumption and for exchange with industrial commodities through consumer cooperatives.[181] The communists, however, opted for the drastic measures elaborated by Osinskii. Their most convincing argument was the fear that free trade would bring about the collapse of the system of central distribution and the destruction of the national economy along with it.[182] The formation of 'seed and sowing committees' was approved by the congress. In January 1921 the programme to form committees for obligatory sowing at the provincial level, including targets for districts, was approved by law.[183]

The law on the seed and sowing committees may be considered the very last effort to keep the foundations of the war communist economic organization intact. Though it was not implemented, owing to the sudden turn in the policy of the tax in kind which took place in Feburary 1921, it deserves attention in so far as it can be regarded as the logical conclusion of successive steps towards the abolition of the market, which Bolshevik policy had aimed at since the seizure of power.

The ultimate end of the law on the seed committees – though not explicitly stated – was the collectivization of land. The purpose of the law was, in fact, to replace farmers' decisions by central obligatory targets, to be achieved through the redistribution of means and materials of production among the individual units. The seed-sowing committees – composed of not more than five members with the obligatory involvement of the rural population in each province, *uezd* (*raion*) and *volost* – had to conform to the central plan of obligatory sowing elaborated by *Narkomzem*, and VSNKh (with the participation of the Central Statistical Administration), and be approved by *Sovnarkom* before 15 January. Each administrative territorial level was responsible for the disaggregation of the central plans. The plan for sowing was considered a state law. The stocks of seed belonging to farmers for their own needs were defined as the 'inviolable seed fund' subject to regulations as to its maintenance and intraprovincial redistribution. Provincial committees charged with expansion of the acreage under crops, together with agricultural and food procurement sections, were entrusted with deciding how much and what to sow within the guidelines of the central plans.

The law specified the means through which the seed fund had to be formed and maintained. These means included: *razverstka*, dispatch or deposit of seeds in sacks labelled with the name of the owner in collective granaries under the responsibility of agricultural collectives, soviets and *volost* executive committees; redistribution of seeds; designation of private stocks of seeds as 'inviolable seed fund' and their expropriation;

obligation to keep stocks of seeds. The regulations relating to mechanization, improvement of ploughed land, agricultural output and maintenance of soil fertility were declared obligatory. The committees had other
responsibilities, including the correct use of work animals and
implements.

The law also covered special premiums in the form of privileged supply
of means of production as well as consumer goods, higher norms of
foodstuffs remaining with the owner after *razverstka*, and certain special
benefits for the successful fulfilment of other duties. Some Soviet literature
interprets this introduction of premiums as a form of incentives preparing
the way to NEP,[184] but these premiums were not intended to encourage
the initiative of farmers in the exploitation of the land, but mainly to fulfil
the plan as such. The fear that material incentives could favour the
development of capitalist methods and mentalities prevailed and inspired
further qualifications as to the criteria applying to premiums. Firstly,
collectives had priority over individual households in the distribution of
premiums; secondly, premiums for individual farmers were conditional
on attainment 'without any use whatsoever of kulak methods'; thirdly,
means of production were supplied as premiums with a precise guarantee
that they would not be used as means 'of transforming farmers into
kulaks'.

The law emphasized collective methods and goals and tried, therefore,
to channel premiums to this purpose, even at the price of limiting
individual efforts aiming at directly improving the material well-being
and the productivity of the individual farm. By substituting central
decisions for individual decision-making in agriculture, the law pursued
not only the immediate goal of avoiding the reduction of ploughed land,
but also the long-term aim of naturalizing (de-monetizing) the economy
as a whole. The aim was to transform agriculture into a 'state sector' like
industry, and to make possible the central distribution of all products and
materials without the intermediation of the market. The project of de-
monetization of the economy, which Bukharin and Preobrazhenskii
considered not feasible in their programme of communism in 1919 owing
to the existence of the private sector of agriculture, became actual. As
Larin stressed, the further steps in the naturalization of the relation
between town and countryside would have ended in the exclusion of the
need for money.[185] The law on the seed and sowing committees completed
the prerequisites for central planning, a goal that the war economic
organization had pursued but not realized. The central production plans
for industry would have been feasible only if accurate forecasts of supply,
both of foodstuffs, i.e. wage goods, and raw materials had materialized.
Plans in agriculture would have meant planning of consumption with

regard to foodstuffs, and planning of raw material with regard to technical crops. From the point of view of the economy as a whole this would have meant the ability to determine from above the equilibrium between demand and supply. The system of orders to the industrial and agricultural units of production – entailing the diligent application of the guidelines of 'conscious' planners – and the central distribution of all products according to established plans through a bonus system – implying central knowledge of individual preferences – prefigured a very rigid type of central planning with no degree of freedom either for labour or for consumers. This form of planning was never realized, since exogenous constraints put pressure on the leadership and enforced a new course in economic policy. The economic model of war communism was, nonetheless, in fact ready, though it had not been theoretically formalized. Its basic lines were going to sustain long-range communist goals and to provide the basis for future research preparing the way for the Soviet type of planning of the thirties.

8.7 TRANSITION TO THE NEW ECONOMIC POLICY

In summer 1920 peasant revolts again started ravaging the central and south-eastern provinces. Opposition to *prodrazverstka* began as soon as signs of a return to the civil regime of peace appeared. In June 1920 revolts spread in the province of Viatka, and in September to Vladimir.[186] Armed bands raged throughout the province of Tambov. Though these revolts have often appeared in the literature under the name of counter-revolutionary movements, there is now agreement, even in recent Soviet literature, that these were peasants' revolts, sometimes with extensive participation of middle and poor peasants, like the *Antonovshchina* which included about 50,000 people and lasted one year in the province of Tambov.[187] The demobilization of soldiers was an additional factor of unrest. Armed bands scoured across the regions of Middle Volga, Don, Kuban, and Tula.[188] In the province of Ufa resentment against *prodrazverstka* induced Sviderskii to declare, on 11 October 1920 to his colleagues in *Narkomprod*, that *razverstka* had negative consequences and that it was necessary to lower it.[189] *Narkomprod* was compelled to suspend food collection in thirteen provinces.[190] The burden of *razverstka* on the provinces which had mainly supplied it during the civil war could have been lowered only if other sources of supply had been made available. The *Narkomprod* officials, in fact, hoped to increase supplies from Siberia, the Caucasus and the Ukraine. In the summer of 1920 the local food procurement organs in Siberia calculated that 110 million puds of grain were available and that more than 6.5 million puds of meat could also be collected. Six thousand people were sent there for state purchase and twenty thousand followed to help in the threshing campaign. VSNKh provided 500 trucks.[191] But in addition to revolts, transport and other organizational defects hindered the plans of supply. In October 1920 the officials in charge of the transport sections of *Narkomprod* affirmed that supply from Siberia and from the Caucasus could not be fulfilled for lack of fuel, sewing machines to sew the sacks of grain, railwaymen and locomotives, and because of the general disruption of railways owing to damage by troops.[192] In spite of some improvements as compared with the situation of civil war, total shipments remained two and a half times below those of mid 1917.[193] Dramatic forecasts were coupled with the lowering of urban consumption of foodstuffs to about ten puds per head a year, i.e less than what was considered a subsistence norm.[194] The general mood in the countryside at this time was summed up by an old peasant at the Eighth Congress of the Soviets: 'The land belongs to us', he declared, 'but the bread belongs to you; the water belongs to us, but the fish to you; the forests are ours, but the timber is yours.'[195] The new situation of emergency induced Lenin to consider alternatives which a few months before he had rejected.

On 30 November 1920 *Sovnarkom*, instructed by Lenin, decided to set up a commission on the transition to a system of tax in kind. On 8 February 1921, Lenin urgently drafted the main points of a revision of the food procurement policy, which were then taken as a basis for formulation of the tax in kind:

1. To satisfy the wishes of the non-party peasants for the substitution of the tax in kind for the surplus appropriation system (the confiscation of the surplus of grain stocks);
2. to reduce the size of this tax as compared with last year's appropriation rate;
3. to approve the principle of making the tax commensurate with the farmers' effort, reducing the rate for those making the greater effort;
4. to give the farmer more leeway in using his after-tax surpluses in local trade, provided his tax is promptly paid in full.[196]

From a certain point of view, the tax in kind did not represent a startling innovation with respect to *prodrazverstka*, which itself was in practice a levy on the surplus arbitrarily determined by the state. The real novelty was the admission of free trade of the surplus remaining to the peasant after tax deduction.

At the Tenth Congress of the Party in March 1921, Lenin emphasized that the substitution of the tax in kind for the surplus appropriation system was 'primarily and mainly a political question', for it was essentially 'a question of the attitude of the working class to the peasantry'.[197]

The arguments of the Mensheviks and Left Socialist-Revolutionaries, which had not made their way through the barrier of Bolshevik dogmatism at the Eighth Congress of Soviets, became convincing at the beginning of 1921, when the failure of the effort to continue *prodrazverstka* in other food-producing regions induced Lenin to impose a drastic turn in policy. The Ukrainian peasants, against whom Shlikhter had not dared to force the surplus appropriation method in 1919, revolted against the introduction of *prodrazverstka* in 1920–1. Before the plenary session of the Moscow Soviet on 24 February 1921, Lenin admitted that the peasants' revolts in the Ukraine and in Siberia was due to the Soviet procurement policy.[198] People demanded free trade, not a change of government;[199] but, had the government stuck to its policy of appropriation, revolts against Soviet power would have grown. Political concerns were coupled with a more concrete worry that sowings could be reduced even more in the forthcoming sowing seasons, in spite of the sanctions foreseen by the law on the seed-sowing committees. Lenin's concern for the attitude of the non-party peasants could not but be related to his concern for 'who controls whom' in the application of the new rules on sowing.

At the Moscow Soviet Plenary Session on 28 February 1921, Lenin made two important admissions. Firstly, he discarded the idea of collective farming as a way out of the agricultural crisis:

So long as we have no machines, so long as the peasant himself has no wish to change from small-scale to large-scale farming, we are inclined to take this idea into account and we shall take this question before the party congress...[200]

Secondly, Lenin admitted that the Bolsheviks had not yet learned to practise 'thrift', a word which he used as a synonym for 'economics'.[201] This was a significant indication of a new approach to economic problems, by which methods of production should be given more attention than methods of distribution. The new approach in economic policy was made clearer at the Tenth Congress of the Party. Lenin stressed that the peasantry needed incentives to make the sowings. The sort of incentives were reflected in their demands:

We know these demands. But we must verify them and examine all that we know of the farmer's economic demands from the standpoint of economic science. If we go into this, we shall see at once that it will take essentially two things to satisfy the smaller farmer. The first is a certain freedom of exchange, freedom for the small private proprietor, and the second is the need to obtain commodities and products.[202]

Lenin's speech represented an important innovation; an analogous standpoint in 1918 would have led to charges of favouring profiteering. At that time, collective commodity exchange had represented an alternative to market distribution rules. When Lenin presented the question of the tax in kind at the Party Congress from the point of view of free trade, that is, individual commodity exchange, of the remainder of the surplus after taxation, the economic situation of workers in the urban centres was no better than in spring 1918. Strumilin's computation of real wages in Petrograd in January 1918 and in January 1921 – 9.07 versus 2.25 real rubles per day, where the formal *paiok* was respectively 1.37 and 1.90[203] – shows that living standards had declined severely. The increase of the *paiok* was not such as to balance, over the year, the loss of purchasing power of wages. If only necessity and not ideology had called for compulsory measures in food collection in the spring of 1918, the same attitude would have been justified even more in 1921. But then, a new approach to town – countryside relations was born out of the 'mistakes' of war communism, which Lenin finally acknowledged:

... the vastness of our agricultural country with its poor transport system, boundless expanses, varying climate, diverse farming conditions, etc., makes a certain freedom of exchange between local agriculture and local industry, on a local scale, inevitable. In this respect, we are very much to blame for having gone too far; we overdid the nationalization of industry and trade, clamping down on the local exchange of commodities. Was that a mistake? It certainly was.[204]

In 1921 the breaking of the vicious circle of deficiency of grain due to scarcity of industrial products, and vice versa, was sought not only in the policy of concessions,[205] but also in an alternative economic model, in some respects anticipating, or providing the basis for, Bukharin's position of the mid twenties on socialist development. Lenin's approach to economic policy in March 1921 suggested that the new economic model would be based on the local economy. This economy was to start to work again through the reciprocal incentives that the peasant market would offer to industry and industrial demand to agriculture. This idea was put forward by Lenin moderately on 6 April 1921, in the presence of a suspicious assembly of party cells:

[The tax in kind] will undoubtedly improve the peasant's conditions, and give him an assurance and a sense of certainty that he will be free to exchange all his available surplus at least for local handicraft wares.[206]

The steps towards a new economic course were taken in haste and without a precise programme regarding the scope of the new policy measures and their connotations. Faced with the bewilderment of the members of the party cells, some of whom had just come back from crushing the Kronstadt revolt, Lenin was forced to display his certainty that liberalization of trade would have limited scope and that the introduction of the tax in kind would not harm the foundations of socialism.[207] But at the Party Congress, he avowed that the leadership had no idea how much latitude should be given to economic exchange.[208] While drafting the outline of the pamphlet on the tax in kind, Lenin was still wondering whether this reform ought to be presented as a retreat, or as an advance (to commodity exchange),[209] whether its meaning ought to be presented in relation to general tasks or to the specific conditions of the current political situation. It was probably through his own speculations about the consequences and the importance of the change in food procurement policy – the original motivation of which was merely political – that Lenin convinced himself that such a measure gave a new turn to economic policy. The expression 'war communism' was used for the first time in the draft of the pamphlet on the tax in kind, to reject the experience of 1918–21 economic policy as a whole. The words 'new policy' made their appearance for the first time under the heading of the article on the tax in kind.[210] To propagate the meaning of the tax in kind, Lenin affirmed that this measure was one of the forms of transition from that 'peculiar war communism' which had been forced upon the country by extreme want, ruin and war, to regularize the socialist exchange of products.[211]

The novelty contained in the tax in kind was private trade, though other words were used for it. Lenin put the emphasis on local markets as means to motivate agricultural productivity. Long excerpts from articles written by him in the Spring of 1918 on the chief tasks of the day and against the childishness of the left wing formed the foreword of the pamphlet on the tax in kind. The ideological foundations of the new policy were sought in the model of state capitalism, which Lenin had supported at the beginning of 1918 against the left wing of the party. But his allegation of a continuity between the policies of 1918 and 1921 was arbitrary and misleading. In 1918, the focus was on state monopoly capitalism versus workers' control, on state commodity exchange versus a free market in industrial commodities and agricultural products, on centralization versus decentralization as a synonym of anarchy. In 1921, on the contrary, the principle of economic centralization had been already seriously questioned and the possibility of local free markets was taken into account to get out of the economic impasse. Lenin's words on this prospect in 1921 had no precedents:

Local or imported salt, paraffin-oil from the nearest town, the handicraft wood working industry, handicrafts using local raw materials and producing certain, perhaps not very important, but necessary and useful articles for peasants, green coal [the utilization of small local sources for electrification] and so on and so forth – all this must be brought into play in order to stimulate exchange between industry and agriculture at all costs. Those who achieve the best results in this sphere, even *by means of private capitalism* [my italics], even without cooperatives, or without transforming directly this capitalism into state capitalism, still do more for the cause of socialist construction in Russia, than those who 'ponder over' the purity of communism, draw up regulations and instructions for state capitalism and the cooperatives, but do nothing practical to stimulate trade.[212]

The restoration of limited private trade, brought about by the tax in kind, was soon to be the vehicle for restoration of the monetary system. Lenin's draft of the instruction of the Council of Labour and Defence written in May 1921 mentioned that commodity exchange was the test of the relationship between industry and agriculture and the foundation of the whole work of creating a fairly well-regulated monetary system.[213]

The implications of the tax in kind for overall economic organization are such that it seems correct, following the existing literature on the subject, to date the end of the war communism experience on the day of the promulgation of the law on the tax in kind on 21 March 1921.[214] The law abolished the principle of collective responsibility in taxation and replaced collective by individual commodity exchange, on the basis of the individual surplus voluntarily delivered to the distribution centres after taxation. Free trade was allowed 'within the limits of local economic exchange', but only a few days later *Sovnarkom* authorized free trade in the sale and purchase of agricultural products all over the country.[215]

These steps were only the beginning of a new economic course, the development of which was then to proceed gradually, along the policy of revising former laws and regulations.[216] Liberalization, however, concerned methods, not principles. The principle of the superiority of the interests of the *state* versus those of individual and local communities was still safeguarded by the levy on agricultural surpluses. The tax in kind was calculated to yield a fairly large amount of agricultural produce for the state, 240 million puds of cereals, that is, half of the forecast figure for state purchase in 1920, but about 90 per cent of the actual *prodrazverstka* of the 1919–20 food campaign.[217] The principle of state control, which war communism had identified with party control, remained and was reinforced. The end of the war communist experience coincided with the beginning of a militarized ideology of the party, which greatly reduced the potential for internal opposition. While undertaking the difficult and unpredictable – as regards outcome – path towards liberalization, Lenin tried to enforce the utmost cohesion of the party around the leadership. War communism had already contributed to the annihilation of the external political opposition. The majority of the Party Congress approved in March 1921 Lenin's motion on party unity against the anarcho-syndicalist deviation. Factionalism was condemned as harmful and impermissible.[218] Lenin's political comments in the margin of the pamphlet of the tax in kind made it clear to public opinion that the new economic course did not entail political freedom:

We can and we must find other methods of testing the mood of the masses and coming closer to them. We suggest that those who want to play the parliamentary, constituent assembly and non-party conference game, should go abroad ... We have no time for this opposition at 'conference' game. We are surrounded by the world bourgeoisie, who are watching for every sign of vacillation in order to bring back their own men and restore landowners and the bourgeoisie. We will keep in prison the Mensheviks and the Socialist-Revolutionaries, whether avowed or in 'non-party' guise.[219]

The ostracism of the opposition and the concentration of political control around a small leadership prevented the New Economic Policy from evolving toward models of socialism other than a rigid one-party model of social organization.

8.8 SUMMARY

The decree on *prodrazverstka* was issued after the decision to adopt a trade monopoly of basic consumer goods. *Prodrazverstka* extended to the country as a whole the limited scheme of commodity exchange, which proved to be ineffective in 1918, when trade monopoly had not yet been decreed. It was expected to meet the overall state demand for grain, irrespective of the consumption needs of the producers. It therefore assumed implicitly that the state would become the only supplier of consumer goods and foodstuffs to the population on the basis of state fixed prices. Food rations were differentiated according to a so-called class principle favouring industrial workers. Nonetheless, central distribution never provided more than fifty per cent of the subsistence demand in towns. This was the reason why the fight against the illegal or semi-legal market channels was irregular and never quite decisive. It was only by the end of 1920 that serious efforts were made to close the remaining channels of market exchange, while trying to enforce plans of agricultural production through the institution of sowing committees. These efforts were linked with the simultaneous attempt to elaborate a central plan of supply of consumer goods to all industrial workers, whose monetary wages were rapidly depreciating. The central plan of supply was an extreme attempt to rationalize not only the expropriation of the agricultural surplus, but also its production. This last endeavour to solve economic problems through administrative measures was abortive.

Prodrazverstka had caused enormous losses to the peasantry, expropriated of its surplus and often of its basic necessities; to the population, which did not get the equivalent of what was expropriated, because of the waste, robberies and disruption which the distributive system entailed, and to the country as a whole which lost both real and potential agricultural output. If carried on after the end of civil war, *prodrazverstka* might have caused the fall of the Bolshevik Government, already exhausted by the strains of war and eroded by internal conflicts. As the discontent of the peasantry started to be manifested through revolts and unrest, it became clear to many that higher degrees of administrative control could result in a loss of political control. The plan of collective commodity exchange based on the forced expropriation of the agricultural surplus was replaced in a hurry in March 1921, before the sowing season started, by the tax in kind which several parties had vainly advocated in 1920. Although the tax level remained high, fiscal rules replaced administrative rules, meaning that right to ownership and to trade after-tax produce was recognized and that room was going to be left for market incentives in the phase of reconstruction.

The radical change in policy, however, did not entail an ideological revision, the outcome of which could have been disruptive. It rather contributed to the strengthening of party discipline around the leadership, and to the ossification of basic ideological tenets, thus sacrificing the potential development of the new Soviet system into a model of organization, respectful of the interests and rights of individual producers, and open to pragmatic options on the way towards a more equal society.

NOTES

1 *Pravda*, no. 188, 4 September 1918, 3.
2 *Sistematicheskii Sbornik dekretov i rasporiazhenii Pravitel'stva po prodovol'stvennomu delu*, vol. 2, Novgorod 1920, p. 39.
3 *Izvestiia*, no. 280, 12 December 1920, 3.
4 M.I. Davydov, *Bor'ba za khleb*, Moscow, 1971, p. 49.
5 *Ibid.*, p. 131n; this was half a million puds more per month than in April 1918.
6 See p. 406.
7 Among others: M.I. Iskrov, 'O razrabotke V.I. Leninym prodovol'stvennoi politiki v 1918g', *Voprosy Istorii KPSS*, no. 7, 1963, 84; S.P. Trapeznikov, *Agrarnyi vopros i Leninskie agrarnye programmy v trekh russkikh revoliutsiiakh*, Moscow, 1963, p. 463.
8 Larin observed that the activity of the rural poor committees caused armed

revolt 'almost in all *uezds*' of Soviet Russia by the 'same peasants who welcomed the victory of the proletariat', 'Ocherk khoziaistvennogo razvitiia Sovetskoi Rossii', *Prodovol'stvennaia politika v svete oboshchego khoziaistvennogo stroitel'stva Sovetskoi Vlasti, Sbornik materialov*, Moscow, 1920, p. 67. Foreign observers reported cases of strikes and clashes between workers and Red Guards because of the lack of food at the end of 1918 in some important industrial centres, such as the Kolomna works (cf. C.E.B., *The Facts about the Bolsheviks* (Compiled from the Accounts of Trustworthy Eye-Witnesses and the Russian Press), London, 1919, pp. 28–9).

9 *Izvestiia*, no. 24, 2 February 1919, 1. Lenin replied promptly in *Pravda* that there was no difference between Trotskii and himself regarding middle peasants and that neither of them considered the middle peasants to be their enemies (V.I. Lenin, *Collected Works*, 4th edn, 45 vols., London, 1964–70, vol. 36, p. 500).

10 *Trudy II Vserossiiskogo S"ezda Sovnarkhozov*, pp. 96–102.

11 A.S. Kon'kova, *Bor'ba Kommunisticheskoi Partii za soiuz rabochego klassa s bedneishim krest'ianstvom v 1917–1918*, Moscow, 1974, p. 138.

12 E. Medvedev, *Krest'ianstvo Srednego Povolzh'ia v Oktiabr'skoi Revoliutsii*, Kuibyshev, 1970, p. 125.

13 *Materialy po istorii Sovetskogo stroitel'stva: Sovety v epokhu voennogo kommunizma, Sbornik dokumentov*, part 1, 1928, pp. 389, 352–3, 347, 375.

14 *Ibid.*, pp. 394, 339, 345, 374.

15 Lenin, *Collected Works*, vol. 42, p. 108.

16 *Ibid.*, p. 132.

17 *Izvestiia*, no. 64, 25 March 1919, 2.

18 Lenin, 'The Middle Peasant' – speech on gramophone records (about March 1919), in *Collected Works*, vol. 29, p. 246.

19 When asked whether the peasants working in the state farms should be authorized to cultivate their own plot, Lenin replied that this would have meant going back to small farming and rejected it in general terms: Lenin, *Collected Works*, vol. 29, p. 117.

20 Lenin, 'Report to the Eighth Congress of the RKP on Work in the Countryside', in *Collected Works*, vol. 29, p. 206.

21 *Ibid.*, pp. 207–8.

22 E.G. Gimpel'son, *Voennyi kommunizm: politika, praktika, ideologiia*, Moscow, 1973, pp. 58–9.

23 *Sobranie uzakonenii*, 1919, no. 1, art. 10.

24 Cf. Osinskii's interpretation of *prodrazverstka* in *Prodovol'stvennaia politika v svete obshchego khoziaistva stroitel'stva Sovetskoi Vlasti. Sbornik materialov*, Moscow, 1920, pp. 190–1.

25 Cf. Kaganovich's 'Uchet izlishkov ili razverstka' in *Prodovol'stvennaia politika*, pp. 181–3.

26 *Ibid.*, p. 183.

27 *Sobranie uzakonenii*, 1919, no. 1, art. 11; continuity in the policy of food provisions is stressed by some Soviet literature, among others M.I. Iskrov, 'O razrabotke V.I. Leninym prodovol'stvennoi politiki v 1918 g', *Voprosy Istorii KPSS*, no. 7, 1963, p. 85.

28 *Prodovol'stvennaia politika*, p. 196.
29 *Ibid.*, p. 200.
30 A. Sviderskii in *Prodovol'stvennaia politika*, pp. 169–70.
31 Larin, 'Ocherk', pp. 72–3.
32 *Ibid.*, pp. 73–4.
33 Cf. E.G. Gimpel'son, *Velikii Oktiabr' i stanovlenie Sovetskoi sistemy upravleniia narodnym khoziaistvom (noiabr' 1917–1920 gg)*, Moscow, 1977, p. 183.
34 *Prodovol'stvennaia politika*, p. 247.
35 *Krasnyi Arkhiv*, vol. 6, 1939, 41.
36 See on collective farms, pp. 414–18 above.
37 Larin, 'Ocherk', p. 73.
38 *Ibid.*, p. 74.
39 *Vestnik agitatsii i propagandy Ts.K.RKP(b)*, 1920, no. 1, 8, 10.
40 Sviderskii in *Prodovol'stvennaia politika*, p. 171.
41 Cf. E.G. Gimpel'son, 'O politike voennogo kommunizma (1918–1920 gg)', *Voprosy Istorii*, no. 5, 1963, 41.
42 *Prodovol'stvennaia politika*, p. 196; quoted from Tsiurupa's speech to the provincial food procurement organs.
43 *Ibid.*, pp. 246, 251.
44 N. Osinskii, 'Glavnyi nedostatok nashei razverstki' in *Prodovol'stvennaia politika*, p. 236.
45 *Vestnik agitatsii i propagandy*, 1920, no. 1, 6–7; and *Vtoroe Vserossiiskoe prodovol'stvennoe soveshchanie: rezoliutsii*, Moscow, 1920, pp. 1–2, quoted by Davydov, p. 138.
46 M. Frumkin, 'Razverstka kak osnovnoi metod', in *Prodovol'stvennaia politika*, p. 177, and Osinskii, 'Glavnyi nedostatok', p. 190.
47 Osinskii, 'Glavnyi nedostatok', p. 190.
48 *Sbornik statisticheskikh svedenii po Soiuzu SSR 1918–1923*, Moscow, 1924, p. 104. Very small farms (below to desiatins) were concentrated in the Moscow Industrial Region and represented about 64.1 per cent of all farms having sowings in that region. But small farming also started to predominate in the Central Agricultural Regions, where 73.7 per cent of farms had less than four desiatins of sown land in 1920.
49 Cf. L. Kritsman, *Geroicheskii period Velikoi Russkoi Revoliutsii*, Moscow, n.d., probably 1924, p. 67 for 1917 figures (he produces different data for 1920, however) and *Sbornik statisticheskikh svedenii*, p. 104.
50 *ILO Studies in War Economies*, Studies and Reports Series E, 1941, pp. 99–100. *Sobranie uzakonenii*, 1919, no. 41, art. 387, no. 42, art. 399; *Sobranie uzakonenii*, 1920, no. 13, arts. 81, 83, no. 19, art. 102, no. 57, art. 260, no. 59, art. 272. See also the resolution of the Seventh All-Russian Congress of Soviets, *7i Vserossiiskii S"ezd Sovetov Rabochikh Kest'ianskikh, Krasnoarmeiskikh i Kazach'ikh Deputatov, 5–9 Dekabria, 1919 g*, Moscow, 1920, p. 255.
53 For instance, honey and vegetables could be sold on the market: see *Prodovol'stvennaia politika*, pp. 271 and 275.
53 Sviderskii, *Prodovol'stvennaia politika*, p. 167.
54 'Decree of *Sovnarkom* on the Obligatory Delivery of Cattle for Meat', *Prodovol'stvennaia politika*, pp. 275–8.
55 A. Vainshtein, *Oblozhenie i platezhi krest'ianstva*, Moscow, 1924, pp. 63–4.

56 S.G. Strumilin, *Ocherki ekonomicheskoi istorii Rossii i SSSR*, Moscow, 1966, pp. 224–6.

57 *Ekonomicheskaia Zhizn'*, 25 May 1920, 1.

58 *Sobranie uzakonenii*, 1917–18, no. 52, art. 593.

59 *Trudy II S"ezda Sovnarkhozov*, pp. 96–102.

60 *Ibid.*, pp. 391–2.

61 *Sobranie uzakonenii*, 1919, no. 9, art. 87.

62 *Ekonomicheskaia Zhizn'*, 29 June 1920, 1.

63 *Pravda*, no. 278, 19 December 1918, 2.

64 Cf. E. Colombino, *Tre mesi nella Russia dei Soviets*, Milan, 1921, pp. 52–4; V. Vacirca, *Ciò che ho visto nella Russia Sovietista*, Milan, 1921, pp. 22–3; B. Russell, *The Practice and Theory of Bolshevism*, London, 1920, p. 85.

65 *Izvestiia*, no. 90, 29 April 1919, 4. Railway workers even grew rye for their own use: see H.N. Brailsford, *The Russian Workers' Republic*, New York – London, 1921, p. 32.

66 *Izvestiia*, no. 140, 29 June 1919, 3.

67 Cf. Kritsman, *Geroicheskii period*, pp. 51–2.

68 L. Volin, *A Century of Russian Agriculture*, Cambridge, Mass., 1970, p. 156.

69 *Ibid.*

70 I.A. Gladkov, *Ocherki sovetskoi ekonomiki 1917–1920 gg*, Moscow, 1956, p. 359.

71 Kritsman, *Geroicheskii period*, p. 107.

72 *Ekonomicheskaia Zhizn'*, 2 October 1919, 1.

73 Volin, p. 156.

74 *Sovetskoe krestianstvo (kratkii ocherk istorii, 1917–1919)*, pod red. V.P. Danilova, M.P. Kima, N.V. Tropkina, Moscow, 1970, p. 71.

75 *Ekonomicheskaia Zhizn'*, 11 November 1919, and 4 October 1919, 1.

76 Kritsman, *Geroicheskii period*, p. 107.

77 K. Marx and F. Engels, *Sochineniia*, 2nd edn, Moscow, 1964, vol. 36, p. 360.

78 K. Kautsky, *Die Sozialisierung der Landwirtschaft*, Berlin, 1919, p. 63.

79 V.I. Lenin, *Polnoe sobranie sochinenii*, 5th edn, 55 vols., 1958–69, vol. 7, pp. 182–3.

80 Lenin, *Collected Works*, vol. 41, p. 177: Lenin's addenda to Kalinin's article on 'the peasant congress' in *Proletarii*, no. 25, November 1905, explained that 'socialism demands that land and the factories should be handed over to working people organizing large-scale (instead of scattered small-scale) production under a general plan'.

81 Lenin, *Polnoe sobranie sochinenii*, vol. 16, pp. 316–17.

82 Lenin, 'Report on Land' (8 November 1917), in *Collected Works*, vol. 26, p. 260.

83 *Uprochenie Sovetskoi Vlasti*, p. 276, Doc. no. 224.

84 Volin, pp. 78–9.

85 *Ibid.*, p. 130. On a sample of 1,103 villages, 88 per cent distributed land by 'mouth', 10 per cent by 'male peasant', and 2 per cent by workers: see *Sovetskoe krest'ianstvo*, p. 45.

86 Volin, p. 151.

87 *Ibid.*, p. 130.

88 *Agrarnaia Politika Sovetskoi Vlasti, 1917–1918 gg : dokumenty i materialy*, Moscow, 1954, pp. 400, 403–5.

89 *Ibid.*, pp. 411, 415–16.
90 Cf. G. Wesson, *Soviet Communes*, New Jersey, 1963, p. 92; though the Bolsheviks obtained commanding posts through the appointment of Sereda, Meshcheriakov, Petrovskii and others, following the resignation of Kolgayev, a Left Socialist-Revolutionary, in April 1918; see Lenin, *Collected Works*, vol. 44, pp. 85–6 and p. 477, n49.
91 Lenin, *Collected Works*, vol. 28, p. 175.
92 P. Apostol, *L'Artel et la coopération en Russie*, Paris, 1899, p. 23.
93 Volin, pp. 153–4.
94 *The Russian Economist*, vol. 1, September 1920–January 1921, London, 1921, 389.
95 *Ibid.*, 390.
96 Wesson, p. 96.
97 The merging of state farms and communes was solicited by Lenin from July 1918: see Lenin, 'Letter to Sereda', in *Collected Works*, vol. 44, pp. 119–20.
98 *O zemle*, vyp., 1, 36.
99 Volin, p. 154.
100 *The Russian Economist*, vol. 1, 390.
101 Collective farms of the province of Vologda, for instance, received 405 acres (150 desiatins), only one-third of which was put under cultivation: see *The Russian Economist*, vol. 1, 390.
102 Volin, p. 155. As early as December 1919, speaking to the representatives of the Agricultural Communes meeting in Moscow, Lenin acknowledged that little could be done in the productive field because of the many shortages caused by war. But he also added that agricultural communes should not be characterized as those forms of land tenure living upon state subsidies, and invited them to make closer contact with the peasant surroundings, without which assistance given to cooperatives and artels would be – according to Lenin – not only useless but harmful (Lenin, *Collected Works*, vol. 30, pp. 195–204.).
103 *Sistematicheskii Sbornik dekretov i rasporiazhenii Pravitel'stva po prodovol'stvennomu delu*, vol. 2, Novgorod, 1920, pp. 302–3.
104 *Ibid.*, p. 312.
105 *Ibid.*, p. 74.
106 *Ibid.*, pp. 312–13 (instruction to *gubprodkomy* signed by Shmidt, one of *Narkomprod*'s commisars, on 10 April 1919).
107 *Ibid.*, p. 313 (regulation approved by *Glavprodukt* on 10 July 1919).
108 *Ibid.*, pp. 306–7.
109 Cf. M.I. Davydov, *Bor'ba za khleb*, p. 185.
110 *Pravda*, 28 December 1918, 3 and *Izvestiia*, no. 7, 12 January 1919, 3.
111 *Izvestiia*, no. 11, 17 January 1919, 4.
112 Cf. Davydov, p. 101.
113 *Ibid.*, p. 186.
114 *Izvestiia*, no. 7, 12 January 1919, 4 and no. 67, 28 March 1919, 3.
115 *Izvestiia*, no. 75, 6 April 1919, 3.
116 *Izvestiia*, no. 224, 8 October 1919, 2.
117 *Izvestiia*, no. 244, 31 October 1919, 2.
118 *Izvestiia*, no. 69, 30 March 1919, 4.
119 *Izvestiia*, no. 207, 18 September 1919, 1.

120	In 1919 workers had the right to 20 arshins (1 arshin = 28 inches = 70 cm.) of cotton fabrics, 1 arshin of wool, and 4 of flax, while the rural population got respectively 9, one-tenth and one-third arshins. Between July and October 1919 the rural population as a whole was assigned 792,000 puds of sugar, while workers – as a whole – got 738,000 puds, in spite of the fact that the ratio between these two components of the national population was 9 : 1. Cf. N. Osinskii, 'Glavnyi nedostatok', pp. 232–3.

121	S.G. Strumilin, *Zarabotnaia plata i proizvoditel'nost' truda v russkoi promyshlennosti v 1913–1922 gg*, Moscow, 1923, p. 3.

122	*Izvestiia*, no. 227, 11 October 1919, 1.

123	Davydov, pp. 186–7; V. Miliutin, 'Problema raspredeleniia i potrebleniia', *Za 5 let (1917–1922)*, *sbornik Ts.K.R.K.P.*, Moscow, 1922, pp. 305–6.

124	*Sobranie uzakonenii*, 1920, no. 55, art. 239.

125	*Za 5 let*, pp. 305–6. The figures are low, indeed, if compared with what was considered the minimum intake of calories for light work, i.e. 2835: cf. *Statistika Truda*, nos. 5, 6, 7, March–April 1919, 31.

126	*Statisticheskii Ezhegodnik (1918–1920)*, vol. 8, p. 54. As compared with pre-war time, peasant consumption decreased: see Iu. Poliakov, *Perekhod k NEPu i Sovetskoe krest'ianstvo*, Moscow, 1967, p. 78.

127	*Vsetnik Statistiki*, 1919, nos. 9–12, p. 84.

128	NKP, *Prodovol'stvennyi transport, sbornik materialov i zametok k VIII S''ezdu Sovetov*, Moscow, 1920, p. 28.

129	There were seven permanently accounted producing provinces: Tambov, Ufa, Samara, Saratov, Kazan, Orenburg, Viatka. The provinces of Voronezh, Kursk, Orel, Penza, Riazan, Tula, Simbirsk, Perm and Cheliabinsk did not take part in state purchase in 1917–18. The latter did not participate in the 1918–19 food campaign either. In 1919–20 the producing provinces were the same as in 1916–17. Consuming provinces taking part in food procurement underwent more changes. In 1916–17 there were nine provinces: Astrakhan, Vologda, Kostroma, Nizhni-Novgorod, Novgorod, Smolensk, Yaroslavl, Rybinsk, and Briansk. In 1917–18 Kostroma dropped out. In 1918–19 only five consuming provinces took part in food provisioning: Astrakhan, Vologda, Kauzhsk, Mogilev, and Nizhni-Novgorod. From 1919–20, twenty two provinces were included in state purchase: Arkhangel, Astrakhan, Briansk, Vitebsk, Vologda, Vladimir, Gomel, Ivanovo, Kostroma, Kauzhsk, Minsk, Moscow, Nizhgorod, Novgorod, Olonets, Petrograd, Pskov, North Dvinsk, Smolensk, Tver, Cherepovets, and Yaroslavl.

130	See p. 407.

131	See S.G. Wheatcroft, 'The Reliability of Russian Prewar Grain Output Statistics', *Soviet Studies*, 1974, no. 2.

132	P. Popov, *Proizvodstvo khleba v RSFSR i federiruiushchikhsia s neiu respublikakh khlebnaia produktsiia*), Moscow, p. 49; *Statisticheskii ezhegodnik*, 1918–20, 274, *Prodovol'stvennaia politika*, p. 181; *Pravda*, no. 220, 3 October 1920, 1.

133	S.G. Strumilin, *Ocherki ekonomicheskoi istorii Rossii i SSSR*, Moscow, 1966, pp. 220–1 challenged these figures on the basis of a partial investigation in 1922–3 in seven *volosti* of European Russia, which revealed only a 7 per cent reduction of the cultivated area, as compared with the 31 per cent reduction estimated by the 1920 census in the same provinces.

134 Popov, *Proizvodstvo khleba v RSFSR*, p. 28.

135 V.P. Timoshenko, *Agricultural Russia and the Wheat Problem*, Stanford, 1932, p. 161.

136 G.M. Krzhizhanovskii, *Desiat' let khoziaistvennogo stroitel'stva SSSR*, Moscow, 1922, pp. 37, 124, 125.

137 Poliakov, p. 58. This author refers to figures provided by *Sotsialisticheskoi stroitel'stvo SSSR, Statisticheskii ezhegodnik*, Moscow, 1934, p. 176.

138 *Sotsialisticheskoe stroitel'stvo*, pp. 176–7, quoted by Poliakov, p. 58.

139 Cf. Poliakov, p. 60.

140 *Sbornik statisticheskikh svedenii*, p. 131.

141 Popov, *Proizvodstvo khleba v RSFSR*, p. 29.

142 *Sbornik statisticheskikh svedenii*, p. 131; Poliakov, p. 65.

143 One expert commented that Russia became transformed from a wheat–rye–oats–barley country into a rye–wheat–oats–millet (truly rye-producing) country (P. Mesiatsev, *Agrarnaia politika v Rossii*, p. 217, quoted by Poliakov, p. 67).

144 R.A. Vaisberg, *Deng'i i tseny (podpol'nyirynok v period 'voennogo kommunizma')*, Moscow, 1925, pp. 54–9.

145 Cf. P. Popov, *Proizvodstvo khleba v RSFSR*, p. 29, Larin, 'Ocherk', p. 65 and N. Oganovskii, *Ocherki po ekonomicheskoi geografii Rossii*, Part 1, 1923, pp. 231–32.

146 Poliakov, p. 72.

147 G.S. Gordeev, *Sel'skoe khoziaistvo v voine i revoliutsii*, Moscow, 1925, pp. 66, 127.

148 *Sel'skoe khoziaistvo SSSR*, TsSU Institut istorii AN SSSR, August 1962, 263.

149 For this comment see Poliakov, p. 71.

150 Gordeev, *Sel'skoe khoziaistvo v voine i revoliutsii*, pp. 115–16.

151 Cf. Poliakov, p. 88.

152 'Mery po obespecheniiu sel'skogo khoziaistva sredstvami proizvodstva', pod red. M. Sheflera, *Narkomfin*, vyp. 3, 1920, pp. 28–9.

153 According to Osinskii ('Glavnyi nedostatok', in *Prodovol'stvennaia politika*, p. 236), the army received 25 per cent of flour, 40 per cent of fodder, 60 per cent of fish, meat and sugar, 40 per cent of soap and fat, 20 per cent of matches, 100 per cent of tobacco, 15 per cent of salt, and 90 per cent of dry vegetables.

154 For the organization of food supply to the army, see *Grazhdanskaia voina, 1918–1921*, vol. 2, Moscow, 1928, pp. 310–17.

155 *The Russian Economist*, vol. 1, p. 381.

156 *Grazhdanskaia voina*, vol. 2, pp. 322–3, 315.

157 *Izvestiia*, no. 66, 27 March 1919, 1.

158 *Izvestiia*, 26 March 1919, 2. Shlikhter admitted later that the system of food procurement employed in Russia would have been unsuitable for the Ukraine, owing to banditism, uncertainty about the position of the rural poor with regard to Soviet power, and the scarcity and political unreliability of armed troops: see *Khleb i Revoliutsiia. Prodovol'stvennaia politika kommunisticheskoi Partii i Sovetskogo Pravitel'stva v 1917–1922 goda*, Moscow, 1978, pp. 32–5.

159 This was recalled by Trotskii himself before the Tenth Congress of the Party (*10i S"ezd RKP*, p. 191).

160 *Prodovol'stvennaia politika*, pp. 250–1.

161 *Ibid.*, pp. 251–2 (*Prikaz* no. 230, 26 June 1920).

162 This was proposed by Kaganovich who had been working in Simbirsk province, *Prodovol'stvennaia politika*, p. 253.

163 *Postanovlenie Soveta Narodnykh Komissarov ob iz"iatii khlebnykh izlishkov v Sibiri*, reported in *Prodovol'stvennaia politika*, p. 263.

164 E.B. Genkina, 'V.I. Lenin i perekhod k novoi ekonomicheskoi politike', *Voprosy istorii*, 1964, no. 5, 11; and Poliakov, p. 221.

165 *Prodovol'stvennaia politika*, pp. 257–560.

166 *Pravda*, no. 176, 11 August 1920, 1.

167 *Ibid.*, 2 and *Prodovol'stvennaia politika*, p. 262 (contains a mistake in the sum of *razverstka* by regions, which is reported as 446,000 rather than 456,000).

168 *Pravda*, no. 202, 12 September 1920, where the editorial was on the bad harvest; then *Pravda*, no. 204, 15 September 1920, 1; no. 226, 10 October 1920, 1.

169 *Pravda*, no. 204, 15 September 1920, 1.

170 Cf. D.A. Konius, 'Daite krest'ianinu sol'', *Pravda*, no. 220, 3 October 1920, 1.

171 *Pravda*, no. 204, 15 September 1920, 1.

172 *Pravda*, no. 226, 10 October 1920, 1.

173 *Pravda*, no. 247, 4 November 1920, 1.

174 *Pravda*, no. 248, 5 November 1920, 1.

175 *Ekonomicheskaia Zhizn'*, 26 November 1920.

176 *Pravda*, 24 October 1920.

177 *Pravda*, no. 273, 4 December 1920, 2.

178 *Pravda*, no. 248, 5 November 1920, 1.

179 These arguments were raised by P. Bogdanov: see *Ekonomicheskaia Zhizn'*, 16 December 1920, 1.

180 *8i Vserossiiskii S"ezd Sovetov Rabochikh, Krest'ianskikh, Krasnoarmeiskikh i Kazach'ikh Deputatov*. Stenograficheskii Otchet (22–9 Dekabria, 1920 g), Moscow, 1921, pp. 42, 201.

181 *Ibid.*, p. 122.

182 *Ibid.*, pp. 146–7; this argument was used by Osinskii.

183 *S"ezdy Sovetov RSFSR v postanovleniiakh*, Moscow, 1939, pp. 170–5, and *Sobranie uzakonenii*, 1921, no. 1, art. 9, and no. 2, art. 14.

184 E.B. Genkina, *Perekhod Sovetskogo Gosudarstva k novoi ekonomicheskoi politike, 1921–1922*, Moscow, 1954, p. 7; cf. *contra*, Poliakov, p. 225.

185 *Pravda*, no. 250, 7 November 1920, 1.

186 Poliakov, p. 196.

187 Cf. Seth Singleton, 'The Tambov Revolt (1920–1921)', *Slavic Review*, vol. 25, September 1966, 499; *Antonovshchina: Sbornik statei, ocherkov i drugikh materialov*, Tambov, 1923, p. 13; I. Ia. Trifonov, 'Klassy i klassovaia borba v SSSR v nachale Nepa (1921–1923 gg)', *Bor'ba s vooruzhennoi kulatskoi kontrrevoliutsiei*, vol. 1, Leningrad, 1964, pp. 4–5; Poliakov, pp. 205–6.

188 *Sovetskoe krest'ianstvo*, p. 107.

189 From Poliakov, p. 198.

190 *10i S"ezd RKP*, p. 231.

191 Davydov, from archive documents, p. 165n.
192 NKP, *Prodovol'stvennyi transport*, p. 10.
193 *Ibid.*, p. 6.
194 S.G. Strumilin, 'K khoziaistvennomu planu na 1921–22 gg', *Narodnoe Khoziaistvo*, 1921, no. 5, 16–18.
195 Quoted by Hans von Eckardt, *Russia*, London, 1932, p. 381.
196 Lenin, *Collected Works*, vol. 32, p. 133.
197 *Ibid.*, p. 214.
198 *Ibid.*, pp. 156–7 and vol. 42, pp. 272, 273–4.
199 Poliakov, p. 209.
200 Lenin, *Collected Works*, vol. 32, p. 156.
201 *Ibid.*, p. 154.
202 *Ibid.*, p. 217.
203 See Table 8.14 on pp. 422–3.
204 Lenin, *Collected Works*, vol. 32, p. 219.
205 *Ibid.*, pp. 223–4.
206 *Ibid.*, p. 294.
207 *Ibid.*, p. 551, n90, pp. 288, 296. Lenin said that the tax in kind was a transitional measure. On events and causes of the Kronstadt revolt, see: P. Avrich, *Kronstadt 1921*, Princeton, 1971.
208 Lenin, *Collected Works*, vol. 32, p. 234.
209 *Ibid.*, pp. 320–1.
210 'The Plan of the Pamphlet *The Tax in Kind*', *ibid.*, p. 320, and 'The Tax in Kind', *ibid.*, p. 329.
211 *Ibid.*, p. 342.
212 *Ibid.*, 'The Tax in Kind', p. 354.
213 *Ibid.*, p. 384.
214 *Sobranie uzakonenii*, 1921, no. 26, art. 147.
215 *Sobranie uzakonenii*, 1921, no. 26, art. 149.
216 Cf. Carr, *The Bolshevik Revolution*, vol. 2, pp. 702–22 on policies of the transition.
217 The expected amount of the levy was announced by Lenin on 6 April 1921, at the assembly of party cells (*Collected Works*, vol. 32, p. 292).
218 Lenin, *Collected Works*, vol. 32, p. 241.
219 *Ibid.*, p. 362.

9

Military institutions and the militarization of labour

9.1 THE ORGANIZATION OF MILITARY SUPPLY

The process of organization of the Soviet economy was characterized, as has been shown, by ambitious aims, contradictory processes, a great deal of improvisation, a firm belief in the thaumaturgic powers of the state, and, last but not least, a predatory policy for food procurement. The outcome of all this could not be, and was not, a centralized economy, although strenuous effort was made to bend the economy to central orders. The question then arises as to how the Bolsheviks were able to win the civil war and to establish their power firmly, in spite of the widespread political and military opposition. As for any sort of conflict, part of the answer is to be sought in the poor performance of the 'losers', whose lack of common goals, military and political mistakes, scarce determination in waging an unpopular war particularly on the side of the Allied Powers, and poor understanding of the social process of transformation that the country had undergone have been widely explored by a specialized literature. It is beyond the scope of this book to deal with this side of the problem. Another part of the answer, however, is to be found in the performance of the Bolshevik military – economic organization, as distinct from the organization of the civil economy. The latter, as I have indicated, was highly conditioned by the anti-market approach which belonged to the Marxist tradition rather than to a model of war economy. The war economic organization of Germany no doubt provided some empirical grounds for the attempts to build an alternative economic system. But the Russian reality, with its historical background, was far from being able to absorb rules and constraints which could make this system effective, especially in a revolutionary environment. Rigidities, inefficiencies and disorganization of the civil economy could be overcome only by forming, within the overall institutional framework, a military enclave based on its own needs and priorities.

It is the purpose of this last chapter to show how military supply was organized, how labour was induced or forced to sustain the efforts of defence, how difficult it was to establish firm and workable relationships with the overall economic environment and, consequently, how useful the surviving traditional economy, based on handicraftsmanship, was in providing some basic equipment for the Red Army.

The organization of military supply was not solely a matter of improvisation. A system of military institutions working for defence had been developed during the First World War under the Tsarist Government. The First World War had required in all the combatants the intervention of government in the economy. In Russia, the direct assumption by the government had some important precedents. The Russian Government had already actively participated in the promotion of economic development in the past century by a system of preferential orders at home and a regime of subsidies to the metal-working and machine industry.[1] Nonetheless, neither the governmental institutions nor the economy as a whole were able to find the necessary level of coordination to enforce military priorities. 'The whole tragedy of our time', exclaimed Krivoshein at one of the secret meetings of the Tsarist Council of Ministers in 1915, '[is that] everyone talks about unity and about accord with the nation, and meanwhile civil and military authorities cannot agree and have not been able to work together for the whole year'.[2] The basic unreadiness of the Russian economy to adapt rapidly to military needs was revealed by the poor performance of a badly equipped army.[3] The incapacity of industry to cope with military equipment was felt particularly in metal-working, heavily dependent on mining and transport. The output of coal, iron and iron ore decreased remarkably between 1914 and 1915. The production of wagons fell by half.[4] These disruptive factors were particularly important, in so far as the industrial centres were very distant from the source of raw materials and mobilized skilled workers were replaced mainly by inexperienced young men and women.[5] Only in mid 1915 were steps for the coordination of the activities related to war taken, in response to the pressures of industrial and *zemstvo* representatives. A Central War Industrial Committee with nineteen departments was set up in Petrograd. By the end of 1915 war industries committees, promoted by representatives of trade and industry, had been formed in seventy-eight provinces and seventy-four cities. The Central War Industrial Committee was composed of members appointed by the government, and other public bodies (representatives of the council of *zemstvos* and the council of towns) and persons elected by the local war industry committees with a modest representation of workers' deputies. It ascertained military requirements, established priorities and distributed production norms to the provincial committees. The latter were responsible for allocating workers to factories.[6] At the same time the *zemstvos* organized a committee known as *Zemgor* for the supply of the army, which was to arrange for the placement of government workers in existing factories. The government intervened later with the establishment in August 1916 of the Special Council of National Defence and three other councils, for fuel, transport and food supplies attached to ministries. These councils were responsible for issuing regulations on prices, transports and allocation of goods and raw materials. It was hoped that they would be able to enforce central decisions upon the provincial units.[7] Localism, however, a chronic disease in Russia, had deeper roots in history, such as the vast distances between areas, the corruption of the autocracy, the location of the chief industries, and short-sighted central bureaucracy. Despite the proliferation of central committees related to the needs of defence, Russian industry remained recalcitrant in responding to military requirements. Almost all large-scale industry and a significant part of medium-sized industry was put under the direction of the Army and Navy Department and the special committees for defence, industrial committees and the Department of Communications.[8] Data collected during 1916 and early 1917 on the monthly output value for 3,486 enterprises employing two-thirds of the industrial labour force show that some branches produced only a minimal amount for the private market.

Table 9.1. *Total and marketed output of industry, 1916 and early 1917*

	Total output	Output for the market
	(per month in million rubles)	
Textile industry	200.7	123.0
Paper industry	10.0	6.1
Mechanical processing of wood	12.8	1.5
Metal-working, production of machines and tools	186.4	4.8
Processing of organic products	37.3	5.8
Processing of mineral materials	14.4	3.0
Food-processing	123.6	27.3
Chemical industry	71.3	32.5
Metallurgical industry	7.2	0.1
Electrical industry	8.5	0.03

Source: *Rossiia v mirovoi voine, 1914–1918 gg*, Moscow, 1925, p. 70 (quoted by A.L. Sidorov, *Ekonomicheskoe polozhenie Rossii v gody pervoi mirovoi voiny*, Moscow, 1973, p. 370)

Nonetheless, the Government was unable to enforce strictly the measures of control needed to share out resources according to priority. A black market of raw materials developed where private dealers were able to provide all sorts of metals and machines at black market prices.[9]

The reasons which had forced the Tsarist Government to set up a special economic organization in waging war and the difficulties encountered during this process were very much the same as those which compelled the Soviet Government to form a parallel economic organization for supplying the army, in some way independent from VSNKh's structure. The conflicts between the military and the civilian departments of the economy were reflected in the antagonism between Rykov, the head of VSNKh, and Trotskii, the chief organizer of the Red Army, and in the lack of coordination among the production branches, which were expected to assist the efforts of defence. Although partially assimilated into the central framework of *glavki* and *tsentry* controlled by VSNKh, civilian industry was not ready to respond to the immediate requirements of war. Nationalized enterprises, *glavki*, *tsentry*, trusts and *kusty* introduced bureaucratic distortions, the features of which – red tape, sluggishness, conflict of responsibilities and cumbersome hierarchy – hindered implementation of central commands.

Bureaucratic methods were officially and regularly criticized, though their origin was not always identified with the impressive number of economic agencies, which were piling up at a dizzy speed. At the Eighth Congress of the Party, bureaucratism was blamed on the backwardness of Russia, and at the Second Congress of *Sovnarkhozy* on the hostility of the bourgeois economic experts who held some key posts in management.[10] Some deeper causes of bureaucratism, like the massive process of nationalization and centralized management, were criticized by the opposition,[11] but did not obtain the specific attention of the leadership. At the top of VSNKh, a technocratic bias induced the economic experts to blame the shortcomings on the incompleteness of the new economic system, rather than on the excessive strains provoked by the rapid changes and instability of the organization. While this was an incentive for the civil economic organization to further the process of nationalization and naturalization of the economy, the military sphere tried to extend its power over the crucial industries, by-passing the civil organization and its rules.

During civil war the militarized section of the economy developed with a good deal of autonomy in relation to the structure of VSNKh and its *glavki*. In this field, the influence at first of *Sovnarkom* and then of the Council of Labour and Defence (STO) was decisive in keeping the military factories under a special regime, which enabled the war effort to be sustained. In order to make the enforcement of military orders possible other organs were created, first for supervision and then for the direct management of industry. The diversification of economic agencies with their autonomous hierarchies justifies Kritsman's assertion that, during civil war, there was no single centre for the organization of the economy.[12]

The first measures for the reorganization of military supply were undertaken in the summer of 1918. A substantial amount of war materials were still under the management of various institutions, the Chief Artillery Administration,[13] the Chief War-Engineering Administration, and the Chief War Economy Administration, attached to the War Department. In June 1918 the People's Commissariat of War formed the Central Administration of Supply to the Red Army (*Tsentral'noe Upravlenie Snabzheniia*). This organ was put under the direction of a committee formed by all principal supply agencies and the War Commissariat. The Administration of Supply was to coordinate its work with VSNKh and the local *sovnarkhozy*, since a great deal of war materials had been moved to the provinces.[14] The computation of all existing military material was completed by the end of 1918.[15] All military factories and artillery works remained under the control of the War Commissariat. All efforts made by the metal section of VSNKh to incorporate such plants failed.[16] By the end of 1918, fifty specialized military factories were producing weapons and 330 enterprises were producing various items of soldiers' equipment, cloth, boots, etc.[17]

The separation of military from civil economic organization produced a duplication of supply for some time. At the end of October 1918, VSNKh formed the Central Section of Military State Purchase (*Tsentral'nyi Otdel Voennykh Zagotovok*, or in abbreviated form *Tsentrovoenzag*) for the supply of products, transport materials and engineering equipment to the army. The section was made responsible for all military orders for finished products and auxiliary materials. Through it, the orders of the military agencies were distributed among the production sections of VSNKh. Finished products were to be handed over to the section which was responsible for terms of delivery and quality. A division of *Tsentrovoenzag* was responsible for controlling the repair of semi-manufactures, and local sections were planned to implement *in situ* some kinds of production.[18] Initially *Tsentrovoenzag* was given the stocks of items deposited in the warehouses of the former Chief War Administration.[19]

VSNKh would have liked to concentrate in its hands the whole of military supply. Local sections of *Tsentrovoenzag* were formed at the beginning of 1919. The principle of dual subordination was applied, making them responsible both to the central section and to the *sovnarkhoz* presidium. This was a sign of the central administration's weakness and of

VSNKh's inability to enforce a rigid hierarchy at the level of military supply. The *gubsovnarkhozy* were to provide financial means. In the absence of local funds, the central section was supposed to finance the local military industries, following the common rules which applied to the civil sector of the economy; that is, presentation of financial estimates. The local sections of *Tsentrovoenzag* were granted priority in the collection of raw materials and semi-manufactures and the right of control over military output. VSNKh's advice was that the military agencies ought to contact nationalized, private or *kustar'* industry only through the local sections of *Tsentrovoenzag*. The assignment of production orders to private and *kustar'* industry was allowed only if nationalized industry under VSNKh control was unable to fulfil the orders, and was subject to approval by State Control.[20] The bureaucratic nature of such procedures hindered prompt execution of orders. But another cause of slowness in execution was the permanent conflict to which the system of double subordination exposed the local sections of *Tsentrovoenzag*. Soon after the institution of the local sections, VSNKh had to remind the *sovnarkhozy* that these organs were to be considered 'independent organs' responsible for the utilization of local resources and products of military interest.[21]

VSNKh's *Tsentrovoenzag* succeeded only as long as its job concerned the distribution of old stocks. When it started dealing with new output, it encountered the shortcomings of the overall economic structure and its criteria. The assumption that nationalized industry should be the privileged source of military supply did not materialize. The best equipped factories, which were the first to be nationalized, were more subject than other traditional undertakings to stoppage of work due to scarcity of raw materials and energy. The entire operation of the most modern textile factories of Moscow, which were transferred to the supervision of *Tsentrovoenzag*, collapsed when the shortage of fuel and electricity became acute.[22] The *glavk* system was not of much help. *Tsentrotekstil'* was unable to fulfil the orders of *Tsentrovoenzag*, which had to find direct contacts with the provinces.[23] Until April 1919 the impressive structure of *Glavles*, *Glavmaslo* and *Prodamet* had been incapable of ensuring the fulfilment of a single order for transport – engineering equipment and raw materials.[24] VSNKh's results in military supply embittered its relations with *Sovnarkom*. VSNKh attributed its failure to the competition for raw materials among various organs, including war agencies, which it accused of acting independently of the local sections of *Tsentrovoenzag* and of turning their orders over directly to the local factories without respecting the VSNKh hierarchy.[25] *Sovnarkom* increased its efforts to take military industry away from the civil regime and to extend its control over auxiliary production. On 2 November 1918, an

Extraordinary Commission for the Production of Articles for Military Equipments, attached to VSNKh in August 1918 and put under the direction of Krasin,[26] was transformed into the Extraordinary Commission for Supply to the Red Army, *Chrezkomsnabarm*, and made responsible for the connection of war industry with non-war industry. This organ was entrusted with the control and regulation of production and obtained juridical powers over producers.[27] By and large, the sudden intensification of military operations and foreign intervention left no time for indulging in the essays of organization undertaken by VSNKh. The new commission had plenipotentiary powers which allowed it to cut through the details of the VSNKh hierarchy. A regime of direct orders replaced the vertical flow of information and control of the *glavk* structure. Formally, the commission was only in charge of supervisory tasks. But, in fact, its competence went far beyond that. *Chrezkomsnabarm* distributed and financed production orders. It was endowed, initially by law, with twenty million rubles, with the aid of which it was able to undertake direct contacts with industry. Financing did not have to follow the ordinary procedures. Funds were advanced to the enterprises, and the enterprises' liabilities were written off when output was delivered on the agreed terms.[28] *Chrezkomsnabarm* assigned its plenipotentiaries to the factories under its control with the task of inspecting work and facilitating the endowment of labour forces and financial means, in order to increase productivity. The presence of political commissars in the factories did, in fact, help the supply of fuel, foodstuffs and raw materials.[29] The rights of the commission regarding mobilization of labour for the army allowed the commissars to discriminate between the recalled workers on the grounds of their qualifications and abilities.[30] Local extraordinary commissions for supply were formed in the main provinces – Petrograd, Kazan, Nizhni-Novgorod, Samara, Simbirsk, Minsk and Kharkov. They worked in close contact with the local *sovnarkhozy*, on the basis of lists of priorities.[31]

On 30 November 1918, a new organ was formed for the coordination of defence measures: the Council of Workers' and Peasants' Defence, transformed, in April 1920, into the Council of Labour and Defence. The new council was a sort of small cabinet of the commissars directly connected with war affairs.[32] It consisted of Lenin, representing *Sovnarkom*, Stalin, representing the All-Russian Central Executive Committee, and representatives of the Revolutionary Military Councils, of *Chrezkomsnabarm*, of the Railway Commissariat and of *Narkomprod*. VSNKh was not represented as such.[33] The Council of Workers' and Peasants' Defence had full rights in the matter of mobilization of the country's labour and resources. In the course of war communism, the Council of Labour and Defence took various decisions in the economic field. The new political organ received daily information about the output of machinery, munitions, personal equipment and supply of arms to the front. Its agents were sent to the most important military factories. Commissions were set up to study the means of increasing the output of weapons. The number of shifts was increased. Three shifts were imposed on factories producing arms and in some cases also on auxiliary factories.[34] On 5 December 1918, a few days after its formation, the Council of Workers' and Peasants' Defence introduced a premium system in the important small arms works of Tula, as an incentive to increased productivity.[35] Other steps towards the unification of all economic activities connected with war were taken in 1919. On the initiative of the All-Russian Central Executive Committee,[36] *Chrezkomsnabarm* was reinforced by the absorption of the Central Administration of Supply and the Chief Artillery Administration. On 8 July 1919 the Extraordinary Agency of the Council of Defence for Supply to the Red Army, *Chusosnabarm*, was formed, under the plenipotentiary direction of the president of VSNKh; on 4 October 1919, *Chusosnabarm* replaced *Chrezkomsnabarm* in all functions. The formation of *Chusosnabarm* was possibly conceived as a means to bend VSNKh to military priorities, by appointing its president to it. VSNKh as such remained responsible for the coordination of all industrial activity, under the same conditions as the other economic commissariats.[37]

The reorganization of supply to the army coincided with the exhaustion of the stocks of weapons of the former military administrations and with the effort to increase the productivity of military factories. In mid 1919 the Red Army had already 1.5 million men.[38] Taking into account that the output of cartridges during the First World War was about 35 million pieces a month, the Council of Defence planned to achieve an average output of 16–20 million pieces a month. The difficulties arose from the shortage of metals. On 1 November 1918, there were 40 million puds of ferrous metals under *Prodrasmet*. By mid 1919 these stocks were exhausted. By that time also, the dispatch of metals from the Ukraine, released by Germany at the end of 1918, stopped. In 1919 only 20 per cent of the demand for metals was satisfied.[39] The output of ammunition increased in the first three months of 1919; although in April 1919, probably because of lack of metals, it fell below the January output (see Table 9.2).

When the productivity of large-scale industry fell,[40] the Council of Defence handed production orders over to *kustari*. Craftsmen's shops were supplied with empty tubes for the production of cartridges.[41] Craft industry, however, was more important for personal equipment.[42]

In July 1919 the liberation of the Urals allowed the resumption of metal supply to large works. More than eight million puds of metals and metal

Table 9.2. *Output of munitions in the first four months of 1919*

	Rifles	Machine guns	Swords	Cartridges	Shells
January	39,213	480	1,000	19,720,000	24,476
February	50,183	500	1,380	24,358,000	36,783
March	43,673	420	3,480	22,478,000	5,222
April	16,010	325	1,200	16,610,000	6,286

Source: A. Vol'pe, 'Voennaia promyshlennost' v grazhdanskoi voine', in *Grazhdanskaia Voina 1918–1921*, 2 vols., Moscow, 1928, vol. 2, p. 372.

products were dispatched from the Urals until July 1920. The restoration of some channels of supply of raw materials and the capture of metal stocks of the enemy allowed a renewal of the activity of the military factories in mid 1919. In August 1919 a Council of War Industry, *Promvoensovet*, was formed within *Chusosnabarm*. This organ was designed to carry out not only administrative and regulatory work, but also direct control over management. *Promvoensovet* concentrated control over all fields of production related to military supplies: production of arms, auxiliary equipment and personal equipment. Direct management was found to be the only way out of the permanent conflict with the local institutions which more than once refused to deliver raw materials and other products without central authorization. *Chrezkomsnabarm* reported, in fact, that in some cases the intervention of the troops had been required to enforce upon the local institutions the orders related to the supply plan.[43] The administration of transport and war-engineering equipment and aviation work were transferred from VSNKh to *Promvoensovet*. Some other administrations related to artillery and navy works as well as the two chief administrations of metallurgical and metal works passed under its control.[44] The section of supply of *Promvoensovet* was responsible for directing the production of material and personal equipment and for supervising the garment and leather administrations of VSNKh, *Glavodezhda* and *Glavkozh*. The five members who composed the board of *Promvoensovet* were appointed by *Chusosnabarm*, in agreement with the All-Russian Council of Trade Unions.[45] Since it was almost a direct expression of the executive, *Promvoensovet* had broad powers in industrial organization. Single enterprises and groups of enterprises could be transferred on its decision from VSNKh and its organs to the newly formed production centres of war industry. The rights of *Promvoensovet* included opening and closing down military factories, control over fulfilment of orders, approval of financial estimates, and assignment of

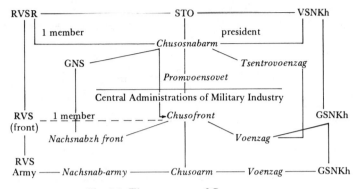

Fig. 9.1 The structure of *Promvoensovet*

Note: RVSR = Revolutionary Military Council, i.e. the chief command of the army at the centre
RVS = local military command[49]
GNS = chief head of supply
Nachsnab = head of military supply
Voenzag = local agencies of *Tsentrovoenzag* (see pp. 470–1)
GSNKh = provincial councils of the national economy
Source: Vol'pe, p. 382.

extra-budgetary funds for the implementation of military orders. VSNKh was merely to execute the orders of payment and had no voice on current loans or extra-budget credits for war orders.[46] The law specified that *Promvoensovet* could make use of the whole industrial organization, including *glavki* and *tsentry*, by agreement with VSNKh.[47] Under *Promvoensovet*, new factories and new agglomerations of the existing ones were formed.[48] By mid 1919 the organization of supply to the army was completed. Its structure is shown in Figure 9.1.

By the end of 1919, Trotskii declared at the Congress of Soviets that the scarcity of small arms, rifles, machine-guns and other military equipment had been overcome completely, and prophetically concluded: 'The test of our military apparatus is the test of our regime as a whole.'[50] The performance of the munitions industry in 1919, was, infact, remarkable (see Table 9.3).

Repair and captures from the enemy increased the availability of weapons. Taking into account repair, Kovalenko calculates a remarkable output of munitions for the crucial years of the civil war (see Table 9.4). No registration was provided for the equipment captured from the enemy. Another unplanned source of supply was the requisition of items destined for railways and kept at railway store-houses.[51]

Table 9.3. *Output of munitions, 1919–21*

	Monthly average output		Total output		
	1919	1st half 1920	1919	1920	1921
Rifles	39,129	25,830	470,155	425,994	245,315
Machine guns	504	313	6,056	4,454	2,900
Small arms	29,771	27,500	357,260	411,365	292,972
Gun powder (pud)	5,314	4,100	63,767	—	76,876

Source: Vol'pe, p. 390

Table 9.4. *Industrial output and repair, 1918–20*

	1918 (2nd half)	1919	1920	Total (round figures)
Rifles	900,000	1,134,712	931,557	2,966,000
Machine guns	8,000	6,270	6,459	21,000
Field guns	2,000	540	230	3,000
Revolvers	75,000	77,560	38,252	190,000
Rifle cartridges	500,000,000	357,260,000	516,315,000	1,616,000,000
Revolver cartridges	1,515,436	1,570,867	589,315	3,676,000
Swords	7,607	56.591	71,369	135,000
Grenades	822,236	725,687	110,089	1,658,000

Source: D.A. Kovalenko, *Oboronnaia promyshlennost' Sovetskoi Rossii v 1918–1920*, Moscow, 1970, p. 392.

Although the ravages of the war had destroyed most of the existing equipment, the factories of the Urals had already been rebuilt by the end of August 1919.[52] In May 1920, when most of Russian territory was under Soviet rule and only the fighting in Poland made it impossible to consider the war as completely over, the Council of Labour and Defence set the target of rounds of ammunition at a monthly production of forty million units.[53] By mid 1920 all factories working for defence had sufficient quantities of mineral fuel. *Promvoensovet* organized direct supplies of metals from the Ukraine and the Urals. The Central Administration of Artillery provided non-ferrous metals, like cartridge brass. All military factories had sufficient lead to last until the end of the year.[54] Nonetheless, the average output of munitions was lower in 1920 than in 1919. The reason may have been lower targets, but, since there is no evidence for that, it could be the decreasing productivity of labour. This fact provides, therefore, a key to the understanding of the special measures on labour mobilization and labour rewards and sanctions which were adopted in 1920.[55]

Supplies of personal equipment were supposed to be coordinated by *Tsentrovoenzag* which was considered the intermediary between army orders and VSNKh's production organs. But the run-down of large-scale industry and the bureaucratic methods applied to production orders and financial estimates made the whole system of supply based on *glavki* and *tsentry* unreliable. The army started relying directly on *kustar'* output. Addressing the Second Congress of *Sovnarkhozy*, Krasin, who was at that time the head of *Chrezkomsnabarm*, categorically refused to stop signing production orders to *kustari* as long as large-scale industry had not been organized in such a way as to show higher standards of efficiency than craft industry.[56] Krasin's premonition of the increasing importance that *kustar'* economy would have for military requirements proved valid. In its first year of existence, *Chusosnabarm* supplied the following quantities of equipment to the Red Army (see Table 9.5):

Table 9.5. *Items of clothing supplied to the Red Army by Chusosnabarm, 1919*

	On orders from the centre[a]	Directly produced and handed over by *Chusosnab*	Total
		(thousand units)	
Overcoats	1,850	1,250	3,100
Sheepskin coats	380	120	500
Padded jackets	410	1,050	1,100
Wadded trousers	990	50	1,040
Leather boots	2,200	1,850	4,050
Felt boots	805	150	955
Cloth shirts	1,510	800	2,310
Cloth trousers	1,460	650	2,110
Summer shirts	210	500	2,600 [?]
Summer trousers	1,700	450	2,150
Body linen	4,450	2,000	6,450
Pants	4,700	2,700	7,000
Sweaters	2,350	—	2,350
Body pants	2,150	—	2,150

[a]Orders were turned over to *kustari* and individuals.
Source: *Grazhdanskaia Voina (1918–1921)*, 2 vols., Moscow, 1928, vol. 2, p. 392

The quota of directly managed production was no more than half the total demand. The difference magnifies the efforts sustained by small producers in this field. In 1919 two million pairs of trousers and more than three million pairs of woollen gloves were ordered from the *kustari*. Of the orders given to *kustari* in the Middle Volga Region in September 1919, 65% came from military agencies.[57] In one small town, more than six hundred tailors worked for the military agencies.[58] The supply of military equipment consistently increased as regards the main items. In 1920 the supply of some items, like summer shirts, pants and body linen, more than doubled.[59] At the end of 1920, *kustari* produced about nine million pairs of trousers to meet the orders from state agencies.[60]

Artels of production were the organizations to which military orders were sent; they were often established by local organs. In the field of textiles they specialized in handicraft work by women, *artels* whose number ranged from about seventy to some thousand.[61] But in the more industrialized provinces, skilled male *kustari* developed auxiliary activities, which were helpful to the military units stationed there. In 1919 a fair number of *kustar' artels* working for the army were reported in Ivanovo-Voznesensk, Samara and the Northern Region. Their range of activities covered the processing of timber, production of building materials, and entrenching tools, mining of iron ore and the mining and processing of mica.[62] Direct contacts with *kustari* involved financing and supply of new materials, fuel and production tools by the agencies which issued production orders.[63] *Kustar'* activity developed to a large extent because it involved a smaller amount of bureaucratic procedure.

After the transfer of *Glavodezhda* (Garment Central Administration) to *Chusosnabarm* the supply of garments was concentrated in the handicrafts sector. In 1920 only two cloth factories were registered under this administration, while the number of *kustari* reached 72,710 at 158 distributing centres and the number of *artels* of production 158,[64] in spite of the lack of support by the central administrations.[65] The request of the district war economic administration of Moscow to employ private labour already furnished with sewing machines[66] gives evidence as late as 1920 of the incapacity of large industry to supply the army with garments, and of the need of the military administration to rely on the same expedients which helped society to smooth out the harshest consequences of a revolutionary transformation of the economic system, which neither people nor structures were prepared to bear.

9.2 THE ORGANIZATION OF LABOUR SUPPLY

The path towards militarization of labour, which some observers have interpreted only as an inherent feature of the war communism ideology and system, may find a more satisfactory explanation in terms of the constraints imposed by low productivity and the lack of material incentives in circumstances of military emergency.

The principle of obligatory labour had been included in the Soviet constitution to affirm the equal dependence of each citizen on his own labour, rather than on other sources of income, such as those deriving from the ownership of the means of production or of landed estates. Obligatory labour was understood as a vehicle of the abolition of class differentiation, but also as a consequence of structural changes leading to the abolition of private property in the means of production. The principle of obligatory labour was therefore not immediately translated into laws and sanctions. The effective measures for the implementation of this principle seem to have been primarily because of the situation of emergency determined by civil war. On 3 September 1918, *Narkomtrud* deprived unemployed persons of the right to refuse employment in other than their specialization. This decision was followed by other measures aiming at full information on the number of unemployed persons as well as persons in employment, but available for transfer into other occupations.[67] These measures can hardly be understood if not in the light of military priorities.

Since the end of 1918, *Chrezkomsnabarm* had decided to exempt from military service the workers of forty-nine plants, adducing production needs.[68] *The ABC of Communism*, which developed the guidelines of the Eighth Party Congress, held in March 1919, stressed the objective conditions which demanded the maximum utilization of labour forces, rather than the principles of the constitution: 'When means of production are nearly exhausted and raw materials are very scarce, everything depends upon the right application of labour power.' The main fields in which labour was considered to be a duty were work on town infrastructures (building, cleaning, repair), emergency work, and transport of timber, peat and other raw materials.[69] On 10 April 1919, *Sovnarkom* proclaimed general mobilization.[70] The Council of Defence passed a decree concerning recalled miners, who were to be considered mobilized at their own posts.[71] Steps towards the extension of this duty were taken in June 1919. Labour cards were introduced for Moscow and Petrograd workers; travel authorizations and ration cards were made dependent on the possession of a document certifying the performance of a job useful to society.[72] Other steps for labour conscription were taken when the situation of raw materials transport made it urgent to use all possible means to get raw materials to the centre. It was noticed that one effect of the distribution of land to the peasants was that they had ceased to be 'labour suppliers'.[73] At the end of 1919, labour conscription was introduced for peasants, in loading, unloading and the provision of all sorts of fuel. The fact that emergency, not plan, determined the adoption of general labour conscription is also suggested by the rapidity of the decision. On 27 December 1919, the decision was taken to form a commission entrusted with working out a plan for general labour conscription. On 30 December the commission started working.[74] On 29 January 1920, the work of the commission had already been translated into a decree. All citizens of the republic were obliged to provide their labour at the request of the authorities in all economic fields, among which the law mentioned fuel, agriculture, construction, roads and foodstuffs.[75] A special administration, *Glavkomtrud*, was established for the coordination of mobilized peasants' labour in forestry, construction and on sugar-beet plantations. In the first half of 1920, 5,800,000 people and 4,160,000 horses were mobilized for the provision of wood fuel.[76] The decree of 29 January 1920 on obligatory labour for all unemployed people also introduced the principle of the obligatory transfer of labour for industrial needs.[77]

But the concentration of labour forces met two obstacles. Firstly, the dismissal of workers from the enterprises shut down did not entail their automatic transfer to other jobs. Many workers had close family ties in the countryside and could return there when dismissed. Secondly, workers who had no other source of income were compelled to lose much of their labour time in the search for food.

During war communism absenteeism grew at an impressive rate. In the wagon factories of Briansk attendance at work fell from 77.9 per cent in January 1919 to 63.5 per cent in June 1919, 59.5 per cent in January 1920 and 58.7 per cent in April 1920. Most of the absences were of skilled and unskilled manual workers and contemporary reports claimed that they had no justification whatsoever.[78] In Moscow, absenteeism reached 40–50 per cent of the enrolled workers in September 1920. There, absences were attributed to a great extent to the black market search for food.[79] In the first quarter of 1920, overall absenteeism in Russia was computed at about 40–50 per cent of the total workforce.[80] In December 1920 Miliutin declared that in electrical industry, the number of workers had decreased about four times, working time about eight times and output sixteen times as compared with pre-war figures.[81]

The decreasing purchasing power of the ruble and the inadequate food rations induced people to take moonlight jobs.[82] Some reports on such activities pointed out their benefits: from 1,000 to 3,000 rubles for one day's extra work.[83]

Moral incentives to increase labour productivity, like the offering of several days' pay to the Red Army,[84] and the communist Saturdays (*subbotniki*) – that is, voluntary overtime labour[85] – were not enough to counterbalance the consequences of material distress, illness and discouragement, as well as poor qualifications, which affected labour productivity. Many skilled workers left their jobs for the army. Twenty-five per cent of all workers, who represented 15 per cent of the total effectives of the Red Army, were metal workers.[86] The departure of qualified workers reduced the level both of skill and of support for Soviet aims among the remaining workers. The strikes in some Petrograd and Briansk factories producing military requirements[87] were a warning against both the 'enforcement' of a policy of moral incentives and the application of authoritarian measures. Workers reacted to distress and compulsion by leaving their jobs. In 1919, 64,702 workers in the military industry left their jobs and 85,151 were engaged.[88] The high labour turnover did not help in the training of workers, and consequently was an obstacle to the implementation of measures, such as piece-work, which could be recommended to increase output. The Central Administration for Rubber, *Glavrezina*, which had adopted since the autumn of 1918 the system of piece-work, admitted that labour productivity had increased at the expense of quality: 50 per cent of the output of tyres had to be reprocessed.[89]

Material incentives were adopted, however, in the form of wage differentiation and bonuses in real terms, depending on the nature of work. In March 1919 the Council of Defence increased the single rations per day in war industry to one funt of bread and forty-eight zolotnik of vegetables (1 *zolotnik* = 4.25 grams), twice the norm for the workers in civil factories.[90]

Industry was divided into civil, reserved and militarized industry, in order to introduce special rationing systems in the most important works and impose differentiation of food distribution. The militarized industry was given the right to ration norms equal to those applying to the Red Army soldiers. About one hundred factories came under this system in March 1919.[91] By 1920, 2,329 enterprises had the same regime.[92] The reserved (or 'iron-clad') industry was granted a reserve of posts – and consequently of rations – irrespective of the effective number of posts filled by workers. Civil industry was left under the regime of the *glavk* to which it belonged. In 1920 the reserve of posts applied to 975 enterprises. The total number of workers falling under the special regime reached about half a million people.[93]

VSNKh tried to tie the system of special rations to the production programmes of some of the crucial branches of the economy. In mid 1920 'shock works' (*udarnye*) were decided upon so that all efforts could be concentrated on securing raw materials, foodstuffs and labour force for the implementation of a production plan. The shock works were selected so as to include all factory-plants forming together a productive complex of complementary units.[94] Twenty-seven factories were selected for shock work on the basis of their technology and equipment. These factories were given adequate supplies of fuel, labour and foodstuffs. Productivity started increasing from August 1920. In the second half of 1920, the percentage of fulfilment of the minimum programme varied between 50 and 106 per cent. On average, productivity increased as compared with the first half of 1920.[95] In one case, the Kulebansk works, the output of rolling stock was about the same as in peace time.[96]

Glavodezhda, the garment administration, was also included after its inclusion into *Chusosnabarm* in the system of shock works. Labour rewards were expressed in terms of premiums in kind – flour, salt, and manufactured goods – tied to fulfilment by more than 125 per cent of the monthly output programme. Special rations were granted for reaching the production norm. The same system was applied to auxiliary factories producing spare parts for machinery, needles, and belt drives.[97] In both cases, however, it was hard to distinguish the role of material incentives in productivity increases. In the case of wagon building, productivity might have been affected by the improved supply of fuel and the introduction of sanctions for absenteeism.[98] In the case of *Glavodezhda*, whose output of overcoats more than doubled in a couple of months – whilst the output of the rest of the range was constant – reports on increased productivity stressed also that steps had been taken for the utilization of prison and concentration camp labour, and of cooperatives and *kustari*.[99]

The main obstacle to the application of a policy of material incentives in the second half of 1920 was, however, the shortage of foodstuffs. Vacancies were very high in the consuming provinces. Vacancies in shock works in the Central Regions reached 39 per cent of total posts in October 1920.[100] Shock works should have had priority in food supply. But this system started collapsing when, owing to pressure from those *glavki* excluded from priority in supply, an increasing number of factories were put under shock work. 'Iron-clad' ration holders numbered 185,859 in December 1919. One year later, they had increased to 268,076.[101] VSNKh reported to the Eighth Congress of Soviets a total number of 1,716 shock works (see Table 9.6).

Though *prodrazverstka* had increased in 1920, a large part of the stocks of foodstuffs were frozen in the provinces for lack of transport. In January 1921 food rations were also decreased in shock works.[102] In the first three months of 1921, absenteeism 'for unknown reasons' reached 37.2 per cent of total absences.[103] Nonetheless, the managers of VSNKh who had formulated the principles of shock works during war were confident that

Table 9.6 *Branch distribution of shock works, 1920*

Branch	Number of shock works
Metal-processing	240
Textiles	408
Food-processing	466
Woodworking	166
Chemicals	92
Minerals	64
Fuel	56
Other	224

Source: *VSNKh, otchet VIII S"ezdu Sovetov*, Moscow, 1921, p. 31.

this system could survive the end of hostilities.[104] Their confidence might be explained by the fact that shock works, because of their exceptional nature, allowed not only material incentives, but also sanctions. In late 1920, a congress of managers of shock works decided to strengthen labour discipline by adopting measures aiming at reducing leave to the minimum.[105] The management of a Kolomna works decided to take off one pound of bread for each day of unjustified absence, three pounds for two days and half the monthly ration for three days.[106] The managers of the shock works agreed that the wage system should be modified in such a way as 'to suppress the present efforts of people to be appointed to lower posts and to induce, vice versa, people to aspire to higher posts'. For this purpose it was proposed that labour norms should be established by technical organs subordinated to managerial directives and that wage rates should be changed by the rates committee[107] only after approval of the technical organs of the enterprise.[108]

Reports from the Kolomna works indicated that productivity had reached peace-time levels after the introduction of sanctions, and that absenteeism had diminished remarkably.[109] All the efforts, however, directed towards increasing labour productivity, whether by material incentives or sanctions, encountered strong hostility from the labour force. Wage differentials based on incentives in kind were considered outrageous amidst hardship shared by all. In December 1919 the Seventh Congress of Soviets affirmed that it was necessary to put an end to the uneven distribution of food among working people and demanded equal rations for all workers.[110] Uneven rationing, in the face of workers' and soviets' demands, was essentially due to scarcity of foodstuffs, which worked against the equalization of rations at sufficiently high levels. Evidence of this may be found in Lenin's marginal notes to the decree of 30 April 1920, which established the distribution of basic food according to categories and qualifications.[111] Lenin invited suggestions for devising a system permitting fewer food coupons and for discrimination between state enterprises and private undertakings, leaving the latter outside the food distribution system.[112] The decree of 30 April 1920 established three categories of labour: physical, administrative, and work on a person's own account. Special norms were allowed for important work and special qualifications.[113] The specialists were excluded from such a regime, since they enjoyed – from 23 May 1919 – a special regime. The specialists, in fact, had their salaries fixed by the boards of the commissariats to which they belonged under the supervision of the People's Commissariats of Labour and State Control and with the endorsement of *Sovnarkom*. It was established that salaries higher than 3,000 rubles per month (which was the maximum for the highest category of workers) could be fixed for outstanding capacities. No upper limit was mentioned.[114] In the industrial field, the Presidium of VSNKh decided on rewards for specialists and individual monetary rewards for special contributions to production.[115]

However, more sophisticated systems of wage differentiation could not be adopted, though interest in this subject had been manifested at the end of 1919, when the trade unions were still willing to discuss 'monetary' rewards. Rewards increasing at progressive rates were considered by the trade unions, particularly under the pressure of the metal-workers.[116] Three systems of monetary rewards were discussed by the economic experts. The first was a straight increase for each output unit above the norm; the second, a higher bonus for each additional unit of output unit above the norm; and the third, increasing rates for the first units above the norm and then decreasing rates, in order to avoid excessive effort.[117] But there were several arguments against these measures: workers could be induced to make excessive efforts; the output norm should be clearly established and this was not possible;[118] in the cases in which the definition of the output norm had been left to workers' organs, it was set at the minimum level; and finally, the example of the metal-workers showed that workers considered rewards independently of labour norms.[119] Representatives of trade unions and some *glavki* agreed that managers of the enterprises must take part in setting the output norm and distribution of rewards if the norm was to be correctly determined.[120] But the debate among trade unionists and economists at the end of 1919[121] became rapidly obsolete and sounded too theoretical amidst the acute inflation of

1920 and the consequent efforts made by workers to avoid the rapid decline in real wages. They demanded the naturalization of wages and imposed it, by simply taking factory products when that was possible. Representatives of the textile workers' union, which met at the end of 1919, demanded bonuses in kind for productivity increases.[122]

If the decree of 30 April 1920 extended the bonus system to all categories of workers, thus partially accepting the workers' requests, penalties were also codified. On 27 April 1920, the system of penalties which some works had already introduced was extended to labour as a whole. Penalties consisted of deductions from regular wages and from any premium, and in the duty to make up for time lost by working on holidays or overtime. Criminal charges were introduced for those managers who failed to keep accurate records of the employees' work. Late arrival at work and tardiness in attending meetings and conferences were punished by reprimands and fines.[123]

All these measures, however, were insufficient to keep workers at their posts. From October 1919 to December 1920 the number of workers belonging to the system of the *Promvoensovet* increased from 122,627 to 175,112.[124] But the size of the industrial labour force decreased considerably. In November 1919 Miliutin had reported that the labour force was 20 per cent less than it was before the war.[125] Five months later, Trotskii reported to the Party Congress that the labour force had diminished by 300,000.[126] As we have seen, his speech opened the way to the 'militarization of labour'. Trotskii provided theoretical arguments, but it was the war that had prepared the way for the enforcement of the extraordinary measures he demanded and which cleared the ground of any opposition at the congress.

While the government extended the duty of labour to all citizens, some armies were being converted into labour armies. Kolchak and Denikin had been defeated at the northern and eastern front. Instead of decreeing the demobilization of the soldiers on the liberated fronts, the military authorities assigned the armies to the most urgent tasks: wood fuel procurement and mining. On 15 January 1920, the third army of the Urals was transformed by decree into the First Revolutionary Labour Army.[127] In the first quarter of 1920, the 'militarization of labour', introduced officially by this decree, allowed the employment of 41,571 soldiers, about 36 per cent of the men in that army fit for work, in transport, extraction of fuel and industrial work. Most of the soldiers were assigned to the transport of timber and to the railways.[128] In April 1920 the Council of Labour and Defence decided to form the Second Revolutionary Labour Army.[129]

Militarization of labour through labour armies primarily concerned peasant soldiers. The work assigned to the Labour Armies, in fact, did not require special skills. The Second Labour Army was ordered to the collection of wood fuel, foodstuffs and fodder, repair of railways and agricultural implements, and to agricultural work. In April 1920, out of more than 115,000 soldiers considered fit for work, only 4,454 could be assigned to industrial work, and only 1,963 to factories.[130] The low percentage of enrolled industrial workers did not allow extensive employment of worker-soldiers in industrial labour by the mere transformation of the armies into labour armies. When Trotskii preached the militarization of labour at the Ninth Congress of the Party, he was talking about industrial labour, since peasant labour had already been militarized. He therefore had no difficulty in accusing the left wing of the party, who opposed this programme, of being inconsistent, since the left wing had never opposed the militarization of peasant labour. Trotskii's theoretical argument for the militarization of industrial labour was that workers had to be directed to productive tasks in accordance with the overall economic plan and that, if they were allowed to choose, this plan would not be implemented.[131]

The Party Congress did not dare to challenge Trotskii's logic. Given the low productivity in civil plants, he had no difficulty in pointing out that arguments based on the low productivity of obligatory labour were equivalent to a rejection of the possibility of building a socialist society.[132] Reports from the Urals affirmed that procurement of wood fuel in April 1920 was twice as much as in February and coal extraction had increased by 50 per cent.[133] Taking the example of the productivity of obligatory labour in these fields, Trotskii ventured the hypothesis that the productivity of obligatory labour could be even higher than the productivity of voluntary labour.[134]

From being an emergency measure, militarization of labour was by the end of the civil war becoming the corner-stone of the programme of reconstruction. Lists of recall, similar to military lists, of all able-bodied workers, including the *kustari*, were applied to industrial labour. In the second half of 1920 all former workers of enterprises included among shock works were mobilized. They were to register at a special military bureau, in order to be appointed to their factory jobs by the People's Commissariat of Labour in agreement with the corresponding regional administrations of the *glavki*. In October 1920, militarization of labour was implemented in nine shock works in Petrograd, twenty in Moscow, eighteen in Nizhni-Novgorod province and fourteen in Ekaterinburg province.[135] Failure to register at the special bureau was considered as desertion.

When the problem of reconstruction was being faced, militarization of labour could have been considered as a temporary necessary measure to overcome immediate problems of disorganization and industrial break-down. It could have been proclaimed as a national necessity and a transitional device. But war, in the mean time, had changed people, their attitudes and feelings. The pre-existing austere sides of an ideology which was committed to levelling out privileges, and to creating equal opportunities for everybody, were bent to the imperative of consolidating power. Two years of severe privations had extinguished the revolutionary ardour of many and sharpened the moral-ideological motivations of the leaders. Despite military victory, civil war widened the gulf between the leadership and the common people. To narrow the gulf, misery needed to be sublimated, necessity to be legitimized, and expediency to be rationalized.

In writing the *Ekonomika* in 1920, Bukharin concluded his remarks against freedom of labour in a socialist society as follows:

In the capitalist regime, compulsion was defended in the name of the 'interests of the totality' while it was in reality in the interest of capitalist groups. Under proletarian dictatorship, compulsion is for the first time really the tool of the majority in the interest of this majority.[136]

Bukharin's assertion was shared by Lenin, as is clear from his comment on it.[137] Trotskii was no less stern:

The principle of compulsory labour service has been replacing the principle of free hiring as radically and as permanently as the socialization of the means of production has replaced capitalist ownership... the elements of material, physical compulsion may be greater or lesser, owing to many conditions.... Such a form of planned distribution [of labour resources] entails the subordination of the distributed ones to the state economic plan. This is the essence of *compulsory labour* service, which inevitably enters the programme of socialist organization of labour as a fundamental element of it.[138]

Lenin discussed the new problems of transition from war to peace and to economic development before the Eighth Congress of Soviets in December 1920. He did not insert the question of compulsion into an economic framework, leaving to Bukharin and Trotskii the honour of providing the first rationalization for the future methods of Soviet planning. Nonetheless, his point about the supremacy of state interests in the formulation of economic policy was as firm and as full of political and social implications as the arguments based on planning constraints. Lenin furnished two corner-stones of Soviet ideology, which were to have fateful consequences for Soviet society: the subjective legitimation of the dictatorship of the proletariat, justifying the case of any means for the realization of its goals, and the objective legitimation, derived from the isolation of the socialist experience from the rest of the world hostile to it. 'It must be borne in mind that although we have now gained a military victory' – declared Lenin to the party members – 'and have secured peace, history teaches us that no big question has ever been settled and no revolution accomplished without a series of wars. And we shall not forget the lesson.'[139] He added:

The dictatorship of the proletariat has been successful because it has been able to combine compulsion with persuasion. The dictatorship of the proletariat does not fear any resort to compulsion and to the most severe, decisive and ruthless forms of coercion by the state. The advanced class, the class most oppressed by capitalism, is entitled to use compulsion, because it is doing so in the interests of the working and exploited people, and because it possesses the means of compulsion and persuasion such as no former classes ever possessed, although they had incomparably greater material facilities for propaganda and agitation than we have.[140]

The durable legacy of war communism to Soviet society was not the use of coercive measures, whose crudest forms did not outlast the war experience, but the ideology which was built on coercion. Once the humanitarian roots of socialism which had been able to survive the sharpest edges of nineteenth-century scientific socialism were wrenched out, they revealed the alarming pallor of a thought eradicated from its soil and deprived of its nourishment.

9.3 SUMMARY

The poor performance and degree of organization achieved by the civil economy were compensated for by the concentration of efforts in the circumscribed sphere of military industry. The defence industry was not submitted to the same rules which applied to civil institutions. Highly centralized military organs, such as *Promvoensovet*, by-passed the cumbersome bureaucratic state hierarchy, thanks to direct financing and control of military orders, direct contacts with *kustari* and a special system of labour bonuses and sanctions.

Priority in supply and restrictive rules on labour mobility were crucial factors for the increase of productivity of the defence industry in 1919. Nonetheless, they had to be backed by material incentives as well. When the implementation of a bonus policy related to productivity became difficult because of the breakdown of the economy as a whole, labour compulsion was rationalized as the only means available for the reconstruction period.

The crude terms in which this rationalization was presented suggest that civil war had definitely marked Soviet ideology and contributed to its divorce from the mainstream of European humanitarian socialism.

NOTES

1 A. Gerschenkron, 'The Rate of Industrial Growth in Russia since 1855', *Journal of Economic History*, vol. 7, Supplement, 1947, 148.
2 M. Cherniavsky, *Prologue to Revolution* (Notes of A.N. Jakhontov on the Secret Meetings of the Council of Ministers, 1918), Englewood Cliffs, N.J., 1967, p. 225. Krivoshein was the acting Minister of agriculture between 1908 and 1915.
3 Cf. N. Nordman, *Peace Problems: Russia's Economics*, London, 1919; N.V. Riasanovsky, *A History of Russia*, 2nd edn, Oxford, 1969, pp. 464–6; J.D. Clarkson, *A History of Russia*, 2nd edn, New York, 1969, pp. 421–3.
4 R. Portal, *La Russie industrielle de 1881 à 1927*, Paris, 1976, p. 150. On the crisis of the metal working industry during the First World War, see also K.N. Tarnovskii, *Formirovanie gosudarstvenno-monopolisticheskogo kapitalizma v Rossii v gody pervoi mirovoi voiny*, Moscow, 1958, pp. 199–212.
5 The journal of the Central War Industry Committee, 28 April 1917, reported that the government sent strikers to the front, though mobilized skilled workers should have remained at their posts.
6 Cf. S. Zagorski, *State control of Industry in Russia during the War*, New Haven, 1928, pp. 70, 89 and H. Seton-Watson, *The Russian Empire, 1801–1917*, Oxford, 1967, pp. 711–12. The nineteen departments were: machinery, metal-working, military equipment, chemicals, linen, cotton, wool, leather and boots, transport, food supply, labour, storage, fuel, finance, road vehicles and aviation, medical and sanitary, invention, legal, auditing.
7 Cf. Seton-Watson, p. 713 and *Ekonomicheskaia Zhizn'*, no. 260, 20 November 1919.
8 I.S. Rozenfel'd, *Promyshlennaia politika SSSR*, Moscow, 1926, p. 71.
9 Portal, p. 156.
10 *8i S"ezd RKP(b)., 18–23 Marta 1919 g*, Moscow, 1933, pp. 63–4; *Trudy II Vserossiiskogo S"ezda Sovnarkhozov*, pp. 30–1.
11 *Trudy II Vserossiiskogo S"ezda Sovnarkhozov*, pp. 25–6, 59, 64–5.
12 L. Kritsman, *Geroicheskii period Velikoi Russkoi Revoliutsii*, Moscow, n.d., probably 1924, p. 204.
13 The CAA registered and distributed products and supervised the provincial military factories (see *Trudy II Vserossiskogo S"ezda Sovnarkhozov*, p. 85).
14 A.V. Venediktov, *Organizatsiia gosudarstvennoi promyshlennosti v SSSR*, vol. 1, Leningrad, 1927, pp. 477–8.
15 D.A. Kovalenko, *Oboronnaia promyshlennost' Sovetskoi Rossii v 1918–1920*, Moscow, 1970, pp. 385–6.
16 VSNKh, *Plenum*, 18 September 1918, p. 73.
17 Kovalenko, p. 386.
18 *Sbornik dekretov i postanovlenii po narodnomu khoziaistvu*, vol. 2, pp. 52–3.
19 *Narodnoe Khoziaistvo*, 1919, no. 4, 47.
20 *Sbornik dekretov*, pp. 53–4.
21 *Ibid.*, pp. 54–5.
22 *Narodnoe Khoziaistvo*, 1919, no. 4, p. 48.
23 *Ibid.*
24 *Ibid.*
25 *Ibid.*, pp. 48–9.

26 Krasin was proposed for this post by Trotskii for his competence. A foreign observer defined him as 'a very shrewd business man, quite unscrupulous and ready to adapt any means to an end' (see H. Boon, *Russia from the Inside*, New York, 1921, p. 35).

27 *Sobranie uzakonenii*, 1918, no. 81, art. 860. According to published archive documents, by the summer of 1918 the programme of the Communist Party was to build up as rapidly as possible an army of three million people: see S.V. Lipitskii, *Voennaia deiatel'nost' TsK RKP(b) 1917–1920*, Moscow, 1973, p. 131.

28 *Trudy II Vserossiiskogo S"ezda Sovnarkhozov*, p. 79.

29 *Narodnoe Khoziaistvo*, 1919, no. 7, 55.

30 *Trudy II Vserossiiskogo S"ezda Sovnarkhozov*, pp. 78–9.

31 Venediktov, pp. 482–3.

32 *Sobranie uzakonenii*, 1918, no. 91–2, art. 924. Ia. M. Sverdlov defined the Council of Defence as 'an organ of extraordinary military dictatorship'; see S.V. Lipitskii, *Leninskoe rukovodstvo oboronoi strany 1917–1920*, Moscow, 1979, p. 120 and T.H. Rigby, *Lenin's Government: Sovnarkom 1917–1922*, Cambridge, 1979, pp. 84–98.

33 However, when Rykov was appointed president of *Chrezkomsnabarm*, VSNKh was indirectly represented in the Council of Workers' and Peasants' Defence, since Rykov remained also the president of VSNKh.

34 I.A. Gladkov, *Voprosy planirovaniia Sovetskogo khoziaistva v 1918–1919 gg*, Moscow, 1951, p. 85.

35 Venediktov, p. 485.

36 On 16 January 1919, Stalin declared that the several administrations of supply were entangling each other, disorganizing and harming the whole business of supply; he proposed uniting them in a single organ: I.V. Stalin, *Sochineniia*, vol. 4, Moscow, 1947, pp. 218, 220.

37 Venediktov, pp. 489–90. *Sobranie uzakonenii*, 1919, no. 35, art. 349 and 1919, no. 98, art. 474.

38 A. Vol'pe, 'Voennaia promyshlennost'', in *Grazhdanskaia voina 1918–1921*, vol. 2, Moscow, 1928, p. 375.

39 Gladkov, *Voprosy planirovaniia*, pp. 95–6.

40 Small munitions were produced in the large works of Lugansk, Simbirsk, Petrograd, Tula and Podol'sk.

41 Gladkov, *Voprosy planirovaniia*, p. 87: two million cartridges were produced by craftsmen in December 1919.

42 See pp. 477–8.

43 *Izvestiia*, no. 55, 12 March 1919, 5.

44 Venediktov, p. 491. According to P. Bogdanov, one of the heads of *Promvoensovet*, the military industry was separated from VSNKh in order to carryout 'a special and vigilant supervision in a particularly difficult economic period', cf. G.P. Bogdanov and A.P. Bogdanov, *Petr Bogdanov*, Moscow, 1970, p. 35.

45 *Narodnoe Khoziaistvo*, 1919, no. 8, 87.

46 *Sbornik dekretov*, vol. 2, pp. 763–5.

47 *Ibid.*

48 Venediktov, p. 491. New products were also made, such as special fuel for aircraft and a new model of tank, called 'Lilliput': cf. Bogdanov and Bogdanov, p. 36.

49 On 24 October 1919, three sorts of *revkomy* (revolutionary military committees) were created by decree: firstly, the *revkomy* of the liberated territories acting as temporary organs of state power; secondly, the *revkomy* of the territories adjacent to the front (20–50 versts), where the provincial executive committees could be temporarily replaced by *revkomy*; and thirdly, the *revkomy* of the home front. The latter could be established by a decision of STO concerning the regional *revkom*, after which the provincial, *uezd*, and *volost revkomy* subordinated to the regional organ were to be formed. The provincial *revkomy* had the right to form land revolutionary soviets, railway revolutionary soviets, etc., in the case of strategic necessity, and to appoint plenipotentiaries to them. The *revkomy* consisted of the president of the executive committee, a member of the executive committee and the local military commander-in-chief. Their members were to be approved by the Central Revolutionary Military Committee of the Republic. In the producing provinces a representative of the provincial organ of *Narkomprod* had by law to enter the composition of the *revkom*. The formation of *revkomy* did not suspend ordinarily the activity of the executive committees of the soviets. The *revkomy* had the right to make use of the existing apparatus, but were financed through their own hierarchy. Their chief task was to help the Red Army in supply, defence and mobilization. The *revkomy* had the right to requisition goods, materials and foodstuffs, subject to agreement with *Narkomprod* (*Izvestiia*, no. 41, 28 October 1919, 1).

50 *7i Vserossiiskii S″ezd Sovetov*, p. 89. By the end of 1919 the Red Army had already 4.4 million soldiers: see Venediktov, p. 624. Foreign reports mentioned that the Soviet army was by that time well organized and disciplined: see Fond (7) 13489 Archives nationaux, Paris; *The Lansing Papers, 1914–1920*, Washington, 1940; c/r report of W.C. Bullitt to the Commission for Peace Negotiations in Paris, on 8 March 1919, p. 81; General Loukomsky, *Memoirs of the Russian Revolution*, Fisher Unwin Ltd, 1922, p. 231.

51 Vol'pe, p. 378.

52 Gladkov, *Voprosy planirovaniia*, p. 99.

53 *Ibid.*, p. 91.

54 Kovalenko, p. 377.

55 See pp. 480–6 above.

56 *Trudy II Vserossiiskogo S″ezda Sovetov*, pp. 93–4.

57 Gladkov, *Voprosy planirovaniia*, p. 105.

58 *Izvestiia*, no. 225, 9 October 1920, 2.

59 *Statisticheskii Ezhegodnik*, (*1918–1920 gg*), vol. 8, vyp. 2, p. 276.

60 D.A. Baevskii, *Ocherki po istorii khoziaistvennogo stroitel'stva perioda grazhdanskoi voiny*, Moscow, 1957, p. 45.

61 See *Narodnoe Khoziaistvo*, 1919, nos. 1–2, pp. 39–40 and *Ekonomicheskaia Zhizn'*, no. 225, 9 October 1919, 3.

62 See *Narodnoe Khoziaistvo*, 1919, nos. 1–2, p. 41; no. 7, 85–7; nos. 9–10, p. 90.

63 *Ekonomicheskaia Zhizn'*, no. 123, 8 June 1919, 3; Gladkov, *Voprosy planirovaniia*, pp. 109–11.

64 *Statisticheskii Ezhegodnik*, p. 275.

65 *Izvestiia*, no. 231, 16 October 1920, 1.

66 *Izvestiia*, no. 225, 9 October 1920, 1. The Central Administration of Fuel

refused to supply the *kustari*, alleging that the supply stations were too far from the site of *kustar'* activities. The board of the textile industry refused to hire unskilled workers for fear of spoiling sophisticated machinery. Such concern – odd in wartime – may possibly be explained by the inexperience of the Soviet managerial staff. In fact, between 85 and 95 per cent of all cotton-spinning machinery was British made and before the revolution was directly managed and technically supervised by British staff and engineers, assistants, carders and weavers (see W.H. Beable, *Commercial Russia*, London, 1918, p. 60).

67 *Sobranie uzakonenii*, 1918, no. 64, art. 704 and cf. E.G. Gimpel'son, *Voennyi kommunizm: politika, praktika, ideologiia*, Moscow, 1973, pp. 91–2.

68 Vol'pe, p. 384.

69 N. Bukharin and E. Preobrazhenskii, *The ABC of Communism*, London, 1969, p. 337.

70 *Izvestiia*, 11 April 1919, 1.

71 *Sobranie uzakonenii*, 1919, no. 14, art. 163.

72 E.H. Carr, *The Bolshevik Revolution, 1917–1923*, 3 vols., London, 1952, vol. 2, p. 609, and p. 617.

73 *Oktiabr' skii perevorot i diktatura proletariata. Sbornik statei*, Moscow, 1919, p. 67.

74 *Sobranie uzakonenii*, 1919, no. 57, art. 543; *Izvestiia*, no. 2, 3 January 1920, 1.

75 *Sobranie uzakonenii*, 1920, no. 8, art. 49.

76 Kritsman, *Geroicheskii period*, p. 106. Between May and December 1920 about 10 per cent of the total work for state purchases and transport of wood was fulfilled by obligatory labour.

77 *Sobranie uzakonenii*, 1920, no. 8, art. 49.

78 *Narodnoe Khoziaistvo*, 1920, nos. 9–10, pp. 4–5. Gimpel'son attributes high absenteeism instead to the increasing percentage of non-proletarian elements in the working class, with a petty-bourgeois individualistic mentality. Cf. Gimpel'son, *Voennyi kommunizm*, pp. 89–90. For details on disciplinary measures adopted by the government against absenteeism, lateness, theft, labour turnover and desertion, see J.B. Sorensen, *The Life and Death of Soviet Trade Unionism, 1917–1928*, New York, 1969, pp. 145–2.

79 *Izvestiia*, no. 217, 30 September 1920, 1.

80 *Izvestiia*, no. 48, 3 March 1920, 1.

81 *Izvestiia*, no. 275, 7 December 1920, 2.

82 *Izvestiia*, no. 217, 30 September 1920, 1.

83 *Krasnaya Gazeta*, 4 July 1920 (quoted by L. Pasvolsky, *The Economics of Communism*, London, 1921, p. 181).

84 Such cases were reported by *Izvestiia*. The pay was converted into foodstuffs. Two days' pay for all the workers of the food industry, for instance, was converted into 200 puds of sugar, considered equivalent to one million rubles (*Izvestiia*, no. 224, 8 October 1920, 1).

85 The cash value of five *subbotniki* between August and September 1919 was estimated to be 1,167,188 rubles (Bukharin and Preobrazhenskii, *The ABC of Communism*, p. 341). On 1 May 1920, 15 million people participated in the Saturday Labour March (Kovalenko, pp. 381–2).

86 Vol'pe, p. 383. There are no complete data on mobilized workers. Partial data show, however, a remarkably high mobilization among skilled workers.

From Petrograd alone, 10,000 workers were mobilized: Kovalenko, p. 379.

87 A. Akselrod, *L'Oeuvre économique des Soviets*, Paris, 1920, p. 61.

88 Vol'pe, p. 386.

89 *Narodnoe Khoziaistvo*, 1919, no. 4, 37.

90 Vol'pe, p. 386.

91 I.A. Gladkov, *Ocherki Sovetskoi ekonomiki 1917–1920gg*, Moscow, 1956, p. 356.

92 Vol'pe p. 385. A special bonus system applied also to workers charged with the task of 'finding machine-tools for the development and reconstruction of the military industry' (see Bogdanov and Bogdanov, p. 36).

93 *Ibid.*, pp. 385–6.

94 *Narodnoe Khoziaistvo*, 1920, nos. 9–10, p. 2.

95 *Izvestiia*, no. 16, 26 January 1921, 3.

96 *Ekonomicheskaia Zhizn'*, no. 221, 3 October 1920, 2.

97 *Izvestiia*, no. 223, 7 October 1920, 1; see also N.I. Bazylev, *Stanovlenie ekonomicheskoi teorii sotsializma SSSR*, Minsk, 1975, p. 159. Bonuses in kind were tied to the percentage fulfilment of collective and individual production norms. The following criteria applied to collective bonuses: 40 per cent of the material incentive funds for 100 per cent fulfilment of the collective output norm, 55 per cent for 125 per cent fulfilment; 70 per cent for 150 per cent; 85 per cent for 175 per cent and 100 per cent for 200 per cent fulfilment of the collective output norm. More effort was required from individual labour. Individual bonuses ranged from 25 per cent of the total fund assigned to this purpose, to 100 per cent according to the fulfilment of output norms.

98 *Izvestiia*, no. 16, 26 January 1921, 3.

99 *Izvestiia*, no. 223, 7 October 1920, 1.

100 *Ekonomicheskaia Zhizn'*, no. 220, 3 October 1920, 2 and no. 221, 5 October 1920, 2.

101 Vol'pe, p. 386.

102 *Izvestiia*, no. 22, 7 February, 1921, 1.

103 V. Sarabianov, *Ekonomika i ekonomicheskaia politika SSSR*, Moscow, 1926, p. 226.

104 *Izvestiia*, no. 19, 29 January 1921, 2.

105 *Narodnoe Khoziaistvo*, 1920, nos. 15–16, pp. 25–7.

106 *Izvestiia*, no. 39 (886), 21 February 1920, 1 and *Narodnoe Khoziaistvo*, 1920, nos. 9–10, p. 6.

107 During war communism, trade unions set the wage rates: see for instance *All-Russian Union of Workers in the Food Manufacturing Industry*, Moscow, 1920; *All-Russian Union of Metal Workers*, Moscow, 1920, p. 12; *All-Russian Union of Civil Servants, Shop Assistants and Clerks*, Moscow, 1920, pp. 11–12. In the factory, the evaluation and standardization of labour was carried out by a special trade union committee, the Wage Committee, elected by workers and employees of the given undertaking under the guidance of the union and directed in its work by the regulations of the regional branch of the union. A standardization bureau, with the participation of higher technical staff, ascertained the standard of output of the workers and groups of workers. A special wage-standardization section attached to the central committee of the union ensured general coordination in this field: A. Lozovsky, *Trade*

Unions in Soviet Russia, Their Development and Present Position, Collection of Trade Unions' Documents compiled by the ILP Information Committee, 1920. See also pp. 182–4 above.

108 *Narodnoe Khoziaistvo*, 1920, nos. 15–16, pp. 25–7.
109 *Narodnoe Khoziaistvo*, 1920, nos. 9–10, p. 6.
110 *8i Vserossiiskii S"ezd Sovetov*, p. 255.
111 *Izvestiia*, no. 94, 4 May 1920, 2.
112 V.I. Lenin, *Collected Works*, 4th edn, 45 vols, London, 1964–70, vol. 42, pp. 136–7.
113 *Izvestiia*, no. 94, 4 May 1920, 2.
114 Lenin, *Collected Works*, vol. 42, pp. 136–7.
115 *Narodnoe Khoziaistvo*, 1920, nos. 1–2, pp. 34–5.
116 *Ekonomicheskaia Zhizn'*, no. 251, 9 November 1919, 1.
117 *Ekonomicheskaia Zhizn'*, no. 257, 16 November 1919, 1.
118 *Ekonomicheskaia Zhizn'*, no. 251, 9 November 1919, 1.
119 *Ekonomicheskaia Zhizn'*, no. 257, 16 November 1919, 1.
120 *Ekonomicheskaia Zhian'*, no. 251, 9 November 1919, 1.
121 On other aspects of the debate see: *Ekonomicheskaia Zhizn'*, no. 266, 27 November 1919, 1; no. 271, 30 November 1919, 1; no. 280, 13 December 1919, 1.
122 *Ekonomicheskaia Zhizn'*, no. 289, 24 December 1919, 1.
123 Cf. L. Pasvolsky, pp. 185–7.
124 Vol'pe, p. 384.
125 *Ekonomicheskaia Zhizn'*, no. 250, 7 November 1919, 1.
126 *9i S"ezd RKP (b)*, p. 81.
127 *Sobranie uzakonenii*, 1920, no. 3, art. 15.
128 *Izvestiia*, no. 78, 14 April 1920, 1; 33,000 soldiers were assigned to timber collection, 5,000 to railways, and 600 to food procurement.
129 *Izvestiia*, no. 86, 23 April 1920, 4.
130 *Izvestiia*, no. 78, 14 April 1920, 1.
131 *9i S"ezd RKP (b)*, pp. 80–2.
132 *Ibid.*, p. 84.
133 *Izvestiia*, no. 78, 14 April 1920, 1.
134 *9i S"ezd RKP (b)*, p. 87.
135 *Izvestiia*, no. 224, 8 October 1920, 4.
136 N. Bukharin, *The Economics of the Transformation Period, with Lenin's Remarks*, New York, 1971, p. 158.
137 *Leninskii sbornik*, vol. 11, 1929, p. 396. Alongside the passage cited Lenin wrote 'that's true' (*Verno!*).
138 L. Trotsky, *Defence of Terrorism: Terrorism and Communism. A Reply to K. Kaustsky*, London 1921, pp. 126, 129, 131.
139 Lenin, *Collected Works*, vol. 31, p. 494.
140 Lenin, *Collected Works*, vol. 31, pp. 496–7.

10

Conclusion

The short but lacerating experience of war communism may be epitomized by Lenin's rhetorical question at the Tenth Party Congress, two and a half years after the seizure of power: 'How could one start a socialist revolution in a country like ours without dreamers?'

War communism, indeed, embodied the inner contradiction of the Bolshevik Revolution, which officially appealed to criteria and principles of scientific socialism but, in fact, stemmed from the contrasting impulses and tensions of a recent economic take-off, dramatically challenged by war. The October Revolution was born out of a dream, in spite of the lesser or greater realism which may have guided the new leadership, in capturing power. This dream united workers' claims for better standards of living, soldiers' prostration before the massacre of war, the peasants' claims to land ownership, the aspirations of young and passionate intellectuals to freedom of expression and creative imagination, and the aspirations of technocrats to modernization of the economic machinery. The leaders of the revolution had no precise ideas about feasible alternatives; they thought, however, that their government would have enough support to establish economic control over production and distribution. But this also belonged to the pre-revolutionary dream.

The co-existence and urgency of each single tension or aspiration which provoked the February Revolution were at the same time the reasons for what Berdiaev defined as the paradox of the Russian fate and revolution. The liberal ideals, the ideals of justice, that is reformism, were considered to be utopian in Russia, while Bolshevism, which seemed to offer a global solution encompassing each problem, appeared less illusory, more realistic and adequate to the situation of 1917.[1]

The reformist method was but a poor message in face of the urgency of claims raised from everywhere. The Messianic perspectives opened by Russian Marxism were believed by the Bolsheviks to be capable of offering a global alternative to the dispersed energies liberated by the

February Revolution. But the variety of social, political and economic claims which in 1917 seemed to join the cause of the revolution could be embodied in a global solution only at the price of avoiding specific, feasible solutions. The revolution in its anarchical phase does not admit the separation of each problem from the general context. This is the phase of deviation from the crucial problems of administration, that is from the patient, methodical and compromisory solution which each problem emerging from the 'whole' requires. In the case of Russia, the revolution offering global solutions was the Bolshevik promise in the spring and summer of 1917. The Bolsheviks, under Lenin's leadership, could successfully ride the tiger of Messianic programmes as long as the revolutionary message was confined to demagogical appeals calling for the 'negation' of the existing political and economic system.

Claims and protests against the existing order were bound to conflict with each other as soon as the 'negation' phase of the revolution was transformed into the active construction of a new order; when the nakedness of utopia was to be clothed with improvisation and expediency by a government which did not have capable administrators, material means and precise projects.

The Bolshevik leadership inherited pre-existing claims and tensions multiplied tenfold by the expectations which it deliberately nourished. Workers demanded wage increases to keep up with inflation, but the redistribution of land according to the criteria desired by the peasants themselves was bound to lower productivity, diminish the marketable output, add inflationary pressure on war-inflated prices and finally jeopardize the policy of state-monopoly prices on grain purchase. The demobilization of the soldiers was bound to make the problems of employment harder and to sharpen the difficulties deriving from land redistribution. The control of inflation was bound to clash with the demands for increases in wages and the purchase prices of grain and for nationalization of factories. Workers' factory management, which was considered a democratic achievement of the revolution rather than an expedient against closures and unemployment (as it often was), was bound to conflict with the hypothesis of central economic control – one of the few clear aims of Marxists who repudiated the market for its 'anarchic' behaviour.

Lenin, who urged the seizure of power 'by people as they are now',[2] that is to say in a backward environment very different from the Marxist image of developed capitalism, was nevertheless convinced that his vanguard party would be able to determine the quality and schedules of change. The first months of Soviet power revealed how far this hypothesis was from reality. Economic and social control required a broad political consensus which the Bolsheviks were not able to gather. Their efforts to conquer the active alliance of the Mensheviks and Socialist-Revolutionaries necessarily damaged the alleged legitimation of the Bolshevik Party as representative of the proletariat as well as the claim for the necessity of the dictatorship of the proletariat in the first phase of the revolution. On 18 January 1918, the first session of the Constituent Assembly rejected the Bolshevik Declaration of Rights by 237 votes to 138.[3] When this occurred, the Bolshevik leadership did not hesitate to close the assembly. The signing of the Brest–Litovsk Treaty not only increased the isolation of the leadership from other parties of the left, but also compromised its internal cohesion. Acceptance of the harsh conditions imposed by the Germans not only ended the Left Socialist-Revolutionaries' support, but also increased the tensions within the Bolshevik Party and induced the left wing to abandon governmental responsibilities. The progressive loss of support was due not only to disagreements as to the Russian participation in the war, but also to the impact that the economic clauses of the treaty had on economic policy.

The loss of the Ukraine, the traditional source of grain for the Central Regions, was used as a justification for adopting a militarized food-procurement policy instead of increasing the purchase price of grain, which was urged by several parties and by some Bolshevik personalities too. The policy of food procurement was carried out with harshness and contempt for the peasants' needs both because the Bolshevik leadership adopted a moralistic attitude to speculation, the economic reasons for which were disregarded, and because the economic interests and needs of the peasantry did not find any legitimation in Marxist ideology. This policy was the greatest impediment to political support in the countryside and a decisive incitement to the organization of counter-revolution and the radicalization of the opposition.

Financial policy was another source of tension. Lenin's conviction that nationalization of the banking system offered the government a means of indirect control over business was not accompanied by any clear policy for the nationalized banks to follow. Fear of inflation induced the leadership to adopt for some time a restrictive financial policy which, in default of normal market relations and other economic measures, jeopardized even more than before the relations between town and countryside and favoured a chaotic barter of industrial commodities for foodstuffs by which workers' organizations and local soviets tried to overcome financial obstacles.

The concentration of industrial financing in the hands of the state and the rapid depreciation of the ruble were an incitement to nationalize industry. Both nationalized and non-nationalized enterprises became dependent on state means. If the limited funds for financing provoked the resentment of the managers of the central administrations against financing private industry, the local *sovnarkhozy* demanded national-ization to avoid closures. In the first months of government, the leadership did not want to speed up nationalization. But this occurred in spite of its wishes. Nationalization was demanded by workers either when their factories had been abandoned by management, or when management ignored the decree on workers' control, or shut down the factory, or dismissed workers due to lack of raw materials and fuel, or when other labour claims were not satisfied. The confiscation of local undertakings by the soviets or *sovnarkhozy* heralded a request for nationalization. In the most peripheral areas (such as the Southern Regions, where the mining of coal and ore was concentrated) the interruption of wage payments after the nationalization of banks, together with the spontaneous taking over of mines and factories by workers and local soviets, impelled the central government to decree nationalization early in 1918. This phase, which lasted until June 1918, was characterized by what VSNKh economists called 'punitive national-ization', that is, by unplanned and decentralized decisions to expropriate which reflected the incapacity of the central government to impose its own plans and schedules. *Glavki* and *tsentry* which could eventually have carried out preparatory work before nationalization within the broad rights of intervention granted to them were by-passed by the 28 June decree on nationalization of large-scale industry. This decision was also unplanned. The Bolshevik leadership resorted to this measure to avoid being compelled to indemnify German shares for enterprises nationalized after 1 July 1918.

The inability of the Bolshevik leadership to control the tensions unleashed by the economic revolution; its panic in face of initiatives tending to safeguard German interests in Russia; and the fear of losing the backing of the proletariat in the large industrial centres which had been conquered by the slogans of bread and peace were the main reasons for a radical turn in economic policy. The beginning of war communism as an experience in economic organization was determined by the decision of *Sovnarkom* to confer extraordinary powers, including the use of arms and troops, on the People's Commissariat for Food Procurement, in order to implement the government's policy of foodstuffs collection. This decision was taken when the leadership began to face the problem of recon-struction of the economy, after the withdrawal of Russian troops from the war. The social and political context of the Brest–Litovsk respite was not such as to justify the adoption of extraordinary measures against the peasants when they demanded a higher price for grain. Nor was the economic framework so calamitous (if compared with the state of the economy two years later, when opposite decisions were adopted), as to justify the harsh measures taken. Other possible courses were increase of the purchase price for grain, partial payment by the peasants for land distribution (or a rent in money or in kind), and/or fiscal measures. The fact is that Lenin believed an extension of the class struggle in the countryside would better help the implementation of central policy than would a resort to economic measures. Rural poor committees were created *ad hoc* by food detachments, Bolshevik Party cells and even factory workers, to help the government discover and expropriate stocks of grain, and to replace local peasants' soviets where their interests were essentially represented by the Socialist-Revolutionaries. The assumption was that the poorest strata of the rural population would collaborate with the central organs of food procurement within the framework of collective commodity exchange, which favoured them as compared with the so-called wealthy ones from whom the surplus was to be extracted. But the socio-economic analysis which supported this policy was not correct. Lenin was convinced that the peasants' social and economic situation was so differentiated as to justify a successful policy of expropriation of the surplus only from the wealthy ones. Facts were different.

The agrarian policy of the Tsarist Government promoted by Stolypin, the process of land distribution enacted by the Bolshevik Revolution itself, and the criteria adopted by the local soviets for land allocation had already entailed a major social and economic unification of the rural population and a solidarity of interests among land-holding peasants that Bolshevism ignored, partly because it never got really in touch with the rural population. The consequence of all this was that the rural poor committees either carried out a policy which was hostile to the peasant–owners as such, or found an agreement with them which circumvented the criteria of commodity exchange followed by the central government. In either case the agricultural surplus was not expropriated on the basis of progressive quotas falling proportionately more on the best-off producers, but on the basis of arbitrary criteria. The identification of the beginning of war communism with the adoption of extraordinary measures in food procurement is based not only on the fact that military means were preferred to economic measures, but also on the fact that from the very beginning the characteristics of the food procurement policy contained some elements peculiar to the war communist economic organization. These elements were the preference for payment in kind, i.e delivery of industrial commodities for grain, and the application of the principle of *collective* commodity exchange, which remained under *prodrazverstka*, the system of obligatory delivery by quotas of agricultural products adopted in January 1919. There is evidence that the government was reluctant to use money in exchange for food not only because in some cases the peasants were unwilling to deliver grain for money, whose purchasing power was falling, but also because money could be used to finance the counter-revolution. The products offered in exchange for grain were consumer goods and production equipment. There is no reason to believe that, in the Russian situation, barter instead of monetary transactions would not have worked if industrial goods had been provided in adequate amounts and acceptable ratios with respect to *individual* grain supply. The purchasing power of money was rapidly falling, in fact, as was the range of products available in the countryside. *Collective* barter did not work, because the amount of industrial goods acquired in exchange for grain was trivial and did not bear any relation to the surplus extracted from each individual farm. The amount of industrial products had to bear a relation to the total supply of grain assigned to a rural district, not to what individual households supplied. The organs in charge of the delivery of industrial commodities were the rural poor committees, who were supposed to hand commodities over to households according to their needs. Collective commodity exchange was disliked by the peasants. The tensions of the countryside joined the anti-revolutionary drive of the dispossessed classes. Peasant revolts alarmed the leadership. In August 1918 there were signs of a revision of the policy in the countryside. The rural poor committees were admonished by Lenin not to harass middle peasants, and the purchase price of grain was increased. But it was too late: with the aid of foreign intervention, civil war spread all over the country. In January 1919 the decree on *prodrazverstka* defined principles and criteria of the appropriation of the agricultural surplus by the state. The principle of *prodrazverstka* was the priority of state demand over individual demand. Elements of coercion became prevalent. Firstly, the state's demand was to be computed, and secondly, it fell upon the village's community to deliver the centrally-assigned quota of agricultural products on the basis of the mutual responsibility of its component households. Collective commodity exchange applied so far as industrial products for exchange were available. In order to form a central fund of industrial products available for exchange, state monopoly of trade was decreed, by which industrial finished products were to be delivered to a central administration subordinate to the People's Commissariat for Food Procurement, which was designed to establish the criteria and mode of exchange.

Industrial products for exchange, however, were not present in significant quantity during war communism. *Prodrazverstka* was, in practice, the policy through which the Bolsheviks financed the war. It was calculated later that the peasants paid in the year 1918–19 under war communism, through deliveries of foodstuffs and raw materials, not less than twice all the levies and payments for land purchase paid in 1912. In 1920 *prodrazverstka* constituted about four-fifths of state revenue. *Prodrazverstka* was not only an emergency measure, since the principle of collective commodity exchange had been applied since March 1918 and the leadership did not interpret the end of civil war as an opportune moment to change the food procurement system radically, but, on the contrary, as an opportunity for rationalizing it. The ideological element which gave the peasants a lower status than the proletariat was important enough to induce the leadership to believe that even a peace economy could be organized in such a way as to shift the main burden of reconstruction on to the peasantry. The committees for obligatory sowing were unable to start operating in 1921 only because peasant revolts warned the leadership that the limits of tolerance had been reached.

Ideological elements were also present in the economic organization as a whole. Centralization, which was the principle which inspired the organization of production and distribution, belonged not only to the war economy organization but also to the communist ideology. In Marxian analysis the evolution of capitalism led to monopoly capitalism. The tendency towards concentration of production interested the Marxists because it was interpreted as a favourable framework for central direction, because it would make the transition from capitalism to communism easier, and because it represented the antithesis of the competitive market which Marxists identified with anarchy. Those Bolsheviks who exerted the major impact on the formation of the war communist organization greeted the inherited structures of state control, the chief and central committees formed by the Tsarist Government, as suitable organs for reducing the scope of the market and replacing market criteria by central orders. *Glavkism* developed within this conception, in which orders, or commands – as Larin defined the directives falling on individual enterprises – were considered to be possible substitutes for market indicators. *Glavki* and *tsentry* were given by the Bolshevik Government larger powers than they had before. They were given the right to requisition products and transfer materials and equipment within their own branch from one enterprise to another, and to shut down enterprises. The *sovnarkhozy*, on the contrary, were deprived of the right to nationalize factories without central approval early in 1918. The vertical administration of industry, therefore, was conceived of and applied before war introduced new reasons for centralization. The major shortcomings of such a system were the lack of economic indicators to replace market indicators and the absence of a central planning organ able to coordinate the independent initiatives of the *glavki* in the field of supply as well as in production.

A real effort of centralization of supply and distribution was made only with respect to military production and its auxiliary industries. Military factories were subordinated to the control of *ad hoc* organizations for supplying the Red Army and were put under one-man management. The organization of war supply developed like an enclave within the structure of *glavki*. A system of incentives in terms of privileged rations and bonuses emerged in connection with the system of military priorities. The concentration of effort on military industry, together with the discretional application of financial rules for supply of personal military equipment from sectors such as the *kustari* which largely escaped the *glavk* administration, allowed the Bolsheviks to support a well equipped army amidst general distress and disorganization.

The system of material incentives and sanctions, however, favouring some factory workers over others, could not much help the economic reconstruction begun after March 1920, since bonuses in kind could not be extended to the whole industrial sector for lack of foodstuffs and other consumer goods. The leadership had, therefore, to resort to other measures. Progressive steps were taken to extend labour conscription.

Obligatory labour was one of the principles of the Soviet Constitution. From the ideological point of view, obligatory labour was justified inasmuch as class differentiation was bound to disappear under socialism together with its sources, i.e., private ownership of the means of production and land, which under capitalism produced other income beyond that used for labour remuneration. As a principle, the obligation to work was meant to affirm the moral pre-eminence of labour in all domains – social, economic, and political – over a system of idle exploitation based on surplus value. Initially, in fact, obligatory labour was decreed only for the bourgeoisie. Under war communism, however, labour conscription rules were not intended to implement the moral principle, but to overcome labour shortage in some crucial fields. The peasants were compelled to offer free labour in cutting and collecting wood for fuel, owing to the transport and fuel crisis. Labour conscription was imposed on the industrial sector only when absenteeism, mainly due to the food crisis, reached 40–50 per cent of the employed labour force, thus jeopardizing the entire production process. Labour conscription was accompanied by ideological rationalizations within that framework of militarized culture which affected deeply some of the leaders. Nonetheless, militarization of labour was rejected by several influential members of the party and by the most authoritative economic experts, and one may suppose that it was not extensively implemented.

Absenteeism remained very high even after the rules for militarization of labour were introduced; this suggests that sanctions did not have much influence or were not rigidly applied. It would, therefore, be more correct not to consider labour conscription as an essential feature of the war communism economic organization, but rather a product of war and a later perversion of ideology in face of the crudest aspects of the unprepared revolution.

The question whether ideology was or was not a determinant factor in shaping the war communist economic system cannot be answered without qualification. Marxist ideology provided some of the background: belief that political means could take the place of economic criteria – which was a *voluntaristic* element; disregard for the peasants' interests, in so far as they aspired to own land; justification of coercion as a necessary element of the revolution; preference for central control as a substitute for the market; and finally the urgency of modernization. Yet the effective shape which the first communist economic organization assumed was highly dependent on specific Russian legacies, on emergency and on social pressure. Measures which have often been considered essential features of the first Bolshevik economic system were only the results of autonomous developments which escaped central control, and which perforce had to be legalized. Such was the naturalization of wages. Severe inflation and the interruption of wage payments, caused by revolutionary disorganization, led workers to seize stocks of finished products from their own factories and exchange them for foodstuffs, or to secure from the factory administration itself some payment in kind. Cases of payment in kind were evident early in 1918. Ideology had an impact in this field to the extent that it did not offer much resistance to such developments, and even appeared to justify them. Marxist ideology assumed, in fact, that money was an expression of capitalism that was bound to disappear with it. The programme of the Communist Party affirmed the goal of the abolition of money. But ideology and the programme did not foresee the immediate disappearance of money. Marx assumed that money would not be needed in a communist society of plenty, when 'commodities' (produced for the market) would be replaced by 'products' (produced for use), and purchase by distribution according to each individual's needs. The Party Programme admitted the need for money in the transition period. In fact, money was widely used in war communism and its importance remained great enough to justify the continuation of 'armouring money', a procedure by which the most important central administrations and departments maintained their control over financial funds which were not allowed to be transferred to other uses.

The extension of the system of payments in kind and distribution of products was due to galloping inflation, and to the application of collective commodity exchange with the peasantry as a precautionary measure of political control over possible counter-revolutionary initiatives.

Wages were never fully paid in kind under war communism and payments in kind were never quite generalized. This practice did not belong to immediate programmes. Initially, the economic institutions complained against individual cases of distribution by factories of their own output to their workers. Until the end of 1919, economic experts and representatives of the trade unions sought agreement on productivity premiums expressed in monetary terms. Only when the purchasing power of the ruble was almost annihilated did the trade unions start pressing for the generalization of wages in kind.

The system of non-monetary clearing balances could not be extended to the whole economy in so far as the non-state sector remained an important source of products for the state sector. The strongest opposition to the extension of non-monetary clearing balances came from the most important People's Commissariats, which tried to safeguard the partial autonomy of supply ensured by monetary funds, which was vital to counter-balance the deficiencies of the state system of supply.

Under war communism, the illegal market supplied from 65 to 70 per cent of the food necessary for survival. There are no data on the market supply of raw materials and fuel. But partial data confirm that a number of institutions and important factories did not rely on central supply to continue working. It may appear curious that several influential members of the party imputed the disorganization of the economy to the black market, since it was the other way around. This bias may be partly explained by the importance attributed by the Bolsheviks to 'voluntarism' and by their resort to 'moralism' as a political answer to people's indignant reactions in the face of the relative plenty of the illegal market as compared with the meagre official rations.

War communism was not an organic system whose features might be considered as integral parts of a whole. One of its peculiarities was the highly changeable territorial, military and economic situation. New institutions had no time to take firm root and display their effects fully. Each new institution was bound to conflict with the existing ones, having neither the capacity to dispossess the former institution altogether of its powers, nor the force quite to replace it, in default of an organic network of established ties and functions.

The *glavki* should have replaced the *sovnarkhozy* within the policy of progressive concentration and centralization of the state economy. But the *sovnarkhozy* not only survived; they even acquired a *de facto* autonomy, which partly helped the country to overcome the disrupting effects of too rapid institutional changes. The local economy remained under the sphere of influence of the *sovnarkhozy* and manifested a higher vitality than large-scale industry on which *glavkism* was based.

Prodrazverstka should have provided the basis for central distribution of foodstuffs and centrally controlled relations between town and country-side. The food procurement organization did succeed in requisitioning fairly significant amounts of foodstuffs – though it may still be questioned whether other methods would not have been less harmful to the economy as a whole – but it did not succeed in its aim, that is, in a regular distribution of the calories necessary for survival. Only part of the requisitioned foodstuffs could be dispatched. Stocks of requisitioned products often lay for a long time in state warehouses and spoiled. Expediency and fraudulent practices prevented the equitable distribution of that part which did reach the large urban centres. The number of ration cards far exceeded the number of people with the right to rations, and there were various abuses in their use.

Obligatory collective commodity exchange was initially designed to compel the peasantry to accept the centrally fixed price ratio between industrial and agricultural products, and at the same time it was to discriminate in favour of the poor strata. But it induced the countryside to revive old methods of production and traditional craftsmanship, thus promoting self-sufficiency of the countryside, reduction of the cultivated area, and concentration of energies in production of peasants' staples.

Wage levelling, one of the principles of the party programme which was never really pursued, was not a feature of war communism. The wage rate differentials were reduced from 5–1 to 4–1, but this concerned only monetary wages, which were not of much importance in 1920; it did not apply to specialists, whose remunerations were determined by other criteria outside trade union control. Industries which adopted piece-work got wages sometimes four times as high as the normal. The anarchical naturalization of wages, in terms of factory-output, produced real differences between wages depending on market prices for each type of product.

Financing by estimates should have helped the Treasury to know in advance the total financial means needed by nationalized industry. But schedules were not respected. Delays occurred at the time of presentation of estimates, approval of them and assignment of financial funds. Enterprises over-estimated their requirements and financial centres revised them downwards. Production programmes were elaborated without precise information about inputs available. Supply did not depend on a single centre, but on individual *glavki* by criteria which did not respect complementarities in production. Thus it happened that scarce materials remained idle in some factories, whilst other factories had a shortage of them. Not only were products wasted, owing to the lack of coordination in supply, but time was wasted too. *Glavki* were daily assaulted by factory commissioners who pressed the state officials for favours.

There are no complete and fully reliable data on the fall of production under war communism. The available data show a dramatic fall in output, particularly in the central regions which remained under Soviet rule and were cut off for a long time from the sources of raw materials and fuel. The output value of the semi-finished products subject to further processing expressed in gold rubles at pre-war prices was in 1920 less than 20 per cent of the corresponding 1912 value (see Table 10.1). Incomplete figures on finished products suggest even worse outcomes (see Table 10.2).

In spite of the very bad economic situation, which the leadership did not ignore (indeed, they discussed and criticized it at the official meetings), revision of the economic organization was not seriously considered, even when military achievements in mid 1920 made this possible and necessary for the forthcoming reconstruction. An explanation may be found in the militarized culture produced by two years of civil war, which induced some people to confront economic problems as military goals, on which all efforts had to be concentrated for success, with labour discipline enforced by one-man management on the model of the army. The militarized culture affected even people who criticized Trotskii's plan of reconstruction. At the end of the civil war, nobody within the Bolshevik Party really wanted to renounce the elements of a militarized economy which each one considered suitable to sustain the effort of reconstruction. *Prodrazverstka* and conscription of peasant labour were not rejected by any of the party members at the Ninth Congress of the Party which greeted the success of the Red Army against the counter-revolution. Victory over the White Armies, on the contrary, consolidated the belief that the peasantry had been definitely won over to the Bolshevik side, in spite of the sacrifices imposed upon it. Disagreements concerned industrial organization, the meaning of planning, and one-man management. In 1920, however, these questions were rather academic and concerned refinements of the existing economic organization rather than modifications of it. Economists with a technical background, such as Larin and Kritsman, believed that the central system of economic administration ought to be improved by rationalizing the system of supply and distribution. The tendencies of the *glavki* to operate in supply as autonomous organs were interpreted as negative with regard to central planning. This question had a theoretical interest. Taking for granted, as all Bolsheviks did at that time, the abolition of the market, the problem to solve was that of finding an alternative mechanism of supply. Larin and Kritsman proposed strengthening the functions and machinery of some existing technical organs – such as the Committee for Utilization and the Committee for Production – in order to concentrate the work of calculating the objective requirements of raw materials and fuel in relation to the productive capacity of the enterprise and its technical (input–output) coefficients. The proposal of Larin and Kritsman over-estimated the organizational capacity of the whole distributive system. Other economic leaders, such as Miliutin and Rykov, were reluctant to accept planning as a method of getting out of the impasse of disorganization and falling productivity. They believed that the *glavk* system, once liberated from the constraints of war, might be capable of carrying the process of reconstruction and output-increase which would prepare the economy for the serious work of planning. The party leaders, such as Trotskii, who during the war had experienced the adverse consequences in the provinces of the vertical organization by *glavki*, proposed to combine a relative decentralization of management with strict planning in priority sectors, such as transport and certain branches of heavy industry. While Larin and Kritsman tried to convince their colleagues of the importance of finding an alternative to market allocation of resources, the party leadership was inclined to rationalize the existing model, giving more room to political decisions and institutionalizing the military practice of concentration of effort on crucial sectors. The confidence of the party in the workability of the economic organization after the end of the war may be partially explained by: (1), the comparatively satisfactory results in military industry, which had been put under special controls since the beginning of the large-scale hostilities; (2), a small increase in output which occurred in some branches because more raw materials and fuel became available; and (3), under-estimation of the adverse effects that the food procurement policy had already produced and was likely to worsen, now that civil war was no longer present to justify it.

Only the rapid deterioration of the economic situation between the autumn and winter of 1920–1, and the increasing peasant hostility to *prodrazverstka*, imposed the abandonment of the war communist economic policy and organization. Some figures showing the evolution of output between 1920 and 1921 may help in understanding both the enthusiasm and the ideological rationalization of the military experience in 1920 and the dramatic change of policy in 1921.[4]

In the third quarter of 1920 output of raw materials and fuel started

Table 10.1. *Value of industrial output of semi-finished products, 1912, 1920, 1921 (gold rubles at pre-war prices)*

Semi-finished products	Year	Centre	Urals	Ukraine	Caucasus	Total (including Crimea, Siberia and Turkestan)[c]
Minerals	1912	5,620.9	3,848.6	2,507.3	15.6	12,420.6
	1920	4,250.9	1,616.6	25.4	—	5,892.9
	1921	—	—	—	—	3,896.0
Mining	1912	697.4	21,226.1	20,674.6	96,089.3	145,124.1
	1920	82.6	1,749.3	—	12,467.7	14,634.0
	1921	140.0	2,385.4	92.2	36,601.9	39,544.3
Metals	1912	99,371.6	92,903.0	209,437.7	9,029.0	410,741.3
	1920	2,766.9	9,063.2	2,982.2	—	14,812.3
	1921	4,012.9	7,249.5	4,300.4	—	15,562.8
Wood	1912	42,363.1	4,008.7	8,184.3	3,150.6	52,556.1
	1920	5,768.2	5,768.2	1,115.0	—	6,883.2
	1921	(5,768.2)	(5,768.2)	(1,115.0)	—	(6,883.2)
Chemicals	1912	15,443.4	4,674.0	16,577.6	951.3	20,117.3
	1920	3,376.9	592.3	—	—	3,969.2
	1921	5,651.2	1,027.5	—	—	6,678.7
Food	1912	272,998.8	31,660.0	163,214.0	33,428.0	470,775.3
	1920	122,265.0	21,382.0	3,702.0	—	147,349.0
	1921	71,250.0	2,470.0	11,685.0	3,895.0	85,405.0
Processing of organic solid materials	1912	2,002.0	—	229.7	—	2,231.7
	1920	257.3	—	—	—	257.3
	1921	450.8	—	18.0	—	468.8
Leather and Fur	1912	21,252.9	1,980.8	4,965.7	594.4	28,793.8
	1920	18,546.3	3,484.1	1,956.5	145.7	24,132.6
	1921	19,845.3	2,032.7	2,918.0	626.6	25,428.9

Cotton	1912	782,551.6	—	—	5,880.4	782,551.6
	1920	29,897.8			—	29,897.8
	1921	40,963.8			—	40,963.8
Wool	1912	201,667.7	7,467.6	17,386.1	601.9	209,135.3
	1920	34,519.0	3,476.5	—	—	37,995.5
	1921	31,389.9	2,897.1	—	—	34,287.0
Silk	1912	41,896.5	—	—	2,488.7	41,896.5
	1920	—	—	—	—	—
	1921	—	—	—	—	—
Flax	1912	46,791.1	5,009.3	57.7	—	51,858.1
	1920	8,954.5	72.5	—	—	9,027.0
	1921	6,070.7	454.3	—	—	6,525.0
Hemp and other fibres	1912	7,548.6	97.5	3,068.8	—	10,714.9
	1920	2,312.8	—	—	—	2,312.8
	1921	—	—	—	—	2,583.0
Paper	1912	3,754.5	106.3	250.5	—	4,111.3
	1920	1,989.2	72.8	—	—	2,062.0
	1921	1,202.8	152.3	2.4	—	1,357.5
Total	1912	1,543,960.1	172,981.9	446,414.0	150,229.2	2,243,027.9
	1920	284,496.7	b	—	—	299,225.6
	1921	213,414.4[a]	b	—	—	269,584.0

[a] The total includes only the regions which are comparable over the three years.
[b] The total output value in the Urals in 1920 and 1921 is reported as exactly equal to the Centre's, which is, of course, wrong.
[c] The totals do not always include output from the Caucasus and the Ukraine.

Source: Statisticheskii spravochnik po narodnomu khoziaistvu, vyp. 2, Promyshlennost', Moscow, 1923, Table no. 8, p. 26

Table 10.2. *Value of industrial output of finished products, 1912, 1920, 1921 (gold rubles at pre-war prices)*

Finished products	Year	Centre	Urals	Ukraine	Caucasus	Total (including Crimea, Siberia and Turkestan)
Minerals	1912	86,377.1	3,050.7	23,134.8	7,828.0	99,498.9
	1920	—	4,163.6	—	—	4,181.7
	1921	—	—	—	—	5,920.1
Mining	1912	14,061.6	27,685.5	173,111.0	31,741.0	296,617.0
	1920	16,234.4	5,350.0	29,271.4	36,000.0	97,981.0
	1921	19,244.4	5,867.1	39,804.3	14,070.0	87,096.5
Oil	1912	24,478.6	—	3,570.8	246,264.8	274,314.2
	1920	966.9	—	—	44,639.4	45,606.3
	1921	8,075.7	—	—	90,203.2	98,278.9
Metals	1912	436,065.2	67,057.1	216,806.3	6,821.0	723,494.1
	1920	—	45,586.8	—	—	45,586.8
	1921	—	—	—	—	71,010.5
Wood	1912	78,295.6	5,746.1	20,548.4	2,808.0	8,000.0 (?)
	1920	—	—	—	—	9,300.0
	1921	—	—	—	—	9,300.0
Chemicals	1912	173,772.4	1,037.0	10,115.6	546.2	175,958.1
	1920	30,772.2	311.4	—	—	31,021.6
	1921	36,115.7	123.7	—	—	36,317.4
Food	1912	433,947.9	12,455.3	555,438.3	43,587.6	1,045,457.9
	1920	62,792.4	1,645.2	26,649.8	—	96,502.8
	1921	59,314.2	59,314.2	—	6,193.5	100,219.6
Processing of organic solid materials	1912	9,387.3	—	858.9	—	10,246.2
	1920	654.1	—	—	—	654.1
	1921	573.8	—	13.5	—	587.3

Leather and Fur	1912	40,889.5	2,380.4	3,345.1	627.8	47,242.7
	1920	41,914.7	4,432.6	6,670.3	1,302.6	54,320.2
	1921	31,737.7	3,401.8	6,382.9	1,688.8	43,471.6
Cotton	1912	599,125.1	—	994.1	245.3	600,364.5
	1920	39,646.9	—	—	—	39,646.9
	1921	44,919.4	—	—	—	44,919.4
Wool	1912	108,037.9	2,052.7	7,363.7	194.8	110,090.6
	1920	37,539.0	1,966.0	—	—	39,505.0
	1921	36,419.2	976.7	—	—	37,395.9
Silk	1912	54,420.9	—	—	—	54,420.9
	1920	1,174.5	—	—	—	1,174.5
	1921	1,704.0	—	—	—	1,704.0
Flax	1912	34,168.8	1,546.2	2.5	—	35,717.7
	1920	12,449.3	94.5	—	—	12,543.8
	1921	9,990.6	481.6	—	—	10,472.2
Hemp and other fibres	1912	12,678.1	498.6	4,577.7	—	17,754.4
	1920	2,434.8	—	3,373.2	—	5,808.0
	1921	—	—	—	—	4,279.3
Knitwear	1912	9,593.4	—	245.1	—	9,838.5
	1920	3,089.6	—	—	—	3,089.6
	1921	3,990.1	—	—	—	3,990.1
Paper	1912	47,691.4	1,335.9	7,864.6	358.7	57,250.6
	1920	13,256.9	399.8	144.9	—	13,801.6
	1921	10,141.4	587.5	96.4	—	10,825.3
Total	1912	2,162,990.8	124,845.5	1,027,976.8	841,023.2	3,566,266.3
	1920	—	—	—	—	500,723.9
	1921	—	—	—	—	566,688.1

Source: *Statisticheskii spravochnik*, Table no. 8, pp. 28–9

increasing, though unevenly, over the entire Soviet territory. Relative to the first quarter of 1920, output rose for coal, oil, shale, cast iron, steel, cement, paper, textiles, locomotives and wagons, the principal items of the chemical industry, and some consumer goods. Accidental factors, however, had an impact on this favourable trend. Transport was made easier owing to the possibility of navigation in the spring of 1920. Some branches enjoyed priority in foodstuffs distribution. Total output increased thanks to the additional output of the captured regions. The output of coal in the Moscow Basin increased because adequate supplies of food were provided and other inputs were concentrated there. Extraction of coal increased in the Donets Basin owing to the proximity of grain-producing regions and the special rations which this made possible. In the other coalfields output fell, owing to shortage of food, poor labour discipline and difficulties of organization. Output of cement increased only because of the additional contribution of the Southern Region and the Caucasus.

The availability of bread grains from the new harvest helped to reduce absenteeism in the fourth quarter of 1920. Over a sample of 165 enterprises in various industries, absenteeism for unknown reasons (generally interpreted as the search for food) fell from 16.0 per cent of total labour time in January 1920 to 6.5 per cent in December 1920. The transport situation improved because the reduction of military transport allowed an increase of commercial freight.

The effort undertaken to restore transport is indicated by the number employed in permanent work, which in 1920 was 161.7 per cent of the 1913 level. But its effects were not immediate: freight carried per verst of the network was 26.6 per cent, locomotives 31.6 per cent and freight wagons 32.3 per cent of pre-war levels. The transport plan (known as Orders nos. 1042 and 1157), which aimed at the complete restoration of the rail network in four and a half years, relied primarily on material incentives, with provision for an increasing number of workers and their families to be fed on the privileged rations of *Narkomprod*.

Confidence in the existing economic organization was badly shaken in the first quarter of 1921. The policy of material incentives in kind could not be maintained when an ever-increasing number of enterprises were given privileged rations. Winter halted navigation and the fuel crisis manifested its effects all over the economy. The output of coal diminished in the Donets and Kuznets fields, in Turkestan and Borovichi. The shortfall in coal and oil could not be compensated for by wood fuel, as it had been to some extent in late 1920. Between January and March 1921 transport fell daily, impeding the dispatch of fuel from other regions such as the Urals, the South and Siberia.

The crucial factor in economic disruption, however, remained food procurement. In the first three months of 1921 the collection of bread grains in the producing provinces fell to less than half the corresponding quantity in 1920: from 37.3 to 15.2 million puds. Only 2.6 million were collected in the consuming provinces, while 21.0 million puds of Siberian grain could not reach the central regions because of transport difficulties, peasant uprisings and banditry.

The consequence of the food crisis was immediately reflected in increasing absenteeism due to 'unknown reasons' which reached alarming levels in the spring of 1921. The output increase in some branches was attributed by the experts of VSNKh to the possibility of wage payment in kind, by giving workers part of the factory output. Output increased, in fact, only in some branches of the food industry and chemical industry, while enterprises of the same branches which did not produce marketable output did not have the same success. The wood fuel collection crisis was also attributed to the impossibility of feeding a large number of workers. Output in the industries heavily dependent on fuel decreased. The trend towards total disruption became inevitable in the spring of 1921.

This was the situation which induced Lenin to start a revision of the Soviet economic organization at the beginning of 1921. The revision began in the same field in which the basis of war communism's economic organization had been established in 1918: food procurement policy. The human, social and economic costs of this policy had been tolerated by the Russian peasants as long as the civil war appeared to imperil the free use of land which the Bolshevik Government had conceded. The end of the war extinguished the only rationale that the food procurement policy could have for the peasants. The failure of *prodrazverstka* entailed the failure of centrally controlled collective commodity exchange as a method of imposing planned relations between town and countryside, industry and agriculture. The tax in kind which replaced *prodrazverstka* did not represent a lesser burden on the peasantry, since its amount was reckoned as about equal to the 1920 *prodrazverstka*.[5] The real novelty brought about by the tax in kind was the acknowledgement that commodity exchange could not be carried out by the centre and that market exchange – though limited and checked by the sphere of state industry – was the only way to gather the necessary energies to start the reconstruction of the country. The admission that the peasants had the right to dispose of their surplus after tax was equivalent to the acceptance of market exchange, marketable output and decentralization of production decisions.

Nonetheless, ideological tenets remained as they were. The New Economic Policy was presented as a 'retreat', as a concession to hard times. Lenin did not want to start an ideological revision. The debate of the mid twenties on industrialization[6] still suffered from the ideological ambiguity which accompanied the first steps of NEP. Preobrazhenskii's model of industrialization did not meet any consistent ideological opposition, though its basic tenets – an artificial price ratio between industrial and agricultural products favouring accumulation at the expense of peasant incomes – had already been experienced in obligatory commodity exchange since August 1918, with dramatic effects on agricultural output. Stalin's appropriation and implementation of Preobrazhenskii's model would only add an essential complement – the collectivization of land, which the party had not dared to impose in the twenties but which the ideology still considered to be a necessary prerequisite for establishing a socialist mode of production to replace the 'anarchy' of the market.

NOTES

1 N. Berdiaev, *Les Sources et le sens du Communisme Russe*, Paris, 1951, p. 221.
2 V.I. Lenin, 'State and Revolution', in *Collected Works*, 4th edn, 45 Vols., London, 1964–70, vol. 25, p. 425.
3 See E.H. Carr, *The Bolshevik Revolution, 1917–1923*, 3 vols., London, 1952, vol. 2, pp. 112–23 on the reasons which led to the closure of the Constituent Assembly.
4 The following data are taken from V. Sarabianov, *Ekonomika i ekonomicheskaia politika SSSR*, Moscow, 1926, pp. 204–47.
5 It is true that the regained territories of the Ukraine and Siberia were included in the tax in kind in 1921, but it is also true that lower output per head and restriction of the cultivated area made expropriation of the surplus in 1921 harder than in 1918.
6 On this debate see A. Erlich, *The Soviet Industrialization Debate, 1924–1928*. Cambridge (Mass.), 1960.

Bibliography

CONGRESSES AND CONFERENCES

5i Vserossiiskii S"ezd Sovetov Rabochikh, Krest'ianskikh, Soldatskikh i Kazach'ikh Deputatov. 4–10 Iulia, 1918 g, Stenograficheskii otchet, Moscow, 1918

6i Vserossiiskii Chrezvychainyi S"ezd Sovetov Rabochikh, Krest'ianskikh, Kazach'ikh i Krasnoarmeiskikh Deputatov. 6–9 Noiabria, 1918 g, Stenograficheskii otchet, Moscow, 1919

7i Vserossiiskii S"ezd Sovetov Rabochikh, Krest'ianskikh, Krasnoarmeiskikh i Kazach'ikh Deputatov, 5–9 Dekabria, 1919 g, Moscow, 1920

8i Vserossiiskii S"ezd Sovetov Rabochikh, Krestianskikh, Krasnoarmeiskikh i Kazach'ikh Deputatov. 22–9 Dekabria, 1920 g, Stenograficheskii otchet, Moscow, 1921

7i S"ezd Rossiiskoi Kommunisticheskoi Partii. 6–8 Marta 1918 g, Stenograficheskii otchet, Moscow, 1923

8i S"ezd RKP(b). 18–23 Marta 1919 g, Moscow, 1933

9i S"ezd Rossiiskoi Kommunisticheskoi Partii. 20 Marta–4 Aprelia 1920 g, Stenograficheskii otchet, Moscow, 1920

10i S"ezd Rossiiskoi Kommunisticheskoi Partii. Stenograficheskii otchet, *8–16 Marta 1921 g,* Moscow, 1921

1i S"ezd Komitetov Derevenskoi Bednoty Soiuza Kommun Severnoi Oblasti Sostoiavshiisia v godovshchinu Velikoi Sotsialisticheskoi Revoliutsii, 3–9 Noiabria, 1918 g, Petrograd, 1918

Trudy I Vserossiiskogo S"ezda Sovetov Narodnogo Khoziaistva, 26 Maia–4 Iunia 1918 g, Stenograficheskii otchet, Moscow, 1918

Trudy II Vserossiiskogo S"ezda Sovetov Narodnogo Khoziaistva, 19 Dekabria–27 Dekabria 1918 g, Moscow, 1919

III Vserossiiskaia Konferentsiia Professional'nykh Soiuzov. Stenograficheskii otchet, Moscow, 1917

IV Vserossiiskaia Konferentsiia Professional'nykh Soiuzov, 12–17 Marta 1918. Protokoly i materialy, Moscow, 1923

Otchet Vserossiiskogo Tsentral'nogo Soveta Professional'nykh Soiuzov za 1919, Moscow, 1920

Rezoliutsii Vserossiiskikh Konferentsii i S"ezdov Profsoiuzov, Petrograd, 1919

Putevoditel' po rezoliutsiiam Vserossiiskikh S"ezdov i Konferentsii Professional'nykh Soiuzov (sos. Iu. Milanov), Moscow, 1924

Vtoroe Vserossiiskoe Prodovol'stvennoe Soveshchanie: Rezoliutsii, Moscow, 1920
Protokoly Zasedanii VSTsIK Sovetov Rabochikh i Soldatskikh Deputatov, Moscow, 1919

COLLECTIONS OF LAWS, DECREES, ETC.

Dekrety Sovetskoi Vlasti, vol. 2, Moscow, 1959.
KPSS v rezoliutsiiakh i resheniiakh s"ezdov, konferentsii i plenumov TsK, vol. 2, 1917–24, Moscow, 1970
Ekonomicheskaia Zhizn' SSSR, khronika sobytii i faktov 1917–1965 v dvukh knigakh, Moscow, 1967
Sobranie uzakonenii i rasporiazhenii Rabochego i Krest'ianskogo Pravitel'stva, 1917–18
Sobranie uzakonenii i rasporiazhenii Rabochego i Krest'ianskogo Pravitel'stva, 1919, 1920, 1921
Sbornik dekretov i postanovlenii po narodnomu khoziaistvu, 2 vols., Moscow, 1918–21 (goes until mid 1919)
Sbornik postanovlenii i rasporiazhenii obshchikh i mestnykh (reguliruiushchikh prodovol'stvennoe delo v Moskve), vyp. 1 (Izd. po 1-e Janvaria 1918 g), Moscow, 1918
Sistematicheskii Sbornik dekretov i rasporiazhenii Pravitel'stva po prodovol'stvennomu delu, vol. 1, Moscow, 1919, vol. 2, Novogorod, 1920
S"ezdy Sovetov RSFSR v postanovleniiakh, Moscow, 1939
VKP(b) v Rezoliutsiiakh, Moscow, 1941
VKP(b) v rezoliutsiiakh i resheniiakh S"ezdov, konferentsii i plenumov TsK, Moscow, 1926, 5th edn.
Uprochenie Sovetskoi Vlasti v Moskve i Moskovskoi Gubernii, Dokumenty i Materialy, Moscow, 1958

STATISTICAL MATERIALS

Sbornik statisticheskikh svedenii po Soiuzu SSR 1918–1923, Moscow, 1924
Sel'skoe khoziaistvo SSSR, TsSU Institut istorii AN SSSR, August 1962
Statisticheskii Ezhegodnik (1918–1920 gg), vol. 8
Statisticheskii sbornik za 1913–1917, Moscow, 1921
Statisticheskii spravochnik po agrarnomu voprosu, vyp. 1, Moscow, 1917
Statisticheskii spravochnik po narodnomu khoziaistvu, vyp. 2, *Promyshlennost',* Moscow, 1923
Ekonomicheskoe rassloenie krest'ianstva v 1917–1919 gg, Trudy TsSU, vol. 6, vyp. 3, Moscow, 1922
Vserossiiskaia perepis' chlenov RKP v 1922 g, vyp. 4, Moscow, 1923

JOURNALS AND NEWSPAPERS

Biulleten' Moskovskogo Soveta Narodnogo Khoziaistva, 1921
Biulleten' VSNKh, 1918
Ekonomicheskaia Zhizn', 1918, 1919, 1920
Ezhednevnyi Biulleten' VIII S"ezda Sovetov, nos. 1–2, 1920
Izvestiia, 1918, 1919, 1920, 1921
Izvestiia Narodnogo Komissariata Finansov, 1918–1920

Kommunist (organ gruppy levykh kommunistov), 1918
Narodnoe Khoziaistvo, 1918, 1919, 1920, 1922
Novyi Luch, 1917, 1918
Novyi Put', 1918
Pravda, 1918, 1919, 1920, 1921
Rabochaia Zhizn', 1919
The Russian Economist, vol. 1, September 1920–January 1921, London, 1921
Vestnik agitatsii i propagandy Ts.K.RKP(b), 1920, no. 1
Vestnik Sel'skogo Khoziaistva, 1919
Vestnik Statistiki, 1920
Znamia, 1920

OTHER DOCUMENTS AND COLLECTIONS OF MATERIALS

Agrarnaia Politika Sovetskoi Vlasti (1917–1918): dokumenty i materialy, Moscow, 1954
All-Russian Union of Civil Servants, Shop Assistants and Clerks, Moscow, 1920
All-Russian Union of Metal Workers, Moscow, 1920
All-Russian Union of Workers in the Food Manufacturing Industry, Moscow, 1920
Antonovshchina: sbornik statei, ocherkov i drugikh materialov, Tambov, 1923.
Bor'ba rabochikh i krest'ian pod rukovodstvom Bol'shevistskoi Partii za ustanovlenie Sovetskoi Vlasti v Tambovskoi Gubernii (1917–1918 gg), sbornik dokumentov, Tambov, 1957
Fonds des Archives Nationaux, Paris, no. 13489
Komitety bednoty. Sbornik materialov, Moscow–Leningrad, 1933, vol. 1
Komitety derevenskoi bednoty Moskovskoi oblasti. Sbornik materialov i dokumentov, pod red. A.V. Shestakova, Moscow, 1938
Krasnyi Arkhiv
Materialy po istorii Sovetskogo stroitel'stva: Sovety v epokhu voennogo kommunizma. Sbornik dokumentov, 1928
Narodnyi Komissariat Finansov: 'K 8 S"ezdu Sovetov', Moscow, 1920
Natsionalizatsiia promyshlennosti i organizatsiia sotsialisticheskogo proizvodstva v Petrograde (1917–1920 gg). Dokumenty i materialy, vol. 1, Leningrad, 1958; vol. 2, Leningrad, 1960
NKP, Prodovol'stvennyi transport, sbornik materialov i zametok k VIII S"ezdu Sovetov, Moscow, 1920
Oktiabr'skii perevorot i diktatura proletariata. Sbornik statei, Moscow, 1919
Piat' let vlasti Sovetov, Moscow, 1922
Prodovol'stvennaia politika v svete obshchego khoziaistva stroitel'stva Sovetskoi Vlasti. Sbornik materialov, Moscow, 1920
Promyshlennost' v usloviiakh Novoi Ekonomicheskoi Politiki, Moscow, 1926
Rabochii kontrol' i natsionalizatsiia promyshlennosti v Kostromskoi Gubernii. Sbornik dokumentov 1917–1918, Kostroma, 1960
Rabochii kontrol' i natsionalizatsiia promyshlennosti Novgorodskoi Gubernii v 1917–1921 gg, Moscow, 1974
The Russian Almanac, London, 1919
Za god: sbornik statei, Moscow, 1918
Za piat' let (1917–1922), Sbornik TsKRKP, Moscow, 1922
Zapiski Instituta Izucheniia Rossii, vol. 2, Prague, 1925
O zemle, vyp. 1, 1921

BOOKS AND ARTICLES

Akselrod, A. *L'Oeuvre économique des Soviets*, Paris, 1920
Aleksinskij, G. *Les Effets économiques et sociaux de la Révolution Bolcheviste et son échec*, Brussels, 1920
Al'skii, M. *Nashi finansy za vremia grazhdanskoi voiny i NEPa*, Moscow, 1925
Anavieroff, N. *Lo sviluppo della Russia sotto il governo bolscevico*, Rome, 1921
Ankudinova, L.E. *Natsionalizatsiia promyshlennosti v SSSR (1917–1920)*, Moscow, 1963
Antonelli, E. *La Russie Bolcheviste*, Paris, 1919
Antoshkin, A. 'Rabochie Trekhgornoi manufaktury v 1917', *Istoriia Proletariata SSSR*, no. 8, 1931
Apostol, P. *L'Artel et la coopération en Russie*, Paris, 1899
Arnold, A.Z. *Banks, Credit and Money in Soviet Russia*, New York, 1937
Arskii, R. (VSNKh), *Regulirovanie Promyshlennosti*, Moscow (no date, presumably 1918–19)
Astrov, N.J. 'The Municipal Government and the All Russian Union of Towns', *The War and the Russian Government*, New Haven, 1929
Atlas, M.S. *Natsionalizatsiia bankov v SSSR*, Moscow, 1948
Atlas, Z.V. 'Iz razvitiia istorii tovaroobmena mezhdu gorodom i derevnei (1918–1921 gg)', *Voprosy ekonomiki*, 1967, no. 9
Ocherki po istorii denezhnogo obrashcheniia v SSSR (1917–1925), Moscow, 1940
Autobiografie dei Bolscevichi, a cura di C. Haupt and J.J. Marie, Rome, 1971
Avdakov, Iu. K. *Organizatsionno-khoziaistvennaia deiatel'nost' VSNKh v pervye gody Sovetskoi Vlasti (1917–1921 gg)*, Moscow, 1971
Avdakov, Iu. K. and Borodin, V.V. *Proizvodstvennye ob"edineniia i ikh rol' v organizatsii upravleniia sovetskoi promyshlennosti*, Moscow, 1973
Avrich, P.H. *The Anarchists in the Revolution*, London, 1973
'The Bolshevik Revolution and Workers' Control in Russian Industry', *Slavic Review*, vol. 22, no. 1, March 1963
Kronstadt 1921, Princeton, NJ, 1971
C.E.B. *The Facts about the Bolsheviks (compiled from the Accounts of Trustworthy Eye-Witnesses and the Russian Press)*, London, 1919
Baevskii, D.A. *Ocherki po istorii khoziaistvennogo stroitel'stva perioda grazhdanskoi voiny*, Moscow, 1957
Rabochii klass v pervye gody Sovetskoi Vlasti (1917–1921 gg), Moscow, 1974
Baykov, A. *The Development of the Soviet Economic System*, Cambridge, 1946
Bazylev, N.I. *Stanovlenie ekonomicheskoi teorii sotsializma v SSSR*, Minsk, 1975
Beable, W.H. *Commercial Russia*, London, 1918
Belevsky, A. and Voronoff, B. *Les organisations publiques et leur rôle pendant la guerre*, Paris, 1917
Berdiaev, N. *Les Sources et le sens du Communisme Russe*, Paris, 1951
Berkevich, A. 'Petrogradskii proletariat v bor'be za khleb v gody voennogo kommunizma', *Bor'ba Klassov*, 1935, nos. 7–8
Bettelheim, C. *Class Struggles in the USSR, First Period: 1917–1923*, Brighton, 1976
Black, C.E. (ed.), *The Transformation of Russian Society: Aspects of Social Change Since 1961*, Cambridge, Mass., 1960

Bogdanov, A. *A Short Course of Economic Science*, London, 1925
Bogdanov, G.P. and Bogdanov, A.P. *Petr Bogdanov*, Moscow, 1970
Bogomazov, G.G. *Marksizm-Leninizm i problemy tovarno-denezhnykh otnoshenii v period stroitel'stva sotsializma v SSSR*, Leningrad, 1974
The Bolsheviks and the October Revolution. Central Committee Minutes of the Russian Social-Democratic Labour Party (Bolsheviks), August 1917–February 1918, London, 1974
Bol'shevistskie voenno-revoliutsionnye komitety, Moscow, 1958
Boon, H. *Russia from the Inside*, New York, 1921
Bor'ba v vooruzhennoi kulatskoi kontrrevoliutsii, vol. 1, Leningrad, 1964
Brailsford, N.N. *The Russian Workers' Republic*, New York–London, 1921
British Parliamentary Account Papers, Report of the Committee to Collect Information on Russia, no. 1, 1921
Brus, W. *Socialist Ownership and Political Systems*, London–Boston, 1975
Buchanan, H.R. 'Lenin and Bukharin on the Transition from Capitalism to Socialism: the Meshchersky Controversy', *Soviet Studies*, vol. 28, no. 1, January 1976
Bukharin, N. *Anarchia e Comunismo Scientifico*, Società Editrice del PC d'Italia, 1922
The Economics of the Transformation Period, with Lenin's Remarks, New York, 1971
Imperialism and World Economy, London, 1972
Bukharin, N. and Preobrazhensky, *The ABC of Communism*, Harmondsworth, 1969
Bunyan, J. *The Origin of Forced Labor in the Soviet System, 1917–1918: Documents and Materials*, Baltimore, 1967
Carr, E.H. *The Bolshevik Revolution, 1917–1923*, 3 vols., London, 1952
The October Revolution, New York, 1971
Chamberlin, W.H. *The Russian Revolution*, New York, 1935
Cherniavsky, M. *Prologue to Revolution* (Notes of A.N. Jakhontov on the Secret Meetings of the Council of Ministers, 1918), Englewood Cliffs, NJ, 1967
Chumak, A.F. 'K voprosu o vovlechenii kustarei i remeslennikov v sotsialisticheskoe stroitel'stvo', *Voprosy istorii KPSS*, no. 7, 1967
Clarkson, J.D. *A History of Russia*, 2nd edn, New York, 1969
Cohen, S.F. *Bukharin and the Bolshevik Revolution*, Oxford, 1980
Cole, G.D.H. *A History of Socialist Thought*, 5 vols., London, 1953–60
Colombino, E. *Tre mesi nella Russia dei Soviets*, Milan, 1921
Crisenoy, C. de, *Lénine face aux Moujiks*, Paris, 1978
Crisp, O. *Studies in the Russian Economy before 1914*, London, 1976
Dan, F.I. *La Politique économique et la situation de la classe ouvrière en Russie Soviétique*, Brussels, 1923
Daniels, R.V. *Red October. The Bolshevik Revolution of 1917*, New York, 1967
'The State and Revolution: a Case Study in the Genesis and Transformation of Communist Ideology', *The American Slavic and East European Review*, vol. 12, February 1953
Danilov, V.P. *Sovetskaia dokolkhoznaia derevniia (Naselenie, zemlepol'zovanie, khoziaistvo)*, Moscow, 1977
Davies, R.W. *Development of the Soviet Budgetary System*, Cambridge, 1958
'Soviet Industrial Production, 1928–1937. The Rival Estimates', *CREES Discussion Papers*, Series SIPS Birmingham, no. 18, 1978

Davydov, *Bor'ba za khleb*, Moscow, 1971
De Basily, N. *Russia Under Soviet Rule*, London, 1938
Demorgny, G. *Les Partis politiques de la Révolution Russe*, Paris, 1919
Demostenov, S.S. 'Food Prices and the Market in Foodstuffs', *Food Supply in Russia during World War* (ed. P. Struve), New Haven, 1930
    Denezhnoe obrashchenie i kredit, vol. 1, Petrograd, 1922
Deutscher, I. *Soviet Trade Unions: Their Place in Soviet Labour Policy*, London–New York, 1950
    The Unfinished Revolution. Russia 1917–1967, London, 1967
Dewar, M. *Labour Policy in the USSR, 1917–1928*, London–New York, 1956
D'iachenko, V.P. *Istoriia finansov SSSR*, Moscow, 1978
    Sovetskie finansy v pervoi faze razvitiia sotsialisticheskogo gosudarstva, Moscow, 1947
Dobb, M. *Soviet Economic Development after 1917*, London, 1951
Dobrotvor, N. 'Moskovskie rabochie v prodotriadakh', *Bor'ba Klassov*, 1934, nos. 7–8
Drobizhev, V.Z. 'Sotsialisticheskoe obobshchestvlenie promyshlennosti v SSSR', *Voprosy Istorii*, 1964, no. 6
Drobizhev, V.Z. and Medvedev, A.B. *Iz istorii sovnarkhozov*, Moscow, 1964
Eckardt, H. von. *Russia*, London, 1932
Egorova, A.E. *Profsoiuzy i fabzavkomy v bor'be za pobedu Oktiabria (mart–oktiabr' 1917g)*, Moscow, 1960
    'Profsoiuzy i fabzavkomy v period podgotovki i provedeniia Oktiabr'skoi Revoliutsii', in *Rabochii klass: vedushchaia sila Oktiabr'skoi Revoliutsii, Sbornik statei*, Moscow, 1976
Ekonomika i politika tverdykh tsen. Sbornik statei, Moscow, 1918
Epstein, E. *Les Banques de Commerce Russes*, Paris, 1925
Erlich, A. *The Soviet Industrialization Debate, 1924–1928*, Cambridge (Mass.), 1960
B.F., *Rukovodstvo po rabochemu kontroliu*, (izd. Soveta Rabochego Kontrolia Tsentralnoi Promyshlennoi Oblasti), Moscow, 1918
Feigel'son, M. 'Kak revoliutsiia reshila prodovol'stvennyi vopros', *Problemy ekonomiki*, no. 3, 1938
Fin, Ia. *Profdvizhenie SSSR*, Moscow, 1928
Finansovaia politika Sovetskoi Vlasti za 10 let. Sbornik statei, Moscow–Leningrad, 1928 (English edition: G.Y. Sokolnykov *et al.*, *Soviet Policy in Public Finance, 1917–1928*, Stanford, 1931)
Frumkin, M. *Chetyre goda prodovol'stvennoi raboty. Stat'i i otchetnye materialy*, Moscow, 1922
Gaponenko, L.S. 'Rabochii klass v Oktiabr'skoi Revoliutsii' (nekotorye itogi issledovanii), *Voprosy Istorii*, 1968, no. 1
Gaponenko, L.S.; Sakharov, A.N.; Sobolev, G.L. 'Velikii Oktiabri' i ego sovremennye burzhuaznye kritiki', *Voprosy Istorii*, no. 1, 1969
Garvi, P.A. *Professional'nye soiuzy v Rossii v pervye gody revoliutsii (1917–1921)*, New York, 1958
Gavronsky, D., *Le Bilan du Bolchevisme Russe*, Paris, 1920
Genkina, E.B. *Perekhod Sovetskogo Gosudarstva k novoi ekonomicheskoi politike, 1921–1922*, Moscow, 1954
Genkina, E.B. 'V.I. Lenin i perekhod k novoi ekonomicheskoi politike', *Voprosy*

Istorii, no. 5, 1964

Gerschenkron, A. *Economic Backwardness in Historical Perspective*, New York, 1965
'The Rate of Industrial Growth in Russia since 1885', *Journal of Economic History*, vol. 7, Supplement, 1947

Gimpel'son, E.G., 'Izmeneniia v sotsial'nom sostave rabochego klassa Sovetskoi Respubliki v 1918–1920 gg', *Iz istorii grazhdanskoi voiny i interventsii 1917–1922 gg*, Moscow, 1974
'Kak slozhilas' Sovetskaia forma proletarskogo gosudarstva', *Voprosy istorii*, no. 9, 1967
Lenin i material'noe stimulirovanie truda v gody grazhdanskoi voiny', *Voprosy Istorii KPSS*, no. 10, 1971
'O politike voennogo kommunizma' (1918–1920 gg), *Voprosy Istorii*, no. 5, 1963
'Sotsial'no-politicheskie izmeneniia v sostave rabochego klassa v pervye gody Sovetskoi Vlasti', *in Rabochii klass: vedushchaia sila Oktiabr'skoi Revoliutsii, Sbornik statei*, Moscow, 1976
Velikii Oktiabr' i stanovlenie Sovetskoi sistemy upravleniia narodnym khoziaistvom (noiabr 1917–1920 gg), Moscow, 1977
Voennyi kommunizm: politika, praktika, ideologiia, Moscow, 1973

Gladkov, I.A. 'Leninskie printsipy rukovodstva sotsialisticheskoi ekonomiki', *Voprosy Istorii KPSS*, no. 3, 1969
Natsionalizatsiia promyshlennosti v Rossii, Moscow, 1954
Ocherki Sovetskoi ekonomiki 1917–1920 gg, Moscow, 1956
Ocherki stroitel'stva Sovetskogo planovogo khoziaistva v 1917–1918 gg, Moscow, 1950
'Vazhnyi etap razrabotki plana postroeniia sotsializma', *Voprosy Istorii*, no. 11, 1967
Voprosy planirovaniia Sovetskogo khoziaistva v 1918–1919 gg, Moscow, 1951

God Proletarskoi Diktatury, Nizhni-Novgorod, 1918

Goode, W.T. *Bolshevism at Work*, London, 1920

Goldstein, J.M. *Russia: her Economic Past and Future*, New York, 1919

Gordeev, G.S. *Sel'skoe khoziaistvo v voine i revoliutsii*, Moscow, 1925

Grazhdanskaia Voina 1918–1921, 2 vols., Moscow, 1928, vol. 2

Grave, B.B. 'Militarizatsiia promyshlennosti i rossiiskii proletariat v gody pervoi mirovoi voiny', *Iz istorii rabochego klassa i revoliutsionnogo dvizheniia*, Moscow, 1958

Grebennikov, P.P. 'Iz istorii bor'by kommunisticheskoi partii protiv pravogo opportunizma i profdvizhenii v period uprocheniia sovetskoi vlasti (noiabr' 1917 g–1918 g)', *Materialy mezhvuzovskoi nauchnoi konferentsii kafedr obshchestvennykh naukh*, Omsk, 1971

Grinevetskii, V.I. *Poslevoennye perspektivy Russkoi promyshlennosti*, Kharkov, 1919

Guest, L.H. *The Struggle for Power in Europe (1917–1921)*, London, 1921

Gurevich, A.I. *Desiat' let profdvizheniia SSSR*, Moscow, 1927

Gusakov, A.D. *Planirovanie denezhnogo obrashcheniia v SSSR*, Moscow, 1974

Haimson, L.H. *The Russian Marxists and the Origins of Bolshevism*, Cambridge, Mass., 1955

Hilferding, R. *Das Finanz Kapital, Marx Studien*, vol. 3, Vienna, 1923

The History of the Civil War in the USSR, ed. M. Gorkii *et al.*, 2 vols., 1946

Hoshiller, M. *Le Mirage due Soviétisme*, Paris, 1921

Ignatenko, T.A. *Sovetskaia istoriografiia rabochego kontrolia i natsionalizatsii promyshlennosti v SSSR (1917–67)*, Moscow, 1971

ILO, *Studies in War Economies*, Studies and Report, Series E, 1941

Iskrov, M.I. 'O razrabotke V.I. Leninym prodovol'stvennoi politiki v 1918 g', *Voprosy Istorii KPSS*, no. 7, 1963

Istoriia VKP(b), pod red. Iaroslavskogo, Moscow, 1930

Istoriia VKP(b), kratkii kurs, Moscow, 1938

Iurkov, I.A. 'Finansovaia politika Sovetskogo Gosudarstva i tovarno-denezhnye otnosheniia v gody grazhdanskoi voiny (1918–1920 gg)', *Voprosy Istorii*, no. 10, 1980

Iurovskii, L.N. *Denezhnaia politika Sovetskoi Vlasti (1917–1927)*, Moscow, 1928

Iustuzov, V.E. 'K voprosu o preemstvennosti novoi ekonomicheskoi politiki i ekonomicheskoi politiki vesny 1918 g', in *Problemy istoriografii i istochnikovedeniia istorii KPSS*, vyp. 1, Leningrad, 1971

Jasny, N. *The Socialized Agriculture of the USSR. Plans and Performance*, Stanford, 1949

Soviet Economists of the Twenties, Cambridge, 1972

Kabanov, V.V. 'Natsionalizatsiia Moskovskogo Narodnogo Banka', *Voprosy Istorii*, no. 4, 1970

Kanev, S. *Oktiabr'skaia Revoliutsiia i krakh anarkhizma*, Moscow, 1974

Kaplan, F.I. *Bolshevik Ideology and the Ethics of Soviet Labour*, London, 1963

Russian Labor and the Bolshevik Party, 1917–1920, Berkeley, 1965

Karabtschevksy, N. *La Révolution et la Russie*, Paris, 1921

Kautsky, K. *Das Erfurter Programm*, Stuttgart–Berlin, 1922

La Révolution sociale, Paris, 1921

Die Sozialisierung der Landwirtschaft, Berlin, 1919

Khesin, S.S. *Matrosy revoliutsii, uchastie voennykh moriakov v bor'be za uprochenie Sovetskoi Vlasti* (Oktiabr' 1917–Marta 1918), Moscow, 1958

Khleb i Revoliutsiia. Prodovol'stvennaia politika Kommunisticheskoi Partii i Sovetskogo Pravitel'stva v 1917–1922 goda, Moscow, 1978

Knipovich, B. 'Napravlenie i itogi agrarnoi politiki 1917–1920', *O zemle*, vyp. 1, 1921

Kondrat'ev, N.D. and Oganovskii, N.P. *Sel'skoe khoziaistvo Rossii v XX veke, Sbornik statistiko-ekonomicheskikh svedenii za 1901–1922 gg*, Moscow, 1923

Kon'kova, A.S. *Bor'ba Kommunisticheskoi Partii za soiuz rabochego klassa s bedneishim krestianstcom v 1917–1918, Moscow, 1971*

Kovalenko, A. 'Bor'ba fabrichno-zavodskikh komitetov Petrograda za rabochii kontrol' and proizvodstvom', *Istoricheskie Zapiski*, vol. 61, 1957

Kovalenko, D.A. *Oboronnaia promyshlennost' Sovetskoi Rossii v 1918–1920*, Moscow, 1970

Kozlov, A.G. *Sovetskie den'gi*, Gosfinizdat, 1939

[Kozlov, A.G. (ed.)] *Finansy i kredit SSSR*, Leningrad, 1938

Kozochkina, E.Z. *Iz istorii organizatsii upravleniia promyshlennosti*, Moscow, 1964

Kritsman, L. *Edinyi khoziaistvennyi plan i komissiia ispol'zovaniia*, 1921

Geroicheskii period Velikoi Russkoi Revoliutsii, Moscow, (no date, probably 1924)

Krzhizhanovskii, G.M. *Desiat' let khoziaistvennogo stroitel'stva SSSR*, Moscow, 1922

Izbrannoe, Moscow, 1957

Labry, R. *L'Industrie russe et la révolution*, Paris, 1919
    Une législation communiste, Paris, 1920
Lansbury, G. *What I Saw in Russia*, London, 1920
    The Lansing Papers, 1914–1920, Washington, 1940
Larin, Iu. and Kritsman, L. *Ocherk khoziaistvennoi zhizni i organizatsiia narodnogo*
    khoziaistva Sovetskoi Rossii, Moscow, 1920
Lawton, L. *An Economic History of Soviet Russia*, Moscow, London, 1928
Leites, K. *Recent Economic Development in Russia*, Oxford, 1922
V.I. Lenin, *Collected Works*, 4th edn, 45 vols., London 1964–70
    Collected Works, 4th edn, vol. 26, Moscow, 1964
    Polnoe sobranie sochinenii, 5th edn, 55 vols., Moscow, 1958–69
    Sochineniia, 3rd edn, Moscow, 1924–37
V.I. *Lenin: vo glave velikogo stroitel'stva* (collection of memoirs), Moscow,
    1960
Leninskaia sistema Partiino-Gosudarstvennogo Kontrolia i ego rol' v stroitel'stve Sotsializma
    (*1917–1932 gg*), Moscow, 1965
Leninskii sbornik, vol. 11, 1929; vol. 18, 1931; vol. 35, 1945
Lescure, J. *La Révolution Russe et le Bolchevisme*, Paris, 1929
Liashchenko, P.I. *Istoriia narodnogo khoziastva SSSR*, vol. 2, Gos. Izd. Politicheskoi
    Literatury, 1948
Liberman, S.I. *Dela i liudi (na sovetskoi stroike)*, New York, 1944
Lipitski, S.V. *Leninskoe rukovodstvo oboronoi strany 1917–1920*, Moscow, 1979
    Voiennaia deiatel'nost' TsK RKP(b) 1917–1920, Moscow, 1973
Lomakin, A. 'Ob osnovnykh etapakh istorii SSSR (1917–1934)', *Vestnik kom-*
    munisticheskoi akademii, 1934, nos. 5–6
Los Rios, F. De, *Mi viaje en la Russia Sovietista*, Madrid, 1922
Lozovsky, A. *Lenin and the Trade Union Movement*, Washington, 1924
    Trade Unions in Soviet Russia: Their Development and Present Position, Collection of
    Russian Trade Unions' Documents compiled by the ILP Information
    Committee, 1920
Mar'iakin, G.L. *Ocherki istorii nalogov u naseleniia v SSSR*, Moscow, 1964
Marx, K. *Capital*, 3 vols., Moscow, 1957
    Critique of the Gotha Program, New York, 1966
    Grundrisse, Harmondsworth, 1973
    Theories of the Surplus-Value, Moscow, 1969
Marx, K. and Engels, F. *Collected Works*, London, 1978
    Selected Works, vol. 1, Moscow, 1962
    Materialy po istorii SSSR, vol. 3, Moscow, 1956
Medvedev, E. *Krest'ianstvo Srednego Povolzh'ia v Oktiabr'skoi Revoliutsii*, Kuibyshev,
    1970
Medvedev, R. *Dopo la Rivoluzione*, Rome, 1978
    La Révolution d'Octobre était-elle inéluctable?, Paris, 1976
'Mery po obespecheniiu sel'skogo khoziaistva sredstvami proizvodstva', pod red.
    M. Sheflera, *Narkomfin*, vyp. 3, 1920
Meyer, A. *Leninism*, Cambridge, Mass., 1957
Miliutin, V.P. *Istoriia ekonomicheskogo razvitiia SSSR*. Moscow–Leningrad, 1929
    Sovremennoe eknonomicheskoe razvitie Rossi i diktatura proletariata (1914–1918 gg),
    Moscow, 1918

Narodnoe khoziaistvo Sovetskoi Rossii, Moscow, 1920
Narodnoe khoziaistvo, Moscow, 1968
Mints, L.I. *Istoriia Velikogo Oktiabria*, Moscow, 1968
Moore, B., Jr, *Soviet Politics: The Dilemma of Power*, New York, 1965
Nasyrin, V.P. 'O nekotorykh voprosakh sotsialisticheskogo preobrazovaniia promyshlennosti v SSSR', *Voprosy istorii*, 1956, no. 5
Nelidov, A.A. *N.K.P. RSFSR i ego mestnye organy v period ustanovleniia i provedeniia v zhizn' prodovol'stvennoi diktatury (leto–osen' 1918)*, Trudy Moskovskogo gosistoriko-arkhivnogo instituta, vol. 19, 1965, 41
Nolde, B.E. (Baron), *Russia in Economic War*, New Haven, 1928
Nordman, N. *Peace Problems: Russia's Economics*, London, 1919
Nove, A. *An Economic History of the USSR*, Harmondsworth, 1969
Oganovskii, N.P. *Individualizatsiia zemledeliia v Rossii i ee posledstviia*, Moscow, 1917
Ocherki po ekonomicheskoi geografii Rossii, 1923
Ol', P.V. *Inostrannye kapitaly v Rossii*, Petrograd, 1922
Orekhova, L.M. 'Pokhod rabochikh v derevne v 1918 g', *Voprosy Istorii KPSS*, 1958, no. 1
Orlov, N. *Prodovol'stvennaia rabota Sovetskoi Vlasti*, Moscow, 1918
Orlov, V.S. 'V.I. Lenin i sozdanie apparata pervogo v mire rabochego-krest'ianskogo pravitel'stva', *Voprosy Istorii*, 1963, no. 4
Osinskii, N. *Stroitel'stvo sotsializma*, Moscow, 1918
Pankratova, A.M. *Fabzavkomy i profsoiuzy v revoliutsii 1917 goda*, Moscow, 1927
Fabzavkomy Rossii v bor'be za sotsialisticheskuiu fabriku, Moscow, 1923
Parliamentary Papers on Bolshevism, United Kingdom, 1919
Pasvolsky, L. *The Economics of Communism*, London, 1921
Pavlevski, J. *Le Niveau de vie en Russie de la Révolution d'Octobre à 1980*, Economica, 1975
Podoviskii, M.I. *God 1917*, Moscow, 1958
Pogrebinskii, A.P. 'Sel'skoe khoziaistvo i prodovol'stvennyi vopros v Rossii v gody pervoi mirovoi voiny', *Istoricheskie Zapiski*, vol. 31, 1950
Poliakov, Iu. A. *Perekhod k NEPu i Sovetskoe krest'anstvo*, Moscow, 1967
Polner, T.J. *Russian Local Government during the War and the Union of Zemstvos*, New Haven, 1930
Popov, P. *Proizvodstvo khleba v RSFSR i federiruiushchikhsia s neiu respublikakh (khlebnaia produktsiia)*, Moscow, 1921
(ed.), *Balans narodnogo khoziaistva SSSR v 1923–24 goda*, Moscow, 1926
Portal, R. *La Russie industrielle de 1881 à 1927*, Paris, 1976
Potekhin, M.N. *Pervyi sovet proletarskoi diktatury*, Leningrad, 1966
Preobrazhenskii, E. *Bumazhnye Den'gi v epokhu proletarskoi diktatury*, 1920
(English translation: *Paper Money during the Proletarian Dictatorship*, Moscow, 1920)
Voprosy finansovoi politiki, 1921
Price, M.P. *My Reminiscences of the Russian Revolution*, London, 1921
Prokopovitch, S.N. *Ocherki khoziaistva Sovetskoi Rossii*, Berlin, 1923 (English translation: *The Economic Condition of Soviet Russia*, London, 1924)
Promyshlennost' v usloviiakh NEP, Moscow, 1925
Rabinovich, A. *Ekonomicheskoe oblozhenie*, 1927

Rabochee dvizhenie v 1917 godu, podg. k pechati V.L. Meller i A.M. Pankratova, Moscow-Leningrad, 1926

Rabochee Vremia i proizvoditel'nost' truda, Novosibirsk, 1963

Radek, C. 'L'evoluzione del socialismo dalla scienza all'azione'. *Documenti della Rivoluzione*, no. 13, (Reprint Feltrinelli), 1970

Rathenau, W. *L'economia nuova*, Turin, 1976

Razumovich, N.N. *Organizatsionno-pravovye formy sotsialistichéskogo obobshchestvleniia promyshlennosti v SSSR, 1917–1920 gg*, Moscow, 1959

Riasanovsky, N. *A History of Russia*, 2nd edn, Oxford, 1969

Rigby, T.H. *Lenin's Government: Sounarkom 1917–22*, Cambridge, 1979.

Roberts, P.C. *Alienation and the Soviet Economy*, Albuquerque, NM, 1971

Roden-Buxton, C. *In a Russian Village*, London, 1922

Rostow, W.W. *The Stages of Economic Growth*, 7th edn, Cambridge, 1969

Rozenfel'd S. *Promyshlennaia politika SSSR*, Moscow, 1926

Russell, B. *The Practice and the Theory of Bolshevism*, London, 1920

Ryss, P. *L'Expérience Russe*, Paris, 1922

Sadoul, J. *Notes sur la Révolution Bolchévique*, Paris, 1919

Samokhvalov, F.V. *Sovety narodnogo khoziaistva v 1917–1923 gg*, Moscow, 1964

Sarabianov, V. *Ekonomika i ekonomicheskaia politika SSSR*, Moscow, 1926

Schapiro, L. *Storia del Partito Comunista Sovietico*, Milan, 1962

Selitskii, V.I. *Massy v bor'be za rabochii kontrol' (mart-iiul' 1917 g)*, Moscow, 1971

Selunskaia, V.M. *Rabochii klass i Oktiabr' v derevne*, Moscow, 1968

Serebrovskii, A.P. *Upravlenie zavodskim predpriiatiiam*, 2nd edn, Moscow, 1919

Seton-Watson, H. *The Russian Empire, 1801–1917*, Oxford, 1967

Shanin, T. *The Awkward Class*, Oxford, 1972

Sidorov, A.L. *Ekonomicheskoe polozhenie Rossii v gody pervoi mirovoi voiny*, Moscow, 1973

Silantiev, N. *Rabochii kontrol' i sovnarkhozy*, Moscow, 1957

Singleton, Seth 'The Tambov Revolt (1920–1921)', *Slavic Review*, vol. 25, September 1966

Smith, S.A. *Red Petrograd: the Revolution in the Factories, 1917–1918*, Cambridge, 1983

Smolinskii, L. 'Grinevetsky e l'industrializzazione Sovietica', *L'Est, Rivista trimestrale*, CESES, 1968, no. 4; 1971, no. 3

Sokol'nikov, G.Y. *et al. Soviet Policy in Public Finance, 1917–1928*, Stanford, 1931 (English edition of *Finansovaia politika Sovetskoi Vlasti za 10 let. Sbornik statei*, Moscow-Leningrad, 1928)

Sokoloff, B. *Les Bolcheviks jugés par eux-mêmes*. Documents des Soviets de 1919, Paris, 1919

Sokolov, S.A. *Revoliutsiia i khleb. Iz istorii Sovetskoi prodovol'stvennoi politiki v 1917–1918*, Saratov, 1967

Sorenson, J.B. *The Life and Death of Soviet Trade Unionism, 1917–1928*, New York, 1969

Sorlin, P. *The Soviet People and Their Society*, Praeger, 1969

Sovetskoe krest'ianstvo (kratkii ocherk istorii, 1917–1919), pod red. V.P. Danilova, M.P. Kima, N.V. Tropkina, Moscow, 1970

Spirin, M. *Klassy i partii v grazhdanskoi voine v Rossii*, Moscow, 1968

Stalin, J.V. *Sochineniia*, vol. 4, Moscow, 1947 *Works*, 13 vols., Moscow, 1952–5

Stepanov, I. *Ot rabochego kontrolia k rabochemu upravleniiu v promyshlennosti i zemledelii*, Moscow, 1918

Strizhkov, Iu. K. *Prodovol'stvennye otriady v gody grazhdanskoi voiny i inostrannoi interventsii, 1917–1921*, Moscow, 1973

Strumilin, S.G. 'K khoziaistvennomu planu na 1921–22 gg', *Narodnoe Khoziaistvo*, 1921, no. 5

Ocherki ekonomicheskoi istorii Rossii i SSSR, Moscow, 1966

Problemy ekonomiki truda, Moscow, 1925

Zarabotnaia plata i proizvoditel'nost' truda v russkoi promyshlennosti v 1913–1922 gg, Moscow, 1923

Sukhanov, N.N. *Zapiski o Revoliutsii*, Berlin–Petersburg–Moscow, 1922–3 English translation: *The Russian Revolution 1917: An Eyewitness Account*. New York, 1962

Sumerin, P.G. *Kombedy v Penzenskoi Gubernii*, Penza, 1960

Sviderskii, A. *Tri goda bor'by s golodom*, Moscow, 1920

Syromolotov, Th. Th. (VSNKh), *Finansirovanie natsional'-promyshlennosti po VSNKh v 1919*, Moscow, 1921

Szamuely, L. *First Models of the Socialist Economic Systems, Principles and Theories*, Budapest, 1974

Tarnovskii, K.N. *Formirovanie gosudarstvenno-monopolisticheskogo kapitalizma v Rossii v gody pervoi mirovoi voiny*, Moscow, 1958

Teoriia i Praktika Sovetskogo Stroia – Respublika Sovetov, vyp. 1, Berlin–Milan, 1920

Timoshenko, V.P. *Agricultural Russia and the Wheat Problem*, Stanford, 1932

Trapeznikov, S.P. *Agrarnyi vopros i Leninskie agrarnye programmy v trekh russkikh revoliutsiiakh*, Moscow, 1963

Trotsky, L. *The History of the Russian Revolution*, London, 1933

Storia della rivoluzione Russa, 2 vols., Milan, 1969

Defense of Terrorism: Terrorism and Communism. A Reply to K. Kautsky. London, 1921

The Trotsky Papers (1917–1919), vol. 1 (ed. Jan M. Meijer), London – The Hague – Paris, 1964

Trukhan, 'Rabochii klass i sotsialisticheskoe obobshchestvlenie promyshlennosti (1917–1919 gg)', in *Rabochii klass: vedushchaia sila Oktiabr'skoi Revoliutsii, Sbornik statei*, Moscow, 1976

'V.I. Lenin o gegemonii proletariata v Oktiabr'skoi Revoliutsii', in *V.I. Lenin ob istoricheskom opyte Velikogo Oktiabria*, Moscow, 1969

Tsyperovitch, G. *Sindikaty i tresty v dorevoliutsionnoi Rossii i SSSR*, Leningrad, 1927

Umnov, A.S. *Grazhdanskaia voina i srednee krest'ianstvo (1918–1920 gg)*, Moscow, 1959

Vacirca, V. *Ciò che heo visto nella Russia Sovietista*, Milan, 1921

Vainshtein, A. 'Metody bezdenezhnogo ucheta khoziaistvennykh predpriiatii', Nar. Kom. Zemledeliia, 1921

Oblozhenie i platezhi krest'ianstva, Moscow, 1924

Vaisberg, R.E. *Den'gi i tseny (podpol'nyi rynok v period 'voennogo kommunizma'*, Moscow, 1925

Venediktov, A.V. *Organizatsiia gosudarstvennoi promyshlennosti v SSSR*, 2 vols.,

Moscow, 1957–61
Venturi, F. *Il populismo russo*, 2 vols., Turin, 1952
Vinogradov, V. *Workers' Control over Production, Past and Present*, Moscow, 1973
Volin, L. *A Century of Russian Agriculture*, Cambridge, Mass., 1970
Volobuev, P.V. *Ekonomicheskaia politika Vremennogo Pravitel'stva*, Moscow, 1962
Volobuev, P.V. and Drobizhev, V,Z. 'Iz istorii goskapitalizma v nachal'nyi period sotsialisticheskogo stroitel'stva v SSSR', *Voprosy Istorii*, 1957, no. 9
Voronetskaia, A.A. 'Organizatsiia Vysshego Soveta Narodnogo Khoziaistva i ego rol' v natsionalizatsii promyshlennosti', *Istoricheskie Zapiski*, 1953, no. 43
Ward, B. 'Wild Socialism in Russia: the Origin' (unpublished article), 1971
Welter, G. *Histoire de la Russie Communiste 1917–1934*, Paris, 1935
Wesson, G. *Soviet Communes*, New Jersey, 1963
Wheatcroft, S.G. 'The Reliability of Russian Prewar Grain Output Statistics', *Soviet Studies*, 1974, no. 2
Wiles, P. *The Political Economy of Communism*, Oxford, 1962
Wolfe, B.D. 'Backwardness and Industrialization in Russian History and Thought', *Slavic Review*, vol. 25, no. 2, June 1967
Three who Made a Revolution, New York, 1964
Zagorsky, S. *La République des Soviets: Bilan économique*, Paris, 1921
State Control of Industry in Russia during the War, New Haven, 1928
Zaitsev, K.I. 'Organization and Policy', in *Food Supply in Russia during World War*, ed. P. Struve, New Haven, 1930
Zvorikine, N. *La Révolution et le Bolchévisme en Russie*, Paris, 1920

Glossary

Chrezkomsnabarm	Extraordinary Commission for Army Supply
Chusosnabarm	Extraordinary Agency of the Council of Supply and Defence to the Army
fabzavkomy	factory-plant committees
glavki	branch chief committees
Glavkustprom	Central Administration for *Kustar'* industry
glavnye pravleniia	central administrations of the nationalized enterprises
Glavprodukt	Chief Administration for Supply of foodstuffs and consumer goods *attached to Narkomprod*
GOELRO	State Commission for the Electrification of Russia
GOSPLAN	State Economic Planning Commission
gubernia	an administrative unit, or province
gubsovnarkhoz	the economic department of the *gubernia* soviet, or provincial economic council
kholkoz	collective farm
kombedy	rural poor committees
kulak	a rich peasant (literally *fist*)
kust	grouping of homogeneous production factories
kustar'	handicraftsman
Narkomfin	People's Commissariat of Finance
Narkomprod	People's Commissariat of Food Procurement
Narkomtrud	People's Commissariat of Labour
Narkomzem	People's Commissariat of Agriculture
Narodnik	a member of the Populist Movement (*Narod*)
NEP	the New Economic Policy
Prodraspred	Section of General Distribution of foodstuffs
prodrazverstka	obligatory delivery of foodstuffs by quota
prombureaux	industrial boards
Promvoensovet	Council of War Industry
smychka	the alliance between the working class and the peasantry
sovkhoz	state farm
sovnarkhoz	local economic council
Sovnarkom	Council of People's Commissars
STO	Council of Labour and Defence
trust	grouping of a number of factories

Tsekomprodarm	Central Commission for the regulation of Food Procurement Supply to the Army
Tsentrovoenzag	Central Section of Military State Purchase
Tsentrozakaz	Central Section of Orders
Ts.I.K.	Central Executive Committee
VSNKh	Supreme Council of the National Economy
zemstvo	elective district council in pre-revolutionary Russia
uezd	an administrative unit equivalent to a county
volost	small rural district
oblast	large region
obsovnarkhoz	regional economic council
paiok	food ration

WEIGHTS AND MEASURES

arshin	28 in. = 0.71 metres
desiatin	2.7 acres = 1.09 hectares
funt	0.90 lb = 0.36 kilograms
sazhen	7 ft = 2.134 metres; cubic sazhen = 343 cubic ft = 9.71 cubic metres
pud	36.11 lb = 16.38 kilograms
verst	0.66 miles = 1.06 kilometres
zolotnik	0.15 oz = 4.26 grams

Index